THE HISTORY
OF ENGLAND

VOLUME III

THE HISTORY

OF ENGLAND

from the Invasion of Julius Caesar

to The Revolution in 1688

IN SIX VOLUMES

BY DAVID HUME, ESQ.

VOLUME III

Based on the Edition of 1778, with the Author's
Last Corrections and Improvements

Liberty Fund

The cuneiform inscription that serves as our logo and as the design motif for our endpapers is the earliest-known written appearance of the word "freedom" (*amagi*), or "liberty." It is taken from a clay document written about 2300 B.C. in the Sumerian city-state of Lagash.

This Liberty Fund edition is based on the edition of 1778, containing the author's last corrections and improvements. The only two recorded sets of that edition in the United States were consulted. One is a complete set at the Humanities Research Center of the University of Texas at Austin. The other is an incomplete set in the Boston Public Library. The publisher acknowledges with thanks the cooperation of both institutions as well as the advice of Professors William B. Todd and David Levy.

Design by Martin Lubin/Betty Binns Graphics. New York, New York.
Editorial services provided by Harkavy Publishing Service, New York, New York.

Library of Congress Cataloging in Publication Data

Hume, David, 1711–1776.
  The history of England.
  "Based on the edition of 1778, with the author's last corrections and improvements."
  Reprint. Originally published: London: T. Cadell, 1778. With new foreword.
  1. Great Britain—History—To 1485. 2. Great Britain—History—Tudors, 1485–1603. 3. Great Britain—History—Stuarts, 1603–1714. I. Title.
DA30 .H9   1983   942   82-25868
ISBN 0-86597-019-X (series)
ISBN 0-86597-020-3 (pbk. series)
ISBN 0-86597-028-9 (Volume III)
ISBN 0-86597-029-7 (Volume III pbk.)

16 19 20 21 22   C 8 7 6 5 4
19 20 21 22 23   P 10 9 8 7 6

CONTENTS

OF THE THIRD VOLUME

XXVI

XXVII

HENRY VIII

*Popularity of the new king – His
ministers – Punishment of Empson and Dudley –
King's marriage – Foreign affairs – Julius the second –
League of Cambray – War with France – Expedition
to Fontarabia – Deceit of Ferdinand – Return of
the English – Leo the Tenth – A parliament –
War with Scotland – Wolsey minister –
His character – Invasion of France –
Battle of Guinegate – Battle of Flouden –
Peace with France*

PAGE 83

XXVIII

*Wolsey's administration – Scotch affairs –
Progress of Francis I. – Jealousy of Henry –
Tournay delivered to France – Wolsey
appointed legate – His manner of
exercising that office – Death of
the emperor Maximilian – Charles, king
of Spain, chosen emperor – Interview between Henry
and Francis near Calais – The emperor Charles arrives
in England – Mediation of Henry – Trial
and condemnation of the
duke of Buckingham*

PAGE 113

XXIX

XXX

XXXI

XXXII

XXXV

XXXVI

MARY

XXXVII

THE HISTORY
OF ENGLAND

VOLUME   III

XXIV
HENRY VII

Accession of Henry VII. –
His title to the crown – King's
prejudice against the house of York –
His joyful reception in London –
His coronation – Sweating sickness –
A parliament – Entail of the crown – King's
marriage – An insurrection – Discontents
of the people – Lambert Simnel –
Revolt of Ireland – Intrigues
of the dutchess of Burgundy –
Lambert Simnel invades England –
Battle of Stoke

THE VICTORY, which the earl of Richmond gained at Bosworth, was entirely decisive; being attended, as well with the total rout and dispersion of the royal army, as with the death of the king himself. Joy for this great success suddenly prompted the soldiers, in the field of battle, to bestow on their victorious general the appellation of king, which he had not hitherto assumed; and the acclamations of *Long live Henry the Seventh*, by a natural and unpremeditated movement, resounded from all quarters. To bestow some appearance of formality on this species of military election, Sir William Stanley brought a crown of ornament, which Richard wore in battle, and which had been found among the spoils; and

3

he put it on the head of the victor. Henry himself remained not in suspence; but immediately, without hesitation, accepted of the magnificent present, which was tendered him. He was come to the crisis of his fortune; and being obliged suddenly to determine himself, amidst great difficulties, which he must have frequently revolved in his mind, he chose that part, which his ambition suggested to him, and to which he seemed to be invited by his present success.

His title to the crown.

There were many titles, on which Henry could found his right to the crown; but no one of them free from great objections, if considered, with respect either to justice or to policy.

During some years, Henry had been regarded as heir to the house of Lancaster, by the party attached to that family; but the title of the house of Lancaster itself was generally thought to be very ill-founded. Henry IV. who had first raised it to royal dignity, had never clearly defined the foundation of his claim; and while he plainly invaded the order of succession, he had not acknowledged the election of the people. The parliament, it is true, had often recognized the title of the Lancastrian princes; but these votes had little authority, being considered as instances of complaisance towards a family in possession of present power: And they had accordingly been often reversed during the late prevalence of the house of York. Prudent men also, who had been willing, for the sake of peace, to submit to any established authority, desired not to see the claims of that family revived; claims, which must produce many convulsions at present, and which disjointed for the future the whole system of hereditary right. Besides, allowing the title of the house of Lancaster to be legal, Henry himself was not the true heir of that family; and nothing but the obstinacy, natural to faction, which never, without reluctance, will submit to an antagonist, could have engaged the Lancastrians to adopt the earl of Richmond as their head. His mother indeed, Margaret, countess of Richmond, was sole daughter and heir of the duke of Somerset, sprung from John of Gaunt, duke of Lancaster. But the descent of the Somerset line was itself illegitimate and even adulterous. And though the duke of Lancaster had obtained the legitimation of his natural children by a patent from Richard II. confirmed in parliament; it might justly be doubted, whether this deed could bestow any title to the crown; since in the patent itself all the privileges

CHAPTER XXIV

conferred by it are fully enumerated, and the succession to the kingdom is expressly excluded.[a] In all settlements of the crown, made during the reigns of the Lancastrian princes, the line of Somerset had been entirely overlooked; and it was not till the failure of the legitimate branch, that men had paid any attention to their claim. And to add to the general dissatisfaction against Henry's title, his mother, from whom he derived all his right, was still alive; and evidently preceded him in the order of succession.

The title of the house of York, both from the plain reason of the case, and from the late popular government of Edward IV. had universally obtained the preference in the sentiments of the people; and Henry might engraft his claim on the rights of that family, by his intended marriage with the princess Elizabeth, the heir of it; a marriage, which he had solemnly promised to celebrate, and to the expectation of which he had chiefly owed all his past successes. But many reasons dissuaded Henry from adopting this expedient. Were he to receive the crown only in right of his consort, his power, he knew, would be very limited; and he must expect rather to enjoy the bare title of king by a sort of courtesy, than possess the real authority which belongs to it. Should the princess die before him without issue, he must descend from the throne, and give place to the next in succession: And even if his bed should be blest with offspring, it seemed dangerous to expect, that filial piety in his children would prevail over the ambition of obtaining present possession of regal power. An act of parliament, indeed, might easily be procured to settle the crown on him during life; but Henry knew how much superior the claim of succession by blood was to the authority of an assembly,[b] which had always been overborne by violence in the shock of contending titles, and which had ever been more governed by the conjunctures of the times, than by any consideration derived from reason or public interest.

There was yet a third foundation, on which Henry might rest his claim, the right of conquest, by his victory over Richard, the present possessor of the crown. But besides that Richard himself was deemed no better than an usurper, the army, which fought against him, consisted chiefly of Englishmen; and a right of con-

[a] Rymer, tom. vii. p. 849. Coke's inst. 4. Inst. part 1. p. 37.   [b] Bacon in Kennet's complete History, p. 579.

quest over England could never be established by such a victory. Nothing also would give greater umbrage to the nation than a claim of this nature; which might be construed as an abolition of all their rights and privileges, and the establishment of absolute authority in the sovereign.[c] William himself, the Norman, though at the head of a powerful and victorious army of foreigners, had at first declined the invidious title of conqueror; and it was not till the full establishment of his authority, that he had ventured to advance so violent and destructive a pretension.

But Henry was sensible, that there remained another foundation of power, somewhat resembling the right of conquest, namely, present possession; and that this title, guarded by vigour and abilities, would be sufficient to secure perpetual possession of the throne. He had before him the example of Henry IV. who, supported by no better pretension, had subdued many insurrections, and had been able to transmit the crown peaceably to his posterity. He could perceive, that this claim, which had been perpetuated through three generations of the family of Lancaster, might still have subsisted, notwithstanding the preferable title of the house of York; had not the scepter devolved into the hands of Henry VI. which were too feeble to sustain it. Instructed by this recent experience, Henry was determined to put himself in possession of regal authority; and to show all opponents, that nothing but force of arms and a successful war should be able to expel him. His claim as heir to the house of Lancaster he was resolved to advance; and never allow to be discussed: And he hoped that this right, favoured by the partizans of that family, and seconded by present power, would secure him a perpetual and an independant authority.

These views of Henry are not exposed to much blame, because founded on good policy, and even on a species of necessity: But there entered into all his measures and counsels another motive, which admits not of the same apology. The violent contentions, which, during so long a period, had been maintained between the rival families, and the many sanguinary revenges, which they had alternately taken on each other, had inflamed the opposite factions to a high pitch of animosity. Henry himself, who had seen most of his near friends and relations perish in battle or by the exe-

King's prejudice against the house of York.

[c] Bacon, p. 579.

CHAPTER XXIV

cutioner, and who had been exposed in his own person to many hardships and dangers, had imbibed a violent antipathy to the York party, which no time or experience were ever able to efface. Instead of embracing the present happy opportunity of abolishing these fatal distinctions, of uniting his title with that of his consort, and of bestowing favour indiscriminately on the friends of both families; he carried to the throne all the partialities which belong to the head of a faction, and even the passions which are carefully guarded against by every true politician in that situation. To exalt the Lancastrian party, to depress the adherents of the house of York, were still the favourite objects of his pursuit: and through the whole course of his reign, he never forgot these early prepossessions. Incapable from his natural temper of a more enlarged and more benevolent system of policy, he exposed himself to many present inconveniences, by too anxiously guarding against that future possible event which might disjoin his title from that of the princess whom he espoused. And while he treated the Yorkists as enemies, he soon rendered them such, and taught them to discuss that right to the crown, which he so carefully kept separate; and to perceive its weakness and invalidity.

To these passions of Henry, as well as to his suspicious politics, we are to ascribe the measures, which he embraced two days after the battle of Bosworth. Edward Plantagenet, earl of Warwic, son of the duke of Clarence, was detained in a kind of confinement at Sherif-Hutton in Yorkshire, by the jealousy of his uncle, Richard; whose title to the throne was inferior to that of the young prince. Warwic had now reason to expect better treatment, as he was no obstacle to the succession either of Henry or Elizabeth; and from a youth of such tender years no danger could reasonably be apprehended. But Sir Robert Willoughby was dispatched by Henry with orders to take him from Sherif-Hutton, to convey him to the Tower, and to detain him in close custody.[d] The same messenger carried directions, that the princess Elizabeth, who had been confined to the same place, should be conducted to London, in order to meet Henry, and there celebrate her nuptials.

Henry himself set out for the capital, and advanced by slow journies. Not to rouse the jealousy of the people, he took care to

[d] Bacon, p. 579. Polydore Virgil, p. 565.

avoid all appearance of military triumph, and so to restrain the insolence of victory, that every thing about him bore the appearance of an established monarch, making a peaceable progress through his dominions, rather than of a prince who had opened *His joyful* his way to the throne by force of arms. The acclamations of the *reception* people were every where loud, and no less sincere and hearty. *in London.* Besides that a young and victorious prince, on his accession, was naturally the object of popularity; the nation promised themselves great felicity from the new scene which opened before them. During the course of near a whole century the kingdom had been laid waste by domestic wars and convulsions; and if at any time the noise of arms had ceased, the sound of faction and discontent still threatened new disorders. Henry, by his marriage with Elizabeth, seemed to ensure a union of the contending titles of the two families; and having prevailed over a hated tyrant, who had anew disjointed the succession even of the house of York, and had filled his own family with blood and murder, he was, everywhere, attended with the unfeigned favour of the people. Numerous and splendid troops of gentry and nobility accompanied his progress. The mayor and companies of London received him as he approached the city: The crouds of people and citizens were zealous in their expressions of satisfaction. But Henry, amidst this general effusion of joy, discovered still the stateliness and reserve of his temper, which made him scorn to court popularity: He entered London in a close chariot, and would not gratify the people with a sight of their new sovereign.

But the king did not so much neglect the favour of the people, as to delay giving them assurances of his marriage with the princess Elizabeth, which he knew to be so passionately desired by the nation. On his leaving Britanny, he had artfully dropped some hints, that, if he should succeed in his enterprize, and obtain the crown of England, he would espouse Anne, the heir of that dutchy; and the report of this engagement had already reached England, and had begotten anxiety in the people, and even in Elizabeth herself. Henry took care to dissipate these apprehensions, by solemnly renewing, before the council and principal nobility, the promise which he had already given to celebrate his nuptials with the English princess. But though bound by honour, as well as by interest, to complete this alliance, he was resolved to

CHAPTER XXIV

postpone it, till the ceremony of his own coronation should be finished, and till his title should be recognized by parliament. Still anxious to support his personal and hereditary right to the throne, he dreaded lest a preceding marriage with the princess should imply a participation of sovereignty in her, and raise doubts of his own title by the house of Lancaster. *His coronation.*

There raged at that time in London, and other parts of the kingdom, a species of malady, unknown to any other age or nation, the Sweating sickness, which occasioned the sudden death of great multitudes; though it seemed not to be propagated by any contagious infection, but arose from the general disposition of the air and of the human body. In less than twenty-four hours the patient commonly died or recovered; but when the pestilence had exerted its fury for a few weeks, it was observed, either from alterations in the air, or from a more proper regimen, which had been discovered, to be considerably abated.*ε* Preparations were then made for the ceremony of Henry's coronation. In order to heighten the splendor of that spectacle he bestowed the rank of knight banneret on twelve persons; and he conferred peerages on three. Jasper earl of Pembroke, his uncle, was created duke of Bedford; Thomas lord Stanley, his father-in-law, earl of Derby; and Edward Courteney, earl of Devonshire. At the coronation likewise there appeared a new institution, which the king had established for security as well as pomp, a band of fifty archers, who were termed yeomen of the guard. But lest the people should take umbrage at this unusual symptom of jealousy in the prince, as if it implied a personal diffidence of his subjects, he declared the institution to be perpetual. The ceremony of coronation was performed by cardinal Bourchier, archbishop of Canterbury. *Sweating sickness.*

30th Oct.

The parliament being assembled at Westminster, the majority immediately appeared to be devoted partizans of Henry; all persons of another disposition, either declining to stand in those dangerous times, or being obliged to dissemble their principles and inclinations. The Lancastrian party had every where been successful in the elections; and even many had been returned, who, during the prevalence of the house of York, had been exposed to the rigour of law, and had been condemned by sentence of attainder *7th Nov. A parliament*

ε Polydore Virgil, p. 567.

and outlawry. Their right to take seats in the house being questioned, the case was referred to all the judges, who assembled in the Exchequer Chamber, in order to deliberate on so delicate a subject. The opinion delivered was prudent, and contained a just temperament between law and expediency.[f] The judges determined, that the members attainted should forbear taking their seat till an act were passed for the reversal of their attainder. There was no difficulty in obtaining this act; and in it were comprehended a hundred and seven persons of the king's party![g]

But a scruple was started of a nature still more important. The king himself had been attainted; and his right of succession to the crown might thence be exposed to some doubt. The judges extricated themselves from this dangerous question, by asserting it as a maxim; "That the crown takes away all defects and stops in blood; and that from the time the king assumed royal authority, the fountain was cleared, and all attainders and corruptions of blood discharged."[h] Besides that the case, from its urgent necessity, admitted of no deliberation; the judges probably thought, that no sentence of a court of judicature had authority sufficient to bar the right of succession; that the heir of the crown was commonly exposed to such jealousy as might often occasion stretches of law and justice against him; and that a prince might even be engaged in unjustifiable measures during his predecessor's reign, without meriting on that account to be excluded from the throne, which was his birthright.

With a parliament so obsequious, the king could not fail of obtaining whatever act of settlement he was pleased to require. He seems only to have entertained some doubt within himself on what claim he should found his pretensions. In his speech to the parliament he mentioned his just title by hereditary right: But lest that title should not be esteemed sufficient, he subjoined his claim by the judgment of God, who had given him victory over his enemies. And again, lest this pretension should be interpreted as assuming a right of conquest, he ensured to his subjects the full enjoyment of their former properties and possessions.

Entail of the crown.

The entail of the crown was drawn, according to the sense of the king, and probably in words, dictated by him. He made no

[f] Bacon, p. 581.   [g] Rot. Parl. I Hen. VII. n. 2, 3, 4–15, 17, 26–65.
[h] Bacon, p. 581.

CHAPTER XXIV

mention in it of the princess Elizabeth, nor of any branch of her family; but in other respects the act was compiled with sufficient reserve and moderation. He did not insist, that it should contain a declaration or recognition of his preceding right; as on the other hand, he avoided the appearance of a new law or ordinance. He chose a middle course, which, as is generally unavoidable in such cases, was not entirely free from uncertainty and obscurity. It was voted, "That the inheritance of the crown should rest, remain, and abide in the king";[i] but whether as rightful heir, or only as present possessor, was not determined. In like manner, Henry was contented that the succession should be secured to the heirs of his body; but he pretended not, in case of their failure, to exclude the house of York, or to give the preference to that of Lancaster: He left that great point ambiguous for the present, and trusted, that, if it should ever become requisite to determine it, future incidents would open the way for the decision.

But even after all these precautions, the king was so little satisfied with his own title, that, in the following year, he applied to papal authority for a confirmation of it; and as the court of Rome gladly laid hold of all opportunities, which the imprudence, weakness, or necessities of princes afforded it to extend its influence, Innocent VIII. the reigning pope, readily granted a bull, in whatever terms the king was pleased to desire. All Henry's titles, by succession, marriage, parliamentary choice, even conquest, are there enumerated; and to the whole the sanction of religion is added; excommunication is denounced against every one who should either disturb him in the present possession, or the heirs of his body. In the future succession, of the crown; and from this penalty, no criminal, except in the article of death, could be absolved but by the pope himself, or his special commissioners. It is difficult to imagine, that the security, derived from this bull, could be a compensation for the defect which it betrayed in Henry's title, and for the danger of thus inviting the pope to interpose in these concerns.

It was natural, and even laudable in Henry to reverse the attainders, which had passed against the partizans of the house of Lancaster: But the revenges, which he exercised against the adher-

---

[i] Bacon, p. 581.

ents of the York family, to which he was so soon to be allied, cannot be considered in the same light. Yet the parliament, at his instigation, passed an act of attainder against the late king himself, against the duke of Norfolk, the earl of Surrey, viscount Lovel, the lords Zouche and Ferrars of Chartley, Sir Walter and Sir James Harrington, Sir William Berkeley, Sir Humphrey Stafford, Catesby, and about twenty other gentlemen, who had fought on Richard's side in the battle of Bosworth. How men could be guilty of treason, by supporting the king in possession against the earl of Richmond, who assumed not the title of king, it is not easy to conceive; and nothing but a servile complaisance in the parliament could have engaged them to make this stretch of justice. Nor was it a small mortification to the people in general, to find, that the king, prompted either by avarice or resentment, could, in the very beginning of his reign, so far violate the cordial union, which had previously been concerted between the parties, and to the expectation of which he had plainly owed his succession to the throne.

The king, having gained so many points of consequence from the parliament, thought it not expedient to demand any supply from them, which the profound peace enjoyed by the nation, and *roth Dec.* the late forfeiture of Richard's adherents, seemed to render somewhat superfluous. The parliament, however, conferred on him during life the duty of tonnage and poundage, which had been enjoyed in the same manner by some of his immediate predecessors; and they added, before they broke up, other money bills of no great moment. The king, on his part, made returns of grace and favour to his people. He published his royal proclamation, offering pardon to all such as had taken arms, or formed any attempts against him; provided they submitted themselves to mercy by a certain day, and took the usual oath of fealty and allegiance. Upon this proclamation many came out of their sanctuaries; and the minds of men were every where much quieted. Henry chose to take wholly to himself the merit of an act of grace, so agreeable to the nation; rather than communicate it with the parliament, (as was his first intention) by passing a bill to that purpose. The earl of Surrey, however, though he had submitted, and delivered himself into the king's hands, was sent prisoner to the Tower.

During this parliament, the king also bestowed favours and

CHAPTER XXIV

honours on some particular persons, who were attached to him. Edward Stafford, eldest son of the duke of Buckingham, attainted in the late reign, was restored to the honours of his family, as well as to its fortune, which was very ample. This generosity, so unusual in Henry, was the effect of his gratitude to the memory of Buckingham, who had first concerted the plan of his elevation, and who by his own ruin had made way for that great event. Chandos of Britanny was created earl of Bath, Sir Giles Daubeny lord Daubeny, and Sir Robert Willoughby lord Broke. These were all the titles of nobility conferred by the king during this session of parliament.[k]

But the ministers, whom Henry most trusted and favoured, were not chosen from among the nobility, or even from among the laity. John Morton, and Richard Fox, two clergymen, persons of industry, vigilance, and capacity, were the men to whom he chiefly confided his affairs and secret counsels. They had shared with him all his former dangers and distresses; and he now took care to make them participate in his good fortune. They were both called to the privy council; Morton was restored to the bishopric of Ely, Fox was created bishop of Exeter. The former soon after, upon the death of Bourchier, was raised to the see of Canterbury. The latter was made privy seal; and successively, bishop of Bath and Wells, Durham, and Winchester. For Henry, as lord Bacon observes, loved to employ and advance prelates; because, having rich bishoprics to bestow, it was easy for him to reward their services: And it was his maxim to raise them by slow steps, and make them first pass through the inferior sees.[l] He probably expected, that, as they were naturally more dependant on him than the nobility, who, during that age, enjoyed possessions and jurisdictions dangerous to royal authority; so the prospect of farther elevation would render them still more active in his service, and more obsequious to his commands.

In presenting the bill of tonnage and poundage, the parliament, anxious to preserve the legal, undisputed succession to the crown, had petitioned Henry, with demonstrations of the greatest zeal, to espouse the princess Elizabeth; but they covered their true reason under the dutiful pretence of their desire to have heirs of

1486.
8th Jan.

[k] Polydore Virgil, p. 566.　[l] Bacon, p. 582.

*King's
marriage.*
his body. He now thought in earnest of satisfying the minds of his
people in that particular. His marriage was celebrated at London;
and that with greater appearance of universal joy, than either his
first entry or his coronation. Henry remarked with much displeasure this general favour borne to the house of York. The
suspicions, which arose from it, not only disturbed his tranquillity
during his whole reign; but bred disgust towards his consort herself, and poisoned all his domestic enjoyments. Though virtuous,
amiable, and obsequious to the last degree, she never met with a
proper return of affection or even of complaisance from her husband; and the malignant ideas of faction still, in his sullen mind,
prevailed over all the sentiments of conjugal tenderness.

The king had been carried along, with such a tide of success,
ever since his arrival in England, that he thought nothing could
withstand the fortune and authority which attended him. He now
resolved to make a progress into the North, where the friends of
the house of York, and even the partizans of Richard, were numerous; in hopes of curing, by his presence and conversation, the
prejudices of the malcontents. When he arrived at Nottingham, he
heard that viscount Lovel, with Sir Humphrey Stafford and
Thomas, his brother, had secretly withdrawn themselves from
their sanctuary at Colchester: But this news appeared not to him
of such importance as to stop his journey; and he proceeded for-
*An in-
surrec-
tion.*
ward to York. He there heard, that the Staffords had levied an
army, and were marching to besiege the city of Worcester: And
that Lovel, at the head of three or four thousand men, was approaching to attack him in York. Henry was not dismayed with this
intelligence. His active courage, full of resources, immediately
prompted him to find the proper remedy. Though surrounded
with enemies in these disaffected counties, he assembled a small
body of troops, in whom he could confide; and he put them under
the command of the duke of Bedford. He joined to them all his
own attendants; but he found that this hasty armament was more
formidable by their spirit and their zealous attachment to him,
than by the arms or military stores with which they were provided.
He therefore gave Bedford orders not to approach the enemy; but
previously to try every proper expedient to disperse them. Bedford published a general promise of pardon to the rebels; which
had a greater effect on their leader than on his followers. Lovel,

who had undertaken an enterprize that exceeded his courage and capacity, was so terrified with the fear of desertion among his troops, that he suddenly withdrew himself; and, after lurking some time in Lancashire, he made his escape into Flanders, where he was protected by the dutchess of Burgundy. His army submitted to the king's clemency; and the other rebels, hearing of this success, raised the siege of Worcester, and dispersed themselves. The Staffords took sanctuary in the church of Colnham, a village near Abingdon; but as it was found, that this church had not the privilege of giving protection to rebels, they were taken thence: The elder was executed at Tyburn; the younger, pleading that he had been misled by his brother, obtained a pardon.[m]

Henry's joy for this success was followed, some time after, by the birth of a prince, to whom he gave the name of Arthur, in memory of the famous British king of that name, from whom, it was pretended, the family of Tudor derived its descent.

20th Sept.

Though Henry had been able to defeat this hasty rebellion, raised by the relics of Richard's partizans, his government was become in general unpopular: The source of public discontent arose chiefly from his prejudices against the house of York, which was generally beloved by the nation, and which, for that very reason, became every day more the object of his hatred and jealousy. Not only a preference on all occasions, it was observed, was given to the Lancastrians; but many of the opposite party had been exposed to great severity, and had been bereaved of their fortunes by acts of attainder. A general resumption likewise had passed of all grants made by the princes of the house of York; and though this rigour had been covered under the pretence, that the revenue was become insufficient to support the dignity of the crown, and though the grants, during the later years of Henry VI. were resumed by the same law, yet the York party, as they were the principal sufferers by the resumption, thought it chiefly levelled against them. The severity, exercised against the earl of Warwic, begat compassion for youth and innocence, exposed to such oppression; and his confinement in the Tower, the very place where Edward's children had been murdered by their uncle, made the public expect a like catastrophe for him, and led them to make a

Discontents of the people.

---

[m] Polydore Virgil, p. 569.

comparison between Henry and that detested tyrant. And when it was remarked, that the queen herself met with harsh treatment, and even after the birth of a son, was not admitted to the honour of a public coronation, Henry's prepossessions were then concluded to be inveterate, and men became equally obstinate in their disgust to his government. Nor was the manner and address of the king calculated to cure these prejudices contracted against his administration; but had, in every thing, a tendency to promote fear, or at best reverence, rather than goodwill and affection.[n] While the high idea, entertained of his policy and vigour, retained the nobility and men of character in obedience; the effects of his unpopular government soon appeared, by incidents of an extraordinary nature.

Lambert Simnel.

There lived in Oxford, one Richard Simon, a priest, who possessed some subtlety, and still more enterprize and temerity. This man had entertained the design of disturbing Henry's government, by raising a pretender to his crown; and for that purpose, he cast his eyes on Lambert Simnel, a youth of fifteen years of age, who was son of a baker, and who, being endowed with understanding above his years, and address above his condition, seemed well fitted to personate a prince of royal extraction. A report had been spread among the people, and received with great avidity, that Richard, duke of York, second son of Edward IV. had, by a secret escape, saved himself from the cruelty of his uncle, and lay somewhere concealed in England. Simon, taking advantage of this rumour, had at first instructed his pupil to assume that name, which he found to be so fondly cherished by the public: But hearing afterwards a new report, that Warwic had made his escape from the Tower, and observing that this news was attended with no less, general satisfaction, he changed the plan of his imposture, and made Simnel personate that unfortunate prince.[o] Though the youth was qualified by nature for the part which he was instructed to act; yet was it remarked, that he was better informed in circumstances relating to the royal family, particularly in the adventure of the earl of Warwic, than he could be supposed to have learned from one of Simon's condition: And it was thence conjectured, that persons of higher rank, partizans of the house of York, had laid the

[n] Bacon, p. 583.   [o] Polydore Virgil, p. 569, 570.

plan of this conspiracy, and had conveyed proper instructions to the actors. The queen-dowager herself was exposed to suspicion; and it was indeed the general opinion, however unlikely it might seem, that she had secretly given her consent to the imposture. This woman was of a very restless disposition. Finding, that, instead of receiving the reward of her services, in contributing to Henry's elevation, she herself was fallen into absolute insignificance, her daughter treated with severity, and all her friends brought under subjection, she had conceived the most violent animosity against him, and had resolved to make him feel the effects of her resentment. She knew, that the impostor, however successful, might easily at last be set aside; and if a way could be found at his risque to subvert the government, she hoped that a scene might be opened, which, though difficult at present exactly to foresee, would gratify her revenge, and be on the whole less irksome to her, than that slavery and contempt, to which she was now reduced.[p]

But whatever care Simon might take to convey instruction to his pupil Simnel, he was sensible, that the imposture would not bear a close inspection; and he was therefore determined to open the first public scene of it in Ireland. That island, which was zealously attached to the house of York, and bore an affectionate regard to the memory of Clarence, Warwic's father, who had been their lieutenant, was improvidently allowed by Henry to remain in the same condition, in which he found it; and all the counsellors and officers, who had been appointed by his predecessor, still retained their authority. No sooner did Simnel present himself to Thomas Fitz-gerald, earl of Kildare, the deputy and claim his protection as the unfortunate Warwic, than that credulous nobleman, not suspecting so bold an imposture, gave attention to him, and began to consult some persons of rank with regard to this extraordinary incident. These he found even more sanguine in their zeal and belief than himself: And in proportion as the story diffused itself among those of lower condition, it became the object of still greater passion and credulity, till the people in Dublin with one consent tendered their allegiance to Simnel, as to the true Plantagenet. Fond of a novelty, which flattered their natural propension, they overlooked the daughters of Edward IV. who stood

[p] Polydore Virgil, p. 570.

Revolt of
Ireland.

before Warwic in the order of succession, they payed the pretended prince attendance as their sovereign, lodged him in the castle of Dublin, crowned him with a diadem taken from a statue of the virgin, and publicly proclaimed him king, by the appellation of Edward VI. The whole island followed the example of the capital; and not a sword was any where drawn in Henry's quarrel.

When this intelligence was conveyed to the king, it reduced him to some perplexity. Determined always to face his enemies in person, he yet scrupled at present to leave England, where, he suspected, the conspiracy was first framed, and where, he knew, many persons of condition, and the people in general, were much disposed to give it countenance. In order to discover the secret source of the contrivance, and take measures against this open revolt, he held frequent consultations with his ministers and counsellors, and laid plans for a vigorous defence of his authority, and the suppression of his enemies.

The first event, which followed these deliberations, gave surprize to the public: It was the seizure of the queen-dowager, the forfeiture of all her lands and revenue, and the close confinement of her person in the nunnery of Bermondesey. This act of authority was covered with a very thin pretence. It was alleged, that, notwithstanding the secret agreement to marry her daughter to Henry, she had yet yielded to the solicitations and menaces of Richard, and had delivered that princess and her sisters into the hands of the tyrant. This crime, which was now become obsolete, and might admit of alleviations, was therefore suspected not to be the real cause of the severity, with which she was treated; and men believed, that the king, unwilling to accuse so near a relation of a conspiracy against him, had cloaked his vengeance or precaution under colour of an offence known to the whole world.[q] They were afterwards the more confirmed in this suspicion, when they found, that the unfortunate queen, though she survived this disgrace several years, was never treated with any more lenity, but was allowed to end her life in poverty, solitude, and confinement.

The next measure of the king's was of a less exceptionable nature. He ordered that Warwic should be taken from the Tower, be led in procession through the streets of London, be conducted

---

[q] Bacon, p. 583. Polydore Virgil, p. 571.

CHAPTER XXIV

to St. Paul's, and there exposed to the view of the whole people. He even gave directions, that some men of rank, attached to the house of York, and best acquainted with the person of this prince, should approach him and converse with him: And he trusted, that these, being convinced of the absurd imposture of Simnel, would put a stop to the credulity of the populace. The expedient had its effect in England: But in Ireland the people still persisted in their revolt, and zealously retorted on the king the reproach of propagating an imposture, and of having shewn a counterfeit Warwic to the public.

Henry had soon reason to apprehend, that the design against him was not laid on such slight foundations as the absurdity of the contrivance seemed to indicate. John, earl of Lincoln, son of John de la Pole, duke of Suffolk, and of Elizabeth, eldest sister to Edward IV, was engaged to take part in the conspiracy. This nobleman, who possessed capacity and courage, had entertained very aspiring views; and his ambition was encouraged by the known intentions of his uncle, Richard, who had formed a design, in case he himself should die without issue, of declaring Lincoln successor to the crown. The king's jealousy against all eminent persons of the York party, and his rigour towards Warwic, had farther struck Lincoln with apprehensions, and made him resolve to seek for safety in the most dangerous counsels. Having fixed a secret correspondence with Sir Thomas Broughton, a man of great interest in Lancashire, he retired to Flanders, where Lovel had arrived a little before him; and he lived, during some time, in the court of his aunt the dutchess of Burgundy, by whom he had been invited over.

Margaret, widow of Charles the Bold, duke of Burgundy, not having any children of her own, attached herself with an entire friendship to her daughter-in-law, married to Maximilian, archduke of Austria; and after the death of that princess, she persevered in her affection to Philip and Margaret, her children, and occupied herself in the care of their education and of their persons. By her virtuous conduct and demeanour, she had acquired great authority among the Flemings, and lived with much dignity, as well as economy, upon that ample dowry, which she inherited from her husband. The resentments of this princess were no less warm than her friendships; and that spirit of faction, which it is so difficult for a social and sanguine temper to guard

Intrigues of the dutchess of Burgundy.

against, had taken strong possession of her heart, and entrenched somewhat on the probity, which shone forth in the other parts of her character. Hearing of the malignant jealousy, entertained by Henry against her family, and his oppression of all its partizans; she was moved with the highest indignation, and she determined to make him repent of that enmity, to which so many of her friends, without any reason or necessity, had fallen victims. After consulting with Lincoln and Lovel, she hired a body of two thousand veteran Germans, under the command of Martin Swart, a brave and experienced officer,[r] and sent them over, together with these two noblemen, to join Simnel in Ireland. The countenance, given by persons of such high rank, and the accession of this military force, much raised the courage of the Irish, and made them entertain the resolution of invading England, where they believed the spirit of disaffection as prevalent as it appeared to be in Ireland. The poverty also, under which they laboured, made it impossible for them to support any longer their new court and army, and inspired them with a strong desire of enriching themselves by plunder and preferment in England.

Henry was not ignorant of these intentions of his enemies; and he prepared himself for defence. He ordered troops to be levied in different parts of the kingdom, and put them under the command of the duke of Bedford, and earl of Oxford. He confined the marquis of Dorset, who, he suspected, would resent the injuries suffered by his mother, the queen dowager: And to gratify the people by an appearance of devotion, he made a pilgrimage to our lady of Walsingham, famous for miracles; and there offered up prayers for success and for deliverance from his enemies.

Being informed that Simnel was landed at Foudrey in Lancashire, he drew together his forces, and advanced towards the enemy as far as Coventry. The rebels had entertained hopes, that the disaffected counties in the North would rise in their favour: But the people in general, averse to join Irish and German invaders, convinced of Lambert's imposture, and kept in awe by the king's reputation for success and conduct, either remained in tranquillity, or gave assistance to the royal army. The earl of Lincoln, therefore, who commanded the rebels, finding no hopes but in

1487.

Lambert Simnel invades England.

---

[r] Polyd. Virg. p. 572, 573.

CHAPTER XXIV

victory, was determined to bring the matter to a speedy decision; and the king, supported by the native courage of his temper, and emboldened by a great accession of volunteers, who had joined him, under the earl of Shrewsbury and lord Strange, declined not the combat. The hostile armies met at Stoke in the county of Nottingham, and fought a battle, which was bloody, and more obstinately disputed than could have been expected from the inequality of their force. All the leaders of the rebels were resolved to conquer or to perish; and they inspired their troops with like resolution. The Germans also, being veteran and experienced soldiers, kept the event long doubtful; and even the Irish, though ill-armed and almost defenceless, showed themselves not defective in spirit and bravery. The king's victory was purchased with loss, but was entirely decisive. Lincoln, Broughton, and Swart, perished in the field of battle, with four thousand of their followers. As Lovel was never more heard of, he was believed to have undergone the same fate. Simnel, with his tutor, Simon, was taken prisoner. Simon, being a priest, was not tried at law, and was only committed to close custody: Simnel was too contemptible to be an object either of apprehension or resentment to Henry. He was pardoned, and made a scullion in the king's kitchen; whence he was afterwards advanced to the rank of a falconer.[s]

6th June. Battle of Stoke.

Henry had now leisure to revenge himself on his enemies. He made a progress into the northern parts, where he gave many proofs of his rigorous disposition. A strict enquiry was made after those who had assisted or favoured the rebels. The punishments were not all sanguinary: The king made his revenge subservient to his avarice. Heavy fines were levied upon the delinquents. The proceedings of the courts, and even the courts themselves, were arbitrary. Either the criminals were tried by commissioners appointed for the purpose, or they suffered punishment by sentence of a court-martial. And as a rumour had prevailed before the battle of Stoke, that the rebels had gained the victory, that the royal army was cut in pieces, and that the king himself had escaped by flight, Henry was resolved to interpret the belief or propagation of this report as a mark of disaffection; and he punished many for that pretended crime. But such, in this age, was the situation of the

[s] Bacon, p. 586. Pol. Virg. p. 574.

English government, that the royal prerogative, which was but imperfectly restrained during the most peaceable periods, was sure, in tumultuous, or even suspicious times, which frequently recurred, to break all bounds of law, and to violate public liberty.

After the king had gratified his rigour by the punishment of his enemies, he determined to give contentment to the people, in a point, which, though a mere ceremony, was passionately desired by them. The queen had been married near two years, but had not yet been crowned; and this affectation of delay had given great discontent to the public, and had been one principal source of the disaffection which prevailed. The king, instructed by experience, now finished the ceremony of her coronation; and to shew a disposition still more gracious, he restored to liberty the marquis of Dorset, who had been able to clear himself of all the suspicions entertained against him.

25th
Nov.

XXV

State of foreign affairs –
State of Scotland – of Spain – of the
Low Countries – of France – of Britanny –
French invasion of Britanny – French
embassy to England – Dissimulation of the
French court – An insurrection in the North –
suppressed – King sends forces into
Britanny – Annexation of Britanny to
France – A parliament – War with France –
Invasion of France – Peace with France –
Perkin Warbec – His imposture – He is
avowed by the dutchess of Burgundy –
and by many of the English nobility –
Trial and execution of Stanley –
A parliament

THE KING acquired great reputation throughout Europe by the vigorous and prosperous conduct of his domestic affairs: But as some incidents, about this time, invited him to look abroad, and exert himself in behalf of his allies, it will be necessary, in order to give a just account of his foreign measures, to explain the situation of the neighbouring kingdoms; beginning with Scotland, which lies most contiguous.

1488.
State of
foreign
affairs.

23

State of Scotland. The kingdom of Scotland had not yet attained that state, which distinguishes a civilized monarchy, and which enables the government, by the force of its laws and institutions alone, without any extraordinary capacity in the sovereign, to maintain itself in order and tranquillity. James III, who now filled the throne, was a prince of little industry and of a narrow genius; and though it behoved him to yield the reins of government to his ministers, he had never been able to make any choice, which could give contentment both to himself and to his people. When he bestowed his confidence on any of the principal nobility, he found, that they exalted their own family to such a height, as was dangerous to the prince, and gave umbrage to the state: When he conferred favour on any person of meaner birth, on whose submission he could more depend, the barons of his kingdom, enraged at the power of an upstart minion, proceeded to the utmost extremities against their sovereign. Had Henry entertained the ambition of conquests, a tempting opportunity now offered of reducing that kingdom to subjection; but as he was probably sensible, that a warlike people, though they might be over-run by reason of their domestic divisions, could not be retained in obedience without a regular military force, which was then unknown in England, he rather intended the renewal of the peace with Scotland, and sent an embassy to James for that purpose. But the Scots, who never desired a durable peace with England, and who deemed their security to consist in constantly preserving themselves in a warlike posture, would not agree to more than a seven years truce, which was accordingly concluded.[']

The European states on the continent were then hastening fast to the situation, in which they have remained, without any material alteration, for near three centuries; and began to unite themselves *State of Spain.* into one extensive system of policy, which comprehended the chief powers of Christendom. Spain, which had hitherto been almost entirely occupied within herself, now became formidable by the union of Aragon and Castile, in the persons of Ferdinand and Isabella, who, being princes of great capacity, employed their force in enterprizes the most advantageous to their combined monarchy. The conquest of Granada from the Moors was then under-

['] Polyd. Virg. p. 575.

CHAPTER XXV

taken, and brought near to a happy conclusion. And in that expedition the military genius of Spain was revived; honour and security were attained; and her princes, no longer kept in awe by a domestic enemy so dangerous, began to enter into all the transactions of Europe, and make a great figure in every war and negociation.

Maximilian, king of the Romans, son of the emperor Frederic, *Of the* had, by his marriage with the heiress of Burgundy, acquired an *Low* interest in the Netherlands; and though the death of his consort *Countries.* had weakened his connexions with that country, he still pretended to the government as tutor to his son Philip, and his authority had been acknowledged by Brabant, Holland, and several of the provinces. But as Flanders and Hainault still refused to submit to his regency, and even appointed other tutors to Philip, he had been engaged in long wars against that obstinate people, and never was able thoroughly to subdue their spirit. That he might free himself from the opposition of France, he had concluded a peace with Lewis XI. and had given his daughter Margaret, then an infant, in marriage to the dauphin; together with Artois, Fanche-Compté, and Charolois, as her dowry. But this alliance had not produced the desired effect. The dauphin succeeded to the crown of France by the appellation of Charles VIII. but Maximilian still found the mutinies of the Flemings fomented by the intrigues of the court of France.

France, during the two preceding reigns, had made a mighty *State of* encrease in power and greatness; and had not other states of Eu- *France.* rope at the same time received an accession of force, it had been impossible to have retained her within her ancient boundaries. Most of the great fiefs, Normandy, Champagne, Anjou, Dauphiny, Guienne, Provence, and Burgundy, had been united to the crown; the English had been expelled from all their conquests; the authority of the prince had been raised to such a height as enabled him to maintain law and order; a considerable military force was kept on foot, and the finances were able to support it. Lewis XI. indeed, from whom many of these advantages were derived, was dead, and had left his son, in early youth and ill educated, to sustain the weight of the monarchy: But having entrusted the government to his daughter, Anne, lady of Beaujeu, a woman of spirit and capacity, the French power suffered no check or decline.

On the contrary, this princess formed the great project, which at last she happily effected, of uniting to the crown Britanny, the last and most independent fief of the monarchy.

Of Britanny. Francis II. duke of Britanny, conscious of his own incapacity for government, had resigned himself to the direction of Peter Landais, a man of mean birth, more remarkable for abilities than for virtue or integrity. The nobles of Britanny, displeased with the great advancement of this favourite, had even proceeded to disaffection against their sovereign; and after many tumults and disorders, they at last united among themselves, and in a violent manner seized, tried, and put to death the obnoxious minister. Dreading the resentment of the prince for this invasion of his authority, many of them retired to France; others, for protection and safety, maintained a secret correspondence with the French ministry, who, observing the great dissentions among the Bretons, thought the opportunity favourable for invading the dutchy; and so much the rather as they could cover their ambition under the specious pretence of providing for domestic security.

Lewis, duke of Orleans, first prince of the blood, and presumptive heir of the monarchy, had disputed the administration with the lady of Beaujeu; and though his pretensions had been rejected by the states, he still maintained cabals with many of the grandees, and laid schemes for subverting the authority of that princess. Finding his conspiracies detected, he took to arms, and fortified himself in Beaugenci; but as his revolt was precipitate, before his confederates were ready to join him, he had been obliged to submit, and to receive such conditions as the French ministry were pleased to impose upon him. Actuated however by his ambition, and even by his fears, he soon retired out of France, and took shelter with the duke of Britanny, who was desirous of strengthening himself against the designs of the lady of Beaujeu by the friendship and credit of the duke of Orleans. This latter prince also, perceiving the ascendant which he soon acquired over the duke of Britanny, had engaged many of his partizans to join him at that court, and had formed the design of aggrandizing himself by a marriage with Anne, the heir of that opulent dutchy.

The barons of Britanny, who saw all favour engrossed by the duke of Orleans and his train, renewed a stricter correspondence with France, and even invited the French king to make an invasion

CHAPTER XXV

on their country. Desirous however of preserving its independency, they had regulated the number of succours, which France was to send them, and had stipulated that no fortified place in Britany should remain in the possession of that monarchy: A vain precaution, where revolted subjects treat with a power so much superior! The French invaded Britany with forces three times more numerous than those which they had promised to the barons; and advancing into the heart of the country, laid siege to Ploermel. To oppose them, the duke raised a numerous, but ill-disciplined army, which he put under the command of the duke of Orleans, the count of Dunois, and others of the French nobility. The army, discontented with this choice, and jealous of their confederates, soon disbanded, and left their prince with too small a force to keep the field against his invaders. He retired to Vannes; but being hotly pursued by the French, who had now made themselves masters of Ploermel, he escaped to Nantz; and the enemy, having previously taken and garrisoned Vannes, Dinant, and other places, laid close siege to that city. The barons of Britany, finding their country menaced with total subjection, began gradually to withdraw from the French army, and to make peace with their sovereign.

French invasion of Britanny.

This desertion, however, of the Bretons discouraged not the court of France from pursuing her favourite project of reducing Britany to subjection. The situation of Europe appeared favourable to the execution of this design. Maximilian was indeed engaged in close alliance with the duke of Britany, and had even opened a treaty for marrying his daughter; but he was on all occasions so indigent, and at that time so disquieted by the mutinies of the Flemings, that little effectual assistance could be expected from him. Ferdinand was entirely occupied in the conquest of Granada; and it was also known, that, if France would resign to him Rousillon and Cerdagne, to which he had pretensions, she could at any time engage him to abandon the interests of Britany. England alone was both enabled by her power, and engaged by her interests, to support the independency of that dutchy; and the most dangerous opposition was therefore, by Anne of Beaujeu, expected from that quarter. In order to cover her real designs, no sooner was she informed of Henry's success against Simnel and his partizans, than she dispatched ambassadors to the court of London, and made professions of the greatest trust and confidence in that monarch.

French embassy to England. The ambassadors, after congratulating Henry on his late victory, and communicating to him, in the most cordial manner, as to an intimate friend, some successes of their master against Maximilian, came in the progress of their discourse to mention the late transactions in Britanny. They told him that the duke having given protection to French fugitives and rebels, the king had been necessitated, contrary to his intention and inclination, to carry war into that dutchy: That the honour of the crown was interested not to suffer a vassal so far to forget his duty to his liege lord; nor was the security of the government less concerned to prevent the consequences of this dangerous temerity: That the fugitives were no mean or obscure persons; but, among others, the duke of Orleans, first prince of the blood, who, finding himself obnoxious to justice for treasonable practices in France, had fled into Britanny; where he still persevered in laying schemes of rebellion against his sovereign: That the war being thus, on the part of the French monarch, entirely defensive, it would immediately cease, when the duke of Britanny, by returning to his duty, should remove the causes of it: That their master was sensible of the obligations, which the duke, in very critical times, had conferred on Henry; but it was known also, that, in times still more critical, he or his mercenary counsellors had deserted him, and put his life in the utmost hazard: That his sole refuge in these desperate extremities had been the court of France, which not only protected his person, but supplied him with men and money, with which, aided by his own valour and conduct, he had been enabled to mount the throne of England: That France, in this transaction, had, from friendship to Henry, acted contrary to what, in a narrow view, might be esteemed her own interest; since, instead of an odious tyrant, she had contributed to establish on a rival throne a prince endowed with such virtue and abilities: And that as both the justice of the cause and the obligations conferred on Henry thus preponderated on the side of France, she reasonably expected that, if the situation of his affairs did not permit him to give her assistance, he would at least preserve a neutrality between the contending parties.[u]

[u] Bacon, p. 589.

CHAPTER XXV

This discourse of the French ambassadors was plausible; and to give it greater weight, they communicated to Henry, as in confidence, their master's intention, after he should have settled the differences with Britanny, to lead an army into Italy, and make good his pretensions to the kingdom of Naples: A project, which, they knew, would give no umbrage to the court of England. But all these artifices were in vain employed against the penetration of the king. He clearly saw, that France had entertained the view of subduing Britanny; but he also perceived, that she would meet with great, and, as he thought, insuperable difficulties in the execution of her project. The native force of that dutchy, he knew, had always been considerable, and had often, without any foreign assistance, resisted the power of France; the natural temper of the French nation, he imagined, would make them easily abandon any enterprize, which required perseverance; and as the heir of the crown was confederated with the duke of Britanny, the ministers would be still more remiss in prosecuting a scheme, which must draw on them his resentment and displeasure. Should even these internal obstructions be removed, Maximilian, whose enmity to France was well known, and who now paid his addresses to the heiress of Britanny, would be able to make a diversion on the side of Flanders; nor could it be expected that France, if she prosecuted such ambitious projects, would be allowed to remain in tranquillity by Ferdinand and Isabella. Above all, he thought, the French court could never expect, that England, so deeply interested to preserve the independancy of Britanny, so able by her power and situation to give effectual and prompt assistance, would permit such an accession of force to her rival. He imagined, therefore, that the ministers of France, convinced of the impracticability of their scheme, would at last embrace pacific views, and would abandon an enterprize so obnoxious to all the potentates of Europe.

This reasoning of Henry was solid, and might justly engage him in dilatory and cautious measures: But there entered into his conduct another motive, which was apt to draw him beyond the just bounds, because founded on a ruling passion. His frugality, which by degrees degenerated into avarice, made him averse to all warlike enterprizes and distant expeditions, and engaged him previously to try the expedient of negociation. He dispatched Urswic, his almoner, a man of address and abilities, to make offer of his mediation to the contending parties: An offer, which, he thought, if accepted by France, would soon lead to a composure of all differences; if refused or eluded, would at least discover the perseverance of that court in her ambitious projects. Urswic found the lady of Beaüjeu, now dutchess of Bourbon, engaged in the siege of Nantz, and had the satisfaction to find that his master's offer of mediation was readily embraced, and with many expressions of confidence and moderation. That able princess concluded, that the duke of Orleans, who governed the court of Britanny, foreseeing that every accommodation must be made at his expence, would use all his interest to have Henry's proposal rejected; and would by that means make an apology for the French measures, and draw on the Bretons the reproach of obstinacy and injustice. The event justified her prudence. When the English ambassador made the same offer to the duke of Britanny, he received for answer, in the name of that prince, that having so long acted the part of protector and guardian to Henry, during his youth and adverse fortune, he had expected, from a monarch of such virtue, more effectual assistance in his present distresses, than a barren offer of mediation, which suspended not the progress of the French arms: That if Henry's gratitude were not sufficient to engage him in such a measure, his prudence, as king of England, should discover to him the pernicious consequences attending the conquest of Britanny, and its annexation to the crown of France: That that kingdom, already too powerful, would be enabled, by so great an accession of force, to display, to the ruin of England, that hostile disposition, which had always subsisted between those rival nations: That Britanny, so useful an ally, which, by its situation, gave the English an entrance into the heart of France; being annexed to that kingdom, would be equally enabled from its situation to disturb, either by pyracies or naval armaments, the commerce and peace of England: And that, if the duke rejected Henry's mediation, it proceeded neither from an inclination to a war, which he experienced to be ruinous to him, nor from a confidence in his own force, which he knew to be much inferior to that of the enemy; but on the contrary, from a sense of his present necessities, which must engage the king to act the part of his confederate, not that of a mediator.

When this answer was reported to the king, he abandoned not

*Dissimu-
lation
of the
French
court.*

CHAPTER XXV

the plan which he had formed: He only concluded, that some more time was requisite to quell the obstinacy of the Bretons and make them submit to reason. And when he learned that the people of Britanny, anxious for their duke's safety, had formed a tumultuary army of 60,000 men, and had obliged the French to raise the siege of Nantz, he fortified himself the more in his opinion, that the court of France would at last be reduced, by multiplied obstacles and difficulties, to abandon the project of reducing Britanny to subjection. He continued therefore his scheme of negotiation, and thereby exposed himself to be deceived by the artifices of the French ministry; who, still pretending pacific intentions, sent lord Bernard Daubigni. a Scotch man of quality, to London, and pressed Henry not to be discouraged in offering his mediation to the court of Britanny. The king on his part dispatched another embassy, consisting of Urswic, the abbot of Abingdon, and Sir Richard Tonstal, who carried new proposals for an amicable treaty. No effectual succours, meanwhile, were provided for the distressed Bretons. Lord Woodville, brother to the queen dowager, having asked leave to raise underhand a body of volunteers and to transport them into Britanny, met with a refusal from the king, who was desirous of preserving the appearance of a strict neutrality. That nobleman, however, still persisted in his purpose. He went over to the Isle of Wight, of which he was governor; levied a body of 400 men; and having at last obtained, as is supposed, the secret permission of Henry, sailed with them to Britanny. This *28th* enterprize proved fatal to the leader, and brought small relief to *July.* the unhappy duke. The Bretons rashly engaged in a general action with the French at St. Aubin, and were discomfited. Woodville and all the English were put to the sword; together with a body of Bretons, who had been accoutered in the garb of Englishmen, in order to strike a greater terror into the French, to whom the martial prowess of that nation was always formidable.[w] The duke of Orleans, the prince of Orange, and many other persons of rank were taken prisoners: And the military force of Britanny was totally broken. The death of the duke, which followed soon after, *9th Sept.* threw affairs into still greater confusion, and seemed to threaten the state with a final subjection.

[w] Argertíe Hist. de Fretagne, liv. xii.

Though the king did not prepare against these events, so hurtful to the interests of England, with sufficient vigour and precaution, he had not altogether overlooked them. Determined to maintain a pacific conduct, as far as the situation of affairs would permit, he yet knew the warlike temper of his subjects, and observed, that their ancient and inveterate animosity to France was now revived by the prospect of this great accession to her power and grandeur. He resolved therefore to make advantage of this disposition, and draw some supplies from the people, on pretence of giving assistance to the duke of Britanny. He had summoned a parliament at Westminster;[x] and he soon persuaded them to grant him a considerable subsidy.[y] But this supply, though voted by parliament, involved the king in unexpected difficulties. The counties of Durham and York, always discontented with Henry's government, and farther provoked by the late oppressions, under which they had laboured, after the suppression of Simnel's rebellion, resisted the commissioners who were appointed to levy the tax. The commissioners, terrified with this appearance of sedition, made application to the earl of Northumberland, and desired of him advice and assistance in the execution of their office. That nobleman thought the matter of importance enough to consult the king; who, unwilling to yield to the humours of a discontented populace, and foreseeing the pernicious consequence of such a precedent, renewed his orders for strictly levying the imposition. Northumberland summoned together the justices and chief freeholders, and delivered the king's commands in the most imperious terms, which, he thought, would inforce obedience, but which tended only to provoke the people, and make them believe him the adviser of those orders which he delivered to them.[z] They flew to arms, attacked Northumberland in his house, and put him to death. Having incurred such deep guilt, their mutinous humour prompted them to declare against the king himself; and being instigated by John Achamber, a seditious fellow of low birth, they chose Sir John Egremond their leader, and prepared themselves for a vigorous resistance. Henry was not dismayed with an insurrection so precipitate and ill-supported. He immediately levied a

An insurrection in the North,

[x] 9th November, 1487.   [y] Polydore Virgil, p. 579, says, that this imposition was a capitation tax; the other historians say, it was a tax of two shillings in the pound.   [z] Bacon, p. 595.

force which he put under the command of the earl of Surrey, whom he had freed from confinement, and received into favour. His intention was to send down these troops, in order to check the progress of the rebels; while he himself should follow with a greater body, which would absolutely insure success. But Surrey thought himself strong enough to encounter alone a raw and un-armed multitude; and he succeeded in the attempt. The rebels *suppressed.* were dissipated; John Achamber was taken prisoner, and after-wards executed with some of his accomplices; Sir John Egremond fled to the dutchess of Burgundy, who gave him protection; the greater number of the rebels received a pardon.

Henry had probably expected, when he obtained this grant from parliament, that he should be able to terminate the affair of Britany by negociation, and that he might thereby fill his coffers with the money levied by the imposition. But as the distresses of the Bretons still multiplied, and became every day more urgent; he found himself under the necessity of taking more vigorous mea-sures, in order to support them. On the death of the duke, the French had revived some antiquated claims to the dominion of the dutchy; and as the duke of Orleans was now captive in France, their former pretence for hostilities could no longer serve as a *1489.* cover to their ambition. The king resolved therefore to engage as auxiliary to Britany; and to consult the interests, as well as desires of his people, by opposing himself to the progress of the French power. Besides entering into a league with Maximilian, and an-other with Ferdinand, which were distant resources, he levied a body of troops, to the number of 6000 men, with an intention of transporting them into Britany. Still anxious, however, for the re-payment of his expences, he concluded a treaty with the young dutchess, by which she engaged to deliver into his hands two sea-port towns, there to remain till she should entirely refund the charges of the armament.[a] Though he engaged for the service of these troops during the space of ten months only, yet was the *King* dutchess obliged, by the necessity of her affairs, to submit to such *sends* rigid conditions, imposed by an ally, so much concerned in interest *forces* to protect her. The forces arrived under the command of lord *into* Willoughby of Broke; and made the Bretons, during some time, *Britany.*

[a] Du Tillet, Recueil des Traites.

masters of the field. The French retired into their garrisons; and expected by dilatory measures to waste the fire of the English, and disgust them with the enterprize. The scheme was well laid, and met with success. Lord Broke found such discord and confusion in the counsels of Britanny, that no measures could be concerted for any undertaking; no supply obtained; no provisions, carriages, artillery, or military stores procured. The whole court was rent into factions: No one minister had acquired the ascendant: And whatever project was formed by one, was sure to be traversed by another. The English, disconcerted in every enterprize, by these animosities and uncertain counsels, returned home as soon as the time of their service was elapsed; leaving only a small garrison in those towns which had been configured into their hands. During their stay in Britanny, they had only contributed still farther to waste the country; and by their departure, they left it entirely at the mercy of the enemy. So feeble was the succour, which Henry in this important conjuncture afforded his ally, whom the invasion of a foreign enemy, concurring with domestic dissensions, had reduced to the utmost distress.

The great object of the domestic dissensions in Britanny was the disposal of the young dutchess in marriage. The mareschal Rieux, favoured by Henry, seconded the suit of the lord d'Albret, who led some forces to her assistance. The chancellor Montauban, observing the aversion of the dutchess to this suitor, insisted, that a petty prince, such as d'Albret, was unable to support Anne in her present extremities; and he recommended some more powerful *1490.* alliance, particularly that of Maximilian, king of the Romans. This party at last prevailed; the marriage with Maximilian was celebrated by proxy; and the dutchess thenceforth assumed the title of queen of the Romans. But this magnificent appellation was all she gained by her marriage. Maximilian, destitute of troops and money, and embarrassed with the continual revolts of the Flemings, could send no succour to his distressed consort: While d'Albret, enraged at the preference given to his rival, deserted her cause, and received the French into Nantz, the most important place in the dutchy, both for strength and riches.

The French court now began to change their scheme with regard to the subjection of Britanny. Charles had formerly been affianced to Margaret daughter of Maximilian; who, though too

CHAPTER XXV

young for the consummation of her marriage, had been sent to Paris to be educated, and at this time bore the title of queen of France. Besides the rich dowry, which she brought the king, she was, after her brother Philip, then in early youth, heir to all the dominions of the house of Burgundy; and seemed in many respects the most proper match, that could be chosen for the young monarch. These circumstances had so blinded both Maximilian and Henry, that they never suspected any other intentions in the French court, nor were they able to discover, that engagements, seemingly so advantageous and so solemnly entered into, could be infringed and set aside. But Charles began to perceive, that the conquest of Britany, in opposition to the natives, and to all the great powers of Christendom, would prove a difficult enterprize; and that even, if he should over-run the country and make himself master of the fortresses, it would be impossible for him long to retain possession of them. The marriage alone of the dutchess could fully re-annex that fief to the crown; and the present and certain enjoyment of so considerable a territory seemed preferable to the prospect of inheriting the dominions of the house of Burgundy; a prospect which became every day more distant and precarious. Above all, the marriage of Maximilian and Anne, appeared destructive to the grandeur and even security of the French monarchy; while that prince, possessing Flanders on the one hand, and Britany on the other, might thus, from both quarters, make inroads into the heart of the country. The only remedy for these evils was therefore concluded to be the dissolution of the two marriages, which had been celebrated, but not consummated; and the espousal of the dutchess of Britany by the king of France.

It was necessary, that this expedient, which had not been foreseen by any court in Europe, and which they were all so much interested to oppose, should be kept profound secret, and should be discovered to the world only by the full execution of it. The measures of the French ministry in the conduct of this delicate enterprize were wise and political. While they pressed Britany with all the rigours of war, they secretly gained the count of Dunois, who possessed great authority with the Bretons; and having also engaged in their interests the prince of Orange, cousin-german to the dutchess, they gave him his liberty, and sent him into Britany. These partizans, supported by other emissaries of

France, prepared the minds of men for the great revolution projected and displayed, though still with many precautions, all the advantages of a union with the French monarchy. They represented to the barons of Britanny, that their country, harassed during so many years with perpetual war, had need of some repose, and of a solid and lasting peace with the only power that was formidable to them: That their alliance with Maximilian was not able to afford them even present protection, and by closely uniting them to a power, which was rival to the greatness of France, fixed them in perpetual enmity with that potent monarchy: That their vicinity exposed them first to the inroads of the enemy; and the happiest event, which, in such a situation, could befal them, would be to attain a peace, though by a final subjection to France, and by the loss of that liberty, transmitted to them from their ancestors: And that any other expedient, compatible with the honour of the state, and their duty to their sovereign, was preferable to a scene of such disorder and devastation.

These suggestions had influence with the Bretons: But the chief difficulty lay in surmounting the prejudices of the young dutchess herself. That princess had imbibed a strong prepossession against the French nation, particularly against Charles, the author of all the calamities, which, from her earliest infancy, had befallen her family. She had also fixed her affections on Maximilian; and as she now deemed him her husband, she could not, she thought, without incurring the greatest guilt, and violating the most solemn engagements, contract a marriage with any other *1491.* person. In order to overcome her obstinacy, Charles gave the duke of Orleans his liberty, who, though formerly a suitor to the dutchess, was now contented to ingratiate himself with the king, by employing in his favour all the interest which he still possessed in Britanny. Mareschal Rieux and chancellor Montauban were reconciled by his mediation; and these rival ministers now concurred with the prince of Orange and the count of Dunois, in pressing the conclusion of a marriage with Charles. By their suggestion, Charles advanced with a powerful army and invested Rennes, at that time the residence of the dutchess; who, assailed on *Annex-* all hands, and finding none to support her in her inflexibility, at *ation of* last opened the gates of the city, and agreed to espouse the king of *Britanny* France. She was married at Langey in Touraine; conducted to St. *to France.*

CHAPTER XXV

Dennis, where she was crowned; thence made her entry into Paris, amidst the joyful acclamations of the people, who regarded this marriage as the most prosperous event that could have befallen the monarchy.

The triumph and success of Charles was the most sensible mortification to the king of the Romans. He had lost a considerable territory, which he thought he had acquired, and an accomplished princess whom he had espoused; he was affronted in the person of his daughter Margaret, who was sent back to him, after she had been treated during some years as queen of France; he had reason to reproach himself with his own supine security, in neglecting the consummation of his marriage, which was easily practicable for him, and which would have rendered the tye indissoluble: These considerations threw him into the most violent rage, which he vented in very indecent expressions; and he threatened France with an invasion from the united arms of Austria, Spain, and England.

The king of England had also just reason to reproach himself with misconduct in this important transaction, and though the affair had terminated in a manner which he could not precisely foresee, his negligence, in leaving his most useful ally so long exposed to the invasion of superior power, could not but appear on reflection the result of timid caution and narrow politics. As he valued himself on his extensive foresight and profound judgment, the ascendant acquired over him, by a raw youth, such as Charles, could not but give him the highest displeasure; and prompt him to seek vengeance, after all remedy for his miscarriage was become absolutely impracticable. But he was farther actuated by avarice, a motive still more predominant with him than either pride or revenge; and he sought, even from his present disappointments, the gratification of this ruling passion. On pretence of a French war, *7th July.* he issued a commission for levying a *Benevolence* on his people;[b] a species of taxation, which had been abolished by a recent law of Richard III. This violence (for such it really was) fell chiefly on the commercial part of the nation, who were possessed of the ready money. London alone contributed to the amount of near 10,000

[b] Rymer, vol. xii. p. 446. Bacon says that the benevolence was levied with consent of parliament, which is a mistake.

pounds. Archbishop Morton, the chancellor, instructed the commissioners to employ a dilemma, in which every one might be comprehended: If the persons applied to, lived frugally, they were told, that their parsimony must necessarily have enriched them: If their method of living were splendid and hospitable, they were concluded to be opulent on account of their expences. This device was by some called chancellor Morton's fork, by others his crutch.

So little apprehensive was the king of a parliament on account of his levying this arbitrary imposition, that he soon after summoned that assembly to meet at Westminster; and he even expected to enrich himself farther by working on their passions and prejudices. He knew the displeasure, which the English had conceived against France, on account of the acquisition of Britanny; and he took care to insist on that topic, in the speech, which he himself pronounced to the parliament. He told them, that France, elated with her late successes, had even proceeded to a contempt of England, and had refused to pay the tribute, which Lewis XI. had stipulated to Edward IV. That it became so warlike a nation as the English to be rouzed by this indignity, and not to limit their pretensions merely to repelling the present injury: That for his part, he was determined to lay claim to the crown itself of France, and to maintain by force of arms so just a title, transmitted to him by his gallant ancestors: That Crecy, Poictiers, and Azincour were sufficient to instruct them in their superiority over the enemy; nor did he despair of adding new names to the glorious catalogue: That a king of France had been prisoner in London, and a king of England had been crowned at Paris; events which should animate them to an emulation of like glory with that which had been enjoyed by their forefathers: That the domestic dissentions of England had been the sole cause of her losing these foreign dominions; and her present internal union would be the effectual means of recovering them: That where such lasting honour was in view, and such an important acquisition, it became not brave men to repine at the advance of a little treasure: And that for his part, he was determined to make the war maintain itself, and hoped, by the invasion of so opulent a kingdom as France, to encrease, rather than diminish, the riches of the nation.[e]

27th Oct.

A parliament.

---

[e] Bacon, p. 601.

CHAPTER XXV

Notwithstanding these magnificent vaunts of the king, all men of penetration concluded, from the personal character of the man, and still more, from the situation of affairs, that he had no serious intention of pushing the war to such extremities as he pretended. France was not now in the same condition as when such successful inroads had been made upon her by former kings of England. The great fiefs were united to the crown; the princes of the blood were desirous of tranquillity; the nation abounded with able captains and veteran soldiers; and the general aspect of her affairs seemed rather to threaten her neighbours, than to promise them any considerable advantages against her. The levity and vain-glory of Maximilian were supported by his pompous titles; but were ill seconded by military power, and still less, by any revenue, proportioned to them. The politic Ferdinand, while he made a show of war, was actually negociating for peace; and rather than expose himself to any hazard, would accept of very moderate concessions from France. Even England was not free from domestic discontents; and in Scotland, the death of Henry's friend and ally, James III. who had been murdered by his rebellious subjects, had made way for the succession of his son, James IV. who was devoted to the French interest, and would surely be alarmed at any important progress of the English arms. But all these obvious considerations had no influence on the parliament. Inflamed by the ideas of subduing France, and of enriching themselves by the spoils of that kingdom, they gave into the snare prepared for them, and voted the supply which the king demanded. Two fifteenths were granted him; and the better to enable his vassals and nobility to attend him, an act was passed, empowering them to sell their estates, without paying any fines for alienation.

The nobility were universally seized with a desire of military glory; and having credulously swallowed all the boasts of the king, they dreamed of no less than carrying their triumphant banners to the gates of Paris, and putting the crown of France on the head of their sovereign. Many of them borrowed large sums, or sold off manors, that they might appear in the field with greater splendour, and lead out their followers in more complete order. The king crossed the sea, and arrived at Calais on the sixth of October, with an army of twenty-five thousand foot and sixteen hundred horse, which he put under the command of the duke of Bedford

1492.

6th Oct.
War with
France.

and the earl of Oxford: But as some inferred, from his opening the campaign in so late a season, that peace would soon be concluded between the crowns, he was desirous of suggesting a contrary inference. "He had come over," he said, "to make an entire conquest of France, which was not the work of one summer. It was therefore of no consequence at what season he began the invasion; especially as he had Calais ready for winter quarters." As if he had seriously intended this enterprize, he instantly marched into the enemy's country and laid siege to Bulloigne: But notwithstanding this appearance of hostility, there had been secret advances made towards peace above three months before; and commissioners had been appointed to treat of the terms. The better to reconcile the minds of men to this unexpected measure, the king's ambassadors arrived in the camp from the Low Countries, and informed him, that Maximilian was in no readiness to join him; nor was any assistance to be expected from that quarter. Soon after, messengers came from Spain, and brought news of a peace concluded between that kingdom and France, in which Charles had made a cession of the counties of Roussillon and Cerdagne to Ferdinand. Though these articles of intelligence were carefully dispersed throughout the army, the king was still apprehensive, lest a sudden peace, after such magnificent promises and high expectations, might expose him to reproach. In order the more effectually to cover the intended measures, he secretly engaged the marquis of Dorset, together with twenty-three persons of distinction, to present him a petition for agreeing to a treaty with France. The pretence was founded on the late season of the year, the difficulty of supplying the army at Calais during winter, the obstacles which arose in the siege of Bulloigne, the desertion of those allies whose assistance had been most relied on: Events which might, all of them, have been foreseen before the embarkation of the forces.

Invasion of France.

In consequence of these preparatory steps, the bishop of Exeter and lord Daubeney were sent to confer at Estaples with the mareschal de Cordes, and to put the last hand to the treaty. A few days sufficed for that purpose: The demands of Henry were wholly pecuniary; and the king of France, who deemed the peaceable possession of Britanny an equivalent for any sum, and who was all on fire for his projected expedition ·into Italy, readily agreed to the proposals made him. He engaged to pay Henry

3rd Nov. Peace with France.

CHAPTER XXV

745,000 crowns, near 400,000 pounds sterling of our present money; partly as a reimbursement of the sums advanced to Britanny, partly as arrears of the pension due to Edward IV. And he stipulated a yearly pension to Henry and his heirs of 25,000 crowns. Thus the king, as remarked by his historian made profit upon his subjects for the war; and upon his enemies for the peace.[d] And the people agreed, that he had fulfilled his promise, when he said to the parliament, that he would make the war maintain itself. Maximilian was, if he pleased, comprehended in Henry's treaty; but he disdained to be in any respect beholden to an ally, of whom, he thought, he had reason to complain: He made a separate peace with France, and obtained restitution of Artois, Franchecompté, and Charolois, which had been ceded as the dowry of his daughter, when she was affianced to the king of France.

The peace, concluded between England and France, was the more likely to continue, because Charles, full of ambition and youthful hopes, bent all his attention to the side of Italy, and soon after undertook the conquest of Naples; an enterprize which Henry regarded with the greater indifference, as Naples lay remote from him, and France had never, in any age, been successful in that quarter. The king's authority was fully established at home; and every rebellion, which had been attempted against him, had hitherto tended only to confound his enemies, and consolidate his power and influence. His reputation for policy and conduct was daily augmenting; his treasures had encreased even from the most unfavourable events; the hopes of all pretenders to his throne were cut off, as well by his marriage, as by the issue which it had brought him. In this prosperous situation, the king had reason to flatter himself with the prospect of durable peace and tranquillity: But, his inveterate and indefatigable enemies, whom he had wantonly provoked, raised him an adversary, who long kept him in inquietude, and sometimes even brought him into danger.

The dutchess of Burgundy, full of resentment for the depression of her family and its partizans, rather irritated than discouraged by the ill success of her past enterprizes, was determined at last to disturb that government, which she found it so difficult to subvert. By means of her emissaries, she propagated a report, that

[d] Bacon, p. 605. Pol. Virg. p. 586.

her nephew, Richard Plantagenet, duke of York, had escaped from the Tower when his elder brother was murdered, and that he still lay somewhere concealed: And finding this rumour, however improbable, to be greedily received by the people, she had been looking out for some young man, proper to personate that unfortunate prince.

Perkin Warbec.   There was one Osbec, or Warbec, a renegado Jew of Tournay, who had been carried by some business to London in the reign of Edward IV. and had there a son born to him. Having had opportunities of being known to the king, and obtaining his favour, he prevailed with that prince, whose manners were very affable, to stand godfather to his son, to whom he gave the name of Peter, corrupted, after the Flemish manner, into Peterkin, or Perkin. It was by some believed, that Edward, among his amorous adventures, had a secret commerce with Warbec's wife; and people thence accounted for that resemblance, which was afterwards remarked between young Perkin and that monarch.[e] Some years after the birth of this child, Warbec returned to Tournay; where Perkin, his son, did not long remain, but by different accidents was carried from place to place, and his birth and fortunes became thereby unknown, and difficult to be traced by the most diligent enquiry. The variety of his adventures had happily favoured the natural versatility and sagacity of his genius; and he seemed to be a youth perfectly fitted to act any part, or assume any character. In this light he had been represented to the dutchess of Burgundy, who, struck with the concurrence of so many circumstances suited to her purpose, desired to be made acquainted with the man, on *His im-* whom she already began to ground her hopes of success. She *posture.* found him to exceed her most sanguine expectations; so comely did he appear in his person, so graceful in his air, so courtly in his address, so full of docility and good sense in his behaviour and conversation. The lessons, necessary to be taught him, in order to his personating the duke of York, were soon learned by a youth of such quick apprehension, but as the season seemed not then favourable for his enterprize, Margaret, in order the better to conceal him, sent him, under the care of lady Brampton, into Portugal, where he remained a year, unknown to all the world.

[e] Bacon, p. 606.

CHAPTER XXV

The war, which was then ready to break out between France and England, seemed to afford a proper opportunity for the discovery of this new phaenomenon; and Ireland, which still retained its attachments to the house of York, was chosen as the proper place for his first appearance.[f] He landed at Corke; and immediately affirming the name of Richard Plantagenet, drew to him partizans among that credulous people. He wrote letters to the earls of Desmond and Kildare, inviting them to join his party: He dispersed everywhere the strange intelligence of his escape from the cruelty of his uncle Richard: And men, fond of every thing new and wonderful, began to make him the general subject of their discourse, and even the object of their favour.

The news soon reached France; and Charles, prompted by the secret solicitations of the dutchess of Burgundy, and the intrigues of one Frion, a secretary of Henry's, who had deserted his service, sent Perkin an invitation to repair to him at Paris. He received him with all the marks of regard due to the duke of York; settled on him a handsome pension, assigned him magnificent lodgings, and in order to provide at once for his dignity and security, gave him a guard for his person, of which lord Congresal accepted the office of captain. The French courtiers readily embraced a fiction, which their sovereign thought it his interest to adopt: Perkin, both by his deportment and personal qualities, supported the prepossession, which was spread abroad of his royal pedigree: And the whole kingdom was full of the accomplishments, as well as the singular adventures and misfortunes of the young Plantagenet. Wonders of this nature are commonly augmented at a distance. From France, the admiration and credulity diffused themselves into England: Sir George Nevil, Sir John Taylor, and above a hundred gentlemen more, came to Paris, in order to offer their services to the supposed duke of York, and to share his fortunes: And the impostor had now the appearance of a court attending him, and began to entertain hopes of final success in his undertakings.

When peace was concluded between France and England at Estaples, Henry applied to have Perkin put into his hands; but Charles, resolute not to betray a young man, of whatever birth, whom he had invited into his kingdom, would agree only to dismiss

[f] Polyd. Virg. p. 589.

him. The pretended Richard retired to the dutchess of Burgundy, and craving her protection and assistance, offered to lay before her all the proofs of that birth, to which he laid claim. The princess affected ignorance of his pretensions; even put on the appearance of distrust; and having, as she said, been already deceived by Simnel, she was determined never again to be reduced by any impostor. She desired before all the world to be instructed in his reasons for assuming the name which he bore; seemed to examine every circumstance with the most scrupulous nicety; put many particular questions to him; affected astonishment at his answers; and at last, after long and severe scrutiny, burst out into joy and admiration at his wonderful deliverance, embraced him as her nephew, the true image of Edward, the sole heir of the Plantagenets, and the legitimate successor to the English throne. She immediately assigned him an equipage, suited to his pretended birth; appointed him a guard of thirty halberdiers; engaged every one to pay court to him; and on all occasions honoured him with the appellation of the *White Rose of England*. The Flemings, moved by the authority which Margaret, both from her rank and personal character, enjoyed among them, readily adopted the fiction of Perkin's royal descent: No surmise of his true birth was as yet heard of: Little contradiction was made to the prevailing opinion: And the English, from their great communication with the Low Countries, were every day more and more prepossessed in favour of the impostor.

It was not the populace alone of England that gave credit to Perkin's pretensions. Men of the highest birth and quality, disgusted at Henry's government, by which they found the nobility depressed, began to turn their eyes towards the new claimant; and some of them even entered into a correspondence with him. Lord Fitzwater, Sir Simon Mountfort, Sir Thomas Thwaites betrayed their inclination towards him: Sir William Stanley himself, lord chamberlain, who had been so active in raising Henry to the throne, moved either by blind credulity or a restless ambition, entertained the project of a revolt in favour of his enemy.[g] Sir Robert Clifford and William Barley were still more open in their measures: They went over to Flanders, were introduced by the dutchess of Burgundy to the acquaintance of Perkin, and made

He is avowed by the dutchess of Burgundy,

1493.

and by many of the English nobility.

[g] Bacon, p. 608.

him a tender of their services. Clifford wrote back to England, that he knew perfectly the person of Richard duke of York, that this young man was undoubtedly that prince himself, and that no circumstance of his story was exposed to the least difficulty. Such positive intelligence, conveyed by a person of rank and character, was sufficient with many to put the matter beyond question, and excited the attention and wonder even of the most indifferent. The whole nation was held in suspence; a regular conspiracy was formed against the king's authority; and a correspondence settled between the malcontents in Flanders and those in England.

The king was informed of all these particulars; but agreeably to his character, which was both cautious and resolute, he proceeded deliberately, though steadily, in counter-working the projects of his enemies. His first object was to ascertain the death of the real duke of York, and to confirm the opinion that had always prevailed with regard to that event. Five persons had been employed by Richard in the murder of his nephews, or could give evidence with regard to it; Sir James Tirrel, to whom he had committed the government of the Tower for that purpose, and who had seen the dead princes; Forrest, Dighton, and Slater, who perpetrated the crime; and the priest who buried the bodies. Tirrel and Dighton alone were alive, and they agreed in the same story; but as the priest was dead, and as the bodies were supposed to have been removed by Richard's orders, from the place where they were first interred, and could not now be found, it was not in Henry's power to put the fact, so much as he wished, beyond all doubt and controversy.

He met at first with more difficulty, but was in the end more successful, in detecting who this wonderful person was that thus boldly advanced pretensions to his crown. He dispersed his spies all over Flanders and England; he engaged many to pretend that they had embraced Perkin's party; he directed them to insinuate themselves into the confidence of the young man's friends; in proportion as they conveyed intelligence of any conspirator, he bribed his retainers, his domestic servants, nay sometimes his confessor, and by these means traced up some other confederate; Clifford himself he engaged by the hope of rewards and pardon, to betray the secrets committed to him; the more trust he gave to any of his spies, the higher resentment did he feign against them;

some of them he even caused to be publicly anathematized, in order the better to procure them the confidence of his enemies: And in the issue, the whole plan of the conspiracy was clearly laid before him; and the pedigree, adventures, life, and conversation of the pretended duke of York. This latter part of the story was immediately published for the satisfaction of the nation: The conspirators he reserved for a slower and surer vengeance.

1494.   Meanwhile, he remonstrated with the archduke, Philip, on account of the countenance and protection, which was afforded in his dominions to so infamous an impostor; contrary to treaties subsisting between the sovereigns, and to the mutual amity which had so long been maintained by the subjects of both states. Margaret had interest enough to get his application rejected; on pretence that Philip had no authority over the demesnes of the dutchess dowager. And the king, in resentment of this injury, cut off all commerce with the Low-Countries, banished the Flemings, and recalled his own subjects from these provinces. Philip retaliated by like edicts; but Henry knew, that so mutinous a people as the Flemings would not long bear, in compliance with the humours of their prince, to be deprived of the beneficial branch of commerce which they carried on with England.

He had it in his power to inflict more effectual punishment on his domestic enemies; and when his projects were sufficiently matured, he failed not to make them feel the effects of his resentment. Almost in the same instant, he arrested Fitzwater, Mountfort, and Thwaites, together with William Daubeney, Robert Ratcliff, Thomas Cressenor, and Thomas Astwood. All these were arraigned, convicted, and condemned for high treason, in adhering and promising aid to Perkin. Mountfort, Ratcliff, and Daubeney were immediately executed: Fitzwater was sent over to Calais, and detained in custody; but being detected in practising on his keeper for an escape, he soon after underwent the same fate. The rest were pardoned, together with William Worseley, dean of St. Paul's, and some others, who had been accused and examined, but not brought to public trial.[h]

Greater and more solemn preparations were deemed requisite for the trial of Stanley, lord chamberlain, whose authority in the

[h] Polydore Virgil, p. 592.

CHAPTER XXV

nation, whose domestic connexions with the king, as well as his former services, seemed to secure him against any accusation or punishment. Clifford was directed to come over privately to England, and to throw himself at the king's feet, while he sat in council; craving pardon for past offences, and offering to atone for them by any services, which should be required of him. Henry then told him, that the best proof he could give of penitence, and the only service he could now render him, was the full confession of his guilt, and the discovery of all his accomplices, however distinguished by rank or character. Encouraged by this exhortation, Clifford accused Stanley then present, as his chief abettor; and offered to lay before the council the full proof of his guilt. Stanley himself could not discover more surprize than was affected by Henry on the occasion. He received the intelligence as absolutely false and incredible; that a man, to whom he was in a great measure beholden for his crown, and even for his life; a man, to whom, by every honour and favour, he had endeavoured to express his gratitude; whose brother, the earl of Derby, was his own father-in-law; to whom he had even committed the trust of his person, by creating him lord chamberlain: That this man, enjoying his full confidence and affection, not actuated by any motive of discontent or apprehension, should engage in a conspiracy against him. Clifford was therefore exhorted to weigh well the consequences of his accusation; but as he persisted in the same positive asseverations, Stanley was committed to custody, and was soon after examined before the council.[i] He denied not the guilt imputed to him by Clifford; he did not even endeavour much to extenuate it; whether he thought that a frank and open confession would serve as an atonement, or trusted to his present connexions, and his former services, for pardon and security. But princes are often apt to regard great services as a ground of jealousy, especially if accompanied with a craving and restless disposition, in the person who has performed them. The general discontent also, and mutinous humour of the people, seemed to require some great example of severity. And as Stanley was one of the most opulent subjects in the kingdom, being possessed of above three thousand pounds a-year in land, and forty thousand marks in plate and

Trial and execution of Stanley.

1495.

[i] Bacon, p. 611. Polyd. Virg. p. 593.

money, besides other property of great value, the prospect of so rich a forfeiture was deemed no small motive for Henry's proceeding to extremities against him. After six weeks delay, which was interposed in order to shew that the king was restrained by doubts and scruples; the prisoner was brought to his trial, condemned, and presently after beheaded. Historians are not agreed with regard to the crime which was proved against him. The general report is, that he should have said in confidence to Clifford, that, if he were sure the young man, who appeared in Flanders, was really son to king Edward, he never would bear arms against him. The sentiment might disgust Henry, as implying a preference of the house of York to that of Lancaster, but could scarcely be the ground, even in those arbitrary times, of a sentence of high treason against Stanley. It is more probable, therefore, as is asserted by some historians, that he had expressly engaged to assist Perkin, and had actually sent him some supply of money.

The fate of Stanley made great impression on the kingdom, and struck all the partizans of Perkin with the deepest dismay. From Clifford's desertion, they found that all their secrets were betrayed; and as it appeared, that Stanley, while he seemed to live in the greatest confidence with the king, had been continually surrounded by spies, who reported and registered every action in which he was engaged, nay, every word which fell from him, a general distrust took place, and all mutual confidence was destroyed, even among intimate friends and acquaintance. The jealous and severe temper of the king, together with his great reputation for sagacity and penetration, kept men in awe, and quelled not only the movements of sedition, but the very murmurs of faction. Libels, however, creeped out against Henry's person and administration; and being greedily propagated by every secret art, showed that there still remained among the people a considerable root of discontent, which wanted only a proper opportunity to discover itself.

But Henry continued more intent on encreasing the terrors of his people, than on gaining their affections. Trusting to the great success which attended him in all his enterprizes, he gave every day, more and more, a loose to his rapacious temper, and employed the arts of perverted law and justice, in order to exact fines and compositions from his people. Sir William Capel, alderman of

CHAPTER XXV

London, was condemned on some penal statutes to pay the sum of 2743 pounds, and was obliged to compound for sixteen hundred and fifteen. This was the first noted case of the kind; but it became a precedent, which prepared the way for many others. The management, indeed, of these arts of chicanery, was the great secret of the king's administration. While he depressed the nobility, he exalted and honoured and caressed the lawyers; and by that means both bestowed authority on the laws, and was enabled, whenever he pleased, to pervert them to his own advantage. His government was oppressive; but it was so much the less burthensome, as, by his extending royal authority, and curbing the nobles, he became in reality the sole oppressor in his kingdom.

As Perkin found, that the king's authority daily gained ground among the people, and that his own pretensions were becoming obsolete, he resolved to attempt something, which might revive the hopes and expectations of his partizans. Having collected a band of outlaws, pirates, robbers, and necessitous persons of all nations, to the number of 600 men, he put to sea, with a resolution of making a descent in England, and of exciting the common people to arms, since all his correspondence with the nobility was cut off by Henry's vigilance and severity. Information being brought him, that the king had made a progress to the north, he cast anchor on the coast of Kent, and sent some of his retainers ashore, who invited the country to join him. The gentlemen of Kent assembled some troops to oppose him; but they purposed to do more essential service than by repelling the invasion: They carried the semblance of friendship to Perkin, and invited him to come, himself, ashore, in order to take the command over them. But the wary youth, observing that they had more order and regularity in their movements than could be supposed in new levied forces, who had taken arms against established authority, refused to entrust himself into their hands; and the Kentish troops, despairing of success in their stratagem, fell upon such of his retainers, as were already landed; and besides some whom they slew, they took a hundred and fifty prisoners. These were tried and condemned; and all of them executed, by orders from the king, who was resolved to use no lenity towards men of such desperate fortunes.[k]

[k] Polydore Virgil, p. 595.

This year a parliament was summoned in England, and another in Ireland; and some remarkable laws were passed in both
countries. The English parliament enacted, that no person, who
should by arms or otherwise assist the king for the time being,
should ever afterwards, either by course of law or act of parliament, be attainted for such an instance of obedience. This statute
might be exposed to some censure, as favourable to usurpers; were
there any precise rule, which always, even during the most factious
times, could determine the true successor, and render every one
inexcusable, who did not submit to him. But as the titles of princes
are then the great subject of dispute, and each party pleads topics
in its own favour, it seems but equitable to secure those who act in
support of public tranquillity, an object at all times of undoubted
benefit and importance. Henry, conscious of his disputed title,
promoted this law, in order to secure his partizans against all
events; but as he had himself observed a contrary practice with
regard to Richard's adherents, he had reason to apprehend, that,
during the violence which usually ensues on public convulsions,
his example, rather than his law, would, in case of a new revolution, be followed by his enemies. And the attempt to bind the
legislature itself, by prescribing rules to future parliaments, was
contradictory to the plainest principles of political government.

The parliament also passed an act, impowering the king to
levy, by course of law, all the sums which any person had agreed
to pay by way of benevolence: A statute, by which that arbitrary
method of taxation was indirectly authorized and justified.

The king's authority appeared equally prevalent and uncon-
troled in Ireland. Sir Edward Poynings had been sent over to that
country, with an intention of quelling the partizans of the house of
York, and of reducing the natives to subjection. He was not supported by forces sufficient for that enterprize: The Irish, by flying
into their woods, and morasses, and mountains, for some time
eluded his efforts: But Poynings summoned a parliament at Dublin, where he was more successful. He passed that memorable
statute, which still bears his name, and which establishes the authority of the English government in Ireland. By this statute, all
the former laws of England were made to be of force in Ireland;
and no bill can be introduced into the Irish parliament, unless it
previously receive the sanction of the council of England. This

CHAPTER XXV

latter clause seems calculated for ensuring the dominion of the English; but was really granted at the desire of the Irish commons, who intended, by that means, to secure themselves from the tyranny of their lords, particularly of such lieutenants or deputies as were of Irish birth.[l]

While Henry's authority was thus established throughout his dominions, and general tranquillity prevailed, the whole continent was thrown into combustion by the French invasion of Italy, and by the rapid success which attended Charles in that rash and ill-concerted enterprize. The Italians, who had entirely lost the use of arms, and who, in the midst of continual wars, had become every day more unwarlike, were astonished to meet an enemy, that made the field of battle, not a pompous tournament, but a scene of blood, and sought at the hazard of their own lives the death of their enemy. Their effeminate troops were dispersed every where on the approach of the French army: Their best fortified cities opened their gates: Kingdoms and states were in an instant over-turned: And through the whole length of Italy, which the French penetrated without resistance, they seemed rather to be taking quarters in their own country, than making conquests over an enemy. The maxims, which the Italians, during that age, followed in negociations, were as ill calculated to support their states, as the habits to which they were addicted in war: A treacherous, deceit-ful, and inconsistent system of politics prevailed; and even those small remains of fidelity and honour, which were preserved in the councils of the other European princes, were ridiculed in Italy, as proofs of ignorance and rusticity. Ludovico, duke of Milan, who invited the French to invade Naples, had never desired or ex-pected their success; and was the first that felt terror from the prosperous issue of those projects, which he himself had con-certed. By his intrigues a league was formed among several poten-tates to oppose the progress of Charles's conquests and secure their own independency. This league was composed of Ludovico himself, the pope, Maximilian king of the Romans, Ferdinand of Spain, and the republic of Venice. Henry too entered into the confederacy; but was not put to any expence or trouble in con-sequence of his engagement. The king of France, terrified by so

[l] Sir John Davis, p. 235.

powerful a combination, retired from Naples with the greater part
of his army, and returned to France. The forces, which he left in
his new conquest were, partly by the revolt of the inhabitants,
partly by the invasion of the Spaniards, soon after subdued; and
the whole kingdom of Naples suddenly returned to its allegiance
under Ferdinand, son to Alphonso, who had been suddenly expelled by the irruption of the French. Ferdinand died soon after;
and left his uncle, Frederic, in full possession of the throne.

XXVI

Perkin retires to Scotland –
Insurrection in the west – Battle of
Blackheath – Truce with Scotland – Perkin
taken prisoner – Perkin executed –
The earl of Warwic executed – Marriage
of prince Arthur with Catharine of Arragon –
His death – Marriage of the princess
Margaret with the king of Scotland –
Oppressions of the people – A parliament –
Arrival of the king of Castile – Intrigues
of the earl of Suffolk – Sickness of the
king – His death –
and character – His laws

AFTER PERKIN WAS REPULSED from the coast of Kent, he retired   *1495.*
into Flanders; but as he found it impossible to procure
subsistence for himself and his followers, while he remained in
tranquillity, he soon after made an attempt upon Ireland, which
had always appeared forward to join every invader of Henry's
authority. But Poynings had now put the affairs of that island in
so good a posture, that Perkin met with little success; and being
tired of the savage life, which he was obliged to lead, while skulking
among the wild Irish, he bent his course towards Scotland, and

presented himself to James IV. who then governed that kingdom. He had been previously recommended to this prince by the king of France, who was disgusted at Henry for entering into the general league against him; and this recommendation was even seconded by Maximilian, who, though one of the confederates, was also displeased with the king, on account of his prohibiting in England all commerce with the Low Countries. The countenance given to Perkin by these princes procured him a favourable reception with the king of Scotland, who assured him, that, whatever he were, he never should repent putting himself in his hands:[m] The insinuating address and plausible behaviour of the youth himself, seem even to have gained him credit and authority. James, whom years had not yet taught distrust or caution, was seduced to believe the story of Perkin's birth and adventures; and he carried his confidence so far as to give him in marriage the lady Catherine Gordon, daughter of the earl of Huntley, and related to himself; a young lady too, eminent for virtue as well as beauty.

Perkin retires to Scotland.

1496.

There subsisted at that time a great jealousy between the courts of England and Scotland; and James was probably the more forward on that account to adopt any fiction, which, he thought, might reduce his enemy to distress or difficulty. He suddenly resolved to make an inroad into England, attended by some of the borderers; and he carried Perkin along with him, in hopes, that the appearance of the pretended prince might raise an insurrection in the northern counties. Perkin himself dispersed a manifesto, in which he set forth his own story, and craved the assistance of all his subjects in expelling the usurper, whose tyranny and maladministration, whose depression of the nobility by the elevation of mean persons, whose oppression of the people by multiplied impositions and vexations, had justly, he said, rendered him odious to all men. But Perkin's pretensions, attended with repeated disappointments, were now become stale in the eyes even of the populace; and the hostile dispositions, which subsisted between the kingdoms, rendered a prince, supported by the Scots, but an unwelcome present to the English nation. The ravages also, committed by the borderers, accustomed to licence and disorder, struck a terror into all men; and made the people prepare rather

[m] Bacon, p. 615. Polydore Virgil, p. 596, 597.

for repelling the invaders than for joining them. Perkin, that he might support his pretensions to royal birth, feigned great compassion for the misery of his plundered subjects; and publicly remonstrated with his ally against the depredations exercised by the Scottish army:[n] But James told him, that he doubted his concern was employed only in behalf of an enemy, and that he was anxious to preserve what never should belong to him. That prince now began to perceive, that his attempt would be fruitless; and hearing of an army, which was on its march to attack him, he thought proper to retreat into his own country.

The king discovered little anxiety to procure either reparation or vengeance for this insult committed on him by the Scottish nation: His chief concern was to draw advantage from it, by the pretence which it might afford him to levy impositions on his own subjects. He summoned a parliament, to whom he made bitter complaints against the irruption of the Scots, the absurd imposture countenanced by that nation, the cruel devastations committed in the northern counties, and the multiplied insults thus offered both to the king and kingdom of England. The parliament made the expected return to this discourse, by granting a subsidy to the amount of 120,000 pounds, together with two fifteenths. After making this grant, they were dismissed.

The vote of parliament for imposing the tax was without much difficulty procured by the authority of Henry; but he found it not so easy to levy the money upon his subjects. The people, who were acquainted with the immense treasures which he had amassed, could ill brook the new impositions raised on every slight occasion; and it is probable, that the flaw, which was universally known to be in his title, made his reign the more subject to insurrections and rebellions. When the subsidy began to be levied in Cornwal, the inhabitants, numerous and poor, robust and courageous, murmured against a tax, occasioned by a sudden inroad of the Scots, from which they esteemed themselves entirely secure, and which had usually been repelled by the force of the northern counties. Their ill-humour was farther incited by one Michael Joseph, a farrier of Bodmin, a notable prating fellow, who, by thrusting himself forward on every occasion, and being loudest in every

1497.

Insurrection in the West.

[n] Polydore Virgil, p. 598.

complaint against the government, had acquired an authority among those rude people. Thomas Flammoc too, a lawyer, who had become the oracle of the neighbourhood, encouraged the sedition, by informing them, that the tax, though imposed by parliament, was entirely illegal; that the northern nobility were bound, by their tenures, to defend the nation against the Scots; and that if these new impositions were tamely submitted to, the avarice of Henry and of his ministers would soon render the burden intolerable to the nation. The Cornish, he said, must deliver to the king a petition, seconded by such a force as would give it authority; and in order to procure the concurrence of the rest of the kingdom, care must be taken, by their orderly deportment, to shew that they had nothing in view but the public good, and the redress of all those grievances under which the people had so long laboured.

Encouraged by these speeches, the multitude flocked together, and armed themselves with axes, bills, bows, and such weapons as country people are usually possessed of. Flammoc and Joseph were chosen their leaders. They soon conducted the Cornish through the county of Devon, and reached that of Somerset. At Taunton the rebels killed, in their fury, an officious and eager commissioner of the subsidy, whom they called the provost of Perin. When they reached Wells, they were joined by lord Audley, a nobleman of an ancient family, popular in his deportment, but vain, ambitious, and restless in his temper. He had from the beginning maintained a secret correspondence with the first movers of the insurrection; and was now joyfully received by them as their leader. Proud of the countenance given them by so considerable a nobleman, they continued their march; breathing destruction to the king's ministers and favourites, particularly to Morton, now a cardinal, and Sir Reginald Bray, who were deemed the most active instruments in all his oppressions. Notwithstanding their rage against the administration, they carefully followed the directions given them by their leaders; and as they met with no resistance, they committed, during their march, no violence or disorder.

The rebels had been told by Flammoc, that the inhabitants of Kent, as they had ever, during all ages, remained unsubdued, and had even maintained their independence during the Norman conquest, would surely embrace their party, and declare themselves for a cause, which was no other than that of public good and general liberty. But the Kentish people had very lately distinguished themselves by repelling Perkin's invasion; and as they had received from the king many gracious acknowledgments for this service, their affections were, by that means, much conciliated to his government. It was easy, therefore, for the earl of Kent, lord Abergavenny, and lord Cobham, who possessed great authority in those parts, to retain the people in obedience; and the Cornish rebels, though they pitched their camp near Eltham, at the very gates of London, and invited all the people to join them, got reinforcement from no quarter. There wanted not discontents every where, but no one would take part in so rash and ill-concerted an enterprise; and besides, the situation, in which the king's affairs then stood, discouraged even the boldest and most daring.

Henry, in order to oppose the Scots, had already levied an army, which he put under the command of lord Daubeney, the chamberlain; and as soon as he heard of the Cornish insurrection, he ordered it to march southwards, and suppress the rebels. Not to leave the northern frontier defenceless, he dispatched thither the earl of Surrey, who assembled the forces on the borders, and made head against the enemy. Henry found here the concurrence of the three most fatal incidents that can befal a monarchy; a foreign enemy, a domestic rebellion, and a pretender to his crown; but he enjoyed great resources in his army and treasure, and still more, in the intrepidity and courage of his own temper. He did not, however, immediately give full scope to his military spirit. On other occasions, he had always hastened to a decision, and it was a usual saying with him, *that he desired but to see his rebels:* But as the Cornish mutineers behaved in an inoffensive manner, and committed no spoil on the country; as they received no accession of force on their march or in their encampment; and as such hasty and popular tumults might be expected to diminish every moment by delay; he took post in London, and assiduously prepared the means of ensuring victory.

After all his forces were collected, he divided them into three bodies, and marched out to assail the enemy. The first body, commanded by the earl of Oxford, and under him by the earls of Essex and Suffolk, were appointed to place themselves behind the hill on

Battle of Blackheath.

which the rebels were encamped: The second and most considerable, Henry put under the command of lord Daubeney, and ordered him to attack the enemy in front, and bring on the action. The third, he kept as a body of reserve about his own person, and took post in St. George's fields; where he secured the city, and *June 22d.* could easily, as occasion served, either restore the fight or finish the victory. To put the enemy off their guard, he had spread a report that he was not to attack them till some days after; and the better to confirm them in this opinion, he began not the action till near the evening. Daubeney beat a detachment of the rebels from Deptford-bridge; and before their main body could be in order to receive him, he had gained the ascent of the hill, and placed himself in array before them. They were formidable from their numbers, being sixteen thousand strong, and were not defective in valour; but being tumultuary troops, ill armed, and not provided with cavalry or artillery, they were but an unequal match for the king's forces. Daubeney began the attack with courage, and even with a contempt of the enemy, which had almost proved fatal to him. He rushed into the midst of them, and was taken prisoner; but soon after was released by his own troops. After some resistance, the rebels were broken, and put to flight.[o] Lord Audley, Flammoc, and Joseph, their leaders, were taken, and all three executed. The latter seemed even to exult in his end, and boasted, with a preposterous ambition, that he should make a figure in history. The rebels, being surrounded on every side by the king's troops, were almost all made prisoners; and immediately dismissed without farther punishment: Whether, that Henry was satisfied with the victims who had fallen in the field, and who amounted to near two thousand, or that he pitied the ignorance and simplicity of the multitude, or favoured them on account of their inoffensive behaviour, or was pleased that they had never, during their insurrection, disputed his title, and had shewn no attachment to the house of York, the highest crime, of which, in his eyes, they could have been guilty.

The Scottish king was not idle during these commotions in England. He levied a considerable army, and sat down before the

[o] Polydore Virgil, p. 601.

castle of Norham in Northumberland; but found that place, by the precaution of Fox, bishop of Durham, so well provided both with men and ammunition, that he made little or no progress in the siege. Hearing that the earl of Surrey had collected some forces and was advancing upon him, he retreated into his own country, and left the frontiers exposed to the inroads of the English general, who besieged and took Aiton, a small castle lying a few miles beyond Berwic. These unsuccessful or frivolous attempts on both sides prognosticated a speedy end to the war; and Henry, notwithstanding his superior force, was no less desirous than James of terminating the differences between the nations. Not to depart, however, from his dignity, by making the first advances, he employed in this friendly office Peter Hialas, a man of address and learning, who had come to him as ambassador from Ferdinand and Isabella, and who was charged with a commission of negociating the marriage of the infanta Catherine, their daughter, with Arthur prince of Wales.[p]

Hialas took a journey northwards, and offered his mediation between James and Henry, as minister of a prince, who was in alliance with both potentates. Commissioners were soon appointed to meet, and confer on terms of accommodation. The first demand of the English was, that Perkin should be put into their hands: James replied, that he himself was no judge of the young man's pretensions, but having received him as a supplicant, and promised him protection, he was determined not to betray a man, who had trusted to his good faith and his generosity. The next demand of the English met with no better reception: They required reparation for the ravages committed by the late inroads into England: The Scottish commissioners replied, that the spoils were like water spilt upon the ground, which could never be recovered, and that Henry's subjects were better able to bear the loss, than their master's to repair it. Henry's commissioners next proposed, that the two kings should have an interview at Newcastle, in order to adjust all differences; but James said, that he meant to treat of a peace, not to go a begging for it. Lest the conferences should break off altogether without effect, a truce was concluded

Truce with Scotland.

[p] Polydore Virgil, p. 603.

for some months; and James, perceiving, that, while Perkin remained in Scotland, he himself never should enjoy a solid peace with Henry, privately desired him to depart the kingdom.

Access was now barred Perkin into the Low Countries, his usual retreat in all his disappointments. The Flemish merchants, who severely felt the loss resulting from the interruption of commerce with England, had made such interest in the archduke's council, that commissioners were sent to London, in order to treat of an accommodation. The Flemish court agreed, that all English rebels should be excluded the Low Countries; and in this prohibition the demesnes of the dutchess-dowager were expressly comprehended. When this principal article was agreed to, all the other terms were easily adjusted. A treaty of commerce was finished, which was favourable to the Flemings, and to which they long gave the appellation of *Intercursus magnus,* the great treaty. And when the English merchants returned to their usual abode at Antwerp, they were publickly received, as in procession, with joy and festivity.

Perkin was a Fleming by descent, though born in England; and it might therefore be doubted whether he were included in the treaty between the two nations: But as he must dismiss all his English retainers if he took shelter in the Low Countries, and as he was sure of a cold reception, if not bad usage, among people who were determined to keep on terms of friendship with the court of England; he thought fit rather to hide himself, during some time, in the wilds and fastnesses of Ireland. Impatient however of a retreat, which was both disagreeable and dangerous, he held consultations with his followers, Herne, Skelton, and Astley, three broken tradesmen: By their advice, he resolved to try the affections of the Cornish, whose mutinous disposition, notwithstanding the king's lenity, still subsisted, after the suppression of their rebellion. No sooner did he appear at Bodmin in Cornwal, than the populace, to the number of three thousand, flocked to his standard; and Perkin, elated with this appearance of success, took on him, for the first time, the appellation of Richard IV. king of England. Not to suffer the expectations of his followers to languish, he presented himself before Exeter; and by many fair promises, invited that city to join him. Finding that the inhabitants shut their gates against him, he laid siege to the place; but being unprovided with artillery, ammunition, and every thing requisite for

CHAPTER XXVI

the attempt, he made no progress in his undertaking. Messengers were sent to the king, informing him of this insurrection: The citizens of Exeter meanwhile were determined to hold out to the last extremity, in expectation of receiving succour from the well-known vigilance of that monarch.

When Henry was informed, that Perkin was landed in England, he expressed great joy, and prepared himself with alacrity to attack him, in hopes of being able, at length, to put a period to pretensions, which had so long given him vexation and inquietude. All the courtiers, sensible that their activity on this occasion would be the most acceptable service which they could render the king, displayed their zeal for the enterprize, and forwarded his preparations. The lords Daubeney, and Broke, with Sir Rice ap Thomas, hastened forward with a small body of troops to the relief of Exeter. The earl of Devonshire, and the most considerable gentlemen in the county of that name, took arms of their own accord, and marched to join the king's generals. The duke of Buckingham put himself at the head of a troop, consisting of young nobility and gentry, who served as volunteers, and who longed for an opportunity of displaying their courage and their loyalty. The king himself prepared to follow with a considerable army; and thus all England seemed united against a pretender, who had at first engaged their attention and divided their affections.

Perkin, informed of these great preparations, immediately raised the siege of Exeter, and retired to Taunton. Though his followers now amounted to the number of near seven thousand, and seemed still resolute to maintain his cause, he himself despaired of success, and secretly withdrew to the sanctuary of Beaulieu in the new forest. The Cornish rebels submitted to the king's mercy, and found that it was not yet exhausted in their behalf. Except a few persons of desperate fortunes, who were executed, and some others who were severely fined, all the rest were dismissed with impunity. Lady Catherine Gordon, wife to Perkin, fell into the hands of the victor, and was treated with a generosity, which does him honour. He soothed her mind with many marks of regard, placed her in a reputable station about the queen, and assigned her a pension, which she enjoyed even under his successor.

Henry deliberated what course to take with Perkin himself. *1498.*

Some counselled him to make the privileges of the church yield to reasons of state, to take him by violence from the sanctuary, to inflict on him the punishment due to his temerity, and thus at once to put an end to an imposture which had long disturbed the government, and which the credulity of the people and the artifices of malcontents were still capable of reviving. But the king deemed not the matter of such importance as to merit so violent a remedy. He employed some persons to deal with Perkin, and persuade him, under promise of pardon, to deliver himself into the king's hands.[q]

Perkin taken prisoner. The king conducted him in a species of mock triumph to London. As Perkin passed along the road, and through the streets of the city, men of all ranks flocked about him, and the populace treated with the highest derision his fallen fortunes. They seemed desirous of revenging themselves, by their insults, for the shame, which their former belief of his impostures had thrown upon them. Though the eyes of the nation were generally opened with regard to Perkin's real parentage, Henry required of him a confession of his life and adventures; and he ordered the account of the whole to be dispersed, soon after, for the satisfaction of the public. But as his regard to decency made him entirely suppress the share which the dutchess of Burgundy had had in contriving and conducting the imposture, the people, who knew that she had been the chief instrument in the whole affair, were inclined, on account of the silence on that head, to pay the less credit to the authenticity of the narrative.

1499. But Perkin, though his life was granted him, was still detained in custody; and keepers were appointed to guard him. Impatient of confinment, he broke from his keepers, and flying to the sanctuary of Shyne, put himself into the hands of the prior of that monastery. The prior had obtained great credit by his character of sanctity; and he prevailed on the king again to grant a pardon to Perkin. But in order to reduce him to still greater contempt, he was set in the stocks at Westminster and Cheapside, and obliged in both places to read aloud to the people the confession, which had formerly been published in his name. He was then confined to the Tower, where his habits of restless intrigue and enterprize followed him. He insinuated himself into the intimacy of four ser-

[q] Polydore Virgil, p. 606.

CHAPTER XXVI

vants of Sir John Digby, lieutenant of the Tower; and by their means, opened a correspondence with the earl of Warwic, who was confined in the same prison. This unfortunate prince, who had from his earliest youth been shut up from the commerce of men, and who was ignorant even of the most common affairs of life, had fallen into a simplicity which made him susceptible of any impression. The continued dread also of the more violent effects of Henry's tyranny, joined to the natural love of liberty, engaged him to embrace a project for his escape, by the murder of the lieutenant; and Perkin offered to conduct the whole enterprize. The conspiracy escaped not the king's vigilance: It was even very generally believed, that the scheme had been laid by himself, in order to draw Warwic and Perkin into the snare: But the subsequent execution of two of Digby's servants for the contrivance, seems to clear the king of that imputation, which was indeed founded more on the general idea entertained of his character, than on any positive evidence.

Perkin, by this new attempt, after so many enormities, had rendered himself totally unworthy of mercy: and he was accordingly arraigned, condemned, and soon after hanged at Tyburn, persisting still in the confession of his imposture.[r] It happened about that very time, that one Wilford, a cordwainer's son, encouraged by the surprising credit given to other impostures, had undertaken to personate the earl of Warwic; and a priest had even ventured from the pulpit to recommend his cause to the people, who seemed still to retain a propensity to adopt it. This incident served Henry as a pretence for his severity towards that prince. He was brought to trial, and accused, not of contriving his escape (for as he was committed for no crime, the desire of liberty must have been regarded as natural and innocent), but of forming designs to disturb the government, and raise an insurrection among the people. Warwic confessed the indictment, was condemned, and the sentence was executed upon him.

This violent act of tyranny, the great blemish of Henry's reign, by which he destroyed the last remaining male of the line of Plantagenet, begat great discontent among the people, who saw an unhappy prince, that had long been denied all the privileges of his

Perkin executed.

The earl of Warwic executed. 21st Nov.

[r] See note [A] at the end of the volume.

high birth, even been cut off from the common benefits of nature, now at last deprived of life itself, merely for attempting to shake off that oppression under which he laboured. In vain did Henry endeavour to alleviate the odium of this guilt, by sharing it with his ally, Ferdinand of Arragon, who, he said, had scrupled to give his daughter Catherine in marriage to Arthur, while any male descendant of the house of York remained. Men, on the contrary, felt higher indignation at seeing a young prince sacrificed, not to law and justice, but to the jealous politics of two subtle and crafty tyrants.

But though these discontents festered in the minds of men, they were so checked by Henry's watchful policy and steady severity, that they seemed not to weaken his government; and foreign princes, deeming his throne now entirely secure, paid him rather the greater deference and attention. The archduke, Philip, in particular, desired an interview with him; and Henry, who had passed over to Calais, agreed to meet him in St. Peter's church near that city. The archduke, on his approaching the king, made haste to alight, and offered to hold Henry's stirrup; a mark of condescension, which that prince would not admit of. He called the king *father, patron, protector;* and by his whole behaviour expressed a strong desire of conciliating the friendship of England. The duke of Orleans had succeeded to the crown of France by the appellation of Lewis XII. and having carried his arms into Italy, and subdued the dutchy of Milan, his progress begat jealousy in Maximilian, Philip's father, as well as in Ferdinand, his father-in-law. By the counsel, therefore, of these monarchs, the young prince endeavoured by every art to acquire the amity of Henry, whom they regarded as the chief counterpoise to the greatness of France. No particular plan however of alliance seems to have been concerted between these two princes in their interview: All passed in general professions of affection and regard; at least, in remote projects of a closer union, by the future intermarriages of their children, who were then in a state of infancy.

1500. The Pope too, Alexander VI. neglected not the friendship of a monarch, whose reputation was spread over Europe. He sent a nuncio into England, who exhorted the king to take part in the great alliance projected for the recovery of the Holy Land, and to

CHAPTER XXVI

lead in person his forces against the infidels. The general frenzy for crusades was now entirely exhausted in Europe; but it was still thought a necessary piece of decency to pretend zeal for those pious enterprizes. Henry regretted to the nuncio the distance of his situation, which rendered it inconvenient for him to expose his person in defence of the Christian cause. He promised, however, his utmost assistance by aids and contributions; and rather than the pope should go alone to the holy wars, unaccompanied by any monarch, he even promised to overlook all other considerations, and to attend him in person. He only required as a necessary condition, that all differences should previously be adjusted among Christian princes, and that some sea-port towns in Italy should be consigned to him for his retreat and security. It was easy to conclude, that Henry had determined not to intermeddle in any war against the Turk: But as a great name, without any real assistance, is sometimes of service, the knights of Rhodes, who were at that time esteemed the bulwark of Christendom, chose the king protector of their order.

But the prince, whose alliance Henry valued the most, was Ferdinand of Arragon, whose vigorous and steady policy, always attended with success, had rendered him, in many respects, the most considerable monarch in Europe. There was also a remarkable similarity of character between these two princes: Both were full of craft, intrigue, and design; and though a resemblance of this nature be a slender foundation for confidence and amity, where the interests of the parties in the least interfere; such was the situation of Henry and Ferdinand, that no jealousy ever on any occasion arose between them. The king had now the satisfaction of completing a marriage, which had been projected and negociated during the course of seven years, between Arthur prince of Wales and the infanta Catherine, fourth daughter of Ferdinand and Isabella; he near sixteen years of age, she eighteen. But this marriage proved in the issue unprosperous. The young prince, a few months after, sickened and died, much regretted by the nation. Henry, desirous to continue his alliance with Spain, and also unwilling to restore Catherine's dowry, which was two hundred thousand ducats, obliged his second son, Henry, whom he created prince of Wales, to be contracted to the infanta. The prince made

1501.
Marriage of prince Arthur with Catherine of Arragon.
12th Nov.

1502.
2d April.
His death.

all the opposition, of which a youth of twelve years of age was capable; but as the king persisted in his resolution, the espousals were at length, by means of the pope's dispensation, contracted between the parties: An event, which was afterwards attended with the most important consequences.

Marriage of the princess Margaret with the king of Scotland.

The same year, another marriage was celebrated, which was also, in the next age, productive of great events: The marriage of Margaret, the king's elder daughter, with James king of Scotland. This alliance had been negociated during three years, though interrupted by several broils; and Henry hoped, from the completion of it, to remove all source of discord with that neighbouring kingdom, by whose animosity England had so often been infested. When this marriage was deliberated on in the English council, some objected, that England might, by means of that alliance, fall under the dominion of Scotland. "No," replied Henry, "Scotland, in that event, will only become an accession to England." Amidst these prosperous incidents, the king met with a domestic calamity, which made not such impression on him as it merited: His queen died in childbed; and the infant did not long survive her. This princess was deservedly a favourite of the nation; and the general affection for her encreased, on account of the harsh treatment, which, it was thought, she met with from her consort.

1503. 11th Feb.

The situation of the king's affairs, both at home and abroad, was now, in every respect, very fortunate. All the efforts of the European princes, both in war and negociation, were turned to the side of Italy; and the various events, which there arose, made Henry's alliance be courted by every party, yet interested him so little as never to touch him with concern or anxiety. His close connexions with Spain and Scotland ensured his tranquillity; and his continued successes over domestic enemies, owing to the prudence and vigour of his conduct, had reduced the people to entire submission and obedience. Uncontrouled, therefore, by apprehension or opposition of any kind, he gave full scope to his natural propensity; and avarice, which had ever been his ruling passion, being encreased by age, and encouraged by absolute authority, broke all restraints of shame or justice. He had found two ministers, Empson and Dudley, perfectly qualified to second his rapacious and tyrannical inclinations, and to prey upon his de-

Oppressions of the people.

fenceless people. These instruments of oppression were both law-yers, the first of mean birth, of brutal manners, of an unrelenting temper; the second better born, better educated, and better bred, but equally unjust, severe, and inflexible. By their knowledge in law, these men were qualified to pervert the forms of justice to the oppression of the innocent; and the formidable authority of the king supported them in all their iniquities.

It was their usual practice at first to observe so far the appear-ance of law as to give indictments to those whom they intended to oppress: Upon which the persons were committed to prison, but never brought to trial; and were at length obliged, in order to recover their liberty, to pay heavy fines and ransoms, which were called mitigations and compositions. By degrees, the very appear-ance of law was neglected: The two ministers sent forth their precepts to attach men, and summon them before themselves and some others, at their private houses, in a court of commission, where, in a summary manner, without trial or jury, arbitrary de-crees were issued, both in pleas of the crown and controversies between private parties. Juries themselves, when summoned, proved but small security to the subject; being brow-beaten by these oppressors; nay, fined, imprisoned, and punished, if they gave sentence against the inclination of the ministers. The whole system of the feudal law, which still prevailed, was turned into a scheme of oppression. Even the king's wards, after they came of age, were not suffered to enter into possession of their lands with-out paying exorbitant fines. Men were also harassed with informa-tions of intrusion upon scarce colourable titles. When an outlawry in a personal action was issued against any man, he was not allowed to purchase his charter of pardon, except on the payment of a great sum; and if he refused the composition required of him, the strict law, which, in such cases, allows forfeiture of goods, was rigorously insisted on. Nay, without any colour of law, the half of men's lands and rents were seized during two years, as a penalty in case of outlawry. But the chief means of oppression, employed by these ministers, were the penal statutes, which, without consid-eration of rank, quality, or services, were rigidly put in execution against all men: Spies, informers, and inquisitors were rewarded and encouraged in every quarter of the kingdom: And no differ-ence was made whether the statute were beneficial or hurtful, recent or obsolete, possible or impossible to be executed. The sole end of the king and his ministers was to amass money, and bring every one under the lash of their authority.[s]

Through the prevalence of such an arbitrary and iniquitous administration, the English, it may safely be affirmed, were considerable losers by their ancient privileges, which secured them from all taxations, except such as were imposed by their own consent in parliament. Had the king been impowered to levy general taxes at pleasure, he would naturally have abstained from these oppressive expedients, which destroyed all security in private property, and begat an universal diffidence throughout the nation. In vain did the people look for protection from the parliament, which was

pretty frequently summoned during this reign. That assembly was so overawed, that, at this very time, during the greatest rage of Henry's oppressions, the commons chose Dudley their speaker, the very man who was the chief instrument of his iniquities. And though the king was known to be immensely opulent, and had no pretence of wars or expensive enterprizes of any kind, they

granted him the subsidy, which he demanded. But so insatiable was his avarice, that next year he levied a new benevolence, and renewed that arbitrary and oppressive method of taxation. By all these arts of accumulation, joined to a rigid frugality in his expence, he so filled his coffers, that he is said to have possessed in ready money the sum of 1,800,000 pounds: A treasure almost incredible, if we consider the scarcity of money in those times.[t]

But while Henry was enriching himself by the spoils of his oppressed people, there happened an event abroad, which engaged his attention, and was even the object of his anxiety and concern. Isabella, queen of Castile, died about this time; and it was foreseen, that by this incident the fortunes of Ferdinand, her husband, would be much affected. The king was not only attentive to

---

[s] Bacon, 629, 630. Hollingshed, p. 504. Polyd. Virg. p. 613, 615.   [t] Silver was during this reign 37 shillings and sixpence a pound, which makes Henry's treasure near three millions of our present money. Besides, many commodities have become above thrice as dear by the encrease of gold and silver in Europe. And what is a circumstance of still greater weight, all other states were then very poor, in comparison of what they are at present: These circumstances make Henry's treasure appear very great; and may lead us to conceive the oppressions of his government.

the fate of his ally, and watchful lest the general system of Europe should be affected by so important an event: He also considered the similarity of his own situation with that of Ferdinand, and regarded the issue of these transactions as a precedent for himself. Joan, the daughter of Ferdinand by Isabella, was married to the archduke Philip, and being, in right of her mother, heir of Castile, seemed entitled to dispute with Ferdinand the present possession of that kingdom. Henry knew, that notwithstanding his own pretensions by the house of Lancaster, the greater part of the nation was convinced of the superiority of his wife's title; and he dreaded lest the prince of Wales, who was daily advancing towards manhood, might be tempted by ambition to lay immediate claim to the crown. By his perpetual attention to depress the partizans of the York family, he had more closely united them into one party, and encreased their desire of shaking off that yoke, under which they had so long laboured, and of taking every advantage, which his oppressive government should give his enemies against him. And as he possessed no independent force like Ferdinand, and governed a kingdom more turbulent and unruly, which he himself, by his narrow politics, had confirmed in factious prejudices; he apprehended that his situation would prove in the issue still more precarious.

Nothing at first could turn out more contrary to the king's wishes than the transactions in Spain. Ferdinand, as well as Henry, had become very unpopular, and from a like cause, his former exactions and impositions; and the states of Castile discovered an evident resolution of preferring the title of Philip and Joan. In *1506.* order to take advantage of these favourable dispositions, the archduke, now king of Castile, attended by his consort, embarked for Spain during the winter season; but meeting with a violent tempest in the channel, was obliged to take shelter in the harbour of Weymouth. Sir John Trenchard, a gentleman of authority in the *Arrival* county of Dorset, hearing of a fleet upon the coast, had assembled *of the* some forces; and being joined by Sir John Cary, who was also at the *king of* head of an armed body, he came to that town. Finding that Philip, *Castile.* in order to relieve his sickness and fatigue, was already come ashore, he invited him to his house; and immediately dispatched a messenger, to inform the court of this important incident. The king sent in all haste the earl of Arundel to compliment Philip on his arrival in England, and to inform him, that he intended to pay him a visit in person, and to give him a suitable reception in his dominions. Philip knew, that he could not now depart without the king's consent; and therefore, for the sake of dispatch, he resolved to anticipate his visit, and to have an interview with him at Windsor. Henry received him with all the magnificence possible, and with all the seeming cordiality; but he resolved, notwithstanding, to draw some advantage from this involuntary visit, paid him by his royal guest.

Intrigues of the earl of Suffolk. Edmond de la Pole, earl of Suffolk, nephew to Edward IV. and brother to the earl of Lincoln, slain in the battle of Stoke, had some years before killed a man in a sudden fit of passion, and had been obliged to apply to the king for a remission of the crime. The king had granted his request; but being little indulgent to all persons connected with the house of York, he obliged him to appear openly in court and plead his pardon. Suffolk, more resenting the affront than grateful for the favour, had fled into Flanders, and taken shelter with his aunt, the dutchess of Burgundy: But being promised forgiveness by the king, he returned to England, and obtained a new pardon. Actuated, however, by the natural inquietude of his temper, and uneasy from debts which he had contracted by his great expence at prince Arthur's wedding, he again made an elopement into Flanders. The king, well acquainted with the general discontent which prevailed against his administration, neglected not this incident, which might become of importance; and he employed his usual artifices to elude the efforts of his enemies. He directed Sir Robert Curson, governor of the castle of Hammes, to desert his charge, and to insinuate himself into the confidence of Suffolk, by making him a tender of his services. Upon information secretly conveyed by Curson, the king seized William Courtney, eldest son to the earl of Devonshire, and married to the lady Catherine, sister of the queen; William de la Pole, brother to the earl of Suffolk; Sir James Tirrel, and Sir James Windham, with some persons of inferior quality; and he committed them to custody. Lord Abergavenny and Sir Thomas Green were also apprehended; but were soon after released from their confinement. William de la Pole was long detained in prison: Courtney was attainted and, though not executed, he recovered not his liberty during the king's life-time. But Henry's chief sever-

CHAPTER XXVI

ity fell upon Sir James Windham, and Sir James Tirrel, who were brought to their trial, condemned, and executed: The fate of the latter gave general satisfaction, on account of his participation in the murder of the young princes, sons of Edward IV. Notwithstanding these discoveries and executions, Curson was still able to maintain his credit with the earl of Suffolk: Henry, in order to remove all suspicion, had ordered him to be excommunicated, together with Suffolk himself, for his pretended rebellion. But after that traitor had performed all the services expected from him, he suddenly deserted the earl, and came over to England, where the king received him with unusual marks of favour and confidence. Suffolk, astonished at this instance of perfidy, finding that even the dutchess of Burgundy, tired with so many fruitless attempts, had become indifferent to his cause, fled secretly into France, then into Germany, and returned at last into the Low-Countries: where he was protected, though not countenanced, by Philip, then in close alliance with the king.

Henry neglected not the present opportunity of complaining to his guest of the reception which Suffolk had met with in his dominions. "I really thought," replied the king of Castile, "that your greatness and felicity had set you far above apprehensions from any person of so little consequence: But to give you satisfaction, I shall banish him my state." "I expect that you will carry your complaisance farther," said the king; "I desire to have Suffolk put into my hands, where alone I can depend upon his submission and obedience." "That measure," said Philip, "will reflect dishonour upon you as well as myself. You will be thought to have treated me as a prisoner." "Then the matter is at an end," replied the king, "for I will take that dishonour upon me; and so your honour is saved."[u] The king of Castile found himself under a necessity of complying, but he first exacted Henry's promise that he would spare Suffolk's life. That nobleman was invited over to England by Philip; as if the king would grant him a pardon, on the intercession of his friend and ally. Upon his appearance, he was committed to the Tower; and the king of Castile, having fully satisfied Henry, as well by his concession, as by signing a treaty of commerce between England and Castile, which was advantageous to the former king-   *1507.*

---

[u] Bacon, p. 633.

dom,[w] was at last allowed to depart after a stay of three months. He landed in Spain, was joyfully received by the Castilians, and put in possession of the throne. He died soon after; and Joan, his widow, falling into deep melancholy, Ferdinand was again enabled to re-instate himself in authority, and to govern, till the day of his death, the whole Spanish monarchy.

1508.

The king survived these transactions two years; but nothing memorable occurs in the remaining part of his reign, except his affiancing his second daughter Mary to the young archduke Charles, son of Philip of Castile. He entertained also some in-tentions of marriage for himself, first with the queen-dowager of Naples, relict of Ferdinand; afterwards with the dutchess dowager of Savoy, daughter of Maximilian, and sister of Philip. But the decline of his health put an end to all such thoughts; and he began to cast his eye towards that future existence, which the iniquities and severities of his reign rendered a very dismal prospect to him. To allay the terrors, under which he laboured, he endeavoured, by distributing alms and founding religious houses, to make atone-ment for his crimes, and to purchase, by the sacrifice of part of his ill-gotten treasures, a reconciliation with his offended Maker. Re-morse even seized him at intervals for the abuse of his authority by Empson and Dudley; but not sufficient to make him stop the rapacious hand of those oppressors. Sir William Capel was again fined two thousand pounds under some frivolous pretence, and was committed to the Tower for daring to murmur against the iniquity. Harris, an alderman of London, was indicted, and died of vexation before his trial came to an issue. Sir Laurence Ailmer, who had been mayor, and his two sheriffs, were condemned in heavy fines, and sent to prison till they made payment. The king gave countenance to all these oppressions; till death, by its nearer approaches, impressed new terrors upon him; and he then or-dered, by a general clause in his will, that restitution should be made to all those whom he had injured. He died of a consumption at his favourite palace of Richmond, after a reign of twenty-three years and eight months, and in the fifty-second year of his age.[x]

Sickness of the king.

1509.
His death,
22d April.

and character.

The reign of Henry VII. was, in the main, fortunate for his people at home, and honourable abroad. He put an end to the civil

[w] Rymer, vol. xiii. p. 142.   [x] Dugd. baronage, II. p. 237.

wars with which the nation had long been harassed, he maintained peace and order in the state, he depressed the former exorbitant power of the nobility, and, together with the friendship of some foreign princes, he acquired the consideration and regard of all. He loved peace without fearing war; though agitated with continual suspicions of his servants and ministers, he discovered no timidity, either in the conduct of his affairs, or in the day of battle; and though often severe in his punishments, he was commonly less actuated by revenge than by maxims of policy. The services, which he rendered the people, were derived from his views of private advantage, rather than the motives of public spirit; and where he deviated from interested regards, it was unknown to himself, and ever from the malignant prejudices of faction, or the mean projects of avarice; not from the sallies of passion, or allurements of pleasure; still less, from the benign motives of friendship and generosity. His capacity was excellent, but somewhat contracted by the narrowness of his heart; he possessed insinuation and address, but never employed these talents, except where some great point of interest was to be gained; and while he neglected to conciliate the affections of his people, he often felt the danger of resting his authority on their fear and reverence alone. He was always extremely attentive to his affairs; but possessed not the faculty of seeing far into futurity; and was more expert at providing a remedy for his mistakes than judicious in avoiding them: Avarice was, on the whole, his ruling passion;[y] and he remains an instance, almost singular, of a man, placed in a high station, and possessed of talents for great affairs, in whom that passion predominated above ambition. Even among private persons, avarice is commonly nothing but a species of ambition, and is chiefly incited by the prospect of that regard, distinction, and consideration, which attend on riches.

The power of the kings of England had always been somewhat

---

[y] As a proof of Henry's attention to the smallest profits, Bacon tells us, that he had seen a book of accompts kept by Epsom, and subscribed in almost every leaf by the king's own hand. Among other articles was the following. "*Item,* Received of such a one five marks for a pardon, which, if it do not pass, the money to be repayed, or the party otherwise satisfied." Opposite to the memorandum, the king had writ with his own hand, "otherwise satisfied." Bacon, p. 630.

irregular or discretionary; but was scarcely ever so absolute during any former reign, at least after the establishment of the great charter, as during that of Henry. Besides the advantages, derived from the personal character of the man, full of vigour, industry, and severity, deliberate in all projects, steady in every purpose, and attended with caution, as well as good fortune, in every enterprize; he came to the throne after long and bloody civil wars, which had destroyed all the great nobility, who alone could resist the encroachments of his authority: The people were tired with discord and intestine convulsions, and willing to submit to usurpations, and even to injuries, rather than plunge themselves anew into like miseries: The fruitless efforts made against him served always, as is usual, to confirm his authority: As he ruled by a faction, and the lesser faction, all those on whom he conferred offices, sensible that they owed every thing to his protection, were willing to support his power, though at the expence of justice and national privileges. These seem the chief causes which at this time bestowed on the crown so considerable an addition of prerogative, and rendered the present reign a kind of epoch in the English constitution.

This prince, though he exalted his prerogative above law, is celebrated by his historian for many good laws, which he made be enacted for the government of his subjects. Several considerable regulations, indeed, are found among the statutes of this reign, both with regard to the police of the kingdom, and its commerce: *His laws.* But the former are generally contrived with much better judgment than the latter. The more simple ideas of order and equity are sufficient to guide a legistator in every thing that regards the internal administration of justice: But the principles of commerce are much more complicated, and require long experience and deep reflection to be well understood in any state. The real consequence of a law or practice is there often contrary to first appearances. No wonder, that, during the reign of Henry VII. these matters were frequently mistaken; and it may safely be affirmed, that even in the age of lord Bacon, very imperfect and erroneous ideas were formed on that subject.

Early in Henry's reign, the authority of the Star Chamber, which was before founded on common law, and ancient practice, was in some cases confirmed by act of parliament:[z] Lord Bacon

---

[z] See note [B] at the end of the volume.

CHAPTER XXVI

extols the utility of this court; but men began, even during the age of that historian, to feel that so arbitrary a jurisdiction was incompatible with liberty; and in proportion as the spirit of independance still rose higher in the nation, the aversion to it encreased, till it was entirely abolished by act of parliament in the reign of Charles I. a little before the commencement of the civil wars.

Laws were passed in this reign, ordaining the king's suit for murder to be carried on within a year and day.[a] Formerly, it did not usually commence till after; and as the friends of the person murdered, often, in the interval, compounded matters with the criminal, the crime frequently passed unpunished. Suits were given to the poor *in forma pauperis,* as it is called: That is, without paying dues for the writs, or any fees to the council:[b] A good law at all times, especially in that age, when the people laboured under the oppression of the great; but a law difficult to be carried into execution. A law was made against carrying off any woman by force.[c] The benefit of clergy was abridged;[d] and the criminal, on the first offence, was ordered to be burned in the hand with a letter denoting his crime; after which he was punished capitally for any new offence. Sheriffs were no longer allowed to fine any person, without previously summoning him before their court.[e] It is strange, that such a practice should ever have prevailed. Attaint of juries was granted in cases which exceeded forty pounds value.[f] A law which has an appearance of equity, but which was afterwards found inconvenient. Actions popular were not allowed to be eluded by fraud or covin. If any servant of the king's conspired against the life of the steward, treasurer, or comptroller of the king's household, this design, though not followed by any overt act, was made liable to the punishment of felony.[g] This statute was enacted for the security of archbishop Morton, who found himself exposed to the enmity of great numbers.

There scarcely passed any session during this reign without some statute against engaging retainers, and giving them badges or liveries;[h] a practice, by which they were, in a manner, inlisted under some great lord, and were kept in readiness to assist him in all wars, insurrections, riots, violences, and even in bearing evi-

---

[a] 3 H. 7. cap. 1.   [b] 11 H. 7. cap. 12.   [c] 3 H. 7. cap. 2.   [d] 4 H. 7. cap. 13.
[e] 11 H. 7. cap. 15.   [f] Ibid. cap. 24. 19 H. 7. cap. 3.   [g] 3 H. 7. cap. 13.
[h] 3 H. 7. cap. 1. & 12. 11 H. 7. cap. 3. 19 H. 7. cap. 14.

dence for him in courts of justice.[i] This disorder, which had prevailed during many reigns, when the law could give little protection to the subject, was then deeply rooted in England; and it
required all the vigilance and rigour of Henry to extirpate it.
There is a story of his severity against this abuse; and it seems to
merit praise, though it is commonly cited as an instance of his
avarice and rapacity. The earl of Oxford, his favourite general, in
whom he always placed great and deserved confidence, having
splendidly entertained him at his castle of Heningham, was desirous of making a parade of his magnificence at the departure of
his royal guest; and ordered all his retainers, with their liveries and
badges, to be drawn up in two lines, that their appearance might
be the more gallant and splendid. "My lord," said the king, "I have
heard much of your hospitality; but the truth far exceeds the
report. These handsome gentlemen and yeomen, whom I see on
both sides of me, are, no doubt, your menial servants." The earl
smiled, and confessed that his fortune was too narrow for such
magnificence. "They are most of them," subjoined he, "my retainers, who are come to do me service at this time, when they
know I am honoured with your majesty's presence." The king
started a little, and said, "By my faith, my lord, I thank you for your
good cheer, but I must not allow my laws to be broken in my sight.
My attorney must speak with you." Oxford is said to have payed no
less than fifteen thousand marks, as a composition for his offence.

The encrease of the arts, more effectually than all the severities
of law, put an end to this pernicious practice. The nobility, instead
of vying with each other, in the number and boldness of their
retainers, acquired by degrees a more civilized species of emulation, and endeavoured to excel in the splendour and elegance of
their equipage, houses, and tables. The common people, no longer
maintained in vicious idleness by their superiors, were obliged to
learn some calling or industry, and became useful both to themselves and to others. And it must be acknowledged, in spite of those
who declaim so violently against refinement in the arts, or what
they are pleased to call luxury, that, as much as an industrious
tradesman is both a better man and a better citizen than one of
those idle retainers, who formerly depended on the great families;

[i] 3 H. 7. cap. 12. 11 H. 7. cap. 25.

so much is the life of a modern nobleman more laudable than that of an ancient baron.[k]

But the most important law in its consequences, which was enacted during the reign of Henry, was that by which the nobility and gentry acquired a power of breaking the ancient entails, and of alienating their estates.[l] By means of this law, joined to the beginning luxury and refinements of the age, the great fortunes of the barons were gradually dissipated, and the property of the commons encreased in England. It is probable, that Henry foresaw and intended this consequence, because the constant scheme of his policy consisted in depressing the great, and exalting churchmen, lawyers, and men of new families, who were more dependant on him.

This king's love of money naturally led him to encourage commerce, which encreased his customs; but, if we may judge by most of the laws enacted during his reign, trade and industry were rather hurt than promoted by the care and attention given to them. Severe laws were made against taking interest for money, which was then denominated usury.[m] Even the profits of exchange were prohibited, as favouring of usury,[n] which the superstition of the age zealously proscribed. All evasive contracts, by which profits could be made from the loan of money, were also carefully guarded against.[o] It is needless to observe how unreasonable and iniquitous these laws, how impossible to be executed, and how hurtful to trade, if they could take place. We may observe, however, to the praise of this king, that sometimes, in order to promote commerce, he lent to merchants sums of money, without interest; when he knew, that their stock was not sufficient for those enterprizes, which they had in view.[p]

Laws were made against the exportation of money, plate, or bullion:[q] A precaution, which serves to no other purpose than to make more be exported. But so far was the anxiety on this head carried, that merchants alien, who imported commodities into the

[k] See note [C] at the end of the volume. [l] 4 H. 7. cap. 24. The practice of breaking entails by means of a fine and recovery was introduced in the reign of Edward the IVth; But it was not, properly speaking, law, till the statute of Henry the VIIth; which, by correcting some abuses that attended that practice, gave indirectly a sanction to it. [m] 3 H. 7. cap. 5. [n] Ibid. cap. 6. [o] 7 H. 7. cap. 8. [p] Polyd. Virg. [q] 4 H. 7. cap. 23.

kingdom, were obliged to invest, in English commodities, all the money acquired by their sales, in order to prevent their conveying it away in a clandestine manner.[r]

It was prohibited to export horses; as if that exportation did not encourage the breed, and render them more plentiful in the kingdom.[s] In order to promote archery no bows were to be sold at a higher price than six shillings and four-pence,[t] reducing money to the denomination of our time. The only effect of this regulation must be either that the people would be supplied with bad bows or none at all. Prices were also affixed to woollen cloth,[u] to caps and hats:[w] And the wages of labourers were regulated by law.[x] It is evident, that these matters ought always to be left free, and be entrusted to the common course of business and commerce. To some it may appear surprising, that the price of a yard of scarlet cloth should be limited to six and twenty shillings, money of our age; that of a yard of coloured cloth to eighteen; higher prices than these commodities bear at present: and that the wages of a trades-man, such as a mason, bricklayer, tyler, &c. should be regulated at near ten-pence a-day; which is not much inferior to the present wages given in some parts of England. Labour and commodities have certainly risen since the discovery of the West-Indies; but not so much in every particular as is generally imagined. The greater industry of the present times has encreased the number of trades-men and labourers, so as to keep wages nearer a par than could be expected from the great encrease of gold and silver. And the additional art, employed in the finer manufactures, has even made some of these commodities fall below their former value. Not to mention, that merchants and dealers, being contented with less profit than formerly, afford the goods cheaper to their customers. It appears by a statute of this reign,[y] that goods bought for six-teenpence would sometimes be sold by the merchants for three shillings. The commodities, whose price has chiefly risen, are butcher's meat, fowl, and fish (especially the latter), which cannot be much augmented in quantity by the encrease of art and indus-try. The profession, which then abounded most, and was some-times embraced by persons of the lowest rank, was the church: By

[r] 3 H. 7. cap. 8.   [s] 11 H. 7. cap. 13.   [t] 3 H. 7. cap. 12.   [u] 4 H. 7. cap. 8.
[w] Ibid. cap. 9.   [x] 11 H. 7. cap. 22.   [y] 4 H. 7. cap. 9.

CHAPTER XXVI

a clause of a statute, all clerks or students of the university were forbidden to beg, without a permission from the vice-chancellor.[z]

One great cause of the low state of industry during this period, was the restraints put upon it; and the parliament, or rather the king (for he was the prime mover in every thing), enlarged a little some of these limitations; but not to the degree that was requisite. A law had been enacted during the reign of Henry IV,[a] that no man could bind his son or daughter to an apprenticeship, unless he were possessed of twenty shillings a-year in land; and Henry VII. because the decay of manufactures was complained of in Norwich from the want of hands, exempted that city from the penalties of the law.[b] Afterwards, the whole county of Norfolk obtained a like exemption with regard to some branches of the woollen manufacture.[c] These absurd limitations proceeded from a desire of promoting husbandry, which however is never more effectually encouraged than by the encrease of manufactures. For a like reason, the law enacted against inclosures, and for the keeping up of farm houses,[d] scarcely deserves the high praises bestowed on it by lord Bacon. If husbandmen understand agriculture, and have a ready vent for their commodities, we need not dread a diminution of the people, employed in the country. All methods of supporting populousness, except by the interest of the proprietors, are violent and ineffectual. During a century and a half after this period, there was a frequent renewal of laws and edicts against depopulation; whence we may infer, that none of them were ever executed. The natural course of improvement at last provided a remedy.

One check to industry in England was the erecting of corporations; an abuse which is not yet entirely corrected. A law was enacted, that corporations should not pass any by-laws without the consent of three of the chief officers of state.[e] They were prohibited from imposing tolls at their gates.[f] The cities of Glocester and Worcester had even imposed tolls on the Severne, which were abolished.[g]

There is a law of this reign,[h] containing a preamble, by which it appears, that the company of merchant adventurers in London

[z] 11 H. 7. cap. 22.   [a] 7 H. 7. cap. 17.   [b] 11 H. 7. cap. 11.   [c] 12 H. 7. cap. 1.   [d] 4 H. 7. cap. 19.   [e] 19 H. 7. cap. 7.   [f] Ibid. cap. 8.   [g] Ib. cap. 18.   [h] 12 H. 7. cap. 6.

had, by their own authority, debarred all the other merchants of the kingdom, from trading to the great marts in the Low Countries, unless each trader previously paid them the sum of near seventy pounds. It is surprising that such a by-law (if it deserve the name) could ever be carried into execution, and that the authority of parliament should be requisite to abrogate it.

It was during this reign, on the second of August 1492, a little before sun set, that Christopher Columbus, a Genoese, set out from Spain on his memorable voyage for the discovery of the western world; and a few years after, Vasquez de Gama, a Portuguese, passed the Cape of Good Hope, and opened a new passage to the East Indies. These great events were attended, with important consequences to all the nations of Europe, even to such as were not immediately concerned in those naval enterprizes. The enlargement of commerce and navigation encreased industry and the arts every where: The nobles dissipated their fortunes in expensive pleasures: Men of an inferior rank both acquired a share in the landed property, and created to themselves a considerable property of a new kind, in stock, commodities, art, credit, and correspondence. In some nations the privileges of the commons encreased, by this encrease of property: In most nations, the kings, finding arms to be dropped by the barons, who could no longer endure their former rude manner of life, established standing armies, and subdued the liberties of their kingdoms: But in all places, the condition of the people, from the depression of the petty tyrants, by whom they had formerly been oppressed, rather than governed, received great improvement, and they acquired, if not entire liberty, at least the most considerable advantages of it. And as the general course of events thus tended to depress the nobles and exalt the people, Henry VII. who also embraced that system of policy, has acquired more praise, than his institutions, strictly speaking, seem of themselves to deserve, on account of any profound wisdom attending them.

It was by accident only, that the king had not a considerable share in those great naval discoveries, by which the present age was so much distinguished. Columbus, after meeting with many repulses from the courts of Portugal and Spain, sent his brother, Bartholomew, to London, in order to explain his projects to Henry, and crave his protection for the execution of them. The

CHAPTER XXVI

king invited him over to England; but his brother, being taken by pyrates, was detained in his voyage; and Columbus, meanwhile, having obtained the countenance of Isabella, was supplied with a small fleet, and happily executed his enterprize. Henry was not discouraged by this disappointment: He fitted out Sebastian Cabot, a Venetian, settled in Bristol; and sent him westwards in 1498, in search of new countries. Cabot discovered the main land of America towards the sixtieth degree of northern latitude: He sailed southwards along the coast, and discovered Newfoundland, and other countries: But returned to England, without making any conquest or settlement. Elliot and other merchants in Bristol made a like attempt in 1502.[i] The king expended fourteen thousand pounds in building one ship called the *Great Harry*.[k] She was, properly speaking, the first ship in the English navy. Before this period, when the prince wanted a fleet, he had no other expedient than hiring or pressing ships from the merchants.

But though this improvement of navigation, and the discovery of both the Indies, was the most memorable incident that happened during this or any other period, it was not the only great event, by which the age was distinguished. In 1453, Constantinople was taken by the Turks; and the Greeks, among whom some remains of learning were still preserved, being scattered by these barbarians, took shelter in Italy, and imported, together with their admirable language, a tincture of their science and of their refined taste in poetry and eloquence. About the same time, the purity of the Latin tongue was revived, the study of antiquity became fashionable, and the esteem for literature gradually propagated itself throughout every nation in Europe. The art of printing, invented about that time, extremely facilitated the progress of all these improvements: The invention of gunpowder changed the whole art of war: Mighty innovations were soon after made in religion, such as not only affected those states that embraced them, but even those that adhered to the ancient faith and worship: And thus a general revolution was made in human affairs throughout this part of the world; and men gradually attained that situation, with regard to commerce, arts, science, government, police, and cultivation, in which they have ever since persevered. Here there-

[i] Rymer, vol. xiii, p. 37.   [k] Stowe, p. 484.

fore commences the useful, as well as the more agreeable part of modern annals; certainty has place in all the considerable, and even most of the minute parts of historical narration; a great variety of events, preserved by printing, give the author the power of selecting, as well as adorning, the facts, which he relates; and as each incident has a reference to our present manners and situation, instructive lessons occur every moment during the course of the narration. Whoever carries his anxious researches into preceding periods is moved by a curiosity, liberal indeed and commendable; not by any necessity for acquiring knowledge of public affairs, or the arts of civil government.

XXVII

HENRY VIII

---

*Popularity of the new king –
His ministers – Punishment of Empson
and Dudley – King's marriage – Foreign
affairs – Julius II. – League of Cambray –
War with France – Expedition to Fontarabia –
Deceit of Ferdinand – Return of the
English – Leo X. – A parliament – War with
Scotland – Wolsey minister – His
character – Invasion of France – Battle
of Guinegate – Battle of Flouden –
Peace with France*

THE DEATH OF HENRY VII. had been attended with as open and visible a joy among the people as decency would permit; and the accession and coronation of his son, Henry VIII. spread universally a declared and unfeigned satisfaction. Instead of a monarch, jealous, severe, and avaricious, who, in proportion as he advanced in years, was sinking still deeper in those unpopular vices; a young prince of eighteen had succeeded to the throne, who, even in the eyes of men of sense, gave promising hopes of his future conduct, much more in those of the people, always enchanted with novelty, youth and royal dignity. The beauty and vigour of his person, accompanied with dexterity in every manly exercise, was farther adorned with a blooming and ruddy countenance, with a lively air, with the appearance of spirit and activity in all his demeanour.[l] His father, in order to remove him from the knowledge of public business, had hitherto occupied him entirely in the pursuits of literature; and the proficiency which he made, gave no bad prognostic of his parts and capacity.[m] Even the vices of vehemence, ardour, and impatience, to which he was subject, and which afterwards degenerated into tyranny, were considered only as faults, incident to unguarded youth, which would be corrected, when time had brought him to greater moderation and maturity. And as the contending titles of York and Lancaster were now at last fully united in his person, men justly expected from a prince, obnoxious to no party, that impartiality of administration, which had long been unknown in England.

These favourable prepossessions of the public were encouraged by the measures which Henry embraced in the commencement of his reign. His grandmother, the countess of Richmond and Derby, was still alive; and as she was a woman much celebrated for prudence and virtue, he wisely shewed great deference to her opinion in the establishment of his new council. The members were, Warham, archbishop of Canterbury, and chancellor; the earl of Shrewsbury, steward; lord Herbert, chamberlain; Sir Thomas Lovel, master of the wards and constable of the Tower; Sir Edward Poynings, comptroller; Sir Henry Marney, afterwards lord Marney; Sir Thomas Darcy, afterwards lord Darcy; Thomas Ruthal, doctor of laws; and Sir Henry Wyat.[n] These men had long been accustomed to business under the late king, and were the least unpopular of all the ministers employed by that monarch.

His ministers.

But the chief competitors for favour and authority under the new king, were the earl of Surrey, treasurer, and Fox, bishop of Winchester, secretary and privy seal. This prelate, who enjoyed great credit during all the former reign, had acquired such habits of caution and frugality as he could not easily lay aside; and he still opposed, by his remonstrances, those schemes of dissipation and expence, which the youth and passions of Henry rendered agreeable to him. But Surrey was a more dexterous courtier; and though few had borne a greater share in the frugal politics of the late king, he knew how to conform himself to the humour of his new master;

---

[l] T. Mori. Lucubr. p. 182.   [m] Father Paul, lib. 1.   [n] Herbert, Stowe, p. 486. Hollingshed, p. 799.

CHAPTER XXVII

and no one was so forward in promoting that liberality, pleasure, and magnificence, which began to prevail under the young monarch.[o] By this policy he ingratiated himself with Henry; he made advantage, as well as the other courtiers, of the lavish disposition of his master; and he engaged him in such a course of play and idleness as rendered him negligent of affairs, and willing to entrust the government of the state entirely into the hands of his ministers. The great treasures amassed by the late king, were gradually dissipated in the giddy expences of Henry. One party of pleasure succeeded to another: Tilts, tournaments and carousals were exhibited with all the magnificence of the age: And as the present tranquillity of the public permitted the court to indulge itself in every amusement, serious business was but little attended to. Or if the king intermitted the course of his festivity, he chiefly employed himself in an application to music and literature, which were his favourite pursuits, and which were well adapted to his genius. He had made such proficiency in the former art, as even to compose some pieces of church-music which were sung in his chapel.[p] He was initiated in the elegant learning of the ancients. And though he was so unfortunate as to be seduced into a study of the barren controversies of the Schools, which were then fashionable, and had chosen Thomas Aquinas for his favourite author, he still discovered a capacity fitted for more useful and entertaining knowledge.

The frank and careless humour of the king, as it led him to dissipate the treasures, amassed by his father, rendered him negligent in protecting the instruments whom that prince had employed in his extortions. A proclamation being issued to encourage complaints, the rage of the people was let loose on all informers, who had so long exercised an unbounded tyranny over the nation:[q] They were thrown into prison, condemned to the pillory, and most of them lost their lives by the violence of the populace. Empson and Dudley, who were most exposed to public hatred, were immediately summoned before the council, in order to answer for their conduct, which had rendered them so obnoxious. Empson made a shrewd apology for himself, as well as for his associate. He told the council, that, so far from his being justly exposed to censure for his

Punishment of Empson and Dudley.

[o] Lord Herbert, [p] Ibid. [q] Herbert, Stowe, p. 486. Hollingshed, p. 799. Polyd. Virg. lib. 27.

past conduct, his enemies themselves grounded their clamour on actions, which seemed rather to merit reward and approbation: That a strict execution of law was the crime, of which he and Dudley were accused; though that law had been established by general consent, and though they had acted in obedience to the king, to whom the administration of justice was entrusted by the constitution: That it belonged not to them, who were instruments in the hands of supreme power, to determine what laws were recent or obsolete, expedient or hurtful; since they were all alike valid, so long as they remained unrepealed by the legislature: That it was natural for a licentious populace to murmur against the restraints of authority; but all wise states had ever made their glory consist in the just distribution of rewards and punishments, and had annexed the former to the observance and enforcement of the laws, the latter to their violation and infraction: And that a sudden overthrow of all government might be expected, where the judges were committed to the mercy of the criminals, the rulers to that of the subjects.[r]

Notwithstanding this defence, Empson and Dudley were sent to the Tower; and soon after brought to their trial. The strict execution of laws, however obsolete, could never be imputed to them as a crime in a court of judicature; and it is likely, that, even where they had exercised arbitrary power, the king, as they had acted by the secret commands of his father, was not willing that their conduct should undergo too severe a scrutiny. In order, therefore, to gratify the people with the punishment of these obnoxious ministers, crimes very improbable, or indeed absolutely impossible, were charged upon them; that they had entered into a conspiracy against the sovereign, and had intended, on the death of the late king, to have seized by force the administration of government. The jury were so far moved by popular prejudices, joined to court influence, as to give a verdict against them; which was afterwards confirmed by a bill of attainder in parliament,[s]

[r] Herbert, Hollingshed, p. 804.   [s] This parliament met on the 21st January, 1510. A law was there enacted, in order to prevent some abuses which had prevailed during the late reign. The forfeiture upon the penal statutes was reduced to the term of three years. Costs and damages were given against informers upon acquittal of the accused: More severe punishments were enacted against perjury: The false inquisitions procured by Empson

and, at the earnest desire of the people, was executed by warrant from the king. Thus, in those arbitrary times, justice was equally violated, whether the king sought power and riches, or courted popularity.

Henry, while he punished the instruments of past tyranny, had yet such deference to former engagements as to deliberate, immediately after his accession, concerning the celebration of his marriage with the infanta Catherine, to whom he had been affianced during his father's lifetime. Her former marriage with his brother, *King's* and the inequality of their years, were the chief objections, urged *mar-* against his espousing her: But on the other hand, the advantages *riage.* of her known virtue, modesty, and sweetness of disposition were insisted on; the affection which she bore to the king; the large dowry to which she was entitled as princess of Wales; the interest of cementing a close alliance with Spain; the necessity of finding some confederate to counterbalance the power of France; the expediency of fulfilling the engagements of the late king. When these considerations were weighed, they determined the council, though contrary to the opinion of the primate, to give Henry their advice for celebrating the marriage. The countess of Richmond, *3d* who had concurred in the same sentiments with the council, died *June.* soon after the marriage of her grandson.

The popularity of Henry's government, his undisputed title, his extensive authority, his large treasures, the tranquillity of his subjects, were circumstances which rendered his domestic administration easy and prosperous: The situation of foreign affairs was *Foreign* no less happy and desirable. Italy continued still, as during the late *affairs.* reign, to be the center of all the wars and negociations of the European princes; and Henry's alliance was courted by all parties; at the same time, that he was not engaged by any immediate interest or necessity to take part with any. Lewis XII. of France, after his conquest of Milan, was the only great prince that possessed any territory in Italy; and could he have remained in tranquillity, he was enabled by his situation to prescribe laws to all the Italian princes and republics, and to hold the balance among them. But the desire of making a conquest of Naples, to which he had the

---

and Dudley, were declared null and invalid. Traverses were allowed; and the time of tendering them enlarged. 1 H. 8. c. 8, 10, 11, 12.

same title or pretensions with his predecessor, still engaged him in new enterprizes; and as he foresaw opposition from Ferdinand, who was connected both by treaties and affinity with Frederic of Naples, he endeavoured, by the offers of interest, to which the ears of that monarch were ever open, to engage him in an opposite confederacy. He settled with him a plan for the partition of the kingdom of Naples and the expulsion of Frederic: A plan, which the politicians of that age regarded as the most egregious imprudence in the French monarch, and the greatest perfidy in the Spanish. Frederic, supported only by subjects, who were either discontented with his government, or indifferent about his fortunes, was unable to resist so powerful a confederacy, and was deprived of his dominions: But he had the satisfaction to see Naples immediately prove the source of contention among his enemies. Ferdinand gave secret orders to his general, Gonsalvo, whom the Spaniards honour with the appellation of the *great captain,* to attack the armies of France, and make himself master of all the dominions of Naples. Gonsalvo prevailed in every enterprize, defeated the French in two pitched battles, and ensured to his prince the entire possession of that kingdom. Lewis, unable to procure redress by force of arms, was obliged to enter into a fruitless negociation with Ferdinand for the recovery of his share of the partition; and all Italy, during some time, was held in suspence between these two powerful monarchs.

There has scarcely been any period, when the balance of power was better secured in Europe, and seemed more able to maintain itself without any anxious concern or attention of the princes. Several great monarchies were established; and no one so far surpassed the rest as to give any foundation, or even pretence, for jealousy. England was united in domestic peace, and by its situation happily secured from the invasion of foreigners. The coalition of the several kingdoms of Spain had formed one powerful monarchy, which Ferdinand administered with arts, fraudulent indeed and deceitful, but full of vigour and ability. Lewis XII. a gallant and generous prince, had, by espousing Anne of Britanny, widow to his predecessor, preserved the union with that principality, on which the safety of his kingdom so much depended. Maximilian, the emperor, besides the hereditary dominions of the Austrian family, maintained authority in the empire, and notwithstanding the levity of his character, was able to unite the German princes in any great plan of interest, at least of defence. Charles, prince of Castile, grandson to Maximilian and Ferdinand, had already succeeded to the rich dominions of the house of Burgundy; and being as yet in early youth, the government was entrusted to Margaret of Savoy, his aunt, a princess endowed with signal prudence and virtue. The internal force of these several powerful states, by balancing each other, might long have maintained general tranquillity, had not the active and enterprising genius of Julius II. an ambitious pontiff, first excited the flames of *Julius* war and discord among them. By his intrigues, a league had been *II.* formed at Cambray,[*f*] between himself, Maximilian, Lewis, and Ferdinand; and the object of this great confederacy was to overwhelm, *Cambray.* by their united arms, the commonwealth of Venice. Henry, without any motive from interest or passion, allowed his name to be inserted in the confederacy. This oppressive and iniquitous league was but too successful against the republic.

League of
Cambray.

The great force and secure situation of the considerable monarchies prevented any one from aspiring to any conquest of moment; and though this consideration could not maintain general peace, or remedy the natural inquietude of men, it rendered the princes of this age more disposed to desert engagements and change their alliances, in which they were retained by humour and caprice, rather than by any natural or durable interest. Julius had *1510.* no sooner humbled the Venetian republic, than he was inspired with a nobler ambition, that of expelling all foreigners from Italy, or, to speak in the stile affected by the Italians of that age, the freeing of that country entirely from the dominion of Barbarians.[*u*] He was determined to make the tempest fall first upon Lewis; and in order to pave the way for this great enterprize, he at once fought for a ground of quarrel with that monarch, and courted the alliance of other princes. He declared war against the duke of Ferrara, the confederate of Lewis. He solicited the favour of England, by sending Henry a sacred rose, perfumed with musk and anointed with chrism.[*w*] He engaged in his interests Bambridge, archbishop of York, and Henry's ambassador at Rome, whom he soon after created a cardinal. He drew over Ferdinand to his party, though that monarch, at first, made no declaration of his intentions. And what he chiefly valued, he formed a treaty with the Swiss cantons,

---

[*f*] In 1508. [*u*] Guicciard. lib. 8. [*w*] Spelman, Concil. vol. ii. p. 725.

who, enraged by some neglects put upon them by Lewis, accompanied with contumelious expressions, had quitted the alliance of France, and waited for an opportunity of revenging themselves on that nation.

1511.   While the French monarch repelled the attacks of his enemies, he thought it also requisite to make an attempt on the pope himself, and to despoil him, as much as possible, of that sacred character, which chiefly rendered him formidable. He engaged some cardinals, disgusted with the violence of Julius, to desert him; and by their authority, he was determined, in conjunction with Maximilian, who still adhered to his alliance, to call a general council, which might reform the church, and check the exorbitancies of the Roman pontiff. A council was summoned at Pisa, which from the beginning bore a very inauspicious aspect, and promised little success to its adherents. Except a few French bishops, who unwillingly obeyed the king's commands in attending the council, all the other prelates kept aloof from an assembly, which they regarded as the offspring of faction, intrigue, and worldly politics. Even Pisa, the place of their residence, showed them signs of contempt; which engaged them to transfer their session to Milan, a city under the dominion of the French monarch. Notwithstanding this advantage, they did not experience much more respectful treatment from the inhabitants of Milan; and found it necessary to make another remove to Lyons.[x] Lewis himself fortified these violent prejudices in favour of papal authority, by the symptoms, which he discovered, of regard, deference, and submission to Julius, whom he always spared, even when fortune had thrown into his hands the most inviting opportunities of humbling him. And as it was known, that his consort, who had great influence over him, was extremely disquieted in mind, on account of his dissensions with the holy father, all men prognosticated to Julius final success in this unequal contest.

The enterprizing pontiff knew his advantages, and availed himself of them with the utmost temerity and insolence. So much had he neglected his sacerdotal character, that he acted in person at the siege of Mirandola, visited the trenches, saw some of his attendants killed by his side, and, like a young soldier, cheerfully bore all the rigours of winter and a severe season, in pursuit of

[x] Guicciardini, lib. 10.

military glory:[y] Yet was he still able to throw, even on his most moderate opponents, the charge of impiety and prophaneness. He summoned a council at the Lateran: He put Pisa under an interdict, and all the places which gave shelter to the schismatical council: He excommunicated the cardinals and prelates who attended it: He even pointed his spiritual thunder against the princes who adhered to it: He freed their subjects from all oaths of allegiance, and gave their dominions to every one, who could take possession of them.

Ferdinand of Arragon, who had acquired the sirname of Catholic, regarded the cause of the pope and of religion only as a cover to his ambition and selfish politics: Henry, naturally sincere and sanguine in his temper, and the more so on account of his youth and inexperience, was moved with a hearty desire of protecting the pope from the oppression, to which he believed him exposed from the ambitious enterprizes of Lewis. Hopes had been given him by Julius, that the title of *most Christian King,* which had hitherto been annexed to the crown of France, and which was regarded as its most precious ornament, should, in reward of his services, be transferred to that of England.[z] Impatient also of acquiring that distinction in Europe, to which his power and opulence entitled him, he could not long remain neuter amidst the noise of arms; and the natural enmity of the English against France, as well as their ancient claims upon that kingdom, led Henry to join that alliance, which the pope, Spain, and Venice had formed against the French monarch. A herald was sent to Paris, to exhort Lewis not to wage impious war against the sovereign pontiff; and when he returned without success, another was sent to demand the ancient patrimonial provinces, Anjou, Maine, Guienne, and Normandy. This message was understood to be a declaration of war; and a parliament being summoned, readily granted supplies for a purpose so much favoured by the English nation.[a]

Buonaviso, an agent of the pope's at London, had been corrupted by the court of France, and had previously revealed to Lewis all the measures, which Henry was concerting against him. But this infidelity did the king inconsiderable prejudice, in comparison of the treachery, which he experienced from the selfish

1512.

War with France. 4th Feb.

[y] Guicciardini, lib. 9.   [z] Guicciard. lib. 11. P. Daniel, vol. ii. p. 1893. Herbert. Hollingshed, p. 831.   [a] Herbert. Hollingshed, p. 811.

purposes of the ally, on whom he chiefly relied for assistance. Ferdinand, his father-in-law, had so long persevered in a course of crooked politics; that he began even to value himself on his dexterity in fraud and artifice; and he made a boast of those shameful successes. Being told one day, that Lewis, a prince of a very different character, had complained of his having once cheated him: "he lies, the drunkard!" said he, "I have cheated him above twenty times." This prince considered his close connexions with Henry, only as the means which enabled him the better to take advantage of his want of experience. He advised him not to invade France by the way of Calais, where he himself should not have it in his power to assist him: He exhorted him rather to send forces to Fontarabia, whence he could easily make a conquest of Guienne, a province, in which, it was imagined, the English had still some adherents. He promised to assist this conquest by the junction of a Spanish army. And so forward did he seem to promote the interests of his son-in-law, that he even sent vessels to England, in order to transport over the forces which Henry had levied for that purpose. The marquis of Dorset commanded this armament, which consisted of ten thousand men, mostly infantry; lord Howard, son of the earl of Surrey, lord Broke, lord Ferrars, and many others of the young gentry and nobility, accompanied him in this service. All were on fire to distinguish themselves by military achievements, and to make a conquest of importance for their master. The secret purpose of Ferdinand in this unexampled generosity was suspected by no body.

Expedition to Fontarabia.

The small kingdom of Navarre lies on the frontiers between France and Spain; and as John d'Albret, the sovereign, was connected by friendship and alliance with Lewis, the opportunity seemed favourable to Ferdinand, while the English forces were conjoined with his own, and while all adherents to the council of Pisa lay under the sentence of excommunication, to put himself in possession of these dominions. No sooner, therefore, was Dorset landed in Guipiscoa, than the Spanish monarch declared his readiness to join him with his forces, to make with united arms an invasion of France, and to form the siege of Bayonne, which opened the way into Guienne:[b] But he remarked to the English general how dangerous it might prove to leave behind them the kingdom of Navarre, which, being in close alliance with France,

---

[b] Herbert. Hollingshed, p. 813.

CHAPTER XXVII

could easily give admittance to the enemy, and cut off all communication between Spain and the combined armies. To provide
against so dangerous an event, he required, that John should stipulate a neutrality in the present war; and when that prince expressed his willingness to enter into any engagement for that purpose, he also required, that security should be given for the strict
observance of it. John having likewise agreed to this condition,
Ferdinand demanded, that he should deliver into his hands six of
the most considerable places of his dominions, together with his
eldest son as a hostage. These were not terms to be proposed to a
sovereign; and as the Spanish monarch expected a refusal, he gave
immediate orders to the duke of Alva, his general, to make an
invasion on Navarre, and to reduce that kingdom. Alva soon made
himself master of all the smaller towns; and being ready to form
the siege of Pampeluna, the capital, he summoned the marquis of
Dorset to join him with the English army, and concert together all
their operations.

Dorset began to suspect, that the interests of his master were
very little regarded in all these transactions; and having no orders
to invade the kingdom of Navarre, or make war any where but in
France, he refused to take any part in the enterprize. He remained
therefore in his quarters at Fontarabia; but so subtle was the contrivance of Ferdinand, that, even while the English army lay in that
situation, it was almost equally serviceable to his purpose, as if it
had acted in conjunction with his own. It kept the French army in
awe, and prevented it from advancing to succour the kingdom of
Navarre; so that Alva, having full leisure to conduct the siege,
made himself master of Pampeluna, and obliged John to seek for
shelter in France. The Spanish general applied again to Dorset,
and proposed to conduct with united counsels the operations of
the *holy league,* so it was called, against Lewis: But as he still declined forming the siege of Bayonne, and rather insisted on the
invasion of the principality of Bearne, a part of the king of Navarre's dominions, which lies on the French side of the Pyrenees,
Dorset, justly suspicious of his sinister intentions, represented,
that, without new orders from his master, he could not concur in
such an undertaking. In order to procure these orders, Ferdinand
dispatched Martin de Ampios to London; and persuaded Henry,
that, by the refractory and scrupulous humour of the English
general, the most favourable opportunities were lost, and that it

*Deceit of
Ferdinand.*

was necessary he should, on all occasions, act in concert with the Spanish commander, who was best acquainted with the situation of the country, and the reasons of every operation. But before orders to this purpose reached Spain, Dorset had become extremely impatient; and observing that his farther stay served not to promote the main undertaking, and that his army was daily perishing by want and sickness, he demanded shipping from Ferdinand to transport them back into England. Ferdinand, who was bound by treaty to furnish him with this supply, whenever demanded, was at length, after many delays, obliged to yield to his importunity; and Dorset, embarking his troops, prepared himself for the voyage. Meanwhile, the messenger arrived with orders from Henry, that *Return of the English.* the troops should remain in Spain; but the soldiers were so discontented with the treatment which they had met with, that they mutinied, and obliged their commanders to set sail for England. Henry was much displeased with the ill success of this enterprize; and it was with difficulty, that Dorset, by explaining the fraudulent conduct of Ferdinand, was at last able to appease him.

There happened this summer an action at sea, which brought not any more decisive advantage to the English. Sir Thomas Knevet, master of horse, was sent to the coast of Britanny with a fleet of forty-five sail; and he carried with him Sir Charles Brandon, Sir John Carew, and many other young courtiers, who longed for an opportunity of displaying their valour. After they had committed some depredations, a French fleet of thirty-nine sail issued from Brest, under the command of Primauget, and began an engagement with the English. Fire seized the ship of Primauget, who, finding his destruction inevitable, bore down upon the vessel of the English admiral, and grappling with her, resolved to make her share his fate. Both fleets stood some time in suspence, as spectators of this dreadful engagement; and all men saw with horror the flames which consumed both vessels, and heard the cries of fury and despair, which came from the miserable combatants. At last, the French vessel blew up; and at the same time destroyed the English.[c] The rest of the French fleet made their escape into different harbours.

[c] Polydore Virgil, lib. 27. Stowe, p. 490. Lanquet's Epitome of chronicles, fol. 273.

CHAPTER XXVII

The war, which England waged against France, though it brought no advantage to the former kingdom, was of great prejudice to the latter; and by obliging Lewis to withdraw his forces for the defence of his own dominions, lost him that superiority, which his arms, in the beginning of the campaign, had attained in Italy. Gaston de Foix, his nephew, a young hero, had been entrusted with the command of the French forces; and in a few months performed such feats of military art and prowess, as were sufficient to render illustrious the life of the oldest captain.[d] His career finished with the great battle of Ravenna, which, after the most obstinate conflict, he gained over the Spanish and papal armies. He perished the very moment his victory was complete; and with him perished the fortune of the French arms in Italy. The Swiss, who had rendered themselves extremely formidable by their bands of disciplined infantry, invaded the Milanese with a numerous army, and raised up that inconstant people to a revolt against the dominion of France. Genoa followed the example of the dutchy; and thus Lewis, in a few weeks, entirely lost his Italian conquests, except some garrisons; and Maximilian Sforza, the son of Ludovic, was reinstated in possession of Milan.

1513.

Julius discovered extreme joy on the discomfiture of the French; and the more so, as he had been beholden for it to the Swiss, a people, whose councils, he hoped, he should always be able to influence and govern. The pontiff survived this success a very little time; and in his place was chosen John de Medicis, who took the appellation of Leo X. and proved one of the most illustrious princes that ever sat on the papal throne. Humane, beneficent, generous, affable; the patron of every art, and friend of every virtue;[e] he had a soul no less capable of forming great designs than his predecessor, but was more gentle, pliant, and artful in employing means for the execution of them. The sole defect, indeed, of his character was too great finesse and artifice; a fault, which, both as a priest and an Italian, it was difficult for him to avoid. By the negociations of Leo, the emperor Maximilian was detached from the French interest; and Henry, notwithstanding his disappointments in the former campaign, was still encouraged to prosecute his warlike measures against Lewis.

21st Feb. Leo X.

[d] Guicciard. lib. 10.　　[e] Father Paul, lib. 1.

Henry had summoned a new session of parliament,[f] and obtained a supply for his enterprize. It was a poll-tax, and imposed
different sums, according to the station and riches of the person.
A duke payed ten marks, an earl five pounds, a baron four pounds,
a knight four marks; every man valued at eight hundred pounds
in goods, four marks. An imposition was also granted of two fifteenths and four tenths.[g] By these supplies, joined to the treasure,
which had been left by his father, and which was not yet entirely
dissipated, he was enabled to levy a great army, and render himself
formidable to his enemy. The English are said to have been much
encouraged in this enterprize, by the arrival of a vessel in the
Thames under the papal banner. It carried presents of wine and
hams to the king, and the more eminent courtiers; and such fond
devotion was at that time entertained towards the court of Rome,
that these trivial presents were every where received with the greatest triumph and exultation.

In order to prevent all disturbances from Scotland, while Henry's arms should be employed on the continent, Dr. West, dean
of Windsor, was dispatched on an embassy to James, the king's
brother-in-law; and instructions were given him to accommodate
all differences between the kingdoms, as well as to discover the
intentions of the court of Scotland.[h] Some complaints had already
been made on both sides. One Barton, a Scotchman, having suffered injuries from the Portugueze, for which he could obtain no
redress, had procured letters of marque against that nation; but he
had no sooner put to sea, than he was guilty of the grossest abuses,
committed depredations upon the English, and much infested the
narrow seas.[i] Lord Howard and Sir Edward Howard, admirals, and
sons of the earl of Surrey, sailing out against him, fought him in
a desperate action, where the pyrate was killed; and they brought
his ships into the Thames. As Henry refused all satisfaction for this
act of justice, some of the borderers, who wanted but a pretence
for depredations, entered England under the command of lord
Hume, warden of the marches, and committed great ravages on
that kingdom. Notwithstanding these mutual grounds of dissatis-

[f] 4th November, 1512.   [g] Stowe.   [h] Polydore Virgil, lib. 27.   [i] Stowe, p.
489. Hollingshed, p. 811.

CHAPTER XXVII

faction, matters might easily have been accommodated, had it not been for Henry's intended invasion of France, which rouzed the jealousy of the Scotish nation.[k] The ancient league, which subsisted between France and Scotland, was conceived to be the strongest band of connexion; and the Scots universally believed, that, were it not for the countenance which they received from this foreign alliance, they had never been able so long to maintain their independence against a people so much superior. James was farther incited to take part in the quarrel by the invitations of Anne, queen of France, whose knight he had ever in all tournaments professed himself, and who summoned him, according to the ideas of romantic gallantry, prevalent in that age, to take the field in her defence, and prove himself her true and valorous champion. The remonstrances of his consort and of his wisest counsellors were in vain opposed to the martial ardour of this prince. He first sent a squadron of ships to the assistance of France; the only fleet which Scotland seems ever to have possessed. And though he still made professions of maintaining a neutrality, the English ambassador easily foresaw, that a war would in the end prove inevitable; and he gave warning of the danger to his master, who sent the earl of Surrey to put the borders in a posture of defence, and to resist the expected invasion of the enemy.

War with Scotland.

Henry, all on fire for military fame, was little discouraged by this appearance of a diversion from the north; and so much the less, as he flattered himself with the assistance of all the considerable potentates of Europe in his invasion of France. The pope still continued to thunder out his excommunications against Lewis, and all the adherents of the schismatical council: The Swiss cantons made professions of violent animosity against France: The ambassadors of Ferdinand and Maximilian had signed with those of Henry a treaty of alliance against that power, and had stipulated the time and place of their intended invasion: And though Ferdinand disavowed his ambassador, and even signed a truce for a twelvemonth with the common enemy; Henry was not yet fully convinced of his selfish and sinister intentions, and still hoped for his concurrence after the expiration of that term. He had now got

[k] Buchanan, lib. 13. Drummond in the life of James IV.

a minister who complied with all his inclinations, and flattered him in every scheme, to which his sanguine and impetuous temper was inclined.

Wolsey minis- ter.

Thomas Wolsey, dean of Lincoln, and almoner to the king, surpassed in favour all his ministers, and was fast advancing towards that unrivalled grandeur, which he afterwards attained. This man was son of a butcher at Ipswich; but having got a learned education, and being endowed with an excellent capacity, he was admitted into the marquis of Dorset's family as tutor to that nobleman's children, and soon gained the friendship and countenance of his patron.[l] He was recommended to be chaplain to Henry VII. and being employed by that monarch in a secret negociation, which regarded his intended marriage with Margaret of Savoy, Maximilian's daughter, he acquitted himself to the king's satisfaction, and obtained the praise both of diligence and dexterity in his conduct.[m] That prince, having given him a commission to Maximilian, who at that time resided in Brussels, was surprized, in less than three days after, to see Wolsey present himself before him; and supposing that he had protracted his departure, he began to reprove him for the dilatory execution of his orders. Wolsey informed him, that he had just returned from Brussels, and had successfully fulfilled all his majesty's commands. "But on second thoughts," said the king, "I found that somewhat was omitted in your orders; and have sent a messenger after you, with fuller instructions." "I met the messenger," replied Wolsey, "on my return: But as I had reflected on that omission, I ventured of myself to execute what, I knew, must be your majesty's intentions." The death of Henry, soon after this incident, retarded the advancement of Wolsey, and prevented his reaping any advantage from the good opinion, which that monarch had entertained of him: But thenceforwards he was looked on at court as a rising man; and Fox, bishop of Winchester, cast his eye upon him as one, who might be serviceable to him in his present situation.[n] This prelate, observing that the earl of Surrey had totally eclipsed him in favour, resolved to introduce Wolsey to the young prince's familiarity, and hoped, that he might rival Surrey in his insinuating arts, and yet

[l] Stowe, p. 997.   [m] Cavendish, Fiddes's life of Wolsey. Stowe.   [n] Antiq. Brit. Eccles. p. 309. Polydore Virgil, lib. 27.

be content to act in the cabinet a part subordinate to Fox himself, who had promoted him. In a little time, Wolsey gained so much on the king, that he supplanted both Surrey in his favour, and Fox in his trust and confidence. Being admitted to Henry's parties of pleasure, he took the lead in every jovial conversation, and promoted all that frolic and entertainment, which he found suitable to the age and inclination of the young monarch. Neither his own years, which were near forty, nor his character of a clergyman, were any restraint upon him, or engaged him to check, by any useless severity, the gaiety, in which Henry, who had small propension to debauchery, passed his careless hours. During the intervals of amusement he introduced business, and insinuated those maxims of conduct which he was desirous his master should adopt. He observed to him, that, while he entrusted his affairs into the hands of his father's counsellors, he had the advantage indeed of employing men of wisdom and experience, but men who owed not their promotion to his favour, and who scarcely thought themselves accountable to him for the exercise of their authority: That by the factions, and cabals, and jealousies, which had long prevailed among them, they more obstructed the advancement of his affairs, than they promoted it by the knowledge, which age and practice had conferred upon them: That while he thought proper to pass his time in those pleasures, to which his age and royal fortune invited him, and in those studies, which would in time enable him to sway the scepter with absolute authority, his best system of government would be to entrust his authority into the hands of some one person, who was the creature of his will, and who could entertain no view but that of promoting his service: And that if this minister had also the same relish for pleasure with himself, and the same taste for science, he could more easily, at intervals, account to him for his whole conduct, and introduce his master gradually into the knowledge of public business, and thus, without tedious constraint or application, initiate him in the science of government.[o]

Henry entered into all the views of Wolsey; and finding no one so capable of executing this plan of administration as the person who proposed it, he soon advanced his favourite, from being the

[o] Cavendish, p. 12. Stowe, p. 499.

His
character.

companion of his pleasures, to be a member of his council; and from being a member of his council, to be his sole and absolute minister. By this rapid advancement and uncontrouled authority, the character and genius of Wolsey had full opportunity to display itself. Insatiable in his acquisitions, but still more magnificent in his expence: Of extensive capacity, but still more unbounded enterprize: Ambitious of power, but still more desirous of glory: Insinuating, engaging, persuasive; and, by turns, lofty, elevated, commanding: Haughty to his equals, but affable to his dependants; oppressive to the people, but liberal to his friends; more generous than grateful; less moved by injuries than by contempt; he was framed to take the ascendant in every intercourse with others, but exerted this superiority of *nature* with such ostentation as exposed him to envy, and made every one willing to recal the original inferiority or rather meanness of his *fortune*.

The branch of administration, in which Henry most exerted himself, while he gave his entire confidence to Wolsey, was the military, which, as it suited the natural gallantry and bravery of his temper, as well as the ardour of his youth, was the principal object of his attention. Finding that Lewis had made great preparations both by sea and land to resist him, he was no less careful to levy a formidable army, and equip a considerable fleet for the invasion of France. The command of the fleet was entrusted to Sir Edward Howard: who, after scouring the channel for some time, presented himself before Brest, where the French navy then lay; and he challenged them to a combat. The French admiral, who expected from the Mediterranean a reinforcement of some gallies under the command of Prejeant de Bidoux, kept within the harbour, and saw with patience the English burn and destroy the country in the neighbourhood. At last Prejeant arrived with six gallies, and put into Conquet, a place within a few leagues of Brest; where he secured himself behind some batteries, which he had planted on rocks, that lay on each side of him. Howard was, notwithstanding, determined to make an attack upon him; and as he had but two gallies, he took himself the command of one, and gave the other to lord Ferrars. He was followed by some row-barges and some crayers under the command of Sir Thomas Cheyney, Sir William Sidney, and other officers of distinction. He immediately fastened on Prejeant's ship, and leaped on board of her, attended by one

25th
April.

CHAPTER XXVII

Carroz, a Spanish cavalier, and seventeen Englishmen. The cable, meanwhile, which fastened his ship to that of the enemy, being cut, the admiral was thus left in the hands of the French; and as he still continued the combat with great gallantry, he was pushed over-board by their pikes.[p] Lord Ferrars, seeing the admiral's galley fall off, followed with the other small vessels; and the whole fleet was so discouraged by the loss of their commander, that they retired from before Brest.[q] The French navy came out of harbour; and even ventured to invade the coast of Sussex. They were repulsed, and Prejeant, their commander, lost an eye by the shot of an arrow. Lord Howard, brother to the deceased admiral, succeeded to the command of the English fleet; and little memorable passed at sea during this summer.

Great preparations had been making at land, during the whole winter, for an invasion on France by the way of Calais; but the summer was well advanced before every thing was in sufficient readiness for the intended enterprize. The long peace which the kingdom had enjoyed, had somewhat unfitted the English for military expeditions; and the great change, which had lately been introduced in the art of war, had rendered it still more difficult to enure them to the use of the weapons now employed in action. The Swiss, and after them the Spaniards, had shown the advantage of a stable infantry, who fought with pike and sword, and were able to repulse even the heavy-armed cavalry, in which the great force of the armies formerly consisted. The practice of fire-arms was become common; though the caliver, which was the weapon now in use, was so inconvenient, and attended with so many disadvan-tages, that it had not entirely discredited the bow, a weapon in which the English excelled all European nations. A considerable part of the forces, which Henry levied for the invasion of France, consisted of archers; and as soon as affairs were in readiness, the vanguard of the army, amounting to 8000 men, under the com-mand of the earl of Shrewsbury, sailed over to Calais. Shrewsbury

[p] It was a maxim of Howard's, that no admiral was good for any thing that was not brave even to a degree of madness. As the sea-service requires much less plan and contrivance and capacity than the land, this maxim has great plausibility and appearance of truth: Though the fate of Howard himself may serve as a proof that even there courage ought to be tempered with discretion.   [q] Stowe, p. 491. Herbert, Hollingshed, p. 816.

was accompanied by the earl of Derby, the lords Fitzwater, Hastings, Cobham, and Sir Rice ap Thomas, captain of the light horse. Another body of 6000 men soon after followed under the command of lord Herbert, the chamberlain, attended by the earls of Northumberland and Kent, the lords Audley and Delawar, together with Carew, Curson, and other gentlemen.

The king himself prepared to follow with the main body and rear of the army; and he appointed the queen regent of the kingdom during his absence. That he might secure her administration from all disturbance, he ordered Edmond de la Pole, earl of Suffolk, to be beheaded in the Tower, the nobleman who had been attainted and imprisoned during the late reign. Henry was led to commit this act of violence by the dying commands, as is imagined, of his father, who told him, that he never would be free from danger, while a man of so turbulent a disposition as Suffolk was alive. And as Richard de la Pole, brother of Suffolk, had accepted of a command in the French service, and foolishly attempted to revive the York faction, and to instigate them against the present government he probably, by that means, drew more suddenly the king's vengeance on this unhappy nobleman.

30th June.

At last, Henry, attended by the duke of Buckingham and many others of the nobility, arrived at Calais, and entered upon his French expedition, from which he fondly expected so much success and glory.[r] Of all those allies, on whose assistance he relied, the Swiss alone fully performed their engagements. Being put in motion by a sum of money sent them by Henry, and incited by their victories obtained in Italy, and by their animosity against France, they were preparing to enter that kingdom with an army of twenty-five thousand men; and no equal force could be opposed to their incursion. Maximilian had received an advance of 120,000 crowns from Henry, and had promised to reinforce the Swiss with 8000 men, but failed in his engagements. That he might make atonement to the king, he himself appeared in the Low Countries, and joined the English army with some German and Flemish soldiers, who were useful in giving an example of discipline to Henry's new levied forces. Observing the disposition of the Eng-

Invasion of France.

[r] Polydore Virgil, lib. 27. Belcarius, lib. 14.

CHAPTER XXVII

lish monarch to be more bent on glory than on interest, he inlisted himself in his service, wore the cross of St. George, and received pay, a hundred crowns a day, as one of his subjects and captains. But while he exhibited this extraordinary spectacle, of an emperor of Germany serving under a king of England, he was treated with the highest respect by Henry, and really directed all the operations of the English army.

Before the arrival of Henry and Maximilian in the camp, the earl of Shrewsbury and lord Herbert had formed the siege of Teroüane, a town situated on the frontiers of Picardy; and they began to attack the place with vigour. Teligni and Crequi commanded in the town, and had a garrison not exceeding two thousand men; yet made they such stout resistance as protracted the siege a month, and they at last found themselves more in danger from want of provisions and ammunition, than from the assaults of the besiegers. Having conveyed intelligence of their situation to Lewis, who had advanced to Amiens with his army, that prince gave orders to throw relief into the place. Fontrailles appeared at the head of 800 horsemen, each of whom carried a sack of gunpowder behind him, and two quarters of bacon. With this small force he made a sudden and unexpected irruption into the English camp, and surmounting all resistance, advanced to the fossee of the town, where each horseman threw down his burden. They immediately returned at the gallop, and were so fortunate as again to break through the English, and to suffer little or no loss in this dangerous attempt.[s] *16th Aug.*

But the English had, soon after, full revenge for the insult. Henry had received intelligence of the approach of the French horse, who had advanced to protect another incursion of Fontrailles; and he ordered some troops to pass the Lis, in order to oppose them. The cavalry of France, though they consisted chiefly of gentlemen, who had behaved with great gallantry in many desperate actions in Italy, were, on sight of the enemy, seized with so unaccountable a panic, that they immediately took to flight; and were pursued by the English. The duke of Longueville, who commanded the French, Bussi d'Amboise, Clermont, Imbercourt, the *Battle of Guinegate.*

[s] Hist. de Chev. Bayard, chap. 57. Memoires de Bellai.

chevalier Bayard, and many other officers of distinction, were made prisoners.[f] This action, or rather rout, is sometimes called the battle of Guinegate, from the place where it was fought; but more commonly the *Battle of Spurs,* because the French, that day, made more use of their spurs than of their swords or military weapons.

After so considerable an advantage, the king, who was at the head of a complete army of above 50,000 men, might have made incursions to the gates of Paris, and spread confusion and desolation every where. It gave Lewis great joy, when he heard, that the English, instead of pushing their victory, and attacking the dismayed troops of France, returned to the siege of so inconsiderable a place as Terouane. The governors were obliged soon after to capitulate; and Henry found his acquisition of so little moment, though gained at the expence of some blood, and what, in his present circumstances, was more important, of much valuable time, that he immediately demolished the fortifications. The anxieties of the French were again revived with regard to the motions of the English. The Swiss at the same time had entered Burgundy with a formidable army, and laid siege to Dijon, which was in no condition to resist them. Ferdinand himself, though he had made a truce with Lewis, seemed disposed to lay hold of every advantage which fortune should present to him. Scarcely ever was the French monarchy in greater danger, or less in a condition to defend itself against those powerful armies, which on every side assailed or threatened it. Even many of the inhabitants of Paris, who believed themselves exposed to the rapacity and violence of the enemy, began to dislodge, without knowing what place could afford them greater security.

But Lewis was extricated from his present difficulties by the manifold blunders of his enemies. The Swiss allowed themselves to be seduced into a negociation by Tremoille, governor of Burgundy; and without making enquiry, whether that nobleman had any powers to treat, they accepted of the conditions which he offered them. Tremoille, who knew that he should be disavowed

[f] Memoires de Bellai, liv. 1. Polydore Virgil, liv. 27. Hollingshed, p. 822. Herbert.

CHAPTER XXVII

by his master, stipulated whatever they were pleased to demand; and thought himself happy, at the expence of some payments, and very large promises, to get rid of so formidable an enemy.[u]

The measures of Henry showed equal ignorance in the art of war with that of the Swiss in negociation. Tournay was a great and rich city, which, though it lay within the frontiers of Flanders, belonged to France, and afforded the troops of that kingdom a passage into the heart of the Netherlands. Maximilian, who was desirous of freeing his grandson from so troublesome a neighbour, advised Henry to lay siege to the place; and the English monarch, not considering that such an acquisition nowise advanced his conquests in France, was so imprudent as to follow this interested counsel. The city of Tournay, by its ancient charters, being exempted from the burthen of a garrison, the burghers, against the remonstrance of their sovereign, strenuously insisted on maintaining this dangerous privilege; and they engaged, by themselves, to make a vigorous defence against the enemy.[w] Their courage failed them when matters came to trial; and after a few days siege, the place was surrendered to the English. The bishop of Tournay was lately dead; and as a new bishop was already elected by the chapter, but not installed in his office, the king bestowed the administration of the see on his favourite, Wolsey, and put him in immediate possession of the revenues, which were considerable.[x] Hearing of the retreat of the Swiss, and observing the season to be far advanced, he thought proper to return to England; and he carried the greater part of his army with him. Success had attended him in every enterprize; and his youthful mind was much elated with this seeming prosperity; but all men of judgment, comparing the advantages of his situation with his progress, his expence with his acquisitions, were convinced, that this campaign, so much vaunted, was, in reality, both ruinous and inglorious to him.[y] *24th Sept.*

The success, which, during this summer, had attended Henry's arms in the North, was much more decisive. The king of Scotland had assembled the whole force of his kingdom; and having passed the Tweed with a brave, though a tumultuary army of above

---

[u] Memoires du mareschal de Fleuranges, Bellarius, lib. 14.   [w] Memoires de Fleuranges.   [x] Strype's Memorials, vol. i. p. 5, 6.   [y] Guicciardini.

50,000 men, he ravaged those parts of Northumberland which lay nearest that river, and he employed himself in taking the castles of Norham, Etal, Werke, Ford, and other places of small importance. Lady Ford, being taken prisoner in her castle, was presented to James, and so gained on the affections of that prince, that he wasted in pleasure the critical time, which, during the absence of his enemy, he should have employed in pushing his conquests. His troops, lying in a barren country, where they soon consumed all the provisions, began to be pinched with hunger; and as the authority of the prince was feeble, and military discipline, during that age, extremely relaxed, many of them had stolen from the camp, and retired homewards. Meanwhile, the earl of Surrey, having collected a force of 26,000 men, of which 5000 had been sent over from the king's army in France, marched to the defence of the country, and approached the Scots, who lay on some high ground near the hills of Cheviot. The river Till ran between the armies, and prevented an engagement: Surrey therefore sent a herald to the Scottish camp, challenging the enemy to descend into the plain of Milfield, which lay towards the south; and there, appointing a day for the combat, to try their valour on equal ground. As he received no satisfactory answer, he made a feint of marching towards Berwick; as if he intended to enter Scotland, to lay waste the borders, and cut off the provisions of the enemy. The Scottish army, in order to prevent his purpose, put themselves in motion; and having set fire to the huts in which they had quartered, they descended from the hills. Surrey, taking advantage of the smoke, which was blown towards him, and which concealed his movements, passed the Till with his artillery and vanguard at the bridge of Twisel, and sent the rest of his army to seek a ford higher up the river.

An engagement was now become inevitable, and both sides prepared for it with tranquillity and order.[z] The English divided their army into two lines: Lord Howard led the main body of the first line, Sir Edmond Howard the right wing, Sir Marmaduke Constable the left. The earl of Surrey himself commanded the main body of the second line, lord Dacres the right wing, Sir

1515.

9th Sept.

---

[z] Buchanan, lib. 13. Drummond. Herbert. Polydore Virgil, lib. 27. Stowe, p. 493. Paulus Jovius.

CHAPTER XXVII

Edward Stanley the left. The front of the Scots presented three *Battle of* divisions to the enemy: The middle was led by the king himself: *Flouden.* The right by the earl of Huntley, assisted by lord Hume: The left by the earls of Lenox and Argyle. A fourth division under the earl of Bothwel made a body of reserve. Huntley began the battle; and after a sharp conflict, put to flight the left wing of the English, and chaced them off the field: But on returning from the pursuit, he found the whole Scottish army in great disorder. The division under Lenox and Argyle, elated with the success of the other wing, had broken their ranks, and notwithstanding the remonstrances and entreaties of La Motte, the French ambassador, had rushed headlong upon the enemy. Not only Sir Edmond Howard, at the head of his division, received them with great valour; but Dacres, who commanded in the second line, wheeling about during the action, fell upon their rear, and put them to the sword without resistance. The division under James and that under Bothwel, animated by the valour of their leaders, still made head against the English, and throwing themselves into a circle, protracted the ac-tion, till night separated the combatants. The victory seemed yet undecided, and the numbers that fell on each side, were nearly equal, amounting to above 5000 men: But the morning discovered where the advantage lay. The English had lost only persons of small note; but the flower of the Scottish nobility had fallen in battle, and their king himself, after the most diligent enquiry, could no where be found. In searching the field, the English met with a dead body, which resembled him, and was arrayed in a similar habit; and they put it in a leaden coffin, and sent it to London. During some time it was kept unburied; because James died under sentence of excommunication, on account of his con-federacy with France, and his opposition to the holy see:[a] But upon Henry's application, who pretended that this prince had, in the instant before his death, discovered signs of repentance, abso-lution was given him, and his body was interred. The Scots, how-ever, still asserted, that it was not James's body, which was found on the field of battle, but that of one Elphinston, who had been arrayed in arms resembling their king's, in order to divide the attention of the English, and share the danger with his master. It

[a] Buchanan, lib. 13. Herbert.

was believed that James had been seen crossing the Tweed at Kelso; and some imagined that he had been killed by the vassals of lord Hume, whom that nobleman had instigated to commit so enormous a crime. But the populace entertained the opinion that he was still alive, and having secretly gone in pilgrimage to the holy land, would soon return, and take possession of the throne. This fond conceit was long entertained among the Scots.

The king of Scotland and most of his chief nobles being slain in the field of Flouden, so this battle was called, an inviting opportunity was offered to Henry of gaining advantages over that kingdom, perhaps of reducing it to subjection. But he discovered on this occasion a mind truly great and generous. When the queen of Scotland, Margaret, who was created regent during the infancy of her son, applied for peace, he readily granted it; and took compassion of the helpless condition of his sister and nephew. The earl of Surrey, who had gained him so great a victory, was restored to the title of duke of Norfolk, which had been forfeited by his father, for engaging on the side of Richard III. Lord Howard was honoured with the title of earl of Surrey. Sir Charles Brandon the king's favourite, whom he had before created viscount Lisle, was now raised to the dignity of duke of Suffolk. Wolsey, who was both his favourite and his minister, was created bishop of Lincoln. Lord Herbert obtained the title of earl of Worcester. Sir Edward Stanley, that of lord Monteagle.

1514.

Though peace with Scotland gave Henry security on that side, and enabled him to prosecute in tranquillity his enterprize against France, some other incidents had happened, which more than counterbalanced this fortunate event, and served to open his eyes with regard to the rashness of an undertaking, into which his youth and high fortune had betrayed him.

Lewis, fully sensible of the dangerous situation, to which his kingdom had been reduced during the former campaign, was resolved, by every expedient, to prevent the return of like perils, and to break the confederacy of his enemies. The pope was nowise disposed to push the French to extremity; and provided they did not return to take possession of Milan, his interests rather led him to preserve the balance among the contending parties. He accepted, therefore, of Lewis's offer to renounce the council of

CHAPTER XXVII

Lyons; and he took off the excommunication, which his predecessor and himself had fulminated against that king and his kingdom. Ferdinand was now fast declining in years; and as he entertained no farther ambition than that of keeping possession of Navarre, which he had subdued by his arms and policy, he readily hearkened to the proposals of Lewis for prolonging the truce another year; and he even showed an inclination of forming a more intimate connexion with that monarch. Lewis had dropped hints of his intention to marry his second daughter, Renée, either to Charles, prince of Spain, or his brother, Ferdinand, both of them grandsons of the Spanish monarch; and he declared his resolution of bestowing on her, as her portion, his claim to the dutchy of Milan. Ferdinand not only embraced these proposals with joy; but also engaged the emperor, Maximilian, in the same views, and procured his accession to a treaty, which opened so inviting a prospect of aggrandizing their common grandchildren.

When Henry was informed of Ferdinand's renewal of the truce with Lewis, he fell into a violent rage, and loudly complained, that his father-in-law had first, by high promises and professions, engaged him in enmity with France, and afterwards, without giving him the least warning, had now again sacrificed his interests to his own selfish purposes, and had left him exposed alone to all the danger and expence of the war. In proportion to his easy credulity and his unsuspecting reliance on Ferdinand was the vehemence with which he exclaimed against the treatment which he met with; and he threatened revenge for this egregious treachery and breach of faith.[b] But he lost all patience when informed of the other negociation, by which Maximilian was also seduced from his alliance, and in which proposals had been agreed to, for the marriage of the prince of Spain with the daughter of France. Charles, during the lifetime of the late king, had been affianced to Mary, Henry's younger sister; and as the prince now approached the age of puberty, the king had expected the immediate completion of the marriage, and the honourable settlement of a sister, for whom he had entertained a tender affection. Such a complication, there-

[b] Petrus de Angleria Epist. 545, 546.

fore, of injuries gave him the highest displeasure, and inspired him with a desire of expressing his disdain towards those who had imposed on his youth and inexperience, and had abused his too great facility.

The duke of Longueville, who had been made prisoner at the battle of Guinegate, and who was still detained in England, was ready to take advantage of all these dispositions of Henry, in order to procure a peace and even an alliance, which he knew to be passionately desired by his master. He represented to the king, that Anne, queen of France, being lately dead, a door was thereby opened for an affinity, which might tend to the advantage of both kingdoms, and which would serve to terminate honourably all the differences between them: That she had left Lewis no male children; and as he had ever entertained a strong desire of having heirs to the crown, no marriage seemed more suitable to him than that with the princess of England, whose youth and beauty afforded the most flattering hopes in that particular: That though the marriage of a princess of sixteen, with a king of fifty-three, might seem unsuitable; yet the other advantages, attending the alliance, were more than a sufficient compensation for this inequality: And that Henry, in loosening his connexions with Spain, from which he had never reaped any advantage, would contract a close affinity with Lewis, a prince, who, through his whole life, had invariably maintained the character of probity and honour.

As Henry seemed to hearken to this discourse with willing ears, Longueville informed his master of the probability, which he discovered, of bringing the matter to a happy conclusion; and he received full powers for negociating the treaty. The articles were easily adjusted between the monarchs. Lewis agreed that Tournay should remain in the hands of the English; that Richard de la Pole should be banished to Metz, there to live on a pension assigned him by Lewis; that Henry should receive payment of a million of crowns, being the arrears due by treaty to his father and himself; and that the princess Mary should bring four hundred thousand crowns as her portion, and enjoy as large a jointure as any queen of France, even the former, who was heiress of Britanny. The two princes also agreed on the succours, with which they should mutu-

Peace with France. 7th August.

CHAPTER XXVII

ally supply each other, in case either of them were attacked by an enemy.[c]

In consequence of this treaty, Mary was sent over to France with a splendid retinue, and Lewis met her at Abbeville, where the espousals were celebrated. He was enchanted with the beauty, grace, and numerous accomplishments of the young princess; and being naturally of an amorous disposition, which his advanced age had not entirely cooled, he was seduced into such a course of gaiety and pleasure, as proved very unsuitable to his declining state of health.[d] He died in less than three months after the marriage, to the extreme regret of the French nation, who, sensible of his tender concern for their welfare, gave him with one voice the honourable appellation of *father of his people.* *9th Octob.*

1515. 1st Jan.

Francis, duke of Angouleme, a youth of one and twenty, who had married Lewis's elder daughter, succeeded him on the throne; and by his activity, valour, generosity, and other virtues, gave prognostics of a happy and glorious reign. This young monarch had been extremely struck with the charms of the English princess; and even during his predecessor's life-time, had payed her such assiduous court, as made some of his friends apprehend, that he had entertained views of gallantry towards her. But being warned, that, by indulging this passion, he might probably exclude himself from the throne, he forbore all farther addresses; and even watched the young dowager with a very careful eye during the first months of her widowhood. Charles Brandon, duke of Suffolk, was at that time in the court of France, the most comely personage of his time, and the most accomplished in all the exercises, which were then thought to befit a courtier and a soldier. He was Henry's chief favourite; and that monarch had even once entertained thoughts of marrying him to his sister, and had given indulgence to the mutual passion, which took place between them. The queen asked Suffolk, whether he had now the courage, without farther reflection, to espouse her; and she told him, that her brother would more easily forgive him for not asking his consent, than for acting contrary to his orders. Suffolk declined not so inviting an offer; and their nuptials were secretly celebrated at Paris. Francis,

[c] Du Tillet.   [d] Brantome Eloge de Louis XII.

who was pleased with this marriage, as it prevented Henry from forming any powerful alliance by means of his sister,[e] interposed his good offices in appeasing him: And even Wolsey, having entertained no jealousy of Suffolk, who was content to participate in the king's pleasures, and had no ambition to engage in public business, was active in reconciling the king to his sister and brother-in-law; and he obtained them permission to return to England.

[e] Petrus de Angleria, Epist. 544.

XXVIII

Wolsey's administration –
Scotch affairs – Progress of Francis I. –
Jealousy of Henry – Tournay delivered
to France – Wolsey appointed legate –
His manner of exercising that office –
Death of the emperor Maximilian –
Charles, king of Spain, chosen emperor – Interview
between Henry and Francis near Calais –
The emperor Charles arrives in England –
Mediation of Henry – Trial and condemnation
of the duke of Buckingham

THE NUMEROUS ENEMIES, whom Wolsey's sudden elevation, his aspiring character, and his haughty deportment had raised him, served only to rivet him faster in Henry's confidence; who valued himself on supporting the choice which he had made, and who was incapable of yielding either to the murmurs of the people or to the discontents of the great. That artful prelate likewise, well acquainted with the king's imperious temper, concealed from him the absolute ascendant, which he had acquired; and while he secretly directed all public councils, he ever pretended a blind submission to the will and authority of his master. By entering into the king's pleasures, he preserved his affection; by conducting his business, he gratified his indolence; and by his unlimited complaisance in both capacities, he prevented all that jealousy, to which his exorbitant acquisitions, and his splendid ostentatious train of life should naturally have given birth. The archbishopric of York falling vacant by the death of Bambridge, Wolsey was promoted to that see, and resigned the bishopric of Lincoln. Besides enjoying the administration of Tournay, he got possession, on easy leases, of the revenues of Bath, Worcester, and Hereford, bishoprics filled by Italians, who were allowed to reside abroad, and who were glad to compound for this indulgence, by yielding a considerable share of their income. He held in commendam the abbey of St. Albans, and many other church preferments. He was even allowed to unite with the see of York, first that of Durham, next that of Winchester; and there seemed to be no end of his acquisitions. His farther advancement in ecclesiastical dignity served him as a pretence for engrossing still more revenues: The pope, observing his great influence over the king, was desirous of engaging him in his interests, and created him a cardinal. No churchman, under colour of exacting respect to religion, ever carried to a greater height the state and dignity of that character. His train consisted of eight hundred servants, of whom many were knights and gentlemen: Some even of the nobility put their children into his family as a place of education; and in order to gain them favour with their patron, allowed them to bear offices as his servants. Whoever was distinguished by any art or science paid court to the cardinal; and none paid court in vain. Literature, which was then in its infancy, found in him a generous patron; and both by his public institutions and private bounty, he gave encouragement to every branch of erudition.[f] Not content with this munificence, which gained him the approbation of the wise, he strove to dazzle the eyes of the populace, by the splendor of his equipage and furniture, the costly embroidery of his liveries, the lustre of his apparel. He was the first clergyman in England that wore silk and gold, not only on his habit, but also on his saddles and the trappings of his horses.[g] He caused his cardinal's hat to be borne aloft by a person of rank; and when he came to the king's chapel, would permit it to be laid on no place but the altar. A priest, the tallest and

[f] Erasm. Epist. lib. 2. epist. 1. lib. 16. epist. 3   [g] Polydore Virgil, lib. 27. Stowe, p. 501. Holingshed, p. 847.

CHAPTER XXVIII

most comely he could find, carried before him a pillar of silver, on whose top was placed a cross. But not satisfied with this parade, to which he thought himself entitled as cardinal, he provided another priest of equal stature and beauty, who marched along, bearing the cross of York, even in the diocese of Canterbury; contrary to the ancient rule and the agreement between the prelates of these rival sees.[h] The people made merry with the cardinal's ostentation; and said they were now sensible, that one crucifix alone was not sufficient for the expiation of his sins and offences.

Warham, chancellor and archbishop of Canterbury, a man of a moderate temper, averse to all disputes, chose rather to retire from public employment, than maintain an unequal contest with the haughty cardinal. He resigned his office of chancellor; and the great seal was immediately delivered to Wolsey. If this new accumulation of dignity encreased his enemies, it also served to exalt his personal character, and prove the extent of his capacity. A strict administration of justice took place during his enjoyment of this high office; and no chancellor ever discovered greater impartiality in his decisions, deeper penetration of judgment, or more enlarged knowledge of law and equity.[i]

The duke of Norfolk, finding the king's money almost entirely exhausted by projects and pleasures, while his inclination for expence still continued, was glad to resign his office of treasurer, and retire from court. His rival, Fox, bishop of Winchester, reaped no advantage from his absence; but partly overcome by years and infirmities, partly disgusted at the ascendant acquired by Wolsey, withdrew himself wholly to the care of his diocese. The duke of Suffolk had also taken offence, that the king, by the cardinal's persuasion, had refused to pay a debt, which he had contracted during his residence in France; and he thenceforth affected to live in privacy. These incidents left Wolsey to enjoy without a rival the whole power and favour of the king; and they put into his hands every kind of authority. In vain, did Fox, before his retirement, warn the king "not to suffer the servant to be greater than his master:" Henry replied, "that he well knew how to retain all his subjects in obedience;" but he continued still an unlimited deference in every thing to the directions and counsels of the cardinal.

[h] Polydore Virgil, lib. 27.   [i] Sir Thomas More. Stowe, p. 504.

The public tranquillity was so well established in England, the obedience of the people so entire, the general administration of justice, by the cardinal's means,[k] so exact, that no domestic occurrence happened considerable enough to disturb the repose of the king and his minister: They might even have dispensed with giving any strict attention to foreign affairs, were it possible for men to enjoy any situation in absolute tranquillity, or abstain from projects and enterprizes, however fruitless and unnecessary.

Scotch affairs. The will of the late king of Scotland, who left his widow regent of the kingdom, and the vote of the convention of states, which confirmed that destination, had expressly limited her authority to the condition of her remaining unmarried:[l] But notwithstanding this limitation, a few months after her husband's death, she espoused the earl of Angus, of the name of Douglas, a young nobleman of great family and promising hopes. Some of the nobility now proposed the electing of Angus to the regency, and recommended this choice as the most likely means of preserving peace with England: But the jealousy of the great families, and the fear of exalting the Douglasses, begat opposition to this measure. Lord Hume in particular, the most powerful chieftain in the kingdom, insisted on recalling the duke of Albany, son to a brother of James III. who had been banished into France, and who, having there married, had left posterity, that were the next heirs to the crown, and the nearest relations to their young sovereign. Albany, though first prince of the blood, had never been in Scotland, was totally unacquainted with the manners of the people, ignorant of their situation, unpractised in their language; yet such was the favour attending the French alliance, and so great the authority of Hume, that this prince was invited to accept the reins of government. Francis, careful not to give offence to the king of England, detained Albany some time in France; but at length, sensible how important it was to keep Scotland in his interests, he permitted him to go over, and take possession of the regency: He even renewed the ancient league with that kingdom, though it implied such a close connexion, as might be thought somewhat to intrench on his alliance with England.

[k] Erasm. lib. 2. epist. 1. Cavendish, Hall.   [l] Buchanan, lib. 14. Drummond, Herbert.

CHAPTER XXVIII

When the regent arrived in Scotland, he made enquiries concerning the state of the country, and character of the people; and he discovered a scene, with which he was hitherto but little acquainted. That turbulent kingdom, he found, was rather to be considered as a confederacy, and that not a close one, of petty princes, than a regular system of civil polity; and even the king, much more a regent, possessed an authority very uncertain and precarious. Arms, more than laws, prevailed; and courage, preferably to equity or justice, was the virtue most valued and respected. The nobility, in whom the whole power resided, were so connected by hereditary alliances, or so divided by inveterate enmities, that it was impossible, without employing an armed force, either to punish the most flagrant guilt, or give security to the most entire innocence. Rapine and violence, when exercised on a hostile tribe, instead of making a person odious among his own clan, rather recommended him to their esteem and approbation; and by rendering him useful to the chieftain, entitled him to a preference above his fellows. And though the necessity of mutual support served as a close cement of amity among those of the same kindred, the spirit of revenge against enemies, and the desire of prosecuting the deadly feuds (so they were called), still appeared to be passions the most predominant among that uncultivated people.

The persons, to whom Albany, on his arrival, first applied for information with regard to the state of the country, happened to be inveterate enemies of Hume;[m] and they represented that powerful nobleman as the chief source of public disorders, and the great obstacle to the execution of the laws, and the administration of justice. Before the authority of the magistrate could be established, it was necessary, they said, to make an example of this great offender; and by the terror of his punishment, teach all lesser criminals to pay respect to the power of their sovereign. Albany, moved by these reasons, was induced to forget Hume's past services, to which he had, in a great measure, been indebted for the regency; and he no longer bore towards him that favourable countenance, with which he was wont to receive him. Hume perceived the alteration, and was incited, both by regard to his own safety and from motives of revenge, to take measures in opposition to the

[m] Buchanan, lib. 14. Drummond.

regent. He applied himself to Angus and the queen dowager, and represented to them the danger, to which the infant prince was exposed, from the ambition of Albany, next heir to the crown, to whom the states had imprudently entrusted the whole authority of government. By his persuasion, Margaret formed the design of carrying off the young king, and putting him under the protection of her brother; and when that conspiracy was detected, she herself, attended by Hume and Angus, withdrew into England, where she was soon after delivered of a daughter.

Henry, in order to check the authority of Albany and the French party, gave encouragement to these malcontents, and assured them of his support. Matters being afterwards in appearance accommodated between Hume and the regent, that nobleman returned into his own country; but mutual suspicions and jealousies still prevailed. He was committed to custody, under the care of the earl of Arran, his brother-in-law; and was, for some time, detained prisoner in his castle. But having persuaded Arran to enter into the conspiracy with him, he was allowed to make his escape; and he openly levied war upon the regent. A new accommodation ensued, not more sincere than the foregoing; and Hume was so imprudent as to entrust himself, together with his brother, into the hands of that prince. They were immediately seized, committed to custody, brought to trial, condemned, and executed. No legal crime was proved against these brothers: It was only alleged, that, at the battle of Flouden, they had not done their duty in supporting the king; and as this backwardness could not, from the course of their past life, be ascribed to cowardice, it was commonly imputed to a more criminal motive. The evidence, however, of guilt, produced against them, was far from being valid or convincing; and the people, who hated them while living, were much dissatisfied with their execution.

Such violent remedies often produce, for some time, a deceitful tranquillity; but as they destroy mutual confidence, and beget the most inveterate animosities, their consequences are commonly fatal, both to the public, and to those who have recourse to them. The regent, however, took advantage of the present calm which prevailed; and being invited over by the French king, who was, at that time, willing to gratify Henry, he went into France; and was engaged to remain there for some years. During the absence of the regent, such confusions prevailed in Scotland, and such mutual enmity, rapine, and violence among the great families, that that kingdom was for a long time utterly disabled both from offending its enemies and assisting its friends. We have carried on the Scottish history some years beyond the present period; that, as that country had little connexion with the general system of Europe, we might be the less interrupted in the narration of those more memorable events, which were transacted in the other kingdoms.

It was foreseen, that a young, active prince, like Francis, and of so martial a disposition, would soon employ the great preparations, which his predecessor, before his death, had made for the conquest of Milan. He had been observed even to weep at the recital of the military exploits of Gaston de Foix; and these tears of emulation were held to be sure presages of his future valour. He renewed the treaty which Lewis had made with Henry; and having left every thing secure behind him, he marched his armies towards the south of France; pretending, that his sole purpose was to defend his kingdom against the incursions of the Swiss. This formidable people still retained their animosity against France; and having taken Maximilian, duke of Milan, under their protection, and in reality reduced him to absolute dependance, they were determined, from views both of honour and of interest, to defend him against the invader.[n] They fortified themselves in all those vallies of the Alps, through which, they thought, the French must necessarily pass; and when Francis, with great secrecy, industry, and perseverance, made his entrance into Piedmont by another passage, they were not dismayed, but descended into the plain, though unprovided with cavalry, and opposed themselves to the progress of the French arms. At Marignan near Milan, they fought with Francis one of the most furious and best contested battles, that is to be met with in the history of these later ages; and it required all the heroic valour of this prince to inspire his troops with courage sufficient to resist the desperate assault of those mountainiers. After a bloody action in the evening, night and darkness parted the combatants; but next morning, the Swiss renewed the attack with unabated ardour; and it was not till they had lost all their bravest troops that they could be prevailed on to retire.

Progress of Francis I.

13th Sept.

[n] Memoires du Bellai, lib. 1. Guicciardini, lib. 12.

The field was strowed with twenty thousand slain on both sides; and the mareschal Trivulzio, who had been present at eighteen pitched battles, declared that every engagement, which he had yet seen, was only the play of children; the action of Marignan was a combat of heroes.[o] After this great victory, the conquest of the Milaneze was easy and open to Francis.

Jealousy of Henry. The success and glory of the French monarch began to excite jealousy in Henry; and his rapid progress, though in so distant a country, was not regarded without apprehensions by the English ministry. Italy was, during that age, the seat of religion, of literature, and of commerce; and as it possessed alone that lustre, which has since been shared out among other nations, it attracted the attention of all Europe, and every acquisition, which was made there, appeared more important than its weight in the balance of power was, strictly speaking, entitled to. Henry also thought, that he had reason to complain of Francis for sending the duke of Albany into Scotland, and undermining the power and credit of his sister, the queen dowager.[p] The repairing of the fortifications of Teroüenne was likewise regarded as a breach of treaty. But above all, what tended to alienate the court of England, was the disgust which Wolsey had entertained against the French monarch.

Henry, on the conquest of Tournay, had refused to admit Lewis Gaillart, the bishop elect, to the possession of the temporalities, because that prelate declined taking the oath of allegiance to his new sovereign; and Wolsey was appointed, as above related, administrator of the bishopric. As the cardinal wished to obtain the free and undisturbed enjoyment of this revenue, he applied to Francis, and desired him to bestow on Gaillart some see of equal value in France, and to obtain his resignation of Tournay. Francis, who still hoped to recover possession of that city, and who feared, that the full establishment of Wolsey in the bishopric would prove an obstacle to his purpose, had hitherto neglected to gratify the haughty prelate; and the bishop of Tournay, by applying to the court of Rome, had obtained a bull for his settlement in the see. Wolsey, who expected to be indulged in every request, and who exacted respect from the greatest princes, resented the slight put

[o] Histoire de la Ligue de Cambrey.   [p] Pere Daniel, vol. iii. p. 31.

upon him by Francis; and he pushed his master to seek an occasion of quarrel with that monarch.[q]

Maximilian, the emperor, was ready to embrace every overture for a new enterprize; especially if attended with an offer of money, of which he was very greedy, very prodigal, and very indigent. Richard Pace, formerly secretary to cardinal Bambridge, and now secretary of state, was dispatched to the court of Vienna, and had a commission to propose some considerable payments to Maximilian:[r] He thence made a journey into Switzerland; and by like motives engaged some of the cantons to furnish troops to the emperor. That prince invaded Italy with a considerable army; but being repulsed from before Milan, he retreated with his army into Germany, made peace with France and Venice, ceded Verona to that republic for a sum of money, and thus excluded himself, in some measure, from all future access into Italy. And Henry found, that, after expending five or six hundred thousand ducats, in order to gratify his own and the cardinal's humour, he had only weakened his alliance with Francis, without diminishing the power of that prince.

There were many reasons, which engaged the king not to proceed farther at present in his enmity against France: He could hope for assistance from no power in Europe. Ferdinand, his father-in-law, who had often deceived him, was declining through age and infirmities; and a speedy period was looked for to the long and prosperous reign of that great monarch. Charles, prince of Spain, sovereign of the Low Countries, desired nothing but peace with Francis, who had it so much in his power, if provoked, to obstruct his peaceable accession to that rich inheritance, which was awaiting him. The pope was overawed by the power of France, and Venice was engaged in a close alliance with that monarchy.[s] Henry therefore was constrained to remain in tranquillity during some time; and seemed to give himself no concern with regard to the affairs of the continent. In vain did Maximilian endeavour to allure him into some expence, by offering to make a resignation of the imperial crown in his favour. The artifice was too gross to succeed even with a prince so little politic as Henry; and Pace, his

[q] Polydore Virgil, lib. 27.   [r] Petrus de Angleria, epist. 568.   [s] Guicciardini, lib. 12.

envoy, who was perfectly well acquainted with the emperor's motives and character, gave him warning that the sole view of that prince, in making him so liberal an offer, was to draw money from him.

1516.   While an universal peace prevailed in Europe, that event happened, which had so long been looked for, and from which such important consequences were expected, the death of Ferdinand the Catholic, and the succession of his grandson, Charles, to his extensive dominions. The more Charles advanced in power and authority, the more was Francis sensible of the necessity he himself lay under of gaining the confidence and friendship of Henry; and he took at last the only method by which he could obtain success, the paying of court, by presents and flattery, to the haughty cardinal.

1518.   Bonnivet, admiral of France, was dispatched to London, and he was directed to employ all his insinuation and address, qualities in which he excelled, to procure himself a place in Wolsey's good graces. After the ambassador had succeeded in his purpose, he took an opportunity of expressing his master's regret, that, by mistakes and misapprehensions, he had been so unfortunate as to lose a friendship, which he so much valued as that of his eminence. Wolsey was not deaf to these honourable advances from so great a monarch; and he was thenceforth observed to express himself, on all occasions, in favour of the French alliance. The more to engage him in his interests, Francis entered into such confidence with him, that he asked his advice even in his most secret affairs; and had recourse to him in all difficult emergencies as to an oracle of wisdom and profound policy. The cardinal made no secret to the king of this private correspondence; and Henry was so prepossessed in favour of the great capacity of his minister, that, he said, he verily believed he would govern Francis as well as himself.[t]

When matters seemed sufficiently prepared, Bonnivet opened to the cardinal his master's desire of recovering Tournay; and Wolsey immediately, without hesitation, engaged to effect his purpose. He took an opportunity of representing to the king and council, that Tournay lay so remote from Calais, that it would be very difficult, if not impossible, in case of war, to keep the commu-

---

[t] Polydore Virgil, lib. 27.

nication open between these two places: That as it was situated on the frontiers both of France and the Netherlands, it was exposed to attacks from both these countries, and must necessarily, either by force or famine, fall into the hands of the first assailant: That even in time of peace, it could not be preserved without a large garrison, to restrain the numerous and mutinous inhabitants, ever discontented with the English government: And that the possession of Tournay, as it was thus precarious and expensive, so was it entirely useless, and afforded little or no means of annoying, on occasion, the dominions either of Charles or of Francis.

These reasons were of themselves convincing, and were sure of meeting with no opposition, when they came from the mouth of the cardinal. A treaty therefore was entered into for the ceding of Tournay; and in order to give to that measure a more graceful appearance, it was agreed, that the dauphin and the princess Mary, both of them infants, should be betrothed, and that this city should be considered as the dowry of the princess. Such kinds of agreement were then common among sovereigns, though it was very rare, that the interests and views of the parties continued so steady as to render the intended marriages effectual. But as Henry had been at considerable expence in building a citadel at Tournay, Francis agreed to pay him 600,000 crowns at twelve annual payments, and to put into his hands eight hostages, all of them men of quality, for the performance of the article." And lest the cardinal should think himself neglected in these stipulations, Francis promised him a yearly pension of twelve thousand livres, as an equivalent for his administration of the bishopric of Tournay.

Tournay ceded to France.

The French monarch having succeeded so well in this negociation, began to enlarge his views, and to hope for more considerable advantages, by practising on the vanity and self-conceit of the favourite. He redoubled his flatteries to the cardinal, consulted him more frequently in every doubt or difficulty, called him in each letter, *father, tutor, governor,* and professed the most unbounded deference to his advice and opinion. All these caresses were preparatives to a negociation for the delivery of Calais, in consideration of a sum of money to be paid for it; and if we may

---

" Memoires du Bellay, lib. 1.

credit Polydore Virgil, who bears a particular ill-will to Wolsey, on account of his being dispossessed of his employment and thrown into prison by that minister, so extraordinary a proposal met with a favourable reception from the cardinal. He ventured not, however, to lay the matter before the council: He was content to sound privately the opinion of the other ministers, by dropping hints in conversation, as if he thought Calais a useless burthen to the kingdom:[w] But when he found, that all men were strongly riveted in a contrary persuasion, he thought it dangerous to proceed any farther in his purpose; and as he fell, soon after, into new connexions with the king of Spain, the great friendship between Francis and him began gradually to decline.

Wolsey appointed legate. The pride of Wolsey was now farther encreased by a great accession of power and dignity. Cardinal Campeggio had been sent as legate into England, in order to procure a tithe from the clergy, for enabling the pope to oppose the progress of the Turks; a danger which was become real, and was formidable to all Christendom, but on which the politics of the court of Rome had built so many interested projects, that it had lost all influence on the minds of men. The clergy refused to comply with Leo's demands: Campeggio was recalled; and the king desired of the pope, that Wolsey, who had been joined in this commission, might alone be invested with the legantine power; together with the right of visiting all the clergy and monasteries, and even with suspending all the laws of the church during a twelvemonth. Wolsey, having obtained this new dignity, made a new display of that state and parade, to which he was so much addicted. On solemn feast-days, he was not content without saying mass after the manner of the pope himself: Not only he had bishops and abbots to serve him; he even engaged the first nobility to give him water and the towel. He affected a rank superior to what had ever been claimed by any churchman in England. Warham, the primate, having written him a letter, in which he subscribed himself, *your loving brother,* Wolsey complained of his presumption, in thus challenging an equality with him. When Warham was told what offence he had given, he made light of the matter. "Know ye not," said he, "that this man is drunk with too much prosperity."

[w] Polydore Virgil, lib. 27.

CHAPTER XXVIII

But Wolsey carried the matter much farther than vain pomp *His* and ostentation. He erected an office, which he called the leg- *manner* antine court; and as he was now, by means of the pope's commis- *of exer-* sion and the king's favour, invested with all power, both ec- *cising* clesiastical and civil, no man knew what bounds were to be set to *that of-* the authority of his new tribunal. He conferred on it a kind of *fice.* inquisitorial and censorial powers even over the laity, and directed it to enquire into all matters of conscience; into all conduct which had given scandal; into all actions, which, though they escaped the law, might appear contrary to good morals. Offence was taken at this commission, which was really unbounded; and the people were the more disgusted, when they saw a man, who indulged himself in pomp and pleasure, so severe in repressing the least appearance of licentiousness in others. But to render his court more obnoxious, Wolsey made one John Allen judge in it, a person of scandalous life,[x] whom he himself, as chancellor, had, it is said, condemned for perjury: And as it is pretended, that this man either extorted fines from every one whom he was pleased to find guilty, or took bribes to drop prosecutions, men concluded, and with some appearance of reason, that he shared with the cardinal those wages of iniquity. The clergy, and in particular the monks, were exposed to this tyranny; and as the libertinism of their lives often gave a just handle against them, they were obliged to pur- chase an indemnity, by paying large sums of money to the legate or his judge. Not content with this authority, Wolsey pretended, by virtue of his commission, to assume the jurisdiction of all the bish- ops' courts; particularly that of judging of Wills and Testaments; and his decisions in those important points were deemed not a little arbitrary. As if he himself were pope, and as if the pope could absolutely dispose of every ecclesiastical preferment, he presented to whatever priories or benefices he pleased, without regard to the right of election in the monks, or of patronage in the nobility and gentry.[y]

[x] Strype's Memorials, vol. i. p. 125.   [y] Polydore Virgil, lib. 27. This whole narrative has been copied by all the historians from the author here cited: There are many circumstances, however, very suspicious, both because of the obvious partiality of the historian, and because the parliament, when they afterwards examined Wolsey's conduct, could find no proof of any material offence he had ever committed.

No one durst carry to the king any complaint against these usurpations of Wolsey, till Warham ventured to inform him of the discontents of his people. Henry professed his ignorance of the whole matter. "A man," said he, "is not so blind any where as in his own house: But do you, farther," added he to the primate, "go to Wolsey, and tell him, if any thing be amiss, that he amend it." A reproof of this kind was not likely to be effectual: It only served to augment Wolsey's enmity to Warham: But one London having prosecuted Allen, the legate's judge, in a court of law, and having convicted him of malversation and iniquity, the clamour at last reached the king's ears; and he expressed such displeasure to the cardinal as made him ever after more cautious in exerting his authority.

While Henry, indulging himself in pleasure and amusement, entrusted the government of his kingdom to this imperious minister, an incident happened abroad, which excited his attention.

Maximilian the emperor died; a man, who, of himself, was indeed of little consequence; but as his death left vacant the first station among christian princes, it set the passions of men in agitation, and proved a kind of era in the general system of Europe. The kings of France and Spain immediately declared themselves candidates for the Imperial crown; and employed every expedient of money or intrigue, which promised them success in so great a point of ambition. Henry also was encouraged to advance his pretensions; but his minister, Pace, who was dispatched to the electors, found that he began to solicit too late, and that the votes of all these princes were already pre-engaged either on one side or the other.

Francis and Charles made profession from the beginning of carrying on this rivalship with emulation, but without enmity; and Francis in particular declared, that his brother Charles and he were, fairly and openly, suitors to the same mistress: The more fortunate, added he, will carry her; the other must rest contented.[z]

But all men apprehended, that this extreme moderation, however reasonable, would not be of long duration; and that incidents would certainly occur to sharpen the minds of the candidates against each other. It was Charles who at length prevailed, to the great disgust of the French monarch, who still continued to the last

[z] Belcaria, lib. 16. Guicciardin, lib. 13.

CHAPTER XXVIII

in the belief, that the majority of the electoral college was engaged in his favour. And as he was some years superior in age to his rival, and, after his victory at Marignan, and conquest of the Milanese, much superior in renown, he could not suppress his indignation, at being thus, in the face of the world, after long and anxious expectation, disappointed in so important a pretension. From this competition, as much as from opposition of interests, arose that emulation between those two great monarchs; which, while it kept their whole age in movement, sets them in so remarkable a contrast to each other: Both of them princes endowed with talents and abilities; brave, aspiring, active, warlike; beloved by their servants and subjects, dreaded by their enemies, and respected by all the world: Francis, open, frank, liberal, munificent, carrying these virtues to an excess which prejudiced his affairs: Charles, political, close, artful, frugal; better qualified to obtain success in wars and in negociations, especially the latter. The one, the more amiable man; the other, the greater monarch. The king, from his over-sights and indiscretions, naturally exposed to misfortunes; but qualified, by his spirit and magnanimity, to extricate himself from them with honour: The emperor, by his designing, interested character, fitted, in his greatest successes, to excite jealousy and opposition even among his allies, and to rouze up a multitude of enemies, in the place of one whom he had subdued. And as the personal qualities of these princes thus counterpoised each other, so did the advantages and disadvantages of their dominions. Fortune alone, without the concurrence of prudence or valour, never reared up of a sudden so great a power as that which centered in the emperor Charles. He reaped the succession of Castile, of Arragon, of Austria, of the Netherlands: He inherited the conquest of Naples, of Granada: Election entitled him to the empire: Even the bounds of the globe seemed to be enlarged a little before his time, that he might possess the whole treasure, as yet entire and unrifled, of the new world. But though the concurrence of all these advantages formed an empire, greater and more extensive than any known in Europe since that of the Romans, the kingdom of France alone, being close, compact, united, rich, populous, and being interposed between all the provinces of the emperor's dominions, was able to make a vigorous opposition to his progress, and maintain the contest against him.

Henry possessed the felicity of being able, both by the native force of his kingdom and its situation, to hold the balance between those two powers; and had he known to improve, by policy and prudence, his singular and inestimable advantage, he was really, by means of it, a greater potentate than either of those mighty monarchs, who seemed to strive for the dominion of Europe. But this prince was, in his character, heedless, inconsiderate, capricious, impolitic; guided by his passions or his favourite; vain, imperious, haughty; sometimes actuated by friendship for foreign powers, oftener by resentment, seldom by his true interest. And thus, though he exulted in that superiority which his situation in Europe gave him, he never employed it to his own essential and durable advantage, or to that of his kingdom.

1520.
Interview
between
Henry
and
Francis
at Calais.

Francis was well acquainted with Henry's character, and endeavoured to accommodate his conduct to it. He solicited an interview near Calais; in expectation of being able, by familiar conversation, to gain upon his friendship and confidence. Wolsey earnestly seconded this proposal; and hoped, in the presence of both courts, to make parade of his riches, his splendor, and his influence over both monarchs.[a] And as Henry himself loved show and magnificence, and had entertained a curiosity of being personally acquainted with the French king, he chearfully adjusted all the preliminaries of this interview. The nobility of both nations vyed with each other in pomp and expence: Many of them involved themselves in great debts, and were not able, by the penury of their whole lives, to repair the vain splendour of a few days. The duke of Buckingham, who, though very rich, was somewhat addicted to frugality, finding his preparations for this festival amount to immense sums, threw out some expressions of displeasure against the cardinal, whom he believed the author of that measure.[b] An imprudence which was not forgotten by this minister.

The
emperor
Charles
arrives in
England.
25th
May.

While Henry was preparing to depart for Calais, he heard that the emperor was arrived at Dover; and he immediately hastened thither with the queen, in order to give a suitable reception to his royal guest. That great prince, politic though young, being in-

[a] Polydore Virgil, lib. 27.   [b] Polydore Virgil, lib. xxvii. Herbert. Hollingshed. p. 855.

CHAPTER XXVIII

formed of the intended interview between Francis and Henry, was apprehensive of the consequences, and was resolved to take the opportunity, in his passage from Spain to the Low Countries, to make the king still a higher compliment, by paying him a visit in his own dominions. Besides the marks of regard and attachment which he gave to Henry, he strove, by every testimony of friendship, by flattery, protestations, promises, and presents, to gain on the vanity, the avarice, and the ambition of the cardinal. He here instilled into this aspiring prelate the hope of attaining the papacy; and as that was the sole point of elevation, beyond his present greatness, it was sure to attract his wishes with the same ardour, as if fortune had never yet favoured him with any of her presents. In confidence of reaching this dignity by the emperor's assistance, he secretly devoted himself to that monarch's interests; and Charles was perhaps the more liberal of his promises, because Leo was a very young man; and it was not likely, that, for many years, he should be called upon to fulfil his engagements. Henry easily observed this courtship payed to his minister; but instead of taking umbrage at it, he only made it a subject of vanity; and believed, that, as his favour was Wolsey's sole support, the obeisance of such mighty monarchs to his servant, was in reality a more conspicuous homage to his own grandeur.

The day of Charles's departure, Henry went over to Calais with the queen and his whole court; and thence proceeded to Guisnes, a small town near the frontiers. Francis, attended in like manner, came to Ardres, a few miles distant; and the two monarchs met, for the first time, in the fields, at a place situated between these two towns, but still within the English pale: For Francis agreed to pay this compliment to Henry, in consideration of that prince's passing the sea, that he might be present at the interview. Wolsey, to whom both kings had entrusted the regulation of the ceremonial, contrived this circumstance, in order to do honour to his master. The nobility both of France and England here displayed their magnificence with such emulation and profuse expence, as procured to the place of interview the name of *the field of the cloth of gold*.

The two monarchs, after saluting each other in the most cordial manner, retired into a tent which had been erected on purpose, and they held a secret conference together. Henry here proposed to make some amendments on the articles of their former alliance;

30th May.

and he began to read the treaty, *I Henry king:* These were the first words; and he stopped a moment. He subjoined only the words *of England,* without adding, *France,* the usual style of the English monarchs.[c] Francis remarked this delicacy, and expressed by a smile his approbation of it.

He took an opportunity soon after of paying a compliment to Henry of a more flattering nature. That generous prince, full of honour himself, and incapable of distrusting others, was shocked at all the precautions which were observed, whenever he had an interview with the English monarch: The number of their guards and attendants was carefully reckoned on both sides: Every step was scrupulously measured and adjusted: And if the two kings intended to pay a visit to the queens, they departed from their respective quarters at the same instant, which was marked by the firing of a culverin; they passed each other in the middle point between the places; and the moment that Henry entered Ardres, Francis put himself into the hands of the English at Guisnes. In order to break off this tedious ceremonial, which contained so many dishonourable implications, Francis, one day, took with him two gentlemen and a page, and rode directly into Guisnes. The guards were surprized at the presence of the monarch, who called aloud to them, *You are all my prisoners: Carry me to your master.* Henry was equally astonished at the appearance of Francis; and taking him in his arms, "My brother," said he, "you have here played me the most agreeable trick in the world, and have showed me the full confidence I may place in you: I surrender myself your prisoner from this moment." He took from his neck a collar of pearls, worth 15000 angels;[d] and putting it about Francis's, begged him to wear it for the sake of his prisoner. Francis agreed, but on condition that Henry should wear a bracelet, of which he made him a present, and which was double in value to the collar.[e] The king went next day to Ardres, without guards or attendants; and confidence being now fully established between the monarchs, they employed the rest of the time entirely in tournaments and festivals.

A defiance had been sent by the two kings to each other's court, and through all the chief cities in Europe, importing, that Henry

[c] Memoires de Fleuranges.   [d] An angel was then estimated at seven shillings, or near twelve of our present money.   [e] Memoires de Fleuranges.

and Francis, with fourteen aids, would be ready, in the plains of Picardy, to answer all comers, that were gentlemen, at tilt, tournament, and barriers. The monarchs, in order to fulfil this challenge, advanced into the field on horseback, Francis surrounded with Henry's guards, and Henry with those of Francis. They were gorgeously apparelled; and were both of them the most comely personages of their age, as well as the most expert in every military exercise. They carried away the prize at all trials in those rough and dangerous pastimes; and several horses and riders were overthrown by their vigour and dexterity. The ladies were the judges in these feats of chivalry, and put an end to the rencounter, whenever they judged it expedient. Henry erected a spacious house of wood and canvas, which had been framed in London; and he there feasted the French monarch. He had placed a motto on this fabric, under the figure of an English archer embroidered on it, *Cui adhæreo præst; He prevails whom I favour.* [f] Expressing his own situation, as holding in his hands the balance of power among the potentates of Europe. In these entertainments, more than in any serious business, did the two kings pass their time, till their departure.

Henry paid then a visit to the emperor and Margaret of Savoy at Gravelines, and engaged them to go along with him to Calais, and pass some days in that fortress. The artful and politic Charles here completed the impression, which he had begun to make on Henry and his favourite, and effaced all the friendship, to which the frank and generous nature of Francis had given birth. As the house of Austria began sensibly to take the ascendant over the French monarchy, the interests of England required, that some support should be given to the latter, and above all, that any important wars should be prevented, which might bestow on either of them a decisive superiority over the other. But the jealousy of the English against France has usually prevented a cordial union between these nations: And Charles, sensible of this hereditary animosity, and desirous farther to flatter Henry's vanity, had made him an offer (an offer in which Francis was afterwards obliged to concur); that he should be entirely arbiter in any dispute or difference that might arise between the monarchs. But the

24th June.

[f] Mezeray.

masterpiece of Charles's politics was the securing of Wolsey in his interests, by very important services, and still higher promises. He renewed assurances of assisting him in obtaining the papacy; and he put him in present possession of the revenues belonging to the sees of Badajox and Palencia in Castile. The acquisitions of Wolsey were now become so exorbitant, that, joined to the pensions from foreign powers, which Henry allowed him to possess, his revenues were computed nearly to equal those which belonged to the crown itself; and he spent them with a magnificence, or rather an ostentation, which gave general offence to the people; and even lessened his master in the eyes of all foreign nations.[g]

War between Charles and Francis.

1521. Mediation of Henry.

The violent personal emulation and political jealousy, which had taken place between the emperor and the French king, soon broke out in hostilities. But while these ambitious and warlike princes were acting against each other in almost every part of Europe, they still made professions of the strongest desire of peace; and both of them incessantly carried their complaints to Henry, as to the umpire between them. The king, who pretended to be neutral, engaged them to send their ambassadors to Calais, there to negociate a peace under the mediation of Wolsey and the pope's nuncio. The emperor was well apprized of the partiality of these mediators; and his demands in the conference were so unreasonable, as plainly proved him conscious of the advantage. He required the restitution of Burgundy, a province, which many years before had been ceded to France by treaty, and which, if in his possession, would have given him entrance into the heart of that kingdom: And he demanded to be freed from the homage, which his ancestors had always done for Flanders and Artois, and which he himself had, by the treaty of Noyon, engaged to renew. On Francis's rejecting these terms, the congress of Calais broke up,

24th Nov.

and Wolsey, soon after, took a journey to Bruges, where he met with the emperor. He was received with the same state, magnificence, and respect, as if he had been the king of England himself; and he concluded in his master's name an offensive alliance with the pope and the emperor against France. He stipulated, that England should next summer invade that kingdom with forty thousand men; and he betrothed to Charles the princess Mary, the king's only child, who had now some prospect of inheriting the

[g] Polydore Virgil. Hall.

crown. This extravagant alliance, which was prejudicial to the interests, and might have proved fatal to the liberty and independence of the kingdom, was the result of the humours and prejudices of the king, and the private views and expectations of the cardinal.

The people saw every day new instances of the uncontrouled authority of this minister. The duke of Buckingham, constable of England, the first nobleman both for family and fortune in the kingdom, had imprudently given disgust to the cardinal; and it was not long before he found reason to repent of his indiscretion. He seems to have been a man full of levity and rash projects; and being infatuated with judicial astrology, he entertained a commerce with one Hopkins, a carthusian friar, who encouraged him in the notion of his mounting one day the throne of England. He was descended by a female from the duke of Gloucester, youngest son of Edward III.; and though his claim to the crown was thereby very remote, he had been so unguarded as to let fall some expressions, as if he thought himself best intitled, in case the king should die without issue, to possess the royal dignity. He had not even abstained from threats against the king's life, and had provided himself with arms, which he intended to employ, in case a favourable opportunity should offer. He was brought to a trial; and the duke of Norfolk, whose son, the earl of Surrey, had married Buckingham's daughter, was created lord steward, in order to preside at this solemn procedure. The jury consisted of a duke, a marquis, seven earls, and twelve barons; and they gave their verdict against Buckingham, which was soon after carried into execution. There is no reason to think the sentence unjust;[h] but as Buckingham's crimes seemed to proceed more from indiscretion than deliberate malice, the people who loved him, expected that the king would grant him a pardon, and imputed their disappointment to the animosity and revenge of the cardinal. The king's own jealousy, however, of all persons allied to the crown, was, notwithstanding his undoubted title, very remarkable during the whole course of his reign; and was alone sufficient to render him implacable against Buckingham. The office of constable, which this nobleman inherited from the Bohuns, earls of Hereford, was forfeited, and was never after revived in England.

Trial and condemnation of the duke of Buckingham.

[h] Herbert. Hall. Stowe, 513. Holingshed, p. 862.

XXIX

Digression concerning the ecclesiastical state – Origin of the reformation – Martin Luther – Henry receives the title of defender of the faith – Causes of the progress of the reformation – War with France – Invasion of France – War with Scotland – A parliament – Invasion of France – Italian wars – The king of France invades Italy – Battle of Pavia and Captivity of Francis – Francis recovers his liberty – Sack of Rome – League with France

1521.

DURING SOME YEARS, many parts of Europe had been agitated with those religious controversies, which produced the reformation, one of the greatest events in history: But as it was not till this time, that the king of England publicly took part in the quarrel, we had no occasion to give any account of its rise and progress. It will now be necessary to explain these theological disputes; or what is more material, to trace from their origin those abuses, which so generally diffused the opinion, that a reformation of the church or ecclesiastical order was become highly expedient, if not absolutely necessary. We shall be better enabled to comprehend the subject, if we take the matter a little higher, and reflect a moment on the reasons, why there must be an ecclesiastical

CHAPTER XXIX

order, and a public establishment of religion in every civilized community. The importance of the present occasion will, I hope, excuse this short digression.

Most of the arts and professions in a state are of such a nature, that, while they promote the interest of the society, they are also useful or agreeable to some individuals; and in that case, the constant rule of the magistrate, except, perhaps, on the first introduction of any art, is, to leave the profession to itself, and trust its encouragement to those who reap the benefit of it. The artizans, finding their profits to rise by the favour of their customers, encrease, as much as possible, their skill and industry; and as matters are not disturbed by any injudicious tampering, the commodity is always sure to be at all times nearly proportioned to the demand.

Digression concerning the ecclesiastical state.

But there are also some callings, which, though useful and even necessary in a state, bring no particular advantage or pleasure to any individual; and the supreme power is obliged to alter its conduct with regard to the retainers of those professions. It must give them public encouragement in order to their subsistence; and it must provide against that negligence, to which they will naturally be subject, either by annexing peculiar honours to the profession, by establishing a long subordination of ranks and a strict dependance, or by some other expedient. The persons, employed in the finances, armies, fleets, and magistracy, are instances of this order of men.

It may naturally be thought, at first sight, that the ecclesiastics belong to the first class, and that their encouragement, as well as that of lawyers and physicians, may safely be entrusted to the liberality of individuals, who are attached to their doctrines, and who find benefit or consolation from their spiritual ministry and assistance. Their industry and vigilance will, no doubt, be whetted by such an additional motive; and their skill in the profession, as well as their address in governing the minds of the people, must receive daily encrease, from their encreasing practice, study, and attention.

But if we consider the matter more closely, we shall find, that this interested diligence of the clergy is what every wise legislator will study to prevent; because in every religion, except the true, it is highly pernicious, and it has even a natural tendency to pervert the true, by infusing into it a strong mixture of superstition, folly, and delusion. Each ghostly practitioner, in order to render himself more precious and sacred in the eyes of his retainers, will inspire them with the most violent abhorrence of all other sects, and continually endeavour, by some novelty, to excite the languid devotion of his audience. No regard will be paid to truth, morals, or decency in the doctrines inculcated. Every tenet will be adopted that best suits the disorderly affections of the human frame. Customers will be drawn to each conventicle by new industry and address in practising on the passions and credulity of the populace. And in the end, the civil magistrate will find, that he has dearly paid for his pretended frugality, in saving a fixed establishment for the priests; and that in reality the most decent and advantageous composition, which he can make with the spiritual guides, is to bribe their indolence, by assigning stated salaries to their profession, and rendering it superfluous for them to be farther active, than merely to prevent their flock from straying in quest of new pastures. And in this manner ecclesiastical establishments, though commonly they arose at first from religious views, prove in the end advantageous to the political interests of society.

But we may observe, that few ecclesiastical establishments have been fixed upon a worse foundation than that of the church of Rome, or have been attended with circumstances more hurtful to the peace and happiness of mankind.

The large revenues, privileges, immunities, and powers of the clergy rendered them formidable to the civil magistrate, and armed with too extensive authority an order of men, who always adhere closely together, and who never want a plausible pretence for their encroachments and usurpations. The higher dignities of the church served, indeed, to the support of gentry and nobility; but by the establishment of monasteries, many of the lowest vulgar were taken from the useful arts, and maintained in those receptacles of sloth and ignorance. The supreme head of the church was a foreign potentate, guided by interests, always different from those of the community, sometimes contrary to them. And as the hierarchy was necessarily solicitous to preserve an unity of faith, rites, and ceremonies, all liberty of thought ran a manifest risque of being extinguished; and violent persecutions, or what was worse, a stupid and abject credulity took place every where.

CHAPTER XXIX

To encrease these evils, the church, though she possessed large revenues, was not contented with her acquisitions, but retained a power of practising farther on the ignorance of mankind. She even bestowed on each individual priest a power of enriching himself by the voluntary oblations of the faithful, and left him still an urgent motive for diligence and industry in his calling. And thus, that church, though an expensive and burthensome establishment, was liable to many of the inconveniencies, which belong to an order of priests, trusted entirely to their own art and invention for attaining a subsistence.

The advantages, attending the Romish hierarchy, were but a small compensation for its inconveniencies. The ecclesiastical privileges, during barbarous times, had served as a cheque on the despotism of kings. The union of all the western churches under the supreme pontiff facilitated the intercourse of nations, and tended to bind all the parts of Europe into a close connection with each other. And the pomp and splendor of worship which belonged to so opulent an establishment, contributed, in some respect, to the encouragement of the fine arts, and began to diffuse a general elegance of taste, by uniting it with religion.

It will easily be conceived, that, though the balance of evil prevailed in the Romish church, this was not the chief reason, which produced the reformation. A concurrence of incidents must have contributed to forward that great revolution.

Leo X. by his generous and enterprizing temper, had much exhausted his treasury, and was obliged to employ every invention, which might yield money, in order to support his projects, pleasures, and liberalities. The scheme of selling indulgences was suggested to him, as an expedient which had often served in former times to draw money from the christian world, and make devout people willing contributors to the grandeur and riches of the court of Rome. The church, it was supposed, was possessed of a great stock of merit, as being entitled to all the good works of all the saints, beyond what were employed in their own justification; and even to the merits of Christ himself, which were infinite and unbounded: And from this unexhausted treasury, the pope might retail particular portions, and by that traffic acquire money, to be employed in pious purposes, in resisting the infidels, or subduing

Origin of the reformation.

schismatics. When the money came into his exchequer, the greater part of it was usually diverted to other purposes.[i]

It is commonly believed, that Leo, from the penetration of his genius, and his familiarity with ancient literature, was fully acquainted with the ridicule and falsity of the doctrines, which, as supreme pontiff, he was obliged by his interest to promote: It is the less wonder, therefore, that he employed for his profit those pious frauds, which his predecessors, the most ignorant and credulous, had always, under plausible pretences, made use of for their selfish purposes. He published the sale of a general indulgence;[k] and as his expences had not only exhausted his usual revenue, but even anticipated the money expected from this extraordinary expedient, the several branches of it were openly given away to particular persons, who were entitled to levy the imposition. The produce, particularly, of Saxony and the countries bordering on the Baltic, was assigned to his sister Magdalene, married to Cibo, natural son of Innocent VIII. and she, in order to enhance her profit, had farmed out the revenue to one Arcemboldi, a Genoese, once a merchant, now a bishop, who still retained all the lucrative arts of his former profession.[l] The Austin friars had usually been employed in Saxony to preach the indulgences, and from this trust had derived both profit and consideration: But Arcemboldi, fearing, lest practice might have taught them means to secrete the money,[m] and expecting no extraordinary success from the ordinary methods of collection, gave this occupation to the Dominicans. These monks, in order to prove themselves worthy of the distinction conferred on them, exaggerated the benefits of indulgences by the most unbounded panegyrics; and advanced doctrines on that head, which, though not more ridiculous than those already received, were not as yet entirely familiar to the ears of the people.[n] To add to the scandal, the collectors of this revenue are said to have lived very licentious lives, and to have spent in taverns, gaming-houses, and places still more infamous, the money, which devout persons had saved from their usual expences, in order to purchase a remission of their sins.[o]

All these circumstances might have given offence, but would

[i] Father Paul and Sleidan.   [k] In 1517.   [l] Father Paul, Sleidan.   [m] Father Paul, lib. 1.   [n] See note [D] at the end of the volume.   [o] Father Paul, lib. 1.

CHAPTER XXIX

have been attended with no event of any importance, had there not arisen a man, qualified to take advantage of the incident. Martin Luther, an Austin friar, professor in the university of Wittemberg, resenting the affront put upon his order, began to preach against these abuses in the sale of indulgences; and being naturally of a fiery temper, and provoked by opposition, he proceeded even to decry indulgences themselves; and was thence carried, by the heat of dispute, to question the authority of the pope, from which his adversaries derived their chief arguments against him.[p] Still as he enlarged his reading, in order to support these tenets, he discovered some new abuse or error in the church of Rome; and finding his opinions greedily hearkened to, he promulgated them by writing, discourse, sermon, conference; and daily encreased the number of his disciples. All Saxony, all Germany, all Europe, were in a very little time filled with the voice of this daring innovator; and men, roused from that lethargy, in which they had so long sleeped, began to call in question the most ancient and most received opinions. The elector of Saxony, favourable to Luther's doctrine, protected him from the violence of the papal jurisdiction: The republic of Zuric even reformed their church according to the new model: Many sovereigns of the empire, and the imperial diet itself, showed a favourable disposition towards it: And Luther, a man naturally inflexible, vehement, opinionative, was become incapable, either from promises of advancement, or terrors of severity, to relinquish a sect, of which he was himself the founder, and which brought him a glory, superior to all others, the glory of dictating the religious faith and principles of multitudes.

The rumour of these innovations soon reached England; and as there still subsisted in that kingdom great remains of the Lollards, whose principles resembled those of Luther, the new doctrines secretly gained many partizans among the laity of all ranks and denominations. But Henry had been educated in a strict attachment to the church of Rome, and he bore a particular prejudice against Luther, who, in his writings, spoke with contempt of Thomas Aquinas, the king's favourite author: He opposed himself therefore to the progress of the Lutheran tenets, by all the influence which his extensive and almost absolute authority conferred

Martin Luther.

[p] Father Paul, Sleidan.

upon him: He even undertook to combat them with weapons not usually employed by monarchs, especially those in the flower of their age, and force of their passions. He wrote a book in Latin against the principles of Luther; a performance, which, if allowance be made for the subject and the age, does no discredit to his capacity. He sent a copy of it to Leo, who received so magnificent a present with great testimony of regard; and conferred on him the title of *defender of the faith;* an appellation still retained by the kings of England. Luther, who was in the heat of controversy, soon published an answer to Henry; and without regard to the dignity of his antagonist, treated him with all the acrimony of style, to which, in the course of his polemics, he had so long been accustomed. The king, by this ill usage, was still more prejudiced against the new doctrines; but the public, who naturally favour the weaker party, were inclined to attribute to Luther the victory in the dispute.[q] And as the controversy became more illustrious, by Henry's entering the lists, it drew still more the attention of mankind; and the Lutheran doctrine daily acquired new converts in every part of Europe.

Henry receives the title of defender of the faith.

The quick and surprising progress of this bold sect may justly in part be ascribed to the late invention of printing, and revival of learning: Not that reason bore any considerable share, in opening men's eyes with regard to the impostures of the Romish Church: For of all branches of literature, philosophy had, as yet, and till long afterwards, made the most inconsiderable progress; neither is there any instance that argument has ever been able to free the people from that enormous load of absurdity, with which superstition has every where overwhelmed them: Not to mention, that the rapid advance of the Lutheran doctrine, and the violence, with which it was embraced, prove sufficiently, that it owed not its success to reason and reflection. The art of printing and the revival of learning forwarded its progress in another manner. By means of that art, the books of Luther and his sectaries, full of vehemence, declamation, and a rude eloquence, were propagated more quickly, and in greater numbers. The minds of men, somewhat awakened from a profound sleep of so many centuries, were prepared for every novelty, and scrupled less to tread in any unusual

Causes of the progress of the reformation.

[q] Father Paul, lib. 1.

CHAPTER XXIX

path, which was opened to them. And as copies of the Scriptures and other ancient monuments of the christian faith became more common, men perceived the innovations, which were introduced after the first centuries; and though argument and reasoning could not give conviction, an historical fact, well supported, was able to make impression on their understandings. Many of the powers, indeed, assumed by the church of Rome, were very ancient, and were prior to almost every political government established in Europe: But as the ecclesiastics would not agree to possess their privileges as matters of civil right, which time might render valid, but appealed still to a divine origin, men were tempted to look into their primitive charter; and they could, without much difficulty, perceive its defect in truth and authenticity.

In order to bestow on this topic the greater influence, Luther and his followers, not satisfied with opposing the pretended divinity of the Romish church, and displaying the temporal inconveniencies of that establishment, carried matters much farther, and treated the religion of their ancestors, as abominable, detestable, damnable; foretold by sacred writ itself as the source of all wickedness and pollution. They denominated the pope antichrist, called his communion the scarlet whore, and gave to Rome the appellation of Babylon; expressions, which, however applied, were to be found in Scripture, and which were better calculated to operate on the multitude than the most solid arguments. Excited by contest and persecution on the one hand, by success and applause on the other, many of the reformers carried to the greatest extremities their opposition to the church of Rome; and in contradiction to the multiplied superstitions, with which that communion was loaded, they adopted an enthusiastic strain of devotion, which admitted of no observances, rites, or ceremonies, but placed all merit in a mysterious species of faith, in inward vision, rapture, and ecstacy. The new sectaries, seized with this spirit, were indefatigable in the propagation of their doctrine, and set at defiance all the anathemas and punishments, with which the Roman pontiff endeavoured to overwhelm them.

That the civil power, however, might afford them protection against the ecclesiastical jurisdiction, the Lutherans advanced doctrines favourable, in some respect, to the temporal authority of sovereigns. They inveighed against the abuses of the court of

Rome, with which men were at that time generally discontented; and they exhorted princes to reinstate themselves in those powers, of which the encroaching spirit of the ecclesiastics, especially of the sovereign pontiff, had so long bereaved them. They condemned celibacy and monastic vows, and thereby opened the doors of the convents to those who were either tired of the obedience and chastity, or disgusted with the licence, in which they had hitherto lived. They blamed the excessive riches, the idleness, the libertinism of the clergy; and pointed out their treasures and revenues as lawful spoil to the first invader. And as the ecclesiastics had hitherto conducted a willing and a stupid audience, and were totally unacquainted with controversy, much more with every species of true literature; they were unable to defend themselves against men, armed with authorities, quotations, and popular topics, and qualified to triumph in every altercation or debate. Such were the advantages, with which the reformers began their attack on the Romish hierarchy; and such were the causes of their rapid and astonishing success.

1st Decemb. Leo X. whose oversights and too supine trust in the profound ignorance of the people had given rise to this sect, but whose sound judgment, moderation, and temper, were well qualified to retard its progress, died in the flower of his age, a little after he received the king's book against Luther; and he was succeeded in the papal chair, by Adrian, a Fleming, who had been tutor to the emperor Charles. This man was fitted to gain on the reformers by the integrity, candour, and simplicity of manners, which distinguished his character; but, so violent were their prejudices against the church, he rather hurt the cause by his imprudent exercise of those virtues. He frankly confessed, that many abominable and detestable practices prevailed in the court of Rome; and by this sincere avowal, he gave occasion of much triumph to the Lutherans. This pontiff also, whose penetration was not equal to his good intentions, was seduced to concur in that league, which Charles and Henry had formed against France;[r] and he thereby augmented the scandal, occasioned by the practice of so many preceding popes, who still made their spiritual arms subservient to political purposes.

[r] Guicciardini, lib. 14.

CHAPTER XXIX

The emperor, who knew, that Wolsey had received a disappointment in his ambitious hopes by the election of Adrian, and who dreaded the resentment of that haughty minister, was solicitous to repair the breach made in their friendship by this incident. He paid another visit to England; and besides flattering the vanity of the king and the cardinal, he renewed to Wolsey all the promises, which he had made him, of seconding his pretensions to the papal throne. Wolsey, sensible that Adrian's great age and infirmities promised a speedy vacancy, dissembled his resentment, and was willing to hope for a more prosperous issue to the next election. The emperor renewed the treaty made at Bruges, to which some articles were added; and he agreed to indemnify both the king and Wolsey for the revenue, which they should lose by a breach with France. The more to ingratiate himself with Henry and the English nation, he gave to Surrey, admiral of England, a commission for being admiral of his dominions; and he himself was installed knight of the garter at London. After a stay of six weeks in England, he embarked at Southampton, and in ten days arrived in Spain, where he soon pacified the tumults which had arisen in his absence.[s]

The king declared war against France; and this measure was founded on so little reason, that he could allege nothing as a ground of quarrel, but Francis's refusal to submit to his arbitration, and his sending Albany into Scotland. This last step had not been taken by the French king, till he was quite assured of Henry's resolution to attack him. Surrey landed some troops at Cherbourg in Normandy; and after laying waste the country, he sailed to Morlaix, a rich town in Britanny, which he took and plundered. The English merchants had great property in that place, which was no more spared by the soldiers, than the goods of the French. Surrey then left the charge of the fleet to the vice-admiral; and sailed to Calais, where he took the command of the English army, destined for the invasion of France. This army, when joined by forces from the Low-Countries, under the command of the count de Buren, amounted in the whole to 18,000 men.

The French had made it a maxim in almost all their wars with the English, since the reign of Charles V. never, without great

1522.

26th May.

War with France.

Invasion of France.

[s] Petrus de Angleria, epist. 765.

necessity, to hazard a general engagement; and the duke of Vendome, who commanded the French army, now embraced this wise policy. He supplied the towns most exposed, especially Boulogne, Montreuil, Teroüenne, Hedin, with strong garrisons and plenty of provisions: He himself took post at Abbeville, with some Swiss and French infantry, and a body of cavalry: The count of Guise encamped under Montreuil with six thousand men. These two bodies were in a situation to join upon occasion; to throw supply into any town that was threatened; and to harass the English in every movement. Surrey, who was not provided with magazines, first divided his troops for the convenience of subsisting them; but finding that his quarters were every moment beaten up by the activity of the French generals, he drew together his forces, and laid siege to Hedin. But neither did he succeed in this enterprize. The garrison made vigorous sallies upon his army: The French forces assaulted him from without: Great rains fell: Fatigue and bad weather threw the soldiers into dysenteries: And Surrey was obliged to raise the siege, and put his troops into winter-quarters about the end of October. His rear guard was attacked at Pas in Artois, and five or six hundred men were cut off; nor could all his efforts make him master of one place within the French frontier.

The allies were more successful in Italy. Lautrec, who commanded the French, lost a great battle at Bicocca near Milan; and was obliged to retire with the remains of his army. This misfortune, which proceeded from Francis's negligence in not supplying Lautrec with money,[t] was followed by the loss of Genoa. The castle of Cremona was the sole fortress in Italy, which remained in the hands of the French.

Europe was now in such a situation, and so connected by different alliances and interests, that it was almost impossible for war to be kindled in one part, and not diffuse itself throughout the whole: But of all the leagues among kingdoms, the closest was that which had so long subsisted between France and Scotland; and the English, while at war with the former nation, could not hope to remain long unmolested on the northern frontier. No sooner had Albany arrived in Scotland, than he took measures for kindling a war with England; and he summoned the whole force of the kingdom to

War with Scotland.

[t] Guicciardini, lib. 14.

CHAPTER XXIX

meet in the fields of Rosline.[u] He thence conducted the army southwards into Annandale; and prepared to pass the borders at Solway-Frith. But many of the nobility were disgusted with the regent's administration; and observing, that his connexions with Scotland were feeble in comparison of those which he maintained with France, they murmured, that, for the sake of foreign interests, their peace should so often be disturbed, and war, during their king's minority, be wantonly entered into with a neighbouring nation, so much superior in force and riches. The Gordons, in particular, refused to advance any farther; and Albany, observing a general discontent to prevail, was obliged to conclude a truce with lord Dacres, warden of the English West marches. Soon after, he departed for France; and lest the opposite faction should gather force in his absence, he sent thither before him the earl of Angus, husband to the queen dowager.

Next year, Henry, that he might take advantage of the regent's absence, marched an army into Scotland under the command of Surrey, who ravaged the Merse and Teviotdale without opposition, and burned the town of Jedburgh. The Scots had neither king nor regent to conduct them: The two Humes had been put to death: Angus was in a manner banished: No nobleman of vigour or authority remained, who was qualified to assume the government: And the English monarch, who knew the distressed situation of the country, determined to push them to extremity, in hopes of engaging them, by the sense of their present weakness, to make a solemn renunciation of the French alliance, and to embrace that of England.[w] He even gave them hopes of contracting a marriage between the lady Mary, heiress of England, and their young monarch; an expedient, which would for ever unite the two kingdoms:[x] And the queen dowager, with her whole party, recommended every where the advantages of this alliance, and of a confederacy with Henry. They said, that the interests of Scotland had too long been sacrificed to those of the French nation, who, whenever they found themselves reduced to difficulties, called for the assistance of their allies; but were ready to abandon them, as soon as they found their advantage in making peace with England:

1523.

---

[u] Buchanan, lib. 14. Drummond. Pitscottie.   [w] Buchanan, lib. 14. Herbert.   [x] Le Grand, vol. iii. p. 39.

HISTORY OF ENGLAND

That where a small state entered into so close a confederacy with a greater, it must always expect this treatment, as a consequence of the unequal alliance; but there were peculiar circumstances in the situation of the kingdoms, which, in the present case, rendered it inevitable: That France was so distant and so divided from them by sea, that she scarcely could, by any means, and never could in time, send succours to the Scots, sufficient to protect them against ravages from the neighbouring kingdom: That nature had, in a manner, formed an alliance between the two British nations; having enclosed them in the same island; given them the same manners, language, laws, and form of government; and prepared everything for an intimate union between them: And that, if national antipathies were abolished, which would soon be the effect of peace, these two kingdoms, secured by the ocean and by their domestic force, could set at defiance all foreign enemies, and remain for ever safe and unmolested.

The partizans of the French alliance, on the other hand, said, that the very reasons, which were urged in favour of a league with England, the vicinity of the kingdom and its superior force, were the real causes, why a sincere and durable confederacy could never be formed with that hostile nation: That among neighbouring states, occasions of quarrel were frequent; and the more powerful would be sure to seize every frivolous pretence for oppressing the weaker, and reducing it to subjection: That as the near neighbourhood of France and England had kindled a war almost perpetual between them, it was the interest of the Scots, if they wished to maintain their independance, to preserve their league with the former kingdom, which balanced the force of the latter: That if they deserted that old and salutary alliance, on which their importance in Europe chiefly depended, their ancient enemies, stimulated both by interest and by passion, would soon invade them with superior force, and bereave them of all their liberties: Or if they delayed the attack, the insidious peace, by making the Scots forget the use of arms, would only prepare the way for a slavery more certain and more irretrievable.[y]

The arguments employed by the French party, being seconded by the natural prejudices of the people, seemed most prevalent:

[y] Buchanan, lib. 14.

CHAPTER XXIX

And when the regent himself, who had been long detained beyond his appointed time by the danger from the English fleet, at last appeared among them, he was able to throw the balance entirely on that side. By authority of the convention of states, he assembled an army, with a view of avenging the ravages committed by the English in the beginning of the campaign; and he led them southwards towards the borders. But when they were passing the Tweed at the bridge of Melross, the English party raised again such opposition, that Albany thought proper to make a retreat. He marched downwards, along the banks of the Tweed, keeping that river on his right; and fixed his camp opposite to Werk-Castle, which Surrey had lately repaired. He sent over some troops to besiege this fortress, who made a breach in it, and stormed some of the outworks: But the regent, hearing of the approach of an English army, and discouraged by the advanced season, thought proper to disband his forces and retire to Edinburgh. Soon after he went over to France, and never again returned to Scotland. The Scottish nation, agitated by their domestic factions, were not, during several years, in a condition to give any more disturbance to England; and Henry had full leisure to prosecute his designs on the continent.

The reason, why the war against France proceeded so slowly on the part of England was the want of money. All the treasures of Henry VII. were long ago dissipated; the king's habits of expence still remained; and his revenues were unequal even to the ordinary charge of government, much more to his military enterprizes. He had last year caused a general survey to be made of the kingdom; the numbers of men, their years, profession, stock, revenue;[2] and expressed great satisfaction on finding the nation so opulent. He then issued privy seals to the most wealthy, demanding loans of particular sums: This act of power, though somewhat irregular and tyrannical, had been formerly practised by kings of England; and the people were now familiarized to it. But Henry, this year, carried his authority much farther. He published an edict for a general tax upon his subjects, which he still called a loan; and he levied five shillings in the pound upon the clergy, two shillings upon the laity. This pretended loan, as being more regular,

[2] Herbert. Stowe, p. 514.

was really more dangerous to the liberties of the people; and was a precedent for the king's imposing taxes without consent of parliament.

15th April.
A par-
liament.

Henry soon after summoned a parliament, together with a convocation; and found neither of them in a disposition to complain of the infringement of their privileges. It was only doubted, how far they would carry their liberality to the king. Wolsey, who had undertaken the management of the affair, began with the convocation; in hopes, that their example would influence the parliament to grant a large supply. He demanded a moiety of the ecclesiastical revenues to be levied in five years, or two shillings in the pound during that time; and though he met with opposition, he reprimanded the refractory members in such severe terms, that his request was at last complied with. The cardinal afterwards, attended by several of the nobility and prelates, came to the house of commons; and in a long and elaborate speech laid before them the public necessities, the danger of an invasion from Scotland, the affronts received from France, the league in which the king was engaged with the pope and the emperor; and he demanded a grant of 800,000 pounds, divided into four yearly payments; a sum computed from the late survey or valuation, to be equal to four shillings in the pound of one year's revenue, or one shilling in the pound yearly, according to the division proposed.[a] So large a grant was unusual from the commons; and though the cardinal's demand was seconded by Sir Thomas More the speaker, and several other members attached to the court, the house could not be prevailed with to comply.[b] They only voted two shillings in the pound on all who enjoyed twenty pounds a year and upwards; one shilling on all who possessed between twenty pounds and forty shillings a year; and on the other subjects above sixteen years of age a groat a-head. This last sum was divided into two yearly payments; the former into four, and was not therefore at the outmost above six-pence in the pound. The grant of the commons was but the moiety of the sum demanded; and the cardinal, therefore, much mortified with the disappointment, came again to the

[a] This survey or valuation is liable to much suspicion, as fixing the rents a great deal too high: Unless the sum comprehend the revenues of all kinds, industry as well as land and money.   [b] Herbert, Stowe, 518. Parliamentary History. Strype, vol. i. p. 49.

CHAPTER XXIX

house, and desired to reason with such as refused to comply with
the king's request. He was told, that it was a rule of the house never
to reason but among themselves; and his desire was rejected. The
commons, however, enlarged a little their former grant, and voted
an imposition of three shillings in the pound on all possessed of
fifty pounds a year, and upwards.[c] The procedings of this house of
commons evidently discover the humour of the times: They were
extremely tenacious of their money, and refused a demand of
the crown, which was far from being unreasonable; but they allowed an encroachment on national privileges to pass uncensured,
though its direct tendency was to subvert entirely the liberties of
the people. The king was so dissatisfied with this saving disposition
of the commons, that, as he had not called a parliament during
seven years before, he allowed seven more to elapse, before he
summoned another. And on pretence of necessity, he levied, in
one year, from all who were worth forty pounds, what the parliament had granted him payable in four years;[d] a new invasion of
national privileges. These irregularities were commonly ascribed
to the cardinal's counsels, who, trusting to the protection afforded
him by his ecclesiastical character, was the less scrupulous in his
encroachments on the civil rights of the nation.

That ambitious prelate received this year a new disappointment in his aspiring views. The pope, Adrian VI. died;
and Clement VII. of the family of Medicis, was elected in his
place, by the concurrence of the imperial party. Wolsey could now
perceive the insincerity of the emperor, and he concluded that
that prince would never second his pretensions to the papal chair.
As he highly resented this injury, he began thenceforth to es-
trange himself from the imperial court, and to pave the way for
an union between his master and the French king. Meanwhile, he
concealed his disgust; and after congratulating the new pope
on his promotion, applied for a continuation of the legantine
powers, which the two former popes had conferred upon him.
Clement, knowing the importance of gaining his friendship,
granted him a commission for life; and by this unusual concession,
he in a manner transferred to him the whole papal authority
in England. In some particulars, Wolsey made a good use of

[c] See note [E] at the end of the volume.   [d] Speed. Hall. Herbert.

this extensive power. He erected two colleges, one at Oxford, another at Ipswich, the place of his nativity: He sought, all over Europe, for learned men to supply the chairs of these colleges: And in order to bestow endowments on them, he suppressed some smaller monasteries, and distributed the monks into other convents. The execution of this project became the less difficult for him, because the Romish church began to perceive, that she over-abounded in monks, and that she wanted some supply of learning, in order to oppose the inquisitive, or rather disputative, humour of the reformers.

The confederacy against France seemed more formidable than ever, on the opening of the campaign.[e] Adrian, before his death, had renewed the league with Charles and Henry. The Venetians had been induced to desert the French alliance, and to form engagements for securing Francis Sforza, brother to Maximilian, in possession of the Milanese. The Florentines, the dukes of Ferrara and Mantua, and all the powers of Italy combined in the same measure. The emperor in person menaced France with a powerful invasion on the side of Guienne: The forces of England and the Netherlands hovered over Picardy: A numerous body of Germans were preparing to ravage Burgundy: But all these perils from foreign enemies were less threatening than a domestic conspiracy, which had been formed, and which was now come to full maturity, against the French monarch.

Charles duke of Bourbon, constable of France, was a prince of the most shining merit; and, besides distinguishing himself in many military enterprizes, he was adorned with every accomplishment, which became a person of his high station. His virtues, embellished with the graces of youth, had made such impression on Louise of Savoy, Francis's mother, that, without regard to the inequality of their years, she made him proposals of marriage; and meeting with a repulse, she formed schemes of unrelenting vengeance against him. She was a woman, false, deceitful, vindictive, malicious; but, unhappily for France, had, by her capacity, which was considerable, acquired an absolute ascendant over her son. By her instigation, Francis put many affronts on the constable, which it was difficult for a gallant spirit to endure; and at last he permit-

[e] Guicciardini, lib. 14.

ted Louise to prosecute a lawsuit against him, by which, on the most frivolous pretences, he was deprived of his ample possessions; and inevitable ruin was brought upon him.

Bourbon, provoked at all these indignities, and thinking, that, if any injuries could justify a man in rebelling against his prince and country, he must stand acquitted, had entered into a secret correspondence with the emperor and the king of England.[f] Francis, pertinacious in his purpose of recovering the Milanese, had intended to lead his army in person into Italy; and Bourbon, who feigned sickness, in order to have a pretence for staying behind, purposed, as soon as the king should have passed the Alps, to raise an insurrection among his numerous vassals, by whom he was extremely beloved, and to introduce foreign enemies into the heart of the kingdom. Francis got intimation of his design; but as he was not expeditious enough in securing so dangerous a foe, the constable made his escape;[g] and entering into the emperor's service, employed all the force of his enterprizing spirit and his great talents for war to the prejudice of his native country.

The king of England, desirous that Francis should undertake his Italian expedition, did not openly threaten Picardy this year with an invasion; and it was late before the duke of Suffolk, who commanded the English forces, passed over to Calais. He was attended by the lords Montacute, Herbert, Ferrars, Morney, Sandys, Berkeley, Powls, and many other noblemen and gentlemen.[h] The English army, reinforced by some troops, drawn from the garrison of Calais, amounted to about 12,000 men; and having joined an equal number of Flemings under the count de Buren, they prepared for an invasion of France. The siege of Boulogne was first proposed; but that enterprize appearing difficult, it was thought more advisable to leave this town behind them. The frontier of Picardy was very ill provided with troops; and the only defence of that province was the activity of the French officers, who infested the allied army in their march, and threw garrisons, with great expedition, into every town, which was threatened by them. After coasting the Somme, and passing Hedin, Montreüil, Dourlens, the English and Flemings presented themselves before Bray, a place of small force, which commanded a bridge over that

24th Aug.

Invasion of France.

[f] Memoires du Bellay, liv. 2.   [g] Belcarius, lib. 17.   [h] Herbert.

river. Here they were resolved to pass, and, if possible, to take up winter-quarters in France; but Crequi threw himself into the town, and seemed resolute to defend it. The allies attacked him with vigour and success; and when he retreated over the bridge, they pursued him so hotly, that they allowed him not time to break it down, but passed it along with him, and totally routed his army. They next advanced to Montdidier, which they besieged and took by capitulation. Meeting with no opposition, they proceeded to the river Oise, within eleven leagues of Paris, and threw that city into great consternation; till the duke of Vendôme hastened with some forces to its relief. The confederates, afraid of being surrounded, and of being reduced to extremities during so advanced a season, thought proper to retreat. Montdidier was abandoned: And the English and Flemings, without effecting any thing, retired into their respective countries.

France defended herself from the other invasions with equal facility and equal good fortune. Twelve thousand Lansquenets broke into Burgundy under the command of the count of Furstenberg. The count of Guise, who defended that frontier, had nothing to oppose to them but some militia, and about nine hundred heavy-armed cavalry. He threw the militia into the garrison-towns; and with his cavalry, he kept the field, and so harassed the Germans, that they were glad to make their retreat into Lorraine. Guise attacked them as they passed the Meuse, put them into disorder, and cut off the greater part of their rear.

The emperor made great preparations on the side of Navarre; and though that frontier was well guarded by nature, it seemed now exposed to danger from the powerful invasion which threatened it. Charles besieged Fontarabia, which a few years before had fallen into Francis's hands; and when he had drawn thither Lautrec, the French general, he of a sudden raised the siege, and sat down before Bayonne. Lautrec, aware of that stratagem, made a sudden march, and threw himself into Bayonne, which he defended with such vigour and courage, that the Spaniards were constrained to raise the siege. The emperor would have been totally unfortunate on this side, had he not turned back upon Fontarabia, and, contrary to the advice of all his generals, sitten down, in the winter season, before that city, well fortified and strongly garrisoned. The cowardice or misconduct of the governor saved

CHAPTER XXIX

him from the shame of a new disappointment. The place was surrendered in a few days; and the emperor, having finished this enterprize, put his troops into winter-quarters.

So obstinate was Francis in prosecuting his Italian expedition, that, notwithstanding these numerous invasions, with which his kingdom was menaced on every side, he had determined to lead in person a powerful army to the conquest of Milan. The intelligence of Bourbon's conspiracy and escape stopped him at Lyons; and fearing some insurrection in the kingdom from the intrigues of a man so powerful and so much beloved, he thought it prudent to remain in France, and to send forward his army, under the command of admiral Bonnivet. The dutchy of Milan had been purposely left in a condition somewhat defenceless, with a view of alluring Francis to attack it, and thereby facilitating the enterprizes of Bourbon; and no sooner had Bonnivet passed the Tefin, than the army of the league, and even Prosper Colonna, who commanded it, a prudent general, were in the utmost confusion. It is agreed, that if Bonnivet had immediately advanced to Milan, that great city, on which the whole dutchy depends, would have opened its gates without resistance: But as he wasted his time in frivolous enterprizes, Colonna had opportunity to reinforce the garrison, and to put the place in a posture of defence. Bonnivet was now obliged to attempt reducing the city by blockade and famine; and he took possession of all the posts, which commanded the passages to it. But the army of the league, meanwhile, was not unactive; and they so straitened and harassed the quarters of the French, that it seemed more likely the latter should themselves perish by famine, than reduce the city to that extremity. Sickness and fatigue and want had wasted them to such a degree, that they were ready to raise the blockade; and their only hopes consisted in a great body of Swiss, which was levied for the service of the French king, and whose arrival was every day expected. But these mountaineers no sooner came within sight of the French camp, than they stopped from a sudden caprice and resentment; and instead of joining Bonnivet, they sent orders to a great body of their countrymen, who then served under him, immediately to begin their march, and to return home in their company.[i] After this desertion of the

Italian wars.

1524.

---

[i] Guicciardini, lib. 15. Memoires du Bellai, liv. 2.

Swiss, Bonnivet had no other choice, but that of making his retreat, as fast as possible, into France.

The French being thus expelled Italy, the pope, the Venetians, the Florentines were satisfied with the advantage obtained over them, and were resolved to prosecute their victory no farther. All these powers, especially Clement, had entertained a violent jealousy of the emperor's ambition; and their suspicions were extremely augmented, when they saw him refuse the investiture of Milan, a fief of the empire, to Francis Sforza, whose title he had acknowledged, and whose defence he had embraced.[k] They all concluded, that he intended to put himself in possession of that important dutchy, and reduce Italy to subjection: Clement in particular, actuated by this jealousy, proceeded so far in opposition to the emperor, that he sent orders to his nuncio at London to mediate a reconciliation between France and England. But affairs were not yet fully ripe for this change. Wolsey, disgusted with the emperor, but still more actuated by vain-glory, was determined that he himself should have the renown of bringing about that great alteration; and he engaged the king to reject the pope's mediation. A new treaty was even concluded between Henry and Charles for the invasion of France. Charles stipulated to supply the duke of Bourbon with a powerful army, in order to conquer Provence and Dauphiny: Henry agreed to pay him a hundred thousand crowns for the first month; after which, he might either chuse to continue the same monthly payments, or invade Picardy with a powerful army. Bourbon was to possess these provinces with the title of king; but to hold them in fee of Henry as king of France. The dutchy of Burgundy was to be given to Charles: The rest of the kingdom to Henry.

This chimerical partition immediately failed of execution in the article which was most easily performed: Bourbon refused to acknowledge Henry as king of France. His enterprize, however, against Provence still took place. A numerous army of Imperialists invaded that country under his command and that of the marquis of Pescara. They laid siege to Marseilles, which, being weakly garrisoned, they expected to reduce in a little time: But the citizens defended themselves with such valour and obstinacy, that Bour-

[k] Guicciardini, lib. 15.

CHAPTER XXIX

bon and Pescara, who heard of the French king's approach with a numerous army, found themselves under a necessity of raising the siege; and they led their forces, weakened, baffled, and disheartened, into Italy.

Francis might now have enjoyed in safety the glory of repulsing all his enemies, in every attempt which they had hitherto made for invading his kingdom: But as he received intelligence, that the king of England, discouraged by his former fruitless enterprizes, and disgusted with the emperor, was making no preparations for any attempt on Picardy, his ancient ardour seized him for the conquest of Milan; and, notwithstanding the advanced season, he was immediately determined, contrary to the advice of his wisest counsellors, to lead his army into Italy.

He passed the Alps at Mount Cenis, and no sooner appeared in Piedmont, than he threw the whole Milanese into consternation. The forces of the emperor and Sforza retired to Lodi; and had Francis been so fortunate as to pursue them, they had abandoned that place, and had been totally dispersed:[l] But his ill fate led him to besiege Pavia, a town of considerable strength, well garrisoned, and defended by Leyva, one of the bravest officers in the Spanish service. Every attempt, which the French king made to gain this important place, proved fruitless. He battered the walls, and made breaches; but by the vigilance of Leyva, new retrenchments were instantly thrown up behind the breaches: He attempted to divert the course of the Tesin, which ran by one side of the city, and defended it; but an inundation of the river destroyed in one night all the mounds, which the soldiers, during a long time, and with infinite labour, had been erecting. Fatigue and the bad season (for it was the depth of winter) had wasted the French army. The imperial generals mean while were not unactive. Pescara and Lannoy, viceroy of Naples, assembled forces from all quarters. Bourbon, having pawned his jewels, went into Germany, and with the money, aided by his personal interest, levied a body of twelve thousand Lansquenets, with which he joined the imperialists. This whole army advanced to raise the siege of Pavia; and the danger to the French became every day more imminent.

The state of Europe was such, during that age, that, partly from

The king of France invades Italy.

1525.

---

[l] Guicciardini, lib. 15. Du Bellay, lib. 2.

want of commerce and industry every where, except in Italy and the Low-Countries, partly from the extensive privileges still possessed by the people in all the great monarchies, and their frugal maxims in granting money, the revenues of the princes were extremely narrow, and even the small armies, which they kept on foot, could not be regularly paid by them. The imperial forces, commanded by Bourbon, Pescara, and Lannoy, exceeded not twenty thousand men; they were the only body of troops maintained by the emperor (for he had not been able to levy any army for the invasion of France, either on the side of Spain or Flanders). Yet so poor was that mighty monarch, that he could transmit no money for the payment of this army; and it was chiefly the hopes of sharing the plunder of the French camp, which had made them advance, and kept them to their standards. Had Francis raised the siege before their approach, and retired to Milan, they must immediately have disbanded; and he had obtained a complete victory, without danger or bloodshed. But it was the character of this monarch, to become obstinate in proportion to the difficulties which he encountered; and having once said, that he would take Pavia or perish before it, he was resolved rather to endure the utmost extremities than depart from this resolution.

24th Feb. Battle of Pavia, and captivity of Francis.
The imperial generals, after cannonading the French camp for several days, at last made a general assault, and broke into the entrenchments. Leyva sallied from the town, and encreased the confusion among the besiegers. The Swiss infantry, contrary to their usual practice, behaved in a dastardly manner, and deserted their post. Francis's forces were put to rout; and he himself, surrounded by his enemies, after fighting with heroic valour, and killing seven men with his own hand, was at last obliged to surrender himself prisoner. Almost the whole army, full of nobility and brave officers, either perished by the sword, or were drowned in the river. The few, who escaped with their lives, fell into the hands of the enemy.

The emperor received this news by Pennalosa, who passed through France, by means of a safe-conduct, granted him by the captive king. The moderation, which he displayed on this occasion, had it been sincere, would have done him honour. Instead of rejoicing, he expressed sympathy with Francis's ill fortune, and discovered his sense of those calamities, to which the greatest mon-

CHAPTER XXIX

archs are exposed.[m] He refused the city of Madrid permission to make any public expressions of triumph; and said that he reserved all his exultation, till he should be able to obtain some victory over the infidels. He sent orders to his frontier garrisons to commit no hostilities upon France. He spoke of concluding immediately a peace on reasonable terms. But all this seeming moderation was only hypocrisy, so much the more dangerous as it was profound. And he was wholly occupied in forming schemes, how, from this great incident, he might draw the utmost advantage, and gratify that exorbitant ambition, by which, in all his actions, he was ever governed.

The same Pennalosa, in passing through France, carried also a letter from Francis to his mother, whom he had left regent, and who then resided at Lyons. It contained only these few words, *Madam, all is lost, except our honour.* The princess was struck with the greatness of the calamity. She saw the kingdom without a sovereign, without an army, without generals, without money; surrounded on every side by implacable and victorious enemies: And her chief resource, in her present distresses, were the hopes, which she entertained, of peace and even of assistance from the king of England.

Had the king entered into the war against France from any concerted political views, it is evident, that the victory of Pavia, and the captivity of Francis, were the most fortunate incidents that could have befallen him, and the only ones that could render his schemes effectual. While the war was carried on in the former feeble manner, without any decisive advantage, he might have been able to possess himself of some frontier town, or perhaps of a small territory, of which he could not have kept possession, without expending much more than its value. By some signal calamity alone, which annihilated the power of France, could he hope to acquire the dominion of considerable provinces, or dismember that great monarchy, so affectionate to its own government and its own sovereigns. But as it is probable, that Henry had never before carried his reflections so far, he was startled at this important event, and became sensible of his own danger, as well as that of all Europe, from the loss of a proper counterpoise to the

[m] Vera, Hist. de Carl. V.

Henry embraces the alliance of France.

power of Charles. Instead of taking advantage, therefore, of the distressed condition of Francis, he was determined to lend him assistance in his present calamities; and as the glory of generosity, in raising a fallen enemy, concurred with his political interests, he hesitated the less in embracing these new measures.

Some disgusts also had previously taken place between Charles and Henry, and still more between Charles and Wolsey; and that powerful minister waited only for a favourable opportunity of revenging the disappointments which he had met with. The behaviour of Charles, immediately after the victory of Pavia, gave him occasion to revive the king's jealousy and suspicions. The emperor so ill supported the appearance of moderation, which he at first assumed, that he had already changed his usual style to Henry; and instead of writing to him with his own hand, and subscribing himself *your affectionate son and cousin;* he dictated his letters to a secretary, and simply subscribed himself *Charles.*[n] Wolsey also perceived a diminution in the caresses and professions, with which the emperor's letters to him were formerly loaded; and this last imprudence, proceeding from the intoxication of success, was probably more dangerous to Charles's interests than the other.

Henry, though immediately determined to embrace new measures, was careful to save appearances in the change; and he caused rejoicings to be every where made on account of the victory of Pavia, and the captivity of Francis. He publicly dismissed a French envoy, whom he had formerly allowed, notwithstanding the war, to reside at London:[o] But upon the regent of France's submissive applications to him, he again opened a correspondence with her; and besides assuring her of his friendship and protection, he exacted a promise, that she never would consent to the dismembering of any province from the monarchy for her son's ransom. With the emperor, however, he put on the appearance of vigour and enterprize; and in order to have a pretence for breaking with him, he dispatched Tonstal, bishop of London, to Madrid, with proposals for a powerful invasion of France. He required, that Charles should immediately enter Guienne at the head of a great army, in order to put him in possession of that province; and he demanded the payment of large sums of money, which that

[n] Guicciardini, lib. 16.   [o] Du Bellay, liv. iii. Stowe, p. 221. Baker, p. 273.

CHAPTER XXIX

prince had borrowed from him in his last visit at London. He knew, that the emperor was in no condition of fulfilling either of these demands; and that he had as little inclination to make him master of such considerable territories upon the frontiers of Spain.

Tonstal likewise, after his arrival at Madrid, informed his master, that Charles, on his part, urged several complaints against England; and in particular was displeased with Henry, because last year he had neither continued his monthly payments to Bourbon, nor invaded Picardy, according to his stipulations. Tonstal added, that, instead of expressing an intention to espouse Mary, when she should be of age, the emperor had hearkened to proposals, for marrying his niece Isabella, princess of Portugal; and that he had entered into a separate treaty with Francis, and seemed determined to reap alone all the advantages of the success, with which fortune had crowned his arms.

The king, influenced by all these motives, concluded at Moore his alliance with the regent of France, and engaged to procure her son his liberty on reasonable conditions:[p] The regent also, in another treaty, acknowledged the kingdom Henry's debtor for one million eight hundred thousand crowns, to be discharged in half-yearly payments of fifty thousand crowns: After which, Henry was to receive, during life, a yearly pension of a hundred thousand. A large present of a hundred thousand crowns was also made to Wolsey, for his good offices, but covered under the pretence of arrears due on the pension granted him for relinquishing the administration of Tournay. *30th Aug.*

Meanwhile, Henry, foreseeing that this treaty with France might involve him in a war with the emperor, was also determined to fill his treasury by impositions upon his own subjects; and as the parliament had discovered some reluctance in complying with his demands, he followed, as is believed, the counsel of Wolsey, and resolved to make use of his prerogative alone for that purpose. He issued commissions to all the counties of England, for levying four shillings in the pound upon the clergy, three shillings and four pence upon the laity; and so uncontroulable did he deem his authority, that he took no care to cover, as formerly, this arbitrary exaction, even under the slender pretence of a loan. But he soon *Discontents of the English.*

[p] Du Tillet, Recueil des Traites de Leonard, tom. 2. Herbert.

found, that he had presumed too far on the passive submission of his subjects. The people, displeased with an exaction beyond what was usually levied in those days, and farther disgusted with the illegal method of imposing it, broke out in murmurs, complaints, opposition to the commissioners; and their refractory disposition threatened a general insurrection. Henry had the prudence to stop short, in that dangerous path, into which he had entered. He sent letters to all the counties; declaring, that he meant no force by this last imposition, and that he would take nothing from his subjects but by way of *benevolence*. He flattered himself, that his condescension in employing that disguise would satisfy the people, and that no one would dare to render himself obnoxious to royal authority, by refusing any payment required of him in this manner. But the spirit of opposition, once roused, could not so easily be quieted at pleasure. A lawyer in the city objecting the statute of Richard III. by which benevolences were for ever abolished, it was replied by the court, that, Richard being an usurper, and his parliament a factious assembly, his statutes could not bind a lawful and *absolute* monarch, who held his crown by hereditary right, and needed not to court the favour of a licentious populace.[q] The judges even went so far as to affirm positively, that the king might exact by commission any sum he pleased; and the privy council gave a ready assent to this decree, which annihilated the most valuable privilege of the people, and rendered all their other privileges precarious. Armed with such formidable authority, of royal prerogative and a pretence of law, Wolsey sent for the mayor of London, and desired to know what he was willing to give for the supply of his majesty's necessities. The mayor seemed desirous, before he should declare himself, to consult the common council: but the cardinal required, that he and all the aldermen should separately confer with himself about the benevolence; and he eluded by that means the danger of a formed opposition. Matters, however, went not so smoothly in the country. An insurrection was begun in some places; but as the people were not headed by any considerable person, it was easy for the duke of Suffolk, and the earl of Surrey, now duke of Norfolk, by employing persuasion and authority, to induce the ringleaders to lay down their arms, and

[q] Herbert. Hall.

surrender themselves prisoners. The king, finding it dangerous to punish criminals, engaged in so popular a cause, was determined, notwithstanding his violent, imperious temper, to grant them a general pardon; and he prudently imputed their guilt, not to their want of loyalty or affection, but to their poverty. The offenders were carried before the star-chamber; where, after a severe charge brought against them by the king's council, the cardinal said, "That, notwithstanding their grievous offence, the king, in consideration of their necessities, had granted them his gracious pardon, upon condition, that they would find sureties for their future good behaviour." But they replying, that they had no sureties, the cardinal first, and after him the duke of Norfolk, said, that they would be bound for them. Upon which they were dismissed.[r]

These arbitrary impositions, being imputed, though on what grounds is unknown, to the counsels of the cardinal, encreased the general odium, under which he laboured; and the clemency of the pardon, being ascribed to the king, was considered as an atonement on his part for the illegality of the measure. But Wolsey, supported both by royal and papal authority, proceeded, without scruple, to violate all ecclesiastical privileges, which, during that age, were much more sacred than civil; and having once prevailed in that unusual attempt of suppressing some monasteries, he kept all the rest in awe, and exercised over them an arbitrary jurisdiction. By his commission as legate, he was impowered to visit them, and reform them, and chastise their irregularities; and he employed his usual agent, Allen, in the exercise of this authority. The religious houses were obliged to compound for their guilt, real or pretended, by paying large sums to the cardinal or his deputy; and this oppression was carried so far, that it reached at last the king's ears, which were not commonly open to complaints against his favourite. Wolsey had built a splendid palace at Hampton-court, which he probably intended, as well as that of York-place in Westminster, for his own residence; but fearing the encrease of envy on account of this magnificence, and desirous to appease the king, he made him a present of the building, and told him, that, from the first, he had erected it for his use.

The absolute authority, possessed by the king, rendered his

[r] Herbert. Hall. Stowe, p. 525. Holingshed, p. 891.

domestic government, both over his people and his ministers, easy and expeditious: The conduct of foreign affairs alone required effort and application; and they were now brought to such a situation, that it was no longer safe for England to remain entirely neutral. The feigned moderation of the emperor was of short duration; and it was soon obvious to all the world, that his great dominions, far from gratifying his ambition, were only regarded as the means of acquiring an empire more extensive. The terms which he demanded of his prisoner, were such as must for ever have annihilated the power of France, and destroyed the balance of Europe. These terms were proposed to Francis, soon after the battle of Pavia, while he was detained in Pizzichitone; and as he had hitherto trusted somewhat to the emperor's generosity, the disappointment excited in his breast the most lively indignation. He said, that he would rather live and die a prisoner, than agree to dismember his kingdom; and that, even were he so base as to submit to such conditions, his subjects would never permit him to carry them into execution.

Francis was encouraged to persist in demanding more moderate terms, by the favourable accounts, which he heard of Henry's dispositions towards him, and of the alarm, which had seized all the chief powers in Italy, upon his defeat and captivity. He was uneasy, however, to be so far distant from the emperor with whom he must treat; and he expressed his desire (which was complied with) to be removed to Madrid, in hopes that a personal interview would operate in his favour, and that Charles, if not influenced by his ministers, might be found possessed of the same frankness of disposition, by which he himself was distinguished. He was soon convinced of his mistake. Partly from want of exercise, partly from reflexions on his present melancholy situation, he fell into a languishing illness; which begat apprehensions in Charles, lest the death of his captive should bereave him of all those advantages, which he purposed to extort from him. He then paid him a visit in the castle of Madrid; and as he approached the bed in which Francis lay, the sick monarch called to him, "You come, Sir, to visit your prisoner." "No," replied the emperor, "I come to visit my brother, and my friend, who shall soon obtain his liberty." He soothed his afflictions with many speeches of a like nature, which

Francis removed to Madrid.

had so good an effect, that the king daily recovered;[s] and thenceforth employed himself in concerting with the ministers of the emperor the terms of his treaty.

At last the emperor, dreading a general combination against him, was willing to abate somewhat of his rigour; and the treaty of Madrid was signed, by which, it was hoped, an end would be finally put to the differences between these great monarchs. The principal condition was the restoring of Francis's liberty, and the delivery of his two eldest sons as hostages to the emperor for the cession of Burgundy: If any difficulty should afterwards occur in the execution of this last article, from the opposition of the states, either of France or of that province, Francis stipulated, that, in six weeks time, he should return to his prison, and remain there till the full performance of the treaty. There were many other articles in this famous convention, all of them extremely severe upon the captive monarch; and Charles discovered evidently his intention of reducing Italy, as well as France, to subjection and dependance.

Many of Charles's ministers foresaw, that Francis, how solemn soever the oaths, promises, and protestations exacted of him, never would execute a treaty, so disadvantageous, or rather ruinous and destructive, to himself, his posterity, and his country. By putting Burgundy, they thought, into the emperor's hands, he gave his powerful enemy an entrance into the heart of the kingdom: By sacrificing his allies in Italy, he deprived himself of foreign assistance; and arming his oppressor with the whole force and wealth of that opulent country, rendered him absolutely irresistible. To these great views of interest, were added the motives, no less cogent, of passion and resentment; while Francis, a prince, who piqued himself on generosity, reflected on the rigour with which he had been treated during his captivity, and the severe terms which had been exacted of him for the recovery of his liberty. It was also foreseen, that the emulation and rivalship, which had so long subsisted between these two monarchs, would make him feel the strongest reluctance on yielding the superiority to an antagonist, who, by the whole tenor of his conduct, he would be apt to think, had shewn himself so little worthy of that advantage,

1526.
14th
Jan.

[s] Herbert, De Vera, Sandoval.

which fortune, and fortune alone, had put into his hands. His ministers, his friends, his subjects, his allies, would be sure, with one voice, to inculcate on him, that the first object of a prince, was the preservation of his people; and that the laws of honour, which, with a private man, ought to be absolutely supreme, and superior to all interests, were, with a sovereign, subordinate to the great duty of ensuring the safety of his country. Nor could it be imagined, that Francis would be so romantic in his principles, as not to hearken to a casuistry, which was so plausible in itself, and which so much flattered all the passions, by which, either as a prince or a man, he was strongly actuated.

18th March. Francis recovers his liberty.

Francis, on entering his own dominions, delivered his two eldest sons as hostages into the hands of the Spaniards. He mounted a Turkish horse, and immediately putting him to the gallop, he waved his hand, and cried aloud several times, *I am yet a king.* He soon reached Bayonne, where he was joyfully received by the regent and his whole court. He immediately wrote to Henry; acknowledging that to his good offices alone he owed his liberty, and protesting, that he should be entirely governed by his counsels in all transactions with the emperor. When the Spanish envoy demanded his ratification of the treaty of Madrid, now that he had fully recovered his liberty, he declined the proposal; under colour, that it was previously necessary to assemble the States both of France and of Burgundy, and to obtain their consent. The States of Burgundy soon met; and declaring against the clause, which contained an engagement for alienating their province, they expressed their resolution of opposing, even by force of arms, the execution of so ruinous and unjust an article. The Imperial minister then required, that Francis, in conformity to the treaty of Madrid, should now return to his prison; but the French monarch,

22nd May.

instead of complying, made public the treaty, which, a little before, he had secretly concluded at Cognac, against the ambitious schemes and usurpations of the emperor.[t]

The pope, the Venetians, and other Italian states, who were deeply interested in these events, had been held in the most anxious suspence with regard to the resolutions, which Francis should take, after the recovery of his liberty; and Clement, in particular,

[t] Guicciardini, lib. 17.

CHAPTER XXIX

who suspected, that this prince would never execute a treaty so hurtful to his interests, and even destructive of his independency, had very frankly offered him a dispensation from all his oaths and engagements. Francis remained not in suspence; but entered immediately into the confederacy proposed to him. It was stipulated, by that king, the pope, the Venetians, the Swiss, the Florentines, and the duke of Milan, among other articles, that they would oblige the emperor to deliver up the two young princes of France on receiving a reasonable sum of money; and to restore Milan to Sforza, without farther condition or incumbrance. The king of England was invited to accede, not only as a contracting party, but as protector of the *holy league,* so it was called: And if Naples should be conquered from the emperor, in prosecution of this confederacy, it was agreed, that Henry should enjoy a principality in that kingdom of the yearly revenue of 30,000 ducats: And that cardinal Wolsey, in consideration of the services, which he had rendered to Christendom, should also, in such an event, be put in possession of a revenue of 10,000 ducats.

Francis was desirous, that the appearance of this great confederacy should engage the emperor to relax somewhat in the extreme rigour of the treaty of Madrid; and while he entertained these hopes, he was the more remiss in his warlike preparations; nor did he send in due time reinforcement to his allies in Italy. The *1527.* duke of Bourbon had got possession of the whole Milanese, of which the emperor intended to grant him the investiture; and having levied a considerable army in Germany, he became formidable to all the Italian potentates; and not the less so, because Charles, destitute, as usual, of money, had not been able to remit any pay to the forces. The general was extremely beloved by his troops; and in order to prevent those mutinies, which were ready to break out every moment, and which their affection alone for him had hitherto restrained, he led them to Rome, and promised to enrich them by the plunder of that opulent city. He was himself *6th* killed, as he was planting a scaling ladder against the walls; but his *May.* soldiers, rather enraged than discouraged by his death, mounted to the assault with the utmost valour, and entering the city, sword *Sack of* in hand, exercised all those brutalities, which may be expected *Rome.* from ferocity excited by resistance, and from insolence which takes place when that resistance is no more. This renowned city, exposed by her renown alone to so many calamities, never endured in any age, even from the barbarians, by whom she was often subdued, such indignities as she was now compelled to suffer. The unrestrained massacre and pillage, which continued for several days, were the least ills, to which the unhappy Romans were exposed." Whatever was respectable in modesty or sacred in religion, seemed but the more to provoke the insults of the soldiery. Virgins suffered violation in the arms of their parents, and upon those very altars, to which they had fled for protection. Aged prelates, after enduring every indignity, and even every torture, were thrown into dungeons, and menaced with the most cruel death, in order to make them reveal their secret treasures, or purchase liberty by exorbitant ransoms. Clement himself, who had trusted for protection to the sacredness of his character, and neglected to make his escape in time, was taken captive; and found that his dignity, which procured him no regard from the Spanish soldiers, did but draw on him the insolent mockery of the German, who, being generally attached to the Lutheran principles, were pleased to gratify their animosity by the abasement of the sovereign pontiff.

When intelligence of this great event was conveyed to the emperor, that young prince, habituated to hypocrisy, expressed the most profound sorrow for the success of his arms: He put himself and all his court in mourning: He stopped the rejoicings for the birth of his son Philip: And knowing that every artifice, however gross, is able, when seconded by authority, to impose upon the people, he ordered prayers, during several months, to be put up in the churches for the Pope's liberty; which, all men knew, a letter under his hand could in a moment have procured.

The concern, expressed by Henry and Francis for the calamity of their ally, was more sincere. These two monarchs, a few days before the sack of Rome, had concluded a treaty^w at Westminster, in which, besides renewing former alliances, they agreed to send ambassadors to Charles, requiring him to accept of two millions of crowns as the ranson of the French princes, and to repay the money, borrowed from Henry; and in case of refusal, the ambassadors, attended by heralds, were ordered to denounce war against him. This war, it was agreed, to prosecute in the Low Countries,

---

" Guicciardini, lib. 18. Bellay. Stowe, p. 527. ^{w} 30th April.

CHAPTER XXIX

with an army of thirty thousand infantry and fifteen hundred men at arms, two-thirds to be supplied by Francis, the rest by Henry. And in order to strengthen the alliance between the princes, it was stipulated, that either Francis or his son, the duke of Orleans, as should afterwards be agreed on, should espouse the princess Mary, Henry's daughter. No sooner did the monarchs receive intelligence of Bourbon's enterprize, than they changed, by a new treaty, the scene of the projected war from the Netherlands to Italy; and hearing of the pope's captivity, they were farther stimulated to undertake the war with vigour for restoring him to liberty. Wolsey himself crossed the sea, in order to have an interview with Francis, and to concert measures for that purpose; and he displayed all that grandeur and magnificence with which he was so much intoxicated. He was attended by a train of a thousand horse. The cardinal of Lorraine, and the chancellor Alançon, met him at Boulogne: Francis himself, besides granting to that haughty prelate the power of giving, in every place where he came, liberty to all prisoners, made a journey as far as Amiens to meet him, and even advanced some miles from the town, the more to honour his reception. It was here stipulated, that the duke of Orleans should espouse the princess Mary; and as the emperor seemed to be taking some steps towards assembling a general council, the two monarchs agreed not to acknowledge it, but, during the interval of the pope's captivity, to govern the churches in their respective dominions, by their own authority. Wolsey made some attempts to get his legantine power extended over France, and even over Germany; but finding his efforts fruitless, he was obliged, though with great reluctance, to desist from these ambitious enterprizes.[x]

29th May.

11th July.

The more to cement the union between these princes, a new treaty was, some time after, concluded at London; in which Henry agreed finally to renounce all claims to the crown of France; claims, which might now indeed be deemed chimerical, but which often served as a pretence for exciting the unwary English to wage war upon the French nation. As a return for this concession, Francis bound himself and his successors to pay for ever fifty thousand crowns a year to Henry and his successors; and that greater solemnity might be given to this treaty, it was agreed, that the parlia-

18th Sept.

League with France.

[x] Burnet, book 3. coll. 12, 13.

ments and great nobility of both kingdoms should give their assent to it. The mareschal Montmorency, accompanied by many persons of distinction, and attended by a pompous equipage, was sent over to ratify the treaty; and was received at London with all the parade, which suited the solemnity of the occasion. The terror of the emperor's greatness had extinguished the ancient animosity between the nations; and Spain, during more than a century, became, though a more distant power, the chief object of jealousy to the English.

This cordial union between France and England, though it added influence to the joint embassy, which they sent to the emperor, was not able to bend that monarch to submit entirely to the conditions insisted on by the allies. He departed indeed from his demand of Burgundy as the ransom of the French princes; but he required, previously to their liberty, that Francis should evacuate Genoa, and all the fortresses held by him in Italy: And he declared his intention of bringing Sforza to a trial, and confiscating the dutchy of Milan, on account of his pretended treason. The English and French heralds, therefore, according to agreement, declared war against him, and set him at defiance. Charles answered the English herald with moderation; but to the French, he reproached his master with breach of faith, reminded him of the private conversation which had passed between them at Madrid before their separation, and offered to prove by single combat, that he had acted dishonourably. Francis retaliated this challenge by giving Charles the lie; and, after demanding security of the field, he offered to maintain his cause by single combat. Many messages passed to and fro between them; but though both princes were undoubtedly brave, the intended duel never took place. The French and Spaniards, during that age, zealously disputed which of the monarchs incurred the blame of this failure; but all men of moderation every where lamented the power of fortune, that the prince the more candid, generous, and sincere, should, by unhappy incidents, have been reduced to so cruel a situation, that nothing but his violation of treaty could preserve his people, and that he must ever after, without being able to make a proper reply, bear to be reproached with breach of promise by a rival, inferior to him both in honour and virtue.

CHAPTER XXIX

But though this famous challenge between Charles and Francis had no immediate consequence with regard to these monarchs themselves, it produced a considerable alteration on the manners of the age. The practice of challenges and duels, which had been part of the ancient barbarous jurisprudence, which was still preserved on very solemn occasions, and which was sometimes countenanced by the civil magistrate, began thenceforth to prevail in the most trivial incidents; and men, on any affront or injury, thought themselves entitled, or even required in honour, to take revenge on their enemies, by openly vindicating their right in single combat. These absurd, though generous maxims, shed much of the best blood in Christendom during more than two centuries; and notwithstanding the severity of law and authority of reason, such is the prevailing force of custom, they are far from being as yet entirely exploded.

XXX

Scruples concerning the king's
marriage – The king enters into these
scruples – Anne Boleyn – Henry applies
to the pope for a divorce – The pope
favourable – The emperor threatens him –
The pope's ambiguous conduct – The
cause evoked to Rome – Wolsey's fall –
Commencement of the reformation in
England – Foreign affairs – Wolsey's
death – A parliament – Progress of the
reformation – A parliament – King's final
breach with Rome – A parliament

NOTWITHSTANDING the submissive deference, paid to papal authority before the reformation, the marriage of Henry with Catherine of Arragon, his brother's widow, had not passed, without much scruple and difficulty. The prejudices of the people were in general bent against a conjugal union between such near relations; and the late king, though he had betrothed his son, when that prince was but twelve years of age, gave evident proofs of his intention to take afterwards a proper opportunity of annulling the contract.[y] He ordered the young prince, as soon as he came of age,

1527.
Scruples
concerning
the king's
marriage.

[y] Morison's Apomaxis, p. 13.

CHAPTER XXX

to enter a protestation against the marriage;[z] and on his death-bed he charged him, as his last injunction, not to finish an alliance, so unusual, and exposed to such insuperable objections. After the king's accession, some members of the privy council, particularly Warham, the primate, openly declared against the resolution, of completing the marriage; and though Henry's youth and dissipation kept him, during some time, from entertaining any scruples with regard to the measure which he had embraced, there happened incidents, sufficient to rouse his attention, and to inform him of the sentiments, generally entertained on that subject. The states of Castile had opposed the emperor Charles's espousals with Mary, Henry's daughter; and among other objections, had insisted on the illegitimate birth of the young princess.[a] And when the negociations were afterwards opened with France, and mention was made of betrothing her to Francis or the duke of Orleans, the bishop of Tarbe, the French ambassador, revived the same objection.[b] But though these events naturally raised some doubts in Henry's mind, there concurred other causes, which tended much to encrease his remorse, and render his conscience more scrupulous.

The queen was older than the king by no less than six years: and the decay of her beauty, together with particular infirmities and diseases, had contributed, notwithstanding her blameless character and deportment, to render her person unacceptable to him. Though she had borne him several children, they all died in early infancy, except one daughter; and he was the more struck with this misfortune, because the curse of being childless is the very threatening, contained in the Mosaical law, against those who espouse their brother's widow. The succession too of the crown was a consideration, that occurred to every one, whenever the lawfulness of Henry's marriage was called in question; and it was apprehended, that if doubts of Mary's legitimacy concurred with the weakness of her sex, the king of Scots, the next heir, would advance his pretensions, and might throw the kingdom into confusion. The evils, as yet recent, of civil wars and convulsions, arising from a disputed title, made great impression on the minds of men, and rendered

The king enters into these scruples.

[z] Morison, p. 13. Heylin's Queen Mary, p. 2.   [a] Lord Herbert, Fiddes's life of Wolsey.   [b] Rymer, vol. xiv. 192, 203. Heylin, p. 3.

the people universally desirous of any event, which might obviate so irreparable a calamity. And the king was thus impelled, both by his private passions, and by motives of public interest, to seek the dissolution of his inauspicious, and, as it was esteemed, unlawful marriage with Catherine.

Henry afterwards affirmed, that his scruples arose entirely from private reflection; and that on consulting his confessor, the bishop of Lincoln, he found the prelate possessed with the same doubts and difficulties. The king himself, being so great a casuist and divine, next proceeded to examine the question more carefully by his own learning and study; and having had recourse to Thomas of Aquine, he observed that this celebrated doctor, whose authority was great in the church and absolute with him, had treated of that very case, and had expressly declared against the lawfulness of such marriages.[c] The prohibitions, said Thomas, contained in Leviticus, and among the rest, that of marrying a brother's widow, are moral, eternal, and founded on a divine sanction; and though the pope may dispense with the rules of the church, the laws of God cannot be set aside by any authority less than that which enacted them. The archbishop of Canterbury was then applied to; and he was required to consult his brethren: All the prelates of England, except Fisher, bishop of Rochester, unanimously declared, under their hand and seal, that they deemed the king's marriage unlawful.[d] Wolsey also fortified the king's scruples;[e] partly with a view of promoting a total breach with the emperor, Catherine's nephew; partly desirous of connecting the king more closely with Francis, by marrying him to the dutchess of Alençon, sister to that monarch; and perhaps too somewhat disgusted with the queen herself, who had reproved him for certain freedoms, unbefitting his character and station.[f] But Henry was carried forward, though perhaps not at first excited, by a motive more forcible than even the suggestions of that powerful favourite.

Anne Boleyn.

Anne Boleyn, who lately appeared at court, had been appointed maid of honour to the queen; and having had frequent opportunities of being seen by Henry, and of conversing with him,

[c] Burnet, Fiddes.   [d] Burnet, vol. i. p. 38. Stowe, p. 548.   [e] Le Grand, vol. iii, p. 46, 166, 168. Saunders. Heylin, p. 4.   [f] Burnet, vol. i. p. 38. Strype, vol. i. p. 88.

CHAPTER XXX

she had acquired an entire ascendant over his affections. This young lady, whose grandeur and misfortunes have rendered her so celebrated, was daughter of Sir Thomas Boleyn, who had been employed by the king in several embassies, and who was allied to all the principal nobility in the kingdom. His wife, mother to Anne, was daughter of the duke of Norfolk; his own mother was daughter of the earl of Ormond; his grandfather Sir Geoffry Boleyn, who had been mayor of London, had espoused one of the daughters and co-heirs of lord Hastings.[g] Anne herself, though then in very early youth, had been carried over to Paris by the king's sister, when the princess espoused Lewis XII. of France; and upon the demise of that monarch, and the return of his dowager into England, this damsel, whose accomplishments even in her tender years were always much admired, was retained in the service of Claude, queen of France, spouse to Francis; and after the death of that princess, she passed into the family of the dutchess of Alençon, a woman of singular merit. The exact time, when she returned to England, is not certainly known; but it was after the king had entertained doubts with regard to the lawfulness of his marriage with Catherine; if the account is to be credited, which he himself afterwards gave of that transaction. Henry's scruples had made him break off all conjugal commerce with the queen; but as he still supported an intercourse of civility and friendship with her, he had occasion, in the frequent visits which he paid her, to observe the beauty, the youth, the charms of Anne Boleyn. Finding the accomplishments of her mind nowise inferior to her exterior graces, he even entertained the design of raising her to the throne; and was the more confirmed in this resolution, when he found that her virtue and modesty prevented all hopes of gratifying his passion in any other manner. As every motive, therefore, of inclination and policy, seemed thus to concur in making the king desirous of a divorce from Catherine, and as his prospect of success was inviting, he resolved to make applications to Clement, and he sent Knight, his secretary, to Rome for that purpose.

Henry applies to the pope for a divorce.

That he might not shock the haughty claims of the pontiff, he resolved not to found the application on any general doubts concerning the papal power to permit marriage in the nearer degrees

[g] Camden's preface to the life of Elizabeth Burnet, vol. i. p. 44.

of consanguinity; but only to insist on particular grounds of nullity in the bull, which Julius had granted for the marriage of Henry and Catherine. It was a maxim in the court of Rome, that, if the pope be surprised into any concession, or grant any indulgence upon false suggestions, the bull may afterwards be annulled; and this pretence had usually been employed, wherever one pope had recalled any deed, executed by any of his predecessors. But Julius's bull, when examined, afforded abundant matter of this kind; and any tribunal, favourable to Henry, needed not want a specious colour for gratifying him in his applications for a divorce. It was said in the preamble, that the bull had been granted upon his solicitation; though it was known, that, at that time, he was under twelve years of age: It was also affirmed, as another motive for the bull, that the marriage was requisite, in order to preserve peace between the two crowns; though it is certain, that there was not then any ground or appearance of quarrel between them. These false premises in Julius's bull seemed to afford Clement a sufficient reason or pretence for annulling it, and granting Henry a dispensation for a second marriage.[h]

The pope favour-able. But though the pretext for this indulgence had been less plausible, the pope was in such a situation, that he had the strongest motives to embrace every opportunity of gratifying the English monarch. He was then a prisoner in the hands of the emperor, and had no hopes of recovering his liberty on any reasonable terms, except by the efforts of the league, which Henry had formed with Francis and the Italian powers, in order to oppose the ambition of Charles. When the English Secretary, therefore, solicited him in private, he received a very favourable answer; and a dispensation was forthwith promised to be granted to his master.[i] Soon after, the march of a French army into Italy, under the command of Lautrec, obliged the Imperialists to restore Clement to his liberty; and he retired to Orvietto, where the Secretary, with Sir Gregory Caffali, the king's resident at Rome, renewed their applications to him. They still found him full of high professions of friendship, gratitude, and attachment to the king; but not so prompt in granting his request as they expected. The emperor, who had got intel-

[h] Collier, Eccles. Hist. vol. ii. p. 25. from the Cott. Lib. Vitel. p. 9.
[i] Burnet, vol. i. p. 47.

ligence of Henry's application to Rome, had exacted a promise from the pope, to take no steps in the affair before he communicated them to the Imperial ministers; and Clement, embarrassed by this promise, and still more overawed by the emperor's forces in Italy, seemed willing to postpone those concessions desired of him by Henry. Importuned, however, by the English ministers, he at last put into their hands a *commission* to Wolsey, as legate, in conjunction with the archbishop of Canterbury, or any other English prelate, to examine the validity of the king's marriage, and of Julius's dispensation:[k] He also granted them a provisional *dispensation* for the king's marriage with any other person; and promised to issue a *decretal bull,* annulling the marriage with Catherine. But he represented to them the dangerous consequences, which must ensue to him, if these concessions should come to the emperor's knowledge; and he conjured them not to publish those papers, or make any further use of them, till his affairs were in such a situation as to secure his liberty and independance. And his secret advice was, whenever they should find the proper time for opening the scene, that they should prevent all opposition, by proceeding immediately to a conclusion, by declaring the marriage with Catherine invalid, and by Henry's instantly espousing some other person. Nor would it be so difficult, he said, for himself to confirm these proceedings, after they were passed, as previously to render them valid, by his consent and authority.[l]

When Henry received the commission and dispensation from his ambassadors, and was informed of the pope's advice, he laid the whole before his ministers, and asked their opinion in so delicate a situation. The English counsellors considered the danger of proceeding in the manner pointed out to them. Should the pope refuse to ratify a deed, which he might justly call precipitate and irregular, and should he disavow the advice which he gave in so clandestine a manner, the king would find his second marriage totally invalidated; the children, which it might bring him, declared illegitimate; and his marriage with Catherine more firmly rivetted than ever.[m] And Henry's apprehensions of the possibility, or even probability, of such an event, were much confirmed

1528.

---

[k] Rymer, vol. xiv. 237.   [l] Collier, from Cott. Lib. Vitel. B. 10.   [m] Burnet, vol. l. p. 51.

when he reflected on the character and situation of the sovereign pontiff.

Clement was a prince of excellent judgment, whenever his timidity, to which he was extremely subject, allowed him to make full use of those talents and that penetration with which he was endowed.[n] The captivity, and other misfortunes, which he had undergone, by entering into a league against Charles, had so affected his imagination, that he never afterwards exerted himself with vigour in any public measure; especially if the interest or inclination of that potentate stood in opposition to him. The Imperial forces were, at that time, powerful in Italy, and might return to the attack of Rome, which was still defenceless, and exposed to the same calamities with which it had already been overwhelmed. And besides these dangers, Clement fancied himself exposed to perils, which threatened, still more immediately, his person and his dignity.

The emperor threatens him.

Charles, apprized of the timid disposition of the holy father, threw out perpetual menaces of summoning a general council; which he represented as necessary to reform the church, and correct those enormous abuses, which the ambition and avarice of the court of Rome had introduced into every branch of ecclesiastical administration. The power of the sovereign pontiff himself, he said, required limitation; his conduct called aloud for amendment; and even his title to the throne, which he filled, might justly be called in question. That pope had always passed for the natural son of Julian of Medicis, who was of the sovereign family of Florence; and though Leo X. his kinsman, had declared him legitimate, upon a pretended promise of marriage between his father and mother, few believed that declaration to be founded on any just reason or authority.[o] The canon law, indeed, had been entirely silent with regard to the promotion of bastards to the papal throne; but, what was still dangerous, the people had entertained a violent prepossession, that this stain in the birth of any person was incompatible with so holy an office. And in another point, the canon law was express and positive, that no man, guilty of simony, could attain that dignity. A severe bull of Julius II. had added new sanctions to this law, by declaring, that a simoniacal election could not

[n] Father Paul, lib. i. Guicciardini.   [o] Father Paul, lib. i.

CHAPTER XXX

be rendered valid, even by a posterior consent of the cardinals. But unfortunately Clement had given to cardinal Colonna a billet, containing promises of advancing that cardinal, in case he himself should attain the papal dignity by his concurrence: And this billet, Colonna, who was in entire dependance on the emperor, threatened every moment to expose to public view.*

While Charles terrified the pope with these menaces, he also allured him by hopes, which were no less prevalent over his affections. At the time when the emperor's forces sacked Rome, and reduced Clement to captivity, the Florentines, passionate for their ancient liberty, had taken advantage of his distresses, and revolting against the family of Medicis, had entirely abolished their authority in Florence, and re-established the democracy. The better to protect themselves in their freedom, they had entered into the alliance with France, England, and Venice, against the emperor; and Clement found, that, by this interest, the hands of his confederates were tied from assisting him in the restoration of his family; the event, which, of all others, he most passionately desired. The emperor alone, he knew, was able to effect this purpose; and therefore, whatever professions he made of fidelity to his allies, he was always, on the least glimpse of hope, ready to embrace every proposal of a cordial reconciliation with that monarch.*

These views and interests of the pope were well known in England; and as the opposition of the emperor to Henry's divorce was foreseen, both on account of the honour and interests of Catherine his aunt, and the obvious motive of distressing an enemy, it was esteemed dangerous to take any measure of consequence, in expectation of the subsequent concurrence of a man of Clement's character, whose behaviour always contained so much duplicity, and who was at present so little at his own disposal. The safest measure seemed to consist in previously engaging him so far, that he could not afterwards recede, and in making use of his present ambiguity and uncertainty, to extort the most important concessions from him. For this purpose, Stephen Gardiner, the cardinal's secretary, and Edward Fox, the king's almoner, were dispatched to Rome, and were ordered to solicit a commission from the pope, of such a nature as would oblige him

10th Feb.

p Ibid. *q* Father Paul.

to confirm the sentence of the commissioners, whatever it should be, and disable him, on any account, to recal the commission, or evoke the cause to Rome.[r]

The pope's ambiguous conduct.

But the same reasons, which made the king so desirous of obtaining this concession, confirmed the pope in the resolution of refusing it: He was still determined to keep the door open for an agreement with the emperor, and he made no scruple of sacrificing all other considerations to a point, which he deemed the most essential and important to his own security, and to the greatness of his family. He granted, therefore, a new commission, in which cardinal Campeggio was joined to Wolsey, for the trial of the king's marriage; but he could not be prevailed on to insert the clause desired of him. And though he put into Gardiner's hand a letter, promising not to recal the present commission; this promise was found, on examination, to be couched in such ambiguous terms, as left him still the power, whenever he pleased, of departing from it.[s]

Campeggio lay under some obligations to the king; but his dependance on the pope was so much greater, that he conformed himself entirely to the views of the latter; and though he received his commission in April, he delayed his departure under so many pretences, that it was October before he arrived in England. The first step, which he took, was to exhort the king to desist from the prosecution of his divorce; and finding that this counsel gave offence, he said, that his intention was also to exhort the queen to take the vows in a convent, and that he thought it his duty, previously to attempt an amicable composure of all differences.[t] The more to pacify the king, he shewed to him, as also to the cardinal, the decretal bull, annulling the former marriage with Catherine; but no entreaties could prevail on him to make any other of the king's council privy to the secret.[u] In order to atone, in some degree, for this obstinacy, he expressed to the king and the cardinal, the pope's great desire of satisfying them in every reasonable demand; and in particular, he showed, that their request for suppressing some more monasteries, and converting them into

---

[r] Lord Herbert. Burnet, vol. i. p. 29. in the collect. Le Grand, vol. iii. p. 28. Strype, vol. i. p. 93. with App. No 23, 24, &c. [s] Lord Herbert, p. 221. Burnet, p. 59. [t] Herbert, p. 225. [u] Burnet, p. 58.

cathedrals and episcopal sees, had obtained the consent of his holiness.[w]

These ambiguous circumstances, in the behaviour of the pope and the legate, kept the court of England in suspense, and determined the king to wait with patience the issue of such uncertain councils. Fortune meanwhile seemed to promise him a more sure and expeditious way of extricating himself from his present difficulties. Clement was seized with a dangerous illness; and the intrigues, for electing his successor, began already to take place among the cardinals. Wolsey, in particular, supported by the interest of England and of France, entertained hopes of mounting the throne of St. Peter;[x] and it appears, that if a vacancy had then happened, there was a probability of his reaching that summit of his ambition. But the pope recovered, though after several relapses; and he returned to the same train of false and deceitful politics, by which he had hitherto amused the court of England. He still flattered Henry with professions of the most cordial attachment, and promised him a sudden and favourable issue to his process: He still continued his secret negociations with Charles, and persevered in the resolution of sacrificing all his promises, and all the interests of the Romish religion, to the elevation of his family. Campeggio, who was perfectly acquainted with his views and intentions, protracted the decision by the most artful delays; and gave Clement full leisure to adjust all the terms of his treaty with the emperor.

The emperor, acquainted with the king's extreme earnestness in this affair, was determined, that he should obtain success by no other means than by an application to him, and by deserting his alliance with Francis, which had hitherto supported, against the superior force of Spain, the tottering state of the French monarchy. He willingly hearkened, therefore, to the applications of Catherine, his aunt; and promising her his utmost protection, exhorted her never to yield to the malice and persecutions of her enemies. The queen herself was naturally of a firm and resolute temper; and was engaged by every motive to persevere in protesting against the injustice to which she thought herself exposed.

[w] Rymer, vol. xiv. p. 270. Strype, vol. i. p. 110, 111. Append. No. 28.
[x] Burnet, vol. i. p. 63.

1529.

The imputation of incest, which was thrown upon her marriage
with Henry, struck her with the highest indignation: The illegitimacy of her daughter, which seemed a necessary consequence,
gave her the most just concern: The reluctance of yielding to a
rival, which, she believed, had supplanted her in the king's affections, was a very natural motive. Actuated by all these considerations, she never ceased soliciting her nephew's assistance, and
earnestly entreating an evocation of the cause to Rome, where
alone, she thought, she could expect justice. And the emperor, in
all his negociations with the pope, made the recal of the commission, which Campeggio and Wolsey exercised in England, a fundamental article.ʸ

*31st
May.
Trial of
the king's
marriage.*
The two legates, meanwhile, opened their court at London,
and cited the king and queen to appear before it. They both
presented themselves; and the king answered to his name, when
called: But the queen, instead of answering to hers, rose from her
seat, and throwing herself at the king's feet, made a very pathetic
harangue, which her virtue, her dignity, and her misfortunes rendered the more affecting. She told him, that she was a stranger in
his dominions, without protection, without council, without assistance; exposed to all the injustice, which her enemies were pleased
to impose upon her: That she had quitted her native country
without other resource, than her connexions with him and his
family, and had expected, that, instead of suffering thence any
violence or iniquity, she was assured in them of a safeguard against
every misfortune: That she had been his wife during twenty years,
and would here appeal to himself, whether her affectionate submission to his will had not merited better treatment, than to be
thus, after so long a time, thrown from him with so much indignity: That she was conscious—he himself was assured—that her
virgin honour was yet unstained, when he received her into his
bed, and that her connexions with his brother had been carried no
farther than the ceremony of marriage: That their parents, the
kings of England and Spain, were esteemed the wisest princes of
their time, and had undoubtedly acted by the best advice, when
they formed the agreement for that marriage, which was now
represented as so criminal and unnatural: And that she acquiesced

ʸ Herbert, p. 225. Burnet, vol. i. p. 69.

CHAPTER XXX

in their judgment, and would not submit her cause to be tried by a court, whose dependance on her enemies was too visible, ever to allow her any hopes of obtaining from them an equitable or impartial decision.[z] Having spoken these words, she rose, and making the king a low reverence, she departed from the court, and never would again appear in it.

After her departure, the king did her the justice to acknowledge, that she had ever been a dutiful and affectionate wife, and that the whole tenor of her behaviour had been conformable to the strictest rules of probity and honour. He only insisted on his own scruples, with regard to the lawfulness of their marriage; and he explained the origin, the progress, and the foundation of those doubts, by which he had been so long and so violently agitated. He acquitted cardinal Wolsey from having any hand in encouraging his scruples; and he craved a sentence of the court, agreeable to the justice of his cause.

The legates, after citing the queen anew, declared her *contumacious,* notwithstanding her appeal to Rome; and then proceeded to the examination of the cause. The first point which came before them, was, the proof of prince Arthur's consummation of his marriage with Catherine; and it must be confessed, that no stronger arguments could reasonably be expected of such a fact after so long an interval. The age of the prince, who had passed his fifteenth year, the good state of his health, the long time that he had cohabited with his consort, many of his expressions to that very purpose; all these circumstances form a violent presumption in favour of the king's assertion.[a] Henry himself, after his brother's death, was not allowed for some time to bear the title of prince of Wales, in expectation of her pregnancy: The Spanish ambassador, in order the better to ensure possession of her jointure, had sent over to Spain, proofs of the consummation of her marriage:[b] Julius's bull itself was founded on the supposition, that Arthur had *perhaps* had knowledge of the princess: In the very treaty, fixing Henry's marriage, the consummation of the former marriage with prince Arthur, is acknowledged on both sides.[c] These particulars were all laid before the court, accompanied with many reasonings

[z] Burnet, vol. i. p. 73. Hall. Stowe, p. 543.   [a] Herbert.   [b] Burnet, vol. ii. p. 35.   [c] Rymer, vol. xiii. p. 81.

concerning the extent of the pope's authority, and against his power of granting a dispensation to marry within the prohibited degrees. Campeggio heard these doctrines with great impatience; and notwithstanding his resolution to protract the cause, he was often tempted to interrupt and silence the king's council, when they insisted on such disagreeable topics. The trial was spun out till the 23d of July; and Campeggio chiefly took on him the part of conducting it. Wolsey, though the elder cardinal, permitted him to act as president of the court; because it was thought, that a trial, managed by an Italian cardinal, would carry the appearance of greater candour and impartiality, than if the king's own minister and favourite had presided in it. The business now seemed to be drawing near to a period; and the king was every day in expectation of a sentence in his favour; when, to his great surprize, Campeggio, on a sudden, without any warning, and upon very frivolous pretences,[d] prorogued the court, till the first of October. The evocation, which came a few days after from Rome, put an end to all the hopes of success, which the king had so long and so anxiously cherished.[e]

The cause evoked to Rome.

During the time, that the trial was carried on before the legates at London, the emperor had by his ministers earnestly solicited Clement to evoke the cause; and had employed every topic of hope or terror, which could operate either on the ambition or timidity of the pontiff. The English ambassadors, on the other hand, in conjunction with the French, had been no less earnest in their applications, that the legates should be allowed to finish the trial; but, though they employed the same engines of promises and menaces, the motives, which they could set before the pope, were not so urgent or immediate as those which were held up to him by the emperor.[f] The dread of losing England, and of fortifying the Lutherans by so considerable an accession, made small impression on Clement's mind, in comparison of the anxiety for his personal safety, and the fond desire of restoring the Medicis to their dominion in Florence. As soon, therefore, as he had adjusted all terms with the emperor, he laid hold of the pretence of justice, which required him, as he asserted, to pay regard to the queen's appeal; and suspending the commission of the legates, he adjourned the

---

[d] Burnet, vol. i. p. 76, 77.   [e] Herbert, p. 254.   [f] Burnet, vol. i. p. 75.

CHAPTER XXX

cause to his own personal judgment at Rome. Campeggio had beforehand received private orders, delivered by Campana, to burn the decretal bull, with which he was entrusted.

Wolsey had long foreseen this measure as the sure forerunner of his ruin. Though he had at first desired, that the king should rather marry a French princess than Anne Boleyn, he had employed himself with the utmost assiduity and earnestness to bring the affair to a happy issue:[g] He was not therefore to be blamed for the unprosperous event, which Clement's partiality had produced. But he had sufficient experience of the extreme ardour and impatience of Henry's temper, who could bear no contradiction, and was wont, without examination or distinction, to make his ministers answerable for the success of those transactions with which they were entrusted. Anne Boleyn also, who was prepossessed against him, had imputed to him the failure of her hopes; and as she was newly returned to court, whence she had been removed, from a regard to decency, during the trial before the legates, she had naturally acquired an additional influence on Henry, and she served much to fortify his prejudices against the cardinal.[h] Even the queen and her partizans, judging of Wolsey by the part which he had openly acted, had expressed great animosity against him; and the most opposite factions seemed now to combine in the ruin of this haughty minister. The high opinion itself, which Henry had entertained of the cardinal's capacity, tended to hasten his downfall; while he imputed the bad success of that minister's undertakings, not to ill fortune or to mistake, but to the malignity or infidelity of his intentions. The blow, however, fell not instantly on his head. The king, who probably could not justify by any good reason his alienation from his ancient favourite, seems to have remained some time in suspence; and he received him, if not with all his former kindness, at least with the appearance of trust and regard.

But constant experience evinces how rarely a high confidence and affection receives the least diminution, without sinking into absolute indifference, or even running into the opposite extreme. The king now determined to bring on the ruin of the cardinal with a motion almost as precipitate as he had formerly employed in his

Wolsey's fall.

18th Oct.

[g] Collier, vol. ii. p. 45. Burnet, vol. i. p. 53. [h] Cavendish, p. 40.

elevation. The dukes of Norfolk and Suffolk were sent to require the great seal from him; and on his scrupling to deliver it,[i] without a more express warrant, Henry wrote him a letter, upon which it was surrendered, and it was delivered by the king to Sir Thomas More, a man, who, besides the ornaments of an elegant literature, possessed the highest virtue, integrity, and capacity.

Wolsey was ordered to depart from York-Place, a palace which he had built in London, and which, though it really belonged to the see of York, was seized by Henry, and became afterwards the residence of the kings of England, by the title of Whitehall. All his furniture and plate were also seized: Their riches and splendor befitted rather a royal than a private fortune. The walls of his palace were covered with cloth of gold or cloth of silver: He had a cupboard of plate of massy gold: There were found a thousand pieces of fine holland belonging to him. The rest of his riches and furniture was in proportion; and his opulence was probably no small inducement to this violent persecution against him.

The cardinal was ordered to retire to Asher, a country seat which he possessed near Hampton Court. The world, that had paid him such abject court during his prosperity, now entirely deserted him on this fatal reverse of all his fortunes. He himself was much dejected with the change; and from the same turn of mind, which had made him be so vainly elated with his grandeur, he felt the stroke of adversity with double rigour.[k] The smallest appearance of his return to favour threw him into transports of joy, unbecoming a man. The king had seemed willing, during some time, to intermit the blows, which overwhelmed him. He granted him his protection, and left him in possession of the sees of York and Winchester. He even sent him a gracious message, accompained with a ring, as a testimony of his affection. Wolsey, who was on horseback when the messenger met him, immediately alighted; and throwing himself on his knees in the mire, received in that humble attitude these marks of his majesty's gracious disposition towards him.[l]

But his enemies, who dreaded his return to court, never ceased plying the king with accounts of his several offences; and Anne

[i] Cavendish, p. 41.   [k] Strype, vol. i. p. 114, 115. App. No 31, &c   [l] Stowe, p. 547.

CHAPTER XXX

Boleyn in particular contributed her endeavours, in conjunction with her uncle the duke of Norfolk, to exclude him from all hopes of ever being reinstated in his former authority. He dismissed therefore his numerous retinue: and as he was a kind and beneficent master, the separation passed not without a plentiful effusion of tears on both sides.[m] The king's heart, notwithstanding some gleams of kindness, seemed now totally hardened against his old favourite. He ordered him to be indicted in the Star Chamber, where a sentence was passed against him. And not content with this severity, he abandoned him to all the rigour of the parliament, *November.* which now, after a long interval, was again assembled. The house of lords voted a long charge against Wolsey, consisting of forty-four articles; and accompanied it with an application to the king for his punishment, and his removal from all authority. Little opposition was made to this charge in the upper house: No evidence of any part of it was so much as called for; and as it chiefly consists of general accusations, it was scarcely susceptible of any.[n] The articles were sent down to the house of commons; where Thomas Cromwel, formerly a servant of the cardinal's, and who had been raised by him from a very low station, defended his unfortunate patron with such spirit, generosity, and courage, as acquired him great honour, and laid the foundation of that favour, which he afterwards enjoyed with the king.

Wolsey's enemies, finding that either his innocence or his caution prevented them from having any just ground of accusing him, had recourse to a very extraordinary expedient. An indictment was laid against him, that, contrary to a statute of Richard II. commonly called the statute of provisors, he had procured bulls from Rome, particularly one investing him with the legantine power, which he had exercised with very extensive authority. He confessed the indictment, pleaded ignorance of the statute, and threw himself on the king's mercy. He was perhaps within reach of the law; but besides that this statute had fallen into disuse, nothing could be more rigorous and severe than to impute to him as a crime, what he had openly, during the course of so many years, practised with the consent and approbation of the king, and the acquiescence of the parliament and kingdom. Not to mention,

[m] Cavendish. Stowe, p. 549   [n] See note [F] at the end of the volume.

what he always asserted,[o] and what we can scarcely doubt of, that he had obtained the royal licence in the most formal manner, which, had he not been apprehensive of the dangers attending any opposition to Henry's lawless will, he might have pleaded in his own defence before the judges. Sentence, however, was pronounced against him, "That he was out of the king's protection; his lands and goods forfeited; and that his person might be committed to custody." But this prosecution of Wolsey was carried no farther. Henry even granted him a pardon for all offences; restored him part of his plate and furniture; and still continued, from time to time, to drop expressions of favour and compassion towards him.

Commencement of the reformation in England. The complaints against the usurpations of the ecclesiastics had been very ancient in England, as well as in most other European kingdoms; and as this topic was now become popular every where, it had paved the way for the Lutheran tenets, and reconciled the people, in some measure, to the frightful idea of heresy and innovation. The commons, finding the occasion favourable, passed several bills, restraining the impositions of the clergy; one for the regulating of mortuaries; another against the exactions for the probates of wills;[p] a third against non-residence and pluralities, and against churchmen's being farmers of land. But what appeared chiefly dangerous to the ecclesiastical order, were the severe invectives thrown out, almost without opposition, in the house, against the dissolute lives of the priests, their ambition, their avarice, and their endless encroachments on the laity. Lord Herbert[q] has even preserved the speech of a gentleman of Gray's-Inn, which is of a singular nature, and contains such topics as we should little expect to meet with during that period. The member insists upon the vast variety of theological opinions, which prevailed in different nations and ages; the endless inextricable controversies maintained by the several sects; the impossibility, that any man, much less the people, could ever know, much less examine, the tenets and principles of every sect; the necessity of ignorance and a suspense of judgment with regard to all those objects of dispute: And upon the whole, he infers, that the only

[o] Cavendish, p. 72.   [p] These exactions were quite arbitrary, and had risen to a great height. A member said in the house, that a thousand marks had been exacted from him on that account. Hall, fol. 188, Strype, vol. i. p. 73.   [q] P. 293.

CHAPTER XXX

religion obligatory on mankind is the belief of one supreme Being, the author of nature; and the necessity of good morals, in order to obtain his favour and protection. Such sentiments would be deemed latitudinarian, even in our time, and would not be advanced, without some precaution, in a public assembly. But though the first broaching of religious controversy might encourage the sceptical turn in a few persons of a studious disposition; the zeal, with which men soon after attached themselves to their several parties, served effectually to banish for a long time all such obnoxious liberties.

The bills for regulating the clergy met with some opposition in the house of lords. Bishop Fisher in particular imputed these measures of the commons to their want of faith; and to a formed design, derived from heretical and Lutheran principles, of robbing the church of her patrimony, and overturning the national religion. The duke of Norfolk reproved the prelate in severe, and even somewhat indecent terms. He told him, that the greatest clerks were not always the wisest men. But Fisher replied, that he did not remember any fools in his time, who had proved great clerks. The exceptions taken at the bishop of Rochester's speech stopped not there. The commons, by the mouth of Sir Thomas Audley, their speaker, made complaints to the king of the reflections thrown upon them; and the bishop was obliged to put a more favourable construction on his words.[r]

Henry was not displeased, that the court of Rome and the clergy should be sensible, that they were entirely dependant on him, and that his parliament, if he were willing to second their inclinations, was sufficiently disposed to reduce the power and privileges of the ecclesiastics. The commons gratified the king in another particular of moment: They granted him a discharge of all those debts, which he had contracted since the beginning of his reign: and they grounded this bill, which occasioned many complaints, on a pretence of the king's great care of the nation, and of his regularly employing all the money, which he had borrowed, in the public service. Most of the king's creditors consisted of friends to the cardinal, who had been engaged by their patron to contribute to the supply of Henry's necessities; and the present cour-

[r] Parliamentary History, vol. iii. p. 59. Burnet, vol. ii. p. 82.

tiers were well pleased to take the opportunity of mulcting them.[5] Several also approved of an expedient, which, they hoped, would ever after discredit a method of supply, so irregular and so unparliamentary.

Foreign affairs. The domestic transactions of England were at present so interesting to the king, that they chiefly engaged his attention; and he regarded foreign affairs only in subordination to them. He had declared war against the emperor; but the mutual advantages reaped by the commerce between England and the Netherlands, had engaged him to stipulate a neutrality with those provinces; and except by money contributed to the Italian wars, he had in effect exercised no hostility against any of the imperial dominions. A general peace was this summer established in Europe. Margaret of Austria and Louisa of Savoy met at Cambray, and settled the terms of pacification between the French king and the emperor. Charles accepted of two millions of crowns in lieu of Burgundy; and he delivered up the two princes of France, whom he had retained as hostages. Henry was, on this occasion, so generous to his friend and ally Francis, that he sent him an acquittal of near 600,000 crowns, which that prince owed him. Francis's Italian confederates were not so well satisfied as the king with the peace of Cambray: They were almost wholly abandoned to the will of the emperor; and seemed to have no means of security left, but his equity and moderation. Florence, after a brave resistance, was subdued by the imperial arms, and finally delivered over to the dominion of the family of Medicis. The Venetians were better treated: They were only obliged to relinquish some acquisition, which they had made on the coast of Naples. Even Francis Sforza obtained the investiture of Milan, and was pardoned for all past offences. The emperor in person passed into Italy with a magnificent train, and received the imperial crown from the hands of the pope at Bologna. He was but twenty-nine years of age; and having already, by his vigour and capacity, succeeded in every enterprize, and reduced to captivity the two greatest potentates in Europe, the one spiritual, the other temporal, he attracted the eyes of all men; and many prognostications were formed of his growing empire.

[5] Burnet, vol. ii. p. 83.

CHAPTER XXX

But though Charles seemed to be prosperous on every side, and though the conquest of Mexico and Peru now began to prevent that scarcity of money, under which he had hitherto laboured, he found himself threatened with difficulties in Germany; and his desire of surmounting them was the chief cause of his granting such moderate conditions to the Italian powers. Sultan Solyman, the greatest and most accomplished prince that ever sat on the Ottoman throne, had almost entirely subdued Hungary, had besieged Vienna, and though repulsed, still menaced the hereditary dominions of the house of Austria with conquest and subjection. The Lutheran princes of the empire, finding that liberty of conscience was denied them, had combined in a league for their own defence at Smalcalde; and because they protested against the votes passed in the imperial diet, they thenceforth received the appellation of *protestants*. Charles had undertaken to reduce them to obedience; and on pretence of securing the purity of religion, he had laid a scheme for aggrandizing his own family, by extending its dominion over all Germany.

The friendship of Henry was one material circumstance yet wanting to Charles, in order to ensure success in his ambitious enterprizes; and the king was sufficiently apprized, that the concurrence of that prince would at once remove all the difficulties, which lay in the way of his divorce; that point, which had long been the object of his most earnest wishes. But besides that the interests of his kingdom seemed to require an alliance with France, his haughty spirit could not submit to a friendship imposed on him by constraint; and as he had ever been accustomed to receive courtship, deference, and solicitation from the greatest potentates, he could ill brook that dependance, to which this unhappy affair seemed to have reduced him. Amidst the anxieties with which he was agitated, he was often tempted to break off all connexions with the court of Rome; and though he had been educated in a superstitious reverence to papal authority, it is likely, that his personal experience of the duplicity and selfish politics of Clement, had served much to open his eyes in that particular. He found his prerogative firmly established at home: He observed, that his people were in general much disgusted with clerical usurpations, and disposed to reduce the powers and privileges of the ecclesiastical order: He knew that they had cordially taken part with him in his prosecution of the divorce, and highly resented the unworthy treatment, which, after so many services and such devoted attachment, he had received from the court of Rome. Anne Boleyn also could not fail to use all her efforts, and employ every insinuation, in order to make him proceed to extremities against the pope; both as it was the readiest way to her attaining royal dignity, and as her education in the court of the duchess of Alençon, a princess inclined to the reformers, had already disposed her to a belief of the new doctrines. But notwithstanding these inducements, Henry had strong motives still to desire a good agreement with the sovereign pontiff. He apprehended the danger of such great innovations: He dreaded the reproach of heresy: He abhorred all connexions with the Lutherans, the chief opponents of the papal power: And having once exerted himself with such applause, as he imagined, in defence of the Romish communion, he was ashamed to retract his former opinions, and betray from passion such a palpable inconsistency. While he was agitated by these contrary motives, an expedient was proposed, which, as it promised a solution of all difficulties, was embraced by him with the greatest joy and satisfaction.

The universities consulted about the king's marriage.

Dr. Thomas Cranmer, fellow of Jesus-College in Cambridge, was a man remarkable in that university for his learning, and still more, for the candour and disinterestedness of his temper. He fell one evening by accident into company with Gardiner, now secretary of state, and Fox, the king's almoner; and as the business of the divorce became the subject of conversation, he observed, that the readiest way, either to quiet Henry's conscience or extort the pope's consent, would be to consult all the universities of Europe with regard to this controverted point: If they agreed to approve of the king's marriage with Catharine, his remorses would naturally cease; if they condemned it, the pope would find it difficult to resist the solicitations of so great a monarch, seconded by the opinion of all the learned men in Christendom.[t] When the king was informed of the proposal, he was delighted with it; and swore, with more alacrity than delicacy, that Cranmer had got the right sow by the ear: He sent for that divine; entered into conversation with him; conceived a high opinion of his virtue and understanding;

[t] Fox, p. 1860, 2d edit. Burnet, vol. i. p. 79. Speed, p. 769. Heylin, p. 5.

CHAPTER XXX

engaged him to write in defence of the divorce; and immediately, in prosecution of the scheme proposed, employed his agents to collect the judgments of all the universities in Europe.

Had the question of Henry's marriage with Catharine been examined by the principles of sound philosophy, exempt from superstition, it seemed not liable to much difficulty. The natural reason, why marriages in certain degrees is prohibited by the civil laws, and condemned by the moral sentiments, of all nations, is derived from men's care to preserve purity of manners; while they reflect, that, if a commerce of love were authorized between near relations, the frequent opportunities of intimate conversation, especially during early youth, would introduce an universal dissoluteness and corruption. But as the customs of countries vary considerably, and open an intercourse, more or less restrained, between different families, or between the several members of the same family, we find, that the moral precept, varying with its cause, is susceptible, without any inconvenience, of very different latitude in the several ages and nations of the world. The extreme delicacy of the Greeks permitted no communication between persons of different sexes, except where they lived under the same roof; and even the apartment of a step-mother, and her daughters, were almost as much shut up against visits from the husband's sons, as against those from any stranger or more distant relation: Hence, in that nation, it was lawful for a man to marry, not only his niece, but his half-sister by the father: A liberty unknown to the Romans, and other nations, where a more open intercourse was authorized between the sexes. Reasoning from this principle, it would appear, that the ordinary commerce of life, among great princes, is so obstructed by ceremony and numerous attendants, that no ill consequence would result, among them, from marrying a brother's widow; especially if the dispensation of the supreme priest be previously required, in order to justify what may in common cases be condemned, and to hinder the precedent from becoming too common and familiar. And as strong motives of public interest and tranquillity may frequently require such alliances between the foreign families, there is the less reason for extending towards them the full rigour of the rule, which has place among individuals.ᵘ

ᵘ See note [G] at the end of the volume.

1530.   But in opposition to these reasons, and many more which might be collected, Henry had custom and precedent on his side, the principle by which men are almost wholly governed in their actions and opinions. The marrying of a brother's widow was so unusual, that no other instance of it could be found in any history or record of any Christian nation; and though the popes were accustomed to dispense with more essential precepts of morality, and even permitted marriages within other prohibited degrees, such as those of uncle and niece, the imaginations of men were not yet reconciled to this particular exercise of his authority. Several universities of Europe, therefore, without hesitation, as well as without interest or reward,[w] gave verdict in the king's favour; not only those of France, Paris, Orleans, Bourges, Tolouse, Angiers, which might be supposed to lie under the influence of their prince, ally to Henry; but also those of Italy, Venice, Ferrara, Padua; even Bologna itself, though under the immediate jurisdiction of Clement. Oxford alone[x] and Cambridge[y] made some difficulty; because these universities, alarmed at the progress of Lutheranism, and dreading a defection from the holy see, scrupled to give their sanction to measures, whose consequences, they feared, would prove fatal to the ancient religion. Their opinion, however, conformable to that of the other universities of Europe, was at last obtained; and the king, in order to give more weight to all these authorities, engaged his nobility to write a letter to the pope, recommending his cause to the holy father, and threatening him with the most dangerous consequences in case of a denial of justice.[z] The convocations too, both of Canterbury and York, pronounced the king's marriage invalid, irregular, and contrary to the law of God, with which no human power had authority to dispense.[a] But Clement, lying still under the influence of the emperor, continued to summon the king to appear, either by himself or proxy, before his tribunal at Rome; and the king, who knew that he could expect no fair trial there, refused to submit to such a condition, and would not even admit of any citation, which he regarded as a high insult, and a violation of his royal prerogative. The father of Anne Bol-

---

[w] Herbert, Burnet.   [x] Wood, hist. and an. Ox. lib. i. p. 225.   [y] Burnet, vol. i. p. 6.   [z] Rymer, vol. xiv. 405. Burnet, vol. i. p. 95.   [a] Rymer, vol. xiv. p. 454, 472.

CHAPTER XXX

eyn, created earl of Wiltshire, carried to the pope the king's reasons for not appearing by proxy; and, as the first instance of disrespect from England, refused to kiss his holiness's foot, which he very graciously held out to him for that purpose.[b]

The extremities, to which Henry was pushed, both against the pope and the ecclesiastical order, were naturally disagreeable to cardinal Wolsey; and as Henry foresaw his opposition, it is the most probable reason that can be assigned for his renewing the prosecution against his ancient favourite. After Wolsey had remained some time at Asher, he was allowed to remove to Richmond, a palace which he had received as a present from Henry, in return for Hampton-Court: But the courtiers, dreading still his vicinity to the king, procured an order for him to remove to his see of York. The cardinal knew it was in vain to resist: He took up his residence at Cawood in Yorkshire, where he rendered himself extremely popular in the neighbourhood, by his affability and hospitality;[c] but he was not allowed to remain long unmolested in this retreat. The earl of Northumberland received orders, without regard to Wolsey's ecclesiastical character, to arrest him for high treason, and to conduct him to London, in order to his trial. The cardinal, partly from the fatigues of his journey, partly from the agitation of his anxious mind, was seized with a disorder which turned into a dysentery; and he was able, with some difficulty, to reach Leicester-abbey. When the abbot and the monks advanced to receive him with much respect and reverence, he told them, that he was come to lay his bones among them; and he immediately took to his bed, whence he never rose more. A little before he expired, he addressed himself in the following words to Sir William Kingston, constable of the Tower, who had him in custody. "I pray you, have me heartily recommended unto his royal majesty, and beseech him on my behalf to call to his remembrance all matters that have passed tween us from the beginning, especially with regard to his business with the queen; and then will he know in his conscience whether I have offended him.

"He is a prince of a most royal carriage, and hath a princely heart: and rather than he will miss for want any part of his will, he will endanger the one half of his kingdom.

Nov. 28.

[b] Burnet, vol. i. p. 94.   [c] Cavendish. Stowe, p. 554.

"I do assure you, that I have often kneeled before him, sometimes three hours together, to persuade him from his will and appetite; but could not prevail: had I but served God as diligently as I have served the king, he would not have given me over in my grey hairs. But this is the just reward that I must receive for my indulgent pains and study, not regarding my service to God, but only to my prince. Therefore, let me advise you, if you be one of the privy-council, as by your wisdom you are fit, take care what you put into the king's head: For you can never put it out again."[d]

Wolsey's death

Thus died this famous cardinal, whose character seems to have contained as singular a variety, as the fortune to which he was exposed. The obstinacy and violence of the king's temper may alleviate much of the blame, which some of his favourite's measures have undergone; and when we consider, that the subsequent part of Henry's reign was much more criminal than that which had been directed by Wolsey's counsels, we shall be inclined to suspect those historians of partiality, who have endeavoured to load the memory of this minister with such violent reproaches. If, in foreign politics, he sometimes employed his influence over the king for his private purposes, rather than his master's service, which, he boasted, he had solely at heart; we must remember, that he had in view the papal throne; a dignity, which, had he attained it, would have enabled him to make Henry a suitable return for all his favours. The cardinal of Amboise, whose memory is respected in France, always made this apology for his own conduct, which was, in some respect, similar to Wolsey's; and we have reason to think, that Henry was well acquainted with the views by which his minister was influenced, and took a pride in promoting them. He much regretted his death, when informed of it; and always spoke favourably of his memory: A proof, that humour more than reason, or any discovery of treachery, had occasioned the last persecutions against him.

1531. 16 January. A parliament.

A new session of parliament was held, together with a convocation; and the king here gave strong proofs of his extensive authority, as well as of his intention to turn it to the depression of the clergy. As an ancient statute, now almost obsolete, had been employed to ruin Wolsey, and render his exercise of the legantine

[d] Cavendish.

CHAPTER XXX

power criminal, notwithstanding the king's permission; the same law was now turned against the ecclesiastics. It was pretended, that every one, who had submitted to the legantine court, that is, the whole church, had violated the statute of provisors; and the attorney-general accordingly brought an indictment against them.[e] The convocation knew, that it would be in vain to oppose reason or equity to the king's arbitrary will, or plead that their ruin would have been the certain consequence of not submitting to Wolsey's commission, which was procured by Henry's consent, and supported by his authority. They chose therefore to throw themselves on the mercy of their sovereign; and they agreed to pay 118,840 pounds for a pardon.[f] A confession was likewise extorted from them, that *the king was the protector and the supreme head of the church and clergy of England;* though some of them had the dexterity to get a clause inserted, which invalidated the whole submission, and which ran in these terms, *in so far as is permitted by the law of Christ.*

The commons, finding that a pardon was granted the clergy, began to be apprehensive for themselves, lest either they should afterwards be brought into trouble on account of their submission to the legantine court, or a supply, in like manner, be extorted from them, in return for their pardon. They therefore petitioned the king, to grant a remission to his lay subjects; but they met with a repulse. He told them, that if he ever chose to forgive their offence, it would be from his own goodness, not from their application, lest he should seem to be compelled to it. Some time after, when they despaired of obtaining this concession, he was pleased to issue a pardon to the laity; and the commons expressed great gratitude for that act of clemency.[g]

By this strict execution of the statute of provisors, a great part of the profit, and still more of the power, of the court of Rome was cut off; and the connexions between the pope and the English clergy were, in some measure, dissolved. The next session found both king and parliament in the same dispositions. An act was passed against levying the annates or first fruits;[h] being a year's rent of all the bishoprics that fell vacant: a tax which was imposed

1532.

15 January.

[e] Antiq. Brit. Eccles. p. 325. Burnet, vol. i. p. 106   [f] Hollingshed, p. 923. [g] Hall's chronicle. Hollingshed, p. 923. Baker, p. 208.   [h] Burnet, vol. i. Collect. No 41. Strype, vol. i. p. 144.

Progress of the reformation. by the court of Rome for granting bulls to the new prelates, and which was found to amount to considerable sums. Since the second of Henry VII. no less than one hundred and sixty thousand pounds had been transmitted to Rome, on account of this claim; which the parliament, therefore, reduced to five per cent. on all the episcopal benefices. The better to keep the pope in awe, the king was entrusted with a power of regulating these payments, and of confirming or infringing this act at his pleasure: And it was voted, that any censures, which should be passed by the court of Rome, on account of that law, should be entirely disregarded, and that mass should be said, and the sacraments administered, as if no such censures had been issued.

This session the commons preferred to the king a long complaint against the abuses and oppressions of the ecclesiastical courts; and they were proceeding to enact laws for remedying them, when a difference arose, which put an end to the session, before the parliament had finished all their business. It was become a custom for men to make such settlements, or trust deeds, of their lands by will, that they defrauded, not only the king, but all other lords, of their wards, marriages, and reliefs; and by the same artifice the king was deprived of his premier seisin, and the profits of the livery, which were no inconsiderable branches of his revenue. Henry made a bill be drawn to moderate, not remedy altogether, this abuse: He was contented, that every man should have the liberty of disposing in this manner of the half of his land; and he told the parliament in plain terms, "If they would not take a reasonable thing, when it was offered, he would search out the extremity of the law; and then would not offer them so much again." The lords came willingly into his terms; but the commons rejected the bill: A singular instance, where Henry might see, that his power and authority, though extensive, had yet some boundaries. The commons, however, found reason to repent of their victory. The king made good his threats: he called together the judges and ablest lawyers, who argued the question in chancery; and it was decided, that a man could not by law bequeath any part of his lands, in prejudice of his heir.[i]

*1532.
10
April.*

The parliament being again assembled after a short pro-

---

[i] Burnet, vol. i. p. 116. Hall. Parliamentary history.

CHAPTER XXX

rogation, the king caused the two oaths to be read to them, that which the bishops took to the pope, and that to the king, on their installation; and as a contradiction might be suspected between them, while the prelates seemed to swear allegiance to two sovereigns;[k] the parliament shewed their intention of abolishing the oath to the pope, when their proceedings were suddenly stopped by the breaking out of the plague at Westminster, which occasioned a prorogation. It is remarkable, that one Temse ventured this session to move, that the house should address the king, to take back the queen, and stop the prosecution of his divorce. This motion made the king send for Audley, the speaker: and explain to him the scruples, with which his conscience had long been burdened; scruples, he said, which had proceeded from no wanton appetite, which had arisen after the fervours of youth were past, and which were confirmed by the concurring sentiments of all the learned societies in Europe. Except in Spain and Portugal, he added, it was never heard of, that any man had espoused two sisters; but he himself had the misfortune, he believed, to be the first Christian man that had ever married his brother's widow.[l]

After the prorogation, Sir Thomas More, the chancellor, foreseeing that all the measures of the king and parliament led to a breach with the church of Rome, and to an alteration of religion, with which his principles would not permit him to concur, desired leave to resign the great seal; and he descended from his high station with more joy and alacrity than he had mounted up to it. The austerity of this man's virtue, and the sanctity of his manners, had no wise encroached on the gentleness of his temper, or even diminished that frolic and gaiety, to which he was naturally inclined. He sported with all the varieties of fortune into which he was thrown; and neither the pride, naturally attending a high station, nor the melancholy incident to poverty and retreat, could ever lay hold of his serene and equal spirit. While his family discovered symptoms of sorrow on laying down the grandeur and magnificence, to which they had been accustomed, he drew a subject of mirth from their distresses; and made them ashamed of losing even a moment's chearfulness, on account of such trivial misfortunes. The king, who had entertained a high opinion of his virtue,

[k] Burnet, vol. i. p. 123, 124.   [l] Herbert. Hall, fol. 205.

received his resignation with some difficulty; and he delivered the great seal soon after to Sir Thomas Audley.

During these transactions in England, and these invasions of the papal and ecclesiastical authority, the court of Rome was not without solicitude; and she entertained just apprehensions of losing entirely her authority in England; the kingdom, which, of all others, had long been the most devoted to the holy see, and which had yielded it the most ample revenue. While the imperial cardinals pushed Clement to proceed to extremities against the king, his more moderate and impartial counsellors represented to him the indignity of his proceedings; that a great monarch, who had signalized himself, both by his pen and his sword, in the cause of the pope, should be denied a favour, which he demanded on such just grounds, and which had scarcely ever before been refused to any person of his rank and station. Notwithstanding these remonstrances, the queen's appeal was received at Rome; the king was cited to appear; and several consistories were held, to examine the validity of their marriage. Henry was determined not to send any proxy to plead his cause before this court: He only dispatched Sir Edward Karne and Dr. Bonner, in quality of excusators, so they were called, to carry his apology, for not paying that deference to the papal authority. The prerogatives of his crown, he said, must be sacrificed, if he allowed appeals from his own kingdom; and as the question regarded conscience, not power or interest, no proxy could supply his place, or convey that satisfaction, which the dictates of his own mind alone could confer. In order to support himself in this measure, and add greater security to his intended defection from Rome, he procured an interview with Francis at *11th* *Oct.* Boulogne and Calais, where he renewed his personal friendship, as well as public alliance, with that monarch, and concerted all measures for their mutual defence. He even employed arguments, by which, he believed, he had persuaded Francis to imitate his example in withdrawing his obedience from the bishop of Rome, and administering ecclesiastical affairs without having farther recourse to that see. And being now fully determined in his own mind, as well as resolute to stand all consequences, he privately *14th* *Nov.* celebrated his marriage with Anne Boleyn, whom he had previously created marchioness of Pembroke. Rouland Lee, soon after raised to the bishopric of Coventry, officiated at the marriage. The duke of Norfolk, uncle to the new queen, her father, mother, and brother, together with Dr. Cranmer, were present at the ceremony.[m] Anne became pregnant soon after her marriage: and this event, both gave great satisfaction to the king, and was regarded by the people as a strong proof of the queen's former modesty and virtue.

The parliament was again assembled: and Henry, in conjunction with the great council of the nation, proceeded still in those gradual and secure steps, by which they loosened their connexions with the see of Rome, and repressed the usurpations of the Roman pontiff. An act was made against all appeals to Rome in causes of matrimony, divorces, wills, and other suits cognizable in ecclesiastical courts; appeals esteemed dishonourable to the kingdom, by subjecting it to a foreign jurisdiction; and found to be very vexatious, by the expence and the delay of justice, which necessarily attended them.[n] The more to show his disregard to the pope, Henry, finding the new queen's pregnancy to advance, publicly owned his marriage; and in order to remove all doubts with regard to its lawfulness, he prepared measures for declaring, by a formal sentence, the invalidity of his marriage with Catherine: A sentence which ought naturally to have preceded his espousing of Anne.[o]

The king, even amidst his scruples and remorses on account of his first marriage, had always treated Catherine with respect and distinction; and he endeavoured, by every soft and persuasive art, to engage her to depart from her appeal to Rome, and her opposition to his divorce. Finding her obstinate in maintaining the justice of her cause, he had totally forborne all visits and intercourse with her; and had desired her to make choice of any one of his palaces, in which she should please to reside. She had fixed her abode for some time at Amphill near Dunstable; and it was in this latter town that Cranmer, now created archbishop of Canterbury, on the death of Warham,[p] was appointed to open his court for examining the validity of her marriage. The near neighbourhood of the place was chosen, in order to deprive her of all plea of ignorance: and as she made no answer to the citation, either by herself or proxy, she was declared *contumacious;* and the primate

*1533.
4th Feb.
A parlia-
ment.*

*12th
April.*

*10th
May.*

---

[m] Herbert, p. 340, 341.   [n] 24 Hen. VIII. c. 12.   [o] Collier, vol. ii. p. 31, and Records, No 8.   [p] See note [H] at the end of the volume.

proceeded to the examination of the cause. The evidences of Arthur's consummation of his marriage were anew produced; the opinions of the universities were read, together with the judgment pronounced two years before by the convocations both of Canterbury and York; and after these preliminary steps, Cranmer proceeded to a sentence, and annulled the king's marriage with Catherine, as unlawful and invalid. By a subsequent sentence, he ratified the marriage with Anne Boleyn, who soon after was publicly crowned Queen, with all the pomp and dignity suited to that ceremony.[q] To complete the king's satisfaction on the conclusion of this intricate and vexatious affair, she was safely delivered of a daughter, who received the name of Elizabeth, and who afterwards swayed the scepter with such renown and felicity. Henry was so much delighted with the birth of this child, that soon after he conferred on her the title of princess of Wales;[r] a step somewhat irregular, as she could only be presumptive, not apparent heir of the crown. But he had, during his former marriage, thought proper to honour his daughter Mary with that title; and he was determined to bestow, on the offspring of his present marriage, the same mark of distinction, as well as to exclude the elder princess from all hopes of the succession. His regard for the new queen seemed rather to encrease than diminish by his marriage; and all men expected to see the entire ascendant of one who had mounted a throne, from which her birth had set her at so great a distance, and who, by a proper mixture of severity and indulgence, had long managed so intractable a spirit as that of Henry. In order to efface, as much as possible, all marks of his first marriage, Lord Mountjoy was sent to the unfortunate and divorced queen, to inform her, that she was thenceforth to be treated only as princess-dowager of Wales; and all means were employed to make her acquiesce in that determination. But she continued obstinate in maintaining the validity of her marriage; and she would admit no person to her presence, who did not approach her with the accustomed ceremonial. Henry, forgetting his wonted generosity towards her, employed menaces against such of her servants as complied with her commands in this particular; but was never able to make her relinquish her title and pretensions.[s]

7th
Sept.

[q] Heylin, p. 6.   [r] Burnet, vol. i. p. 134.   [s] Herbert, p. 326. Burnet, vol. i. p. 132.

CHAPTER XXX

When intelligence was conveyed to Rome of these transactions, so injurious to the authority and reputation of the holy see, the conclave was in a rage, and all the cardinals of the Imperial faction urged the pope to proceed to a definitive sentence, and to dart his spiritual thunders against Henry. But Clement proceeded no farther than to declare the nullity of Cranmer's sentence, as well as that of Henry's second marriage; threatening him with excommunicaton, if, before the first of November ensuing, he did not replace every thing in the condition in which it formerly stood.' An event had happened, from which the pontiff expected a more amicable conclusion of the difference, and which hindered him from carrying matters to extremity against the king.

The pope had claims upon the dutchy of Ferrara for the sovereignty of Reggio and Modena;" and having submitted his pretensions to the arbitration of the emperor, he was surprized to find a sentence pronounced against him. Enraged at this disappointment, he hearkened to proposals of amity from Francis; and when that monarch made overtures of marrying the duke of Orleans, his second son, to Catherine of Medicis, niece of the pope, Clement gladly embraced an alliance, by which his family was so much honoured. An interview was even appointed between the pope and French king at Marseilles; and Francis, as a common friend, there employed his good offices in mediating an accommodation between his new ally and the king of England.

Had this connexion of France with the court of Rome taken place a few years sooner, there had been little difficulty in adjusting the quarrel with Henry. The king's request was an ordinary one; and the same plenary power of the pope, which had granted a dispensation for his espousing of Catherine, could easily have annulled the marriage. But, in the progress of the quarrel, the state of affairs was much changed on both sides. Henry had shaken off much of that reverence, which he had early imbibed for the apostolic see; and finding, that his subjects of all ranks had taken part with him, and willingly complied with his measures for breaking off foreign dependance, he had begun to relish his spiritual authority, and would scarcely, it was apprehended, be induced to renew his submissions to the Roman pontiff. The pope, on the other hand, now ran a manifest risque of infringing his authority

' Le Grand, vol. iii. p. 566.   " Burnet, vol. ii. p. 133. Guicciardini.

by a compliance with the king; and as a sentence of divorce could no longer be rested on nullities in Julius's bull, but would be construed as an acknowledgment of papal usurpations, it was foreseen, that the Lutherans would thence take occasion of triumph, and would perservere more obstinately in their present principles. But notwithstanding these obstacles, Francis did not despair of mediating an agreement. He observed that the king had still some remains of prejudice in favour of the catholic church, and was apprehensive of the consequences, which might ensue from too violent innovations. He saw the interest that Clement had in preserving the obedience of England, which was one of the richest jewels in the papal crown. And he hoped, that these motives on both sides would facilitate a mutual agreement, and would forward the effects of his good offices.

1534.

King's first prevailed on the pope to promise, that, if the king would send a proxy to Rome, and thereby submit his cause to the holy see, he should appoint commissioners to meet at Cambray, and form the process; and he should immediately afterwards pronounce the sentence of divorce, required of him. Bellay, bishop of Paris, was next dispatched to London, and obtained a promise from the king, that he would submit his cause to the Roman consistory, provided the cardinals of the Imperial faction were excluded from it. The prelate carried this verbal promise to Rome; and the pope agreed, that, if the king would sign a written agreement to the same purpose, his demands should be fully complied with. A day was appointed for the return of the messengers; and all Europe regarded this affair, which had threatened a violent rupture between England and the Romish church, as drawing towards an amicable conclusion.[w] But the greatest affairs often depend on the most frivolous incidents. The courier, who carried the king's written promise, was detained beyond the day appointed: News was brought to Rome that a libel had been published in England against the court of Rome, and a farce acted before the king in derision of the pope and cardinals.[x] The pope and cardinals entered into the consistory enflamed with anger; and by a precipitate sentence, the marriage of Henry and Catherine was pronounced valid, and Henry declared to be excommu-

*King's
final
breach
with
Rome.*

*23d
March.*

---

[w] Father Paul, lib. 1.   [x] Father Paul, lib. 1.

nicated, if he refused to adhere to it. Two days after, the courier arrived; and Clement, who had been hurried from his usual prudence, found, that, though he heartily repented of this hasty measure, it would be difficult for him to retract it, or replace affairs on the same footing as before.

It is not probable, that the pope, had he conducted himself with ever so great moderation and temper, could hope, during the life-time of Henry, to have regained much authority or influence in England. That monarch was of a temper both impetuous and obstinate; and having proceeded so far in throwing off the papal *15th* yoke, he never could again have been brought tamely to bend his *Jan.* neck to it. Even at the time, when he was negociating a reconciliation with Rome, he either entertained so little hopes of success, or was so indifferent about the event, that he had assembled a Parliament, and continued to enact laws totally destructive of the papal *A par-* authority. The people had been prepared by degrees for this great *liament.* innovation. Each preceding session had retrenched somewhat from the power and profits of the pontiff. Care had been taken, during some years, to teach the nation, that a general council was much superior to a pope. But now a bishop preached every Sunday at Paul's cross, in order to inculcate the doctrine, that the pope was entitled to no authority at all beyond the bounds of his own diocese.[y] The proceedings of the parliament showed that they had entirely adopted this opinion; and there is reason to believe, that the king, after having procured a favourable sentence from Rome, which would have removed all doubts with regard to his second marriage and the succession, might indeed have lived on terms of civility with the Roman pontiff, but never would have surrendered to him any considerable share of his assumed prerogative. The importance of the laws, passed this session, even before intelligence arrived of the violent resolutions taken at Rome, is sufficient to justify this opinion.

All payments made to the apostolic chamber; all provisions, bulls, dispensations, were abolished: Monasteries were subjected to the visitation and government of the king alone: The law for punishing heretics was moderated; the ordinary was prohibited from imprisoning or trying any person upon suspicion alone, with-

[y] Burnet, vol. i. p. 144.

out presentment by two lawful witnesses; and it was declared that to speak against the pope's authority was no heresy: Bishops were to be appointed, by a *congé d'élire* from the crown, or in case of the dean and chapter's refusal, by letters patent; and no recourse was to be had to Rome for palls, bulls, or provisions: Campeggio and Ghinucci, two Italians, were deprived of the bishoprics of Salisbury and Worcester, which they had hitherto enjoyed:[z] The law, which had been formerly made against paying annates or first fruits, but which had been left in the king's power to suspend or enforce, was finally established: And a submission, which was exacted two years before from the clergy, and which had been obtained with great difficulty, received this session the sanction of parliament.[a] In this submission, the clergy acknowledged, that convocations ought to be assembled by the king's authority only; they promise to enact no new canons without his consent; and they agree, that he should appoint thirty-two commissioners, in order to examine the old canons, and abrogate such as should be found prejudicial to his royal prerogative.[b] An appeal was also allowed from the bishop's court to the king in Chancery.

But the most important law, passed this session, was that which regulated the succession to the crown: The marriage of the king with Catherine was declared unlawful, void, and of no effect: The primate's sentence, annulling it, was ratified: And the marriage with queen Anne was established and confirmed. The crown was appointed to descend to the issue of this marriage, and failing them to the king's heirs for ever. An oath likewise was enjoined to be taken in favour of this order of succession, under the penalty of imprisonment during the king's pleasure, and forfeiture of goods and chattels. And all slander against the king, queen, or their issue, was subjected to the penalty of misprision of treason. After these compliances, the parliament was prorogued; and those acts, so contemptuous towards the pope, and so destructive of his authority, were passed at the very time that Clement pronounced his hasty sentence against the king. Henry's resentment against queen Catherine, on account of her obstinacy, was the reason why he excluded her daughter from all hopes of succeeding to the crown;

30th March.

---

[z] Le Neve's Fasti Eccles. Angl.   [a] 25 H. 8. c. 19.   [b] Collier, vol. ii. p. 69, 70.

CHAPTER XXX

contrary to his first intentions, when he began the process of divorce, and of dispensation for a second marriage.

The king found his ecclesiastical subjects as compliant as the laity. The convocation ordered, that the act against appeals to Rome, together with the king's appeal from the pope to a general council, should be affixed to the doors of all the churches in the kingdom: And they voted that the bishop of Rome had, by the law of God, no more jurisdiction in England than any other foreign bishop; and that the authority, which he and his predecessors had there exercised, was only by usurpation and by the sufferance of English princes. Four persons alone opposed this vote in the lower house, and one doubted. It passed unanimously in the upper. The bishops went so far in their complaisance, that they took out new commissions from the crown, in which all their spiritual and episcopal authority was expressly affirmed to be derived ultimately from the civil magistrate, and to be entirely dependent on his good pleasure.[c]

The oath regarding the succession was generally taken throughout the kingdom. Fisher, bishop of Rochester, and Sir Thomas More, were the only persons of note, that entertained scruples with regard to its legality. Fisher was obnoxious on account of some practices, into which his credulity, rather than any bad intentions, seems to have betrayed him. But More was the person of greatest reputation in the kingdom for virtue and integrity; and as it was believed, that his authority would have influence on the sentiments of others, great pains were taken to convince him of the lawfulness of the oath. He declared, that he had no scruple with regard to the succession, and thought that the parliament had full power to settle it: He offered to draw an oath himself, which would ensure his allegiance to the heir appointed; but he refused the oath prescribed by law; because the preamble of that oath asserted the legality of the king's marriage with Anne, and thereby implied, that his former marriage with Catherine was unlawful and invalid. Cranmer, the primate, and Cromwel, now secretary of state, who highly loved and esteemed More, entreated him to lay aside his scruples; and their friendly importunity seemed to weigh more with him, than all the penalties attending his refusal.[d] He per-

[c] Collier's Eccles. Hist. vol. ii.   [d] Burnet, vol. i. p. 156.

sisted, however, in a mild, though firm manner, to maintain his resolution; and the king, irritated against him as well as Fisher, ordered both to be indicted upon the statute, and committed prisoners to the Tower.

3d
Novem. The parliament, being again assembled, conferred on the king the title of the only supreme *head* on earth of the church of England; as they had already invested him with all the real power belonging to it. In this memorable act, the parliament granted him power, or rather acknowledged his inherent power, "to visit, and repress, redress, reform, order, correct, restrain, or amend all errors, heresies, abuses, offences, contempts, and enormities, which fell under any spiritual authority or jurisdiction."[e] They also declared it treason to attempt, imagine, or speak evil against the king, queen, or his heirs, or to endeavour depriving them of their dignities or titles. They gave him a right to all the annates and tythes of benefices, which had formerly been paid to the court of Rome. They granted him a subsidy and a fifteenth. They attainted More and Fisher for misprision of treason. And they completed the union of England and Wales, by giving to that principality all the benefit of the English laws.

Thus the authority of the popes, like all exorbitant power, was ruined by the excess of its acquisitions, and by stretching its pretensions beyond what it was possible for any human principles or prepossessions to sustain. Indulgences had in former ages tended extremely to enrich the holy see; but being openly abused, they served to excite the first commotions and opposition in Germany. The prerogative of granting dispensations had also contributed much to attach all the sovereign princes and great families in Europe to the papal authority; but meeting with an unlucky concurrence of circumstances, was now the cause, why England separated herself from the Romish communion. The acknowledgment of the king's supremacy introduced there a greater simplicity in the government, by uniting the spiritual with the civil power, and preventing disputes about limits, which never could be exactly determined between the contending jurisdictions. A way was also prepared for checking the exorbitancies of superstition, and breaking those shackles, by which all human reason, policy, and

[e] 26 H. 8. c. i.

CHAPTER XXX

industry had so long been encumbered. The prince, it may be supposed, being head of the religion, as well as of the temporal jurisdiction of the kingdom, though he might sometimes employ the former as an engine of government, had no interest, like the Roman pontiff, in nourishing its excessive growth; and, except when blinded by his own ignorance or bigotry, would be sure to retain it within tolerable limits, and prevent its abuses. And on the whole, there followed from this revolution many beneficial consequences; though perhaps neither foreseen nor intended by the persons who had the chief hand in conducting it.

While Henry proceeded with so much order and tranquillity in changing the national religion, and while his authority seemed entirely secure in England, he was held in some inquietude by the state of affairs in Ireland and in Scotland.

The earl of Kildare was deputy of Ireland, under the duke of Richmond, the king's natural son, who bore the title of lieutenant; and as Kildare was accused of some violences against the family of Ossory, his hereditary enemies, he was summoned to answer for his conduct. He left his authority in the hands of his son, who, hearing that his father was thrown into prison, and was in danger of his life, immediately took up arms, and joining himself to Oneale, Ocarrol, and other Irish nobility, committed many ravages, murdered Allen, archbishop of Dublin, and laid siege to that city. Kildare meanwhile died in prison, and his son, persevering in his revolt, made applications to the emperor, who promised him assistance. The king was obliged to send over some forces to Ireland, which so harassed the rebels, that this young nobleman, finding the emperor backward in fulfilling his promises, was reduced to the necessity of surrendering himself prisoner to Lord Leonard Gray, the new deputy, brother to the marquis of Dorset. He was carried over to England, together with his five uncles; and after trial and conviction, they were all brought to public justice; though two of the uncles, in order to save the family, had pretended to join the king's party.

The earl of Angus had acquired the entire ascendant in Scotland; and having gotten possession of the king's person, then in early youth, he was able, by means of that advantage, and by employing the power of his own family, to retain the reins of government. The queen-dowager, however, his consort, bred him great disturbance. For having separated herself from him, on account of some jealousies and disgusts, and having procured a divorce, she had married another man of quality, of the name of Stuart; and she joined all the discontented nobility, who opposed Angus's authority. James himself was dissatisfied with the slavery, to which he was reduced; and by secret correspondence, he incited first Walter Scot, then the earl of Lenox, to attempt, by force of arms, the freeing him from the hands of Angus. Both enterprizes failed of success; but James, impatient of restraint, found means at last of escaping to Stirling, where his mother then resided; and having summoned all the nobility to attend him, he overturned the authority of the Douglasses, and obliged Angus and his brother to fly into England, where they were protected by Henry. The king of Scotland, being now arrived at years of majority, took the government into his own hands; and employed himself with great spirit and valour, in repressing those feuds, ravages, and disorders, which, though they disturbed the course of public justice, served to support the martial spirit of the Scots, and contributed, by that means, to maintain national independency. He was desirous of renewing the ancient league with the French nation; but finding Francis in close union with England, and on that account somewhat cold in hearkening to his proposals, he received the more favourably the advances of the emperor, who hoped, by means of such an ally, to breed disturbance to England. He offered the Scottish king the choice of three princesses, his own near relations, and all of the name of Mary; his sister the dowager of Hungary, his niece a daughter of Portugal, or his cousin the daughter of Henry, whom he pretended to dispose of unknown to her father. James was more inclined to the latter proposal, had it not, upon reflection, been found impracticable; and his natural propensity to France at last prevailed over all other considerations. The alliance with Francis necessarily engaged James to maintain peace with England. But though invited by his uncle, Henry, to confer with him at Newcastle, and concert common measures for repressing the ecclesiastics in both kingdoms, and shaking off the yoke of Rome, he could not be prevailed on, by entering England, to put himself in the king's power. In order to have a pretext for refusing the conference, he applied to the pope, and obtained a brief, forbidding him to engage in any personal negociations with

CHAPTER XXX

an enemy of the holy see. From these measures, Henry easily concluded, that he could very little depend on the friendship of his nephew. But those events took not place till some time after our present period.

XXXI

Religious principles of the people –
of the king – of the ministers – Farther progress
of the reformation – Sir Thomas More – The maid
of Kent – Trial and execution of Fisher bishop of
Rochester – of Sir Thomas More – King
excommunicated – Death of Queen Catherine –
Suppression of the lesser monasteries –
A Parliament – A convocation – Translation of the
Bible – Disgrace of Queen Anne – Her trial – and
execution – A Parliament – A convocation –
Discontents among the people – Insurrection –
Birth of prince Edward and death of
Queen Jane – Suppression of the greater
monasteries – Cardinal Pole

HE ANCIENT and almost uninterrupted opposition of interests between the laity and clergy in England, and between the English clergy and the court of Rome, had sufficiently prepared the nation for a breach with the sovereign pontiff; and men had penetration enough to discover abuses, which were plainly calculated for the temporal advantages of the hierarchy, and which they found destructive of their own. These subjects seemed proportioned to human understanding; and even the people, who felt the

1534.
Religious
prin-
ciples of
the
people.

CHAPTER XXXI

power of interest in their own breasts, could perceive the purpose of those numerous inventions, which the interested spirit of the Roman pontiff had introduced into religion. But when the reformers proceeded thence to dispute concerning the nature of the sacraments, the operations of grace, the terms of acceptance with the Deity, men were thrown into amazement, and were, during some time, at a loss how to chuse their party. The profound ignorance in which both the clergy and laity formerly lived, and their freedom from theological altercations, had produced a sincere, but indolent acquiescence in received opinions; and the multitude were neither attached to them by topics of reasoning, nor by those prejudices and antipathies against opponents, which have ever a more natural and powerful influence over them. As soon therefore as a new opinion was advanced, supported by such an authority as to call up their attention, they felt their capacity totally unfitted for such disquisitions; and they perpetually fluctuated between the contending parties. Hence the quick and violent movements by which the people were agitated, even in the most opposite directions; Hence their seeming prostitution, in sacrificing to present power the most sacred principles: And hence the rapid progress during some time, and the sudden as well as entire check soon after, of the new doctrines. When men were once settled in their particular sects, and had fortified themselves in a habitual detestation of those who were denominated heretics, they adhered with more obstinacy to the principles of their education; and the limits of the two religions thenceforth remained fixed and unchangeable.

Nothing more forwarded the first progress of the reformers, than the offer, which they made, of submitting all religious doctrines to private judgment, and the summons given every one to examine the principles formerly imposed upon him. Though the multitude were totally unqualified for this undertaking, they yet were highly pleased with it. They fancied, that they were exercising their judgment, while they opposed, to the prejudices of ancient authority, more powerful prejudices of another kind. The novelty itself of the doctrines; the pleasure of an imaginary triumph in dispute; the fervent zeal of the reformed preachers, their patience, and even alacrity, in suffering persecution, death, and torments; a disgust at the restraints of the old religion; an indignation against the tyranny and interested spirit of the ecclesiastics; these motives were prevalent with the people, and by such considerations were men so generally induced, during that age, to throw off the religion of their ancestors.

But in proportion as the practice of submitting religion to private judgment was acceptable to the people, it appeared, in some respects, dangerous to the rights of sovereigns, and seemed to destroy that implicit obedience, on which the authority of the civil magistrate is chiefly founded. The very precedent, of shaking so ancient and deep founded an establishment as that of the Romish hierarchy, might, it was apprehended, prepare the way for other innovations. The republican spirit, which naturally took place among the reformers, encreased this jealousy. The furious insurrections of the populace, excited by Muncer and other anabaptists in Germany,[f] furnished a new pretence for decrying the reformation. Nor ought we to conclude, because protestants in our time prove as dutiful subjects as those of any other communion, that therefore such apprehensions were altogether without any shadow of plausibility. Though the liberty of private judgment be tendered to the disciples of the reformation, it is not in reality accepted of; and men are generally contented to acquiesce implicitly in those establishments, however new, into which their early education has thrown them.

No prince in Europe was possessed of such absolute authority as Henry, not even the pope himself, in his own capital, where he united both the civil and ecclesiastical powers;[g] and there was small likelihood, that any doctrine, which lay under the imputation of encouraging sedition, could ever pretend to his favour and countenance. But besides this political jealousy, there was another reason, which inspired this imperious monarch with an aversion to the reformers. He had early declared his sentiments against Luther; and having entered the lists in those scholastic quarrels, he had received, from his courtiers and theologians, infinite applause for his performance. Elated by this imaginary success, and blinded by a natural arrogance and obstinacy of temper, he had entertained the most lofty opinion of his own erudition; and he received with impatience, mixed with contempt, any contradiction to his

Of the king.

[f] Sleidan, lib. 4. & 5.   [g] See note [I] at the end of the volume.

CHAPTER XXXI

sentiments. Luther also had been so imprudent, as to treat in a very indecent manner his royal antagonist; and though he afterwards made the most humble submissions to Henry, and apologized for the vehemence of his former expressions, he never could efface the hatred, which the king had conceived against him and his doctrines. The idea of heresy still appeared detestable as well as formidable to that prince; and whilst his resentment against the see of Rome had corrected one considerable part of his early prejudices, he had made it a point of honour never to relinquish the remainder. Separate as he stood from the catholic church and from the Roman pontiff, the head of it, he still valued himself on maintaining the catholic doctrine, and on guarding, by fire and sword, the imagined purity of his speculative principles.

Henry's ministers and courtiers were of as motley a character as his conduct; and seemed to waver, during this whole reign, between the ancient and the new religion. *Of the ministers.* The queen, engaged by interest as well as inclination, favoured the cause of the reformers: Cromwel, who was created secretary of state, and who was daily advancing in the king's confidence, had embraced the same views; and as he was a man of prudence and abilities, he was able, very effectually, though in a covert manner, to promote the late innovations: Cranmer, archbishop of Canterbury, had secretly adopted the protestant tenets; and he had gained Henry's friendship by his candour and sincerity; virtues which he possessed in as eminent a degree as those times, equally distracted with faction, and oppressed by tyranny, could easily permit. On the other hand, the duke of Norfolk adhered to the ancient faith; and by his high rank, as well as by his talents, both for peace and war, he had great authority in the king's council: Gardiner, lately created bishop of Winchester, had inlisted himself in the same party; and the suppleness of his character, and dexterity of his conduct, had rendered him extremely useful to it.

All these ministers, while they stood in the most irreconcilable opposition of principles to each other, were obliged to disguise their particular opinions, and to pretend an entire agreement with the sentiments of their master. Cromwel and Cranmer still carried the appearance of a conformity to the ancient speculative tenets; but they artfully made use of Henry's resentment to widen the breach with the see of Rome. Norfolk and Gardiner feigned an assent to the king's supremacy, and to his renunciation of the sovereign pontiff; but they encouraged his passion for the catholic faith, and instigated him to punish those daring heretics, who had presumed to reject his theological principles. Both sides hoped, by their unlimited compliance, to bring him over to their party: The king meanwhile, who held the balance between the factions, was enabled, by the courtship payed him both by protestants and catholics, to assume an unbounded authority: And though in all his measures he was really driven by his ungoverned humour, he casually steered a course, which led more certainly to arbitrary power, than any which the most profound politics could have traced out to him. Artifice, refinement, and hypocrisy, in his situation, would have put both parties on their guard against him, and would have taught them reserve in complying with a monarch, whom they could never hope thoroughly to have gained: But while the frankness, sincerity, and openness of Henry's temper were generally known, as well as the dominion of his furious passions; each side dreaded to lose him by the smallest opposition, and flattered themselves that a blind compliance with his will would throw him, cordially and fully, into their interests.

The ambiguity of the king's conduct, though it kept the courtiers in awe, served in the main, to encourage the protestant doctrine among his subjects, and promoted that spirit of innovation, with which the age was generally seized, and which nothing but an entire uniformity, as well as a steady severity in the administration, could be able to repress. There were some Englishmen, Tindal, Joye, Constantine, and others, who, dreading the exertion of the king's authority, had fled to Antwerp;[h] where the great privileges possessed by the Low Country provinces, served, during some time, to give them protection. These men employed themselves in writing English books, against the corruptions of the church of Rome; against images, reliques, pilgrimages; and they excited the curiosity of men with regard to that question, the most important in theology, the terms of acceptance with the Supreme Being. In conformity to the Lutherans and other protestants, they asserted, that salvation was obtained by faith alone; and that the most infal-

Farther progress of the reformation.

[h] Burnet, vol. i. p. 159.

CHAPTER XXXI

lible road to perdition[i] was a reliance on *good works;* by which terms they understood, as well the moral duties, as the ceremonial and monastic observances. The defenders of the ancient religion, on the other hand, maintained the efficacy of *good works;* but though they did not exclude from this appellation the social virtues, it was still the superstitions, gainful to the church, which they chiefly extolled and recommended. The books, composed by these fugitives, having stolen over to England, began to make converts every where; but it was a translation of the scriptures by Tindal, that was esteemed the most dangerous to the established faith. The first edition of this work, composed with little accuracy, was found liable to considerable objections; and Tindal, who was poor, and could not afford to lose a great part of the impression, was longing for an opportunity of correcting his errors, of which he had been made sensible. Tonstal, then bishop of London, soon after of Durham, a man of great moderation, being desirous to discourage, in the gentlest manner, these innovations, gave private orders for buying up all the copies, that could be found at Antwerp; and he burned them publicly in Cheapside. By this measure, he supplied Tindal with money, enabled him to print a new and correct edition of his work, and gave great scandal to the people, in thus committing to the flames the word of God.[k]

The disciples of the reformation met with little severity during the ministry of Wolsey, who, though himself a clergyman, bore too small a regard to the ecclesiastical order, to serve as an instrument of their tyranny: It was even an article of impeachment against him,[l] that by his connivance he had encouraged the growth of heresy, and that he had protected and acquitted some notorious offenders. Sir Thomas More, who succeeded Wolsey as Chancellor, is at once an object deserving our compassion, and an instance of the usual progress of men's sentiments during that age. This man, whose elegant genius and familiar acquaintance with the

Sir Thomas More.

[i] Sacrilegium est et impietas velle placere Deo per opera et non per solam fidem. *Luther adversus regem.* Ita vides quam dives sit homo christianus sive baptizatus, qui etiam volens not potest perdere salutem suam quantiscunque peccatis. Nulla enim peccata possunt eum damnare nisi incredulitas. *Id. de captivitate Babylonica.*   [k] Hall, fol. 186. Fox, vol. i. p. 138. Burnet, vol. i. p. 159.   [l] Articles of impeachment in Herbert. Burnet.

noble spirit of antiquity, had given him very enlarged sentiments, and who had in his early years advanced principles, which even at present would be deemed somewhat too free, had, in the course of events, been so irritated by polemics, and thrown into such a superstitious attachment to the ancient faith, that few inquisitors have been guilty of greater violence in their prosecution of heresy. Though adorned with the gentlest manners, as well as the purest integrity, he carried to the utmost height his aversion to heterodoxy; and James Bainham, in particular, a gentleman of the Temple, experienced from him the greatest severity. Bainham, accused of favouring the new opinions, was carried to More's house; and having refused to discover his accomplices, the chancellor ordered him to be whipped in his presence, and afterwards sent him to the Tower, where he himself saw him put to the torture. The unhappy gentleman, overcome by all these severities, abjured his opinions; but feeling afterwards the deepest compunction for his apostacy, he openly returned to his former tenets, and even courted the crown of martyrdom. He was condemned as an obstinate and relapsed heretic, and was burned in Smithfield.[m]

Many were brought into the bishops' courts for offences, which appear trivial, but which were regarded as symbols of the party: Some for teaching their children the Lord's prayer in English; others for reading the new testament in that language, or for speaking against pilgrimages. To harbour the persecuted preachers, to neglect the fasts of the church, to declaim against the vices of the clergy, were capital offences. One Thomas Bilney, a priest, who had embraced the new doctrine, had been terrified into an abjuration; but was so haunted by remorse, that his friends dreaded some fatal effects of his despair. At last, his mind seemed to be more relieved: but this appearing calm proceeded only from the resolution, which he had taken, of expiating his past offence, by an open confession of the truth, and by dying a martyr to it. He went through Norfolk, teaching the people to beware of idolatry, and of trusting for their salvation either to pilgrimages or to the cowle of St. Francis, to the prayers of the saints, or to images. He was soon seized, tried in the bishop's court, and condemned as a relapsed heretic; and the writ was sent down to burn him. When

[m] Fox. Burnet, vol. i. p. 165.

CHAPTER XXXI

brought to the stake, he discovered such patience, fortitude, and devotion, that the spectators were much affected with the horrors of his punishment; and some mendicant friars, who were present, fearing that his martyrdom would be imputed to them, and make them lose those alms, which they received from the charity of the people, desired him publicly to acquit them[n] of having any hand in his death. He willingly complied; and by this meekness gained the more on the sympathy of the people. Another person, still more heroic, being brought to the stake for denying the real presence, seemed almost in a transport of joy; and he tenderly embraced the faggots, which were to be the instruments of his punishment, as the means of procuring him eternal rest. In short, the tide turning towards the new doctrine, those severe executions, which, in another disposition of men's minds, would have suffced to suppress it, now served only to diffuse it the more among the people, and to inspire them with horror against the unrelenting persecutors.

But though Henry neglected not to punish the protestant doctrine, which he deemed heresy, his most formidable enemies, he knew, were the zealous adherents to the ancient religion, chiefly the monks, who, having their immediate dependance on the Roman pontiff, apprehended their own ruin to be the certain consequence of abolishing his authority in England. Peyto, a friar, preaching before the king, had the assurance to tell him, "That many lying prophets had deceived him, but he as a true Micajah, warned him, that the dogs would lick his blood, as they had done Ahab's."[o] The king took no notice of the insult; but allowed the preacher to depart in peace. Next Sunday he employed Dr. Corren to preach before him; who justified the king's proceedings, and gave Peyto the appellations of a rebel, a slanderer, a dog, and a traitor. Elston, another friar of the same house, interrupted the preacher, and told him, that he was one of the lying prophets, who sought to establish by adultery the succession of the crown; but that he himself would justify all that Peyto had said. Henry silenced the petulant friar; but showed no other mark of resentment than ordering Peyto and him to be summoned before the council, and to be rebuked for their offence.[p] He even here bore patiently

---

[n] Burnet, vol. i. p. 164.   [o] Strype, vol. i. p. 167.   [p] Collier, vol. ii. p. 86. Burnet, vol. i. p. 151.

some new instances of their obstinacy and arrogance: When the earl of Essex, a privy counsellor, told them, that they deserved for their offence to be thrown into the Thames; Elston replied, that the road to heaven lay as near by water as by land.[q]

The maid of Kent.

But several monks were detected in a conspiracy, which, as it might have proved more dangerous to the king, was on its discovery attended with more fatal consequences to themselves. Elizabeth Barton, of Aldington in Kent, commonly called the *holy Maid of Kent,* had been subject to hysterical fits, which threw her body into unusual convulsions; and having produced an equal disorder in her mind, made her utter strange sayings, which, as she was scarcely conscious of them during the time, had soon after entirely escaped her memory. The silly people in the neighbourhood were struck with these appearances, which they imagined to be supernatural; and Richard Masters, vicar of the parish, a designing fellow, founded on them a project, from which he hoped to acquire both profit and consideration. He went to Warham, archbishop of Canterbury, then alive; and having given him an account of Elizabeth's revelations, he so far wrought on that prudent, but superstitious prelate, as to receive orders from him to watch her in her trances, and carefully to note down all her future sayings. The regard, paid her by a person of so high a rank, soon rendered her still more the object of attention to the neighbourhood; and it was easy for Masters to persuade them, as well as the maid herself, that her ravings were inspirations of the Holy Ghost. Knavery, as is usual, soon after succeeding to delusion, she learned to counterfeit trances; and she then uttered, in an extraordinary tone, such speeches as were dictated to her by her spiritual director. Masters associated with him Dr. Bocking, a canon of Canterbury; and their design was to raise the credit of an image of the virgin, which stood in a chapel belonging to Masters, and to draw to it such pilgrimages as usually frequented the more famous images and reliques. In prosecution of this design, Elizabeth pretended revelations, which directed her to have recourse to that image for a cure; and being brought before it, in the presence of a great multitude, she fell anew into convulsions; and after distorting her limbs and countenance during a competent time, she

[q] Stowe, p. 562.

CHAPTER XXXI

affected to have obtained a perfect recovery by the intercession of the virgin.[r] This miracle was soon bruited abroad; and the two priests, finding the imposture to succeed beyond their own expectations, began to extend their views, and to lay the foundation of more important enterprizes. They taught their penitent to declaim against the new doctrines, which she denominated heresy; against innovations in ecclesiastical government; and against the king's intended divorce from Catherine. She went so far as to assert, that, if he prosecuted that design, and married another, he should not be a king a month longer, and should not an hour longer enjoy the favour of the Almighty, but should die the death of a villain. Many monks throughout England, either from folly or roguery, or from faction, which is often a complication of both, entered into the delusion; and one Deering, a friar, wrote a book of the revelations and prophecies of Elizabeth.[s] Miracles were daily added, to encrease the wonder; and the pulpit every where resounded with accounts of the sanctity and inspirations of the new prophetess. Messages were carried from her to queen Catherine, by which that princess was exhorted to persist in her opposition to the divorce; the pope's ambassadors gave encouragement to the popular credulity; and even Fisher, bishop of Rochester, though a man of sense and learning, was carried away by an opinion so favourable to the party which he had espoused.[t] The king at last began to think the matter worthy of his attention: and having ordered Elizabeth and her accomplices to be arrested, he brought them before the star-chamber, where they freely, without being put to the torture, made confession of their guilt. The parliament, in the session held the beginning of this year, passed an act of attainder against some who were engaged in this treasonable imposture;[u] and Elizabeth herself, Masters, Bocking, Deering, Rich, Risby, Gold, suffered for their crime. The bishop of Rochester, Abel, Addison, Lawrence, and others were condemned for misprision of treason; because they had not discovered some criminal speeches which they heard from Elizabeth:[w] And they were thrown into prison. The better to undeceive the multitude, the forgery of many of the prophetess's miracles was detected: and even the

[r] Stowe, p. 570. Blanquet's Epitome of Chronicles. [s] Strype, vol. i. p. 181. [t] Collier, vol. ii. p. 87. [u] 25 Hen. VIII. c. 12. Burnet, vol. i. p. 149. Hall, fol. 220. [w] Godwin's Annals, p. 53.

scandalous prostitution of her manners was laid open to the public. Those passions, which so naturally insinuate themselves amidst the warm intimacies maintained by the devotees of different sexes, had taken place between Elizabeth and her confederates; and it was found, that a door to her dormitory, which was said to have been miraculously opened, in order to give her access to the chapel, for the sake of frequent converse with heaven, had been contrived by Bocking and Masters for less refined purposes.

1535.   The detection of this imposture, attended with so many odious circumstances, both hurt the credit of the ecclesiastics, particularly the monks, and instigated the king to take vengeance on them. He suppressed three monasteries of the Observantine friars; and finding that little clamour was excited by this act of power, he was the more encouraged to lay his rapacious hands on the remainder. Meanwhile, he exercised punishment on individuals, who were obnoxious to him. The parliament had made it treason to endeavour depriving the king of his dignity or titles: They had lately added to his other titles, that of supreme head of the church: It was inferred, that to deny his supremacy was treason; and many priors and ecclesiastics lost their lives for this new species of guilt. It was certainly a high instance of tyranny to punish the mere delivery of a political opinion, especially one that nowise affected the king's temporal right, as a capital offence, though attended with no overt act; and the parliament, in passing this law, had overlooked all the principles, by which a civilized, much more a free people, should be governed: But the violence of changing so suddenly the whole system of government, and making it treason to deny what, during many ages, it had been heresy to assert, is an event which may appear somewhat extraordinary. Even the stern unrelenting mind of Henry was, at first, shocked with these sanguinary measures; and he went so far as to change his garb and dress; pretending sorrow for the necessity by which he was pushed to such extremities. Still impelled, however, by his violent temper, and desirous of striking a terror into the whole nation, he proceeded, by making examples of Fisher and More, to consummate his lawless tyranny.

Trial and execution of Fisher, bishop of Rochester.   John Fisher, bishop of Rochester, was a prelate, eminent for learning and morals, still more than for his ecclesiastical dignities, and for the high favour, which he had long enjoyed with the king.

CHAPTER XXXI

When he was thrown into prison, on account of his refusing the oath which regarded the succession, and his concealment of Elizabeth Barton's treasonable speeches, he had not only been deprived of all his revenues, but stripped of his very cloaths, and, without consideration of his extreme age, he was allowed nothing but rags, which scarcely sufficed to cover his nakedness.[x] In this condition, he lay in prison above a twelvemonth; when the pope, willing to recompense the sufferings of so faithful an adherent, created him a cardinal; though Fisher was so indifferent about that dignity, that, even if the purple were lying at his feet, he declared that he would not stoop to take it. This promotion of a man, merely for his opposition to royal authority, rouzed the indignation of the king; and he resolved to make the innocent person feel the effects of his resentment. Fisher was indicted for denying the king's supremacy, was tried, condemned, and beheaded.

22d June.

The execution of this prelate was intended as a warning to More, whose compliance, on account of his great authority both abroad and at home, and his high reputation for learning and virtue, was anxiously desired by the king. That prince also bore as great personal affection and regard to More, as his imperious mind, the sport of passions, was susceptible of towards a man, who in any particular opposed his violent inclinations. But More could never be prevailed on to acknowledge any opinion so contrary to his principles as that of the king's supremacy; and though Henry exacted that compliance from the whole nation, there was, as yet, no law obliging any one to take an oath to that purpose. Rich, the solicitor general, was sent to confer with More, then a prisoner, who kept a cautious silence with regard to the supremacy: He was only inveigled to say, that any question with regard to the law, which established that prerogative, was a two-edged sword: If a person answer one way, it will confound his soul; if another, it will destroy his body. No more was wanted to sound an indictment of high treason against the prisoner. His silence was called malicious, and made a part of his crime; and these words, which had casually dropped from him, were interpreted as a denial of the supremacy.[y] Trials were mere formalities during this reign: The jury gave sen-

Of Sir Thomas More.

[x] Fuller's Church Hist. book 5. p. 203.   [y] More's Life of Sir Thomas More. Herbert, p. 393.

tence against More, who had long expected this fate, and who needed no preparation to fortify him against the terrors of death. Not only his constancy, but even his cheerfulness, nay, his usual facetiousness, never forsook him; and he made a sacrifice of his life to his integrity with the same indifference that he maintained in any ordinary occurrence. When he was mounting the scaffold, he said to one, "Friend, help me up, and when I come down again, let me shift for myself." The executioner asking him forgiveness, he granted the request, but told him, "You will never get credit by beheading me, my neck is so short." Then laying his head on the block, he bade the executioner stay till he put aside his beard: "For," said he, "it never committed treason." Nothing was wanting to the glory of this end, except a better cause, more free from weakness and superstition. But as the man followed his principles and sense of duty, however misguided, his constancy and integrity are not the less objects of our admiration. He was beheaded in the fifty-third year of his age.

6th July.

When the execution of Fisher and More was reported at Rome, especially that of the former, who was invested with the dignity of cardinal, every one discovered the most violent rage against the king; and numerous libels were published, by the wits and orators of Italy, comparing him to Caligula, Nero, Domitian, and all the most unrelenting tyrants of antiquity. Clement VII. had died about six months after he pronounced sentence against the king; and Paul III. of the name of Farnese, had succeeded to the papal throne. This pontiff, who, while cardinal, had always favoured Henry's cause, had hoped, that, personal animosities being buried with his predecessor, it might not be impossible to form an agreement with England: And the king himself was so desirous of accommodating matters, that, in a negociation, which he entered into with Francis a little before this time, he required, that that monarch should conciliate a friendship between him and the court of Rome. But Henry was accustomed to prescribe, not to receive terms; and even while he was negociating for peace, his usual violence often carried him to commit offences, which rendered the quarrel totally incurable. The execution of Fisher was regarded by Paul, as so capital an injury, that he immediately passed censures against the king, citing him and all his adherents to appear in Rome within ninety days, in order to answer for their crimes: If

30th Aug.

CHAPTER XXXI

they failed, he excommunicated them; deprived the king of his *King* crown; layed the kingdom under an interdict; declared his issue by *excom-* Anne Boleyn illegitimate; dissolved all leagues which any catholic *muni-* princes had made with him; gave his kingdom to any invader; *cated.* commanded the nobility to take arms against him; freed his sub- jects from all oaths of allegiance; cut off their commerce with foreign states; and declared it lawful for any one to seize them, to make slaves of their persons, and to convert their effects to his own use.[z] But though these censures were passed, they were not at that time openly denounced: The pope delayed the publication, till he should find an agreement with England entirely desperate; and till the emperor, who was at that time hard pressed by the Turks and the protestant princes in Germany, should be in a condition to carry the sentence into execution.

The king knew that he might expect any injury, which it should be in Charles's power to inflict; and he therefore made it the chief object of his policy to incapacitate that monarch from wreaking his resentment upon him.[a] He renewed his friendship with Francis, and opened negociations for marrying his infant-daughter, Eliz- abeth, with the duke of Angouleme, third son of Francis. These two monarchs also made advances to the princes of the protestant league in Germany, ever jealous of the emperor's ambition: And Henry, besides remitting them some money, sent Fox, bishop of Hereford, as Francis did Bellay, lord of Langley, to treat with them. But during the first fervours of the reformation, an agree- ment in theological tenets was held, as well as a union of interests, to be essential to a good correspondence among states; and though both Francis and Henry flattered the German princes with hopes of their embracing the confession of Augsbourg, it was looked upon as a bad symptom of the sincerity that they exercised such extreme rigour against all preachers of the reformation in their respective dominions.[b] Henry carried the feint so far, that, while he thought himself the first theologian in the world, he yet invited over Melancthon, Bucer, Sturmius, Draco, and other German di- vines, that they might confer with him, and instruct him in the foundation of their tenets. These theologians were now of great importance in the world; and no poet or philosopher, even in

[z] Sanders, p. 148.   [a] Herbert, p. 350, 351.   [b] Sleidan, lib. 10.

ancient Greece, where they were treated with most respect, had ever reached equal applause and admiration with those wretched composers of metaphysical polemics. The German princes told the king, that they could not spare their divines; and as Henry had no hopes of agreement with such zealous disputants, and knew that in Germany the followers of Luther would not associate with the disciples of Zuinglius, because, though they agreed in every thing else, they differed in some minute particulars with regard to the eucharist, he was the more indifferent on account of this refusal. He could also foresee, that, even while the league of Smalkalde did not act in concert with him, they would always be carried by their interests to oppose the emperor: And the hatred between Francis and that monarch was so inveterate, that he deemed himself sure of a sincere ally in one or other of these potentates.

1536.

During these negociations an incident happened in England, which promised a more amicable conclusion of those disputes, and seemed even to open the way for a reconciliation between Henry and Charles. Queen Catherine was seized with a lingering illness, which at last brought her to her grave: She died at Kimbolton in the county of Huntingdon, in the fiftieth year of her age. A little before she expired, she wrote a very tender letter to the king; in which she gave him the appellation of *her most dear Lord, King, and Husband.* She told him, that, as the hour of her death was now approaching, she laid hold of this last opportunity to inculcate on him the importance of his religious duty, and the comparative emptiness of all human grandeur and enjoyment: That though his fondness towards these perishable advantages had thrown her into many calamities, as well as created to himself much trouble, she yet forgave him all past injuries, and hoped that his pardon would be ratified in heaven: And that she had no other request to make, than to recommend to him his daughter, the sole pledge of their loves; and to crave his protection for her maids and servants. She concluded with these words, *I make this vow, that mine eyes desire you above all things.*[c] The king was touched even to the shedding of tears, by this last tender proof of Catherine's affection; but queen Anne is said to have expressed her joy for the death of a rival beyond what decency or humanity could permit.[d]

6th Jan. Death of queen Catherine.

[c] Herbert, p. 403.   [d] Burnet, vol. i. p. 192.

CHAPTER XXXI

The emperor thought, that, as the demise of his aunt had removed all foundation of personal animosity between him and Henry, it might not now be impossible to detach him from the alliance of France, and to renew his own confederacy with England, from which he had formerly reaped so much advantage. He sent Henry proposals for a return to ancient amity, upon these conditions;[e] that he should be reconciled to the see of Rome, that he should assist him in his war with the Turk, and that he should take part with him against Francis, who now threatened the dutchy of Milan. The king replied, that he was willing to be on good terms with the emperor, provided that prince would acknowledge, that the former breach of friendship came entirely from himself: As to the conditions proposed; the proceedings against the bishop of Rome were so just, and so fully ratified by the parliament of England, that they could not now be revoked; when Christian princes should have settled peace among themselves, he would not fail to exert that vigour, which became him, against the enemies of the faith; and after amity with the emperor was once fully restored, he should then be in a situation, as a common friend both to him and Francis, either to mediate an agreement between them, or to assist the injured party.

What rendered Henry more indifferent to the advances made by the emperor, was, both his experience of the usual duplicity and insincerity of that monarch, and the intelligence which he received of the present transactions in Europe. Francis Sforza, duke of Milan, had died without issue; and the emperor maintained, that the dutchy, being a fief of the empire, was devolved to him, as head of the Germanic body: not to give umbrage, however to the states of Italy, he professed his intention of bestowing that principality on some prince, who should be obnoxious to no party, and he even made offer of it, to the duke of Angouleme, third son of Francis. The French monarch, who pretended that his own right to Milan was now revived upon Sforza's death, was content to substitute his second son, the duke of Orleans, in his place; and the emperor pretended to close with this proposal. But his sole intention in that liberal concession was to gain time, till he should put himself in a warlike posture, and be able to carry an invasion into Francis's

[e] Du Bellay, liv. 5. Herbert. Burnet, vol. iii. in Coll. No 50.

dominions. The ancient enmity between these princes broke out anew in bravadoes, and in personal insults on each other, ill-becoming persons of their rank, and still less suitable to men of such unquestioned bravery. Charles soon after invaded Provence in person, with an army of fifty thousand men; but met with no success. His army perished with sickness, fatigue, famine, and other disasters; and he was obliged to raise the siege of Marseilles, and retire into Italy with the broken remains of his forces. An army of Imperialists, near 30,000 strong, which invaded France on the side of the Netherlands, and laid siege to Peronne, made no greater progress, but retired upon the approach of a French army. And Henry had thus the satisfaction to find, both that his ally, Francis, was likely to support himself without foreign assistance, and that his own tranquillity was fully ensured by these violent wars and animosities on the continent.

If any inquietude remained with the English court, it was solely occasioned by the state of affairs in Scotland. James, hearing of the dangerous situation of his ally, Francis, generously levied some forces; and embarking them on board vessels, which he had hired for that purpose, landed them safely in France. He even went over in person; and making haste to join the camp of the French king, which then lay in Provence, and to partake of his danger, he met that prince at Lyons, who, having repulsed the emperor, was now returning to his capital. Recommended by so agreeable and sea-sonable an instance of friendship, the king of Scots paid his ad-dresses to Magdalen, daughter of the French monarch; and this prince had no other objection to the match, than what arose from the infirm state of his daughter's health, which seemed to threaten her with an approaching end. But James having gained the affec-tions of the princess, and obtained her consent, the father would no longer oppose the united desires of his daughter and his friend: They were accordingly married, and soon after set sail for Scot-land, where the young queen, as was foreseen, died in a little time after her arrival. Francis, however, was afraid, lest his ally, Henry, whom he likewise looked on as his friend, and who lived with him on a more cordial footing than is usual among great princes, should be displeased, that this close confederacy between France and Scotland was concluded without his participation. He there-fore dispatched Pommeraye to London, in order to apologize for

CHAPTER XXXI

this measure; but Henry, with his usual openness and freedom, expressed such displeasure, that he refused even to confer with the ambassador; and Francis was apprehensive of a rupture with a prince, who regulated his measures more by humour and passion than by the rules of political prudence. But the king was so fettered by the opposition, in which he was engaged against the pope and the emperor, that he pursued no farther this disgust against Francis; and in the end every thing remained in tranquillity both on the side of France and of Scotland.

The domestic peace of England seemed to be exposed to more hazard, by the violent innovations in religion; and it may be affirmed, that, in this dangerous conjuncture, nothing ensured public tranquillity so much as the decisive authority acquired by the king, and his great ascendant over all his subjects. Not only the devotion paid to the crown, was profound during that age: The personal respect, inspired by Henry, was considerable; and even the terrors, with which he over-awed every one, were not attended with any considerable degree of hatred. His frankness, his sincerity, his magnificence, his generosity, were virtues which counterbalanced his violence, cruelty, and impetuosity. And the important rank, which his vigour, more than his address, acquired him in all foreign negociations, flattered the vanity of Englishmen, and made them the more willingly endure those domestic hardships, to which they were exposed. The king, conscious of his advantages, was now proceeding to the most dangerous exercise of his authority; and after paving the way for that measure by several preparatory expedients, he was at last determined to suppress the monasteries, and to put himself in possession of their ample revenues.

The great encrease of monasteries, if matters be considered merely in a political light, will appear the radical inconvenience of the catholic religion; and every other disadvantage, attending that communion, seems to have an inseparable connection with these religious institutions. Papal usurpations, the tyranny of the inquisition, the multiplicity of holidays; all these fetters on liberty and industry were ultimately derived from the authority and insinuation of monks, whose habitations, being established every where, proved so many seminaries of superstition and of folly. This order of men was extremely enraged against Henry; and regarded the abolition of the papal authority in England, as the removal of the sole protection, which they enjoyed, against the rapacity of the crown and of the courtiers. They were now subjected to the king's visitation; the supposed sacredness of their bulls from Rome was rejected; the progress of the reformation abroad, which had every where been attended with the abolition of the monastic orders, gave them reason to apprehend like consequences in England; and though the king still maintained the doctrine of purgatory, to which most of the convents owed their origin and support, it was foreseen, that, in the progress of the contest, he would every day be led to depart wider from ancient institutions, and be drawn nearer the tenets of the reformers, with whom his political interests naturally induced him to unite. Moved by these considerations, the friars employed all their influence to enflame the people against the king's government; and Henry, finding their safety irreconcilable with his own, was determined to seize the present opportunity, and utterly destroy his declared enemies.

Cromwel, secretary of state, had been appointed vicar-general, or vicegerent, a new office, by which the king's supremacy, or the absolute, uncontroulable power, assumed over the church, was delegated to him. He employed Layton, London, Price, Gage, Petre, Bellasis, and others, as commissioners, who carried on, every where, a rigorous enquiry with regard to the conduct and deportment of all the friars. During times of faction, especially of the religious kind, no equity is to be expected from adversaries; and as it was known, that the king's intention in this visitation was to find a pretence for abolishing monasteries, we may naturally conclude, that the reports of the commissioners are very little to be relied on. Friars were encouraged to bring in informations against their brethren; the slightest evidence was credited; and even the calumnies, spread abroad by the friends of the reformation, were regarded as grounds of proof. Monstrous disorders are therefore said to have been found in many of the religious houses: Whole convents of women abandoned to lewdness: Signs of abortions procured, of infants murdered, of unnatural lusts between persons of the same sex. It is indeed probable, that the blind submission of the people, during those ages, would render the friars and nuns more unguarded, and more dissolute, than they are in any Roman Catholic country at present: But still, the reproaches, which it is safest to credit, are such as point at vices, naturally

CHAPTER XXXI

connected with the very institution of convents, and with the monastic life. The cruel and inveterate factions and quarrels, therefore, which the commissioners mentioned, are very credible
among men, who, being confined together within the same walls,
never can forget their mutual animosities, and who, being cut off
from all the most endearing connections of nature, are commonly
cursed with hearts more selfish, and tempers more unrelenting,
than fall to the share of other men. The pious frauds, practised to
encrease the devotion and liberality of the people, may be regarded as certain, in an order founded on illusions, lies, and superstition. The supine idleness also, and its attendant, profound ignorance, with which the convents were reproached, admit of no
question; and though monks were the true preservers, as well as
inventors, of the dreaming and captious philosophy of the schools,
no manly or elegant knowledge could be expected among men,
whose lives, condemned to a tedious uniformity, and deprived of
all emulation, afforded nothing to raise the mind, or cultivate the
genius.

Some few monasteries, terrified with this rigorous inquisition
carried on by Cromwel and his commissioners, surrendered their
revenues into the king's hands; and the monks received small
pensions as the reward of their obsequiousness. Orders were given
to dismiss such nuns and friars as were below four and twenty,
whose vows were, on that account, supposed not to be binding.
The doors of the convents were opened, even to such as were
above that age; and every one recovered his liberty who desired it.
But as all these expedients did not fully answer the king's purpose,
he had recourse to his usual instrument of power, the parliament;
and in order to prepare men for the innovations projected, the
report of the visitors was published, and a general horror was
endeavoured to be excited in the nation against institutions, which,
to their ancestors, had been the objects of the most profound
veneration.

The king, though determined utterly to abolish the monastic
order, resolved to proceed gradually in this great work; and he
gave directions to the parliament to go no further at present, than
to suppress the lesser monasteries, which possessed revenues below two hundred pounds a year.*f* These were found to be the most

4th Feb.

A parliament.

---

f 27 Hen. VIII. c. 28.

corrupted, as lying less under the restraint of shame, and being exposed to less scrutiny;[g] and it was deemed safest to begin with them, and thereby prepare the way for the greater innovations projected. By this act three hundred and seventy-six monasteries were suppressed, and their revenues, amounting to thirty-two thousand pounds a year, were granted to the king; besides their goods, chattels, and plate, computed at a hundred thousand pounds more.[h] It does not appear, that any opposition was made to this important law: So absolute was Henry's authority! A court, called the court of augmentation of the king's revenue, was erected for the management of these funds. The people naturally concluded, from this circumstance, that Henry intended to proceed in despoiling the church of her patrimony.[i]

Suppression of the lesser monasteries.

The act formerly passed, empowering the king to name thirty-two commissioners for framing a body of canon-law, was renewed; but the project was never carried into execution. Henry thought, that the present perplexity of that law encreased his authority, and kept the clergy in still greater dependance.

Farther progress was made in completing the union of Wales with England: The separate jurisdictions of several great lords or marchers, as they were called, which obstructed the course of justice in Wales, and encouraged robbery and pillaging, were abolished; and the authority of the king's courts was extended every where. Some jurisdictions of a like nature in England were also abolished[k] this session.

The commons, sensible that they had gained nothing by opposing the king's will, when he formerly endeavoured to secure the profits of wardships and liveries, were now contented to frame a law,[l] such as he dictated to them. It was enacted, that the possession of land shall be adjudged to be in those who have the use of it, not in those to whom it is transferred in trust.

14th April.

After all these laws were passed, the king dissolved the parliament; a parliament memorable, not only for the great and im-

[g] Burnet, vol. i. p. 193.   [h] It is pretended, see Hollingshed, p. 939, that ten thousand monks were turned out on the dissolution of the lesser monasteries. If so, most of them must have been Mendicants: For the revenue could not have supported near that number. The Mendicants, no doubt, still continued their former profession.   [i] 27 Hen. VIII. c. 27.   [k] 27 Hen. VIII. c. 4.   [l] 27 Hen. VIII. c. 10.

CHAPTER XXXI

portant innovations which it introduced, but also for the long time it had sitten, and the frequent prorogations which it had undergone. Henry had found it so obsequious to his will, that he did not chuse, during those religious ferments, to hazard a new election; and he continued the same parliament above six years: A practice, at that time, unusual in England.

The convocation, which sat during this session, was engaged in a very important work, the deliberating on the new translation which was projected of the scriptures. The translation given by Tindal, though corrected by himself in a new edition, was still complained of by the clergy, as inaccurate and unfaithful; and it was now proposed to them, that they should themselves publish a translation, which would not be liable to those objections.

A convocation.

The friends of the reformation asserted, that nothing could be more absurd than to conceal, in an unknown tongue, the word of God itself, and thus to counteract the will of heaven, which, for the purpose of universal salvation, had published that salutary doctrine to all nations: That if this practice were not very absurd, the artifice at least was very gross, and proved a consciousness, that the glosses and traditions of the clergy stood in direct opposition to the original text, dictated by Supreme Intelligence: That it was now necessary for the people, so long abused by interested pretensions, to see with their own eyes, and to examine whether the claims of the ecclesiastics were founded on that charter, which was on all hands acknowledged to be derived from heaven: And that, as a spirit of research and curiosity was happily revived, and men were now obliged to make a choice among the contending doctrines of different sects, the proper materials for decision, and above all, the holy scriptures, should be set before them; and the revealed will of God, which the change of language had somewhat obscured, be again, by their means, revealed to mankind.

The favourers of the ancient religion maintained, on the other hand, that the pretence of making the people see with their own eyes, was a mere cheat, and was itself a very gross artifice, by which the new preachers hoped to obtain the guidance of them, and to seduce them from those pastors, whom the laws, whom ancient establishments, whom heaven itself had appointed for their spiritual direction: That the people were, by their ignorance, their stupidity, their necessary avocations, totally unqualified to chuse their own principles; and it was a mockery to set materials before them, of which they could not possibly make any proper use: That even in the affairs of common life, and in their temporal concerns, which lay more within the compass of human reason, the laws had, in a great measure, deprived them of the right of private judgment, and had, happily for their own and the public interest, regulated their conduct and behaviour: That theological questions were placed far beyond the sphere of vulgar comprehensions; and ecclesiastics themselves, though assisted by all the advantages of education, erudition, and an assiduous study of the science, could not be fully assured of a just decision; except by the promise made them in scripture, that God would be ever present with his church, and that the gates of hell should not prevail against her: That the gross errors, adopted by the wisest heathens, proved how unfit men were to grope their own way, through this profound darkness; nor would the scriptures, if trusted to every man's judgment, be able to remedy; on the contrary, they would much augment, those fatal illusions: That sacred writ itself was involved in so much obscurity, gave rise to so many difficulties, contained so many appearing contradictions, that it was the most dangerous weapon, that could be entrusted into the hands of the ignorant and giddy multitude: That the poetical style, in which a great part of it was composed, at the same time that it occasioned uncertainty in the sense, by its multiplied tropes and figures, was sufficient to kindle the zeal of fanaticism, and thereby throw civil society into the most furious cumbustion: That a thousand sects must arise, which would pretend, each of them, to derive its tenets from the scripture; and would be able, by specious arguments, or even without specious arguments, to seduce silly women and ignorant mechanics, into a belief of the most monstrous principles: And that if ever this disorder, dangerous to the magistrate himself, received a remedy, it must be from the tacit acquiescence of the people in some new authority; and it was evidently better, without farther contest or enquiry, to adhere peaceably to ancient, and therefore the more secure, establishments.

These latter arguments, being more agreeable to ecclesiastical governments, would probably have prevailed in the convocation, had it not been for the authority of Cranmer, Latimer, and some other bishops, who were supposed to speak the king's sense of the matter. A vote was passed for publishing a new translation of the scriptures; and in three years' time the work was finished, and printed at Paris. This was deemed a great point gained by the reformers, and a considerable advancement of their cause. Farther progress was soon expected, after such important successes.

But while the retainers to the new religion were exulting in their prosperity, they met with a mortification, which seemed to blast all their hopes: Their patroness, Anne Boleyn, possessed no longer the king's favour; and soon after lost her life, by the rage of that furious monarch. Henry had persevered in his love to this *Disgrace* lady, during six years that his prosecution of the divorce lasted; *of queen* and the more obstacles he met with to the gratification of his *Anne.* passion, the more determined zeal did he exert in pursuing his purpose. But the affection, which had subsisted, and still encreased, under difficulties, had not long attained secure possession of its object, when it languished from satiety; and the king's heart was apparently estranged from his consort. Anne's enemies soon perceived the fatal change; and they were forward to widen the breach, when they found that they incurred no danger by interposing in those delicate concerns. She had been delivered of a dead son; and Henry's extreme fondness for male issue being thus, for the present, disappointed, his temper, equally violent and superstitious, was disposed to make the innocent mother answerable for the misfortune.ᵐ But the chief means which Anne's enemies employed to inflame the king against her, was his jealousy.

Anne, though she appears to have been entirely innocent, and even virtuous, in her conduct, had a certain gaiety, if not levity, of character, which threw her off her guard, and made her less circumspect than her situation required. Her education in France rendered her the more prone to those freedoms; and it was with difficulty she conformed herself to that strict ceremonial, practised in the court of England. More vain than haughty, she was pleased to see the influence of her beauty on all around her, and she indulged herself in an easy familiarity with persons, who were formerly her equals, and who might then have pretended to her friendship and good graces. Henry's dignity was offended with these popular manners; and though the lover had been entirely

ᵐ Burnet, vol. i. p. 196.

blind, the husband possessed but too quick discernment and pene-tration. Ill instruments interposed, and put a malignant inter-pretation on the harmless liberties of the queen: The viscountess of Rocheford, in particular, who was married to the queen's brother, but who lived on bad terms with her sister-in-law, insin-uated the most cruel suspicions into the king's mind; and as she was a woman of a profligate character, she paid no regard either to truth or humanity in those calumnies which she suggested. She pretended, that her own husband was engaged in a criminal corre-spondence with his sister; and not content with this imputation, she poisoned every action of the queen's, and represented each instance of favour, which she conferred on any one, as a token of affection. Henry Norris, groom of the stole, Weston and Brereton, gentlemen of the king's chamber, together with Mark Smeton, groom of the chamber, were observed to possess much of the queen's friendship; and they served her with a zeal and attach-ment, which, though chiefly derived from gratitude, might not improbably be seasoned with some mixture of tenderness for so amiable a princess. The king's jealousy laid hold of the slightest circumstance; and finding no particular object on which it could fasten, it vented itself equally on every one that came within the verge of its fury.

Had Henry's jealousy been derived from love, though it might on a sudden have proceeded to the most violent extremities, it would have been subject to many remorses and contrarieties; and might at last have served only to augment that affection, on which it was founded. But it was more a stern jealousy, fostered entirely by pride: His love was transferred to another object. Jane, daugh-ter of Sir John Seymour, and maid of honour to the queen, a young lady of singular beauty and merit, had obtained an entire as-cendant over him; and he was determined to sacrifice every thing to the gratification of this new appetite. Unlike to most monarchs, who judge lightly of the crime of gallantry, and who deem the young damsels of their court rather honoured than disgraced by their passion, he seldom thought of any other attachment than that of marriage; and in order to attain this end, he underwent more difficulties, and committed greater crimes, than those which he sought to avoid, by forming that legal connexion. And having thus entertained the design of raising his new mistress to his bed

CHAPTER XXXI

and throne, he more willingly hearkened to every suggestion, which threw any imputation of guilt on the unfortunate Anne Boleyn.

The king's jealousy first appeared openly in a tilting at Green- *1st* wich, where the queen happened to drop her handkerchief; an *May.* incident probably casual, but interpreted by him as an instance of gallantry to some of her paramours.[n] He immediately retired from the place; sent orders to confine her to her chamber; arrested Norris, Brereton, Weston, and Smeton, together with her brother, Rocheford; and threw them into prison. The queen, astonished at these instances of his fury, thought that he meant only to try her; but finding him in earnest, she reflected on his obstinate un- relenting spirit, and she prepared herself for that melancholy doom, which was awaiting her. Next day, she was sent to the Tower; and on her way thither, she was informed of her supposed offences, of which she had hitherto been ignorant: She made ear- nest protestations of her innocence; and when she entered the prison, she fell on her knees, and prayed God so to help her, as she was not guilty of the crime imputed to her. Her surprise and confusion threw her into hysterical disorders; and in that situation, she thought that the best proof of her innocence was to make an entire confession, and she revealed some indiscretions and levities, which her simplicity had equally betrayed her to commit and to avow. She owned, that she had once rallied Norris on his delaying his marriage, and had told him, that he probably expected her, when she should be a widow: She had reproved Weston, she said, for his affection to a kinswoman of hers, and his indifference towards his wife: But he told her, that she had mistaken the object of his affection, for it was herself: Upon which, she defied him.[o] She affirmed, that Smeton had never been in her chamber but twice, when he played on the harpsichord: But she acknowledged, that he had once had the boldness to tell her, that a look sufficed him. The king, instead of being satisfied with the candour and sincerity of her confession, regarded these indiscretions only as preludes to greater and more criminal intimacies.

Of all those multitudes, whom the beneficence of the queen's temper had obliged, during her prosperous fortune, no one durst

[n] Burnet, vol. i. p. 198.   [o] Strype, vol. i. p. 281.

interpose between her and the king's fury; and the person, whose advancement every breath had favoured, and every countenance had smiled upon, was now left neglected and abandoned. Even her uncle, the duke of Norfolk, preferring the connexions of party to the ties of blood, was become her most dangerous enemy; and all the retainers to the catholic religion hoped, that her death would terminate the king's quarrel with Rome, and leave him again to his natural and early bent, which had inclined him to maintain the most intimate union with the apostolic see. Cranmer alone; of all the queen's adherents, still retained his friendship for her; and, as far as the king's impetuosity permitted him, he endeavoured to moderate the violent prejudices, entertained against her.

The queen herself wrote Henry a letter from the Tower, full of the most tender expostulations, and of the warmest protestations of innocence.[p] This letter had no influence on the unrelenting mind of Henry, who was determined to pave the way for his new marriage by the death of Anne Boleyn. Norris, Weston, Brereton, and Smeton, were tried; but no legal evidence was produced against them. The chief proof of their guilt consisted in a hear-say from one lady Wingfield, who was dead. Smeton was prevailed on, by the vain hopes of life, to confess a criminal correspondence with the queen;[q] but even her enemies expected little advantage from this confession: For they never dared to confront him with her; and he was immediately executed; as were also Brereton and Weston. Norris had been much in the king's favour; and an offer of life was made him, if he would confess his crime, and accuse the queen: But he generously rejected the proposal; and said, that in his conscience he believed her entirely guiltless: But, for his part, he could accuse her of nothing, and he would rather die a thousand deaths than calumniate an innocent person.

Her trial: The queen and her brother were tried by a jury of peers, consisting of the duke of Suffolk, the marquis of Exeter, the earl of Arundel, and twenty-three more: Their uncle, the duke of Norfolk, presided as high steward. Upon what proof or pretence the crime of incest was imputed to them is unknown: The chief evidence, it is said, amounted to no more than that Rocheford had been seen to lean on her bed before some company. Part of the

[p] See note [J] at the end of the volume.   [q] Burnet, vol. i. p. 202.

CHAPTER XXXI

charge against her was, that she had affirmed to her minions, that the king never had her heart; and had said to each of them apart, that she loved him better than any person whatsoever: *Which was to the slander of the issue begotten between the king and her.* By this strained interpretation, her guilt was brought under the statute of the 25th of this reign; in which it was declared criminal to throw any slander upon the king, queen, or their issue. Such palpable absurdities were, at that time, admitted; and they were regarded by the peers of England as a sufficient reason for sacrificing an innocent queen to the cruelty of their tyrant. Though unassisted by counsel, she defended herself with presence of mind; and the spectators could not forbear pronouncing her entirely innocent. Judgment, however, was given by the court, both against the queen and lord Rocheford; and her verdict contained, that she should be burned or beheaded at the king's pleasure. When this dreadful sentence was pronounced, she was not terrified, but lifting up her hands to heaven, said, "O, Father! O, Creator! thou who art the way, the truth, and the life, thou knowest that I have not deserved this fate." And then turning to the judges, made the most pathetic declarations of her innocence.

Henry, not satisfied with this cruel vengeance, was resolved entirely to annul his marriage with Anne Boleyn, and to declare her issue illegitimate: He recalled to his memory, that, a little after her appearance in the English court, some attachment had been acknowledged between her and the earl of Northumberland, then lord Piercy; and he now questioned the nobleman with regard to these engagements. Northumberland took an oath before the two archbishops, that no contract or promise of marriage had ever passed between them: He received the sacrament upon it, before the duke of Norfolk and others of the privy council; and this solemn act he accompanied with the most solemn protestations of veracity.[r] The queen, however, was shaken by menaces of executing the sentence against her in its greatest rigour, and was prevailed on to confess in court, some lawful impediments to her marriage with the king.[s] The afflicted primate, who sat as judge, thought himself obliged by this confession, to pronounce the marriage null and invalid. Henry, in the transports of his fury, did not

[r] Herbert, p. 384.   [s] Heylin, p. 94.

perceive that his proceedings were totally inconsistent, and that, if her marriage were, from the beginning, invalid, she could not possibly be guilty of adultery.

and ex-
ecution.

The queen now prepared for suffering the death to which she was sentenced. She sent her last message to the king, and acknowledged the obligations which she owed him, in thus uniformly continuing his endeavours for her advancement: From a private gentlewoman, she said, he had first made her a marchioness, then a queen, and now, since he could raise her no higher in this world, he was sending her to be a saint in heaven. She then renewed the protestations of her innocence, and recommended her daughter to his care. Before the lieutenant of the Tower, and all who approached her, she made the like declarations; and continued to behave herself with her usual serenity, and even with chearfulness. "The executioner," she said to the lieutenant, "is, I hear, very expert; and my neck is very slender." Upon which she grasped it in her hand, and smiled. When brought, however, to the scaffold,

19th
May.

she softened her tone a little with regard to her protestations of innocence. She probably reflected, that the obstinacy of queen Catherine, and her opposition to the king's will, had much alienated him from the lady Mary: Her own maternal concern, therefore, for Elizabeth, prevailed in these last moments over that indignation, which the unjust sentence, by which she suffered, naturally excited in her. She said, that she was come to die, as she was sentenced, by the law: She would accuse none, nor say any thing of the ground upon which she was judged. She prayed heartily for the king; called him a most merciful and gentle prince; and acknowledged, that he had always been to her a good and gracious sovereign; and if any one should think proper to canvass her cause, she desired him to judge the best.[f] She was beheaded by the executioner of Calais, who was sent for as more expert than any in England. Her body was negligently thrown into a common chest of elm-tree, made to hold arrows; and was buried in the Tower.

The innocence of this unfortunate queen cannot reasonably be called in question. Henry himself, in the violence of his rage, knew not whom to accuse as her lover; and though he imputed guilt to her brother, and four persons more, he was able to bring proof

[f] Burnet, vol. i. p. 205.

against none of them. The whole tenour of her conduct forbids us to ascribe to her an abandoned character, such as is implied in the king's accusation: Had she been so lost to all prudence and sense of shame, she must have exposed herself to detection, and afforded her enemies some evidence against her. But the king made the most effectual apology for her, by marrying Jane Seymour the very day after her execution.[u] His impatience to gratify this new passion caused him to forget all regard to decency; and his cruel heart was not softened a moment by the bloody catastrophe of a person, who had so long been the object of his most tender affections.

The lady Mary thought the death of her step-mother a proper opportunity for reconciling herself to the king, who, besides other causes of disgust, had been offended with her, on account of the part which she had taken in her mother's quarrel. Her advances were not at first received; and Henry exacted from her some farther proofs of submission and obedience: He required this young princess, then about twenty years of age, to adopt his theological tenets; to acknowledge his supremacy; to renounce the pope; and to own her mother's marriage to be unlawful and incestuous. These points were of hard digestion with the princess; but after some delays, and even refusals, she was at last prevailed on to write a letter to her father,[w] containing her assent to the articles required of her: Upon which she was received into favour. But notwithstanding the return of the king's affection to the issue of his first marriage, he divested not himself of kindness towards the lady Elizabeth; and the new queen, who was blest with a singular sweetness of disposition, discovered strong proofs of attachment towards her.

The trial and conviction of queen Anne, and the subsequent events, made it necessary for the king to summon a new parliament; and he here, in his speech, made a merit to his people, that, notwithstanding the misfortunes attending his two former marriages, he had been induced, for their good, to venture on a third. The speaker received this profession with suitable gratitude; and he took thence occasion to praise the king for his wonderful gifts of grace and nature: He compared him, for justice and prudence,

8th June. A parliament.

[u] Ibidem, p. 297.   [w] Burnet, vol. i. p. 207. Strype, vol. i. p. 285.

to Solomon; for strength and fortitude to Sampson; and for beauty and comeliness to Absalom. The king very humbly replied, by the mouth of the chancellor, that he disavowed these praises; since, if he were really possessed of such endowments, they were the gift of Almighty God only. Henry found that the parliament was no less submissive in deeds than complaisant in their expressions, and that they would go the same lengths as the former in gratifying even his most lawless passions. His divorce from Anne Boleyn was ratified;[x] that queen, and all her accomplices, were attainted; the issue of both his former marriages were declared illegitimate, and it was even made treason to assert the legitimacy of either of them; to throw any slander upon the present king, queen, or their issue, was subjected to the same penalty; the crown was settled on the king's issue by Jane Seymour, or any subsequent wife; and in case he should die without children, he was impowered, by his will or letters patent, to dispose of the crown: An enormous authority, especially when entrusted to a prince so violent and capricious in his humour. Whoever, being required, refused to answer upon oath to any article of this act of settlement, was declared to be guilty of treason, and by this clause a species of political inquisition was established in the kingdom, as well as the accusations of treason multiplied to an unreasonable degree. The king was also empowered to confer on any one, by his will or letters patent, any castles, honours, liberties, or franchises; words which might have been extended to the dismembering of the kingdom, by the erection of principalities and independant jursidictions. It was also, by another act, made treason to marry, without the king's consent, any princess related in the first degree to the crown. This act was occasioned by the discovery of a design, formed by Thomas Howard, brother of the duke of Norfolk, to espouse the lady Margaret Douglas, niece to the king, by his sister the queen of Scots and the earl of Angus. Howard, as well as the young lady, was committed to the Tower. She recovered her liberty soon after; but he died in

---

[x] The parliament, in annulling the king's marriage with Anne Boleyn, gives this as a reason, "For that his highness had chosen to wife the excellent and virtuous lady Jane, who for her convenient years, excellent beauty, and pureness of flesh and blood, would be apt, God willing, to conceive issue by his highness."

confinement. An act of attainder passed against him this session of parliament.

Another accession was likewise gained to the authority of the crown: The king or any of his successors was empowered to repeat or annul, by letters patent, whatever act of parliament had been passed before he was four and twenty years of age. Whoever maintained the authority of the bishop of Rome, by word or writ, or endeavoured in any manner to restore it in England, was subjected to the penalty of a premunire; that is, his goods were forfeited, and he was put out of the protection of law. And any person who possessed any office, ecclesiastical or civil, or received any grant or charter from the crown, and yet refused to renounce the pope by oath, was declared to be guilty of treason. The renunciation prescribed runs in the style of *So help me God, all saints, and the holy evangelists.*[y] The pope, hearing of Anne Boleyn's disgrace and death, had hoped that the door was opened to a reconciliation, and had been making some advances to Henry: But this was the reception he met with. Henry was now become indifferent with regard to papal censures; and finding a great encrease of authority, as well as of revenue, to accrue from his quarrel with Rome, he was determined to persevere in his present measures. This parliament also, even more than any foregoing, convinced him how much he commanded the respect of his subjects, and what confidence he might repose in them. Though the elections had been made on a sudden, without any preparation or intrigue, the members discovered an unlimited attachment to his person and government.[z]

The extreme complaisance of the convocation, which sat at the same time with the parliament, encouraged him in his resolution of breaking entirely with the court of Rome. There was secretly a great division of sentiments in the minds of this assembly; and as the zeal of the reformers had been augmented by some late successes, the resentment of the catholics was no less excited by their fears and losses: But the authority of the king kept every one submissive and silent; and the new-assumed prerogative, the supremacy, with whose limits no one was fully acquainted, restrained even the most furious movements of theological rancour. Crom-

A convocation.

[y] 28 Hen. VIII. c. 10.   [z] Burnet, vol. i. p. 212.

wel presided as vicar-general; and though the catholic party expected, that, on the fall of queen Anne, his authority would receive
a great shock, they were surprized to find him still maintain the
same credit as before. With the vicar-general concurred Cranmer
the primate, Latimer bishop of Worcester, Shaxton of Salisbury,
Hilsey of Rochester, Fox of Hereford, Barlow of St. David's. The
opposite faction was headed by Lee archbishop of York, Stokesley
bishop of London, Tonstal of Durham, Gardiner of Winchester,
Longland of Lincoln, Sherbone of Chichester, Nix of Norwich,
and Kite of Carlisle. The former party, by their opposition to the
pope, seconded the king's ambition and love of power: The latter
party, by maintaining the ancient theological tenets, were more
conformable to his speculative principles: And both of them had
alternately the advantage of gaining on his humour, by which he
was more governed than by either of these motives.

The church in general was averse to the reformation; and the
lower house of convocation framed a list of opinions, in the whole
sixty-seven, which they pronounced erroneous, and which was a
collection of principles, some held by the ancient Lollards, others
by the modern protestants, or Gospellers, as they were sometimes
called. These opinions they sent to the upper house to be censured; but in the preamble of their representation, they discovered
the servile spirit, by which they were governed. They said, "that
they intended not to do or speak any thing which might be un-
pleasant to the king, whom they acknowledge their supreme head,
and whose commands they were resolved to obey; renouncing the
pope's usurped authority, with all his laws and inventions, now
extinguished and abolished; and addicting themselves to Almighty
God and his laws, and unto the king and the laws made within this
kingdom."[a]

The convocation came at last, after some debate, to decide
articles of faith; and their tenets were of as motley a kind as the
assembly itself, or rather as the king's system of theology, by which
they were resolved entirely to square their principles. They determined the standard of faith to consist in the Scriptures and the
three creeds, the Apostolic, Nicene, and Athanasian; and this article was a signal victory to the reformers: Auricular confession and

[a] Collier, vol. ii. p. 119.

CHAPTER XXXI

penance were admitted, a doctrine agreeable to the catholics: No
mention was made of marriage, extreme unction, confirmation, or
holy orders, as sacraments; and in this omission the influence of
the protestants appeared: The real presence was asserted, conformably to the ancient doctrine: The terms of acceptance were
established to be the merits of Christ, and the mercy and good
pleasure of God, suitably to the new principles.

So far the two sects seem to have made a fair partition, by
alternately sharing the several clauses. In framing the subsequent
articles, each of them seems to have thrown in its ingredient. The
catholics prevailed in asserting, that the use of images was war-
ranted by Scripture; the protestants, in warning the people against
idolatry, and the abuse of these sensible representations. The ancient faith was adopted in maintaining the expedience of praying
to saints; the late innovations in rejecting the peculiar patronage
of saints to any trade, profession, or course of action. The former
rites of worship, the use of holy water, and the ceremonies practised on Ash-wednesday, Palm-sunday, Good friday, and other
festivals, were still maintained; but the new refinements, which
made light of these institutions, were also adopted, by the convocation's denying that they had any immediate power of remitting sin, and by its asserting that their sole merit consisted in
promoting pious and devout dispositions in the mind.

But the article, with regard to purgatory, contains the most
curious jargon, ambiguity, and hesitation, arising from the mixture of opposite tenets. It was to this purpose: "Since according to
due order of charity, and the book of Maccabees, and divers ancient authors, it is a very good and charitable deed to pray for souls
departed; and since such a practice has been maintained in the
church from the beginning; all bishops and teachers should instruct the people not to be grieved for the continuance of the same.
But since the place where departed souls are retained, before they
reach Paradise, as well as the nature of their pains, is left uncertain
by Scripture; all such questions are to be submitted to God, to
whose mercy it is meet and convenient to commend the deceased,
trusting that he accepteth our prayers for them."[b]

These articles, when framed by the convocation, and corrected

[b] Collier, vol. ii. p. 122, & seq. Fuller. Burnet, vol. i. p. 215.

by the king, were subscribed by every member of that assembly; while, perhaps, neither there nor throughout the whole kingdom, could one man be found, except Henry himself, who had adopted precisely these very doctrines and opinions. For though there be not any contradiction in the tenets abovementioned, it had happened in England, as in all countries where factious divisions have place; a certain creed was embraced by each party, few neuters were to be found, and these consisted only of speculative or whimsical people, of whom two persons could scarcely be brought to an agreement in the same dogmas. The protestants, all of them, carried their opposition to Rome farther than those articles: None of the catholics went so far: And the king, by being able to retain the nation in such a delicate medium, displayed the utmost power of an imperious despotism, of which any history furnishes an example. To change the religion of a country, even when seconded by a party, is one of the most perilous enterprizes, which any sovereign can attempt, and often proves the most destructive to royal authority. But Henry was able to set the political machine in that furious movement, and yet regulate and even stop its career: He could say to it, Thus far shalt thou go and no farther: And he made every vote of his parliament and convocation subservient, not only to his interests and passions, but even to his greatest caprices; nay, to his most refined and most scholastic subtilties.

The concurrence of these two national assemblies served, no doubt, to encrease the king's power over the people, and raised him to an authority more absolute, than any prince, in a simple monarchy, even by means of military force, is ever able to attain. But there are certain bounds, beyond which the most slavish submission cannot be extended. All the late innovations, particularly the dissolution of the smaller monasteries, and the imminent danger to which all the rest were exposed,[c] had bred discontent among the people, and had disposed them to revolt. The expelled monks, wandering about the country, excited both the piety and compassion of men; and as the ancient religion took hold of the populace by powerful motives, suited to vulgar capacity, it was able, now that it was brought into apparent hazard, to raise the strongest zeal in its favour.[d] Discontents had even reached some of the nobility and

Discontents among the people.

[c] See note [K] at the end of the volume.   [d] Strype, vol. i. p. 249.

gentry, whose ancestors had founded the monasteries, and who placed a vanity in those institutions, as well as reaped some benefit from them, by the provisions which they afforded them for their younger children. The more superstitious were interested for the souls of their forefathers, which, they believed, must now lie, during many ages, in the torments of purgatory, for want of masses to relieve them. It seemed unjust to abolish pious institutions for the faults, real or pretended, of individuals. Even the most moderate and reasonable deemed it somewhat iniquitous, that men, who had been invited into a course of life by all the laws, human and divine, which prevailed in their country, should be turned out of their possessions, and so little care be taken of their future subsistence. And when it was observed, that the rapacity and bribery of the commissioners and others, employed in visiting the monasteries, intercepted much of the profits resulting from these confiscations, it tended much to encrease the general discontent.[e]

But the people did not break into open sedition, till the complaints of the secular clergy concurred with those of the regular. As Cromwel's person was little acceptable to the ecclesiastics; the authority, which he exercised, being so new, so absolute, so unlimited, inspired them with disgust and terror. He published, in the king's name, without the consent either of parliament or convocation, an ordonance, by which he retrenched many of the ancient holydays; prohibited several superstitions, gainful to the clergy, such as pilgrimages, images, reliques, and even ordered the incumbents in the parishes to set apart a considerable portion of their revenue for repairs, and for the support of exhibitioners and the poor of their parish. The secular priests, finding themselves thus reduced to a grievous servitude, instilled into the people those discontents, which they had long harboured in their own bosoms.

The first rising was in Lincolnshire. It was headed by Dr. Mackrel, prior of Barlings, who was disguised like a mean mechanic, and who bore the name of captain Cobler. This tumultuary army amounted to above 20,000 men;[f] but notwithstanding their number, they showed little disposition of proceeding to extremities against the king, and seemed still overawed by his authority. They acknowledged him to be supreme head of the church of England;

Insurrection.

[e] Burnet, vol. i. p. 223.　[f] Ibid. p. 227. Herbert.

but they complained of suppressing the monasteries, of evil counsellors, of persons meanly born raised to dignity, of the danger to
which the jewels and plate of their parochial churches were exposed: And they prayed the king to consult the nobility of the
realm concerning the redress of these grievances.[g] Henry was little
disposed to entertain apprehensions of danger, especially from a
low multitude, whom he despised. He sent forces against the rebels
under the command of the duke of Suffolk; and he returned them
a very sharp answer to their petition. There were some gentry,
whom the populace had constrained to take part with them, and
who kept a secret correspondence with Suffolk. They informed
him, that resentment against the king's reply was the chief cause,
which retained the malcontents in arms, and that a milder answer
would probably suppress the rebellion. Henry had levied a great
force at London, with which he was preparing to march against the
rebels; and being so well supported by power, he thought, that,
without losing his dignity, he might now show them some greater
condescension. He sent a new proclamation, requiring them to
return to their obedience, with secret assurances of pardon. This
expedient had its effect: The populace was dispersed: Mackrel and
some of their leaders fell into the king's hands, and were executed:
The greater part of the multitude retired peaceably to their usual
occupations: A few of the more obstinate fled to the north, where
they joined the insurrection that was raised in those parts.

The northern rebels, as they were more numerous, were also,
on other accounts, more formidable than those of Lincolnshire;
because the people were there more accustomed to arms, and
because of their vicinity to the Scots, who might make advantage
of these disorders. One Aske, a gentleman, had taken the command of them, and he possessed the art of governing the populace.
Their enterprize they called the *Pilgrimage of Grace:* Some priests
marched before in the habits of their order, carrying crosses in
their hands: In their banners was woven a crucifix, with the representation of a chalice, and of the five wounds of Christ:[h] They wore
on their sleeve an emblem of the five wounds, with the name of
Jesus wrought in the middle: They all took an oath, that they had
entered into the pilgrimage of grace from no other motive, than

6th
Octob.

---

[g] Herbert, p. 410. [h] Fox, vol. ii. p. 992.

their love to God, their care of the king's person and issue, their desire of purifying the nobility, of driving base-born persons from about the king, of restoring the church, and of suppressing heresy. Allured by these fair pretences, about 40,000 men from the counties of York, Durham, Lancaster, and those northern provinces, flocked to their standard; and their zeal, no less than their numbers, inspired the court with apprehensions.

The earl of Shrewsbury, moved by his regard for the king's service, raised forces, though at first without any commission, in order to oppose the rebels. The earl of Cumberland repulsed them from his castle of Skipton: Sir Ralph Evers defended Scarborow-castle against them:[i] Courtney, marquis of Exeter, the king's cousin-german, obeyed orders from court, and levied troops. The earls of Huntingdon, Derby, and Rutland, imitated his example. The rebels, however, prevailed in taking both Hull and York: They had laid siege to Pomfret castle, into which the archbishop of York and lord Darcy had thrown themselves. It was soon surrendered to them; and the prelate and nobleman, who secretly wished success to the insurrection, seemed to yield to the force imposed on them, and joined the rebels.

The duke of Norfolk was appointed general of the king's forces against the northern rebels; and as he headed the party at court, which supported the ancient religion, he was also suspected of bearing some favour to the cause, which he was sent to oppose. His prudent conduct, however, seems to acquit him of this imputation. He encamped near Doncaster, together with the earl of Shrewsbury; and as his army was small, scarcely exceeding five thousand men, he made choice of a post, where he had a river in front, the ford of which he purposed to defend against the rebels. They had intended to attack him in the morning; but during the night, there fell such violent rains as rendered the river utterly unpassable; and Norfolk wisely laid hold of the opportunity to enter into treaty with them. In order to open the door for negociation, he sent them a herald; whom Aske, their leader, received with great ceremony; he himself sitting in a chair of state, with the archbishop of York on one hand, and lord Darcy on the other. It was agreed, that two gentlemen should be dispatched to the king with proposals from

[i] Stowe, p. 574. Baker, p. 258.

the rebels; and Henry purposely delayed giving an answer, and allured them with hopes of entire satisfaction, in expectation that necessity would soon oblige them to disperse themselves. Being informed, that his artifice had, in a great measure, succeeded, he required them instantly to lay down their arms and submit to mercy; promising a pardon to all except six whom he named, and four whom he reserved to himself the power of naming. But though the greater part of the rebels had gone home for want of subsistence, they had entered into the most solemn engagements to return to their standards, in case the king's answer should not prove satisfactory. Norfolk, therefore, soon found himself in the same difficulty as before; and he opened again a negociation with the leaders of the multitude. He engaged them to send three hundred persons to Doncaster, with proposals for an accommodation; and he hoped, by intrigue and separate interests, to throw dissention among so great a number. Aske himself had intended to be one of the deputies, and he required a hostage for his security: But the king, when consulted, replied, that he knew no gentleman or other, whom he esteemed so little as to put him in pledge for such a villain. The demands of the rebels were so exorbitant, that Norfolk rejected them, and they prepared again to decide the contest by arms. They were as formidable as ever both by their numbers and spirit; and notwithstanding the small river, which lay between them and the royal army, Norfolk had great reason to dread the effects of their fury. But while they were preparing to pass the ford, rain fell a second time in such abundance, as made it impracticable for them to execute their design; and the populace, partly reduced to necessity by want of provisions, partly struck with superstition at being thus again disappointed by the same accident, suddenly dispersed themselves. The duke of Norfolk, who had received powers for that end, forwarded the dispersion, by the promise of a general amnesty; and the king ratified this act of clemency. He published, however, a manifesto against the rebels, and an answer to their complaints; in which he employed a very lofty style, suited to so haughty a monarch. He told them, that they ought no more to pretend giving a judgement with regard to government, than a blind man with regard to colours: "And we," he added, "with our whole council, think it right

9th Dec.

strange, that ye, who be but brutes and inexpert folk, do take upon you to appoint us, who be meet or not for our council."

As this pacification was not likely to be of long continuance, Norfolk was ordered to keep his army together, and to march into the northern parts, in order to exact a general submission. Lord Darcy, as well as Aske, was sent for to court; and the former, upon his refusal or delay to appear, was thrown into prison. Every place was full of jealousy and complaints. A new insurrection broke out, headed by Musgrave and Tilby; and the rebels besieged Carlisle with 8000 men. Being repulsed by that city, they were encountered in their retreat by Norfolk, who put them to flight; and having *1537.* made prisoners of all their officers, except Musgrave, who escaped, he instantly put them to death by martial law, to the number of seventy persons. An attempt, made by Sir Francis Bigot and Halam to surprize Hull, met with no better success; and several other risings were suppressed by the vigilance of Norfolk. The king, enraged by these multiplied revolts, was determined not to adhere to the general pardon, which he had granted; and from a movement of his usual violence, he made the innocent suffer for the guilty. Norfolk, by command from his master, spread the royal banner, and, wherever he thought proper, executed martial law in the punishment of offenders. Besides Aske, leader of the first insurrection, Sir Robert Constable, Sir John Bulmer, Sir Thomas Piercy, Sir Stephen Hamilton, Nicholas Tempest, William Lumley, and many others, were thrown into prison; and most of them were condemned and executed. Lord Hussey was found guilty as an accomplice in the insurrection of Lincolnshire, and was executed at Lincoln. Lord Darcy, though he pleaded compulsion, and appealed, for his justification, to a long life, spent in the service of the crown, was beheaded on Tower-hill. Before his execution, he accused Norfolk of having secretly encouraged the rebels; but Henry, either sensible of that nobleman's services and convinced of his fidelity, or afraid to offend one of such extensive power and great capacity, rejected the information. Being now satiated with punishing the rebels, he published anew a general pardon, to which he faithfully adhered;[k] and he erected by patent a court of

---

[k] Herbert, p. 428.

justice at York, for deciding law-suits in the northern counties: A demand which had been made by the rebels.

October 12. Birth of Prince Edward, and death of Q. Jane.

Soon after this prosperous success, an event happened, which crowned Henry's joy, the birth of a son, who was baptized by the name of Edward. Yet was not his happiness without allay: The queen died two days after.[l] But a son had so long been ardently wished for by Henry, and was now become so necessary, in order to prevent disputes with regard to the succession, after the acts declaring the two princesses illegitimate, that the king's affliction was drowned in his joy, and he expressed great satisfaction on the occasion. The prince, not six days old, was created prince of Wales, duke of Cornwal, and earl of Chester. Sir Edward Seymour, the queen's brother, formerly made Lord Beauchamp, was raised to the dignity of earl of Hertford. Sir William Fitz Williams, high admiral, was created earl of Southampton; Sir William Paulet, Lord St. John; Sir John Russel, Lord Russel.

1538.

The suppression of the rebellion and the birth of a son, as they confirmed Henry's authority at home, encreased his consideration among foreign princes, and made his alliance be courted by all parties. He maintained, however, a neutrality in the wars, which were carried on, with various success, and without any decisive event, between Charles and Francis; and though inclined more to favour the latter, he determined not to incur, without necessity, either hazard or expence on his account. A truce, concluded about this time between these potentates, and afterwards prolonged for ten years, freed him from all anxiety on account of his ally, and re-established the tranquillity of Europe.

Henry continued desirous of cementing a union with the German protestants; and for that purpose, he sent Christopher Mount to a congress which they held at Brunswick; but that minister made no great progress in his negociation. The princes wished to know, what were the articles in their confession which Henry disliked; and they sent new ambassadors to him, who had orders both to negociate and to dispute. They endeavoured to convince the king, that he was guilty of a mistake, in administering the eucharist in one kind only, in allowing private masses, and in requiring the

---

[l] Strype, vol. ii. p. 5.

CHAPTER XXXI

celibacy of the clergy.[m] Henry would by no means acknowledge any error in these particulars; and was displeased that they should pretend to prescribe rules to so great a monarch and theologian. He found arguments and syllogisms enow to defend his cause; and he dismissed the ambassador without coming to any conclusion. Jealous also least his own subjects should become such theologians as to question his tenets, he used great precaution in publishing that translation of the scripture which was finished this year. He would only allow a copy of it to be deposited in some parish churches, where it was fixed by a chain: And he took care to inform the people by proclamation, "That this indulgence was not the effect of his duty, but of his goodness and his liberality to them; who therefore should use it moderately, for the encrease of virtue, not of strife: And he ordered that no man should read the Bible aloud, so as to disturb the priest, while he sang mass, nor presume to expound doubtful places, without advice from the learned." In this measure, as in the rest, he still halted half way between the catholics and the protestants.

There was only one particular, in which Henry was quite decisive; because he was there impelled by his avarice, or more properly speaking, his rapacity, the consequence of his profusion: This measure was the entire destruction of the monasteries. The *Suppression of the greater monasteries.* present opportunity seemed favourable for that great enterprize, while the suppression of the late rebellion fortified and encreased the royal authority; and as some of the abbots were suspected of having encouraged the insurrection, and of corresponding with the rebels, the king's resentment was farther incited by that motive. A new visitation was appointed of all the monasteries in England; and a pretence only being wanted for their suppression, it was easy for a prince, possessed of such unlimited power, and seconding the present humour of a great part of the nation, to find or feign one. The abbots and monks knew the danger, to which they were exposed; and having learned, by the example of the lesser monasteries, that nothing could withstand the king's will, they were most of them induced, in expectation of better treatment, to make a voluntary resignation of their houses. Where

[m] Collier, vol. ii. p. 145. from the Cott. Lib. Cleopatra, E. 5. fol. 173.

promises failed of effect, menaces and even extreme violence were employed; and as several of the abbots, since the breach with Rome, had been named by the court, with a view to this event, the king's intentions were the more easily effected. Some also, having secretly embraced the doctrine of the reformation, were glad to be freed from their vows; and on the whole the design was conducted with such success, that, in less than two years, the king had got possession of all the monastic revenues.

In several places, particularly in the county of Oxford, great interest was made to preserve some convents of women, who, as they lived in the most irreproachable manner, justly merited, it was thought, that their houses should be saved from the general destruction.[n] There appeared also great difference between the case of nuns and that of friars; and the one institution might be laudable, while the other was exposed to much blame. The males of all ranks, if endowed with industry, might be of service to the public; and none of them could want employment, suited to his station and capacity. But a woman of a family, who failed of a settlement in the married state, an accident to which such persons were more liable than women of lower station, had really no rank which she properly filled: and a convent was a retreat both honourable and agreeable, from the inutility and often want, which attended her situation. But the king was determined to abolish monasteries of every denomination; and probably thought, that these ancient establishments would be the sooner forgotten, if no remains of them, of any kind, were allowed to subsist in the kingdom.

The better to reconcile the people to this great innovation, stories were propagated of the detestable lives of the friars in many of the convents; and great care was taken to defame those whom the court had determined to ruin. The reliques also and other superstitions, which had so long been the object of the people's veneration, were exposed to their ridicule; and the religious spirit, now less bent on exterior observances and sensible objects, was encouraged in this new direction. It is needless to be prolix in an enumeration of particulars: Protestant historians mention on this occasion with great triumph the sacred repositories of convents; the parings of St. Edmond's toes; some of the coals that roasted St.

[n] Burnet, vol. i. p. 328.

CHAPTER XXXI

Laurence; the girdle of the Virgin shown in eleven several places; two or three heads of St. Ursula; the felt of St. Thomas of Lancaster, an infallible cure for the head-ach; part of St. Thomas of Canterbury's shirt, much reverenced by big-bellied women; some reliques, an excellent preventive against rain; others, a remedy to weeds in corn. But such fooleries, as they are to be found in all ages and nations, and even took place during the most refined periods of antiquity, form no particular or violent reproach to the catholic religion.

There were also discovered, or said to be discovered, in the monasteries some impostures of a more artificial nature. At Hales, in the county of Gloucester, there had been shown, during several ages, the blood of Christ brought from Jerusalem; and it is easy to imagine the veneration with which such a relique was regarded. A miraculous circumstance also attended this miraculous relique; the sacred blood was not visible to any one in mortal sin, even when set before him; and till he had performed good works sufficient for his absolution, it would not deign to discover itself to him. At the dissolution of the monastery, the whole contrivance was detected. Two of the monks, who were let into the secret, had taken the blood of a duck, which they renewed every week: They put it in a phial, one side of which consisted of thin and transparent chrystal, the other of thick and opaque. When any rich pilgrim arrived, they were sure to show him the dark side of the phial, till masses and offerings had expiated his offences; and then finding his money, or patience, or faith, nearly exhausted, they made him happy by turning the phial.[o]

A miraculous crucifix had been kept at Boxley in Kent, and bore the appellation of the *Rood of Grace*. The lips, and eyes, and head of the image moved on the approach of its votaries. Hilsey, bishop of Rochester, broke the crucifix at St. Paul's cross, and showed to the whole people the springs and wheels by which it had been secretly moved. A great wooden idol revered in Wales, called Darvel Gatheren, was also brought to London, and cut in pieces: And by a cruel refinement in vengeance, it was employed as fuel to burn friar Forest,[p] who was punished for denying the suprem-

[o] Herbert, p. 431, 432. Stowe, p. 575. [p] Goodwin's Annals. Stowe, p. 575. Herbert. Baker, p. 286.

acy, and for some pretended heresies. A finger of St. Andrew's, covered with a thin plate silver, had been pawned by a convent for a debt of forty pounds; but as the king's commissioners refused to pay the debt, people made themselves merry with the poor creditor, on account of his pledge.

But of all the instruments of ancient superstition, no one was so zealously destroyed as the shrine of Thomas a Becket, commonly called St. Thomas of Canterbury. This saint owed his canonization to the zealous defence, which he had made for clerical privileges; and on that account also, the monks had extremely encouraged the devotion of pilgrimages towards his tomb, and numberless were the miracles, which, they pretended, his reliques wrought in favour of his devout votaries. They raised his body once a year; and the day on which this ceremony was performed, which was called the day of his translation, was a general holiday: Every fiftieth year there was celebrated a jubilee to his honour, which lasted fifteen days: Plenary indulgences were then granted to all that visited his tomb; and a hundred thousand pilgrims have been registered at a time in Canterbury. The devotion towards him had quite effaced in that place the adoration of the Deity: nay, even that of the Virgin. At God's altar, for instance, there were offered in one year three pounds two shillings and six pence; at the Virgin's, sixty-three pounds five shillings and six pence; at St. Thomas's, eight hundred and thirty-two pounds twelve shillings and three pence. But next year, the disproportion was still greater: There was not a penny offered at God's altar; the Virgin's gained only four pounds one shilling and eight pence; but St. Thomas had got for his share nine hundred and fifty-four pounds six shillings and three pence.[q] Lewis VII, of France had made a pilgrimage to this miraculous tomb, and had bestowed on the shrine a jewel, esteemed the richest in Christendom. It is evident, how obnoxious to Henry a saint of this character must appear, and how contrary to all his projects for degrading the authority of the court of Rome. He not only pillaged the rich shrine, dedicated to St. Thomas: he made the saint himself be cited to appear in court, and be tried and condemned as a traitor: He ordered his name to be struck out of the calendar; the office for his festival to be expunged from all breviaries; his bones to be burned, and the ashes to be thrown in the air.

[q] Burnet, vol. i. p. 244.

CHAPTER XXXI

On the whole, the king, at different times, suppressed six hundred and forty-five monasteries: Of which twenty-eight had abbots, that enjoyed a seat in parliament. Ninety colleges were demolished in several counties; two thousand three hundred and seventy-four chantries and free chapels: A hundred and ten hospitals. The whole revenue of these establishments amounted to one hundred and sixty-one thousand one hundred pounds.[r] It is worthy of observation, that all the lands and possessions and revenue of England had, a little before this period, been rated at four millions a year; so that the revenues of the monks, even comprehending the lesser monasteries, did not exceed the twentieth part of the national income: A sum vastly inferior to what is commonly apprehended. The lands belonging to the convents, were usually let at very low rent; and the farmers, who regarded themselves as a species of proprietors, took always care to renew their leases before they expired.[s]

Great murmurs were every where excited on account of these violences; and men much questioned, whether priors and monks, who were only trustees or tenants for life, could, by any deed, however voluntary, transfer to the king the entire property of their estates. In order to reconcile the people to such mighty innovations, they were told, that the king would never thenceforth have occasion to levy taxes, but would be able from the abbey lands alone, to bear, during war as well as peace, the whole charges of government.[t] While such topics were employed to appease the populace, Henry took an effectual method of interesting the nobility and gentry in the success of his measures:[u] He either made a gift of the revenues of convents to his favourites and courtiers, or sold them at low prices, or exchanged them for other lands on very disadvantageous terms. He was so profuse in these liberalities, that he is said to have given a woman the whole revenue of a convent, as a reward for making a pudding, which happened to gratify his palate.[w] He also settled pensions on the abbots and priors, proportioned to their former revenues or to their merits; and gave each monk a yearly pension of eight marks: He erected six new bishoprics, Westminster, Oxford, Peterborow, Bristol, Chester, and Gloucester; of which five subsist at this day: And by all these means

[r] Lord Herbert, Camden, Speed.   [s] See note [L] at the end of the volume.   [t] Coke's 4th Inst. fol. 44.   [u] Dugdale's Warwickshire, p. 800.
[w] Fuller.

of expence and dissipation, the profit, which the king reaped by the seizure of church lands, fell much short of vulgar opinion. As the ruin of convents had been foreseen some years before it happened, the monks had taken care to secrete most of their stock, furniture, and plate; so that the spoils of the great monasteries bore not, in these respects, any proportion to those of the lesser.

Beside the lands, possessed by the monasteries, the regular clergy enjoyed a considerable part of the benefices of England, and of the tythes, annexed to them; and these were also at this time transferred to the crown, and by that means passed into the hands of laymen: An abuse which many zealous churchmen regard as the most criminal sacrilege. The monks were formerly much at their ease in England, and enjoyed revenues, which exceeded the regular and stated expence of the house. We read of the abbey of Chertsey in Surrey, which possessed 744 pounds a year, though it contained only fourteen monks: That of Furnese, in the county of Lincoln, was valued at 960 pounds a year, and contained but thirty.[x] In order to dissipate their revenues, and support popularity, the monks lived in a hospitable manner; and besides the poor, maintained from their offals, there were many decayed gentlemen, who passed their lives in travelling from convent to convent, and were entirely subsisted at the tables of the friars. By this hospitality, as much as by their own inactivity, did the convents prove nurseries of idleness; but the king, not to give offence by too sudden an innovation, bound the new proprietors of abbey lands, to support the ancient hospitality. But this engagement was fulfilled in very few places, and for a very short time.

It is easy to imagine the indignation, with which the intelligence of all these acts of violence was received at Rome; and how much the ecclesiastics of that court, who had so long kept the world in subjection by high sounding epithets, and by holy execrations, would now vent their rhetoric against the character and conduct of Henry. The pope was at last incited to publish the bull, which had been passed against that monarch; and in a public manner he delivered over his soul to the devil, and his dominions to the first invader. Libels were dispersed, in which he was anew compared to the most furious persecutors in antiquity; and the preference was

[x] Burnet, vol. i. p. 237.

CHAPTER XXXI

now given to their side: He had declared war with the dead, whom the pagans themselves respected; was at open hostility with heaven; and had engaged in professed enmity with the whole host of saints and angels. Above all, he was often reproached with his resemblance to the emperor Julian, whom, it was said, he imitated in his apostacy and learning, though he fell short of him in morals. Henry could distinguish in some of these libels the stile and animosity of his kinsman, Pole; and he was thence incited to vent his rage, by every possible expedient, on that famous cardinal.

Reginald de la Pole, or Reginald Pole, was descended from the royal family, being fourth son of the countess of Salisbury, daughter of the duke of Clarence. He gave in early youth indications of that fine genius, and generous disposition, by which, during his whole life, he was so much distinguished; and Henry, having conceived great friendship for him, intended to raise him to the highest ecclesiastical dignities; and, as a pledge of future favours, he conferred on him the deanry of Exeter,[y] the better to support him in his education. Pole was carrying on his studies in the university of Paris, at the time when the king solicited the suffrages of that learned body in favour of his divorce; but though applied to by the English agent, he declined taking any part in the affair. Henry bore this neglect with more temper than was natural to him; and he appeared unwilling, on that account, to renounce all friendship with a person, whose virtues and talents, he hoped, would prove useful, as well as ornamental, to his court and kingdom. He allowed him still to possess his deanry, and gave him permission to finish his studies at Padua: He even paid him some court, in order to bring him into his measures; and wrote to him, while in that university, desiring him to give his opinion freely, with regard to the late measures taken in England, for abolishing the papal authority. Pole had now contracted an intimate friendship with all persons eminent for dignity or merit in Italy, Sadolet, Bembo, and other revivers of true taste and learning; and he was moved by these connections, as well as by religious zeal, to forget, in some respect, the duty which he owed to Henry, his benefactor, and his sovereign. He replied, by writing a treatise of *the unity of the church,* in which he inveighed against the king's supremacy, his divorce,

Cardinal Pole.

[y] Goodwin's Annals.

his second marriage; and he even exhorted the emperor to revenge on him the injury done to the Imperial family, and to the
catholic cause. Henry, though provoked beyond measure at this
outrage, dissembled his resentment; and he sent a message to Pole,
desiring him to return to England, in order to explain certain
passages in his book, which he found somewhat obscure and difficult. Pole was on his guard against this insidious invitation, and was
determined to remain in Italy, where he was universally beloved.

The pope and emperor thought themselves obliged to provide
for a man of Pole's eminence and dignity, who, in support of their
cause, had sacrificed all his pretensions to fortune in his own
country. He was created a cardinal; and though he took not higher
orders than those of a deacon, he was sent legate into Flanders
about the year 1536.[z] Henry was sensible, that Pole's chief intention in chusing that employment, was to foment the mutinous
disposition of the English catholics; and he therefore remonstrated in so vigorous a manner with the queen of Hungary, regent
of the Low Countries, that she dismissed the legate, without allowing him to exercise his functions. The enmity, which he bore to
Pole, was now as open, as it was violent; and the cardinal, on his
part, kept no farther measures in his intrigues against Henry. He
is even suspected of having aspired to the crown, by means of a
marriage with the lady Mary; and the king was every day more
alarmed by informations, which he received, of the correspondence maintained in England by that fugitive. Courtney, marquis
of Exeter, had entered into a conspiracy with him; Sir Edward
Nevil, brother to the lord Abergavenny, Sir Nicholas Carew, master of horse, and knight of the garter; Henry de la Pole, lord
Montacute, and Sir Geoffrey de la Pole, brothers to the cardinal.
These persons were indicted, and tried, and convicted, before lord
Audley, who presided in the trial, as high steward, they were all
executed, except Sir Geoffrey de la Pole, who was pardoned; and
he owed this grace to his having first carried to the king secret
intelligence of the conspiracy. We know little concerning the justice or iniquity of the sentence pronounced against these men: We
only know, that the condemnation of a man, who was, at that time,

[z] Herbert.

CHAPTER XXXI

prosecuted by the court, forms no presumption of his guilt; though, as no historian of credit mentions, in the present case, any complaint occasioned by these trials, we may presume, that sufficient evidence was produced against the marquis of Exeter, and his associates.[a]

[a] Herbert in Kennet, p. 216.

XXXII

Disputation with Lambert –
A Parliament – Law of the
six articles – Proclamations made equal to
laws – Settlement of the succession –
King's projects of marriage – He marries
Anne of Cleves – He dislikes her –
A Parliament – Fall of Cromwel – His
execution – King's divorce from Anne
of Cleves – His marriage with Catherine
Howard – State of affairs in Scotland –
Discovery of the Queen's dissolute
life – A Parliament –
Ecclesiastical affairs

1538.

THE ROUGH HAND of Henry seemed well adapted for rending asunder those bands, by which the ancient superstition had fastened itself on the kingdom; and though, after renouncing the pope's supremacy and suppressing monasteries, most of the political ends of reformation were already attained, few people expected that he would stop at those innovations. The spirit of opposition, it was thought, would carry him to the utmost extremities against the church of Rome; and lead him to declare war against the whole doctrine and worship, as well as discipline, of that

CHAPTER XXXII

mighty hierarchy. He had formerly appealed from the pope to a general council; but now, when a general council was summoned to meet at Mantua, he previously renounced all submission to it, as summoned by the pope, and lying entirely under subjection to that spiritual usurper. He engaged his clergy to make a declaration to the like purpose; and he had prescribed to them many other deviations from ancient tenets and practices. Cranmer took advantage of every opportunity to carry him on in this course; and while queen Jane lived, who favoured the reformers, he had, by means of her insinuation and address, been successful in his endeavours. After her death, Gardiner, who was returned from his embassy to France, kept the king more in suspence; and by feigning an unlimited submission to his will, was frequently able to guide him to his own purposes. Fox, bishop of Hereford, had supported Cranmer in his schemes for a more thorough reformation; but his death had made way for the promotion of Bonner, who, though he had hitherto seemed a furious enemy to the court of Rome, was determined to sacrifice every thing to present interest, and had joined the confederacy of Gardiner, and the partizans of the old religion. Gardiner himself, it is believed, had secretly entered into measures with the pope, and even with the emperor; and in concert with these powers, he endeavoured to preserve, as much as possible, the ancient faith and worship.

Henry was so much governed by passion, that nothing could have retarded his animosity and opposition against Rome, but some other passion, which stopped his career, and raised him new objects of animosity. Though he had gradually, since the commencement of his scruples with regard to his first marriage, been changing the tenets of that theological system, in which he had been educated, he was no less positive and dogmatical in the few articles which remained to him, than if the whole fabric had continued entire and unshaken. And though he stood alone in his opinion, the flattery of courtiers had so enflamed his tyrannical arrogance, that he thought himself entitled to regulate, by his own particular standard, the religious faith of the whole nation. The point, on which he chiefly rested his orthodoxy, happened to be the real presence; that very doctrine, in which, among the numberless victories of superstition over common sense, her triumph is the most signal and egregious. All departure from this principle he held to be heretical and detestable; and nothing, he thought, would be more honourable for him, than while he broke off all connexions with the Roman pontiff, to maintain, in this essential article, the purity of the catholic faith.

Disputation with Lambert.

There was one Lambert,[b] a school-master in London, who had been questioned and confined for unsound opinions by archbishop Warham; but, upon the death of that prelate, and the change of counsels at court, he had been released. Not terrified with the danger which he had incurred, he still continued to promulgate his tenets; and having heard Dr. Taylor, afterwards bishop of Lincoln, defend in a sermon the corporal presence, he could not forbear expressing to Taylor his dissent from that doctrine; and he drew up his objections under ten several heads. Taylor communicated the paper to Dr. Barnes, who happened to be a Lutheran, and who maintained that though the substance of bread and wine remained in the sacrament, yet the real body and blood of Christ were there also, and were, in a certain mysterious manner, incorporated with the material elements. By the present laws and practice Barnes was no less exposed to the stake than Lambert; yet such was the persecuting rage which prevailed, that he determined to bring this man to condign punishment; because, in their common departure from the ancient faith, he had dared to go one step farther than himself. He engaged Taylor to accuse Lambert before Cranmer and Latimer, who, whatever their private opinion might be on these points, were obliged to conform themselves to the standard of orthodoxy, established by Henry. When Lambert was cited before these prelates, they endeavoured to bend him to a recantation; and they were surprised, when instead of complying, he ventured to appeal to the king.

The king, not displeased with an opportunity, where he could at once exert his supremacy, and display his learning, accepted the appeal; and resolved to mix, in a very unfair manner, the magistrate with the disputant. Public notice was given, that he intended to enter the lists with the schoolmaster: Scaffolds were erected in Westminster-hall, for the accommodation of the audience: Henry appeared on his throne, accompanied with all the ensigns of majesty: The prelates were placed on his right hand: The temporal

[b] Fox, vol. ii. p. 396.

peers on his left. The judges and most eminent lawyers had a place assigned them behind the bishops: The courtiers of greatest distinction behind the peers: And in the midst of this splendid assembly was produced the unhappy Lambert, who was required to defend his opinions against his royal antagonist.[c]

The bishop of Chichester opened the conference, by saying, that Lambert, being charged with heretical pravity, had appealed from his bishop to the king; as if he expected more favour from this application, and as if the king could ever be induced to protect a heretic: That though his majesty had thrown off the usurpations of the see of Rome; had disincorporated some idle monks, who lived like drones in a bee-hive; had abolished the idolatrous worship of images; had published the bible in English, for the instruction of all his subjects; and had made some lesser alterations, which every one must approve of; yet was he determined to maintain the purity of the catholic faith, and to punish with the utmost severity all departure from it: And that he had taken the present opportunity, before so learned and grave an audience, of convincing Lambert of his errors; but if he still continued obstinate in them, he must expect the most condign punishment.[d]

After this preamble, which was not very encouraging, the king asked Lambert, with a stern countenance, what his opinion was of Christ's corporal presence in the sacrament of the altar; and when Lambert began his reply with some compliment to his majesty, he rejected the praise with disdain and indignation. He afterwards pressed Lambert with arguments, drawn from Scripture and the schoolmen: The audience applauded the force of his reasoning, and the extent of his erudition: Cranmer seconded his proofs by some new topics: Gardiner entered the lists as a support to Cranmer: Tonstal took up the argument after Gardiner: Stokesley brought fresh aid to Tonstal: Six bishops more appeared successively in the field after Stokesley. And the disputation, if it deserve the name, was prolonged for five hours; till Lambert, fatigued, confounded, brow-beaten, and abashed, was at last reduced to silence. The king, then returning to the charge, asked him whether he were convinced? and he proposed, as a concluding argument, this interesting question, Whether he were resolved to live or to

[c] Fox, vol. ii. p. 426.   [d] Goodwin's Annals.

die? Lambert, who possessed that courage which consists in obstinacy, replied, that he cast himself wholly on his majesty's clemency: The king told him, that he would be no protector of heretics; and therefore, if that were his final answer, he must expect to be committed to the flames. Cromwel, as vicegerent pronounced the sentence against him.[e]

Lambert, whose vanity had probably incited him the more to persevere on account of the greatness of this public appearance, was not daunted by the terrors of the punishment, to which he was condemned. His executioners took care to make the sufferings of a man who had personally opposed the king, as cruel as possible: He was burned at a slow fire; his legs and thighs were consumed to the stumps; and when there appeared no end of his torments, some of the guards, more merciful than the rest, lifted him on their halberts, and threw him into the flames, where he was consumed. While they were employed in this friendly office, he cried aloud several times, *None but Christ, none but Christ;* and these words were in his mouth when he expired.[f]

Some few days before this execution, four Dutch anabaptists, three men and a woman, had faggots tied to their backs at Paul's Cross, and were burned in that manner. And a man and a woman of the same sect and country were burned in Smithfield.[g]

1539.

It was the unhappy fate of the English, during this age, that, when they laboured under any grievance, they had not the satisfaction of expecting redress from parliament: On the contrary, they had reason to dread each meeting of that assembly, and were then sure of having tyranny converted into law, and aggravated, perhaps, with some circumstance, which the arbitrary prince and his ministers had not hitherto devised, or did not think proper, of themselves, to carry into execution. This abject servility never appeared more conspicuously than in a new parliament, which the king now assembled, and which, if he had been so pleased, might have been the last that ever sat in England. But he found them too useful instruments of dominion, ever to entertain thoughts of giving them a total exclusion.

A parliament. 28th April.

[e] See note [M] at the end of the volume.   [f] Fox's Acts and Monuments, p. 427. Burnet.   [g] Stowe, p. 556.

CHAPTER XXXII

The chancellor opened the parliament by informing the house of lords, that it was his majesty's earnest desire to extirpate from his kingdom all diversity of opinion in matters of religion; and as this undertaking was, he owned, important and arduous, he desired them to chuse a committee from among themselves, who might draw up certain articles of faith, and communicate them afterwards to the parliament. The lords named the vicar general, Cromwel, now created a peer, the archbishops of Canterbury and York, the bishops of Durham, Carlisle, Worcester, Bath and Wells, Bangor, and Ely. The house might have seen what a hopeful task they had undertaken: This small committee itself was agitated with such diversity of opinion, that it could come to no conclusion. The duke of Norfolk then moved in the house, that since there were no hopes of having a report from the committee, the articles of faith, intended to be established, should be reduced to six; and a new committee be appointed to draw an act with regard to them. As this peer was understood to speak the sense of the king, his motion was immediately complied with; and, after a short prorogation, the bill of the *six articles,* or the bloody bill, as the protestants justly termed it, was introduced, and having passed the two houses, received the royal assent.

In this law, the doctrine of the real presence was established, the communion in one kind, the perpetual obligation of vows of chastity, the utility of private masses, the celibacy of the clergy, and the necessity of auricular confession. The denial of the first article, with regard to the real presence, subjected the person to death by fire, and to the same forfeiture as in cases of treason; and admitted not the privilege of abjuring: An unheard-of severity, and unknown to the inquisition itself. The denial of any of the other five articles, even though recanted, was punishable by the forfeiture of goods and chattels, and imprisonment during the king's pleasure: An obstinate adherence to error, or a relapse, was adjudged to be felony, and punishable with death. The marriage of priests was subjected to the same punishment. Their commerce with women was, on the first offence, forfeiture and imprisonment; on the second, death. The abstaining from confession, and from receiving the eucharist at the accustomed times, subjected the person to fine, and to imprisonment during the king's pleasure; and if the

Law of the six articles.

criminal persevered after conviction, he was punishable by death and forfeiture, as in cases of felony.[h] Commissioners were to be appointed by the king, for enquiring into these heresies and irregular practices; and the criminals were to be tried by a jury.

The king, in framing this law, laid his oppressive hand on both parties; and even the catholics had reason to complain, that the friars and nuns, though dismissed their convent, should be capriciously restrained to the practice of celibacy:[i] But as the protestants were chiefly exposed to the severity of the statute, the misery of adversaries, according to the usual maxims of party, was regarded by the adherents to the ancient religion, as their own prosperity and triumph. Cranmer had the courage to oppose this bill in the house; and though the king desired him to absent himself, he could not be prevailed on to give this proof of compliance.[k] Henry was accustomed to Cranmer's freedom and sincerity; and being convinced of the general rectitude of his intentions, gave him an unusual indulgence in this particular, and never allowed even a whisper against him. That prelate, however, was now obliged, in obedience to the statute, to dismiss his wife, the niece of Osiander, a famous divine of Nuremburg;[l] and Henry, satisfied with this proof of submission, showed him his former countenance and favour. Latimer and Shaxton threw up their bishoprics on account of the law, and were committed to prison.

*Procla-
mations
made
equal to
laws.*

The parliament, having thus resigned all their religious liberties, proceeded to an entire surrender of their civil; and without scruple or deliberation they made by one act a total subversion of the English constitution. They gave to the king's proclamation the same force as to a statute enacted by parliament; and to render the matter worse, if possible, they framed this law, as if it were only declaratory, and were intended to explain the natural extent of royal authority. The preamble contains, that the king had formerly set forth several proclamations which froward persons had wilfully contemned, not considering what a king by his royal power may do; that this licence might encourage offenders not only to disobey the laws of Almighty God, but also to dishonour the king's most royal majesty, *who may full ill bear it;* that sudden emergencies often

[h] 31 Hen. VIII. c. 14. Herbert in Kennet, p. 219.   [i] See note [N] at the end of the volume.   [k] Burnet, vol. i. p. 249, 270. Fox, vol. ii. p. 1037.
[l] Herbert in Kennet, p. 219.

occur, which require speedy remedies, and cannot await the slow assembling and deliberations of parliament; and that, though the king was empowered, by his authority, derived from God, to consult the public good on these occasions, yet the opposition of refractory subjects might push him to extremity and violence: For these reasons, the parliament, that they might remove all occasion of doubt, ascertained by a statute this prerogative of the crown, and enabled his majesty, with the advice of his council, to set forth proclamations, enjoining obedience under whatever pains and penalties he should think proper: And these proclamations were to have the force of perpetual laws.[m]

What proves either a stupid or a wilful blindness in the parliament is, that they pretended, even after this statute, to maintain some limitations in the government; and they enacted, that no proclamation should deprive any person of his lawful possessions, liberties, inheritances, privileges, franchises; not yet infringe any common law or laudable custom of the realm. They did not consider, that no penalty could be inflicted on the disobeying of proclamations, without invading some liberty or property of the subject; and that the power of enacting new laws, joined to the dispensing power, then exercised by the crown, amounted to a full legislative authority. It is true, the kings of England had always been accustomed, from their own authority, to issue proclamations, and to exact obedience to them; and this prerogative was, no doubt, a strong symptom of absolute government: But still there was a difference between a power, which was exercised on a particular emergence, and which must be justified by the present expedience or necessity; and an authority conferred by a positive statute, which could no longer admit of controul or limitation.

Could any act be more opposite to the spirit of liberty than this law, it would have been another of the same parliament. They passed an act of attainder, not only against the marquis of Exeter, the lords Montacute, Darcy, Hussey, and others, who had been legally tried and condemned; but also against some persons, of the highest quality, who had never been accused, or examined, or convicted. The violent hatred, which Henry bore to cardinal Pole, had extended itself to all his friends and relations; and his mother

---

[m] 31 Hen. VIII. c. 8.

in particular, the countess of Salisbury, had, on that account, become extremely obnoxious to him. She was also accused of having employed her authority with her tenants, to hinder them from reading the new translation of the Bible; of having procured bulls from Rome, which, it is said, had been seen at Coudray, her country seat; and of having kept a correspondence with her son, the cardinal: But Henry found, either that these offences could not be proved, or that they would not by law be subjected to such severe punishments as he desired to inflict upon her. He resolved, therefore, to proceed in a more summary and more tyrannical manner; and for that purpose, he sent Cromwel, who was but too obsequious to his will, to ask the judges, whether the parliament could attaint a person, who was forth-coming, without giving him any trial, or citing him to appear before them?[n] The judges replied, that it was a dangerous question, and that the high court of parliament ought to give the example to inferior courts, of proceeding according to justice: No inferior court could act in that arbitrary manner, and they thought that the parliament never would. Being pressed to give a more explicit answer, they replied, that, if a person were attainted in that manner, the attainder could never afterwards be brought in question, but must remain good in law. Henry learned by this decision, that such a method of proceeding, though directly contrary to all the principles of equity, was yet practicable; and this being all he was anxious to know, he resolved to employ it against the countess of Salisbury. Cromwel showed to the house of peers a banner, on which were embroidered the five wounds of Christ, the symbol, chosen by the northern rebels; and this banner, he affirmed, was found in the countess's house.[o] No other proof seems to have been produced, in order to ascertain her guilt: The parliament, without farther enquiry, passed a bill of attainder against her; and they involved in the same bill, without any better proof, as far as appears, Gertrude marchioness of Exeter, Sir Adrian Fortescue, and Sir Thomas Dingley. These two gentlemen were executed. The marchioness was pardoned, and survived the king; the countess received a reprieve.

The only beneficial act, passed this session, was that by which the parliament confirmed the surrender of the monasteries; yet

[n] Coke's 4th Inst. p. 37, 38.   [o] Rymer, vol. xiv. p. 652.

even this act contains much falsehood, much tyranny, and were it not that all private rights must submit to public interest, much injustice and iniquity. The scheme of engaging the abbots to surrender their monasteries had been conducted, as may easily be imagined, with many invidious circumstances: Arts of all kinds had been employed; every motive, that could work on the frailty of human nature, had been set before them; and it was with great difficulty that these dignified conventuals were brought to make a concession, which most of them regarded as destructive of their interests, as well as sacrilegious and criminal in itself.[p] Three abbots had shown more constancy than the rest, the abbots of Colchester, Reading, and Glastenbury; and in order to punish them for their opposition, and make them an example to others, means had been found to convict them of treason; they had perished by the hands of the executioner, and the revenue of the convents had been forfeited.[q] Besides, though none of these violences had taken place, the king knew, that a surrender made by men, who were only tenants for life, would not bear examination; and he was therefore resolved to make all sure by his usual expedient, an act of parliament. In the preamble to this act, the parliament asserts, that all the surrenders, made by the abbots, had been, "without constraint, of their own accord, and according to due course of common law." And in consequence, the two houses confirm the surrenders, and secure the property of the abbey lands to the king and his successors for ever.[r] It is remarkable, that all the mitred abbots still sat in the house of peers; and that none of them made any protests against this injurious statute.

In this session, the rank of all the great officers of state was fixed: Cromwel, as vicegerent, had the precedency assigned him above all of them. It was thought singular, that a blacksmith's son, for he was no other, should have place next the royal family; and that a man, possessed of no manner of literature, should be set at the head of the church.

As soon as the act of the six articles had passed, the catholics were extremely vigilant in informing against offenders; and no less than five hundred persons were in a little time thrown into prison.

[p] Collier, vol. ii. p. 158. & seq.   [q] 31 Hen. VIII. c. 10.   [r] 31 Hen. VIII. c. 13.

But Cromwel, who had not had interest to prevent that act, was able, for the present, to elude its execution. Seconded by the duke of Suffolk, and chancellor Audley, as well as by Cranmer, he remonstrated against the cruelty of punishing so many delinquents; and he obtained permission to set them at liberty. The uncertainty of the king's humour gave each party an opportunity of triumphing in his turn. No sooner had Henry passed this law, which seemed to inflict so deep a wound on the reformers, than he granted a general permission, for every one to have the new translation of the Bible in his family: A concession regarded by that party, as an important victory.

Henry's projects of marriage. But as Henry was observed to be much governed by his wives, while he retained his fondness for them, the final prevalence of either party seemed much to depend on the choice of the future queen. Immediately after the death of Jane Seymour, the most beloved of all his wives, he began to think of a new marriage. He first cast his eye towards the dutchess-dowager of Milan, niece to the emperor; and he made proposals for that alliance. But meeting with difficulties, he was carried, by his friendship for Francis, rather to think of a French princess. He demanded the dutchess-dowager of Longueville, daughter of the duke of Guise, a prince of the house of Lorraine; but Francis told him, that the lady was already betrothed to the king of Scotland. The king, however, would not take a refusal: He had set his heart extremely on the match: The information, which he had received, of the dutchess's accomplishments and beauty, had prepossessed him in her favour; and having privately sent over Meautys to examine her person, and get certain intelligence of her conduct, the accounts, which that agent brought him, served farther to inflame his desires. He learned, that she was big made; and he thought her, on that account, the more proper match for him, who was now become somewhat corpulent. The pleasure too of mortifying his nephew, whom he did not love, was a farther incitement to his prosecution of this match; and he insisted, that Francis should give him the preference to the king of Scots. But Francis, though sensible that the alliance of England was of much greater importance to his interests, would not affront his friend and ally; and to prevent farther solicitation, he immediately sent the princess to Scotland. Not to shock, however, Henry's humour, Francis made him an offer of Mary of Bourbon, daughter of the duke of Vendome; but as the king was informed, that James had formerly rejected this princess, he would not hear any farther of such a proposal. The French monarch then offered him the choice of the two younger sisters of the queen of Scots; and he assured him, that they were nowise inferior either in merit or size to their elder sister, and that one of them was even superior in beauty. The king was as scrupulous with regard to the person of his wives, as if his heart had been really susceptible of a delicate passion; and he was unwilling to trust any relations, or even pictures, with regard to the important particular. He proposed to Francis, that they should have a conference at Calais on pretence of business; and that this monarch should bring along with him the two princesses of Guise, together with the finest ladies of quality in France, that he might make a choice among them. But the gallante spirit of Francis was shocked with the proposal. He was impressed with too much regard, he said, for the fair sex, to carry ladies of the first quality, like geldings, to a market, there to be chosen or rejected by the humour of the purchaser.[s] Henry would hearken to none of these niceties, but still insisted on his proposal; which, however, notwithstanding Francis's earnest desire of obliging him, was finally rejected.

The king then began to turn his thoughts towards a German alliance; and as the princes of the Smalcaldic league were extremely disgusted with the emperor on account of his persecuting their religion, he hoped, by matching himself into one of their families, to renew a connexion, which he regarded as so advantageous to him. Cromwel joyfully seconded this intention; and proposed to him Anne of Cleves, whose father, the duke of that name, had great interest among the Lutheran princes, and whose sister, Sibylla, was married to the elector of Saxony, the head of the protestant league. A flattering picture of the princess by Hans Holben determined Henry to apply to her father; and after some negociation, the marriage, notwithstanding the opposition of the elector of Saxony, was at last concluded; and Anne was sent over to England. The king, impatient to be satisfied with regard to the person of his bride, came privately to Rochester, and got a sight of her. He found her big, indeed, and tall, as he could wish; but

He marries Anne of Cleves.

[s] Le Grand, vol. iii. p. 638.

utterly destitute both of beauty and grace; very unlike the pictures and representations, which he had received: He swore she was a great Flanders-mare; and declared, that he never could possibly bear her any affection. The matter was worse, when he found, that she could speak no language but Dutch, of which he was entirely ignorant; and that the charms of her conversation were not likely *Dislikes* to compensate for the homeliness of her person. He returned to *her.* Greenwich very melancholy; and he much lamented his hard fate to Cromwel, as well as to Lord Russel, Sir Anthony Brown, and Sir Anthony Denny. This last gentleman, in order to give him comfort, told him, that his misfortune was common to him with all kings, who could not, like private persons, chuse for themselves; but must receive their wives from the judgment and fancy of others.

It was the subject of debate among the king's counsellors, whether the marriage could not yet be dissolved; and the princess be sent back to her own country. Henry's situation seemed at that time very critical. After the ten years' truce, concluded between the emperor and the king of France, a good understanding was thought to have taken place between these rival monarchs; and such marks of union appeared, as gave great jealousy to the court of England. The emperor, who knew the generous nature of Francis, even put a confidence in him, which is rare, to that degree, among great princes. An insurrection had been raised in the Low-Countries by the inhabitants of Ghent, and seemed to threaten the most dangerous consequences. Charles, who resided at that time in Spain, resolved to go in person to Flanders, in order to appease those disorders; but he found great difficulties in chusing the manner of his passing thither. The road by Italy and Germany was tedious: The voyage through the Channel dangerous, by reason of the English naval power: He asked Francis's permission to pass thro' his dominions; and he entrusted himself into the hands of a rival, whom he had so mortally offended. The French monarch received him at Paris, with great magnificence and courtesy; and though prompted both by revenge and interest, as well as by the advice of his mistress and favourites, to make advantage of the present opportunity, he conducted the emperor safely out of his dominions; and would not so much as speak to him of business

CHAPTER XXXII

during his abode in France, lest his demands should bear the air of violence upon his royal guest.

Henry, who was informed of all these particulars, believed that an entire and cordial union had taken place between these princes; and that their religious zeal might prompt them to sail with combined arms upon England.[t] An alliance with the German princes seemed now, more than ever, requisite for his interest and safety; and he knew, that, if he sent back the princess of Cleves, such an affront would be highly resented by her friends and family. He was therefore resolved, notwithstanding his aversion to her, to complete the marriage; and he told Cromwel, that, since matters had gone so far, he must put his neck into the yoke. Cromwel, who knew how much his own interests were concerned in this affair was very anxious to learn from the king, next morning after the marriage, whether he now liked his spouse any better. The king told him, that he hated her worse than ever; and that her person was more disgusting on a near approach: He was resolved never to meddle with her; and even suspected her not to be a true maid: A point, about which he entertained an extreme delicacy. He continued, however, to be civil to Anne; he even seemed to repose his usual confidence in Cromwel; but though he exerted this command over himself, a discontent lay lurking in his breast, and was ready to burst out on the first opportunity.

1540.
6 January.

A session of parliament was held; and none of the abbots were now allowed a place in the house of peers. The king, by the mouth of the chancellor, complained to the parliament of the great diversity of religions, which still prevailed among his subjects: A grievance, he affirmed, which ought the less to be endured; because the Scriptures were now published in English, and ought universally to be the standard of belief to all mankind. But he had appointed, he said, some bishops and divines to draw up a list of tenets, to which his people were to assent; and he was determined, that Christ, the doctrine of Christ, and the truth, should have the victory. The king seems to have expected more effect in ascertaining truth, from this new book of his doctors, than had ensued from the publication of the Scriptures. Cromwel, as vicar-general, made

1540.
12 April.
A parliament.

[t] Stowe, p. 579.

also in the king's name a speech to the upper house; and the peers, in return, bestowed great flattery on him, and in particular said that he was worthy, by his desert, to be vicar-general of the universe. That minister seemed to be no less in his master's good graces: He received, soon after the sitting of the parliament, the title of earl of Essex, and was installed knight of the garter.

There remained only one religious order in England; the knights of St. John of Jerusalem, or the knights of Malta, as they are commonly called. This order, partly ecclesiastical, partly military, had, by their valour, done great service to Christendom; and had very much retarded, at Jerusalem, Rhodes, and Malta, the rapid progress of the barbarians. During the general surrender of the religious houses in England, they had exerted their spirit, and had obstinately refused to yield up their revenues to the king; and Henry, who would endure no society that professed obedience to the pope, was obliged to have recourse to parliament for the dissolution of this order. Their revenues were large; and formed an addition nowise contemptible to the many acquisitions, which the king had already made. But he had very ill husbanded the great revenue acquired by the plunder of the church. His profuse generosity dissipated faster than his rapacity could supply; and the parliament was surprized this session to find a demand made upon them of four-tenths, and a subsidy of one shilling in the pound during two years: So ill were the public expectations answered, that the crown was never more to require any supply from the people. The commons, though lavish of their liberty, and of the blood of their fellow-subjects, were extremely frugal of their money; and it was not without difficulty so small a grant could be obtained by this absolute and dreaded monarch. The convocation gave the king four shillings in the pound to be levied in two years. The pretext for these grants was the great expence, which Henry had undergone for the defence of the realm, in building forts along the sea-coast, and in equipping a navy. As he had at present no ally on the continent, in whom he reposed much confidence, he relied only on his domestic strength, and was on that account obliged to be more expensive in his preparations against the danger of an invasion.

The king's favour to Cromwel, and his acquiescence in the marriage with Anne of Cleves, were both of them deceitful appearances. His aversion to the queen secretly encreased every day; and having at last broken all restraint, it prompted him at once to seek the dissolution of a marriage so odious to him, and to involve his minister in ruin, who had been the innocent author of it. The fall of Cromwel was hastened by other causes. All the nobility hated a man, who, being of such low extraction, had not only mounted above them by his station of vicar-general, but had engrossed many of the other considerable offices of the crown: Besides enjoying that commission, which gave him a high, and almost absolute authority over the clergy, and even over the laity, he was privy seal, chamberlain, and master of the wards: He had also obtained the order of the garter, a dignity which had ever been conferred only on men of illustrious families, and which seemed to be profaned by its being communicated to so mean a person. The people were averse to him, as the supposed author of the violence on the monasteries: establishments, which were still revered and beloved by the commonalty. The catholics regarded him as the concealed enemy of their religion: The protestants, observing his exterior concurrence with all the persecutions exercised against them, were inclined to bear him as little favour: and reproached him with the timidity, if not treachery, of his conduct. And the king, who found, that great clamours had on all hands arisen against the administration, was not displeased to throw on Cromwel the load of public hatred; and he hoped, by making so easy a sacrifice, to regain the affections of his subjects.

Fall of Cromwel.

But there was another cause, which suddenly set all these motives in action, and brought about an unexpected revolution in the ministry. The king had fixed his affection on Catherine Howard, niece to the duke of Norfolk; and being determined to gratify this new passion, he could find no expedient, but, by procuring a divorce from his present consort, to raise Catherine to his bed and throne. The duke, who had long been engaged in enmity with Cromwel, made the same use of her insinuations to ruin this minister, that he had formerly done of Anne Boleyn's against Wolsey: And when all engines were prepared, he obtained a commission from the king, to arrest Cromwel at the council-table, on an accusation of high treason, and to commit him to the Tower. Immediately after, a bill of attainder was framed against him; and the house of peers thought proper, without trial, examination, or evidence, to condemn to death a man, whom, a few days before, they had declared worthy to be vicar-general of the universe. The house of commons passed the bill, though not without some opposition. Cromwel was accused of heresy and treason; but the proofs of his treasonable practices are utterly improbable, and even absolutely ridiculous.[u] The only circumstance of his conduct, by which he seems to have merited this fate, was his being the instrument of the king's tyranny, in conducting like iniquitous bills, in the preceding session, against the countess of Salisbury and others.

Cromwel endeavoured to soften the king by the most humble supplications; but all to no purpose: It was not the practice of that prince to ruin his ministers and favourites by halves, and though the unhappy prisoner once wrote to him in so moving a strain as even to draw tears from his eyes, he hardened himself against all movements of pity, and refused his pardon. The conclusion of Cromwel's letter ran in these words: "I, a most woful prisoner, am ready to submit to death when it shall please God and your majesty; and yet the frail flesh incites me to call to your grace for mercy and pardon of mine offences. Written at the Tower with the heavy heart and trembling hand of your highness's most miserable prisoner and poor slave, Thomas Cromwel." And a little below, "Most gracious prince, I cry for mercy, mercy, mercy."[w] When brought to the place of execution, he avoided all earnest protestations of his innocence, and all complaints against the sentence pronounced upon him. He knew, that Henry would resent on his son those symptoms of opposition to his will, and that his death alone would not terminate that monarch's vengeance. He was a man of prudence, industry, and abilities; worthy of a better master and of a better fate. Though raised to the summit of power from a low origin, he betrayed no insolence or contempt towards his inferiors; and was careful to remember all the obligations, which, during his more humble fortune, he had owed to any one. He had served as a private sentinel in the Italian wars; when he received some good offices from a Lucquese merchant, who had entirely forgotten his person, as well as the service, which he had rendered him. Cromwel, in his grandeur, happened, at London, to cast his eye on his benefactor, now reduced to poverty, by misfortunes. He immedi-

28th July. His execution.

[u] Burnet, vol. i. p. 278.   [w] Burnet, vol. i. p. 281, 282.

ately sent for him, reminded him of their ancient friendship, and by his grateful assistance, reinstated him in his former prosperity and opulence.[x]

The measures for divorcing Henry from Anne of Cleves, were carried on at the same time with the bill of attainder against Cromwel. The house of peers, in conjunction with the commons, applied to the king by petition, desiring that he would allow his marriage to be examined; and orders were immediately given to lay the matter before the convocation. Anne had formerly been contracted by her father to the duke of Lorraine; but she, as well as the duke, were at that time under age, and the contract had been afterwards annulled by consent of both parties. The king, however, pleaded this precontract as a ground of divorce; and he added two reasons more, which may seem a little extraordinary; that, when he espoused Anne he had not *inwardly* given his consent, and that he had not thought proper to consummate the marriage. The convocation was satisfied with these reasons, and solemnly annulled the marriage between the king and queen: The parliament ratified the decision of the clergy;[y] and the sentence was soon after notified to the princess.

Anne was blest with a happy insensibility of temper, even in the points which the most nearly affect her sex; and the king's aversion towards her, as well as his prosecution of the divorce, had never given her the least uneasiness. She willingly hearkened to terms of accommodation with him; and when he offered to adopt her as his sister, to give her place next the queen and his own daughter, and to make a settlement of three thousand pounds a year upon her; she accepted of the conditions, and gave her consent to the divorce.[z] She even wrote to her brother (for her father was now dead), that she had been very well used in England, and desired him to live on good terms with the king. The only instance of pride which she betrayed was, that she refused to return to her own country after the affront which she had received; and she lived and died in England.

Notwithstanding Anne's moderation, this incident produced a great coldness between the king and the German princes; but as

King's divorce from Anne of Cleves.

---

[x] Burnet, vol. i. p. 172.   [y] See note [O] at the end of the volume.
[z] Herbert, p. 458, 459.

the situation of Europe was now much altered, Henry was the more indifferent about their resentment. The close intimacy, which had taken place between Francis and Charles, had subsisted during a very short time: The dissimilarity of their characters soon renewed, with greater violence than ever, their former jealousy and hatred. While Charles remained at Paris, Francis had been imprudently engaged, by his open temper, and by that satisfaction, which a noble mind naturally feels in performing generous actions, to make in confidence some dangerous discoveries to that interested monarch; and having now lost all suspicion of his rival, he hoped that the emperor and he, supporting each other, might neglect every other alliance. He not only communicated to his guest the state of his negociations with Sultan Solyman and the Venetians: He also laid open the solicitations, which he had received from the court of England, to enter into a confederacy against him.[a] Charles had no sooner reached his own dominions, than he shewed himself unworthy of the friendly reception which he had met with. He absolutely refused to fulfil his promise, and put the duke of Orleans in possession of the Milanese: He informed Solyman and the senate of Venice of the treatment, which they had received from their ally: and he took care that Henry should not be ignorant how readily Francis had abandoned his ancient friend to whom he owed such important obligations, and had sacrificed him to a new confederate: He even poisoned and misrepresented many things, which the unsuspecting heart of the French monarch had disclosed to him. Had Henry possessed true judgment and generosity, this incident alone had been sufficient to guide him in the choice of his ally. But his domineering pride carried him immediately to renounce the friendship of Francis, who had so unexpectedly given the preference to the emperor: And as Charles invited him to a renewal of ancient amity, he willingly accepted of the offer; and thinking himself secure in this alliance, he neglected the friendship both of France and of the German princes.

The new turn, which Henry had taken with regard to foreign affairs, was extremely agreeable to his catholic subjects; and as it had perhaps contributed, among other reasons, to the ruin of

[a] Pere Daniel, Du Tület.

CHAPTER XXXII

Cromwel, it made them entertain hopes of a final prevalence over their antagonist. The marriage of the king with Catherine Howard, which followed soon after his divorce from Anne of Cleves, was also regarded as a favourable incident to their party; and the subsequent events corresponded to their expectations. The king's councils being now directed by Norfolk and Gardiner, a furious persecution commenced against the protestants; and the law of the six articles was executed with rigour. Dr. Barnes, who had been the cause of Lambert's execution, felt, in his turn, the severity of the persecuting spirit; and, by a bill, which passed in parliament, he was, without trial, condemned to the flames, together with Jerome and Gerrard. He discussed theological questions even at the stake; and as the dispute between him and the sheriff, turned upon the invocation of saints, he said, that he doubted whether the saints could pray for us; but if they could, he hoped, in half an hour, to be praying for the sheriff and all the spectators. He next entreated the sheriff to carry to the king his dying request, which he fondly imagined would have authority with that monarch, who had sent him to the stake. The purport of his request was, that Henry, besides repressing superstitious ceremonies, should be extremely vigilant in preventing fornication and common swearing.[b]

8th Aug. His marriage with Catherine Howard.

While Henry was exerting this violence against the protestants, he spared not the catholics who denied his supremacy; and a foreigner, at that time in England, had reason to say, that those who were against the pope were burned, and those who were for him were hanged.[c] The king even displayed, in an ostentatious manner, this tyrannical impartiality, which reduced both parties to subjection, and infused terror into every breast. Barnes, Gerrard, and Jerome had been carried to the place of execution on three hurdles; and along with them there was placed on each hurdle a catholic, who was also executed for his religion. These catholics were Abel, Fetherstone, and Powel, who declared, that the most grievous part of their punishment was the being coupled to such heretical miscreants as suffered with them.[d]

Though the spirit of the English seemed to be totally sunk under the despotic power of Henry, there appeared some symp-

[b] Burnet, vol. i. p. 298. Fox. [c] Fox, vol. ii. p. 529. [d] Saunders, de Schism. Angl.

toms of discontent: An inconsiderable rebellion broke out in York-shire, headed by Sir John Nevil; but it was soon suppressed, and Nevil, with other ringleaders, was executed. The rebels were supposed to have been instigated by the intrigues of cardinal Pole; and the king was instantly determined to make the countess of Salisbury, who already lay under sentence of death, suffer for her son's offences. He ordered her to be carried to execution; and this venerable matron maintained still, in these distressful circumstances, the spirit of that long race of monarchs, from whom she was descended.[e] She refused to lay her head on the block, or submit to a sentence where she had received no trial. She told the executioner, that, if he would have her head, he must win it the best way he could: And thus, shaking her venerable grey locks, she ran about the scaffold; and the executioner followed her with his ax, aiming many fruitless blows at her neck, before he was able to give the fatal stroke. Thus perished the last of the line of Plantagenet, which, with great glory, but still greater crimes and misfortunes, had governed England for the space of three hundred years. Lord Leonard Grey, a man who had formerly rendered service to the crown, was also beheaded for treason, soon after the countess of Salisbury. We know little concerning the grounds of his prosecution.

The insurrection in the North engaged Henry to make a progress thither, in order to quiet the minds of his people, to reconcile them to his government, and to abolish the ancient superstitions, to which those parts were much addicted. He had also another motive for this journey: He purposed to have a conference at York with his nephew the king of Scotland, and, if possible, to cement a close and indissoluble union with that kingdom.

The same spirit of religious innovation, which had seized other parts of Europe, had made its way into Scotland, and had begun, before this period, to excite the same jealousies, fears, and persecutions. About the year 1527, Patric Hamilton, a young man of a noble family, having been created abbot of Ferne, was sent abroad for his education; but had fallen into company with some reformers, and he returned into his own country very ill disposed

27th May.

1541.

State of affairs in Scotland.

[e] Herbert, p. 468.

CHAPTER XXXII

towards that church, of which his birth and his merit entitled
him to attain the highest dignities. The fervour of youth and his
zeal for novelty made it impossible for him to conceal his sentiments; and Campbel, prior of the Dominicans, who, under colour
of friendship and a sympathy in opinion, had insinuated himself
into his confidence, accused him before Beaton, archbishop of St.
Andrews. Hamilton was invited to St. Andrews, in order to maintain, with some of the clergy, a dispute concerning the controverted points; and after much reasoning with regard to justification, free-will, original sin, and other topics of that nature, the
conference ended with their condemning Hamilton to be burned
for his errors. The young man, who had been deaf to the insinuations of ambition, was less likely to be shaken with the fears of
death; while he proposed to himself, both the glory of bearing
testimony to the truth, and the immediate reward attending his
martyrdom. The people, who compassionated his youth, his virtue, and his noble birth, were much moved at the constancy of his
end; and an incident, which soon followed, still more confirmed
them in their favourable sentiments towards him. He had cited
Campbel, who still insulted him at the stake, to answer before the
judgment-seat of Christ; and as that persecutor, either astonished
with these events, or overcome with remorse, or, perhaps, seized
casually with a distemper, soon after lost his senses, and fell into a
fever, of which he died; the people regarded Hamilton as a
prophet, as well as a martyr.[f]

Among the disciples converted by Hamilton, was one friar Forrest, who became a zealous preacher; and who, though he did not
openly discover his sentiments, was suspected to lean towards the
new opinions. His diocesan, the bishop of Dunkel, enjoined him,
when he met with a good epistle or good gospel, which favoured
the liberties of holy church, to preach on it, and let the rest alone.
Forrest replied, that he had read both Old and New Testament,
and had not found an ill epistle, or ill gospel in any part of them.
The extreme attachment to the Scriptures was regarded in those
days as a sure characteristic of heresy; and Forrest was soon after
brought to trial, and condemned to the flames. While the priests

[f] Spotswood's Hist. church of Scotland, p. 62.

were deliberating on the place of his execution, a bystander advised them to burn him in a cellar: For that the smoke of Mr. Patric Hamilton had infected all those on whom it blew.[g]

The clergy were at that time reduced to great difficulties not only in Scotland, but all over Europe. As the reformers aimed at a total subversion of ancient establishments, which they represented as idolatrous, impious, detestable; the priests, who found both their honours and properties at stake, thought that they had a right to resist, by every expedient, these dangerous invaders, and that the same simple principles of equity, which justified a man in killing a pyrate or a robber, would acquit them for the execution of such heretics. A toleration, though it is never acceptable to ecclesiastics, might, they said, be admitted in other cases; but seemed an absurdity, where fundamentals were shaken, and where the possessions, and even the existence of the established clergy were brought in danger. But though the church was thus carried by policy, as well as inclination, to kindle the fires of persecution, they found the success of this remedy very precarious, and observed, that the enthusiastic zeal of the reformers, inflamed by punishment, was apt to prove contagious on the compassionate minds of the spectators. The new doctrine, amidst all the dangers, to which it was exposed, secretly spread itself everywhere; and the minds of men were gradually disposed to a revolution in religion.

But the most dangerous symptom for the clergy in Scotland was, that the nobility, from the example of England, had cast a wishful eye on the church revenues, and hoped, if a reformation took place, to enrich themselves by the plunder of the ecclesiastics. James himself, who was very poor, and was somewhat inclined to magnificence, particularly in building, had been swayed by like motives; and began to threaten the clergy with the same fate that had attended them in the neighbouring country. Henry also never ceased exhorting his nephew to imitate his example; and being moved both by the pride of making proselytes, and the prospect of security, should Scotland embrace a close union with him, he solicited the king of Scots to meet him at York; and he obtained a promise to that purpose.

[g] Spotswood, p. 65.

CHAPTER XXXII

The ecclesiastics were alarmed at this resolution of James, and they employed every expedient, in order to prevent the execution of it. They represented the danger of innovation; the pernicious consequences of aggrandizing the nobility, already too powerful; the hazard of putting himself into the hands of the English, his hereditary enemies, the dependance on them which must ensue upon his losing the friendship of France, and of all foreign powers. To these considerations, they added the prospect of immediate interest, by which they found the king to be much governed: They offered him a present gratuity of fifty thousand pounds: They promised him, that the church should always be ready to contribute to his supply: And they pointed out to him, the confiscation of heretics, as the means of filling his exchequer, and of adding a hundred thousand pounds a year to the crown revenues.[h] The insinuations of his new queen, to whom youth, beauty, and address had given a powerful influence over him, seconded all these reasons; and James was at last engaged, first to delay his journey, then to send excuses to the king of England, who had already come to York, in order to be present at the interview.[i]

Henry, vexed with the disappointment, and enraged at the affront, vowed vengeance against his nephew; and he began, by permitting piracies at sea, and incursions at land, to put his threats in execution. But he received soon after, in his own family, an affront to which he was much more sensible, and which touched him in a point where he always shewed an extreme delicacy. He had thought himself very happy in his new marriage: The agreeable person and disposition of Catherine had entirely captivated his affections; and he made no secret of his devoted attachment to her. He had even publicly, in his chapel, returned solemn thanks to heaven for the felicity which the conjugal state afforded him; and he directed the bishop of Lincoln to compose a form of prayer for that purpose. But the queen's conduct very little merited this tenderness: One Lascelles brought intelligence of her dissolute life

Discovery of the queen's dissolute life.

[h] Buchanan, lib. xiv. Drummond in ja. 5. Pitscotie, ibid. Knox.   [i] Henry had sent some books, richly ornamented, to his nephew, who, as soon as he saw by the titles, that they had a tendency to defend the new doctrines, threw them into the fire, in the presence of the person who brought them: Adding, it was better he should destroy them, than they him. See Epist. Reginald. Pole. part i. p. 172.

to Cranmer; and told him, that his sister, formerly a servant in the family of the old dutchess of Norfolk, with whom Catherine was educated, had given him a particular account of her licentious manners. Derham and Mannoc, both of them servants to the dutchess, had been admitted to her bed; and she had even taken little care to conceal her shame from the other servants of the family. The primate, struck with this intelligence, which it was equally dangerous to conceal or to discover, communicated the matter to the earl of Hertford and to the chancellor. They agreed, that the matter should by no means be buried in silence; and the archbishop himself seemed the most proper person to disclose it to the king. Cranmer, unwilling to speak on so delicate a subject, wrote a narrative of the whole, and conveyed it to Henry, who was infinitely astonished at the intelligence. So confident was he of the fidelity of his consort, that at first he gave no credit to the information; and he said to the privy-seal, to Lord Russel, high admiral, Sir Anthony Brown, and Wriothesley, that he regarded the whole as a falsehood. Cranmer was now in a very perilous situation; and had not full proof been found, certain and inevitable destruction hung over him. The king's impatience, however, and jealousy prompted him to search the matter to the bottom: The privy-seal was ordered to examine Lascelles, who persisted in the information he had given; and still appealed to his sister's testimony. That nobleman next made a journey under pretence of hunting, and went to Sussex, where the woman at that time resided: He found her both constant in her former intelligence, and particular as to the facts; and the whole bore but too much the face of probability. Mannoc and Derham, who were arrested at the same time, and examined by the chancellor, made the queen's guilt entirely certain by their confession; and discovered other particulars, which redounded still more to her dishonour. Three maids of the family were admitted into her secrets, and some of them had even passed the night in bed with her and her lovers. All the examinations were laid before the king, who was so deeply affected, that he remained a long time speechless, and at last burst into tears. He found to his surprise, that his great skill in distinguishing a true maid, of which he boasted in the case of Anne of Cleves, had failed him in that of his present consort. The queen, being next questioned, denied her

CHAPTER XXXII

guilt; but when informed, that a full discovery was made, she confessed, that she had been criminal before marriage; and only insisted, that she had never been false to the king's bed. But as there was evidence, that one Colepepper had passed the night with her alone since her marriage; and as it appeared, that she had taken Derham, her old paramour, into her service, she seemed to deserve little credit in this asseveration; and the king, besides, was not of a humour to make any difference between these degrees of guilt.

Henry found, that he could not, by any means, so fully or expeditiously satiate his vengeance on all these criminals as by assembling a parliament, the usual instrument of his tyranny. The two houses, having received the queen's confession, made an address to the king. They entreated him not to be vexed with this untoward accident, to which all men were subject; but to consider the frailty of human nature, and the mutability of human affairs; and from these views to derive a subject of consolation. They desired leave to pass a bill of attainder against the queen and her accomplices; and they begged him to give his assent to this bill, not in person, which would renew his vexation, and might endanger his health, but by commissioners appointed for that purpose. And as there was a law in force, making it treason to speak ill of the queen, as well as of the king, they craved his royal pardon, if any of them should, on the present occasion, have transgressed any part of the statute.

Having obtained a gracious answer to these requests, the parliament proceeded to vote a bill of attainder for treason against the queen, and the viscountess of Rocheford, who had conducted her secret amours; and in this bill Colepepper, and Derham, were also comprehended. At the same time they passed a bill of attainder for misprision of treason against the old dutchess of Norfolk, Catherine's grandmother; her uncle, lord William Howard, and his lady, together with the countess of Bridgewater, and nine persons more; because they knew the queen's vicious course of life before her marriage, and had concealed it. This was an effect of Henry's usual extravagance, to expect that parents should so far forget the ties of natural affection, and the sentiments of shame and decency, as to reveal to him the most secret disorders of their family. He

1542.
6th
Jan.

himself seems to have been sensible of the cruelty of this proceeding: For he pardoned the dutchess of Norfolk, and most of the
others, condemned for misprision of treason.

However, to secure himself for the future, as well as his successors, from this fatal accident, he engaged the parliament to pass a
law somewhat extraordinary. It was enacted, that any one who
knew, or vehemently suspected any guilt in the queen, might,
within twenty days, disclose it to the king or council, without incurring the penalty of any former law, against defaming the queen;
but prohibiting every one, at the same time, from spreading the
matter abroad, or even privately whispering it to others: It was also
enacted, that, if the king married any woman, who had been incon-
tinent, taking her for a true maid, she should be guilty of treason,
if she did not previously reveal her guilt to him. The people made
merry with this singular clause, and said, that the king must henceforth look out for a widow; for no reputed maid would ever be
persuaded to incur the penalty of the statute.[k] After all these laws
were passed, the queen was beheaded on Tower-hill, together with
lady Rocheford. They behaved in a manner suitable to their dissolute life; and as lady Rocheford was known to be the chief instrument in bringing Anne Boleyn to her end, she died unpitied; and
men were farther confirmed, by the discovery of this woman's
guilt, in the favourable sentiments, which they had entertained of
that unfortunate queen.

The king made no demand of any subsidy from this parliament; but he found means of enriching his exchequer from another quarter: He took farther steps towards the dissolution
of colleges, hospitals, and other foundations of that nature. The
courtiers had been practising on the presidents and governors, to
make a surrender of their revenues to the king; and they had been
successful with eight of them. But there was an obstacle to their
farther progress: It had been provided, by the local statutes of
most of these foundations, that no president, or any number of
fellows, could consent to such a deed without the unanimous vote
of all the fellows; and this vote was not easily obtained. All such
statutes were annulled by parliament; and the revenues of these
houses were now exposed to the rapacity of the king and his fa-

[k] Burnet, vol. i. p. 314.

CHAPTER XXXII

vourites.[1] The church had been so long their prey, that nobody was surprised at any new inroads made upon her. From the regular, Henry now proceeded to make devastations on the secular clergy. He extorted from many of the bishops a surrender of chapter lands; and by this device he pillaged the sees of Canterbury, York, and London, and enriched his greedy parasites and flatterers with their spoils.

The clergy have been commonly so fortunate as to make a concern for their temporal interests go hand in hand with a jealousy for orthodoxy; and both these passions be regarded, by the people, ignorant and superstitious, as proofs of zeal for religion: But the violent and headstrong character of Henry now disjoined these objects. His rapacity was gratified by plundering the church, his bigotry and arrogance by persecuting heretics. Though he engaged the parliament to mitigate the penalties of the six articles, so far as regards the marriage of priests, which was now only subjected to a forfeiture of goods, chattels, and lands during life; he was still equally bent on maintaining a rigid purity in speculative principles. He had appointed a commission, consisting of the two archbishops and several bishops of both provinces, together with a considerable number of doctors of divinity; and by virtue of his ecclesiastical supremacy he had given them in charge to chuse a religion for his people. Before the commissioners had made any progress in this arduous undertaking, the parliament, in 1541, had passed a law, by which they ratified all the tenets, which these divines should thereafter establish with the king's consent: And they were not ashamed of thus expressly declaring that they took their religion upon trust, and had no other rule, in spiritual as well as temporal concerns, than the arbitrary will of their master. There is only one clause of the statute, which may seem at first sight to savour somewhat of the spirit of liberty: It was enacted that the ecclesiastical commissioners should establish nothing repugnant to the laws and statutes of the realm. But in reality this proviso was inserted by the king, to serve his own purposes. By introducing a confusion and contradiction into the laws, he became more master of every one's life and property. And as the ancient independance of the church still gave him jealousy, he was well pleased, under

Ecclesiastic affairs.

---

[1] See note [P] at the end of the volume.

cover of such a clause, to introduce appeals from the spiritual to the civil courts. It was for a like reason, that he would never promulgate a body of canon law; and he encouraged the judges on all occasions to interpose in ecclesiastical causes, wherever they thought the law of royal prerogative concerned. A happy innovation; though at first invented for arbitrary purposes!

The king, armed by the authority of parliament, or rather by their acknowledgment of that spiritual supremacy, which he believed inherent in him, employed his commissioners to select a system of tenets for the assent and belief of the nation. A small volume was soon after published, called, the *Institution of a Christian Man,* which was received by the convocation, and voted to be the standard of orthodoxy. All the delicate points of justification, faith, free-will, good works, and grace, are there defined, with a leaning towards the opinion of the reformers: The sacraments, which a few years before were only allowed to be three, were now encreased to the number of seven, conformable to the sentiments of the catholics. The king's caprice is discernable throughout the whole; and the book is in reality to be regarded as his composition. For Henry while he made his opinion a rule for the nation, would tie his own hands by no canon or authority, not even by any which he himself had formerly established.

The people had occasion soon after to see a farther instance of the king's inconstancy. He was not long satisfied with his Institution of a Christian Man: He ordered a new book to be composed, called, the *Erudition of a Christian Man;* and without asking the assent of the convocation, he published, by his own authority, and that of the parliament, this new model of orthodoxy. It differs from the Institution;[m] but the king was no less positive in his new creed than he had been in the old; and he required the belief of the nation to veer about at his signal. In both these compositions, he was particularly careful to inculcate the doctrine of passive obedience; and he was equally careful to retain the nation in the practice.

While the king was spreading his own books among the people, he seems to have been extremely perplexed, as were also the clergy, what course to take with the Scriptures. A review had been

[m] Collier, vol. ii. p. 190.

CHAPTER XXXII

made by the synod of the new translation of the Bible; and Gardiner had proposed, that, instead of employing English expressions throughout, several Latin words should still be preserved; because they contained, as he pretended, such peculiar energy and significance, that they had no correspondent terms in the vulgar tongue.[n] Among these were *eclesia, poenitentia, pontifex, contritus, holocausta, sacramentum, elementa, ceremonia, mysterium, presbyter, sacrificium, humilitas, satisfactio, peccutum, gratia, hostia, charitae,* &c. But as this mixture would have appeared extremely barbarous, and was plainly calculated for no other purpose than to retain the people in their ancient ignorance, the proposal was rejected. The knowledge of the people, however, at least their disputative turn, seemed to be an inconvenience still more dangerous; and the king and parliament,[o] soon after the publication of the Scriptures, retracted the concession, which they had formerly made; and prohibited all but gentlemen and merchants from perusing them.[p] Even that liberty was not granted, without an apparent hesitation, and a dread of the consequences: These persons were allowed to read, *so it be done quietly and with good order.* And the preamble to the act sets forth, "that many seditious and ignorant persons had abused the liberty granted them of reading the Bible, and that great diversity of opinion, animosities, tumults, and schisms had been occasioned by perverting the sense of the Scriptures." It seemed very difficult to reconcile the king's model for uniformity, with the permission of free enquiry.

The mass-book also passed under the king's revisal; and little alteration was as yet made in it: Some doubtful or fictitious saints only were struck out; and the name of the pope was erased. This latter precaution was likewise used with regard to every new book that was printed, or even old book that was sold. The word, Pope, was carefully omitted or blotted out;[q] as if that precaution could abolish the term from the language, or as if such a persecution of

---

[n] Burnet, vol. i. p. 315.   [o] Which met on the 22d of January, 1543.   [p] 33 Hen. VIII. c. i. The reading of the Bible, however, could not, at that time, have much effect in England, where so few persons had learned to read. There were but 500 copies printed of this first authorized edition of the Bible; a book of which there are now several millions of copies in the kingdom.   [q] Parliamentary history, vol. iii. p. 113.

it did not rather imprint it more strongly in the memory of the people.

The king took care about this time to clear the churches from another abuse, which had creeped into them. Plays, interludes, and farces were there often acted in derision of the former superstitions; and the reverence of the multitude for ancient principles and modes of worship was thereby gradually effaced.[r] We do not hear, that the catholics attempted to retaliate by employing this powerful engine against their adversaries, or endeavoured by like arts to expose that fanatical spirit, by which, it appears, the reformers were frequently actuated. Perhaps the people were not disposed to relish a jest on that side: Perhaps the greater simplicity and the more spiritual abstract worship of the protestants, gave less hold to ridicule, which is commonly founded on sensible representations. It was, therefore, a very agreeable concession, which the king made to the catholic party, to suppress entirely these religious comedies.

Thus Henry laboured incessantly, by arguments, creeds, and penal statutes, to bring his subjects to an uniformity in their religious sentiments: But as he entered, himself, with the greatest earnestness, into all those scholastic disputes, he encouraged the people, by his example, to apply themselves to the study of theology; and it was in vain afterwards to expect, however present fear might restrain their tongues or pens, that they would cordially agree in any set of tenets or opinions prescribed to them.

[r] Burnet, vol. i. p. 318.

XXXIII

War with Scotland –
Victory of Solway – Death of James V. –
Treaty with Scotland – New rupture –
Rupture with France – A Parliament –
Affairs of Scotland – A Parliament –
Campaign in France – A Parliament – Peace
with France and Scotland – Persecutions –
Execution of the earl of Surrey –
Attainder of the duke of Norfolk –
Death of the king – His character –
Miscellaneous transactions

HENRY, BEING DETERMINED to avenge himself on the king of
Scots for slighting the advances, which he had made him,
would gladly have obtained a supply from parliament, in order to
prosecute that enterprize; but as he did not think it prudent to
discover his intentions, that assembly, conformably to their frugal
maxims, would understand no hints; and the king was disappointed in his expectations. He continued, however, to make preparations for war; and as soon as he thought himself in a condition
to invade Scotland, he published a manifesto, by which he endeavoured to justify hostilities. He complained of James's breach
of word, in declining the promised interview; which was the real

1542.
War
with
Scotland.

ground of the quarrel:[s] But in order to give a more specious col-
ouring to the enterprize, he mentioned other injuries; namely,
that his nephew had granted protection to some English rebels and
fugitives, and had detained some territory, which, Henry pretended, belonged to England. He even revived the old claim to the
vassalage of Scotland, and he summoned James to do homage to
him as his liege lord and superior. He employed the duke of
Norfolk, whom he called the scourge of the Scots, to command
in the war; and though James sent the bishop of Aberdeen, and
Sir James Learmont of Darsay, to appease his uncle, he would
hearken to no terms of accommodation. While Norfolk was assembling his army at Newcastle, Sir Robert Bowes, attended by Sir
Ralph Sadler, Sir Ralph Evers, Sir Brian Latoun, and others, made
an incursion into Scotland, and advanced towards Jedburgh, with
an intention of pillaging and destroying that town. The earl of
Angus, and George Douglas, his brother, who had been many
years banished their country, and had subsisted by Henry's
bounty, joined the English army in this incursion; and the forces,
commanded by Bowes, exceeded four thousand men. James had
not been negligent in his preparations for defence, and had posted
a considerable body, under the command of the earl of Huntley,
for the protection of the borders. Lord Hume, at the head of his
vassals, was hastening to join Huntley, when he met with the English army; and an action immediately ensued. During the engagement, the forces under Huntley began to appear; and the English,
afraid of being surrounded and overpowered, took to flight, and
were pursued by the enemy. Evers, Latoun, and some other persons of distinction, were taken prisoners. A few only of small note
fell in the skirmish.[t]

    The duke of Norfolk, meanwhile, began to move from his camp
at Newcastle; and being attended by the earls of Shrewsbury,
Derby, Cumberland, Surrey, Hertford, Rutland, with many others
of the nobility, he advanced to the borders. His forces amounted
to above twenty thousand men; and it required the utmost efforts
of Scotland to resist such a formidable armament. James had assembled his whole military force at Fala and Sautrey, and was
ready to advance as soon as he should be informed of Norfolk's

24th Aug. (margin)

[s] Buchanan, lib. 14. Drummond in James the Fifth.   [t] Buchanan, lib. 14.

CHAPTER XXXIII

invading his kingdom. The English passed the Tweed at Berwic, and marched along the banks of the river as far as Kelso; but hearing that James had collected near thirty thousand men, they repassed the river at that village, and retreated into their own country.[u] The king of Scots, inflamed with a desire of military glory, and of revenge on his invaders, gave the signal for pursuing them, and carrying the war into England. He was surprized to find, that his nobility, who were in general disaffected on account of the preference which he had given to the clergy, opposed this resolution, and refused to attend him in his projected enterprize. Enraged at this mutiny, he reproached them with cowardice, and threatened vengeance; but still resolved, with the forces which adhered to him, to make an impression on the enemy. He sent ten thousand men to the western borders, who entered England at Solway frith; and he himself followed them at a small distance, ready to join them upon occasion. Disgusted, however, at the refractory disposition of his nobles, he sent a message to the army, depriving lord Maxwel, their general, of his commission, and conferring the command on Oliver Sinclair, a private gentleman, who was his favourite. The army was extremely disgusted with this alteration, and was ready to disband; when a small body of English appeared, not exceeding 500 men, under the command of Dacres and Musgrave. A panic seized the Scots, who immediately took to flight, and were pursued by the enemy. Few were killed in this rout; for it was no action; but a great many were taken prisoners, and some of the principal nobility: Among these, the earls of Cassilis and Glencairn; the lords Maxwel, Fleming, Somerville, Oliphant, Grey, who were all sent to London, and given in custody to different noblemen.

24th Nov. Victory at Solway.

The king of Scots, hearing of this disaster, was astonished; and being naturally of a melancholic disposition, as well as endowed with a high spirit, he lost all command of his temper on this dismal occasion. Rage against his nobility, who, he believed, had betrayed him; shame for a defeat by such unequal numbers; regret for the past, fear of the future; all these passions so wrought upon him, that he would admit of no consolation, but abandoned himself wholly to despair. His body was wasted by sympathy with his anx-

[u] Buchanan, lib. 14.

ious mind; and even his life began to be thought in danger. He had no issue living; and hearing that his queen was safely delivered, he asked whether she had brought him a male or female child? Being told, the latter; he turned himself in his bed: "The crown came with a woman," said he, "and it will go with one: Many miseries await this poor kingdom: Henry will make it his own either by force of arms or by marriage." A few days after, he expired, in the flower of his age; a prince of considerable virtues and talents; well fitted, by his vigilance and personal courage, for repressing those disorders, to which his kingdom, during that age, was so much exposed. He executed justice with impartiality and rigour; but as he supported the commonalty and the church against the rapine of the nobility, he escaped not the hatred of that order. The protestants also, whom he opposed, have endeavoured to throw many stains on his memory; but have not been able to fix any considerable imputation upon him.[w]

14th Dec. Death of James the Fifth.

1543.

Henry was no sooner informed of his victory and of the death of his nephew, than he projected, as James had foreseen, the scheme of uniting Scotland to his own dominions, by marrying his son, Edward, to the heiress of that kingdom.[x] He called together the Scottish nobles, who were his prisoners; and after reproaching them, in severe terms, for their pretended breach of treaty, he began to soften his tone, and proposed to them this expedient, by which, he hoped, those disorders, so prejudicial to both states, would for the future be prevented. He offered to bestow on them their liberty without ransom; and only required of them engagements to favour the marriage of the prince of Wales with their young mistress. They were easily prevailed on to give their assent to a proposal, which seemed so natural, and so advantageous to both kingdoms; and being conducted to Newcastle, they delivered to the duke of Norfolk hostages for their return, in case the intended nuptials were not completed: And they thence proceeded to Scotland, where they found affairs in some confusion.

The pope, observing his authority in Scotland to be in danger from the spreading of the new opinions, had bestowed on Beaton, the primate, the dignity of cardinal, in order to confer more influ-

---

[w] See note [Q] at the end of the volume.   [x] Stowe, p. 584. Herbert, Burnet, Buchanan.

CHAPTER XXXIII

ence upon him; and that prelate had long been regarded as prime minister to James, and as the head of that party, which defended the ancient privileges and property of the ecclesiastics. Upon the death of his master, this man, apprehensive of the consequences both to his party and to himself, endeavoured to keep possession of power; and for that purpose, he is accused of executing a deed, which required a high degree of temerity. He forged, it is said, a will for the king, appointing himself, and three noblemen more, regents of the kingdom during the minority of the infant princess.[y] At least, for historians are not well agreed in the circumstances of the fact, he had read to James a paper of that import, to which that monarch, during the delirium which preceded his death, had given an imperfect assent and approbation.[z] By virtue of this will, Beaton had put himself in possession of the government; and having united his interests with those of the queen-dowager, he obtained the consent of the convention of states, and excluded the pretensions of the earl of Arran.

James earl of Arran, of the name of Hamilton, was next heir to the crown by his grandmother, daughter of James III; and on that account seemed best entitled to possess that high office, into which the cardinal had intruded himself. The prospect also of his succession after a princess, who was in such tender infancy, procured him many partizans; and though his character indicated little spirit, activity, or ambition, a propensity, which he had discovered for the new opinions, had attached to him all the zealous promoters of those innovations. By means of these adherents, joined to the vassals of his own family, he had been able to make opposition to the cardinal's administration; and the suspicion of Beaton's forgery, with the accession of the noblemen, who had been prisoners in England, assisted too by some money sent from London, was able to turn the balance in his favour. The earl of Angus and his brother, having taken the present opportunity of returning into their native country, opposed the cardinal with all the credit of that powerful family; and the majority of the convention had now embraced opposite interests to those which formerly prevailed. Arran was declared governor; the cardinal was committed

[y] Sadler's Letters, p. 161. Spotswood, p. 71. Buchanan, lib. 15. [z] John Knox, History of the Reformation.

Treaty with Scotland.

to custody under the care of lord Seton; and a negociation was commenced with Sir Ralph Sadler, the English ambassador, for the marriage of the infant queen with the prince of Wales. The following conditions were quickly agreed on; that the queen should remain in Scotland till she should be ten years of age; that she should then be sent to England to be educated; that six Scottish noblemen should immediately be delivered as hostages to Henry; and that the kingdom, notwithstanding its union with England, should still retain its laws and privileges.[a] By means of these equitable conditions, the war between the nations, which had threatened Scotland with such dismal calamities, seemed to be fully composed, and to be changed into perpetual concord and amity.

But the cardinal-primate, having prevailed on Seton to restore him to his liberty, was able, by his intrigues, to confound all these measures, which appeared so well concerted. He assembled the most considerable ecclesiastics; and having represented to them the imminent danger, to which their revenues and privileges were exposed, he persuaded them to collect privately from the clergy a large sum of money, by which, if entrusted to his management, he engaged to overturn the schemes of their enemies.[b] Besides the partizans, whom he acquired by pecuniary motives, he rouzed up the zeal of those, who were attached to the catholic worship; and he represented the union with England as the sure forerunner of ruin to the church and to the ancient religion. The national antipathy of the Scots to their southern neighbours was also an infallible engine, by which the cardinal wrought upon the people; and though the terror of Henry's arms, and their own inability to make resistance, had procured a temporary assent to the alliance and marriage proposed, the settled habits of the nation produced an extreme aversion to those measures. The English ambassador and his retinue received many insults from persons whom the cardinal had instigated to commit those violences, in hopes of bringing on a rupture: But Sadler prudently dissembled the matter; and waited patiently, till the day appointed for the delivery of the hostages. He then demanded of the regent the performance of that important article; but received for answer, that his authority was very precarious, that the nation had now taken a different impression, and

[a] Sir Ralph Sadler's Letters.   [b] Buchanan, lib. 15.

CHAPTER XXXIII

that it was not in his power to compel any of the nobility to deliver themselves as hostages to the English. Sadler, foreseeing the consequence of this refusal, sent a summons to all those who had been prisoners in England, and required them to fulfil the promise, which they had given, of returning into custody. None of them showed so much sentiment of honour, as to fulfil their engagements, except Gilbert Kennedy, earl of Cassilis. Henry was so well pleased with the behaviour of this nobleman, that he not only received him graciously, but honoured him with presents, gave him his liberty, and sent him back to Scotland, with his two brothers, whom he had left as hostages.[c]

This behaviour of the Scottish nobles, though it reflected dishonour on the nation, was not disagreeable to the cardinal, who foresaw, that all these persons would now be deeply interested to maintain their enmity and opposition to England. And as a war was soon expected with that kingdom, he found it necessary immediately to apply to France, and to crave the assistance of that ancient ally, during the present distresses of the Scottish nation. Though the French king was fully sensible of his interest in supporting Scotland, a demand of aid could not have been made on him at a more unseasonable juncture. His pretensions on the Milanese, and his resentment against Charles, had engaged him in a war with that potentate; and having made great, though fruitless efforts during the preceding campaign, he was the more disabled at present from defending his own dominions, much more from granting any succour to the Scots. Matthew Stuart, earl of Lenox, a young nobleman of a great family, was at that time in the French court; and Francis, being informed, that he was engaged in ancient and hereditary enmity with the Hamiltons, who had murdered his father, sent him over to his native country, as a support to the cardinal and the queen-mother: And he promised, that a supply of money, and, if necessary, even military succours, should soon be dispatched after him. Arran, the governor, seeing all these preparations against him, assembled his friends, and made an attempt to get the person of the infant queen into his custody; but being repulsed, he was obliged to come to an accommodation with his enemies, and to entrust that precious charge to four neutral per-

New rupture.

[c] Buchanan, lib 15.

sons, the heads of potent families, the Grahams, Areskines, Lindseys, and Levingstones. The arrival of Lenox, in the midst of these transactions, served to render the victory of the French party over the English still more undisputable.[d]

Rupture with France.

The opposition, which Henry met with in Scotland from the French intrigues, excited his resentment, and farther confirmed the resolution, which he had already taken, of breaking with France, and of uniting his arms with those of the emperor. He had other grounds of complaint against the French king; which, though not of great importance, yet being recent, were able to overbalance those great injuries, which he had formerly received from Charles. He pretended, that Francis had engaged to imitate his example in separating himself entirely from the see of Rome, and that he had broken his promise in that particular. He was dissatisfied, that James his nephew, had been allowed to marry, first Magdalene of France, then a princess of the house of Guise; and he considered these alliances as pledges, which Francis gave of his intentions to support the Scots against the power of England.[e] He had been informed of some railleries, which the French king had thrown out against his conduct with regard to his wives. He was disgusted, that Francis, after so many obligations which he owed him, had sacrificed him to the emperor; and, in the confidence of friendship, had rashly revealed his secrets to that subtle and interested monarch. And he complained, that regular payments were never made of the sums due to him by France, and of the pension, which had been stipulated. Impelled by all these motives, he alienated himself from his ancient friend and confederate, and formed a league with the emperor, who earnestly courted his alliance. This league, besides stipulations for mutual defence, contained a plan for invading France; and the two monarchs agreed to enter Francis's dominions with an army, each of twenty-five thousand men; and to require that prince to pay Henry all the sums which he owed him, and to consign Boulogne, Montreuil, Terouenne, and Ardres, as a security for the regular payment of his pension for the future: In case these conditions were rejected, the confederate princes agreed to challenge, for Henry, the crown of France, or, in default of it, the dutchies of Normandy,

[d] Buchanan, lib. 15. Drummond.　[e] Pere Daniel.

CHAPTER XXXIII

Aquitaine, and Guienne; for Charles, the dutchy of Burgundy, and some other territories.[f] That they might have a pretence for enforcing these claims, they sent a message to Francis, requiring him to renounce his alliance with Sultan Solyman, and to make reparation for all the prejudice, which Christendom had sustained from that unnatural confederacy. Upon the French king's refusal, war was declared against him by the allies. It may be proper to remark, that the partizans of France objected to Charles his alliance with the heretical king of England, as no less obnoxious than that which Francis had contracted with Solyman: And they observed, that this league was a breach of the solemn promise, which he had given to Clement VII. never to make peace or alliance with England.

While the treaty with the emperor was negociating, the king summoned a new session of parliament, in order to obtain supplies for his projected war with France. The parliament granted him a subsidy to be paid in three years: It was levied in a peculiar manner; but exceeded not three shillings in the pound, upon any individual.[g] The convocation gave the king six shillings in the pound, to be levied in three years. Greater sums were always, even during the establishment of the Catholic religion, exacted from the clergy than from the laity: Which made the emperor Charles say, when Henry dissolved the monasteries, and sold their revenues, or bestowed them on his nobility and courtiers, that he had killed the hen, which brought him the golden eggs.[h]

The parliament also facilitated the execution of the former law, by which the king's proclamations were made equal to statutes: They appointed, that any nine counsellors should form a legal court for punishing all disobedience to proclamations. The total abolition of juries in criminal causes, as well as of all parliaments, seemed, if the king had so pleased, the necessary consequence of

22d Jan. A parliament.

---

[f] Rymer, vol. xiv. p. 768. vol. xv. p. 2.   [g] They who were worth in goods twenty shillings and upwards to five pounds, paid four pence of every pound; from five pounds to ten pounds, eight pence; from ten pounds to twenty pounds, sixteen pence; from twenty and upwards, two shillings. Lands, sees, and annuities, from twenty shillings to five pounds, paid eight pence in the pound; from five pounds to ten pounds, sixteen pence; from ten pounds to twenty pounds, two shillings; from twenty pounds and upwards, three shillings.   [h] Collier, vol. ii. p. 176.

this enormous law. He might issue a proclamation, enjoining the execution of any penal statute, and afterwards try the criminals, not for breach of the statute, but for disobedience to his proclamation. It is remarkable, that lord Mountjoy entered a protest against this law; and it is equally remarkable, that that protest is the only one entered against any public bill during this whole reign.[i]

It was enacted,[k] this session, that any spiritual person, who preached or taught contrary to the doctrine contained in the king's book, the *Erudition of a Christian man,* or contrary to any doctrine which he should *thereafter* promulgate, was to be admitted on the first conviction to renounce his error; on the second, he was required to carry a faggot; which if he refused to do, or fell into a third offence, he was to be burnt. But the laity, for the third offence, were only to forfeit their goods and chattels, and be liable to perpetual imprisonment. Indictment must be laid within a year after the offence, and the prisoner was allowed to bring witnesses for his exculpation. These penalties were lighter than those which were formerly imposed on a denial of the real presence: It was, however, subjoined in this statute, that the act of the six articles was still in force. But in order to make the king more entirely master of his people, it was enacted, that he might hereafter, at his pleasure, change this act, or any provision in it. By this clause, both parties were retained in subjection: So far as regarded religion, the king was invested, in the fullest manner, with the sole legislative authority in his kingdom: And all his subjects were, under the severest penalties, expressly bound to receive implicitly, whatever doctrine he should please to recommend to them.

The reformers began to entertain hopes, that this great power of the crown might still be employed in their favour. The king married Catherine Par, widow of Nevil lord Latimer; a woman of virtue, and somewhat inclined to the new doctrine. By this marriage, Henry confirmed what had formerly been foretold in jest, that he would be obliged to espouse a widow. The king's league with the emperor seemed a circumstance no less favourable to the catholic party; and thus matters remained still nearly balanced between the factions.

The advantages, gained by this powerful confederacy between

---

[i] Burnet, p. 322.   [k] 34 and 35 Hen. VIII. c. 1.

CHAPTER XXXIII

Henry and Charles, were inconsiderable during the present year. The campaign was opened with a victory, gained by the duke of Cleves, Francis's ally, over the forces of the emperor:[1] Francis, in person, took the field early; and made himself master, without resistance, of the whole dutchy of Luxembourg: He afterwards took Landrecy, and added some fortifications to it. Charles, having at last assembled a powerful army, appeared in the Low-Countries; and after taking almost every fortress in the dutchy of Cleves, he reduced the duke to accept of the terms, which he was pleased to prescribe to him. Being then joined by a body of six thousand English, he sat down before Landrecy, and covered the siege with an army of above forty thousand men. Francis advanced at the head of an army not much inferior; as if he intended to give the emperor battle, or oblige him to raise the siege; But while these two rival monarchs were facing each other, and all men were in expectation of some great event; the French king found means of throwing succour into Landrecy, and having thus effected his purpose, he skilfully made a retreat. Charles, finding the season far advanced, despaired of success in his enterprize, and found it necessary to go into winter-quarters.

The vanity of Henry was flattered, by the figure which he made in the great transactions on the continent: But the interests of his kingdom were more deeply concerned in the event of affairs in Scotland. Arran, the governor, was of so indolent and unambitious a character, that, had he not been stimulated by his friends and dependants, he never had aspired to any share in the administration; and when he found himself overpowered by the party of the queen-dowager, the cardinal, and the earl of Lenox, he was glad to accept of any terms of accommodation, however dishonourable. He even gave them a sure pledge of his sincerity, by renouncing the principles of the reformers, and reconciling himself to the Romish communion in the Franciscan church at Stirling. By this weakness and levity he lost his credit with the whole nation, and rendered the protestants, who were hitherto the chief support of his power, his mortal enemies. The cardinal acquired an entire ascendant in the kingdom: The queen-dowager placed implicit confidence in him: The governor was obliged to yield to him in

Affairs of Scotland.

[1] Memoires du Bellay, lib. 10.

every pretension: Lenox alone was become an obstacle to his measures, and reduced him to some difficulty.

The inveterate enmity, which had taken place between the families of Lenox and Arran, made the interests of these two noblemen entirely incompatible; and as the cardinal and the French party, in order to engage Lenox the more in their cause, had flattered him with the hopes of succeeding to the crown after their infant sovereign this rivalship had tended still farther to rouze the animosity of the Hamiltons. Lenox too had been encouraged to aspire to the marriage of the queen-dowager, which would have given him some pretensions to the regency; and as he was become assuming, on account of the services which he had rendered the party, the cardinal found, that, since he must chuse between the friendship of Lenox, and that of Arran, the latter nobleman, who was more easily governed, and who was invested with present authority, was in every respect preferable. Lenox, finding that he was not likely to succeed in his pretensions to the queen-dowager, and that Arran, favoured by the cardinal, had acquired the ascendant, retired to Dunbarton, the governor of which was entirely at his devotion; he entered into a secret correspondence with the English court; and he summoned his vassals and partizans to attend him. All those who were inclined to the protestant religion, or were on any account discontented with the cardinal's administration, now regarded Lenox as the head of their party; and they readily made him a tender of their services. In a little time, he had collected an army of ten thousand men, and he threatened his enemies with immediate destruction. The cardinal had no equal force to oppose to him; but as he was a prudent man, he foresaw, that Lenox could not long subsist so great an army, and he endeavoured to gain time, by opening a negociation with him. He seduced his followers, by various artifices; he prevailed on the Douglasses to change party; he represented to the whole nation the danger of civil wars and commotions: And Lenox, observing the unequal contest, in which he was engaged, was at last obliged to lay down his arms, and to accept of an accommodation with the governor and the cardinal. Present peace was restored; but no confidence took place between the parties. Lenox, fortifying his castles, and putting himself in a posture of defence, waited the

CHAPTER XXXIII

arrival of English succours, from whose assistance alone he expected to obtain the superiority over his enemies.

While the winter season restrained Henry from military operations, he summoned a new parliament; in which a law was passed, such as he was pleased to dictate, with regard to the succession of the crown. After declaring, that the prince of Wales, or any of the king's male issue, were first and immediate heirs to the crown, the parliament restored the two princesses, Mary and Elizabeth, to their right of succession. This seemed a reasonable piece of justice, and corrected what the king's former violence had thrown into confusion; but it was impossible for Henry to do any thing, how laudable soever, without betraying in some circumstance, his usual extravagance and caprice: Though he opened the way for these two princesses to mount the throne, he would not allow the acts to be reversed, which had declared them illegitimate; he made the parliament confer on him a power of still excluding them, if they refused to submit to any conditions, which he should be pleased to impose; and he required them to enact, that, in default of his own issue, he might dispose of the crown, as he pleased, by will or letters patent. He did not probably foresee, that, in proportion as he degraded the parliament, by rendering it the passive instrument of his variable and violent inclinations, he taught the people to regard all its acts as invalid, and thereby defeated even the purposes, which he was so bent to attain.

1544. January 14. A parliament.

An act passed, declaring that the king's usual stile should be "King of England, France, and Ireland, defender of the faith, and on earth the supreme head of the church of England and Ireland." It seemed a palpable inconsistency, to retain the title of Defender of the faith, which the court of Rome had conferred on him, for maintaining its cause against Luther; and yet subjoin his ecclesiastical supremacy, in opposition to the claims of that court.

An act also passed, for the remission of the debt, which the king had lately contracted by a general loan, levied upon the people. It will easily be believed, that, after the former act of this kind, the loan was not entirely voluntary.[m] But there was a peculiar circumstance, attending the present statute, which none but Henry would

[m] 35 Hen. VIII. c. 12.

have thought of; namely, that those who had already gotten payment, either in whole or in part, should refund the money to the exchequer.

The oaths, which Henry imposed for the security of his ecclesiastical model, were not more reasonable than his other measures. All his subjects of any distinction had already been obliged to renounce the pope's supremacy; but as the clauses to which they swore had not been deemed entirely satisfactory, another oath was imposed; and it was added, that all those who had taken the former oaths, should be understood to have taken the new one.[n] A strange supposition! to represent men as bound by an oath, which they had never taken.

The most commendable law, to which the parliament gave their sanction, was that by which they mitigated the law of the six articles, and enacted, that no person should be put to his trial upon an accusation concerning any of the offences comprized in that sanguinary statute, except on the oath of twelve persons before commissioners authorized for the purpose; and that no person should be arrested or committed to ward for any such offence before he was indicted. Any preacher, accused of speaking in his sermon contrary to these articles, must be indicted within forty days.

The king always experienced the limits of his authority, whenever he demanded subsidies, however moderate, from the parliament; and, therefore, not to hazard a refusal, he made no mention this season of a supply: But as his wars both in France and Scotland, as well as his usual prodigality, had involved him in great expence, he had recourse to other methods of filling his exchequer. Notwithstanding the former abolition of his debts, he yet required new loans from his subjects: And he enhanced gold from forty-five shillings to forty-eight an ounce; and silver from three shillings and nine pence to four shillings. His pretence for this innovation, was to prevent the money from being exported; as if that expedient could anywise serve the purpose. He even coined some base money, and ordered it to be current by proclamation. He named commissioners for levying a benevolence, and he extorted about seventy thousand pounds by this expedient. Read,

[n] 35 Hen. VIII. c. 1.

alderman of London,[o] a man somewhat advanced in years, having refused to contribute, or not coming up to the expectation of the commissioners, was inrolled as a foot-soldier in the Scottish wars, and was there taken prisoner. Roach, who had been equally refractory, was thrown into prison, and obtained not his liberty but by paying a large composition.[p] These powers of the prerogative (which at that time passed unquestioned), the compelling of any man to serve in any office, and the imprisoning of any man during pleasure, not to mention the practice of extorting loans, rendered the sovereign in a manner, absolute master of the person and property of every individual.

Early this year the king sent a fleet and army to invade Scotland. The fleet consisted of near two hundred vessels, and carried on board ten thousand men. Dudley lord Lisle commanded the sea-forces; the earl of Hertford the land. The troops were disembarked near Leith; and after dispersing a small body which opposed them, they took the town without resistance, and then marched to Edinburgh. The gates were soon beaten down (for little or no resistance was made); and the English first pillaged, and then set fire to the city. The regent and cardinal were not prepared to oppose so great a force, and they fled to Stirling. Hertford marched eastward; and being joined by a new body under Evers, warden of the east marches, he laid waste the whole country, burned and destroyed Haddington and Dunbar, then retreated into England; having lost only forty men in the whole expedition. The earl of Arran collected some forces; but finding that the English were already departed, he turned them against Lenox, who was justly suspected of a correspondence with the enemy. That nobleman, after making some resistance, was obliged to fly into England; where Henry settled a pension on him, and even gave him his niece, lady Margaret Douglas, in marriage. In return, Lenox stipulated conditions, by which, had he been able to execute them, he must have reduced his country to total servitude.[q]

Henry's policy was blamed in this sudden and violent incursion; by which he inflamed the passions of the Scots, without subduing their spirit; and it was commonly said, that he did too

[o] Herbert. Stowe, p. 588. Baker, p. 292. [p] Goodwin's Annals. Stowe, p. 588. [q] Rymer, vol. xv. p. 23, 29.

much, if he intended to solicit an alliance, and too little, if he meant a conquest.[r] But the reason of his recalling the troops so soon, was his eagerness to carry on a projected enterprize against France, in which he intended to employ the whole force of his kingdom. He had concerted a plan with the emperor, which threatened the total ruin of that monarchy, and must, as a necessary consequence, have involved the ruin of England. These two princes had agreed to invade France with forces amounting to above a hundred thousand men: Henry engaged to set out from Calais: Charles from the Low-countries: They were to enter on no siege; but leaving all the frontier towns behind them, to march directly to Paris, where they were to join their forces, and thence to proceed to the entire conquest of the kingdom. Francis could not oppose, to these formidable preparations, much above forty thousand men.

14th July. Campaign in France.

Henry, having appointed the queen regent during his absence, passed over to Calais with thirty thousand men, accompanied by the dukes of Norfolk and Suffolk, Fitzalan earl of Arundel, Vere earl of Oxford, the earl of Surrey, Paulet lord St. John, lord Ferrers of Chartley, lord Mountjoy, lord Grey of Wilton, Sir Anthony Brown, Sir Francis Bryan, and the most flourishing nobility and gentry of his kingdom. The English army was soon joined by the count de Buren, admiral of Flanders, with ten thousand foot, and four thousand horse; and the whole composed an army, which nothing on that frontier was able to resist. The chief force of the French armies was drawn to the side of Champagne, in order to oppose the Imperialists.

The emperor, with an army of near sixty thousand men, had taken the field much earlier than Henry; and not to lose time, while he waited for the arrival of his confederate, he sat down before Luxembourg, which was surrendered to him: He thence proceeded to Commercy on the Meuse, which he took: Ligny met with the same fate: He next laid siege to St. Disier on the Marne, which, though a weak place, made a brave resistance, under the count of Sancerre, the governor, and the siege was protracted beyond expectation.

The emperor was employed before this town at the time the

[r] Herbert. Burnet.

CHAPTER XXXIII

English forces were assembled in Picardy. Henry, either tempted by the defenceless condition of the French frontier, or thinking that the emperor had first broken his engagement, by forming sieges, or, perhaps, foreseeing at last the dangerous consequences of entirely subduing the French power, instead of marching forward to Paris, sat down before Montreuil and Boulogne. The duke of Norfolk commanded the army before Montreuil: The king himself that before Boulogne. Vervin was governor of the latter place, and under him Philip Corse, a brave old soldier, who encouraged the garrison to defend themselves to the last extremity against the English. He was killed during the course of the siege, and the town *14th Sept.* was immediately surrendered to Henry by the cowardice of Vervin; who was afterwards beheaded for this dishonourable capitulation.

During the course of this siege, Charles had taken St. Disier; and finding the season much advanced, he began to hearken to a treaty of peace with France, since all his schemes for subduing that kingdom were likely to prove abortive. In order to have a pretence for deserting his ally, he sent a messenger to the English camp, requiring Henry immediately to fulfil his engagements, and to meet him with his army before Paris. Henry replied, that he was too far engaged in the siege of Boulogne to raise it with honour, and that the emperor himself had first broken the concert by besieging St. Disier. This answer served Charles as a sufficient reason for concluding a peace with Francis, at Crepy, where no mention was made of England. He stipulated to give Flanders as *18th Sept.* a dowry to his daughter, whom he agreed to marry to the duke of Orleans, Francis's second son; and Francis, in return, withdrew his troops from Piedmont and Savoy, and renounced all claim to Milan, Naples, and other territories in Italy. This peace, so advantageous to Francis, was procured, partly by the decisive victory obtained in the beginning of the campaign by the count of Anguyen over the Imperialists at Cerisolles in Piedmont, partly by the emperor's great desire to turn his arms against the protestant princes in Germany. Charles ordered his troops to separate from the English in Picardy; and Henry, finding himself obliged to raise *30th Sept.* the siege of Montreuil, returned into England. This campaign served, to the populace, as matter of great triumph; but all men of sense concluded, that the king had, as in all his former military enterprizes, made, at a great expence, an acquisition, which was of no importance.

The war with Scotland, meanwhile, was conducted feebly, and with various success. Sir Ralph Evers, now lord Evers, and Sir Bryan Latoun, made an inroad into that kingdom; and having laid waste the counties of Tiviotdale and the Merse, they proceeded to the abbey of Coldingham, which they took possession of, and fortified. The governor assembled an army of eight thousand men, in order to dislodge them from this post; but he had no sooner opened his batteries before the place, than a sudden panic seized him; he left the army, and fled to Dunbar. He complained of the mutiny of his troops, and pretended apprehensions lest they should deliver him into the hands of the English: But his own unwarlike spirit was generally believed to have been the motive of this dishonourable flight. The Scottish army upon the departure of their general, fell into confusion; and had not Angus, with a few of his retainers, brought off the cannon, and protected their rear, the English might have gained great advantages over them. Evers, elated with this success, boasted to Henry, that he had conquered all Scotland to the Forth; and he claimed a reward for this important service. The duke of Norfolk, who knew with what difficulty such acquisitions would be maintained against a warlike enemy, advised the king to grant him, as his reward, the conquests of which he boasted so highly. The next inroad made by the English, shewed the vanity of Evers's hopes. This general led about five thousand men into Tiviotdale, and was employed in ravaging that country; when intelligence was brought him, that some Scottish forces appeared near the abbey of Melross. Angus had roused the governor to more activity; and a proclamation being issued for assembling the troops of the neighbouring counties, a considerable body had repaired thither to oppose the enemy. Norman Lesly, son of the earl of Rothes, had also joined the army with some voluntiers from Fife; and he inspired courage into the whole, as well by this accession of force, as by his personal bravery and intrepidity. In order to bring their troops to the necessity of a steady defence, the Scottish leaders ordered all their cavalry to dismount; and they resolved to wait, on some high grounds near Ancram, the assault of the English. The English, whose past suc-

1545.

17th Feb.

CHAPTER XXXIII

cesses had taught them too much to despise the enemy, thought, when they saw the Scottish horses led off the field, that the whole army was retiring; and they hastened to attack them. The Scots received them in good order; and being favoured by the advantage of the ground, as well as by the surprize of the English, who expected no resistance, they soon put them to flight, and pursued them with considerable slaughter. Evers and Latoun were both killed, and above a thousand men were made prisoners. In order to support the Scots in this war, Francis, some time after, sent over a body of auxiliaries, to the number of three thousand five hundred men, under the command of Montgomery, lord of Lorges.[s] Reinforced by these succours, the governor assembled an army of fifteen thousand men at Haddington, and marched thence to ravage the east borders of England. He laid all waste wherever he came; and having met with no considerable resistance, he retired into his own country, and disbanded his army. The earl of Hertford, in revenge, committed ravages on the middle and west marches, and the war on both sides was signalized rather by the ills inflicted on the enemy, than by any considerable advantage gained by either party.

The war likewise between France and England was not distinguished this year by any memorable event. Francis had equipped a fleet of above two hundred sail, besides gallies; and having embarked some land-forces on board, he sent them to make a descent in England.[t] They sailed to the Isle of Wight, where they found the English fleet lying at anchor in St. Helen's. It consisted not of above a hundred sail; and the admiral thought it most advisable to remain in that road, in hopes of drawing the French into the narrow channels and the rocks, which were unknown to them. The two fleets cannonaded each other for two days; and except the sinking of the Mary Rose, one of the largest ships of the English fleet, the damage on both sides was inconsiderable.

Francis's chief intention, in equipping so great a fleet, was to prevent the English from throwing succours into Boulogne, which he resolved to besiege; and for that purpose, he ordered a fort to be built, by which he intended to block up the harbour. After a considerable loss of time and money, the fort was found so ill

[s] Buchanan, lib. 15. Drummond.   [t] Beleair. Memoires du Bellay.

constructed, that he was obliged to abandon it; and though he had assembled, on that frontier, an army of near forty thousand men, he was not able to effect any considerable enterprize. Henry, in order to defend his possessions in France, had levied fourteen thousand Germans; who, having marched to Fleurines in the bishopric of Liege, found that they could advance no farther. The emperor would not allow them a passage through his dominions: They received intelligence of a superior army on the side of France ready to intercept them. Want of occupation and of pay soon produced a mutiny among them: And having seized the English commissaries as a security for arrears, they retreated into their own country. There seems to have been some want of foresight in this expensive armament.

23d Nov. A parliament. The great expence of these two wars, maintained by Henry, obliged him to summon a new parliament. The commons granted him a subsidy, payable in two years, of two shillings a pound on land.[u] The spirituality voted him six shillings a pound. But the parliament, apprehensive lest more demands should be made upon them, endeavoured to save themselves by a very extraordinary liberality of other people's property: By one vote they bestowed on the king all the revenues of the universities, as well as of the chauntries, free chapels,[w] and hospitals. Henry was pleased with this concession, as it encreased his power; but he had no intention to rob learning of all her endowments; and he soon took care to inform the universities, that he meant not to touch their revenues. Thus these ancient and celebrated establishments owe their existence to the generosity of the king, not to the protection of this servile and prostitute parliament.

The prostitute spirit of the parliament farther appeared in the preamble of a statute;[x] in which they recognize the king to have always been, by the word of God, supreme head of the church of

---

[u] Those who possessed goods or money, above five pound and below ten, were to pay eight pence a pound: Those above ten pound, a shilling.   [w] A chauntry was a little church, chapel, or particular altar in some cathedral church, &c. endowed with lands or other revenues for the maintainance of one or more priests, daily to say mass or perform divine service, for the use of the founders, or such others as they appointed: Free chapels were independant on any church, and endowed for much the same purpose as the former. Jacob's Law Dict.   [x] 37 Hen. VIII. c. 17.

England; and acknowledge, that archbishops, bishops, and other ecclesiastical persons, have no manner of jurisdiction but by his royal mandate: To him alone, say they, and such persons as he shall appoint, full power and authority is given from above to hear and determine all manner of causes ecclesiastical, and to correct all manner of heresies, errors, vices, and sins whatsoever. No mention is here made of the concurrence of a convocation, or even of a parliament. His proclamations are in effect acknowledged to have, not only the force of law, but the authority of revelation; and by his royal power he might regulate the actions of men, controul their words, and even direct their inward sentiments and opinions.

The king made in person a speech to the parliament on proroguing them; in which, after thanking them for their loving attachment to him, which, he said, equalled what was ever paid by their ancestors to any king of England, he complained of their dissentions, disputes, and animosities in religion. He told them, that the several pulpits were become a kind of batteries against each other; and that one preacher called another heretic and anabaptist, which was retaliated by the opprobrious appellations of papist and hypocrite: That he had permitted his people the use of the Scriptures, not in order to furnish them with materials for disputing and railing, but that he might enable them to inform their consciences and instruct their children and families: That it grieved his heart to find how that precious jewel was prostituted, by being introduced into the conversation of every alehouse and tavern, and employed as a pretence for decrying the spiritual and legal pastors: And that he was sorry to observe, that the word of God, while it was the object of so much anxious speculation, had very little influence on their practice; and that, though an imaginary knowledge so much abounded, charity was daily going to decay.[y] The king gave good advice; but his own example, by encouraging speculation and dispute, was ill fitted to promote that peaceable submission of opinion, which he recommended.

24th Dec.

Henry employed in military preparations the money granted by parliament; and he sent over the earl of Hertford, and lord Lisle, the admiral, to Calais, with a body of nine thousand men, two-thirds of which consisted of foreigners. Some skirmishes of small

1546.

[y] Hall, fol. 261. Herbert, p. 534.

moment ensued with the French; and no hopes of any considerable progress could be entertained by either party. Henry, whose animosity against Francis was not violent, had given sufficient vent to his humour by this short war; and finding, that, from his great encrease in corpulence and decay in strength, he could not hope for much longer life, he was desirous of ending a quarrel, which might prove dangerous to his kingdom during a minority. Francis likewise, on his part, was not averse to peace with England; because, having lately lost his son, the duke of Orleans, he revived his ancient claim upon Milan, and foresaw, that hostilities must soon, on that account, break out between him and the emperor. Commissioners, therefore, having met at Campe, a small place between Ardres and Guisnes, the articles were soon agreed on, and the peace signed by them. The chief conditions were, that Henry should retain Boulogne during eight years, or till the former debt due by Francis should be paid. This debt was settled at two millions of livres, besides a claim of 500,000 livres, which was afterwards to be adjusted. Francis took care to comprehend Scotland in the treaty. Thus all that Henry obtained by a war, which cost him above one million three hundred and forty thousand pounds sterling,[z] was a bad and a chargeable security for a debt, which was not a third of the value.

7th June. Peace with France and Scotland.

The king, now freed from all foreign wars, had leisure to give his attention to domestic affairs; particularly to the establishment of uniformity in opinion, on which he was so intent. Though he allowed an English translation of the Bible, he had hitherto been very careful to keep the mass in Latin; but he was at last prevailed on to permit, that the Litany, a considerable part of the service, should be celebrated in the vulgar tongue; and by this innovation, he excited anew the hopes of the reformers, who had been somewhat discouraged by the severe law of the six articles. One petition of the new Litany was a prayer to save us *from the tyranny of the bishop of Rome, and from all his detestable enormities.* Cranmer employed his credit to draw Henry into farther innovations; and he took advantage of Gardiner's absence, who was sent on an embassy to the emperor: But Gardiner, having written to the king, that, if he carried his opposition against the catholic religion to greater ex-

---

[z] Herbert. Stowe.

tremities, Charles threatened to break off all commerce with him, the success of Cranmer's projects was for some time retarded. Cranmer lost this year the most sincere and powerful friend that he possessed at court, Charles Brandon, duke of Suffolk: The queen-dowager of France, consort to Suffolk, had died some years before. This nobleman is one instance, that Henry was not altogether incapable of a cordial and steady friendship; and Suffolk seems to have been worthy of the favour, which, from his earliest youth, he had enjoyed with his master. The king was sitting in council when informed of Suffolk's death; and he took the opportunity both to express his own sorrow for the loss, and to celebrate the merits of the deceased. He declared, that, during the whole course of their friendship, his brother-in-law had never made one attempt to injure an adversary, and had never whispered a word to the disadvantage of any person. "Is there any of you, my lords, who can say as much?" When the king subjoined these words, he looked round in all their faces, and saw that confusion, which the consciousness of secret guilt naturally threw upon them.[a]

Cranmer himself, when bereaved of this support, was the more exposed to those cabals of the courtiers, which the opposition in party and religion, joined to the usual motives of interest, rendered so frequent among Henry's ministers and counsellors. The catholics took hold of the king by his passion for orthodoxy; and they represented to him, that, if his laudable zeal for inforcing the truth met with no better success, it was altogether owing to the primate, whose example and encouragement were, in reality, the secret supports of heresy. Henry, seeing the point at which they aimed, feigned a compliance, and desired the council to make enquiry into Cranmer's conduct; promising that, if he were found guilty, he should be committed to prison, and brought to condign punishment. Every body now considered the primate as lost; and his old friends, from interested views, as well as the opposite party, from animosity, began to show him marks of neglect and disregard. He was obliged to stand several hours among the lacqueys at the door of the council-chamber, before he could be admitted; and when he was at last called in, he was told, that they had determined to send him to the Tower. Cranmer said, that he ap-

[a] Coke's Inst. cap. 99.

pealed to the king himself; and finding his appeal disregarded, he produced a ring, which Henry had given him as a pledge of favour and protection. The council were confounded; and when they came before the king, he reproved them in the severest terms, and told them, that he was well acquainted with Cranmer's merit, as well as with their malignity and envy: But he was determined to crush all their cabals, and to teach them, by the severest discipline, since gentle methods were ineffectual, a more dutiful concurrence in promoting his service. Norfolk, who was Cranmer's capital enemy, apologized for their conduct, and said, that their only intention was to set the primate's innocence in a full light, by bringing him to an open trial: And Henry obliged them all to embrace him, as a sign of their cordial reconciliation. The mild temper of Cranmer rendered this agreement more sincere on his part, than is usual in such forced compliances.[b]

Persecutions.

But though Henry's favour for Cranmer rendered fruitless all accusations against him, his pride and peevishness, irritated by his declining state of health, impelled him to punish with fresh severity all others, who presumed to entertain a different opinion from himself, particularly in the capital point of the real presence. Anne Ascue, a young woman of merit as well as beauty,[c] who had great connexions with the chief ladies at court, and with the queen herself, was accused of dogmatizing on that delicate article; and Henry, instead of shewing indulgence to the weakness of her sex and age, was but the more provoked, that a woman should dare to oppose his theological sentiments. She was prevailed on by Bonner's menaces to make a seeming recantation; but she qualified it with some reserves, which did not satisfy that zealous prelate. She was thrown into prison, and she there employed herself in composing prayers and discourses, by which she fortified her resolution to endure the utmost extremity rather than relinquish her religious principles. She even wrote to the king, and told him, that, as to the Lord's Supper, she believed as much as Christ himself had said of it, and as much of his divine doctrine as the catholic church had required: But while she could not be brought to acknowledge an assent to the king's explications, this declaration availed her

[b] Burnet, vol. i. p. 343, 344. Antiq. Brit. in vita Cranm. [c] Bale, Speed, 780.

CHAPTER XXXIII

nothing, and was rather regarded as a fresh insult. The chancellor, Wriothesely, who had succeeded Audley, and who was much attached to the catholic party, was sent to examine her with regard to her patrons at court, and the great ladies who were in correspondence with her: But she maintained a laudable fidelity to her friends, and would confess nothing. She was put to the torture in the most barbarous manner, and continued still resolute in preserving secrecy. Some authors[d] add an extraordinary circumstance: That the chancellor, who stood by, ordered the lieutenant of the Tower to stretch the rack still farther; but that officer refused compliance: The chancellor menaced him; but met with a new refusal: Upon which that magistrate, who was otherwise a person of merit, but intoxicated with religious zeal, put his own hand to the rack, and drew it so violently that he almost tore her body asunder. Her constancy still surpassed the barbarity of her persecutors, and they found all their efforts to be baffled. She was then condemned to be burned alive; and being so dislocated by the rack, that she could not stand, she was carried to the stake in a chair. Together with her, were conducted Nicholas Belenian, a priest, John Lassels, of the king's household, and John Adams a tailor, who had been condemned for the same crime to the same punishment. They were all tied to the stake; and in that dreadful situation the chancellor sent to inform them, that their pardon was ready drawn and signed, and should instantly be given them, if they would merit it by a recantation. They only regarded this offer as a new ornament to their crown of martyrdom; and they saw with tranquillity the executioner kindle the flames, which consumed them. Wriothesely did not consider, that this public and noted situation interested their honour the more to maintain a steady perseverance.

Though the secrecy and fidelity of Anne Ascue saved the queen from this peril, that princess soon after fell into a new danger, from which she narrowly escaped. An ulcer had broken out in the king's leg, which, added to his extreme corpulency and his bad habit of body, began both to threaten his life, and to render him,

---

[d] Fox, vol. ii. p. 578. Speed, p. 780. Baker, p. 299. But Burnet questions the truth of this circumstance; Fox, however, transcribes her own paper, where she relates it. I must add, in justice to the king, that he disapproved of Wriotheseley's conduct, and commended the lieutenant.

even more than usually, peevish and passionate. The queen attended him with the most tender and dutiful care, and endeavoured, by every soothing art and compliance, to allay those gusts of humour, to which he was become so subject. His favourite topic of conversation was theology; and Catherine, whose good sense enabled her to discourse on any subject, was frequently engaged in the argument; and being secretly inclined to the principles of the reformers, she unwarily betrayed too much of her mind on these occasions. Henry, highly provoked, that she should presume to differ from him, complained of her obstinacy to Gardiner, who gladly laid hold of the opportunity to inflame the quarrel. He praised the king's anxious concern for preserving the orthodoxy of his subjects; and represented, that the more elevated the person was who was chastised, and the more near to his person, the greater terror would the example strike into every one, and the more glorious would the sacrifice appear to posterity. The chancellor, being consulted, was engaged by religious zeal to second these topics; and Henry, hurried on by his own impetuous temper, and encouraged by his counsellors, went so far as to order articles of impeachment to be drawn up against his consort. Wriothesely executed his commands; and soon after brought the paper to him to be signed: For as it was high treason to throw slander upon the queen, he might otherwise have been questioned for his temerity. By some means, this important paper fell into the hands of one of the queen's friends, who immediately carried the intelligence to her. She was sensible of the extreme danger, to which she was exposed; but did not despair of being able, by her prudence and address, still to elude the efforts of her enemies. She paid her usual visit to the king, and found him in a more serene disposition than she had reason to expect. He entered on the subject, which was so familiar to him; and he seemed to challenge her to an argument in divinity. She gently declined the conversation, and remarked, that such profound speculations were ill suited to the natural imbecillity of her sex. Women, she said, by their first creation, were made subject to men: The male was created after the image of God; the female after the image of the male: It belonged to the husband to chuse principles for his wife; the wife's duty was, in all cases, to adopt implicitly the sentiments of her husband: And as to herself, it was doubly her duty, being blest with a husband, who was qualified, by his judgment and learning, not only to chuse principles for his own family, but for the most wise and knowing of every nation. "Not so! by St. Mary," replied the king, "you are now become a doctor, Kate; and better fitted to give than receive instruction." She meekly replied, that she was sensible how little she was intitled to these praises; that though she usually declined not any conversation, however sublime, when proposed by his majesty, she well knew, that her conceptions could serve to no other purpose than to give him a little momentary amusement; that she found the conversation apt to languish when not revived by some opposition, and she had ventured sometimes to feign a contrariety of sentiments, in order to give him the pleasure of refuting her; and that she also purposed, by this innocent artifice, to engage him into topics, whence, she had observed by frequent experience, that she reaped profit and instruction. "And is it so, sweetheart?" replied the king, "then are we perfect friends again." He embraced her with great affection, and sent her away with assurances of his protection and kindness. Her enemies, who knew nothing of this sudden change, prepared next day to convey her to the Tower, pursuant to the king's warrant. Henry and Catherine were conversing amicably in the garden, when the chancellor appeared with forty of the pursuivants. The king spoke to him at some distance from her; and seemed to expostulate with him in the severest manner: She even overheard the appellations of *knave*, *fool*, and *beast*, which he liberally bestowed upon that magistrate, and then ordered him to depart his presence. She afterwards interposed to mitigate his anger: He said to her, "Poor soul! you know not how ill intitled this man is to your good offices." Thenceforth, the queen, having narrowly escaped so great a danger, was careful not to offend Henry's humour by any contradiction; and Gardiner, whose malice had endeavoured to widen the breach, could never afterwards regain his favour and good opinion.[e]

But Henry's tyrannical disposition, soured by ill health, burst out soon after to the destruction of a man, who possessed a much superior rank to that of Gardiner. The duke of Norfolk and his father, during this whole reign, and even a part of the foregoing,

[e] Burnet, vol. i. p. 344. Herbert, p. 560. Speed, p. 780. Fox's Acts and Monuments, vol. ii. p. 58.

had been regarded as the greatest subjects in the kingdom, and had rendered considerable service to the crown. The duke himself had in his youth acquired reputation by naval enterprizes: He had much contributed to the victory gained over the Scots at Flouden: He had suppressed a dangerous rebellion in the North: And he had always done his part with honour in all the expeditions against France. Fortune seemed to conspire with his own industry, in raising him to the greatest elevation. From the favours heaped on him by the crown, he had acquired an immense estate: The king had successively been married to two of his nieces; and the king's natural son, the duke of Richmond, had married his daughter: Besides his descent from the ancient family of the Moubrays, by which he was allied to the throne, he had espoused a daughter of the duke of Buckingham, who was descended by a female from Edward III.: And as he was believed still to adhere secretly to the ancient religion, he was regarded, both abroad and at home, as the head of the catholic party. But all these circumstances, in proportion as they exalted the duke, provoked the jealousy of Henry; and he foresaw danger, during his son's minority, both to the public tranquillity, and to the new ecclesiastical system, from the attempts of so potent a subject. But nothing tended more to expose Norfolk to the king's displeasure, than the prejudices, which Henry had entertained against the earl of Surrey, son of that nobleman.

Surrey was a young man of the most promising hopes, and had distinguished himself by every accomplishment, which became a scholar, a courtier, and a soldier. He excelled in all the military exercises, which were then in request: He encouraged the fine arts by his patronage and example: He had made some successful attempts in poetry; and being smitten with the romantic gallantry of the age, he celebrated the praises of his mistress, by his pen and his lance, in every masque and tournament. His spirit and ambition were equal to his talent and his quality; and he did not always regulate his conduct by the caution and reserve, which his situation required. He had been left governor of Bologne, when that town was taken by Henry; but though his personal bravery was unquestioned, he had been unfortunate in some rencounters with the French. The king, somewhat displeased with his conduct, had sent over Hertford to command in his place; and Surrey was so imprudent as to drop some menacing expressions against the ministers,

CHAPTER XXXIII

on account of this affront, which was put upon him. And as he had refused to marry Hertford's daughter, and even waved every other proposal of marriage; Henry imagined, that he had entertained views of espousing the lady Mary; and he was instantly determined to repress, by the most severe expedients, so dangerous an ambition.

Actuated by all these motives, and perhaps influenced by that old disgust, with which the ill conduct of Catherine Howard had inspired him against her whole family, he gave private orders to arrest Norfolk and Surrey; and they were on the same day confined in the Tower. Surrey being a commoner, his trial was the more expeditious; and as to proofs, neither parliaments nor juries seem ever to have given the least attention to them in any cause of the crown, during this whole reign. He was accused of entertaining in his family some Italians who were *suspected* to be spies; a servant of his had paid a visit to cardinal Pole in Italy, whence he was *suspected* of holding a correspondence with that obnoxious prelate; he had quartered the arms of Edward the Confessor on his scutcheon, which made him be *suspected* of aspiring to the crown, though both he and his ancestors had openly, during the course of many years, maintained that practice, and the heralds had even justified it by their authority. These were the crimes, for which a jury, notwithstanding his eloquent and spirited defence, condemned the earl of Surrey for high treason; and their sentence was soon after executed upon him. *12th Dec.*

1547.

Execution of the earl of Surrey.

The innocence of the duke of Norfolk was still, if possible, more apparent than that of his son; and his services to the crown had been greater. His dutchess, with whom he lived on bad terms, had been so base as to carry intelligence to his enemies of all she knew against him: Elizabeth Holland, a mistress of his, had been equally subservient to the design of the court: Yet with all these advantages his accusers discovered no greater crime, than his once saying, that the king was sickly, and could not hold out long; and the kingdom was likely to fall into disorders, through the diversity of religious opinions. He wrote a pathetic letter to the king, pleading his past services, and protesting his innocence: Soon after, he embraced a more proper expedient for appeasing Henry, by making a submission and confession, such as his enemies required: But nothing could mollify the unrelenting temper of the king. He assembled a *14th Jan.*

Attainder of the duke of Norfolk.

parliament, as the surest and most expeditious instrument of his tyranny, and the house of peers, without examining the prisoner, without trial or evidence, passed a bill of attainder against him, and sent it down to the commons. Cranmer, though engaged for many years in an opposite party to Norfolk, and though he had received many and great injuries from him, would have no hand in so unjust a prosecution; and he retired to his seat at Croydon.[f] The king was now approaching fast towards his end; and fearing lest Norfolk should escape him, he sent a message to the commons, by which he desired them to hasten the bill, on pretence, that Norfolk enjoyed the dignity of earl marshal, and it was necessary to appoint another, who might officiate at the ensuing ceremony of installing his son prince of Wales. The obsequious commons obeyed his directions, though founded on so frivolous a pretence; and the king, having affixed the royal assent to the bill by commissioners, issued orders for the execution of Norfolk on the morning of the twenty-ninth of January. But news being carried to the Tower, that the king himself had expired that night, the lieutenant deferred obeying the warrant; and it was not thought advisable by the council to begin a new reign by the death of the greatest nobleman in the kingdom, who had been condemned by a sentence so unjust and tyrannical.

The king's health had long been in a declining state; but for several days all those near him plainly saw his end approaching. He was become so froward, that no one durst inform him of his condition; and as some persons, during this reign, had suffered as traitors for foretelling the king's death,[g] every one was afraid, lest, in the transports of his fury, he might, on this pretence, punish capitally the author of such friendly intelligence. At last, Sir Anthony Denny ventured to disclose to him the fatal secret, and exhorted him to prepare for the fate, which was awaiting him. He expressed his resignation; and desired that Cranmer might be sent for: But before the prelate arrived he was speechless, though he still seemed to retain his senses. Cranmer desired him to give some sign of his dying in the faith of Christ: He squeezed the prelate's hand, and immediately expired, after a reign of thirty-seven years and nine months; and in the fifty-sixth year of his age.

Death of the king.

[f] Burnet, vol. i. p. 348. Fox.   [g] Lanquet's Epitome of Chronicles in the year 1541.

CHAPTER XXXIII

The king had made his will near a month before his demise; in which he confirmed the destination of parliament, by leaving the crown first to prince Edward, then to the lady Mary, next to the lady Elizabeth: The two princesses he obliged, under the penalty of forfeiting their title to the crown, not to marry without consent of the council, which he appointed for the government of his minor son. After his own children, he settled the succession on Frances Brandon, marchioness of Dorset, elder daughter of his sister, the French queen; then on Eleanor, countess of Cumberland, the second daughter. In passing over the posterity of the queen of Scots, his elder sister, he made use of the power obtained from parliament; but as he subjoined, that, after the failure of the French queen's posterity, the crown should descend to the next lawful heir, it afterwards became a question, whether these words could be applied to the Scottish line. It was thought, that these princes were not the next heirs after the house of Suffolk, but before that house; and that Henry, by expressing himself in this manner, meant entirely to exclude them. The late injuries, which he had received from the Scots, had irritated him extremely against that nation; and he maintained to the last that character of violence and caprice, by which his life had been so much distinguished. Another circumstance of his will may suggest the same reflection with regard to the strange contrarieties of his temper and conduct: He left money for masses to be said for delivering his soul from purgatory; and though he destroyed all those institutions, established by his ancestors and others, for the benefit of their souls; and had even left the doctrine of purgatory doubtful in all the articles of faith, which he promulgated during his later years; he was yet determined, when the hour of death was approaching, to take care, at least, of his own future repose, and to adhere to the safer side of the question.[h]

It is difficult to give a just summary of this prince's qualities: He was so different from himself in different parts of his reign, that, as is well remarked by lord Herbert, his history is his best character and description. The absolute, uncontrouled authority which he maintained at home, and the regard which he acquired among foreign nations, are circumstances, which entitle him, in some

His character.

[h] See his will in Fuller, Heylin, and Rymer, p. 110. There is no reasonable ground to suspect its authenticity.

degree, to the appellation of a *great* prince; while his tyranny and barbarity exclude him from the character of a *good* one. He possessed, indeed, great vigour of mind, which qualified him for exercising dominion over men; courage, intrepidity, vigilance, inflexibility: And though these qualities lay not always under the guidance of a regular and solid judgment, they were accompanied with good parts, and an extensive capacity; and every one dreaded a contest with a man, who was known never to yield or to forgive, and who, in every controversy, was determined, either to ruin himself or his antagonist. A catalogue of his vices would comprehend many of the worst qualities incident to human nature: Violence, cruelty, profusion, rapacity, injustice, obstinacy, arrogance, bigotry, presumption, caprice: But neither was he subject to all these vices in the most extreme degree, nor was he, at intervals altogether destitute of virtues: He was sincere, open, gallant, liberal, and capable at least of a temporary friendship and attachment. In this respect he was unfortunate, that the incidents of his reign served to display his faults in their full light: The treatment, which he met with from the court of Rome, provoked him to violence; the danger of a revolt from his superstitious subjects, seemed to require the most extreme severity. But it must, at the same time, be acknowledged, that his situation tended to throw an additional lustre on what was great and magnanimous in his character: The emulation between the emperor and the French king rendered his alliance, notwithstanding his impolitic conduct, of great importance in Europe: The extensive powers of his prerogative, and the submissive, not to say slavish, disposition of his parliaments, made it the more easy for him to assume and maintain that entire dominion, by which his reign is so much distinguished in the English history.

It may seem a little extraordinary, that, notwithstanding his cruelty, his extortion, his violence, his arbitrary administration, this prince not only acquired the regard of his subjects; but never was the object of their hatred: He seems even in some degree to have possessed, to the last, their love and affection.[i] His exterior qualities were advantageous, and fit to captivate the multitude: His magnificence and personal bravery rendered him illustrious in

[i] Strype, vol. i. p. 389.

CHAPTER XXXIII

vulgar eyes: And it may be said, with truth, that the English in that age were so thoroughly subdued, that, like eastern slaves, they were inclined to admire those acts of violence and tyranny, which were exercised over themselves, and at their own expence.

With regard to foreign states, Henry appears long to have supported an intercourse of friendship with Francis, more sincere and disinterested than usually takes place between neighbouring princes. Their common jealousy of the emperor Charles, and some resemblance in their characters (though the comparison sets the French monarch in a very superior and advantageous light), served as the cement of their mutual amity. Francis is said to have been affected with the king's death, and to have expressed much regret for the loss. His own health began to decline: He foretold, that he should not long survive his friend:[k] And he died in about two months after him.

There were ten parliaments summoned by Henry VIII. and twenty-three sessions held. The whole time, in which these parliaments sat during this long reign, exceeded not three years and a half. It amounted not to a twelvemonth during the first twenty years. The innovations in religion obliged the king afterwards to call these assemblies more frequently: But though these were the most important transactions that ever fell under the cognizance of parliament, their devoted submission to Henry's will, added to their earnest desire of soon returning to their country-seats, produced a quick dispatch of the bills, and made the sessions of short duration. All the king's caprices were, indeed, blindly complied with, and no regard was paid to the safety or liberty of the subject. Besides the violent prosecution of whatever he was pleased to term heresy, the laws of treason were multiplied beyond all former precedent. Even words to the disparagement of the king, queen, or royal issue, were subjected to that penalty; and so little care was taken in framing these rigorous statutes, that they contain obvious contradictions; insomuch that, had they been strictly executed, every man, without exception, must have fallen under the penalty of treason. By one statute,[l] for instance, it was declared treason to assert the validity of the king's marriage, either with Catherine of Arragon, or Anne Boleyn: By another,[m] it was treason to say any-

Miscellaneous transactions.

[k] Le Thou.   [l] 28 Hen. VIII. c. 7.   [m] 34, 35 Hen. VIII. c. 1.

thing to the disparagement or slander of the princesses, Mary and Elizabeth; and to call them spurious would, no doubt, have been construed to their slander. Nor would even a profound silence, with regard to these delicate points, be able to save a person from such penalties. For by the former statute, whoever refused to answer upon oath to any point contained in that act, was subjected to the pains of treason. The king, therefore, needed only propose to any one a question with regard to the legality of either of his first marriages: If the person were silent, he was a traitor by law: If he answered, either in the negative or in the affirmative, he was no less a traitor. So monstrous were the inconsistencies, which arose from the furious passions of the king, and the slavish submission of his parliaments. It is hard to say, whether these contradictions were owing to Henry's precipitancy, or to a formed design of tyranny.

It may not be improper to recapitulate whatever is memorable in the statutes of this reign, whether with regard to government or commerce: Nothing can better show the genius of the age than such a review of the laws.

The abolition of the ancient religion much contributed to the regular execution of justice. While the catholic superstition subsisted, there was no possibility of punishing any crime in the clergy: The church would not permit the magistrate to try the offences of her members, and she could not herself inflict any civil penalties upon them. But Henry restrained these pernicious immunities: The privilege of clergy was abolished for the crimes of petty treason, murder, and felony, to all under the degree of a subdeacon.[n] But the former superstition not only protected crimes in the clergy: It exempted also the laity from punishment, by affording them shelter in the churches and sanctuaries. The parliament abridged these privileges. It was first declared, that no sanctuaries were allowed in cases of high treason;[o] next, in those of murder, felony, rapes, burglary, and petty treason:[p] And it limited them in other particulars.[q] The farther progress of the reformation removed all distinction between the clergy and other subjects; and also abolished entirely the privileges of sanctuaries. These consequences were implied in the neglect of the canon law.

[n] 23 Hen. VIII. c. 1.　[o] 26 Hen. VIII. c. 13.　[p] 32 Hen. VIII c. 12.　[q] 22 Hen. VIII. c. 14.

CHAPTER XXXIII

The only expedient employed to support the military spirit during this age, was the reviving and extending of some old laws, enacted for the encouragement of archery, on which the defence of the kingdom was supposed much to depend. Every man was ordered to have a bow:[r] Butts were ordered to be erected in every parish:[s] And every bowyer was ordered, for each bow of yew which he made, to make two of elm or wich, for the service of the common people.[t] The use of cross-bows and hand-guns was also prohibited.[u] What rendered the English bowmen more formidable was, that they carried halberts with them, by which they were enabled, upon occasion, to engage in close fight with the enemy.[w] Frequent musters or arrays were also made of the people, even during time of peace; and all men of substance were obliged to have a complete suit of armour or harness, as it was called.[x] The martial spirit of the English, during that age, rendered this precaution, it was thought, sufficient for the defence of the nation; and as the king had then an absolute power of commanding the service of all his subjects, he could instantly, in case of danger, appoint new officers, and levy regiments, and collect an army as numerous as he pleased. When no faction or division prevailed among the people, there was no foreign power that ever thought of invading England. The city of London alone could muster fifteen thousand men.[y] Discipline, however, was an advantage wanting to those troops; though the garrison of Calais was a nursery of officers; and Tournay first,[z] Boulogne afterwards, served to encrease the number. Every one, who served abroad, was allowed to alienate his lands without paying any fees.[a] A general permission was granted to dispose of land by will.[b] The parliament was so little jealous of its privileges (which indeed were, at that time, scarcely worth preserving), that there is an instance of one Strode, who, because he had introduced into the lower house some bill regarding tin, was severely treated by the Stannery courts in Cornwal: Heavy fines were imposed on him; and upon his refusal to pay, he was thrown into a dungeon, loaded with irons, and used in such a manner as brought his life in danger: Yet all the notice which the parliament took of this enormity, even in such a paultry court, was

[r] 3 Hen. VIII c. 3.   [s] Ibid.   [t] Ibid.   [u] 3 Hen. VIII. c. 13.   [w] Herbert.
[x] Hall, fol. 234. Stowe, p. 515. Hollingshed, p. 947.   [y] Hall, fol. 235.
Hollingshed, p. 547. Stowe, p. 577.   [z] Hall, fol. 68.   [a] 14 and 15 Hen.
VIII. c. 15.   [b] 34 and 35 Hen. VIII. c. 5.

to enact, that no man could afterwards be questioned for his conduct in parliament.[c] This prohibition, however, must be supposed to extend only to the inferior courts: For as to the king, and privy-council, and star-chamber, they were scarcely bound by any law.

There is a bill of tonnage and poundage, which shews what uncertain ideas the parliament had formed both of their own privileges and of the rights of the sovereign.[d] This duty had been voted to every king since Henry IV. during the term of his own life only: Yet Henry VIII. had been allowed to levy it six years without any law; and though there had been four parliaments assembled during that time, no attention had been given either to grant it to him regularly, or restrain him from levying it. At last, the parliament resolved to give him that supply; but even in this concession, they plainly show themselves at a loss to determine whether they grant it, or whether he has a right of himself to levy it. They say, that the imposition was made to endure during the natural life of the late king, and no longer: They yet blame the merchants who had not paid it to the present king: They observe, that the law for tonnage and poundage was expired; yet make no scruple to call that imposition the king's due: They affirm, that he had sustained great and manifold losses by those who had defrauded him of it; and to provide a remedy, they vote him that supply during his life-time, and no longer. It is remarkable, that, notwithstanding this last clause, all his successors, for more than a century, persevered in the like irregular practice: If a practice may deserve that epithet, in which the whole nation acquiesced, and which gave no offence. But when Charles I. attempted to continue in the same course, which had now received the sanction of many generations, so much were the opinions of men altered, that a furious tempest was excited by it; and historians, partial or ignorant, still represent this measure as a most violent and unprecedented enormity in that unhappy prince.

The king was allowed to make laws for Wales, without consent of parliament.[e] It was forgotten, that, with regard both to Wales and England, the limitation was abolished by the statute, which gave to the royal proclamations the force of laws.

The foreign commerce of England, during this age, was mostly

[c] 4 Hen. VIII. c. 8.   [d] 6 Hen. VIII. c. 14.   [e] 34 Hen. VIII.

CHAPTER XXXIII

confined to the Netherlands. The inhabitants of the Low-Countries bought the English commodities, and distributed them into
other parts of Europe. Hence the mutual dependance of those
countries on each other; and the great loss sustained by both,
in case of a rupture. During all the variations of politics, the
sovereigns endeavoured to avoid coming to this extremity; and
though the king usually bore a greater friendship to Francis, the
nation always leaned towards the emperor.

In 1528, hostilities commenced between England and the Low-
Countries; and the inconvenience was soon felt on both sides.
While the Flemings were not allowed to purchase cloth in England,
the English merchants could not buy it from the clothiers, and the
clothiers were obliged to dismiss their workmen, who began to be
tumultuous for want of bread. The cardinal, to appease them, sent
for the merchants, and ordered them to buy cloth as usual: They
told him, that they could not dispose of it as usual; and notwithstanding his menaces, he could get no other answer from them.[f]
An agreement was at last made to continue the commerce between
the states, even during war.

It was not till the end of this reign that any sallads, carrots,
turnips, or other edible roots were produced in England. The little
of these vegetables, that was used, was formerly imported from
Holland and Flanders.[g] Queen Catherine, when she wanted a
sallad, was obliged to dispatch a messenger thither on purpose.
The use of hops and the planting of them, was introduced
from Flanders about the beginning of this reign, or end of the
preceding.

Foreign artificers, in general, much surpassed the English in
dexterity, industry, and frugality: Hence the violent animosity,
which the latter, on many occasions, expressed against any of the
former who were settled in England. They had the assurance to
complain, that all their customers went to foreign tradesmen; and
in the year 1517, being moved by the seditious sermons of one Dr.
Bele, and the intrigues of Lincoln, a broker, they raised an insurrection. The apprentices, and others of the poorer sort, in London,
began by breaking open the prisons, where some persons were
confined for insulting foreigners. They next proceeded to the

[f] Hall, folio 174.   [g] Anderson, vol. i. p. 338.

house of Meutas, a Frenchman, much hated by them; where they committed great disorders; killed some of his servants; and plundered his goods. The mayor could not appease them; nor Sir Thomas More, late under sheriff, though much respected in the city. They also threatened cardinal Wolsey with some insult; and he thought it necessary to fortify his house, and put himself on his guard. Tired at last with these disorders, they dispersed themselves; and the earls of Shrewsbury and Surrey seized some of them. A proclamation was issued, that women should not meet together to babble and talk, and that all men should keep their wives in their houses. Next day the duke of Norfolk came into the city, at the head of thirteen hundred armed men, and made enquiry into the tumult. Bele and Lincoln, and several others, were sent to the Tower, and condemned for treason. Lincoln and thirteen more were executed. The other criminals, to the number of four hundred, were brought before the king, with ropes about their necks, fell on their knees, and cried for mercy. Henry knew at that time how to pardon; he dismissed them without farther punishment.[h]

So great was the number of foreign artizans in the city, that at least fifteen thousand Flemings alone were at one time obliged to leave it, by an order of council, when Henry became jealous of their favour for queen Catherine.[i] Henry himself confesses, in an edict of the star-chamber, printed among the statutes, that the foreigners starved the natives; and obliged them from idleness to have recourse to theft, murder, and other enormities.[k] He also asserts, that the vast multitude of foreigners raised the price of grain and bread.[l] And to prevent an encrease of the evil, all foreign artificers were prohibited from having above two foreigners in their house, either journeymen or apprentices. A like jealousy arose against the foreign merchants; and to appease it, a law was enacted obliging all denizens to pay the duties imposed upon aliens.[m] The parliament had done better to have encouraged foreign merchants and artizans to come over in greater numbers to England; which might have excited the emulation of the natives, and have improved their skill. The prisoners in the kingdom, for

[h] Stowe, 505. Hollingshed, 840.   [i] Le Grand, vol. iii. p. 232.   [k] 21 Hen. VIII.   [l] Ibid.   [m] 22 Hen. VIII. c. 8.

CHAPTER XXXIII

debts and crimes, are asserted in an act of parliament, to be sixty thousand persons and above;[n] which is scarcely credible. Harrison asserts that 72,000 criminals were executed during this reign for theft and robbery, which would amount nearly to 2000 a-year. He adds, that, in the latter end of Elizabeth's reign, there were not punished capitally 400 in a year: It appears, that, in all England, there are not at present fifty executed for those crimes. If these facts be just, there has been a great improvement in morals since the reign of Henry VIII. And this improvement has been chiefly owing to the encrease of industry and of the arts, which have given maintenance, and, what is almost of equal importance, occupation, to the lower classes.

There is a remarkable clause in a statute passed near the beginning of this reign,[o] by which we might be induced to believe, that England was extremely decayed from the flourishing condition, which it had attained in preceding times. It had been enacted in the reign of Edward II. that no magistrate in town or borough, who by his office ought to keep assize, should, during the continuance of his magistracy, sell, either in wholesale or retail, any wine or victuals. This law seemed equitable, in order to prevent fraud or private views in fixing the assize: Yet the law is repealed in this reign. The reason assigned is, that "since the making of that statute and ordinance, many and the most part of all the cities, boroughs, and towns corporate, within the realm of England, are fallen in ruin and decay, and are not inhabited by merchants, and men of such substance as at the time of making that statute: For at this day, the dwellers and inhabitants of the same cities and boroughs are commonly bakers, vintners, fishmongers, and other victuallers, and there remain few others to bear the offices." Men have such a propensity to exalt past times above the present, that it seems dangerous to credit this reasoning of the parliament, without farther evidence to support it. So different are the views in which the same object appears, that some may be inclined to draw an opposite inference from this fact. A more regular police was established in the reign of Henry VIII. than in any former period, and a stricter administration of justice; an advantage which induced the men of landed property to leave the provincial towns,

[n] 3 Hen. VIII. c. 15.   [o] 3 Hen. VIII. c. 8.

and to retire into the country. Cardinal Wolsey, in a speech to parliament, represented it as a proof of the encrease of riches, that the customs had encreased beyond what they were formerly.[p]

But if there were really a decay of commerce, and industry, and populousness in England, the statutes of this reign, except by abolishing monasteries, and retrenching holidays, circumstances of considerable moment, were not in other respects well calculated to remedy the evil. The fixing of the wages of artificers was attempted:[q] Luxury in apparel was prohibited, by repeated statutes;[r] and probably without effect. The chancellor and other ministers were empowered to fix the price of poultry, cheese, and butter.[s] A statute was even passed to fix the price of beef, pork, mutton, and veal.[t] Beef and pork were ordered to be sold at a halfpenny a pound: Mutton and veal at a halfpenny half a farthing, money of that age. The preamble of the statute says, that these four species of butcher's meat were the food of the poorer sort. This act was afterwards repealed.[u]

The practice of depopulating the country, by abandoning tillage, and throwing the lands into pasturage, still continued;[w] as appears by the new laws which were, from time to time, enacted against that practice. The king was entitled to half the rents of the land, where any farm houses were allowed to fall to decay.[x] The unskilful husbandry was probably the cause why the proprietors found no profit in tillage. The number of sheep allowed to be kept in one flock, was restrained to two thousand.[y] Sometimes, says the statute, one proprietor or farmer would keep a flock of twenty-four thousand. It is remarkable, that the parliament ascribes the encreasing price of mutton, to this encrease of sheep: Because say they, the commodity being gotten into few hands, the price of it is raised at pleasure.[z] It is more probable, that the effect proceeded from the daily encrease of money: For it seems almost impossible, that such a commodity could be engrossed.

In the year 1544, it appears that an acre of good land in Cambridgeshire was let at a shilling, or about fifteenpence of our

[p] Hall, folio 110.   [q] 6 Hen. VIII c. 3.   [r] 1 Hen. VIII. c. 14. 6 Hen. VIII. c. 1. 7 Hen. VIII. c. 7.   [s] 25 Hen. VIII. c. 2.   [t] 24 Hen. VIII. c. 3.   [u] 33 Hen. VIII. c. 11.   [w] Strype, vol. i. p. 392.   [x] 6 Hen. VIII. c. 5. 7 Hen. VIII. c. 1.   [y] 25 Hen. VIII. c. 13.   [z] 25 Hen. VIII. c. 13.

CHAPTER XXXIII

present money.[a] This is ten times cheaper than the usual rent at present. But commodities were not above four times cheaper: A presumption of the bad husbandry in that age.

Some laws were made with regard to beggars and vagrants;[b] one of the circumstances in government, which humanity would most powerfully recommend to a benevolent legislator; which seems, at first sight, the most easily adjusted; and which is yet the most difficult to settle in such a manner, as to attain the end without destroying industry. The convents formerly were a support to the poor; but at the same time tended to encourage idleness and beggary.

In 1546, a law was made for fixing the interest of money at 10 per cent.; the first legal interest known in England. Formerly, all loans of that nature were regarded as usurious. The preamble of this very law treats the interest of money as illegal and criminal: And the prejudices still remained so strong, that the law, permitting interest, was repealed in the following reign.

This reign, as well as many of the foregoing and even subsequent reigns, abounds with monopolizing laws, confining particular manufactures to particular towns, or excluding the open country in general.[c] There remain still too many traces of similar absurdities. In the subsequent reign, the corporations, which had been opened by a former law, and obliged to admit tradesmen of different kinds, were again shut up by act of parliament; and every one was prohibited from exercising any trade, who was not of the corporation.[d]

Henry, as he possessed, himself, some talent for letters, was an encourager of them in others. He founded Trinity college in Cambridge, and gave it ample endowments. Wolsey founded Christ Church in Oxford, and intended to call it Cardinal college: But upon his fall, which happened before he had entirely finished his scheme, the king seized all the revenues; and this violence, above all the other misfortunes of that minister, is said to have given him the greatest concern.[e] But Henry afterwards restored the revenues of the college, and only changed the name. The cardinal founded in Oxford the first chair for teaching Greek; and this novelty rent

[a] Anderson, vol. i. p. 374.   [b] 22 Hen. VIII c. 12. 22 Hen. VIII. c. 5.   [c] 21 Hen. VIII c. 12. 25 Hen. VIII. c. 18. 3 & 4 Edw. VI. c. 20. 5 & 6 Edw. VI. c. 24.   [d] 3 & 4 Edw. VI c. 20.   [e] Strype, vol. i. p. 117.

that university into violent factions, which frequently came to blows. The students divided themselves into parties, which bore the names of Greeks and Trojans, and sometimes fought with as great animosity as was formerly exercised by those hostile nations. A new and more correct method of pronouncing Greek being introduced, it also divided the Grecians themselves into parties; and it was remarked, that the catholics favoured the former pronunciation, the protestants gave countenance to the new. Gardiner employed the authority of the king and council to suppress innovations in this particular, and to preserve the corrupt sound of the Greek alphabet. So little liberty was then allowed of any kind! The penalties, inflicted upon the new pronunciation were no less than whipping, degradation, and expulsion; and the bishop declared, that rather than permit the liberty of innovating in the pronunciation of the Greek alphabet, it were better that the language itself were totally banished the universities. The introduction of the Greek language into Oxford, excited the emulation of Cambridge.[f] Wolsey intended to have enriched the library of his college at Oxford, with copies of all the manuscripts that were in the Vatican.[g] The countenance given to letters by this king and his ministers, contributed to render learning fashionable in England: Erasmus speaks with great satisfaction of the general regard paid by the nobility and gentry to men of knowledge.[h] It is needless to be particular in mentioning the writers of this reign, or of the preceding. There is no man of that age, who has the least pretension to be ranked among our classics. Sir Thomas More, though he wrote in Latin, seems to come the nearest to the character of a classical author.

[f] Wood's Hist. & Antiq. Oxon. lib. i. p. 245.　　[g] Ibid. 249.　　[h] Epist. ad Banisium. Also epist. p. 368.

XXXIV

EDWARD VI

State of the regency – Innovations
in the regency – Hertford protector –
Reformation completed – Gardiner's
opposition – Foreign affairs – Progress of
the reformation in Scotland – Assassination
of cardinal Beaton – Conduct of the
war with Scotland – Battle of Pinkey –
A parliament – Farther progress of
the reformation – Affairs of Scotland –
Young queen of Scots sent into France –
Cabals of lord Seymour – Dudley earl of
Warwic – A parliament – Attainder of
lord Seymour – His execution –
Ecclesiastical affairs

THE LATE KING, by the regulations, which he imposed on the government of his infant son, as well as by the limitations of the succession, had projected to reign even after his decease; and he imagined, that his ministers, who had always been so obsequious to him during his life-time, would never afterwards depart from the plan, which he had traced out to them. He fixed the majority of the prince at the completion of his eighteenth year; and as Edward was then only a few months past nine, he appointed sixteen executors; to whom, during the minority, he entrusted

1547.
State of
the re-
gency.

the government of the king and kingdom. Their names were, Cranmer, archbishop of Canterbury; lord Wriothesely, chancellor; lord St. John, great master; lord Russel, privy seal; the earl of Hertford, chamberlain; viscount Lisle, admiral; Tonstal, bishop of Durham; Sir Anthony Brown, master of horse; Sir William Paget, secretary of state; Sir Edward North, chancellor of the court of augmentations; Sir Edward Montague, chief justice of the common pleas; judge Bromley, Sir Anthony Denny, and Sir William Herbert, chief gentlemen of the privy chamber; Sir Edward Wotton, treasurer of Calais; Dr. Wotton, dean of Canterbury. To these executors, with whom was entrusted the whole regal authority, were appointed twelve counsellors, who possessed no immediate power, and could only assist with their advice, when any affair was laid before them. The council was composed of the earls of Arundel and Essex; Sir Thomas Cheyney, treasurer of the household; Sir John Gage, comptroller; Sir Anthony Wingfield, vice-chamberlain; Sir William Petre, secretary of state; Sir Richard Rich, Sir John Baker, Sir Ralph Sadler, Sir Thomas Seymour, Sir Richard Southwel, and Sir Edmund Peckham.[i] The usual caprice of Henry appears somewhat in this nomination; while he appointed several persons of inferior station among his executors, and gave only the place of counsellor to a person of such high rank as the earl of Arundel, and to Sir Thomas Seymour the king's uncle.

Inno-vations in the regency. But the first act of the executors and counsellors was to depart from the destination of the late king in a material article. No sooner were they met, than it was suggested, that the government would lose its dignity, for want of some head, who might represent the royal majesty, who might receive addresses from foreign ambassadors, to whom dispatches from English ministers abroad might be carried, and whose name might be employed in all orders and proclamations: And as the king's will seemed to labour under a defect in this particular, it was deemed necessary to supply it, by chusing a protector; who, though he should possess all the exterior symbols of royal dignity, should yet be bound, in every act of power, to follow the opinion of the executors.[k] This proposal was very disagreeable to chancellor Wriothesely. That magistrate, a

[i] Strype's Memor. vol. ii. p. 457.   [k] Burnet, vol. ii. p. 5.

CHAPTER XXXIV

man of an active spirit and high ambition, found himself, by his office, entitled to the first rank in the regency after the primate; and as he knew, that this prelate had no talent or inclination for state affairs, he hoped, that the direction of public business would of course devolve in a great measure upon himself. He opposed, therefore, the proposal of chusing a protector; and represented that innovation as an infringement of the late king's will, which, being corroborated by act of parliament, ought in every thing to be a law to them, and could not be altered but by the same authority, which had established it. But he seems to have stood alone in the opposition. The executors and counsellors were mostly courtiers, who had been raised by Henry's favour, not men of high birth or great hereditary influence; and as they had been sufficiently accustomed to submission during the reign of the late monarch, and had no pretensions to govern the nation by their own authority, they acquiesced the more willingly in a proposal, which seemed calculated for preserving public peace and tranquillity. It being therefore agreed to name a protector, the choice fell of course on the earl of Hertford, who, as he was the king's maternal uncle, was *Hertford* strongly interested in his safety; and possessing no claims to inherit *protector.* the crown, could never have any separate interest, which might lead him to endanger Edward's person or his authority.[l] The public was informed by proclamation of this change in the administration; and dispatches were sent to all foreign courts to give them intimation of it. All those who were possessed of any office resigned their former commissions, and accepted new ones in the name of the young king. The bishops themselves were constrained to make a like submission. Care was taken to insert in their new commissions, that they held their office during pleasure:[m] And it is there expressly affirmed, that all manner of authority and jurisdiction, as well ecclesiastical as civil, is originally derived from the crown.[n]

The executors, in their next measure, showed a more submissive deference to Henry's will; because many of them found their account in it. The late king had intended, before his death, to make a new creation of nobility, in order to supply the place of

[l] Heylin, Hist. Ref. Edw. VI.   [m] Collier, vol. ii. p. 218. Burnet, vol. ii. p. 6. Strype's Mem. of Cranm. p. 141.   [n] Strype's Mem. of Cranm. p. 141.

those peerages, which had fallen by former attainders, or the failure of issue; and that he might enable the new peers to support their dignity, he had resolved, either to bestow estates on them, or advance them to higher offices. He had even gone so far as to inform them of this resolution; and in his will, he charged his executors to make good all his promises.[o] That they might ascertain his intentions in the most authentic manner, Sir William Paget, Sir Anthony Denny, and Sir William Herbert, with whom Henry had always conversed in a familiar manner, were called before the board of regency; and having given evidence of what they knew concerning the king's promises, their testimony was relied on, and the executors proceeded to the fulfilling of these engagements. Hertford was created duke of Somerset, marschal and lord treasurer; Wriothesely, earl of Southampton; the earl of Essex, marquess of Northampton; viscount Lisle, earl of Warwic; Sir Thomas Seymour, lord Seymour of Sudley, and admiral; Sir Richard Rich, Sir William Willoughby, Sir Edward Sheffield accepted the title of baron.[p] Several to whom the same dignity was offered, refused it; because the other part of the king's promise, the bestowing of estates on these new noblemen, was deferred till a more convenient opportunity. Some of them, however, as also Somerset the protector, were, in the mean time, endowed with spiritual preferments, deaneries and prebends. For among many other invasions of ecclesiastical privileges and property, this irregular practice, of bestowing spiritual benefices on laymen, began now to prevail.

17th Feb.

The earl of Southampton had always been engaged in an opposite party to Somerset; and it was not likely that factions, which had secretly prevailed, even during the arbitrary reign of Henry, should be suppressed in the weak administration, that usually attends a minority. The former nobleman, that he might have the greater leisure for attending to public business, had, of himself and from his own authority, put the great seal in commission, and had empowered four lawyers, Southwell, Tregonel, Oliver, and Bellasis, to execute in his absence the office of chancellor. This measure seemed very exceptionable; and the more so, as, two of the commissioners being canonists, the lawyers suspected, that, by

[o] Fuller, Heylin, and Rymer.   [p] Stowe's Annals, p. 594.

CHAPTER XXXIV

this nomination, the chancellor had intended to discredit the common law. Complaints were made to the council; who, influenced by the protector, gladly laid hold of the opportunity to depress Southampton. They consulted the judges with regard to so unusual a case, and received for answer, that the commission was illegal, and that the chancellor, by his presumption in granting it, had justly forfeited the great seal, and was even liable to punishment. The council summoned him to appear before them. He maintained, that he held his office by the late king's will, founded on an act of parliament, and could not lose it without a trial in parliament; that if the commission, which he had granted, were found illegal, it might be cancelled, and all the ill consequences of it be easily remedied; and that the depriving him of his office for an error of this nature, was a precedent by which any other innovation might be authorized. But the council, notwithstanding these topics of defence, declared that he had forfeited the great seal; that a fine should be imposed upon him; and that he should be confined to his own house during pleasure.[q]

The removal of Southampton encreased the protector's authority, as well as tended to suppress faction in the regency; yet was not Somerset contented with this advantage: His ambition carried him to seek still farther acquisitions. On pretence, that the vote of the executors, choosing him protector, was not a sufficient foundation for his authority, he procured a patent from the young king, by which he entirely overturned the will of Harry VIII, produced a total revolution in the government, and may seem even to have subverted all the laws of the kingdom. He named himself protector with full regal power, and appointed a council, consisting of all the former counsellors, and all the executors, except Southampton: He reserved a power of naming any other counsellors at pleasure: And he was bound to consult with such only as he thought proper. The protector and his council were likewise empowered to act at discretion, and to execute whatever they deemed for the public service, without incurring any penalty or forfeiture from any law, statute, proclamation, or ordinance whatsoever.[r] Even had this patent been more moderate in its concessions, and had it been drawn by direction, from the executors appointed by Henry, its

12 March.

[q] Hollingshed, p. 979.   [r] Burnet, vol. ii. Records, No 6.

legality might justly be questioned; since it seems essential to a trust of this nature to be exercised by the persons entrusted, and not to admit of a delegation to others: But as the patent, by its very tenor, where the executors are not so much as mentioned, appears to have been surreptitiously obtained from a minor King, the protectorship of Somerset was a plain usurpation, which it is impossible by any arguments to justify. The connivance, however, of the executors, and their present acquiescence in the new establishment, made it be universally submitted to; and as the young king discovered an extreme attachment to his uncle, who was also in the main a man of moderation and probity, no objections were made to his power and title. All men of sense, likewise, who saw the nation divided by the religious zeal of the opposite sects, deemed it the more necessary to entrust the government to one person, who might check the exorbitancies of faction, and ensure the public tranquillity. And though some clauses of the patent seemed to imply a formal subversion of all limited government, so little jealousy was then usually entertained on that head, that no exception was ever taken at bare claims or pretensions of this nature, advanced by any person possessed of sovereign power. The actual exercise alone of arbitrary administration, and that in many and great and flagrant and unpopular instances, was able sometimes to give some umbrage to the nation.

Reformation completed.
The extensive authority and imperious character of Henry had retained the partizans of both religions in subjection; but upon his demise, the hopes of the protestants and the fears of the catholics began to revive, and the zeal of these parties produced every where disputes and animosities, the usual preludes to more fatal divisions. The protector had long been regarded as a secret partizan of the reformers; and being now freed from restraint, he scrupled not to discover his intention of correcting all abuses in the ancient religion, and of adopting still more of the protestant innovations. He took care, that all persons, entrusted with the king's education, should be attached to the same principles; and as the young prince discovered a zeal for every kind of literature, especially the theological, far beyond his tender years, all men foresaw, in the course of his reign, the total abolition of the catholic faith in England; and they early began to declare themselves in favour of those tenets, which were likely to become in the end entirely prevalent. After

CHAPTER XXXIV

Southampton's fall, few members of the council seemed to retain any attachment to the Romish communion; and most of the counsellors appeared even sanguine in forwarding the progress of the reformation. The riches, which most of them had acquired from the spoils of the clergy, induced them to widen the breach between England and Rome; and by establishing a contrariety of speculative tenets, as well as of discipline and worship, to render a coalition with the mother church altogether impracticable.[5] Their rapacity also, the chief source of their reforming spirit, was excited by the prospect of pillaging the secular, as they had already done the regular clergy; and they knew, that, while any share of the old principles remained, or any regard to the ecclesiastics, they could never hope to succeed in that enterprize.

The numerous and burthensome superstitions, with which the Romish church was loaded, had thrown many of the reformers, by the spirit of opposition, into an enthusiastic strain of devotion; and all rites, ceremonies, pomp, order, and exterior observances were zealously proscribed by them, as hindrances to their spiritual contemplations, and obstructions to their immediate converse with heaven. Many circumstances concurred to inflame this daring spirit; the novelty itself of their doctrines, the triumph of making proselytes, the furious persecutions to which they were exposed, their animosity against the ancient tenets and practices, and the necessity of procuring the concurrence of the laity, by depressing the hierarchy, and by tendering to them the plunder of the ecclesiastics. Wherever the reformation prevailed over the opposition of civil authority, this genius of religion appeared in its full extent, and was attended with consequences, which, though less durable, were, for some time, not less dangerous than those which were connected with the ancient superstition. But as the magistrate took the lead in England, the transition was more gradual; much of the ancient religion was still preserved; and a reasonable degree of subordination was retained in discipline, as well as some pomp, order, and ceremony in public worship.

The protector, in his schemes for advancing the reformation, had always recourse to the counsels of Cranmer, who, being a man of moderation and prudence, was averse to all violent changes, and

[5] Goodwin's Annals. Heylin.

determined to bring over the people by insensible innovations, to that system of doctrine and discipline, which he deemed the most pure and perfect. He probably also foresaw, that a system, which carefully avoided the extremes of reformation, was likely to be most lasting; and that a devotion, merely spiritual, was fitted only for the first fervours of a new sect, and upon the relaxation of these naturally gave place to the inroads of superstition. He seems therefore to have intended the establishment of a hierarchy, which, being suited to a great and settled government, might stand as a perpetual barrier against Rome, and might retain the reverence of the people, even after their enthusiastic zeal was diminished or entirely evaporated.

The person, who opposed, with greatest authority, any farther advances towards reformation, was Gardiner, bishop of Winchester; who, though he had not obtained a place in the council of regency, on account of late disgusts, which he had given to Henry, was entitled, by his age, experience, and capacity, to the highest *Gardi-* trust and confidence of his party. This prelate still continued to *ner's* magnify the great wisdom and learning of the late king, which, *opposi-* indeed, were generally and sincerely revered by the nation; and he *tion.* insisted on the prudence of persevering, at least till the young king's majority, in the ecclesiastical model, established by that great monarch. He defended the use of images, which were now openly attacked by the protestants; and he represented them as serviceable in maintaining a sense of religion among the illiterate multitude.[t] He even deigned to write an apology for *holy water,* which bishop Ridley had decried in a sermon; and he maintained, that, by the power of the Almighty, it might be rendered an instrument of doing good; as much as the shadow of St. Peter, the hem of Christ's garment, or the spittle and clay laid upon the eyes of the blind.[u] Above all, he insisted, that the laws ought to be observed, that the constitution ought to be preserved inviolate, and that it was dangerous to follow the will of the sovereign, in opposition to an act of parliament.[w]

But though there remained at that time in England an idea of laws and a constitution, sufficient at least to furnish a topic of argument to such as were discontented with any immediate exer-

[t] Fox, vol. ii. p. 712.   [u] Ibid. p. 724.   [w] Collier, vol. ii. p. 228. Fox, vol. ii.

cise of authority; this plea could scarcely, in the present case, be maintained with any plausibility by Gardiner. An act of parliament had invested the crown with a legislative power; and royal proclamations, even during a minority, were armed with the force of laws. The protector, finding himself supported by this statute, was determined to employ his authority in favour of the reformers; and having suspended, during the interval, the jurisdiction of the bishops, he appointed a general visitation to be made in all the dioceses of England.[x] The visitors consisted of a mixture of clergy and laity, and had six circuits assigned them. The chief purport of their instructions was, besides correcting immoralities and irregularities in the clergy, to abolish the ancient superstitions, and to bring the discipline and worship somewhat nearer the practice of the reformed churches. The moderation of Somerset and Cranmer is apparent in the conduct of this delicate affair. The visitors were enjoined to retain for the present all images which had not been abused to idolatry; and to instruct the people not to despise such ceremonies as were not yet abrogated, but only to beware of some particular superstitions, such as the sprinkling of their beds with holy water, and the ringing of bells, or using of consecrated candles, in order to drive away the devil.[y]

But nothing required more the correcting hand of authority, than the abuse of preaching, which was now generally employed, throughout England, in defending the ancient practices and superstitions. The court of augmentation, in order to ease the exchequer of the annuities paid to monks, had commonly placed them in the vacant churches; and these men were led by interest, as well as by inclination, to support those principles, which had been invented for the profit of the clergy. Orders therefore were given to restrain the topics of their sermons: Twelve homilies were published, which they were enjoined to read to the people: And all of them were prohibited, without express permission, from preaching any where but in their parish churches. The purpose of this injunction was to throw a restraint on the catholic divines; while the protestant, by the grant of particular licences, should be allowed unbounded liberty.

Bonner made some opposition to these measures; but soon

[x] Mem. Cranm. p. 146, 147, &c.   [y] Burnet, vol. ii. p. 28.

after retracted and acquiesced. Gardiner was more high spirited and more steady. He represented the peril of perpetual innovations, and the necessity of adhering to some system. " 'Tis a dangerous thing," said he, "to use too much freedom, in researches of this kind. If you cut the old canal, the water is apt to run farther than you have a mind to. If you indulge the humour of novelty, you cannot put a stop to people's demands, nor govern their indiscretions at pleasure. For my part," said he, on another occasion, "my sole concern is to manage the third and last act of my life with decency, and to make a handsome exit off the stage. Provided this point is secured, I am not solicitous about the rest. I am already by nature condemned to death: No man can give me a pardon from this sentence; nor so much as procure me a reprieve. To speak my mind, and to act as my conscience directs, are two branches of liberty, which I can never part with. Sincerity in speech, and integrity in action, are entertaining qualities: They will stick by a man, when every thing else takes its leave; and I must not resign them upon any consideration. The best on it is, if I do not throw them away myself, no man can force them from me: But if I give them up, then am I ruined by myself, and deserve to lose all my preferments."[z] This opposition of Gardiner drew on him the indignation of the council; and he was sent to the Fleet, where he was used with some severity.

One of the chief objections, urged by Gardiner against the new homilies, was that they defined, with the most metaphysical precision, the doctrines of grace, and of justification by faith; points, he thought, which it was superfluous for any man to know exactly, and which certainly much exceeded the comprehension of the vulgar. A famous martyrologist calls Gardiner, on account of this opinion, "An insensible ass, and one that had no feeling of God's spirit in the matter of justification."[a] The meanest protestant imagined at that time, that he had a full comprehension of all those mysterious doctrines; and he heartily despised the most learned and knowing person of the ancient religion, who acknowledged his ignorance with regard to them. It is indeed certain, that the reformers were very fortunate in their doctrine of justification, and

<hr />

[z] Collier, vol. ii. p. 228. ex MS. Col. C. C. Cantab. Bibliotheca Britannica, article GARDINER.   [a] Fox, vol. ii.

might venture to foretel its success, in opposition to all the ceremonies, shows, and superstitions of popery. By exalting Christ and his sufferings, and renouncing all claim to independent merit in ourselves, it was calculated to become popular, and coincided with those principles of panegyric and of self-abasement, which generally have place in religion.

Tonstal, bishop of Durham, having, as well as Gardiner, made some opposition to the new regulations, was dismissed the council; but no farther severity was, for the present, exercised against him. He was a man of great moderation, and of the most unexceptionable character in the kingdom.

The same religious zeal, which engaged Somerset to promote the reformation at home, led him to carry his attention to foreign countries; where the interests of the protestants were now exposed to the most imminent danger. The Roman pontiff, with much reluctance and after long delays, had at last summoned a general council, which was assembled at Trent, and was employed, both in correcting the abuses of the church, and in ascertaining her doctrines. The emperor, who desired to repress the power of the court of Rome, as well as gain over the protestants, promoted the former object of the council; the pope, who found his own greatness so deeply interested, desired rather to employ them in the latter. He gave instructions to his legates, who presided in the council, to protract the debates, and to engage the theologians in argument, and altercation, and dispute concerning the nice points of faith, canvassed before them: A policy, so easy to be executed, that the legates soon found it rather necessary to interpose, in order to appease the animosity of the divines, and bring them at last to some decision.[b] The more difficult task for the legates was to moderate or divert the zeal of the council for reformation, and to repress the ambition of the prelates, who desired to exalt the episcopal authority on the ruins of the sovereign pontiff. Finding this humour become prevalent, the legates, on pretence that the plague had broken out at Trent, transferred of a sudden the council to Bologna, where, they hoped, it would be more under the direction of his holiness.

The emperor, no less than the pope, had learned to make

Foreign affairs.

[b] Father Paul, lib. 2.

religion subservient to his ambition and policy. He was resolved to employ the imputation of heresy as a pretence for subduing the protestant princes, and oppressing the liberties of Germany; but found it necessary to cover his intentions under deep artifice, and to prevent the combination of his adversaries. He separated the Palatine and the elector of Brandenburgh from the protestant confederacy: He took arms against the elector of Saxony, and the landgrave of Hesse: By the fortune of war, he made the former prisoner: He employed treachery and prevarication against the latter, and detained him captive, by breaking a safe-conduct which he had granted him. He seemed to have reached the summit of his ambition; and the German princes, who were astonished with his success, were farther discouraged by the intelligence, which they had received, of the death, first of Henry VIII. then of Francis I. their usual resources in every calamity.[c]

Henry II. who succeeded to the crown of France, was a prince of vigour and abilities; but less hasty in his resolutions than Francis, and less enflamed with rivalship and animosity against the emperor Charles. Though he sent ambassadors to the princes of the Smalcaldic League, and promised them protection, he was unwilling, in the commencement of his reign, to hurry into a war with so great a power as that of the emperor; and he thought that the alliance of those princes was a sure resource, which he could at any time lay hold of.[d] He was much governed by the duke of Guise and the cardinal of Lorraine; and he hearkened to their counsel, in chusing rather to give immediate assistance to Scotland, his ancient ally, which, even before the death of Henry VIII. had loudly claimed the protection of the French monarchy.

Progress of the reformation in Scotland. The hatred between the two factions, the partizans of the ancient and those of the new religion, became every day more violent in Scotland; and the resolution, which the cardinal primate had taken, to employ the most rigorous punishments against the reformers, brought matters to a quick decision. There was one Wishart, a gentleman by birth, who employed himself with great zeal in preaching against the ancient superstitions, and began to give alarm to the clergy, who were justly terrified with the danger of some fatal revolution in religion. This man was celebrated for the

[c] Sleidan.   [d] Pere Daniel.

CHAPTER XXXIV

purity of his morals, and for his extensive learning: But these praises cannot be much depended on; because, we know, that, among the reformers, severity of manners supplied the place of many virtues; and the age was in general so ignorant, that most of the priests in Scotland imagined the New Testament to be a composition of Luther's, and asserted that the Old alone was the word of God.[e] But however the case may have stood with regard to those estimable qualities ascribed to Wishart, he was strongly possessed with the desire of innovation; and he enjoyed those talents, which qualified him for becoming a popular preacher, and for seizing the attention and affections of the multitude. The magistrates of Dundee, where he exercised his mission, were alarmed with his progress; and being unable or unwilling to treat him with rigour, they contented themselves with denying him the liberty of preaching, and with dismissing him the bounds of their jurisdiction. Wishart, moved with indignation, that they had dared to reject him, together with the word of God, menaced them, in imitation of the ancient prophets, with some imminent calamity; and he withdrew to the west country, where he daily encreased the number of his proselytes. Meanwhile, a plague broke out in Dundee; and all men exclaimed, that the town had drawn down the vengeance of Heaven by banishing the pious preacher, and that the pestilence would never cease, till they had made him atonement for their offence against him. No sooner did Wishart hear of this change in their disposition, than he returned to them, and made them a new tender of his doctrine: But lest he should spread the contagion by bringing multitudes together, he erected his pulpit on the top of a gate: The infected stood within; the others without. And the preacher failed not, in such a situation, to take advantage of the immediate terrors of the people, and to enforce his evangelical mission.[f]

The assiduity and success of Wishart became an object of attention to cardinal Beaton; and he resolved, by the punishment of so celebrated a preacher, to strike a terror into all other innovators. He engaged the earl of Bothwel to arrest him; and to deliver him into his hands, contrary to a promise given by Bothwel to that

[e] See note [R] at the end of the volume.   [f] Knox's Hist. of Ref. p. 44. Spotswood.

unhappy man: And being possessed of his prey, he conducted him to St. Andrew's, where, after a trial, he condemned him to the flames for heresy. Arran, the governor, was irresolute in his temper; and the cardinal, though he had gained him over to his party, found, that he would not concur in the condemnation and execution of Wishart. He determined, therefore, without the assistance of the secular arm, to bring that heretic to punishment; and he himself beheld from his window the dismal spectacle. Wishart suffered with the usual patience; but could not forbear remarking the triumph of his insulting enemy. He foretold, that, in a few days, he should, in the very same place, lie as low, as now he was exalted aloft, in opposition to true piety and religion.[g]

Assassination of cardinal Beaton.

This prophecy was probably the immediate cause of the event which it foretold. The disciples of this martyr, enraged at the cruel execution, formed a conspiracy against the cardinal; and having associated to them Norman Lesly, who was disgusted on account of some private quarrel, they conducted their enterprize with great secrecy and success. Early in the morning they entered the cardinal's palace, which he had strongly fortified; and though they were not above sixteen persons, they thrust out a hundred tradesmen and fifty servants, whom they seized separately, before any suspicion arose of their intentions; and having shut the gates, they proceeded very deliberately to execute their purpose on the cardinal. That prelate had been alarmed with the noise which he heard in the castle; and had barricaded the door of his chamber: But finding that they had brought fire in order to force their way, and having obtained, as is believed, a promise of life, he opened the door; and reminding them, that he was a priest, he conjured them to spare him. Two of the assassins rushed upon him with drawn swords; but a third, James Melvil, more calm and more considerate in villany, stopped their career, and bade them reflect, that this sacrifice was the work and judgment of God, and ought to be executed with becoming deliberation and gravity. Then turning the point of his sword towards Beaton, he called to him, "Repent thee, thou wicked cardinal, of all thy sins and iniquities, especially of the murder of Wishart, that instrument of God for the

[g] Spotswood, Buchanan.

conversion of these lands: It is his death, which now cries vengeance upon thee: We are sent by God to inflict the deserved
punishment. For here, before the Almighty, I protest, that it is
neither hatred of thy person, nor love of thy riches, nor fear of thy
power, which moves me to seek thy death: But only because thou
hast been, and still remainest, an obstinate enemy to Christ Jesus,
and his holy gospel." Having spoken these words, without giving
Beaton time to finish that repentance, to which he exhorted him,
he thrust him through the body; and the cardinal fell dead at his
feet.[h] This murder was executed on the 28th of May 1546. The
assassins, being reinforced by their friends to the number of a
hundred and forty persons, prepared themselves for the defence
of the castle, and sent a messenger to London, craving assistance
from Henry. That prince, though Scotland was comprehended in
his peace with France, would not forego the opportunity of disturbing the government of a rival-kingdom; and he promised to
take them under his protection.

It was the peculiar misfortune of Scotland, that five short
reigns had been successively followed by as many long minorities;
and the execution of justice, which the prince was beginning to
introduce, had been continually interrupted by the cabals, factions, and animosities of the great. But besides these inveterate
and ancient evils, a new source of disorder had arisen, the disputes
and contentions of theology, which were sufficient to disturb the
most settled government; and the death of the cardinal, who was
possessed of abilities and vigour, seemed much to weaken the
hands of the administration. But the queen-dowager was a woman
of uncommon talents and virtue; and she did as much to support
the government, and supply the weakness of Arran, the governor,
as could be expected in her situation.

[h] The famous Scotch reformer, John Knox, calls James Melvil, p. 65, a man
most gentle and most modest. It is very horrid, but at the same time
somewhat amusing, to consider the joy and alacrity and pleasure, which
that historian discovers in his narrative of this assassination: And it is
remarkable that in the first edition of his work, these words were printed
on the margin of the page, *The godly Fact and Words of James Melvil.* But the
following editors retrenched them. Knox himself had no hand in the murder of Beaton; but he afterwards joined the assassins, and assisted them in
holding out the castle. See Keith's Hist. of the Ref. of Scotland, p. 43.

Conduct
of the
war with
Scotland.

The protector of England, as soon as the state was brought to some composure, made preparations for war with Scotland; and he was determined to execute, if possible, that project, of uniting the two kingdoms by marriage, on which the late king had been so intent, and which he had recommended with his dying breath to his executors. He levied an army of 18,000 men, and equipped a fleet of sixty sail, one half of which were ships of war, the other laden with provisions and ammunition. He gave the command of the fleet to lord Clinton: He himself marched at the head of the army, attended by the earl of Warwic. These hostile measures were covered with a pretence of revenging some depredations committed by the borderers; but besides, that Somerset revived the ancient claim of the superiority of the English crown over that of Scotland, he refused to enter into negociation on any other condition than the marriage of the young queen with Edward.

The protector, before he opened the campaign, published a manifesto, in which he enforced all the arguments for that measure. He said, that nature seemed originally to have intended this island for one empire; and having cut it off from all communication with foreign states, and guarded it by the ocean, she had pointed out to the inhabitants the road to happiness and to security: That the education and customs of the people concurred with nature; and by giving them the same language, and laws, and manners, had invited them to a thorough union and coalition: That fortune had at last removed all obstacles, and had prepared an expedient, by which they might become one people, without leaving any place for that jealousy either of honour or of interest, to which rival nations are naturally exposed: That the crown of Scotland had devolved on a female: that of England on a male; and happily the two sovereigns, as of a rank, were also of an age, the most suitable to each other: That the hostile dispositions, which prevailed between the nations, and which arose from past injuries, would soon be extinguished, after a long and secure peace had established confidence between them: That the memory of former miseries, which at present inflamed their mutual animosity, would then serve only to make them cherish, with more passion, a state of happiness and tranquillity, so long unknown to their ancestors: That when hostilities had ceased between the kingdoms, the Scottish nobility, who were at present obliged to remain perpetually in a warlike posture, would learn to cultivate the arts of peace, and would soften their minds to a love of domestic order and obedience: That as this situation was desirable to both kingdoms, so particularly to Scotland, which had been exposed to the greatest miseries from intestine and foreign wars, and saw herself every moment in danger of losing her independancy, by the efforts of a richer, and more powerful people: That though England had claims of superiority, she was willing to resign every pretension for the sake of future peace, and desired an union, which would be the more secure, as it would be concluded on terms entirely equal: And that, besides all these motives, positive engagements had been taken for completing this alliance; and the honour and good faith of the nation were pledged to fulfil what her interest and safety so loudly demanded.[i]

Somerset soon perceived, that these remonstrances would have no influence; and that the queen dowager's attachment to France and to the catholic religion would render ineffectual all negociations for the intended marriage. He found himself, therefore, obliged to try the force of arms, and to constrain the Scots by necessity to submit to a measure, for which they seemed to have entertained the most incurable aversion. He passed the borders at Berwic, and advanced towards Edinburgh, without meeting any resistance for some days, except from some small castles, which he obliged to surrender at discretion. The protector intended to have punished the governor and garrison of one of these castles for their temerity in resisting such unequal force: But they eluded his anger by asking only a few hours' respite, till they should prepare themselves for death; after which they found his ears more open to their applications for mercy.[k] *2d Sept.*

The governor of Scotland had summoned together the whole force of the kingdom; and his army, double in number to that of the English, had taken post on advantageous ground, guarded by the banks of the Eske, about four miles from Edinburgh. The English came within sight of them at Faside; and after a skirmish between the horse, where the Scots were worsted, and lord Hume dangerously wounded, Somerset prepared himself for a more

[i] Sir John Haywood in Kennet, p. 279. Heylin, p. 42.   [k] Haywood. Patten.

decisive action. But having taken a view of the Scotish camp with the earl of Warwic, he found it difficult to make an attempt upon it with any probability of success. He wrote, therefore, another letter to Arran; and offered to evacuate the kingdom, as well as to repair all the damages which he had committed, provided the Scots would stipulate not to contract the queen to any foreign prince, but to detain her at home, till she reached the age of chusing a husband for herself. So moderate a demand was rejected by the Scots merely on account of its moderation; and it made them imagine that the protector must either be reduced to great distress or be influenced by fear, that he was now contented to abate so much of his former pretensions. Inflamed also by their priests, who had come to the camp in great numbers, they believed, that the English were detestable heretics, abhorred of God, and exposed to divine vengeance; and that no success could ever crown their arms. They were confirmed in this fond conceit, when they saw the protector change his ground, and move towards the sea; nor did they any longer doubt, that he intended to embark his army, and make his escape on board the ships, which at that very time moved into the bay, opposite to him.[l] Determined therefore to cut off his retreat, they quitted their camp: and passing the river Eske, advanced into the plain. They were divided into three bodies: Angus commanded the vanguard; Arran the main body; Huntley the rear: Their cavalry consisted only of light horse, which were placed on their left flank, strengthened by some Irish archers, whom Argyle had brought over for this service.

10th Sept.

Somerset was much pleased when he saw this movement of the Scottish army; and as the English had usually been superior in pitched battles, he conceived great hopes of success. He ranged his van on the left, farthest from the sea; and ordered them to remain on the high grounds on which he placed them, till the enemy should approach: He placed his main battle and his rear towards the right; and beyond the van he posted lord Grey at the head of the men at arms, and ordered him to take the Scottish van in flank, but not till they should be engaged in close fight with the van of the English.

The battle of Pinkey.

While the Scots were advancing on the plain, they were galled

[l] Hollingshed, p. 985.

with the artillery from the English ships: The eldest son of lord Graham was killed: The Irish archers were thrown into disorder; and even the other troops began to stagger: When lord Grey, perceiving their situation, neglected his orders, left his ground, and at the head of his heavy-armed horse made an attack on the Scottish infantry, in hopes of gaining all the honour of the victory. On advancing, he found a slough and ditch in his way; and behind were ranged the enemy armed with spears, and the field, on which they stood, was fallow ground, broken with ridges, which lay across their front, and disordered the movements of the English cavalry. From all these accidents, the shock of this body of horse was feeble and irregular; and as they were received on the points of the Scottish spears, which were longer than the lances of the English horsemen, they were in a moment pierced, overthrown, and discomfited. Grey himself was dangerously wounded: Lord Edward Seymour, son of the protector, had his horse killed under him: The standard was near being taken: And had the Scots possessed any good body of cavalry, who could have pursued the advantage, the whole English army had been exposed to great danger.[m]

The protector mean-while, assisted by Sir Ralph Sadler and Sir Ralph Vane, employed himself with diligence and success, in rallying the cavalry. Warwic showed great presence of mind in maintaining the ranks of the foot, on which the horse had recoiled: He made Sir Peter Meutas advance, captain of the foot harquebusiers, and Sir Peter Gamboa, captain of some Italian and Spanish harquebusiers on horseback; and ordered them to ply the Scottish infantry with their shot. They marched to the slough, and discharged their pieces full in the face of the enemy: The ships galled them from the flank: The artillery, planted on a height, infested them from the front: The English archers poured in a shower of arrows upon them: And the vanguard, descending from the hill, advanced, leisurely and in good order, towards them. Dismayed with all these circumstances, the Scottish van began to retreat: The retreat soon changed into a flight, which was begun by the Irish archers. The pannic of the van communicated itself to the main body, and passing thence to the rear, rendered the whole field a scene of confusion, terror, flight, and consternation. The English

[m] Patten. Hollingshed, p. 986.

army perceived from the heights the condition of the Scots, and begin the pursuit with loud shouts and acclamations, which added still more to the dismay of the vanquished. The horse in particular, eager to revenge the affront, which they had received in the beginning of the day, did the most bloody execution on the flying enemy; and from the field of battle to Edinburgh, for the space of five miles, the whole ground was strowed with dead bodies. The priests above all, and the monks received no quarter; and the English made sport of slaughtering men, who, from their extreme zeal and animosity, had engaged in an enterprise so ill befitting their profession. Few victories have been more decisive, or gained with smaller loss to the conquerors. There fell not two hundred of the English; and according to the most moderate computation, there perished above ten thousand of the Scots. About fifteen hundred were taken prisoners. This action was called the battle of Pinkey, from a nobleman's seat of that name in the neighbourhood.

The queen-dowager and Arran fled to Stirling, and were scarcely able to collect such a body of forces as could check the incursions of small parties of the English. About the same time, the earl of Lenox and lord Wharton entered the West Marches, at the head of five thousand men, and after taking and plundering Annan, they spread devastation over all the neighbouring counties.[n] Had Somerset prosecuted his advantages, he might have imposed what terms he pleased on the Scottish nation: But he was impatient to return to England, where, he heard, some counsellors, and even his own brother, the admiral, were carrying on cabals against his authority. Having taken the castles of Hume, Dunglass, Eymouth, Fastcastle, Roxborough, and some other small places: and having received the submission of some counties on the borders, he retired from Scotland. The fleet, besides destroying all the shipping along the coast, took Broughty in the Frith of Tay; and having fortified it, they there left a garrison. Arran desired leave to send commissioners in order to treat of a peace; and Somerset, having appointed Berwic for the place of conference, left Warwic with full powers to negociate: But no commissioners from Scotland ever appeared. The overture of the Scots was an artifice, to gain time, till succours should arrive from France.

[n] Hollingshed, p. 992.

CHAPTER XXXIV

The protector, on his arrival in England, summoned a parlia- *4th Nov.*
ment: And being somewhat elated with his success against the
Scots, he procured from his nephew a patent, appointing him to sit
on the throne, upon a stool or bench at the right hand of the king,
and to enjoy the same honours and privileges, that had usually
been possessed by any prince of the blood, or uncle of the kings of
England. In this patent, the king employed his dispensing power,
by setting aside the statute of precedency, enacted during the
former reign.[o] But if Somerset gave offence by assuming too much *A par-*
state, he deserves great praise on account of the laws passed this *liament.*
session, by which the rigour of former statutes was much mitigated, and some security given to the freedom of the constitution.
All laws were repealed, which extended the crime of treason beyond the statute of the twenty-fifth of Edward III.;[p] all laws enacted during the late reign, extending the crime of felony; all the
former laws against Lollardy or heresy, together with the statute of
the six articles. None were to be accused for words, but within a
month after they were spoken. By these repeals several of the most
rigorous laws, that ever had passed in England, were annulled:
and some dawn, both of civil and religious liberty, began to appear
to the people. Heresy, however, was still a capital crime by the
common law, and was subjected to the penalty of burning. Only,
there remained no precise standard, by which that crime could be
defined or determined: A circumstance, which might either be
advantageous or hurtful to public security, according to the disposition of the judges.

A repeal also passed of that law, the destruction of all laws, by
which the king's proclamation was made of equal force with a
statute.[q] That other law likewise was mitigated, by which the king
was empowered to annul every statute passed before the four and
twentieth year of his age: He could prevent their future execution;
but could not recal any past effects, which had ensued from them.[r]

It was also enacted, that all who denied the king's supremacy,
or asserted the pope's, should, for the first offence, forfeit their
goods and chattels, and suffer imprisonment during pleasure; for
the second offence, should incur the penalty of a *praemunire;* and
for the third be attainted of treason. But if any, after the first of
March ensuing, endeavoured, by writing, printing, or any overt act

---

[o] Rymer, vol. xv. p. 164.   [p] 1 Edw. VI. c. 12.   [q] Edw. VI. c. 2.   [r] Ibid.

or deed, to deprive the king of his estate or titles, particularly of his supremacy, or to confer them on any other, he was to be adjudged guilty of treason. If any of the heirs of the crown should usurp upon another, or endeavour to break the order of succession, it was declared treason in them, their aiders and abettors. These were the most considerable acts passed during this session. The members in general discovered a very passive disposition with regard to religion: Some few appeared zealous for the reformation: Others secretly harboured a strong propensity to the catholic faith: But the greater part appeared willing to take any impression, which they should receive from interest, authority, or the reigning fashion.[s]

The convocation met at the same time with the parliament; and as it was found, that their debates were at first cramped by the rigorous statute of the six articles, the king granted them a dispensation from that law, before it was repealed by parliament.[t] The lower house of convocation applied to have liberty of sitting with the commons in parliament; or if this privilege were refused them, which they claimed as their ancient right, they desired, that no law, regarding religion, might pass in parliament without their consent and approbation. But the principles, which now prevailed, were more favourable to the civil than to the ecclesiastical power; and this demand of the convocation was rejected.

1548.

Farther progress of the reformation.

The protector had assented to the repeal of that law, which gave to the king's proclamations the authority of statutes; but he did not intend to renounce that arbitrary or discretionary exercise of power, in issuing proclamations, which had ever been assumed by the crown, and which it is difficult to distinguish exactly from a full legislative power. He even continued to exert this authority in some particulars, which were then regarded as the most momentous. Orders were issued by council, that candles should no longer be carried about on Candlemas day, ashes on Ashwednesday, palms on Palm-sunday.[u] These were ancient religious practices, now termed superstitions: though it is fortunate for mankind, when superstition happens to take a direction so innocent and inoffensive. The severe disposition, which naturally

[s] Heylin, p. 48.   [t] Antiq. Britan. p. 339.   [u] Burnet, vol. ii. p. 59. Collier, vol. ii. p. 241. Heylin, p. 55.

CHAPTER XXXIV

attends all reformers, prompted likewise the council to abolish some gay and showy ceremonies, which belonged to the ancient religion.[w]

An order was also issued by council for the removal of all images from the churches: An innovation which was much desired by the reformers, and which alone, with regard to the populace, amounted almost to a total change of the established religion.[x] An attempt had been made to separate the use of images from their abuse, the reverence from the worship of them; but the execution of this design was found, upon trial, very difficult, if not wholly impracticable.

As private masses were abolished by law, it became necessary to compose a new communion-service; and the council went so far, in the preface which they prefixed to this work, as to leave the practice of auricular confession wholly indifferent.[y] This was a prelude to the entire abolition of that invention, one of the most powerful engines that ever was contrived for degrading the laity, and giving their spiritual guides an entire ascendant over them. And it may justly be said, that, though the priest's absolution, which attends confession, serves somewhat to ease weak minds from the immediate agonies of superstitious terror, it operates only by enforcing superstition itself, and thereby preparing the mind for a more violent relapse into the same disorders.

The people were at that time extremely distracted, by the opposite opinions of their preachers; and as they were totally unable to judge of the reasons advanced on either side, and naturally regarded every thing which they heard at church, as of equal authority, a great confusion and fluctuation resulted from this uncertainty. The council had first endeavoured to remedy the inconvenience, by laying some restraints on preaching; but finding this expedient ineffectual, they imposed a total silence on the preachers, and thereby put an end at once to all the polemics of the pulpit.[z] By the nature of things, this restraint could only be temporary. For in proportion as the ceremonies of public worship, its shews and exterior observances, were retrenched by the reformers, the people were inclined to contract a stronger attachment to

[w] Burnet, vol. ii.   [x] Burnet, vol. ii. p. 60. Collier, vol. ii. p. 241. Heylin, p. 55.   [y] Burnet, vol. ii.   [z] Fuller, Heylin, Burnet.

sermons, whence alone they received any occupation or amusement. The ancient religion, by giving its votaries something to do, freed them from the trouble of thinking: Sermons were delivered only in the principal churches, and at some particular fasts and festivals: And the practice of haranguing the populace, which, if abused, is so powerful an incitement to faction and sedition, had much less scope and influence during those ages.

Affairs of Scotland. The greater progress was made towards a reformation in England, the farther did the protector find himself from all prospect of completing the union with Scotland; and the queen-dowager, as well as the clergy, became the more averse to all alliance with a nation, which had so far departed from all ancient principles. Somerset, having taken the town of Haddington, had ordered it to be strongly garrisoned and fortified, by lord Grey: He also erected some fortifications at Lauder: And he hoped, that these two places, together with Broughty and some smaller fortresses, which were in the hands of the English, would serve as a curb on Scotland; and would give him access into the heart of the country.

Arran, being disappointed in some attempts on Broughty, relied chiefly on the succours expected from France, for the recovery of these places; and they arrived at last in the Frith, to the number of six thousand men; half of them Germans. They were commanded by Desse, and under him by Andelot, Strozzi, Meilleraye, and count Rhingrave. The Scots were at that time so sunk by their misfortunes, that five hundred English horse were able to ravage the whole country without resistance; and make inroads to the gates of the capital:[a] But on the appearance of the French succours, they collected more courage; and having joined Desse with a considerable reinforcement, they laid siege to Haddington.[b] This was an undertaking for which they were by themselves totally unfit; and even with the assistance of the French, they placed their chief hopes of success in starving the garrison. After some vain attempts to take the place by a regular siege, the blockade was formed, and the garrison was repulsed with loss in several sallies which they made upon the besiegers.

The hostile attempts, which the late king and the protector had

[a] Beagué, hist. of the Campagnes 1548 and 1549, p. 6. [b] Hollingshed, p. 993.

CHAPTER XXXIV

made against Scotland, not being steady, regular, nor pushed to the last extremity, had served only to irritate the nation, and to inspire them with the strongest aversion to that union, which was courted in so violent a manner. Even those who were inclined to the English alliance, were displeased to have it imposed on them by force of arms; and the earl of Huntley in particular, said pleasantly, that he disliked not the match, but he hated the manner of wooing.[c] The queen-dowager, finding these sentiments to prevail, called a parliament, in an abbey near Haddington; and it was there proposed, that the young queen, for her greater security, should be sent to France, and be committed to the custody of that ancient ally. Some objected, that this measure was desperate, allowed no resource in case of miscarriage, exposed the Scots to be subjected by foreigners, involved them in perpetual war with England, and left them no expedient, by which they could conciliate the friendship of that powerful nation. It was answered, on the other hand, that the queen's presence was the very cause of war with England; that that nation would desist, when they found, that their views of forcing a marriage had become altogether impracticable; and that Henry, being engaged by so high a mark of confidence, would take their sovereign under his protection, and use his utmost efforts to defend the kingdom. These arguments were aided by French gold, which was plentifully distributed among the nobles. The governor had a pension conferred on him of twelve thousand livres a year, received the title of duke of Chatelrault, and obtained for his son the command of a hundred men at arms.[d] And as the clergy dreaded the consequences of the English alliance, they seconded this measure with all the zeal and industry, which either principle or interest could inspire. It was accordingly determined to send the queen to France; and what was understood to be the necessary consequence, to marry her to the dauphin. Villegaignon, commander of four French gallies lying in the Frith of Forth, set sail as if he intended to return home; but when he reached the open sea, he turned northwards, passed by the Orkneys, and came in on the west coast at Dunbarton: An extraordinary voyage for ships of that fabric.[e] The young queen was there committed to him; and

Young queen of Scots sent into France.

[c] Heylin, p. 46. Patten.   [d] Burnet, vol. ii. p. 83. Buchanan, lib. xv. Keith, p. 55. Thuanus, lib. v. c. 15.   [e] Thuanus, lib. v. c. 15.

being attended by the lords Ereskine and Livingstone, she put to sea, and after meeting with some tempestuous weather, arrived safely at Brest, whence she was conducted to Paris, and soon after she was betrothed to the dauphin.

Somerset, pressed by many difficulties at home, and despairing of success in his enterprize against Scotland, was desirous of composing the differences with that kingdom, and he offered the Scots a ten years' truce; but as they insisted on his restoring all the places which he had taken, the proposal came to nothing. The Scots recovered the fortresses of Hume and Fast-castle by surprize, and put the garrisons to the sword: They repulsed, with loss, the English, who, under the command of lord Seymour, made a descent, first in Fife, then at Montrose: In the former action, James Stuart, natural brother to the queen, acquired honour; on the latter, Areskine of Dun. An attempt was made by Sir Robert Bowes and Sir Thomas Palmer, at the head of a considerable body, to throw relief into Haddington; but these troops, falling into an ambuscade, were almost wholly cut in pieces.[f] And though a small body of two hundred men escaped all the vigilance of the French, and arrived safely in Haddington, with some ammunition and provisions, the garrison was reduced to such difficulties, that the protector found it necessary to provide more effectually for their relief. He raised an army of eighteen thousand men, and adding three thousand Germans, who, on the dissolution of the protestant alliance, had offered their service to England, he gave the command of the whole to the earl of Shrewsbury.[g] D'Essé raised the blockade on the approach of the English; and with great difficulty made good his retreat to Edinburgh, where he posted himself advantageously. Shrewsbury, who had lost the opportunity of attacking him on his march, durst not give him battle in his present situation; and contenting himself with the advantage already gained, of supplying Haddington, he retired into England.

Though the protection of France was of great consequence to the Scots, in supporting them against the invasions of England, *Cabals of lord Seymour.* they reaped still more benefit from the distractions and divisions, which had creeped into the councils of this latter kingdom. Even the two brothers, the protector and admiral, not content with the

[f] Stowe, p. 595. Hollingshed, p. 994.   [g] Hayward, p. 291.

high stations which they severally enjoyed, and the great eminence
to which they had risen, had entertained the most violent jealousy
of each other; and they divided the whole court and kingdom, by
their opposite cabals and pretensions. Lord Seymour was a man of
insatiable ambition; arrogant, assuming, implacable; and though
esteemed of superior capacity to the protector, he possessed not to
the same degree the confidence and regard of the people. By his
flattery and address, he had so insinuated himself into the good
graces of the queen-dowager, that, forgetting her usual prudence
and decency, she married him immediately upon the demise of the
late king: Insomuch that, had she soon proved pregnant, it might
have been doubtful to which husband the child belonged. The
credit and riches of this alliance supported the ambition of the
admiral; but gave umbrage to the dutchess of Somerset, who,
uneasy that the younger brother's wife should have the precedency, employed all her credit with her husband, which was too
great, first to create, then to widen, the breach between the two
brothers.[h]

The first symptoms of this misunderstanding appeared when
the protector commanded the army in Scotland. Secretary Paget,
a man devoted to Somerset, remarked, that Seymour was forming
separate intrigues among the counsellors; was corrupting, by
presents, the king's servants; and even endeavouring, by improper
indulgences and liberalities, to captiviate the affections of the
young monarch. Paget represented to him the danger of this conduct; desired him to reflect on the numerous enemies, whom the
sudden elevation of their family had created; and warned him that
any dissention between him and the protector would be greedily
laid hold of, to effect the ruin of both. Finding his remonstrances
neglected, he conveyed intelligence of the danger to Somerset, and
engaged him to leave the enterprize upon Scotland unfinished, in
order to guard against the attempts of his domestic enemies. In the
ensuing parliament, the admiral's projects appeared still more
dangerous to public tranquillity; and as he had acquired many
partizans, he made a direct attack upon his brother's authority. He
represented to his friends, that formerly, during a minority, the

[h] Hayward, p. 301. Heylin, p. 72. Camden. Thuanus, lib. vi. c. 5. Haynes,
p. 69.

office of protector of the kingdom had been kept separate from that of governor of the king's person; and that the present union of these two important trusts conferred on Somerset an authority, which could not safely be lodged in any subject.[i] The young king was even prevailed on to write a letter to the parliament, desiring that Seymour might be appointed his governor; and that nobleman had formed a party in the two houses, by which he hoped to effect his purpose. The design was discovered before its execution; and some common friends were sent to remonstrate with him, but had so little influence, that he threw out many menacing expressions, and rashly threatened, that, if he were thwarted in his attempt, he would make this parliament the blackest that ever sat in England.[k] The council sent for him, to answer for his conduct; but he refused to attend: They then began to threaten in their turn, and informed him, that the king's letter, instead of availing him any thing to the execution of his views, would be imputed to him as a criminal enterprize, and be construed as a design to disturb the government, by forming a separate interest with a child and minor. They even let fall some menaces of sending him to the Tower for his temerity; and the admiral, finding himself prevented in his design, was obliged to submit, and to desire a reconciliation with his brother.

The mild and moderate temper of Somerset made him willing to forget these enterprizes of the admiral; but the ambition of that turbulent spirit could not be so easily appeased. His spouse, the queen-dowager, died in childbed; but so far from regarding this event as a check to his aspiring views, he founded on it the scheme of a more extraordinary elevation. He made his addresses to the lady Elizabeth, then in the sixteenth year of her age; and that princess, whom even the hurry of business, and the pursuits of ambition, could not, in her more advanced years, disengage entirely from the tender passions, seems to have listened to the insinuations of a man, who possessed every talent proper to captivate the affections of the fair.[l] But as Henry VIII. had excluded his daughters from all hopes of succession, if they married without the consent of his executors, which Seymour could never hope to obtain; it was concluded that he meant to effect his purpose by

[i] Haynes, p. 82, 90.   [k] Ibid. p. 75.   [l] Haynes, p. 95, 96, 102, 108.

CHAPTER XXXIV

expedients still more rash and more criminal. All the other measures of the admiral tended to confirm this suspicion. He continued to attack, by presents, the fidelity of those who had more immediate access to the king's person: He endeavoured to seduce the young prince into his interests: He found means of holding a private correspondence with him: He openly decried his brother's administration; and asserted, that, by enlisting Germans, and other foreigners, he intended to form a mercenary army, which might endanger the king's authority, and the liberty of the people: By promises and persuasion he brought over to his party many of the principal nobility; and had extended his interest all over England: He neglected not even the most popular persons of inferior rank; and had computed, that he could, on occasion, muster an army of 10,000 men, composed of his servants, tenants, and retainers:[m] He had already provided arms for their use; and having engaged in his interests Sir John Sharington, a corrupt man, master of the mint at Bristol, he flattered himself that money would not be wanting. Somerset was well apprized of all these alarming circumstances, and endeavoured, by the most friendly expedients, by intreaty, reason, and even by heaping new favours upon the admiral, to make him desist from his dangerous counsels: But finding all endeavours ineffectual, he began to think of more severe remedies. The earl of Warwic was an ill instrument between the brothers; and had formed the design, by inflaming the quarrel, to raise his own fortune on the ruins of both.

Dudley, earl of Warwic, was the son of that Dudley, minister to Henry VII. who, having, by rapine, extortion, and perversion of law, incurred the hatred of the public, had been sacrificed to popular animosity, in the beginning of the subsequent reign. The late king, sensible of the iniquity, at least illegality, of the sentence, had afterwards restored young Dudley's blood by act of parliament; and finding him endowed with abilities, industry, and activity, he had entrusted him with many important commands, and had ever found him successful in his undertakings. He raised him to the dignity of viscount Lisle, conferred on him the office of admiral, and gave him by his will a place among his executors. Dudley made still farther progress during the minority; and having obtained the

Dudley, earl of Warwic.

[m] Ibid. p. 105, 106.

title of earl of Warwic, and undermined the credit of Southampton, he bore the chief rank among the protector's counsellors.
The victory, gained at Pinkey, was much ascribed to his courage
and conduct; and he was universally regarded as a man equally
endowed with the talents of peace and of war. But all these virtues
were obscured by still greater vices; and exorbitant ambition, an
insatiable avarice, a neglect of decency, a contempt of justice: And
as he found, that lord Seymour, whose abilities and enterprizing
spirit he chiefly dreaded, was involving himself in ruin by his rash
counsels, he was determined to push him on the precipice; and
thereby remove the chief obstacle to his own projected greatness.

When Somerset found, that the public peace was endangered
by his brother's seditious, not to say rebellious, schemes, he was the
more easily persuaded by Warwic to employ the extent of royal
authority against him; and after depriving him of the office of
admiral, he signed a warrant for committing him to the Tower.
Some of his accomplices were also taken into custody, and three
privy counsellors, being sent to examine them, made a report, that
they had met with very full and important discoveries. Yet still the
protector suspended the blow, and showed a reluctance to ruin his
brother. He offered to desist from the prosecution, if Seymour
would promise him a cordial reconciliation; and renouncing all
ambitious hopes, be contented with a private life, and retire into
the country. But as Seymour made no other answer to these
friendly offers than menaces and defiances, he ordered a charge to
be drawn up against him, consisting of thirty-three articles;[n] and
the whole to be laid before the privy council. It is pretended, that
every particular was so incontestibly proved, both by witnesses and
his own hand-writing, that there was no room for doubt; yet did
the council think proper to go in a body to the Tower, in order
more fully to examine the prisoner. He was not daunted by the
appearance: He boldly demanded a fair trial: required to be confronted by the witnesses; desired that the charge might be left with
him, in order to be considered; and refused to answer any inter-
rogatories, by which he might accuse himself.

It is apparent, that, notwithstanding what is pretended, there
must have been some deficiency in the evidence against Seymour,

[n] Burnet, vol. ii. Coll. 31. 2 & 3 Edw. VI. c. 18.

when such demands, founded on the plainest principles of law and equity, were absolutely rejected. We shall indeed conclude, if we carefully examine the charge, that many of the articles were general, and scarcely capable of any proof; many of them, if true, susceptible of a more favourable interpretation; and that, though, on the whole, Seymour appears to have been a dangerous subject, he had not advanced far in those treasonable projects imputed to him. The chief part of his actual guilt seems to have consisted in some unwarrantable practices in the admiralty, by which pyrates were protected, and illegal impositions laid upon the merchants.

But the administration had, at that time, an easy instrument of vengeance, to wit, the Parliament; and needed not to give themselves any concern with regard either to the guilt of the persons whom they prosecuted, or the evidence which could be produced against them. A session of parliament being held, it was resolved to proceed against Seymour by bill of attainder; and the young king being induced, after much solicitation, to give his consent to it, a considerable weight was put on his approbation. The matter was first laid before the upper-house; and several peers, rising up in their places, gave an account of what they knew concerning lord Seymour's conduct and his criminal words or actions. These narratives were received as undoubted evidence; and though the prisoner had formerly engaged many friends and partizans among the nobility, no one had either the courage or equity to move, that he might be heard in his defence, that the testimony against him should be delivered in a legal manner, and that he should be confronted with the witnesses. A little more scruple was made in the house of commons: There were even some members who objected against the whole method of proceeding by bill of attainder, passed in absence; and insisted, that a formal trial should be given to every man before his condemnation. But when a message was sent by the king, enjoining the house to proceed, and offering that the same narratives should be laid before them which had satisfied the peers, they were easily prevailed on to acquiesce.[o] The bill passed in a full house. Near four hundred voted for it; not above nine or ten against it.[p] The sentence was soon after executed, and the prisoner was beheaded on Tower-hill. The warrant

A parliament. 4th Novem.

1549. Attainder of lord Seymour.

March 20.

His execution.

[o] 2 & 3 Edw. VI. c. 18.   [p] Burnet, vol. ii. p. 99.

was signed by Somerset, who was exposed to much blame, on account of the violence of these proceedings. The attempts of the admiral seem chiefly to have been levelled against his brother's usurped authority; and though his ambitious, enterprizing character, encouraged by a marriage with the lady Elizabeth, might have endangered the public tranquillity, the prudence of foreseeing evils at such a distance, was deemed too great; and the remedy was plainly illegal. It could only be said, that this bill of attainder was somewhat more tolerable than the preceding ones, to which the nation had been enured. For here, at least, some shadow of evidence was produced.

Ecclesiastical affairs. All the considerable business transacted this session besides the attainder of lord Seymour, regarded ecclesiastical affairs; which were now the chief object of attention throughout the nation. A committee of bishops and divines had been appointed by the council, to compose a liturgy; and they had executed the work committed to them. They proceeded with moderation in this delicate undertaking: They retained as much of the ancient mass as the principles of the reformers would permit: They indulged nothing to the spirit of contradiction, which so naturally takes place in all great innovations: And they flattered themselves, that they had established a service, in which every denomination of Christians might, without scruple, concur. The mass had always been celebrated in Latin; a practice which might have been deemed absurd, had it not been found useful to the clergy, by impressing the people with an idea of some mysterious unknown virtue in those rites, and by checking all their pretensions to be familiarly acquainted with their religion. But as the reformers pretended, in some few particulars, to encourage private judgment in the laity, the translation of the liturgy, as well as of the Scriptures, into the vulgar tongue, seemed more conformable to the genius of their sect; and this innovation, with the retrenching of prayers to saints, and of some superstitious ceremonies, was the chief difference between the old mass and the new liturgy. The parliament established this form of worship in all the churches, and ordained a uniformity to be observed in all the rites and ceremonies.[q]

There was another material act, which passed this session. The

[q] 2 & 3 Edw. VI. c. 1.

CHAPTER XXXIV

former canons had established the celibacy of the clergy; and though this practice is usually ascribed to the policy of the court of Rome, who thought, that the ecclesiastics would be more devoted to their spiritual head, and less dependant on the civil magistrate, when freed from the powerful tye of wives and children; yet was this institution much forwarded by the principles of superstition inherent in human nature. These principles had rendered the panegyrics on an inviolate chastity so frequent among the ancient fathers, long before the establishment of celibacy. And even this parliament, though they enacted a law, permitting the marriage of priests, yet confess in the preamble, "that it were better for priests and the ministers of the church to live chaste and without marriage, and it were much to be wished they would of themselves abstain." The inconveniencies, which had arisen from the compelling of chastity and the prohibiting of marriage, are the reasons assigned for indulging a liberty in this particular.[r] The ideas of penance also were so much retained in other particulars, that an act of parliament passed, forbidding the use of flesh-meat during Lent and other times of abstinence.[s]

The principal tenets and practices of the catholic religion were now abolished, and the reformation, such as it is enjoyed at present, was almost entirely completed in England. But the doctrine of the real presence, though tacitly condemned by the new communion-service and by the abolition of many ancient rites, still retained some hold on the minds of men; and it was the last doctrine of popery, that was wholly abandoned by the people.[t] The great attachment of the late king to that tenet might, in part, be the ground of this obstinacy; but the chief cause was really the extreme absurdity of the principle itself, and the profound veneration, which of course it impressed on the imagination. The priests likewise were much inclined to favour an opinion, which attributed to them so miraculous a power; and the people, who believed, that they participated of the very body and blood of their Saviour, were loth to renounce so extraordinary, and as they imagined, so salutary a privilege. The general attachment to this dogma was so violent, that the Lutherans, notwithstanding their separation from

[r] 2 & 3 Edw. VI. cap. 21.   [s] 2 & 3 Ed. VI cap. 19. See note [S] at the end of the volume.   [t] Burnet, vol. ii. cap. 104.

Rome, had thought proper, under another name, still to retain it:
And the catholic preachers, in England, when restrained in all
other particulars, could not forbear, on every occasion, inculcating
that tenet. Bonner, for this offence among others, had been tried
by the council, had been deprived of his see, and had been committed to custody. Gardiner also, who had recovered his liberty, appeared anew refractory to the authority, which established the late
innovations; and he seemed willing to countenance that opinion,
much favoured by all the English catholics, that the king was indeed supreme head of the church, but not the council, during a
minority. Having declined to give full satisfaction on this head, he
was sent to the Tower, and threatened with farther effects of the
council's displeasure.

These severities, being exercised on men, possessed of office
and authority, seemed, in that age, a necessary policy, in order to
enforce a uniformity in public worship and discipline: But there
were other instances of persecution, derived from no origin but
the bigotry of theologians; a malady, which seems almost incurable. Though the protestant divines had ventured to renounce
opinions, deemed certain during many ages, they regarded, in
their turn, the new system as so certain, that they would suffer no
contradiction with regard to it; and they were ready to burn in the
same flames, from which they themselves had so narrowly escaped, every one that had the assurance to differ from them. A
commission by act of council was granted to the primate and some
others, to examine and search after all anabaptists, heretics, or
contemners of the book of common prayer.[u] The commissioners
were injoined to reclaim them, if possible; to impose penance on
them; and to give them absolution: Or if these criminals were
obstinate, to excommunicate and imprison them, and to deliver
them over to the secular arm: And in the execution of this charge,
they were not bound to observe the ordinary methods of trial; the
forms of law were dispensed with; and if any statutes happened to
interfere with the powers in the commission, they were over-ruled
and abrogated by the council. Some tradesmen in London were
brought before these commissioners, and were accused of maintaining, among other opinions, that a man regenerate could not
sin, and that, though the outward man might offend, the inward

[u] Burnet, vol. ii. p. 3. Rymer, tom. xv. p. 181.

CHAPTER XXXIV

was incapable of all guilt. They were prevailed on to abjure, and were dismissed. But there was a woman accused of heretical pravity, called Joan Bocher, or Joan of Kent, who was so pertinacious, that the commissioners could make no impression upon her. Her doctrine was, "That Christ was not truly incarnate of the virgin, whose flesh, being the outward man, was sinfully begotten and born in sin; and consequently, he could take none of it. But the word, by the consent of the inward man of the virgin, was made flesh."[w] This opinion, it would seem, is not orthodox; and there was a necessity for delivering the woman to the flames for maintaining it. But the young king, though in such tender years, had more sense than all his counsellors and preceptors; and he long refused to sign the warrant for her execution. Cranmer was employed to persuade him to compliance; and he said, that there was a great difference between errors in other points of divinity, and those which were in direct contradiction to the Apostles creed: These latter were impieties against God, which the prince, being God's deputy, ought to repress; in like manner, as inferior magistrates were bound to punish offences against the king's person. Edward, overcome by importunity, at last submitted, though with tears in his eyes; and he told Cranmer, that, if any wrong were done, the guilt should lie entirely on his head. The primate, after making a new effort to reclaim the woman from her errors, and finding her obstinate against all his arguments, at last committed her to the flames. Some time after, a Dutchman, called Van Paris, accused of the heresy, which has received the name of Arianism, was condemned to the same punishment. He suffered with so much satisfaction, that he hugged and caressed the faggots, that were consuming him; a species of frenzy, of which there is more than one instance among the martyrs of that age.[x]

These rigorous methods of proceeding soon brought the whole nation to a conformity, seeming or real, with the new doctrine and the new liturgy. The lady Mary alone continued to adhere to the mass, and refused to admit the established modes of worship. When pressed and menaced on this head, she applied to the emperor; who, using his interest with Sir Philip Hobby, the English ambassador, procured her a temporary connivance from the council.[y]

[w] Burnet, vol. ii. coll. 35. Strype's Mem. Cranm. p. 181.   [x] Burnet, vol. ii. p. 112. Strype's Mem. Cranm. p. 181.   [y] Heylin, p. 102.

XXXV

Discontents of the people –
Insurrections – Conduct of the war with
Scotland – with France – Factions in
the council – Conspiracy against Somerset –
Somerset resigns the protectorship –
A parliament – Peace with France and
Scotland – Boulogne surrendered –
Persecution of Gardiner – Warwic created
duke of Northumberland – His ambition – Trial
of Somerset – His execution – A parliament –
A new parliament – Succession changed –
The king's sickness – and death

1549.
Discon-
tents of
the people.
THERE IS NO ABUSE SO GREAT, in civil society, as not to be attended with a variety of beneficial consequences; and in the beginnings of reformation, the loss of these advantages is always felt very sensibly, while the benefit, resulting from the change, is the slow effect of time, and is seldom perceived by the bulk of a nation. Scarce any institution can be imagined less favourable, in the main, to the interests of mankind than that of monks and friars; yet was it followed by many good effects, which, having ceased by the suppression of monasteries, were much regretted by

CHAPTER XXXV

the people of England. The monks, always residing in their convents, in the centre of their estates, spent their money in the provinces and among their tenants, afforded a ready market for commodities, were a sure resource to the poor and indigent; and though their hospitality and charity gave but too much encouragement to idleness, and prevented the encrease of public riches, yet did it provide, to many, a relief from the extreme pressures of want and necessity. It is also observable, that, as the friars were limited, by the rules of their institution, to a certain mode of living, they had not equal motives for extortion with other men; and they were acknowledged to have been in England, as they still are in Roman catholic countries, the best and most indulgent landlords. The abbots and priors were permitted to give leases at an undervalue, and to receive, in return, a large present from the tenant; in the same manner as is still practised by the bishops and colleges. But when the abbey-lands were distributed among the principal nobility and courtiers, they fell under a different management: The rents of farms were raised, while the tenants found not the same facility in disposing of the produce; the money was often spent in the capital; and the farmers, living at a distance, were exposed to oppression from their new masters, or to the still greater rapacity of the stewards.

These grievances of the common people were at that time heightened by other causes. The arts of manufacture were much more advanced in other European countries than in England; and even in England these arts had made greater progress than the knowledge of agriculture; a profession, which, of all mechanical employments, requires the most reflection and experience. A great demand arose for wool both abroad and at home: Pasturage was found more profitable than unskilful tillage: Whole estates were laid waste by inclosures: The tenants regarded as a useless burden, were expelled their habitations: Even the cottagers, deprived of the commons, on which they formerly fed their cattle, were reduced to misery: And a decay of people, as well as a diminution of the former plenty, was remarked in the kingdom.[z] This grievance was now of an old date; and Sir Thomas More, alluding

[z] Strype, vol. ii. Repository Q.

to it, observes in his Utopia, that a sheep had become in England a more ravenous animal than a lion or wolf, and devoured whole villages, cities, and provinces.

The general encrease also of gold and silver in Europe, after the discovery of the West-Indies, had a tendency to inflame these complaints. The growing demand in the more commercial countries, had heightened every where the price of commodities, which could easily be transported thither; but in England, the labour of men, who could not so easily change their habitation, still remained nearly at the ancient rates; and the poor complained that they could no longer gain a subsistence by their industry. It was by an addition alone of toil and application they were enabled to procure a maintenance; and though this encrease of industry was at last the effect of the present situation, and an effect beneficial to society, yet was it difficult for the people to shake off their former habits of indolence; and nothing but necessity could compel them to such an exertion of their faculties.

It must also be remarked, that the profusion of Henry VIII. had reduced him, notwithstanding his rapacity, to such difficulties, that he had been obliged to remedy a present necessity, by the pernicious expedient of debasing the coin; and the wars, in which the protector had been involved, had induced him to carry still farther the same abuse. The usual consequences ensued: The good specie was hoarded or exported; base metal was coined at home or imported from abroad in great abundance; the common people, who received their wages in it, could not purchase commodities at the usual rates; a universal dissidence and stagnation of commerce took place; and loud complaints were heard in every part of England.

The protector who loved popularity, and pitied the condition of the people, encouraged these complaints by his endeavours to redress them. He appointed a commission for making enquiry concerning inclosures; and issued a proclamation, ordering all late inclosures to be laid open by a day appointed. The populace, meeting with such countenance from government, began to rise in several places, and to commit disorders, but were quieted by remonstrances and persuasion. In order to give them greater satisfaction, Somerset appointed new commissioners, whom he sent every where, with an unlimited power to hear and determine all causes about inclosures, highways, and cottages.[a] As this commission was disagreeable to the gentry and nobility, they stigmatized it as arbitrary and illegal; and the common people, fearing it would be eluded, and being impatient for immediate redress, could no longer contain their fury, but sought for a remedy by force of arms. The rising began at once in several parts of England, as if an universal conspiracy had been formed by the commonalty. The rebels in Wiltshire were dispersed by Sir William Herbert: Those in the neighbouring counties, Oxford and Glocester, by lord Gray of Wilton. Many of the rioters were killed in the field: Others were executed by martial law. The commotions in Hampshire, Sussex, Kent, and other counties, were quieted by gentler expedients; but the disorders in Devonshire and Norfolk threatened more dangerous consequences.

Insurrections.

The commonalty in Devonshire began with the usual complaints against inclosures and against oppressions from the gentry; but the parish priest of Sampford-Courtenay had the address to give their discontent a direction towards religion; and the delicacy of the subject, in the present emergency, made the insurrection immediately appear formidable. In other counties, the gentry had kept closely united with government; but here many of them took part with the populace; among others, Humphry Arundel, governor of St. Michael's Mount. The rioters were brought into the form of a regular army, which amounted to the number of ten thousand. Lord Russel had been sent against them at the head of a small force; but finding himself too weak to encounter them in the field, he kept at a distance, and began to negociate with them; in hopes of eluding their fury by delay, and of dispersing them by the difficulty of their subsisting in a body. Their demands were, that the mass should be restored, half of the abbey-lands resumed, the law of the six articles executed, holy water and holy bread respected, and all other particular grievances redressed.[b] The council to whom Russel transmitted these demands, sent a haughty answer; commanded the rebels to disperse, and promised them pardon upon their immediate submission. Enraged at this disappointment, they marched to Exeter; carrying before them crosses,

[a] Burnet, vol. ii. p. 115. Strype, vol. ii. p. 171.   [b] Hayward, p. 292. Hollingshed, p. 1003. Fox, vol. ii. p. 666. Mem. Cranm. p. 186.

banners, holy-water, candlesticks, and other implements of ancient superstition; together with the hoste, which they covered
with a canopy.[c] The citizens of Exeter shut their gates; and the
rebels, as they had no cannon, endeavoured to take the place, first
by scalade, then by mining, but were repulsed in every attempt.
Russel meanwhile lay at Honiton, till reinforced by Sir William
Herbert, and lord Gray, with some German horse, and some Italian arquebusiers under Battista Spinola. He then resolved to attempt the relief of Exeter, which was now reduced to extremities.
He attacked the rebels, drove them from all their posts, did great
execution upon them both in the action and pursuit,[d] and took
many prisoners. Arundel and the other leaders were sent to London, tried and executed. Many of the inferior sort were put to
death by martial law:[e] The vicar of St. Thomas, one of the principal
incendiaries, was hanged on the top of his own steeple, arrayed in
his popish weeds, with his beads at his girdle.[f]

The insurrection in Norfolk rose to a still greater height, and
was attended with greater acts of violence. The populace were at
first excited, as in other places, by complaints against inclosures;
but finding their numbers amount to twenty thousand, they grew
insolent, and proceeded to more exorbitant pretensions. They
required the suppression of the gentry, the placing of new counsellors about the king, and the re-establishment of the ancient
rites. One Ket, a tanner, had assumed the government over them,
and he exercised his authority with the utmost arrogance and
outrage. Having taken possession of Moushold-Hill near Norwich,
he erected his tribunal under an old oak, thence called the oak of
reformation; and summoning the gentry to appear before him, he
gave such decrees as might be expected from his character and
situation. The marquis of Northampton was first ordered against
him; but met with a repulse, in an action, where lord Sheffield was
killed.[g] The protector affected popularity, and cared not to appear
in person against the rebels: He therefore sent the earl of Warwic
at the head of 6000 men, levied for the wars against Scotland; and
he thereby afforded his mortal enemy an opportunity of encreasing his reputation and character. Warwic, having tried some

[c] Heylin, p. 76.   [d] Stowe's Annals, p. 597. Hayward, p. 295.   [e] Hayward,
p. 295, 296.   [f] Heylin, p. 76. Hollingshed, p. 1026.   [g] Stowe, p. 597.
Hollingshed, p. 1030–34. Strype, vol. ii. p. 174.

skirmishes with the rebels, at last made a general attack upon them, and put them to flight. Two thousand fell in the action and pursuit: Ket was hanged at Norwich castle; nine of his followers on the boughs of the oak of reformation; and the insurrection was entirely suppressed. Some rebels in Yorkshire, learning the fate of their companions, accepted the offers of pardon, and threw down their arms. A general indemnity was soon after published by the protector.[h]

But though the insurrections were thus quickly subdued in England, and no traces of them seemed to remain, they were attended with bad consequences to the foreign interests of the nation. The forces of the earl of Warwic, which might have made a great impression on Scotland, were diverted from that enterprize; and the French general had leisure to reduce that country to some settlement and composure. He took the fortress of Broughty, and put the garrison to the sword. He straitened the English at Haddington; and though lord Dacres was enabled to throw relief into the place, and to reinforce the garrison, it was found at last very chargeable, and even impracticable, to keep possession of that fortress. The whole country in the neighbourhood was laid waste by the inroads both of the Scots and English, and could afford no supply to the garrison: The place lay above thirty miles from the borders; so that a regular army was necessary to escort any provisions thither: And as the plague had broken out among the troops, they perished daily, and were reduced to a state of great weakness. For these reasons, orders were given to dismantle Haddington, and to convey the artillery and garrison to Berwic; and the earl of Rutland, now created warden of the east marches, executed the orders.

Conduct of the war with Scotland.

The king of France also took advantage of the distractions among the English, and made an attempt to recover Boulogne, and that territory, which Henry VIII. had conquered from France. On other pretences, he assembled an army; and falling suddenly upon the Boulonnois, took the castles of Sellaque, Blackness, and Ambleteuse, though well supplied with garrisons, ammunition, and provisions.[i] He endeavoured to surprize Boulenberg, and was repulsed; but the garrison, not thinking the place tenable after the

With France.

[h] Hayward, p. 297, 298, 299.   [i] Thuanus, lib. vi. c. 6.

loss of the other fortresses, destroyed the works, and retired to Boulogne. The rains, which fell in great abundance during the autumn, and a pestilential distemper, which broke out in the French camp, deprived Henry of all hopes of success against Boulogne itself; and he retired to Paris.[k] He left the command of the army to Gaspar de Coligny, lord of Chatillon, so famous afterwards by the name of admiral Coligny; and he gave him orders to form the siege early in the spring. The active disposition of this general engaged him to make, during the winter, several attempts against the place; but they all proved unsuccessful.

Strozzi, who commanded the French fleet and galleys, endeavoured to make a descent on Jersey; but meeting there with an English fleet, he commenced an action, which seems not to have been decisive, since the historians of the two nations differ in their account of the event.[l]

As soon as the French war broke out, the protector endeavoured to fortify himself with the alliance of the emperor; and he sent over secretary Paget to Brussels, where Charles then kept court, in order to assist Sir Philip Hobby, the resident ambassador, in this negociation. But that prince had formed a design of extending his dominions by acting the part of champion for the catholic religion; and though extremely desirous of accepting the English alliance against France, his capital enemy, he thought it unsuitable to his other pretensions to enter into strict confederacy with a nation, which had broken off all connexions with the church of Rome. He therefore declined the advances of friendship from England; and eluded the applications of the ambassadors. An exact account is preserved of this negociation in a letter of Hobby's; and it is remarkable, that the emperor, in a conversation with the English ministers, asserted that the prerogatives of a king of England were more extensive than those of a king of France.[m] Burnet, who preserves this letter, subjoins, as a parallel instance, that one objection, which the Scots made to marrying their queen with Edward, was, that all their privileges would be swallowed up by the great prerogative of the kings of England.[n]

Somerset, despairing of assistance from the emperor was in-

---

[k] Hayward, p. 300.   [l] Thuan. King Edward's journal, Stowe, p. 597.
[m] Burnet, vol. ii. p. 132, 175.   [n] Idem, p. 133.

CHAPTER XXXV

clined to conclude a peace with France and Scotland; and besides that he was not in a condition to maintain such ruinous wars, he thought, that there no longer remained any object of hostility. The Scots had sent away their queen; and could not, if ever so much inclined, complete the marriage contracted with Edward: And as Henry VIII. had stipulated to restore Boulogne in 1554, it seemed a matter of small moment to anticipate, a few years, the execution of the treaty. But when he proposed these reasons to the council, he met with strong opposition from his enemies, who, seeing him unable to support the war, were determined, for that very reason, to oppose all proposals for a pacification. The factions ran high in the court of England; and matters were drawing to an issue, fatal to the authority of the protector.

After Somerset obtained the patent, investing him with regal authority, he no longer paid any attention to the opinion of the other executors and counsellors; and being elated with his high dignity, as well as with his victory at Pinkey, he thought, that every one ought, in every thing, to yield to his sentiments. All those who were not entirely devoted to him, were sure to be neglected; whoever opposed his will received marks of anger or contempt;[o] and while he shewed a resolution to govern every thing, his capacity appeared not, in any respect, proportioned to his ambition. Warwic, more subtle and artful, covered more exorbitant views under fairer appearances; and having associated himself with Southampton, who had been re-admitted into the council, he formed a strong party, who were determined to free themselves from the slavery, imposed on them by the protector.

Factions in the council.

The malcontent counsellors found the disposition of the nation favourable to their designs. The nobility and gentry were in general displeased with the preference, which Somerset seemed to have given to the people; and as they ascribed all the insults, to which they had been lately exposed, to his procrastination, and to the countenance shown to the multitude, they apprehended a renewal of the same disorders from his present affectation of popularity. He had erected a court of requests in his own house for the relief of the people,[p] and he interposed with the judges in their behalf; a measure which might be deemed illegal, if any exertion

[o] Strype, vol. ii. p. 181.   [p] Ibid. p. 183.

of prerogative, at that time, could with certainty deserve that appellation. And this attempt, which was a stretch of power, seemed the more impolitic, because it disgusted the nobles, the surest support of monarchical authority.

But though Somerset courted the people, the interest, which he had formed with them, was in no degree answerable to his expectations. The catholic party, who retained influence with the lower ranks, were his declared enemies; and took advantage of every opportunity to decry his conduct. The attainder and execution of his brother bore an odious aspect: The introduction of foreign troops into the kingdom, was represented in invidious colours: The great estate, which he had suddenly acquired, at the expence of the church and of the crown, rendered him obnoxious: and the palace, which he was building in the Strand, served, by its magnificence, and still more by other circumstances which attended it, to expose him to the censure of the public. The parish church of St. Mary, with three bishops' houses, was pulled down, in order to furnish ground and materials for this structure: Not content with that sacrilege, an attempt was made to demolish St. Margaret's, Westminster, and to employ the stones to the same purpose; but the parishioners rose in a tumult, and chaced away the protector's tradesmen. He then laid his hands on a chapel in St. Paul's Church-yard, with a cloister, and charnel-house belonging to it; and these edifices, together with a church of St. John of Jerusalem, were made use of to raise his palace. What rendered the matter more odious to the people, was that the tombs and other monuments of the dead were defaced; and the bones, being carried away, were buried in unconsecrated ground.[q]

6th Octob.

Conspiracy against Somerset.

All these imprudences were remarked by Somerset's enemies, who resolved to take advantage of them. Lord St. John, president of the council, the earls of Warwic, Southampton, and Arundel, with five members more, met at Ely-house; and assuming to themselves the whole power of the council, began to act independantly of the protector, whom they represented as the author of every public grievance and misfortune. They wrote letters to the chief nobility and gentry in England, informing them of the present measures, and requiring their assistance: They sent for the mayor

---

[q] Heylin, p. 72, 73. Stowe's Survey of London. Hayward, p. 303.

CHAPTER XXXV

and aldermen of London, and enjoined them to obey their orders, without regard to any contrary orders, which they might receive from the duke of Somerset. They laid the same injunctions on the lieutenant of the Tower, who expressed his resolution to comply with them. Next day, Rich, lord chancellor, the marquis of Northampton, the earl of Shrewsbury, Sir Thomas Cheney, Sir John Gage, Sir Ralph Sadler, and chief justice Montague, joined the malcontent counsellors; and every thing bore a bad aspect for the protector's authority. Secretary Petre, whom he had sent to treat with the council, rather chose to remain with them: The common council of the city, being applied to, declared with one voice their approbation of the new measures, and their resolution of supporting them.[r]

As soon as the protector heard of the defection of the counsellors, he removed the king from Hampton-court, where he then resided, to the castle of Windsor; and, arming his friends and servants, seemed resolute to defend himself against all his enemies. But finding, that no man of rank, except Cranmer and Paget, adhered to him, that the people did not rise at his summons, that the City and Tower had declared against him, that even his best friends had deserted him, he lost all hopes of success, and began to apply to his enemies for pardon and forgiveness. No sooner was this despondency known, than lord Russel, Sir John Baker, speaker of the house of commons, and three counsellors more, who had hitherto remained neuters, joined the party of Warwic, whom every one now regarded as master. The council informed the public, by proclamation, of their actions and intentions; they wrote to the princesses, Mary and Elizabeth, to the same purpose; and they made addresses to the king, in which, after the humblest protestations of duty and submission, they informed him, that they were the council appointed by his father, for the government of the kingdom during his minority; that they had chosen the duke of Somerset protector, under the express condition, that he should guide himself by their advice and direction; that he had usurped the whole authority, and had neglected, and even in every thing opposed, their counsel; that he had proceeded to that height of presumption, as to levy forces against them, and place these forces

[r] Stowe, p. 597, 598. Hollingshed, p. 1057.

Somerset resigns the protector- ship.

about his majesty's person: They therefore begged, that they might be admitted to his royal presence, that he would be pleased to restore them to his confidence, and that Somerset's servants might be dismissed. Their request was complied with: Somerset capitulated only for gentle treatment, which was promised him. He was, however, sent to the Tower,[s] with some of his friends and partizans, among whom was Cecil, afterwards so much distinguished. Articles of indictment were exhibited against him,[t] of which the chief, at least the best founded, is his usurpation of the government, and his taking into his own hands the whole administration of affairs. The clause of his patent, which invested him with absolute power, unlimited by any law, was never objected to him; plainly, because, according to the sentiments of those times, that power was, in some degree, involved in the very idea of regal authority.

The catholics were extremely elated with this revolution; and as they had ascribed all the late innovations to Somerset's authority, they hoped, that his fall would prepare the way for the return of the ancient religion. But Warwic, who now bore chief sway in the council, was entirely indifferent with regard to all these points of controversy; and finding, that the principles of the reformation had sunk deeper into Edward's mind than to be easily eradicated, he was determined to comply with the young prince's inclinations, and not to hazard his new acquired power by any dangerous enterprize. He took care very early to express his intentions of supporting the reformation; and he threw such discouragements on Southampton, who stood at the head of the Romanists, and whom he considered as a dangerous rival, that the high-spirited nobleman retired from the council, and soon after died from vexation and disappointment. The other counsellors, who had concurred in the revolution, received their reward by promotions and new honours. Russel was created earl of Bedford: The marquis of Northampton obtained the office of great chamberlain; and lord Wentworth, besides the office of chamberlain of the household, got two large manors, Stepney and Hackney, which were torne from the see of London.[u] A council of regency was formed, not that which

---

[s] Stowe, p. 600.   [t] Burnet, vol. ii. book i. coll. 46. Hayward, p. 308. Stowe, p. 601. Hollingshed, p. 1059.   [u] Heylin, p. 85. Rymer, tom. xv. p. 226.

CHAPTER XXXV

Henry's will had appointed for the government of the kingdom, and which, being founded on an act of parliament, was the only legal one; but composed chiefly of members, who had formerly been appointed by Somerset, and who derived their seat from an authority, which was now declared usurped and illegal. But such niceties were, during that age, little understood, and still less regarded, in England.

A session of parliament was held; and as it was the usual maxim of that assembly to acquiesce in every administration which was established, the council dreaded no opposition from that quarter, and had more reason to look for a corroboration of their authority. Somerset had been prevailed on to confess, on his knees, before the council, all the articles of charge against him; and he imputed these misdemeanors to his own rashness, folly, and indiscretion, not to any malignity of intention.[w] He even subscribed this confession; and the paper was given in to parliament, who, after sending a committee to examine him, and hear him acknowledge it to be genuine, passed a vote, by which they deprived him of all his offices, and fined him two thousand pounds a year in land. Lord St. John was created treasurer in his place, and Warwic earl marshal. The prosecution against him was carried no farther. His fine was remitted by the king: He recovered his liberty: And Warwic, thinking that he was now sufficiently humbled, and that his authority was much lessened by his late tame and abject behaviour, re-admitted him into the council, and even agreed to an alliance between their families, by the marriage of his own son, lord Dudley, with the lady Jane Seymour, daughter of Somerset.[x]

During this session a severe law was passed against riots.[y] It was enacted, that if any, to the number of twelve persons, should meet together for any matter of state, and being required by a lawful magistrate, should not disperse, it should be treason: and if any broke hedges, or violently pulled up pales about inclosures, without lawful authority, it should be felony: Any attempt to kill a privy counsellor was subjected to the same penalty. The bishops had made an application, complaining, that they were deprived of all their power, by the encroachments of the civil courts, and the

4th Nov. A parliament.

[w] Heylin, p. 84. Hayward, p. 309. Stowe, p. 603.   [x] Hayward, p. 309.   [y] 3 and 4 Edw. VI. c. 5.

present suspension of the canon law; that they could summon no offender before them, punish no vice, or exert the discipline of the church: From which diminution of their authority, they pretended, immorality had every where received great encouragement and encrease. The design of some was, to revive the penitentiary rules of the primitive church. But others thought, that such an authority committed to the bishops, would prove more oppressive than confession, penance, and all the clerical inventions of the Romish superstition. The parliament, for the present, contented themselves with empowering the king to appoint thirty-two commissioners to compile a body of canon laws, which were to be valid, though never ratified by parliament. Such implicit trust did they repose in the crown; without reflecting that all their liberties and properties might be affected by these canons.[z] The king did not live to affix the royal sanction to the new canons. Sir John Sharington, whose crimes and malversations had appeared so egregious at the condemnation of lord Seymour, obtained from parliament a reversal of his attainder.[a] This man sought favour with the more zealous reformers; and bishop Latimer affirmed, that, though formerly he had been a most notorious knave, he was now so penitent, that he had become a very honest man.

1550.
Peace
with
France
and
Scotland.

When Warwic and the council of regency began to exercise their power, they found themselves involved in the same difficulties, that had embarrassed the protector. The wars with France and Scotland could not be supported by an exhausted exchequer; seemed dangerous to a divided nation; and were now acknowledged not to have any object, which even the greatest and most uninterrupted success could attain. The project of peace, entertained by Somerset, had served them as a pretence for clamour against his administration; yet after sending Sir Thomas Cheney to the emperor, and making again a fruitless effort to engage him in the protection of Boulogne, they found themselves obliged to listen to the advances, which Henry made them, by the canal of Guidotti, a Florentine merchant. The earl of Bedford, Sir John Mason, Paget, and Petre, were sent over to Boulogne, with full powers to negociate. The French king absolutely refused to pay

[z] 3 and 4 Edw. VI. c. 2.   [a] Ibid. c. 13.

CHAPTER XXXV

the two millions of crowns, which his predecessor had acknowl- *Boulogne*
edged to be due to the crown of England, as arrears of pensions; *surren-*
and said, that he never would consent to render himself tributary *dered.*
to any prince: But he offered a sum for the immediate restitution
of Boulogne; and four hundred thousand crowns were at last *24th*
agreed on, one half to be paid immediately, the other in August *Mar.*
following. Six hostages were given for the performance of this
article. Scotland was comprehended in the treaty: The English
stipulated to restore Lauder and Dunglas, and to demolish the
fortresses of Roxburgh and Eymouth.[b] No sooner was peace concluded with France, than a project was entertained of a close alliance with that kingdom; and Henry willingly embraced a proposal
so suitable both to his interests and his inclinations. An agreement,
some time after, was formed for a marriage between Edward and
Elizabeth, a daughter of France; and all the articles were, after a
little negociation, fully settled:[c] But this project never took effect.

The intention of marrying the king to a daughter of Henry, a
violent persecutor of the protestants, was no wise acceptable to
that party in England: But in all other respects, the council was
steady in promoting the reformation, and in enforcing the laws
against the Romanists. Several prelates were still addicted to that
communion; and though they made some compliances, in order to
save their bishoprics, they retarded, as much as they safely could,
the execution of the new laws, and gave countenance to such
incumbents as were negligent or refractory. A resolution was
therefore taken to seek pretences for depriving those prelates; and
the execution of this intention was the more easy, as they had all
of them been obliged to take commissions, in which it was declared, that they held their sees during the king's pleasure only. It
was thought proper to begin with Gardiner, in order to strike a
terror into the rest. The method of proceeding against him was
violent, and had scarcely any colour of law or justice. Injunctions
had been given him to inculcate, in a sermon, the duty of obedience to a king, even during his minority; and because he had
neglected this topic, he had been thrown into prison, and had been
there detained during two years, without being accused of any

[b] Burnet, vol. ii. p. 148. Hayward, 310, 311, 312. Rymer, vol. xv. p. 211.
[c] Hayward, p. 318. Heylin, p. 104. Rymer, tom. xv. p. 293.

crime, except disobedience to this arbitrary command. The duke of Somerset, secretary Petre, and some others of the council, were now sent, in order to try his temper, and endeavour to find some grounds for depriving him: He professed to them his intention of conforming to the government, of supporting the king's laws, and of officiating by the new liturgy. This was not the disposition which they expected or desired.[d] A new deputation was therefore sent, who carried him several articles to subscribe. He was required to acknowledge his former misbehaviour, and to confess the justice of his confinement: He was likewise to own, that the king was supreme head of the church; that the power of making and dispensing with holidays was part of the prerogative; that the book of common-prayer was a godly and commendable form; that the king was a complete sovereign in his minority; that the law of the six articles was justly repealed; and that the king had full authority to correct and reform what was amiss in ecclesiastical discipline, government, or doctrine. The bishop was willing to set his hand to all the articles except the first: He maintained his conduct to have been inoffensive; and declared that he would not own himself guilty of faults, which he had never committed.[e]

The council, finding that he had gone such lengths, were determined to prevent his full compliance by multiplying the difficulties upon him, and sending him new articles to subscribe. A list was selected of such points as they thought would be the hardest of digestion; and not content with this rigour, they also insisted on his submission, and his acknowledgment of past errors. To make this subscription more mortifying, they demanded a promise, that he would recommend and publish all these articles from the pulpit: But Gardiner, who saw, that they intended either to ruin or dishonour him, or perhaps both, determined not to gratify his enemies by any farther compliance: He still maintained his innocence; desired a fair trial, and refused to subscribe more articles, till he should recover his liberty. For this pretended offence his bishopric was put under sequestration for three months; and as he then appeared no more compliant than before, a commission was appointed to try, or, more properly speaking, to condemn him. The

[d] Heylin, p. 99. [e] Collier, vol. ii. p. 305, from the council books. Heylin, p. 99.

CHAPTER XXXV

commissioners were, the primate, the bishops of London, Ely, and Lincoln, secretary Petre, Sir James Hales, and some other lawyers. Gardiner objected to the legality of the commission, which was not founded on any statute or precedent, and he appealed from the commissioners to the king. His appeal was not regarded: Sentence was pronounced against him: He was deprived of his bishopric, and committed to close custody: His books and papers were seized; he was secluded from all company; and it was not allowed him either to send or receive any letters or messages.[f]   *1551.*

Gardiner, as well as the other prelates, had agreed to hold his office during the king's pleasure: But the council, unwilling to make use of a concession, which had been so illegally and arbitrarily extorted, chose rather to employ some forms of justice; a resolution, which led them to commit still greater iniquities and severities. But the violence of the reformers did not stop here. Day, bishop of Chichester, Heathe of Worcester, and Voisey of Exeter, were deprived of their bishoprics, on pretence of disobedience. Even Kitchen of Landaff, Capon of Salisbury, and Samson of Coventry, though they had complied in every thing, yet not being supposed cordial in their obedience, were obliged to seek protection, by sacrificing the most considerable revenues of their see to the rapacious courtiers.[g]

These plunderers neglected not even smaller profits. An order was issued by council, for purging the library at Westminster of all missals, legends, and other superstitious volumes, and delivering their garniture to Sir Anthony Aucher.[h] Many of these books were plaited with gold and silver, and curiously embossed; and this finery was probably the superstition that condemned them. Great havoc was likewise made on the libraries at Oxford. Books and manuscripts were destroyed without distinction: The volumes of divinity suffered for their rich binding: Those of literature were condemned as useless: Those of geometry and astronomy were supposed to contain nothing but necromancy.[i] The university had not power to oppose these barbarous violences: They were in danger of losing their own revenues; and expected every moment to be swallowed up by the earl of Warwic and his associates.

[f] Fox, vol. ii. p. 734, & seq. Burnet, Heylin, Collier.   [g] Goodwin de praesul Angl. Heylin, p. 100.   [h] Collier, vol. ii. p. 307, from the council books.
[i] Wood, hist. & antiq. Oxon. lib. 1. p. 271, 272.

Though every one besides yielded to the authority of the council, the lady Mary could never be brought to compliance; and she still continued to adhere to the mass, and to reject the new liturgy. Her behaviour was, during some time, connived at; but, at last, her two chaplains, Mallet and Berkeley, were thrown into prison;[k] and remonstrances were made to the princess herself on account of her disobedience. The council wrote her a letter, by which they endeavoured to make her change her sentiments, and to persuade her, that her religious faith was very ill grounded. They asked her, what warrant there was in Scripture for prayers in an unknown tongue, the use of images, or offering up the sacrament for the dead; and they desired her to peruse St. Austin, and the other ancient doctors, who would convince her of the errors of the Romish superstition, and prove that it was founded merely on false miracles and lying stories.[l] The lady Mary remained obstinate against all this advice, and declared herself willing to endure death rather than relinquish her religion: She only feared, she said, that she was not worthy to suffer martyrdom in so holy a cause: And as for protestant books, she thanked God, that, as she never had, so she hoped never to read any of them. Dreading farther violence, she endeavoured to make an escape to her kinsman Charles; but her design was discovered and prevented.[m] The emperor remonstrated in her behalf, and even threatened hostilities, if liberty of conscience were refused her: But though the council, sensible that the kingdom was in no condition to support, with honour, such a war, was desirous to comply; they found great difficulty to overcome the scruples of the young king. He had been educated in such a violent abhorrence of the mass and other popish rites, which he regarded as impious and idolatrous, that he should participate, he thought, in the sin, if he allowed its commission: And when at last the importunity of Cranmer, Ridley, and Poinet, prevailed somewhat over his opposition, he burst into tears; lamenting his sister's obstinacy, and bewailing his own hard fate, that he must suffer her to continue in such an abominable mode of worship.

The great object, at this time, of antipathy among the protes-

[k] Strype, vol. ii. p. 249.   [l] Fox, vol. ii. Collier, Burnet.   [m] Hayward, p. 315.

tant sects, was popery, or, more properly speaking, the papists. These they regarded as the common enemy, who threatened every moment to overwhelm the evangelical faith, and destroy its partizans by fire and sword: They had not as yet had leisure to attend to the other minute differences among themselves, which afterwards became the object of such furious quarrels and animosities, and threw the whole kingdom into combustion. Several Lutheran divines, who had reputation in those days, Bucer, Peter Martyr, and others, were induced to take shelter in England, from the persecutions, which the emperor exercised in Germany; and they received protection and encouragement. John A-lasco, a Polish nobleman, being expelled his country by the rigours of the catholics, settled, during some time, at Embden in East-Friezland, where he became preacher to a congregation of the reformed. Foreseeing the persecutions which ensued, he removed to England, and brought his congregation along with him. The council, who regarded them as industrious, useful people, and desired to invite over others of the same character, not only gave them the church of Augustine friars for the exercise of their religion, but granted them a charter, by which they were erected into a corporation, consisting of a superintendant and four assisting ministers. This ecclesiastical establishment was quite independent of the church of England, and differed from it in some rites and ceremonies.[n]

These differences among the protestants were matter of triumph to the catholics; who insisted, that the moment men departed from the authority of the church, they lost all criterion of truth and falshood in matters of religion, and must be carried away by every wind of doctrine. The continual variations of every sect of protestants afforded them the same topic of reasoning. The book of Common Prayer suffered in England a new revisal, and some rites and ceremonies, which had given offence, were omitted.[o] The speculative doctrines, or the metaphysics of the religion, were also reduced to forty-two articles. These were intended to obviate farther divisions and variations; and the compiling of them had been postponed till the establishment of the liturgy, which was justly regarded as a more material object to the people. The eternity of hell torments is asserted in this confession of faith; and care is

[n] Mem. Cranm. p. 234.   [o] Mem. Cranm. p. 289.

also taken to inculcate, not only that no heathen, how virtuous soever, can escape an endless state of the most exquisite misery, but also that every one who presumes to maintain, that any pagan can possibly be saved, is himself exposed to the penalty of eternal perdition.[p]

The theological zeal of the council, though seemingly fervent, went not so far as to make them neglect their own temporal concerns, which seem to have ever been uppermost in their thoughts: They even found leisure to attend to the public interest; nay, to the commerce of the nation, which was, at that time, very little the object of general study or attention. The trade of England had anciently been carried on altogether by foreigners, chiefly the inhabitants of the Hanse-towns, or Easterlings, as they were called; and in order to encourage these merchants to settle in England, they had been erected into a corporation by Henry III, had obtained a patent, were endowed with privileges, and were exempted from several heavy duties paid by other aliens. So ignorant were the English of commerce, that this company, usually denominated the merchants of the Stil-yard, engrossed, even down to the reign of Edward, almost the whole foreign trade of the kingdom; and as they naturally employed the shipping of their own country, the navigation of England was also in a very languishing condition. It was therefore thought proper by the council to seek pretences for annulling the privileges of this corporation, privileges which put them nearly on an equal footing with Englishmen in the duties which they paid; and as such patents were, during that age, granted by the absolute power of the king, men were the less surprized to find them revoked by the same authority. Several remonstrances were made against this innovation, by Lubec, Hamburgh, and other Hanse-towns; but the council persevered in their resolution, and the good effects of it soon became visible to the nation. The English merchants, by their very situation as natives, had advantages above foreigners in the purchase of cloth, wool, and other commodities; though these advantages had not hitherto been sufficient to rouze their industry, or engage them to become rivals to this opulent company: But when aliens' duty was also imposed upon all foreigners indiscriminately, the English were

[p] Article xviii.

tempted to enter into commerce; and a spirit of industry began to appear in the kingdom.[q]

About the same time a treaty was made with Gustavus Ericson, king of Sweden, by which it was stipulated, that, if he sent bullion into England, he might export English commodities without paying custom; that he should carry bullion to no other prince; that if he sent ozimus, steel, copper, &c. he should pay custom for English commodities as an Englishman; and that, if he sent other merchandize, he should have free intercourse, paying custom as a stranger.[r] The bullion sent over by Sweden, though it could not be in great quantity, set the mint at work: Good specie was coined: And much of the base metal, formerly issued, was recalled: A circumstance which tended extremely to the encouragement of commerce.

But all these schemes for promoting industry were likely to prove abortive, by the fear of domestic convulsions, arising from the ambition of Warwic. That nobleman, not contented with the station which he had attained, carried farther his pretensions, and had gained partizans, who were disposed to second him in every enterprize. The last earl of Northumberland died without issue; and as Sir Thomas Piercy, his brother, had been attainted on account of the share, which he had in the Yorkshire insurrection during the late reign, the title was at present extinct, and the estate was vested in the crown. Warwic now procured to himself a grant of those ample possessions, which lay chiefly in the North, the most warlike part of the kingdom; and he was dignified with the title of duke of Northumberland. His friend, Paulet, lord St. John, the treasurer, was created, first, earl of Wiltshire, then marquis of Winchester: Sir William Herbert obtained the title of earl of Pembroke. *Warwic created duke of Northumberland.*

But the ambition of Northumberland made him regard all encrease of possessions and titles, either to himself or his partizans, as steps only to farther acquisitions. Finding that Somerset, though degraded from his dignity, and even lessened in the public opinion by his spiritless conduct, still enjoyed a considerable share of popularity, he determined to ruin the man, whom he regarded as the *His ambition.*

[q] Hayward, p. 326. Heylin, p. 108. Strype's Mem. vol. ii. p. 295.   [r] Heylin, p. 109.

chief obstacle to the attainment of his hopes. The alliance, which had been contracted between the families, had produced no cordial union, and only enabled Northumberland to compass with more certainty the destruction of his rival. He secretly gained many of the friends and servants of that unhappy nobleman: He sometimes terrified him by the appearance of danger: Sometimes provoked him by ill usage. The unguarded Somerset often broke out into menacing expressions against Northumberland: At other times, he formed rash projects, which he immediately abandoned: His treacherous confidents carried to his enemy every passionate word, which dropped from him: They revealed the schemes, which they themselves had first suggested:[s] And Northumberland, thinking that the proper season was now come, began to act in an open manner against him.

16th Octob.

In one night, the duke of Somerset, lord Grey, David and John Seymour, Hammond and Neudigate, two of the duke's servants, Sir Ralph Vane and Sir Thomas Palmer, were arrested and committed to custody. Next day, the dutchess of Somerset, with her favourites, Crane and his wife, Sir Miles Partridge, Sir Michael Stanhope, Bannister, and others, was thrown into prison. Sir Thomas Palmer, who had all along acted as a spy upon Somerset, accused him of having formed a design to raise an insurrection in the north, to attack the gens d'armes on a muster day, to secure the Tower, and to raise a rebellion in London: But, what was the only probable accusation, he asserted, that Somerset had once laid a project for murdering Northumberland, Northampton, and Pembroke at a banquet, which was to be given them by lord Paget. Crane and his wife confirmed Palmer's testimony with regard to this last design; and it appears that some rash scheme of that nature had really been mentioned; though no regular conspiracy had been formed, or means prepared for its execution. Hammond confessed, that the duke had armed men to guard him one night in his house at Greenwich.

Trial of Somerset.

Somerset was brought to his trial before the marquis of Winchester, created high steward. Twenty-seven peers composed the jury, among whom were Northumberland, Pembroke, and Northampton, whom decency should have hindered from acting as

---

[s] Heylin, p. 112.

judges in the trial of a man, that appeared to be their capital enemy. Somerset was accused of high treason on account of the projected insurrections, and of felony in laying a design to murder privy-counsellors.

We have a very imperfect account of all state trials during that age, which is a sensible defect in our history: But it appears, that some more regularity was observed in the management of this prosecution than had usually been employed in like cases. The *1st* witnesses were at least examined by the privy-council; and though *Decemb.* they were neither produced in court, nor confronted with the prisoner (circumstances required by the strict principles of equity) their depositions were given in to the jury. The proof seems to have been lame with regard to the treasonable part of the charge; and Somerset's defence was so satisfactory, that the peers gave verdict in his favour: The intention alone of assaulting the privy-counsellors was supported by tolerable evidence; and the jury brought him in guilty of felony. The prisoner himself confessed, that he had expressed his intention of murdering North-umberland and the other lords; but had not formed any resolution on that head: And when he received sentence, he asked pardon of those peers for the designs, which he had hearkened to against them. The people, by whom Somerset was beloved, hearing the first part of his sentence, by which he was acquitted from treason, expressed their joy by loud acclamations: But their satisfaction was suddenly damped, on finding that he was condemned to death for felony.[t]

Care had been taken by Northumberland's emissaries, to pre- *1552.* possess the young king against his uncle; and lest he should relent, no access was given to any of Somerset's friends, and the prince was kept from reflection by a continued series of occupations and amusements. At last the prisoner was brought to the scaffold *His* on Tower-hill, amidst great crowds of spectators, who bore him *execution.* such sincere kindness, that they entertained, to the last moment, *22d Jan.* the fond hopes of his pardon.[u] Many of them rushed in to dip their handkerchiefs in his blood, which they long preserved as a precious relique; and some of them soon after, when North-

[t] Hayward, p. 320, 321, 322. Stowe, p. 606. Hollingshed, p. 1067.
[u] Hayward, p. 324, 325.

umberland met with a like doom, upbraided him with this cruelty, and displayed to him these symbols of his crime. Somerset indeed, though many actions of his life were exceptionable, seems, in general, to have merited a better fate; and the faults, which he committed, were owing to weakness, not to any bad intention. His virtues were better calculated for private than for public life; and by his want of penetration and firmness, he was ill-fitted to extricate himself from those cabals and violences, to which that age was so much addicted. Sir Thomas Arundel, Sir Michael Stanhope, Sir Miles Partridge, and Sir Ralph Vane, all of them Somerset's friends, were brought to their trial, condemned and executed: Great injustice seems to have been used in their prosecution. Lord Paget, chancellor of the dutchy, was, on some pretence, tried in the star-chamber, and condemned in a fine of 6000 pounds, with the loss of his office. To mortify him the more, he was degraded from the order of the garter; as unworthy, on account of his mean birth, to share that honour.[w] Lord Rich, chancellor, was also compelled to resign his office, on the discovery of some marks of friendship, which he had shown to Somerset.

22d Jan. A parliament. The day after the execution of Somerset, a session of parliament was held, in which farther advances were made towards the establishment of the reformation. The new liturgy was authorised; and penalties were enacted against all those who absented themselves from public worship.[x] To use the mass had already been prohibited under severe penalties; so that the reformers, it appears, whatever scope they had given to their own private judgement, in disputing the tenets of the ancient religion, were resolved not to allow the same privilege to others; and the practice, nay the very doctrine of toleration, was, at that time, equally unknown to all sects and parties. To dissent from the religion of the magistrate, was universally conceived to be as criminal as to question his title, or rebel against his authority.

A law was enacted against usury; that is, against taking any interest for money.[y] This act was the remains of ancient superstition; but being found extremely iniquitous in itself, as well as prejudicial to commerce, it was afterwards repealed in the twelfth

[w] Stowe, p. 608.   [x] 5 & 6 Edw. VI. c. 1.   [y] Ibid. c. 20.

CHAPTER XXXV

of Elizabeth. The common rate of interest, notwithstanding the law, was at this time 14 per cent.[z]

A bill was introduced by the ministry into the house of lords, renewing those rigorous statutes of treason, which had been abrogated in the beginning of this reign; and though the peers, by their high station, stood most exposed to these tempests of state, yet had they so little regard to public security, or even to their own true interest, that they passed the bill with only one dissenting voice.[a] But the commons rejected it, and prepared a new bill, that passed into a law, by which it was enacted, that whoever should call the king or any of his heirs, named in the statute of the 35th of the last reign, heretic, schismatic, tyrant, infidel, or usurper of the crown, should forfeit, for the first offence, their goods and chattels, and be imprisoned during pleasure; for the second, should incur a *praemunire;* for the third, should be attainted for treason. But if any should unadvisedly utter such a slander in writing, printing, painting, carving, or graving, he was, for the first offence, to be held a traitor.[b] It may be worthy of notice, that the king and his next heir, the lady Mary, were professedly of different religions; and religions, which threw on each other the imputation of heresy, schism, idolatry, profaneness, blasphemy, wickedness, and all the opprobrious epithets that religious zeal has invented. It was almost impossible, therefore, for the people, if they spoke at all on these subjects, not to fall into the crime, so severely punished by the statute; and the jealousy of the commons for liberty, though it led them to reject the bill of treasons, sent to them by the lords, appears not to have been very active, vigilant, or clear-sighted.

The commons annexed to this bill a clause which was of more importance than the bill itself, that no one should be convicted of any kind of treason, unless the crime were proved by the oaths of two witnesses, confronted with the prisoner. The lords, for some time, scrupled to pass this clause; though conformable to the most obvious principles of equity. But the members of that house trusted for protection to their present personal interest and power, and neglected the noblest and most permanent security, that of laws.

[z] Hayward, p. 318.   [a] Parliamentary Hist. vol. iii. p. 258. Burnet, vol. ii. p. 190.   [b] 5 & 6 Edw. VI. cap. 2.

The house of peers passed a bill, whose object was making a provision for the poor; but the commons, not chusing that a money-bill should begin in the upper-house, framed a new act to the same purpose. By this act, the church-wardens were empowered to collect charitable contributions; and if any refused to give, or dissuaded others from that charity, the bishop of the diocese was impowered to proceed against them. Such large discretionary powers, entrusted to the prelates, seem as proper an object of jealousy as the authority assumed by the peers.[c]

There was another occasion, in which the parliament reposed an unusual confidence in the bishops. They impowered them to proceed against such as neglected the Sundays and holidays.[d] But these were unguarded concessions granted to the church: The general humour of the age rather led men to bereave the ecclesiastics of all power, and even to pillage them of their property: Many clergymen, about this time, were obliged for a subsistence to turn carpenters or taylors, and some kept alehouses.[e] The bishops themselves were generally reduced to poverty, and held both their revenues and spiritual office by a very precarious and uncertain tenure.

Tonstal, bishop of Durham, was one of the most eminent prelates of that age, still less for the dignity of his see, than for his own personal merit; his learning, moderation, humanity, and beneficence. He had opposed, by his vote and authority, all innovations in religion; but as soon as they were enacted, he had always submitted, and had conformed to every theological system, which had been established. His known probity had made this compliance be ascribed, not to an interested or time-serving spirit, but to a sense of duty, which led him to think, that all private opinion ought to be sacrificed to the great concern of public peace and tranquillity. The general regard, paid to his character, had protected him from any severe treatment during the administration of Somerset; but when Northumberland gained the ascendant, he was thrown into prison; and as that rapacious nobleman had formed a design of seizing the revenues of the see of Durham, and of acquiring to himself a principality in the northern counties, he was resolved, in order to effect his purpose, to deprive Tonstal of his bishopric. A

[c] 5 & 6 Edw. VI. cap. 2.   [d] Ibid. cap. 3.   [e] Burnet, vol. ii. p. 202.

CHAPTER XXXV

bill of attainder, therefore, on pretence of misprision of treason, was introduced into the house of peers against the prelate; and it passed with the opposition only of lord Stourton, a zealous catholic, and of Cranmer, who always bore a cordial and sincere friendship to the bishop of Durham. But when the bill was sent down to the commons, they required, that witnesses should be examined, that Tonstal should be allowed to defend himself, and that he should be confronted with his accusers: And when these demands were refused, they rejected the bill.

This equity, so unusual in the parliament during that age, was ascribed by Northumberland and his partizans, not to any regard for liberty and justice, but to the prevalence of Somerset's faction, in a house of commons, which, being chosen during the administration of that nobleman, had been almost entirely filled with his creatures. They were confirmed in this opinion, when they found, that a bill, ratifying the attainder of Somerset and his accomplices, was also rejected by the commons, though it had passed the upper house. A resolution was therefore taken to dissolve the parliament, *15th April.* which had sitten during this whole reign; and soon after to summon a new one.

Northumberland, in order to ensure to himself a house of *A new parliament.* commons entirely obsequious to his will, ventured on an expedient, which could not have been practised, or even imagined, in an age, when there was any idea or comprehension of liberty. He engaged the king to write circular letters to all the sheriffs, in which he enjoined them to inform the freeholders, that they were required to choose men of knowledge and experience for their representatives. After this general exhortation, the king continued in these words: "And yet, nevertheless, our pleasure is, that where our privy-council, or any of them shall, in our behalf, recommend, within their jurisdiction, men of learning and wisdom; in such cases, their directions shall be regarded and followed, as tending to the same end which we desire, that is, to have this assembly composed of the persons in our realm the best fitted to give advice and good counsel."*f* Several letters were sent from the king, recommending members to particular counties, Sir Richard Cotton to Hampshire; Sir William Fitzwilliams and Sir Henry Nevil to Berk-

---

f Strype's Ecclesiastical Memorial, vol. ii. p. 394.

shire; Sir William Drury and Sir Henry Benningfield to Suffolk, &c. But though some counties only received this species of *congé d'elire* from the king; the recommendations from the privy-council and the counsellors, we may fairly presume, would extend to the greater part, if not the whole, of the kingdom.

It is remarkable, that this attempt was made during the reign of a minor king, when the royal authority is usually weakest; that it was patiently submitted to; and that it gave so little umbrage as scarcely to be taken notice of by any historian. The painful and laborious collector above cited, who never omits the most trivial matter, is the only person, that has thought this memorable letter worthy of being transmitted to posterity.

1553.
1st March.

The parliament answered Northumberland's expectations. As Tonstal had in the interval been deprived of his bishopric in an arbitrary manner, by the sentence of lay commissioners, appointed to try him, the see of Durham was by act of parliament divided into two bishoprics, which had certain portions of the revenue assigned them. The regalities of the see, which included the jurisdiction of a count palatine, were given by the king to Northumberland; nor is it to be doubted but that nobleman had also purposed to make rich plunder of the revenue, as was then usual with the courtiers, whenever a bishopric became vacant.

The commons gave the ministry another mark of attachment, which was at that time the most sincere of any, the most cordial, and the most difficult to be obtained: They granted a supply of two subsidies and two fifteenths. To render this present the more acceptable, they voted a preamble, containing a long accusation of Somerset, "for involving the king in wars, wasting his treasure, engaging him in much debt, embasing the coin, and giving occasion for a most terrible rebellion."[g]

The debts of the crown were at this time considerable. The king had received from France 400,000 crowns on delivering Boulogne; he had reaped profit from the sale of some chantry lands; the churches had been spoiled of all their plate and rich ornaments, which, by a decree of council, without any pretence of law or equity, had been converted to the king's use:[h] Yet such had been the rapacity of the courtiers, that the crown owed about 300,000

[g] Edw. VI. cap. 12.   [h] Heylin, p. 95, 132.

CHAPTER XXXV

pounds;[i] and great dilapidations were, at the same time, made of the royal demesnes. The young prince showed among other virtues, a disposition to frugality, which, had he lived, would soon have retrieved these losses: But as his health was declining very fast, the present emptiness of the exchequer was a sensible obstacle to the execution of those projects, which the ambition of Northumberland had founded on the prospect of Edward's approaching end.

That nobleman represented to the prince, whom youth and an infirm state of health made susceptible of any impression, that his two sisters, Mary and Elizabeth, had both of them been declared illegitimate by act of parliament: And though Henry by his will had restored them to a place in the succession, the nation would never submit to see the throne of England filled by a bastard: That they were the king's sisters by the half-blood only; and even if they were legitimate, could not enjoy the crown as his heirs and successors: That the queen of Scots stood excluded by the late king's will; and being an alien, had lost by law all right of inheriting; not to mention, that, as she was betrothed to the dauphin, she would, by her succession, render England, as she had already done Scotland, a province to France: That the certain consequence of his sister Mary's succession, or that of the queen of Scots, was the abolition of the protestant religion, and the repeal of the laws enacted in favour of the reformation, and the re-establishment of the usurpation and idolatry of the church of Rome: That fortunately for England, the same order of succession, which justice required, was also the most conformable to public interest; and there was not on any side any just ground for doubt or deliberation: That when these three princesses were excluded by such solid reasons, the succession devolved on the marchioness of Dorset, elder daughter of the French queen and the duke of Suffolk; That the next heir of the marchioness was the lady Jane Gray, a lady of the most amiable character, accomplished by the best education, both in literature and religion; and every way worthy of a crown: And that even, if her title by blood were doubtful, which there was no just reason to pretend, the king was possessed of the same power, that his father enjoyed; and might leave her the crown by letters patent.

Succession changed.

[i] Strype's Ecclesiastical Memorials, vol. ii. p. 344.

These reasonings made impression on the young prince; and above all, his zealous attachment to the protestant religion made him apprehend the consequences, if so bigotted a catholic as his sister Mary should succeed to the throne. And though he bore a tender affection to the lady Elizabeth, who was liable to no such objection, means were found to persuade him, that he could not exclude the one sister, on account of illegitimacy, without giving also an exclusion to the other.

Northumberland, finding that his arguments were likely to operate on the king, began to prepare the other parts of his scheme. Two sons of the duke of Suffolk by a second venter having died, this season, of the sweating sickness, that title was extinct; and Northumberland engaged the king to bestow it on the marquis of Dorset. By means of this favour and of others, which he conferred upon him, he persuaded the new duke of Suffolk and the dutchess, to give their daughter, the lady Jane, in marriage to his fourth son, the lord Guilford Dudley. In order to fortify himself by farther alliances, he negociated a marriage between the lady Catherine Gray, second daughter of Suffolk, and lord Herbert, eldest son of the earl of Pembroke. He also married his own daughter to lord Hastings, eldest son of the earl of Huntingdon.[k] These marriages were solemnized with great pomp and festivity; and the people, who hated Northumberland, could not forbear expressing their indignation at seeing such public demonstrations of joy, during the languishing state of the young prince's health.

Edward had been seized in the foregoing year, first with the measles, then with the small-pox; but having perfectly recovered from both these distempers, the nation entertained hopes, that they would only serve to confirm his health; and he had afterwards made a progress through some parts of the kingdom. It was suspected, that he had there overheated himself in exercise: He was seized with a cough, which proved obstinate, and gave way neither to regimen nor medicines: Several fatal symptoms of a consumption appeared; and though it was hoped, that, as the season advanced, his youth and temperance might get the better of the malady; men saw with great concern his bloom and vigour

The king's sickness.

[k] Heylin, p. 199. Stowe, p. 609.

CHAPTER XXXV

insensibly decay. The general attachment to the young prince, joined to the hatred borne the Dudleys, made it be remarked, that Edward had every moment declined in health, from the time that lord Robert Dudley had been put about him, in quality of gentleman of the bedchamber.

The languishing state of Edward's health made Northumberland the more intent on the execution of his project. He removed all, except his own emissaries, from about the king: He himself attended him with the greatest assiduity: He pretended the most anxious concern for his health and welfare: And by all these artifices he prevailed on the young prince to give his final consent to the settlement projected. Sir Edward Montague, chief justice of the Common Pleas, Sir John Baker and Sir Thomas Bromley, two judges, with the attorney and solicitor-general, were summoned to the council; where, after the minutes of the intended deed were read to them, the king required them to draw them up in the form of letters patent. They hesitated to obey; and desired time to consider of it. The more they reflected, the greater danger they found in compliance. The settlement of the crown by Henry VIII. had been made in consequence of an act of parliament; and by another act, passed in the beginning of this reign, it was declared treason in any of the heirs, their aiders or abettors, to attempt on the right of another, or change the order of succession. The judges pleaded these reasons before the council. They urged, that such a patent as was intended would be intirely invalid; that it would subject, not only the judges who drew it, but every counsellor who signed it, to the pains of treason; and that the only proper expedient, both for giving sanction to the new settlement, and freeing its partizans from danger, was to summon a parliament, and to obtain the consent of that assembly. The king said, that he intended afterwards to follow that method, and would call a parliament, in which he purposed to have his settlement ratified; but in the mean time, he required the judges, on their allegiance, to draw the patent in the form required. The council told the judges, that their refusal would subject all of them to the pains of treason. Northumberland gave to Montague the appellation of traitor; and said that he would in his shirt fight any man in so just a cause as that of lady Jane's succession. The judges were reduced to great difficulties between the dangers from the law, and those which arose from the violence of present power and authority.[l]

The arguments were canvassed in several different meetings between the council and the judges; and no solution could be found of the difficulties. At last, Montague proposed an expedient, which satisfied both his brethren and the counsellors. He desired, that a special commission should be passed by the king and council, requiring the judges to draw a patent for the new settlement of the crown; and that a pardon should immediately after be granted them for any offence, which they might have incurred by their compliance. When the patent was drawn and brought to the bishop of Ely, chancellor, in order to have the great seal affixed to it, this prelate required, that all the judges should previously sign it. Gosnald at first refused; and it was with much difficulty, that he was prevailed on, by the violent menaces of Northumberland, to comply; but the constancy of Sir James Hales, who, though a zealous protestant, preferred justice on this occasion to the prejudices of his party, could not be shaken by any expedient. The chancellor next required, for his greater security, that all the privy counsellors should set their hands to the patent: The intrigues of Northumberland or the fears of his violence were so prevalent, that the counsellors complied with this demand. Cranmer alone hesitated during some time, but at last yielded to the earnest and pathetic entreaties of the king.[m] Cecil, at that time secretary of state, pretended afterwards, that he only signed as witness to the king's subscription. And thus, by the king's letters patent, the two princesses, Mary and Elizabeth, were set aside; and the crown was settled on the heirs of the dutchess of Suffolk: For the dutchess herself was content to give place to her daughters.

After this settlement was made, with so many inauspicious circumstances, Edward visibly declined every day; and small hopes were entertained of his recovery. To make matters worse, his physicians were dismissed by Northumberland's advice and by an order of council; and he was put into the hands of an ignorant woman, who undertook, in a little time, to restore him to his former state of health. After the use of her medicines, all the bad symptoms encreased to the most violent degree: He felt a difficulty

21st June.

[l] Fuller, book viii. p. 2.   [m] Cranm. Mem. p. 295.

CHAPTER XXXV

of speech and breathing; his pulse failed, his legs swelled, his colour became livid; and many other symptoms appeared of his approaching end. He expired at Greenwich in the sixteenth year of his age, and the seventh of his reign. *And death. 6th July.*

All the English historians dwell with pleasure on the excellent qualities of this young prince; whom the flattering promises of hope, joined to many real virtues, had made an object of tender affection to the public. He possessed mildness of disposition, application to study and business, a capacity to learn and judge, and an attachment to equity and justice. He seems only to have contracted, from his education and from the genius of the age in which he lived, too much of a narrow prepossession in matters of religion, which made him incline somewhat to bigotry and persecution: But as the bigotry of protestants, less governed by priests, lies under more restraints than that of catholics, the effects of this malignant quality were the less to be apprehended, if a longer life had been granted to young Edward.

XXXVI
MARY

Lady Jane Gray proclaimed queen –
Deserted by the people –
The queen proclaimed and acknowledged –
Northumberland executed – Catholic religion
restored – A parliament – Deliberations
with regard to the queen's marriage –
Queen's marriage with Philip – Wyat's
insurrection – Suppressed – Execution of
Lady Jane Gray – A parliament –
Philip's arrival in England

1553. THE TITLE of the princess Mary, after the demise of her brother, was not exposed to any considerable difficulty; and the objections, started by the lady Jane's partizans, were new and unheard-of by the nation. Though all the protestants, and even many of the catholics, believed the marriage of Henry VIII. with Catherine of Arragon to be unlawful and invalid; yet, as it had been contracted by the parties without any criminal intention, had been avowed by their parents, recognized by the nation, and seemingly founded on those principles of law and religion, which then prevailed, few imagined, that their issue ought on that account to be regarded as illegitimate. A declaration to that purpose had indeed been extorted from parliament by the usual violence and caprice of Henry; but as that monarch had afterwards been induced to restore his daughter to the right of succession, her title was now become as legal and parliamentary as it was ever esteemed just and natural. The public had long been familiarized to these sentiments: During all the reign of Edward, the princess was regarded as his lawful successor: And though the protestants dreaded the effects of her prejudices, the extreme hatred, universally entertained against the Dudleys,[n] who, men foresaw, would, under the name of Jane, be the real sovereigns, was more than sufficient to counterbalance, even with that party, the attachment to religion. This last attempt, to violate the order of succession, had displayed Northumberland's ambition and injustice in a full light; and when the people reflected on the long train of fraud, iniquity, and cruelty by which that project had been conducted; that the lives of the two Seymours, as well as the title of the princesses, had been sacrificed to it; they were moved by indignation to exert themselves in opposition to such criminal enterprizes. The general veneration also, paid to the memory of Henry VIII. prompted the nation to defend the rights of his posterity; and the miseries of the ancient civil wars were not so entirely forgotten, that men were willing, by a departure from the lawful heir, to incur the danger of like bloodshed and confusion.

Northumberland, sensible of the opposition which he must expect, had carefully concealed the destination made by the king; and in order to bring the two princesses into his power, he had had the precaution to engage the council, before Edward's death, to write to them in that prince's name, desiring their attendance, on pretence that his infirm state of health required the assistance of their counsel and the consolation of their company.[o] Edward expired before their arrival; but Northumberland, in order to make the princesses fall into the snare, kept the king's death still secret; and the lady Mary had already reached Hoddesden, within half a day's journey of the court. Happily, the earl of Arundel sent her private intelligence, both of her brother's death and of the conspiracy formed against her:[p] She immediately made haste to retire; and she arrived, by quick journies, first at Kenning-hall in Norfolk, then at Framlingham in Suffolk; where she purposed to embark and escape to Flanders, in case she should find it impossible to defend her right of succession. She wrote letters to the nobility and

[n] Sleidan, lib. 25.   [o] Heylin, p. 154.   [p] Burnet, vol. ii. p. 233.

most considerable gentry in every county in England; commanding them to assist her in the defence of her crown and person. And she dispatched a message to the council; by which she notified to them, that her brother's death was no longer a secret to her, promised them pardon for past offences, and required them immediately to give orders for proclaiming her in London.[q]

Northumberland found that farther dissimulation was fruitless: He went to Sion-house,[r] accompanied by the duke of Suffolk, the earl of Pembroke, and others of the nobility; and he approached the lady Jane, who resided there, with all the respect usually paid to the sovereign. Jane was, in a great measure, ignorant of these transactions; and it was with equal grief and surprize, that she received intelligence of them.[s] She was a lady of an amiable person, an engaging disposition, accomplished parts; and being of an equal age with the late king, she had received all her education with him, and seemed even to possess greater facility in acquiring every part of manly and polite literature. She had attained a familiar knowledge of the Roman and Greek languages, besides modern tongues; had passed most of her time in an application to learning; and expressed a great indifference for other occupations and amusements, usual with her sex and station. Roger Ascham, tutor to the lady Elizabeth, having one day paid her a visit, found her employed in reading Plato, while the rest of the family were engaged in a party of hunting in the park; and on his admiring the singularity of her choice, she told him, that she received more pleasure from that author than the others could reap from all their sport and gaiety.[t] Her heart, full of this passion for literature and the elegant arts, and of tenderness towards her husband, who was deserving of her affections, had never opened itself to the flattering allurements of ambition; and the intelligence of her elevation to the throne was no-wise agreeable to her. She even refused to accept of the present; pleaded the preferable title of the two princesses; expressed her dread of the consequences attending an enterprize so dangerous, not to say so criminal; and desired to remain in the private station, in which she was born. Overcome at last by the entreaties, rather than the reasons, of her father and

Lady Jane Gray proclaimed queen.

[q] Fox, vol. iii. p. 14.   [r] Thuanus, lib. xiii. c. 10.   [s] Godwin in Kennet, p. 329, Heylin, p. 149. Burnet, vol. ii. p. 234.   [t] Ascham's works, p. 222, 223.

CHAPTER XXXVI

father-in-law, and above all of her husband, she submitted to their will, and was prevailed on to relinquish her own judgment. It was then usual for the kings of England, after their accession, to pass the first days in the Tower; and Northumberland immediately conveyed thither the new sovereign. All the counsellors were obliged to attend her to that fortress; and by this means became, in reality, prisoners in the hands of Northumberland; whose will they were necessitated to obey. Orders were given by the council to proclaim Jane throughout the kingdom; but these orders were executed only in London, and the neighbourhood. No applause ensued: The people heard the proclamation with silence and concern: Some even expressed their scorn and contempt: and one Pot, a vintner's apprentice, was severely punished for this offence. The protestant teachers themselves, who were employed to convince the people of Jane's title, found their eloquence fruitless; and Ridley, bishop of London, who preached a sermon to that purpose, wrought no effect upon his audience.

The people of Suffolk, meanwhile, paid their attendance on Mary. As they were much attached to the reformed communion, they could not forbear, amidst their tenders of duty, expressing apprehensions for their religion; but when she assured them, that she never meant to change the laws of Edward, they enlisted themselves in her cause with zeal and affection. The nobility and gentry daily flocked to her, and brought her reinforcement. The earls of Bath and Sussex, the eldest sons of lord Wharton and lord Mordaunt, Sir William Drury, Sir Henry Benningfield, Sir Henry Jernegan, persons whose interest lay in the neighbourhood, appeared at the head of their tenants and retainers.[u] Sir Edward Hastings, brother to the earl of Huntingdon, having received a commission from the council to make levies for the lady Jane in Buckinghamshire, carried over his troops, which amounted to four thousand men, and joined Mary. Even a fleet, which had been sent by Northumberland to lie off the coast of Suffolk, being forced into Yarmouth by a storm, was engaged to declare for that princess.

Northumberland, hitherto blinded by ambition, saw at last the danger gather round him, and knew not to what hand to turn

---

[u] Heylin, p. 160. Burnet, vol. ii. p. 237.

himself. He had levied forces, which were assembled at London; but dreading the cabals of the courtiers and counsellors, whose compliance, he knew, had been entirely the result of fear or artifice, he was resolved to keep near the person of the lady Jane, and send Suffolk to command the army. But the counsellors, who wished to remove him,[w] working on the filial tenderness of Jane, magnified to her the danger, to which her father would be exposed; and represented, that Northumberland, who had gained reputation by formerly suppressing a rebellion in those parts, was more proper to command in that enterprize. The duke himself, who knew the slender capacity of Suffolk, began to think, that none but himself was able to encounter the present danger; and he agreed to take on him the command of the troops. The counsellors attended on him at his departure with the highest protestations of attachment, and none more than Arundel, his mortal enemy.[x] As he went along, he remarked the disaffection of the people, which foreboded a fatal issue to his ambitious hopes. "Many," said he to lord Gray, "come out to look at us, but I find not one who cries, *God speed you.*"[y]

The duke had no sooner reached St. Edmond's-bury, than he found his army which did not exceed six thousand men, too weak to encounter the Queen's,[z] which amounted to double the number. He wrote to the council, desiring them to send him a reinforcement; and the counsellors immediately laid hold of the opportunity to free themselves from confinement. They left the Tower, as if they meant to execute Northumberland's commands; but being assembled in Baynard's castle, a house belonging to Pembroke, they deliberated concerning the method of shaking off his usurped tyranny. Arundel began the conference, by representing the injustice and cruelty of Northumberland, the exorbitancy of his ambition, the criminal enterprize which he had projected, and the guilt in which he had involved the whole council; and he affirmed, that the only method of making atonement for their past offences, was by a speedy return to the duty, which they owed to their lawful sovereign.[a] This motion was seconded by Pembroke, who, clapping his hand to his sword, swore he was ready to fight any man

Lady Jane deserted by the people.

---

[w] Godwin, p. 330. Heylin, p. 159. Burnet, vol. ii. p. 239. Fox, vol. iii. p. 15.
[x] Heylin, p. 161. Baker, p. 315. Hollingshed, p. 1086.   [y] Speed, p. 816.
[z] Godwin, p. 331.   [a] Godwin, p. 331, 332. Thuanus, lib. xiii.

CHAPTER XXXVI

that expressed himself of a contrary sentiment. The mayor and aldermen of London were immediately sent for, who discovered great alacrity in obeying the orders they received to proclaim Mary. The people expressed their approbation by shouts of applause. Even Suffolk, who commanded in the Tower, finding resistance fruitless, opened the gates, and declared for the queen. The lady Jane, after the vain pageantry of wearing a crown during ten days, returned to a private life with more satisfaction than she felt when the royalty was tendered to her.[b] And the messengers, who were sent to Northumberland, with order to lay down his arms, found that he had despaired of success, was deserted by all his followers, and had already proclaimed the queen, with exterior marks of joy and satisfaction.[c] The people every where, on the queen's approach to London, gave sensible expressions of their loyalty and attachment. And the lady Elizabeth met her at the head of a thousand horse, which that princess had levied in order to support their joint title against the usurper.[d]

The queen proclaimed and acknowledged.

The queen gave orders for taking into custody the duke of Northumberland, who fell on his knees to the earl of Arundel that arrested him, and abjectly begged his life.[e] At the same time were committed the earl of Warwic his eldest son, lord Ambrose and lord Henry Dudley, two of his younger sons, Sir Andrew Dudley, his brother, the marquis of Northampton, the earl of Huntingdon, Sir Thomas Palmer, and Sir John Gates. The queen afterwards confined the duke of Suffolk, lady Jane Grey, and lord Guilford Dudley. But Mary was desirous, in the beginning of her reign, to acquire popularity by the appearance of clemency; and because the counsellors pleaded constraint as an excuse for their treason, she extended her pardon to most of them. Suffolk himself recovered his liberty; and he owed this indulgence, in a great measure, to the contempt entertained of his capacity. But the guilt of Northumberland was too great, as well as his ambition and courage too dangerous, to permit him to entertain any reasonable hopes of life. When brought to his trial, he only desired permission to ask two questions of the peers, appointed to sit on his jury; whether a man could be guilty of treason that obeyed orders given him by the

[b] Godwin, p. 332. Thuanus, lib. xiii. c. 2.   [c] Stowe, p. 612.   [d] Burnet, vol. ii. p. 240. Heylin, p. 19. Stowe, p. 613.   [e] Burnet, vol. ii. p. 239. Stowe, p. 612. Baker, p. 315. Hollingshed, p. 1088.

council under the great seal? and whether those who were involved in the same guilt with himself, could sit as his judges? Being told, that the great seal of an usurper was no authority, and that persons, not lying under any sentence of attainder, were still innocent in the eye of the law, and might be admitted on any jury;[f] he acquiesced, and pleaded guilty. At his execution, he made profession of the catholic religion, and told the people, that they never would enjoy tranquillity till they returned to the faith of their ancestors: Whether that such were his real sentiments, which he had formerly disguised, from interest and ambition, or that he hoped, by this declaration, to render the queen more favourable to his family.[g] Sir Thomas Palmer, and Sir John Gates suffered with him; and this was all the blood spilled on account of so dangerous and criminal an enterprize against the rights of the sovereign. Sentence was pronounced against the lady Jane and lord Guilford; but without any present intention of putting it in execution. The youth and innocence of the persons, neither of whom had reached their seventeenth year, pleaded sufficiently in their favour.

When Mary first arrived in the Tower, the duke of Norfolk, who had been detained prisoner during all the last reign; Courtney, son of the marquis of Exeter, who, without being charged with any crime, had been subjected to the same punishment ever since his father's attainder; Gardiner, Tonstal, and Bonner, who had been confined for their adhering to the catholic cause, appeared before her, and implored her clemency and protection.[h] They were all of them restored to their liberty, and immediately admitted to her confidence and favour. Norfolk's attainder, notwithstanding that it had passed in Parliament, was represented as null and invalid; because, among other informalities, no special matter had been alledged against him, except wearing a coat of arms, which he and his ancestors, without giving any offence, had always made use of, in the face of the court and of the whole nation. Courtney soon after received the title of earl of Devonshire; and though educated in such close confinement, that he was altogether unacquainted with the world, he soon acquired all the accomplishments of a courtier and a gentleman, and made a considerable figure during

margin note: 22d Aug. Northumberland executed.

[f] Burnet, vol. ii. p. 243. Heylin, p. 18. Baker, p. 316. Hollingshed, p. 1089.   [g] Heylin, p. 19. Burnet, vol. iii. p. 243. Stowe, p. 614.   [h] Heylin, p. 20. Stowe, p. 613. Hollingshed, p. 1088.

the few years, which he lived after he recovered his liberty.[i] Besides performing all those popular acts, which, though they only affected individuals, were very acceptable to the nation, the queen endeavoured to ingratiate herself with the public, by granting a general pardon, though with some exceptions, and by remitting the subsidy voted to her brother by the last parliament.[k]

The joy arising from the succession of the lawful heir, and from the gracious demeanor of the sovereign, hindered not the people from being agitated with great anxiety concerning the state of religion; and as the bulk of the nation inclined to the protestant communion, the apprehensions, entertained concerning the principles and prejudices of the new queen, were pretty general. The legitimacy of Mary's birth had appeared to be somewhat connected with the papal authority; and that princess, being educated with her mother, had imbibed the strongest attachment to the catholic communion, and the highest aversion to those new tenets, whence, she believed, all the misfortunes of her family had originally sprung. The discouragements, which she lay under from her father, though at last they brought her to comply with his will, tended still more to encrease her disgust to the reformers; and the vexations, which the protector and the council gave her, during Edward's reign, had no other effect than to confirm her farther in her prejudices. Naturally of a sour and obstinate temper, and irritated by contradiction and misfortunes, she possessed all the qualities fitted to compose a bigot; and her extreme ignorance rendered her utterly incapable of doubt in her own belief, or of indulgence to the opinions of others. The nation, therefore, had great reason to dread, not only the abolition, but the persecution of the established religion from the zeal of Mary; and it was not long ere she discovered her intentions.

Gardiner, Bonner, Tonstal, Day, Heath, and Vesey, were reinstated in their sees, either by a direct act of power, or, what is nearly the same, by the sentence of commissioners, appointed to review their trial and condemnation. Though the bishopric of Durham had been dissolved by authority of parliament, the queen erected it a-new by letters-patent, and replaced Tonstal in his regalities as well as in his revenue. On pretence of discouraging

Catholic religion restored.

[i] Depeches de Noailles, vol. ii. p. 246, 247.   [k] Stowe, p. 616.

controversy, she silenced, by an act of prerogative, all the preachers throughout England, except such as should obtain a particular licence; and it was easy to foresee, that none but the catholics would be favoured with this privilege. Holgate, archbishop of York, Coverdale, bishop of Exeter, Ridley of London, and Hooper of Glocester, were thrown into prison; whither old Latimer also was sent soon after. The zealous bishops and priests were encouraged in their forwardness to revive the mass, though contrary to the present laws. Judge Hales, who had discovered such constancy in defending the queen's title, lost all his merit by an opposition to those illegal practices; and being committed to custody, was treated with such severity, that he fell into frenzy, and killed himself. The men of Suffolk were brow-beaten; because they presumed to plead the promise, which the queen, when they enlisted themselves in her service, had given them, of maintaining the reformed religion: One, in particular, was set in the pillory, because he had been too peremptory, in recalling to her memory the engagements which she had taken on that occasion. And though the queen still promised, in a public declaration before the council, to tolerate those who differed from her, men foresaw, that this engagement, like the former, would prove but a feeble security, when set in opposition to religious prejudices.

The merits of Cranmer towards the queen, during the reign of Henry had been considerable; and he had successfully employed his good offices in mitigating the severe prejudices which that monarch had entertained against her. But the active part, which he had borne in promoting her mother's divorce, as well as in conducting the reformation, had made him the object of her hatred; and though Gardiner had been equally forward in soliciting and defending the divorce, he had afterwards made sufficient atonement, by his sufferings in defence of the catholic cause. The primate, therefore, had reason to expect little favour during the present reign; but it was by his own indiscreet zeal, that he brought on himself the first violence and persecution. A report being spread, that Cranmer, in order to pay court to the queen, had promised to officiate in the Latin service, the archbishop, to wipe off this aspersion, published a manifesto in his own defence. Among other expressions, he there said, that, as the devil was a liar from the beginning, and the father of lies, he had at this time stirred up his servants to persecute Christ and his true religion:

CHAPTER XXXVI

That this infernal spirit now endeavoured to restore the Latin satisfactory masses, a thing of his own invention and device; and in order to effect his purpose, had falsely made use of Cranmer's name and authority: And that the mass is not only without foundation, either in the Scriptures or in the practice of the primitive church, but likewise discovers a plain contradiction to antiquity and the inspired writings, and is besides replete with many horrid blasphemies.[l] On the publication of this inflammatory paper, Cranmer was thrown into prison, and was tried for the part which he had acted, in concurring with the lady Jane, and opposing the queen's accession. Sentence of high treason was pronounced against him; and though his guilt was shared with the whole privy council, and was even less than that of the greater part of them, this sentence, however severe, must be allowed entirely legal. The execution of it, however, did not follow; and Cranmer was reserved for a more cruel punishment.

Peter Martyr, seeing a persecution gathering against the reformers, desired leave to withdraw;[m] and while some zealous catholics moved for his commitment, Gardiner both pleaded, that he had come over by an invitation from the government, and generously furnished him with supplies for his journey: But as bigotted zeal still encreased, his wife's body, which had been interred at Oxford, was afterwards dug up by public orders, and buried in a dunghill.[n] The bones of Bucer and Fagius, two foreign reformers, were about the same time committed to the flames at Cambridge.[o] John a Lasco was first silenced, then ordered to depart the kingdom with his congregation. The greater part of the foreign protestants followed him; and the nation thereby lost many useful hands for arts and manufactures. Several English protestants also took shelter in foreign parts; and every thing bore dismal aspect for the reformation.

During this revolution of the court, no protection was expected by protestants from the parliament, which was summoned to assemble. A zealous reformer[p] pretends, that great violence and iniquity were used in the elections; but besides that the authority

5th Oct. A parliament.

---

[l] Fox, vol. iii. p. 94. Heylin, p. 25. Godwin, p. 336. Burnet, vol. ii. Coll. No 8. Cranm. Mem. p. 305. Thuanus, lib. xiii. c. 3. [m] Heylin, p. 26. Godwin, p. 336. Cranm. Mem. p. 317. [n] Heylin, p. 26. [o] Saunders de Schism. Anglic. [p] Beale. But Fox, who lived at the time, and is very minute in his narratives, says nothing of the matter. See vol. iii. p. 16.

of this writer is inconsiderable, that practice, as the necessities of government seldom required it, had not hitherto been often employed in England. There still remained such numbers devoted, by opinion or affection, to many principles of the ancient religion, that the authority of the crown was able to give such candidates the preference in most elections; and all those, who hesitated to comply with the court religion, rather declined taking a seat, which, while it rendered them obnoxious to the queen, could afterwards afford them no protection against the violence of prerogative. It soon appeared, therefore, that a majority of the commons would be obsequious to Mary's designs; and as the peers were mostly attached to the court, from interest or expectations, little opposition was expected from that quarter.

In opening the parliament, the court showed a contempt of the laws, by celebrating, before the two houses, a mass of the Holy Ghost, in the Latin tongue, attended with all the ancient rites and ceremonies, though abolished by act of parliament.*q* Taylor, bishop of Lincoln having refused to kneel at this service, was severely handled, and was violently thrust out of the house.*r* The queen, however, still retained the title of supreme head of the church of England; and it was generally pretended, that the intention of the court was only to restore religion to the same condition in which it had been left by Henry; but that the other abuses of popery, which were the most grievous to the nation, would never be revived.

The first bill, passed by the parliament, was of a popular nature, and abolished every species of treason, not contained in the statute of Edward III. and every species of felony, that did not subsist before the first of Henry VIII.*s* The parliament next declared the queen to be legitimate, ratified the marriage of Henry with Catherine of Arragon, and annulled the divorce pronounced by Cranmer,*t* whom they greatly blamed on that account. No mention, however, is made of the pope's authority, as any ground of the marriage. All the statutes of king Edward, with regard to religion, were repealed by one vote.*u* The attainder of the duke of

q Fox, vol. iii. p. 19.   *r* Burnet, vol. ii. p. 252.   *s* Mariae, sess. i. c. 1. By this repeal, though it was in general popular, the clause of 5 & 6 Edw. VI. c. II. was lost, which required the confronting of two witnesses, in order to prove any treason.   *t* Mariae, sess. 2. c. 1.   *u* Mariae, sess. 2. c. 1.

CHAPTER XXXVI

Norfolk was reversed; and this act of justice was more reasonable than the declaring of that attainder invalid, without farther authority. Many clauses of the riot act, passed in the late reign, were revived: A step which eluded, in a great measure, the popular statute enacted at the first meeting of parliament.

Notwithstanding the compliance of the two houses with the queen's inclinations, they had still a reserve in certain articles; and her choice of a husband, in particular, was of such importance to national interest, that they were determined not to submit tamely, in that respect, to her will and pleasure. There were three marriages,[w] concerning which it was supposed that Mary had deliberated after her accession. The first person proposed to her, was Courtney, earl of Devonshire, who, being an Englishman, nearly allied to the crown, could not fail of being acceptable to the nation; and as he was of an engaging person and address, he had visibly gained on the queen's affections,[x] and hints were dropped him of her favourable dispositions towards him.[y] But that nobleman neglected these overtures; and seemed rather to attach himself to the lady Elizabeth, whose youth and agreeable conversation he preferred to all the power and grandeur of her sister. This choice occasioned a great coldness in Mary towards Devonshire; and made her break out in a declared animosity against Elizabeth. The ancient quarrel between their mothers had sunk deep into the malignant heart of the queen; and after the declaration made by parliament in favour of Catherine's marriage, she wanted not a pretence for representing the birth of her sister as illegitimate. The attachment of Elizabeth to the reformed religion offended Mary's bigotry; and as the young princess had made some difficulty in disguising her sentiments, violent menaces had been employed to bring her to compliance.[z] But when the queen found, that Elizabeth had obstructed her views in a point, which, perhaps, touched her still more nearly, her resentment, excited by pride, no longer knew any bounds; and the princess was visibly exposed to the greatest danger.[a]

Cardinal Pole, who had never taken priest's orders, was another party proposed to the queen; and there appeared many reasons to

[w] Thuan. lib. ii. c. 3.   [x] Depeches de Noailles, vol. ii. p. 147, 163, 214, 215. vol. iii. p. 27.   [y] Godwin, p. 339.   [z] Dep. de Noailles, vol. ii. passim. [a] Heylin, p. 31. Burnet, vol. ii. p. 255.

induce her to make choice of this prelate. The high character of Pole for virtue and humanity; the great regard paid him by the catholic church, of which he had nearly reached the highest dignity on the death of Paul III.;[b] the queen's affection for the countess of Salisbury, his mother, who had once been her governess; the violent animosity to which he had been exposed on account of his attachment to the Romish communion; all these considerations had a powerful influence on Mary. But the cardinal was now in the decline of life; and having contracted habits of study and retirement, he was represented to her as unqualified for the bustle of a court, and the hurry of business.[c] The queen, therefore, dropped all thoughts of that alliance: But as she entertained a great regard for Pole's wisdom and virtue, she still intended to reap the benefit of his counsel in the administration of her government. She secretly entered into a negociation with Commendone, an agent of cardinal Dandino, legate at Brussels; she sent assurances to the pope, then Julius III. of her earnest desire to reconcile herself and her kingdoms to the holy see; and she desired that Pole might be appointed legate for the performance of that pious office.[d]

These two marriages being rejected, the queen cast her eye towards the emperor's family, from which her mother was descended, and which, during her own distresses, had always afforded her countenance and protection. Charles V who a few years before was almost absolute master of Germany, had exercised his power in such an arbitrary manner, that he gave extreme disgust to the nation, who apprehended the total extinction of their liberties from the encroachments of that monarch.[e] Religion had served him as a pretence for his usurpations; and from the same principle he met with that opposition, which overthrew his grandeur, and dashed all his ambitious hopes. Maurice, elector of Saxony, enraged that the landgrave of Hesse, who, by his advice, and on his assurances, had put himself into the emperor's hands, should be unjustly detained a prisoner, formed a secret conspiracy among the protestant princes; and covering his intentions with the most artful disguises, he suddenly marched his forces against Charles, and narrowly missed becoming master of his person. The protes-

[b] Father Paul, book iii.   [c] Heylin, p. 31.   [d] Burnet, vol. ii. p. 258.
[e] Thuanus, lib. iv. c. 17.

CHAPTER XXXVI

tants flew to arms in every quarter; and their insurrection, aided by an invasion from France, reduced the emperor to such difficulties, that he was obliged to submit to terms of peace, which insured the independency of Germany. To retrieve his honour, he made an attack on France; and laying siege to Metz, with an army of a hundred thousand men, he conducted the enterprize in person, and seemed determined, at all hazards, to succeed in an undertaking which had fixed the attention of Europe. But the duke of Guise, who defended Metz, with a garrison composed of the bravest nobility of France, exerted such vigilance, conduct, and valour, that the siege was protracted to the depth of winter; and the emperor found it dangerous to persevere any longer. He retired with the remains of his army into the Low-Countries, much dejected with that reverse of fortune, which, in his declining years, had so fatally overtaken him.

No sooner did Charles hear of the death of Edward, and the accession of his kinswoman Mary to the crown of England, than he formed the scheme of acquiring that kingdom to his family; and he hoped, by this incident, to balance all the losses which he had sustained in Germany. His son Philip was a widower; and though he was only twenty-seven years of age, eleven years younger than the queen, this objection, it was thought, would be overlooked, and there was no reason to despair of her still having a numerous issue. The emperor, therefore, immediately sent over an agent to signify his intentions to Mary, who, pleased with the support of so powerful an alliance, and glad to unite herself more closely with her mother's family, to which she was ever strongly attached, readily embraced the proposal. Norfolk, Arundel, and Paget, gave their advice for the match. And Gardiner, who was become prime minister, and who had been promoted to the office of chancellor, finding how Mary's inclinations lay, seconded the project of the Spanish alliance. At the same time, he represented, both to her and the emperor, the necessity of stopping all farther innovations in religion, till the completion of the marriage. He observed, that the parliament, amidst all their compliances, had discovered evident symptoms of jealousy, and seemed at present determined to grant no farther concessions in favour of the catholic religion: That though they might make a sacrifice to their sovereign of some speculative principles, which they did not well comprehend, or of some rites, which seemed not of any great moment, they had imbibed such strong prejudices against the pretended usurpations and exactions of the court of Rome, that they would with great difficulty be again brought to submit to its authority: That the danger of resuming the abbey lands would alarm the nobility and gentry, and induce them to encourage the prepossessions, which were but too general among the people, against the doctrine and worship of the catholic church: That much pains had been taken to prejudice the nation against the Spanish alliance; and if that point were urged, at the same time with farther changes in religion, it would hazard a general revolt and insurrection: That the marriage, being once completed, would give authority to the queen's measures, and enable her afterwards to forward the pious work, in which she was engaged: And that it was even necessary previously to reconcile the people to the marriage, by rendering the conditions extremely favourable to the English, and such as would seem to ensure to them their independency, and the entire possession of their ancient laws and privileges.*f*

The emperor, well acquainted with the prudence and experience of Gardiner, assented to all these reasons; and he endeavoured to temper the zeal of Mary, by representing the necessity of proceeding gradually in the great work of converting the nation. Hearing that cardinal Pole, more sincere in his religious opinions, and less guided by the maxims of human policy, after having sent contrary advice to the queen, had set out on his journey to England, where he was to exercise his legantine commission; he thought proper to stop him at Dillinghen, a town on the Danube; and he afterwards obtained Mary's consent for this detention. The negociation for the marriage mean-while proceeded apace; and Mary's intentions of espousing Philip became generally known to the nation. The commons, who hoped that they had gained the queen by the concessions which they had already made, were alarmed to hear, that she was resolved to contract a foreign alliance; and they sent a committee to remonstrate in strong terms, against that dangerous measure. To prevent farther applications of the same kind, she thought proper to dissolve the parliament.

6th Dec.

A convocation had been summoned at the same time with the

---

f Burnet, vol. ii. p. 261.

parliament; and the majority here also appeared to be of the court religion. An offer was very frankly made by the Romanists, to dispute concerning the points controverted between the two communions; and as transubstantiation was the article, which, of all others, they deemed the clearest, and founded on the most irresistible arguments, they chose to try their strength by defending it. The protestants pushed the dispute as far as the clamour and noise of their antagonists would permit; and they fondly imagined, that they had obtained some advantage, when, in the course of the debate, they obliged the catholics to avow, that, according to their doctrine, Christ had, in his last supper, held himself in his hand, and had swallowed and eaten himself.[g] This triumph, however, was confined only to their own party: The Romanists maintained, that *their* champions had clearly the better of the day; that their adversaries were blind and obstinate heretics; that nothing but the most extreme depravity of heart could induce men to contest such self-evident principles; and that the severest punishments were due to their perverse wickedness. So pleased were they with their superiority in this favourite point, that they soon after renewed the dispute at Oxford; and to show, that they feared no force of learning or abilities, where reason was so evidently on their side, they sent thither Cranmer, Latimer, and Ridley, under a guard, to try whether these renowned controversialists could find any appearance of argument to defend their baffled principles.[h] The issue of the debate was very different from what it appeared to be few years before, in a famous conference, held at the same place, during the reign of Edward.

After the parliament and convocation were dismissed, the new laws with regard to religion, though they had been anticipated, in most places, by the zeal of the catholics, countenanced by government, were still more openly put in execution: The mass was every where reestablished; and marriage was declared to be incompatible with any spiritual office. It has been asserted by some writers, that three fourths of the clergy were, at this time, deprived of their livings; though other historians, more accurate,[i] have estimated the number of sufferers to be far short of this proportion. A vis-

1554.

[g] Collier, vol. ii. p. 356. Fox, vol. iii. p. 22.   [h] Mem. Cranm. p. 354. Heylin, p. 50.   [i] Harmer, p. 138.

itation was appointed, in order to restore more perfectly the mass and the ancient rites. Among other articles, the commissioners were enjoined to forbid the oath of supremacy to be taken by the clergy on their receiving any benefice.[k] It is to be observed, that this oath had been established by the laws of Henry VIII. which were still in force.

Queen's marriage with Philip.

This violent and sudden change of religion inspired the protestants with great discontent; and even affected indifferent spectators with concern, by the hardships, to which so many individuals were on that account exposed. But the Spanish match was a point of more general concern, and diffused universal apprehensions for the liberty and independance of the nation. To obviate all clamour, the articles of marriage were drawn as favourable as possible for the interest and security, and even grandeur of England. It was agreed, that, though Philip should have the title of king, the administration should be entirely in the queen; that no foreigner should be capable of enjoying any office in the kingdom; that no innovation should be made in the English laws, customs, and privileges; that Philip should not carry the queen abroad without her consent, nor any of her children without the consent of the nobility; that sixty thousand pounds a year should be settled as her jointure; that the male issue of this marriage should inherit, together with England, both Burgundy and the Low-Countries; and that, if Don Carlos, Philip's son by his former marriage, should die and his line be extinct, the queen's issue, whether male or female, should inherit Spain, Sicily, Milan, and all the other dominions of Philip.[l] Such was the treaty of marriage signed by count Egmont, and three other ambassadors sent over to England by the emperor.[m]

15th Jan.

These articles, when published, gave no satisfaction to the nation: It was universally said, that the emperor, in order to get possession of England, would verbally agree to any terms; and the greater advantage there appeared in the conditions which he granted, the more certainly might it be concluded, that he had no serious intention of observing them: That the usual fraud and ambition of that monarch might assure the nation of such a con-

---

[k] Collier, vol. ii. p. 364. Fox, vol. iii. p. 38. Heylin, p. 35. Sleidan, lib. 25.
[l] Rymer, xv. p. 377.   [m] Depeches de Noailles, vol. ii. p. 299.

duct; and his son Philip, while he inherited these vices from his father, added to them tyranny, sullenness, pride, and barbarity, more dangerous vices of his own: That England would become a province, and a province to a kingdom which usually exercised the most violent authority over all her dependant dominions. That the Netherlands, Milan, Sicily, Naples groaned under the burthen of Spanish tyranny; and throughout all the new conquests in America there had been displayed scenes of unrelenting cruelty, hitherto unknown in the history of mankind: That the inquisition was a tribunal invented by that tyrannical nation; and would infallibly, with all their other laws and institutions, be introduced into England: And that the divided sentiments of the people with regard to religion would subject multitudes to this iniquitous tribunal, and would reduce the whole nation to the most abject servitude."

These complaints being diffused every where, prepared the people for a rebellion; and had any foreign power given them encouragement, or any great man appeared to head them, the consequences might have proved fatal to the queen's authority. But the king of France, though engaged in hostilities with the emperor, refused to concur in any proposal for an insurrection, lest he should afford Mary a pretence for declaring war against him.° And the more prudent part of the nobility thought, that, as the evils of the Spanish alliance were only dreaded at a distance, matters were not yet fully prepared for a general revolt. Some persons, however, more turbulent than the rest, believed, that it would be safer to prevent than to redress grievances; and they formed a conspiracy to rise in arms, and declare against the queen's marriage with Philip. Sir Thomas Wiat purposed to raise *Wiat's* Kent, Sir Peter Carew, Devonshire; and they engaged the duke of *insur-* Suffolk, by the hopes of recovering the crown for the lady Jane, to *rection.* attempt raising the midland counties.ᵖ Carew's impatience or apprehensions engaged him to break the concert, and to rise in arms before the day appointed: He was soon suppressed by the earl of Bedford, and constrained to fly into France. On this intelligence, Suffolk, dreading an arrest, suddenly left the town, with his brothers, lord Thomas, and lord Leonard Gray; and endeavoured to

" Heylin, p. 32. Burnet, vol. ii. p. 268. Godwin, p. 339. ° Depeches de Noailles, vol. ii. p. 249. vol. iii. p. 17, 58. ᵖ Heylin. p. 33. Godwin, p. 340.

raise the people in the counties of Warwic and Leicester; where his interest lay: But he was so closely pursued by the earl of Huntingdon, at the head of 300 horse, that he was obliged to disperse his followers, and being discovered in his concealment, he was carried prisoner to London.[q] Wiat was at first more successful in his attempt; and having published a declaration at Maidstone in Kent, against the queen's evil counsellors and against the Spanish match, without any mention of religion, the people began to flock to his standard. The duke of Norfolk with Sir Henry Jernegan was sent against him, at the head of the guards and some other troops, reinforced with 500 Londoners commanded by Bret: And he came within sight of the rebels at Rochester, where they had fixed their head-quarters. Sir George Harper here pretended to desert from them; but having secretly gained Bret, these two malcontents so wrought on the Londoners, that the whole body deserted to Wiat, and declared that they would not contribute to enslave their native country. Norfolk, dreading the contagion of the example, immediately retreated with his troops, and took shelter in the city.[r]

After this proof of the dispositions of the people, especially of the Londoners, who were mostly protestants, Wiat was encouraged to proceed: He led his forces to Southwark, where he required of the queen, that she should put the Tower into his hands, should deliver four counsellors as hostages, and in order to ensure the liberty of the nation, should immediately marry an Englishman. Finding that the bridge was secured against him, and that the city was overawed, he marched up to Kingston, where he passed the river with 4000 men; and returning towards London, hoped to encourage his partizans, who had engaged to declare for him. He had imprudently wasted so much time at Southwark, and in his march from Kingston, that the critical season, on which all popular commotions depend, was entirely lost: Though he entered Westminster without resistance, his followers, finding that no person of note joined him, insensibly fell off, and he was at last seized near Temple-Bar by Sir Maurice Berkeley.[s] Four hundred persons are said to have suffered for this rebellion:[t] Four hundred more were conducted before the queen with ropes about their

6th
Feb.

[q] Fox, vol. iii. p. 30.   [r] Heylin, p. 33. Godwin, p. 341. Stowe, p. 619. Baker, p. 318. Hollingshed, p. 1094.   [s] Fox, vol. iii. p. 31. Heylin, p. 34. Burnet, vol. ii. p. 270. Stowe, p. 621.   [t] Depeches de Noailles, vol. ii. p. 124.

CHAPTER XXXVI

necks; and falling on their knees, received a pardon, and were dismissed. Wiat was condemned and executed: As it had been reported, that, on his examination, he had accused the lady Elizabeth and the earl of Devonshire as accomplices, he took care on the scaffold, before the whole people, fully to acquit them of having any share in his rebellion. *Insurrection suppressed.*

The lady Elizabeth had been, during some time, treated with great harshness by her sister; and many studied instances of discouragement and disrespect had been practiced against her. She was ordered to take place at court after the countess of Lenox and the dutchess of Suffolk, as if she were not legitimate:[u] Her friends were discountenanced on every occasion: And while her virtues, which were now become eminent, drew to her the attendance of all the young nobility, and rendered her the favourite of the nation,[w] the malevolence of the queen still discovered itself every day by fresh symptoms, and obliged the princess to retire into the country. Mary seized the opportunity of this rebellion; and hoping to involve her sister in some appearance of guilt, sent for her under a strong guard, committed her to the Tower, and ordered her to be strictly examined by the council. But the public declaration made by Wiat rendered it impracticable to employ against her any false evidence, which might have offered; and the princess made so good a defence, that the queen found herself under a necessity of releasing her.[x] In order to send her out of the kingdom, a marriage was offered her with the duke of Savoy; and when she declined the proposal, she was committed to custody, under a strong guard, at Wodestoke.[y] The earl of Devonshire, though equally innocent, was confined in Fotheringay castle.

But this rebellion proved still more fatal to the lady Jane Gray, as well as to her husband: The duke of Suffolk's guilt was imputed to her; and though the rebels and malcontents seemed chiefly to rest their hopes on the lady Elizabeth and the earl of Devonshire, the queen, incapable of generosity or clemency, determined to remove every person from whom the least danger could be apprehended. Warning was given the lady Jane to prepare for death; a doom which she had long expected, and which the innocence of

[u] Ibid. vol. ii. p. 273, 288.   [w] Ibid. p. 273.   [x] Godwin, p. 343. Burnet, vol. ii. p. 273. Fox, vol. iii. p. 99, 105. Strype's Mem. vol. iii. p. 85.   [y] Depeches de Noailles, vol. iii. p. 226.

her life, as well as the misfortunes, to which she had been exposed, rendered nowise unwelcome to her. The queen's zeal, under colour of tender mercy to the prisoner's soul, induced her to send divines, who harassed her with perpetual disputation; and even a reprieve for three days was granted her, in hopes that she would be persuaded, during that time, to pay, by a timely conversion, some regard to her eternal welfare. The lady Jane had presence of mind, in those melancholy circumstances, not only to defend her religion by all the topics then in use, but also to write a letter to her sister,[z] in the Greek language; in which, besides sending her a copy of the Scriptures in that tongue, she exhorted her to maintain in every fortune, a like steady perseverance. On the day of her execution, her husband, lord Guilford, desired permission to see her; but she refused her consent, and informed him by a message, that the tenderness of their parting would overcome the fortitude of both, and would too much unbend their minds from that constancy, which their approaching end required of them: Their separation, she said, would be only for a moment; and they would soon rejoin each other in a scene, where their affections would be for ever united, and where death, disappointment, and misfortunes could no longer have access to them, or disturb their eternal felicity.[a]

12th Feb.

It had been intended to execute the lady Jane and lord Guilford together on the same scaffold at Tower-hill; but the council, dreading the compassion of the people for their youth, beauty, innocence, and noble birth, changed their orders, and gave directions that she should be beheaded within the verge of the Tower. She saw her husband led to execution; and having given him from the window some token of her remembrance, she waited with tranquillity till her own appointed hour should bring her to a like fate. She even saw his headless body carried back in a cart; and found herself more confirmed by the reports, which she heard of the constancy of his end, than shaken by so tender and melancholy a spectacle. Sir John Gage, constable of the Tower, when he led her to execution, desired her to bestow on him some small present, which he might keep as a perpetual memorial of her: She gave him her table-book, on which she had just written three sentences on

Execution of lady Jane Gray.

---

[z] Fox, vol. iii. p. 35. Heylin, p. 166.   [a] Heylin, p. 167. Baker, p. 319.

CHAPTER XXXVI

seeing her husband's dead body; one in Greek, another in Latin, a third in English.[b] The purport of them was, that human justice was against his body, but divine mercy would be favourable to his soul; that, if her fault deserved punishment, her youth at least, and her imprudence were worthy of excuse; and that God and posterity, she trusted, would show her favour. On the scaffold, she made a speech to the by-standers; in which the mildness of her disposition led her to take the blame wholly on herself, without uttering one complaint against the severity, with which she had been treated. She said, that her offence was not the having laid her hand upon the crown, but the not rejecting it with sufficient constancy: That she had less erred through ambition than through reverence to her parents, whom she had been taught to respect and obey: That she willingly received death, as the only satisfaction, which she could now make to the injured state; and though her infringement of the laws had been constrained, she would show, by her voluntary submission to their sentence, that she was desirous to atone for that disobedience, into which too much filial piety had betrayed her: That she had justly deserved this punishment for being made the instrument, though the unwilling instrument, of the ambition of others: And that the story of her life, she hoped, might at least be useful, by proving that innocence excuses not great misdeeds, if they tend any wise to the destruction of the commonwealth. After uttering these words, she caused herself to be disrobed by her women; and with a steddy serene countenance submitted herself to the executioner.[c]

The duke of Suffolk was tried, condemned, and executed soon after; and would have met with more compassion, had not his temerity been the cause of his daughter's untimely end. Lord Thomas Gray lost his life for the same crime. Sir Nicholas Throgmorton was tried in Guildhall; but there appearing no satisfactory evidence against him, he was able, by making an admirable defence, to obtain a verdict of the jury in his favour. The queen was so enraged at this disappointment, that, instead of releasing him as the law required, she re-committed him to the Tower, and kept him in close confinement during some time. But her resentment

[b] Heylin, p. 167.   [c] Heylin, p. 167. Fox, vol. iii. p. 36, 37. Hollingshed, p. 1099.

stopped not here: The jury, being summoned before the council, were all sent to prison, and afterwards fined, some of them a thousand pounds, others two thousand a-piece.[d] This violence proved fatal to several; among others to Sir John Throgmorton, brother to Sir Nicholas, who was condemned on no better evidence than had formerly been rejected. The queen filled the Tower and all the prisons with nobility and gentry, whom their interest with the nation, rather than any appearance of guilt, had made the objects of her suspicion. And finding, that she was universally hated, she determined to disable the people from resistance, by ordering general musters, and directing the commissioners to seize their arms, and lay them up in forts and castles.[e]

Though the government laboured under so general an odium, the queen's authority had received such an encrease from the suppression of Wiat's rebellion, that the ministry hoped to find a compliant disposition in the new parliament, which was summoned to assemble. The emperor, also, in order to facilitate the same end, had borrowed no less a sum than 400,000 crowns, which he had sent over to England, to be distributed in bribes and pensions among the members: A pernicious practice, of which there had not hitherto been any instance in England. And not to give the public any alarm with regard to the church lands, the queen, notwithstanding her bigotry, resumed her title of supreme head of the church, which she had dropped three months before. Gardiner, the chancellor, opened the session by a speech; in which he asserted the queen's hereditary title to the crown; maintained her right of chusing a husband for herself; observed how proper a use she had made of that right, by giving the preference to an old ally, descended from the house of Burgundy; and remarked the failure of Henry VIII's posterity, of whom there now remained none but the queen and the lady Elizabeth. He added, that, in order to obviate the inconveniencies, which might arise from different pretenders, it was necessary to invest the queen, by law, with a power of disposing of the crown, and of appointing her successor: A power, he said, which was not to be thought unprecedented in England, since it had formerly been conferred on Henry VIII.[f]

A parliament.
5th
April.

---

[d] Fox, vol. iii. p. 99. Stowe, p. 624. Baker, p. 320. Hollingshed, p. 1104, 1121. Strype, vol. iii. p. 120. Dep. de Noailles, vol. iii. p. 173.   [e] Dep. de Noailles, vol. iii. p. 98.   [f] Depeches de Noailles.

CHAPTER XXXVI

The parliament was much disposed to gratify the queen in all her desires; but when the liberty, independency, and very being of the nation were in such visible danger, they could not by any means be brought to compliance. They knew both the inveterate hatred, which she bore to the lady Elizabeth, and her devoted attachment to the house of Austria: They were acquainted with her extreme bigotry, which would lead her to postpone all considerations of justice or national interest to the establishment of the catholic religion: They remarked, that Gardiner had carefully avoided, in his speech, the giving to Elizabeth the appellation of the queen's sister; and they thence concluded, that a design was formed of excluding her as illegitimate: They expected, that Mary, if invested with such a power as she required, would make a will in her husband's favour, and thereby render England for ever a province to the Spanish monarchy: And they were the more alarmed with these projects, as they heard, that Philip's descent from the house of Lancaster was carefully insisted on, and that he was publicly represented as the true and only heir by right of inheritance.

The parliament, therefore, aware of their danger, were determined to keep at a distance from the precipice, which lay before them. They could not avoid ratifying the articles of marriage,[g] which were drawn very favourable for England; but they declined the passing of any such law as the chancellor pointed out to them: They would not so much as declare it treason to imagine or attempt the death of the queen's husband, while she was alive; and a bill introduced for that purpose, was laid aside after the first reading. The more effectually to cut off Philip's hopes of possessing any authority in England, they passed a law, in which they declared, "that her majesty as their only queen, should solely and as a sole queen, enjoy the crown and sovereignty of her realms, with all the pre-eminencies, dignities, and rights thereto belonging, in as large and ample a manner after her marriage as before, without any title or claim accruing to the prince of Spain, either as tenant by courtesy of the realm, or by any other means."[h]

A law passed in this parliament for re-erecting the bishopric of Durham, which had been dissolved by the last parliament of Edward.[i] The queen had already, by an exertion of her power, put

[g] Mar. Parl. 2. cap. 2.   [h] Ibid. cap. 1.   [i] Ibid. cap. 3.

Tonstal in possession of that see: But though it was usual at that time for the crown to assume authority which might seem entirely legislative, it was always deemed more safe and satisfactory to procure the sanction of parliament. Bills were introduced for suppressing heterodox opinions contained in books, and for reviving the law of the six articles, together with those against the Lollards, and against heresy and erroneous preaching: But none of these laws could pass the two houses. A proof, that the parliament had reserves even in their concessions with regard to religion; about which they seem to have been less scrupulous. The queen, therefore, finding that they would not serve all her purposes, finished the session by dissolving them.

5th
May.

Mary's thoughts were now entirely employed about receiving Don Philip, whose arrival she hourly expected. This princess, who had lived so many years in a very reserved and private manner, without any prospect or hopes of a husband, was so smitten with affection for her young consort, whom she had never seen, that she waited with the utmost impatience for the completion of the marriage; and every obstacle was to her a source of anxiety and discontent.[k] She complained of Philip's delays as affected; and she could not conceal her vexation, that, though she brought him a kingdom as her dowry, he treated her with such neglect, that he had never yet favoured her with a single letter.[l] Her fondness was but the more encreased by this supercilious treatment; and when she found that her subjects had entertained the greatest aversion for the event, to which she directed her fondest wishes, she made the whole English nation the object of her resentment. A squadron, under the command of lord Effingham, had been fitted out to convoy Philip from Spain, where he then resided; but the admiral informing her, that the discontents ran very high among the seamen, and that it was not safe for Philip to entrust himself in their hands, she gave orders to dismiss them.[m] She then dreaded, lest the French fleet, being masters of the sea, might intercept her husband; and every rumour of danger, every blast of wind, threw her into panics and convulsions. Her health, and even her understanding, were visibly hurt by this extreme impatience; and she

[k] Strype, vol. iii. p. 125.   [l] Depeches de Noailles, vol. iii. p. 248   [m] Ibid. p. 220.

CHAPTER XXXVI

was struck with a new apprehension, lest her person, impaired by time, and blasted by sickness, should prove disagreeable to her future consort. Her glass discovered to her how hagard she was become; and when she remarked the decay of her beauty, she knew not whether she ought more to desire or apprehend the arrival of Philip.[n]

At last came the moment so impatiently expected; and news was brought the queen of Philip's arrival at Southampton.[o] A few days after, they were married in Westminster; and having made a pompous entry into London, where Philip displayed his wealth with great ostentation, she carried him to Windsor, the palace in which they afterwards resided. The prince's behaviour was ill calculated to remove the prejudices, which the English nation had entertained against him. He was distant and reserved in his address; took no notice of the salutes even of the most considerable noblemen; and so entrenched himself in form and ceremony, that he was in a manner inaccessible:[p] But this circumstance rendered him the more acceptable to the queen, who desired to have no company but her husband's, and who was impatient when she met with any interruption to her fondness. The shortest absence gave her vexation; and when he showed civilities to any other woman, she could not conceal her jealousy and resentment.

19th July. Philip's arrival in England.

Mary soon found, that Philip's ruling passion was ambition; and that the only method of gratifying him and securing his affections, was to render him master of England. The interest and liberty of her people were considerations of small moment, in comparison of her obtaining this favourite point. She summoned a new parliament, in hopes of finding them entirely compliant; and that she might acquire the greater authority over them, she imitated the precedent of the former reign, and wrote circular letters directing a proper choice of members.[q] The zeal of the catholics, the influence of Spanish gold, the powers of prerogative,

12th Nov.

[n] Depeches de Noailles, vol. iii. p. 222, 252, 253. [o] Fox, vol. iii. p. 99. Heylin, p. 39. Burnet, vol. iii. p. 392. Godwin, p. 345. We are told by Sir William Monson, p. 225, that the admiral of England fired at the Spanish navy, when Philip was on board; because they had not lowered their topsails, as a mark of deference to the English navy in the narrow seas. A very spirited behaviour, and very unlike those times. [p] Baker, p. 320. [q] Mem. of Cranm. p. 344. Strype's Eccl. Mem. vol. iii. p. 154, 155.

the discouragement of the gentry, particularly of the protestants; all these causes, seconding the intrigues of Gardiner, had procured her a house of commons, which was, in a great measure, to her satisfaction; and it was thought, from the disposition of the nation, that she might now safely omit, on her assembling the parliament, the title of *supreme head of the church,* though inseparably annexed by law to the crown of England.[r] Cardinal Pole had arrived in Flanders, invested with legantine powers from the pope: In order to prepare the way for his arrival in England, the parliament passed an act, reversing his attainder, and restoring his blood; and the queen, dispensing with the old statute of provisors, granted him permission to act as legate. The cardinal came over; and after being introduced to the king and queen, he invited the parliament to reconcile themselves and the kingdom to the apostolic see, from which they had been so long and so unhappily divided. This message was taken in good part; and both houses voted an address to Philip and Mary, acknowledging that they had been guilty of a most horrible defection from the true church; professing a sincere repentance of their past transgressions; declaring their resolution to repeal all laws enacted in prejudice of the church of Rome; and praying their majesties, that, since they were happily uninfected with that criminal schism, they would intercede with the holy father for the absolution and forgiveness of their penitent subjects.[s] The request was easily granted. The legate, in the name of his holiness, gave the parliament and kingdom absolution, freed them from all censures, and received them again into the bosom of the church. The pope, then Julius III. being informed of these transactions, said, that it was an unexampled instance of his felicity, to receive thanks from the English, for allowing them to do what he ought to give them thanks for performing.[t]

Notwithstanding the extreme zeal of those times, for and against popery, the object always uppermost with the nobility and gentry, was their money and estates: They were not brought to make these concessions in favour of Rome, till they had received repeated assurances, from the pope as well as the queen, that the plunder, which they had made on the ecclesiastics, should never be

[r] Burnet, vol. ii. p. 291. Strype, vol. iii. p. 155.   [s] Fox, vol. iii. p. 3. Heylin, p. 42. Burnet, vol. ii. p. 293. Godwin, p. 247.   [t] Father Paul, lib. iv.

CHAPTER XXXVI

enquired into; and that the abbey and church lands should remain with the present possessors.[u] But not trusting altogether to these promises, the parliament took care, in the law itself,[w] by which they repealed the former statutes enacted against the pope's authority, to insert a clause, in which, besides bestowing validity on all marriages celebrated during the schism, and fixing the right of incumbents to their benefices, they gave security to the possessors of church lands, and freed them from all danger of ecclesiastical censures. The convocation also, in order to remove apprehensions on that head, were induced to present a petition to the same purpose;[x] and the legate, in his master's name, ratified all these transactions. It now appeared, that, notwithstanding the efforts of the queen and king, the power of the papacy was effectually suppressed in England, and invincible barriers fixed against its re-establishment. For though the jurisdiction of the ecclesiastics was, for the present, restored, their property, on which their power much depended, was irretrievably lost, and no hopes remained of recovering it. Even these arbitrary, powerful, and bigotted princes, while the transactions were yet recent, could not regain to the church her possessions so lately ravished from her; and no expedients were left to the clergy for enriching themselves, but those which they had at first practised, and which had required many ages of ignorance, barbarism, and superstition, to produce their effect on mankind.[y]

The parliament, having secured their own possessions, were more indifferent with regard to religion, or even to the lives of their fellow-citizens: They revived the old sanguinary laws against heretics,[z] which had been rejected in the former parliament: They also enacted several statutes against seditious words and rumours;[a] and they made it treason to imagine or attempt the death of Philip, during his marriage with the queen.[b] Each parliament hitherto had been induced to go a step farther than their predecessors; but none of them had entirely lost all regard to national interests. Their hatred against the Spaniards, as well as their suspicion of Philip's pretensions, still prevailed; and though the queen attempted to get her husband declared presumptive heir of the

[u] Heylin, p. 41.   [w] 1 & 2 Phil. & Mar. c. 8.   [x] Heylin, p. 43. 1 & 2 Phil. & Mar. c. 8. Strype, vol. iii. p. 159.   [y] See note [T] at the end of the volume.   [z] 1 & 2 Phil. & Mar. c. 6.   [a] Ibid. c. 3. 9.   [b] Ibid. c. 10.

crown, and to have the administration put into his hands; she failed in all her endeavours, and could not so much as procure the parliament's consent to his coronation.[c] All attempts likewise to obtain subsidies from the commons, in order to support the emperor in his war against France, proved fruitless: The usual animosity and jealousy of the English against that kingdom, seemed to have given place, for the present, to like passions against Spain. Philip, sensible of the prepossessions entertained against him, endeavoured to acquire popularity by procuring the release of several prisoners of distinction; lord Henry Dudley, Sir George Harper, Sir Nicholas Throgmorton, Sir Edmond Warner, Sir William St. Lo, Sir Nicholas Arnold, Harrington, Tremaine, who had been confined from the suspicions or resentment of the court.[d] But nothing was more agreeable to the nation than his protecting the lady Elizabeth from the spite and malice of the queen, and restoring her to liberty. This measure was not the effect of any generosity in Philip, a sentiment of which he was wholly destitute; but of a refined policy, which made him foresee, that, if that princess were put to death, the next lawful heir was the queen of Scots, whose succession would for ever annex England to the crown of France. The earl of Devonshire also reaped some benefit from Philip's affectation of popularity, and recovered his liberty: But that nobleman, finding himself exposed to suspicion, begged permission to travel;[e] and he soon after died at Padua, from poison, as is pretended, given him by the Imperialists. He was the eleventh and last earl of Devonshire of that noble family, one of the most illustrious in Europe.

The queen's extreme desire of having issue, had made her fondly give credit to any appearance of pregnancy; and when the legate was introduced to her, she fancied, that she felt the embryo stir in her womb.[f] Her flatterers compared this motion of the infant to that of John the Baptist, who leaped in his mother's belly at the salutation of the virgin.[g] Dispatches were immediately sent to inform foreign courts of this event: Orders were issued to give public thanks: Great rejoicings were made: The family of the

[c] Godwin, p. 348. Baker, p. 322.   [d] Heylin, p. 39. Burnet, vol. ii. p. 287. Stowe, p. 626. Depeches de Noailles, vol. iv. p. 1, 6, 147.   [e] Heylin, p. 40. Godwin, p. 349.   [f] Depeches de Noailles, vol. iv. p. 25.   [g] Burnet, vol. ii. p. 292. Godwin, p. 348.

young prince was already settled;[h] for the catholics held themselves assured that the child was to be a male: And Bonner, bishop of London, made public prayers be said, that Heaven would please to render him beautiful, vigorous, and witty. But the nation still remained somewhat incredulous; and men were persuaded, that the queen laboured under infirmities, which rendered her incapable of having children. Her infant proved only the commencement of a dropsy, which the disordered state of her health had brought upon her. The belief, however, of her pregnancy was upheld with all possible care; and was one artifice, by which Philip endeavoured to support his authority in the kingdom. The parliament passed a law, which, in case of the queen's demise, appointed him protector during the minority; and the king and queen, finding they could obtain no further concessions, came unexpectedly to Westminster, and dissolved them.

1555.

There happened an incident this session, which must not be passed over in silence. Several members of the lower house, dissatisfied with the measures of the parliament, but finding themselves unable to prevent them, made a secession, in order to show their disapprobation, and refused any longer to attend the house.[i] For this instance of contumacy they were indicted in the King's-bench after the dissolution of parliament: Six of them submitted to the mercy of the court, and paid their fines: The rest traversed; and the queen died before the affair was brought to an issue. Judging of the matter by the subsequent claims of the house of commons, and, indeed, by the true principles of free government, this attempt of the queen's ministers must be regarded as a breach of privilege; but it gave little umbrage at the time, and was never called in question by any house of commons, which afterwards sat during this reign. The count of Noailles, the French ambassador, says, that the queen threw several members into prison for their freedom of speech.[k]

16th Jan.

[h] Heylin, p. 46.   [i] Coke's Institutes, part iv. p. 17. Strype's Memor. vol. i. p. 165.   [k] Vol. v. p. 296.

XXXVII

*Reasons for and against Toleration –
Persecutions – A parliament – The queen's
extortions – The emperor resigns his
crown – Execution of Cranmer – War with
France – Battle of St. Quintin –
Calais taken by the French – Affairs
of Scotland – Marriage of the Dauphin
and the queen of Scots – A parliament –
Death of the queen*

THE SUCCESS, which Gardiner, from his cautious and prudent conduct, had met with in governing the parliament, and engaging them to concur both in the Spanish match, and in the re-establishment of the ancient religion, two points to which, it was believed, they bore an extreme aversion, had so raised his character for wisdom and policy, that his opinion was received as an oracle in the council; and his authority, as it was always great in his own party, no longer suffered any opposition or controul. Cardinal Pole himself, though more beloved on account of his virtue and candour, and though superior in birth and station, had not equal weight in public deliberations; and while his learning, piety, and humanity were extremely respected, he was represented more as a good man than a great minister. A very important question was frequently debated, before the queen and council, by these two

430

CHAPTER XXXVII

ecclesiastics; whether the laws lately revived against heretics should be put in execution, or should only be employed to restrain, by terror, the bold attempts of these zealots? Pole was very sincere in his religious principles; and though his moderation had made him be suspected at Rome of a tendency towards Lutheranism, he was seriously persuaded of the catholic doctrines, and thought that no consideration of human policy ought ever to come in competition with such important interests. Gardiner, on the contrary, had always made his religion subservient to his schemes of safety or advancement; and by his unlimited complaisance to Henry, he had shown, that, had he not been pushed to extremity under the late minority, he was sufficiently disposed to make a sacrifice of his principles to the established theology. This was the well-known character of these two great counsellors; yet such is the prevalence of temper above system, that the benevolent disposition of Pole led him to advise a toleration of the heretical tenets, which he highly blamed; while the severe manners of Gardiner inclined him to support, by persecution, that religion, which, at the bottom, he regarded with great indifference.[l] This circumstance of public conduct was of the highest importance; and from being the object of deliberation in the council, it soon became the subject of discourse throughout the nation. We shall relate, in a few words, the topics, by which each side supported, or might have supported, their scheme of policy; and shall display the opposite reasons, which have been employed, with regard to an argument that ever has been, and ever will be so much canvassed.

The practice of persecution, said the defenders of Pole's opinion, is the scandal of all religion; and the theological animosity, so fierce and violent, far from being an argument of men's conviction in their opposite sects, is a certain proof, that they have never reached any serious persuasion with regard to these remote and sublime subjects. Even those, who are the most impatient of contradiction in other controversies, are mild and moderate in comparison of polemical divines; and wherever a man's knowledge and experience give him a perfect assurance in his own opinion, he regards with contempt, rather than anger, the opposition and mistakes of others. But while men zealously maintain what they

Reasons for and against toleration.

[l] Heylin, p. 47.

neither clearly comprehend, nor entirely believe, they are shaken in their imagined faith, by the opposite persuasion, or even doubts of other men; and vent on their antagonists that impatience, which is the natural result of so disagreeable a state of the understanding. They then easily embrace any pretence for representing opponents as impious and profane; and if they can also find a colour for connecting this violence with the interests of civil government, they can no longer be restrained from giving uncontrouled scope to vengeance and resentment. But surely never enterprize was more unfortunate than that of founding persecution upon policy, or endeavouring, for the sake of peace, to settle an entire uniformity of opinion, in questions which, of all others, are least subjected to the criterion of human reason. The universal and uncontradicted prevalence of one opinion in religious subjects, can be owing at first to the stupid ignorance alone and barbarism of the people, who never indulge themselves in any speculation or enquiry; and there is no expedient for maintaining that uniformity, so fondly sought after, but by banishing for ever all curiosity and all improvement in science and cultivation. It may not, indeed, appear difficult to check, by a steady severity, the first beginnings of controversy; but besides that this policy exposes for ever the people to all the abject terrors of superstition, and the magistrate to the endless encroachments of ecclesiastics, it also renders men so delicate, that they can never endure to hear of opposition; and they will some time pay dearly for that false tranquillity, in which they have been so long indulged. As healthful bodies are ruined by too nice a regimen, and are thereby rendered incapable of bearing the unavoidable incidents of human life; a people, who never were allowed to imagine, that their principles could be contested, fly out into the most outrageous violence, when any event (and such events are common) produces a faction among their clergy, and gives rise to any difference in tenet or opinion. But whatever may be said in favour of suppressing, by persecution, the first beginnings of heresy, no solid argument can be alleged for extending severity towards multitudes, or endeavouring, by capital punishments, to extirpate an opinion, which has diffused itself among men of every rank and station. Besides the extreme barbarity of such an attempt, it commonly proves ineffectual to the purpose intended; and serves only to make men more obstinate in their persuasion, and to encrease the number of their proselytes. The melancholy, with which the fear of death, torture, and persecution inspires the sectaries, is the proper disposition for fostering religious zeal: The prospect of eternal rewards, when brought near, overpowers the dread of temporal punishments: The glory of martyrdom stimulates all the more furious zealots, especially the leaders and preachers: Where a violent animosity is excited by oppression, men naturally pass, from hating the persons of their tyrants, to a more violent abhorrence of their doctrines: And the spectators, moved with pity towards the supposed martyrs, are easily seduced to embrace those principles, which can inspire men with a constancy that appears almost supernatural. Open the door to toleration, mutual hatred relaxes among the sectaries; their attachment to their particular modes of religion decays; the common occupations and pleasures of life succeed to the acrimony of disputation; and the same man, who, in other circumstances, would have braved flames and tortures, is induced to change his sect from the smallest prospect of favour and advancement, or even from the frivolous hope of becoming more fashionable in his principles. If any exception can be admitted to this maxim of toleration, it will only be where a theology altogether new, nowise connected with the ancient religion of the state, is imported from foreign countries, and may easily, at one blow, be eradicated, without leaving the seeds of future innovation. But as this exception would imply some apology for the ancient pagan persecutions, or for the extirpation of Christianity in China and Japan; it ought surely, on account of this detested consequence, to be rather buried in eternal silence and oblivion.

Though these arguments appear entirely satisfactory, yet such is the subtilty of human wit, that Gardiner, and the other enemies to toleration, were not reduced to silence; and they still found topics on which to maintain the controversy. The doctrine, said they, of liberty of conscience, is founded on the most flagrant impiety, and supposes such an indifference among all religions, such an obscurity in theological doctrines, as to render the church and magistrate incapable of distinguishing, with certainty, the dictates of Heaven from the mere fictions of human imagination. If the Divinity reveals principles to mankind, he will surely give a criterion by which they may be ascertained; and a prince, who knowingly allows these principles to be perverted or adulterated, is infinitely more criminal than if he gave permission for the vending of poison, under the shape of food, to all his subjects. Persecution may, indeed, seem better calculated to make hypocrites than converts; but experience teaches us, that the habits of hypocrisy often turn into reality; and the children at least, ignorant of the dissimulation of their parents, may happily be educated in more orthodox tenets. It is absurd, in opposition to considerations of such unspeakable importance, to plead the temporal and frivolous interests of civil society; and if matters be thoroughly examined, even that topic will not appear so universally certain in favour of toleration as by some it is represented. Where sects arise, whose fundamental principle on all sides is to execrate, and abhor, and damn, and extirpate each other; what choice has the magistrate left but to take part, and by rendering one sect entirely prevalent, restore, at least for a time, the public tranquillity? The political body, being here sickly, must not be treated as if it were in a state of sound health; and an affected neutrality in the prince, or even a cool preference, may serve only to encourage the hopes of all the sects, and keep alive their animosity. The protestants, far from tolerating the religion of their ancestors, regard it as an impious and detestable idolatry; and during the late minority, when they were entirely masters, they enacted very severe, though not capital, punishments against all exercise of the catholic worship, and even against such as barely abstained from their profane rites and sacraments. Nor are instances wanting of their endeavours to secure an imagined orthodoxy by the most rigorous executions: Calvin has burned Servetus at Geneva: Cranmer brought Arians and Anabaptists to the stake: And if persecution of any kind be admitted, the most bloody and violent will surely be allowed the most justifiable, as the most effectual. Imprisonments, fines, confiscations, whippings, serve only to irritate the sects, without disabling them from resistance: But the stake, the wheel, and the gibbet, must soon terminate in the extirpation or banishment of all the heretics, inclined to give disturbance, and in the entire silence and submission of the rest.

The arguments of Gardiner, being more agreeable to the cruel bigotry of Mary and Philip, were better received; and though Pole

CHAPTER XXXVII

pleaded, as is affirmed,[m] the advice of the emperor, who recommended it to his daughter-in-law, not to exercise violence against the protestants, and desired her to consider his own example, who, after endeavouring, through his whole life, to extirpate heresy, had, in the end, reaped nothing but confusion and disappointment, the scheme of toleration was entirely rejected. It was determined to let loose the laws in their full vigour against the reformed religion; and England was soon filled with scenes of horror, which have ever since rendered the catholic religion the object of general detestation, and which prove, that no human depravity can equal revenge and cruelty, covered with the mantle of religion.

The persecutors began with Rogers, prebendary of St. Paul's, a man eminent in his party for virtue as well as for learning. Gardiner's plan was first to attack men of that character, whom, he hoped, terror would bend to submission, and whose example, either of punishment or recantation, would naturally have influence on the multitude: But he found a perseverance and courage in Rogers, which it may seem strange to find in human nature, and of which all ages, and all sects, do nevertheless furnish many examples. Rogers, beside the care of his own preservation, lay under other powerful temptations to compliance: He had a wife, whom he tenderly loved, and ten children; yet such was his serenity after his condemnation, that the jailors, it is said, waked him from a sound sleep, when the hour of his execution approached. He had desired to see his wife before he died; but Gardiner told him, that he was a priest; and could not possibly have a wife; thus joining insult to cruelty. Rogers was burnt in Smithfield.[n]

Violent persecutions in England.

Hooper, bishop of Glocester, had been tried at the same time with Rogers; but was sent to his own diocese to be executed. This circumstance was contrived to strike the greater terror into his flock; but it was a source of consolation to Hooper, who rejoiced in giving testimony, by his death, to that doctrine, which he had formerly preached among them. When he was tied to the stake, a

[m] Burnet, vol. ii. Heylin, p. 47. It is not likely, however, that Charles gave any such advice: For he himself was at this very time proceeding with great violence in persecuting the reformed in Flanders. Bentivoglio, part i. lib. 1.   [n] Fox, vol. iii. p. 119. Burnet, vol. ii. p. 302.

stool was set before him, and the queen's pardon laid upon it, which it was still in his power to merit by a recantation: But he ordered it to be removed; and cheerfully prepared himself for that dreadful punishment, to which he was sentenced. He suffered it in its full severity: The wind, which was violent, blew the flame of the reeds from his body: The faggots were green, and did not kindle easily: All his lower parts were consumed, before his vitals were attacked: One of his hands dropped off: With the other he continued to beat his breast: He was heard to pray and to exhort the people; till his tongue, swoln with the violence of his agony, could no longer permit him utterance. He was three quarters of an hour in torture, which he bore with inflexible constancy.[o]

Sanders was burned at Coventry: A pardon was also offered him; but he rejected it, and embraced the stake, saying, "Welcome the cross of Christ; welcome everlasting life." Taylor, parson of Hadley, was punished by fire in that place, surrounded by his ancient friends and parishioners. When tied to the stake, he rehearsed a psalm in English: One of his guards struck him on the mouth, and bade him speak Latin: Another, in a rage, gave him a blow on the head with his halbert, which happily put an end to his torments.

There was one Philpot, archdeacon of Winchester, enflamed with such zeal for orthodoxy, that having been engaged in dispute with an Arian, he spit in his adversary's face, to shew the great detestation, which he had entertained against that heresy. He afterwards wrote a treatise to justify this unmannerly expression of zeal: He said, that he was led to it, in order to relieve the sorrow conceived from such horrid blasphemy, and to signify how unworthy such a miscreant was of being admitted into the society of any Christian.[p] Philpot was a protestant; and falling now into the hands of people as zealous as himself, but more powerful, he was condemned to the flames, and suffered at Smithfield. It seems to be almost a general rule, that, in all religions except the true, no man will suffer martyrdom, who would not also inflict it willingly on all that differ from him. The same zeal for speculative opinions is the cause of both.

[o] Fox, vol. iii. p. 145, &c. Burnet, vol. ii. p. 302. Heylin, p. 48, 49. Godwin, p. 349. [p] Strype, vol. iii. p. 261. and Coll. No 58.

CHAPTER XXXVII

The crime, for which almost all the protestants were condemned, was, their refusal to acknowledge the real presence. Gardiner, who had vainly expected, that a few examples would strike a terror into the reformers, finding the work daily multiply upon him, devolved the invidious office on others, chiefly on Bonner, a man of profligate manners, and of a brutal character, who seemed to rejoice in the torments of the unhappy sufferers.[q] He sometimes whipped the prisoners with his own hands, till he was tired with the violence of the exercise: He tore out the beard of a weaver, who refused to relinquish his religion; and that he might give him a specimen of burning, he held his hand to the candle, till the sinews and veins shrunk and burst.[r]

It is needless to be particular in enumerating all the cruelties practised in England during the course of three years that these persecutions lasted: The savage barbarity on the one hand, and the patient constancy on the other, are so similar in all those martyrdoms, that the narrative, little agreeable in itself, would never be relieved by any variety. Human nature appears not, on any occasion, so detestable, and at the same time so absurd, as in these religious persecutions, which sink men below infernal spirits in wickedness, and below the beasts in folly. A few instances only may be worth preserving, in order, if possible, to warn zealous bigots, for ever to avoid such odious and such fruitless barbarity.

Ferrar, bishop of St. David's, was burned in his own diocese; and his appeal to cardinal Pole was not attended to.[s] Ridley, bishop of London, and Latimer, formerly bishop of Worcester, two prelates celebrated for learning and virtue, perished together in the same flames at Oxford, and supported each other's constancy by their mutual exhortations. Latimer, when tied to the stake, called to his companion, "Be of good cheer, brother; we shall this day kindle such a torch in England, as, I trust in God, shall never be extinguished." The executioners had been so merciful (for that clemency may more naturally be ascribed to them than to the religious zealots) as to tie bags of gunpowder about these prelates, in order to put a speedy period to their tortures: The explosion immediately killed Latimer, who was in extreme old age: Ridley continued alive during some time in the midst of the flames.[t]

[q] Heylin, p. 47, 48.   [r] Fox, vol. iii. p. 187.   [s] Ibid. p. 216.   [t] Burnet, vol. ii. p. 318. Heylin. p. 52.

One Hunter, a young man of nineteen, an apprentice, having been seduced by a priest into a dispute, had unwarily denied the real presence. Sensible of his danger, he immediately absconded; but Bonner, laying hold of his father, threatened him with the greatest severities, if he did not produce the young man to stand his trial. Hunter, hearing of the vexations to which his father was exposed, voluntarily surrendered himself to Bonner, and was condemned to the flames by that barbarous prelate.

Thomas Haukes, when conducted to the stake, agreed with his friends, that, if he found the torture tolerable, he would make them a signal to that purpose in the midst of the flames. His zeal for the cause, in which he suffered, so supported him, that he stretched out his arms, the signal agreed on; and in that posture he expired.[u] This example, with many others of like constancy, encouraged multitudes, not only to suffer, but even to court and aspire to martyrdom.

The tender sex itself, as they have commonly greater propensity to religion, produced many examples of the most inflexible courage, in supporting the profession of it, against all the fury of the persecutors. One execution in particular was attended with circumstances, which, even at that time, excited astonishment, by reason of their unusual barbarity. A woman in Guernsey, being near the time of her labour when brought to the stake, was thrown into such agitation by the torture, that her belly burst, and she was delivered in the midst of the flames. One of the guards immediately snatched the infant from the fire, and attempted to save it: But a magistrate, who stood by, ordered it to be thrown back; being determined, he said, that nothing should survive which sprang from so obstinate and heretical a parent.[w]

The persons condemned to these punishments were not convicted of teaching, or dogmatizing, contrary to the established religion: They were seized merely on suspicion; and articles being offered them to subscribe, they were immediately, upon their refusal, condemned to the flames.[x] These instances of barbarity, so unusual in the nation, excited horror; the constancy of the martyrs was the object of admiration; and as men have a principle of equity

[u] Fox, vol. iii. p. 265.   [w] Ibid. p. 747. Heylin, p. 57. Burnet, vol. ii. p. 337.   [x] Burnet, vol. ii. p. 306.

CHAPTER XXXVII

engraven in their minds, which even false religion is not able totally to obliterate, they were shocked to see persons of probity, of honour, of pious dispositions, exposed to punishments more severe than were inflicted on the greatest ruffians, for crimes subversive of civil society. To exterminate the whole protestant party, was known to be impossible; and nothing could appear more iniquitous, than to subject to torture the most conscientious and courageous among them, and allow the cowards and hypocrites to escape. Each martyrdom, therefore, was equivalent to a hundred sermons against popery; and men either avoided such horrid spectacles, or returned from them full of a violent, though secret, indignation against the persecutors. Repeated orders were sent from the council to quicken the diligence of the magistrates in searching out heretics; and, in some places, the gentry were constrained to countenance, by their presence, those barbarous executions. These acts of violence tended only to render the Spanish government daily more odious; and Philip, sensible of the hatred which he incurred, endeavoured to remove the reproach from himself by a very gross artifice: He ordered his confessor to deliver in his presence a sermon in favour of toleration; a doctrine somewhat extraordinary in the mouth of a Spanish friar.[y] But the court, finding that Bonner, however shameless and savage, would not bear alone the whole infamy, soon threw off the mask; and the unrelenting temper of the queen, as well as of the king, appeared without controul. A bold step was even taken towards introducing the inquisition into England. As the bishops' courts, though extremely arbitrary, and not confined by any ordinary forms of law, appeared not to be invested with sufficient power, a commission was appointed, by authority of the queen's prerogative, more effectually to extirpate heresy. Twenty-one persons were named; but any three were armed with the powers of the whole. The commission runs in these terms; "That since many false rumours were published among the subjects, and many heretical opinions were also spread among them, the commissioners were to enquire into those, either by presentments, by witnesses, or any other political way they could devise, and to search after all heresies; the bringers in, the sellers, the readers of all heretical books: They

[y] Heylin, p. 56.

were to examine and punish all misbehaviours or negligences, in any church or chapel; and to try all priests that did not preach the sacrament of the altar; all persons that did not hear mass, or come to their parish church to service, that would not go in processions, or did not take holy bread or holy water: And if they found any that did obstinately persist in such heresies, they were to put them into the hands of their ordinaries, to be punished according to the spiritual laws: Giving the commissioners full power to proceed, as their discretions and consciences should direct them, and to use all such means as they would invent for the searching of the premises; empowering them also to call before them such witnesses as they pleased, and to force them to make oath of such things as might discover what they sought after." [z] Some civil powers were also given the commissioners to punish vagabonds and quarrelsome persons.

To bring the methods of proceeding in England still nearer to the practice of the inquisition, letters were written to lord North, and others, enjoining them, "To put to the torture such obstinate persons as would not confess, and there to order them at their discretion." [a] Secret spies also, and informers, were employed, according to the practice of that iniquitous tribunal. Instructions were given to the justices of peace, "That they should call secretly before them one or two honest persons within their limits, or more, at their discretion, and command them by oath, or otherwise, that they shall secretly learn and search out such persons as shall evil behave themselves in church, or idly, or shall despise openly by words, the king's or queen's proceedings, or go about to make any commotion, or tell any seditious tales or news. And also that the same persons so to be appointed, shall declare to the same justices of peace, the ill behaviour of lewd disordered persons, whether it shall be for using unlawful games, and such other light behaviour of such suspected persons: And that the same information shall be given secretly to the justices; and the same justices shall call such accused persons before them, and examine them, without declaring by whom they were accused. And that the same justices shall, upon their examination, punish the offenders, according as their offences shall appear, upon the accusement and

---

[z] Burnet, vol. ii. Coll. 32.   [a] Burnet, vol. iii. p. 243.

CHAPTER XXXVII

examination, by their discretion, either by open punishment or by good abearing."[b] In some respects, this tyrannical edict even exceeded the oppression of the inquisition; by introducing into every part of government, the same iniquities, which that tribunal practises for the extirpation of heresy only, and which are, in some measure, necessary, wherever that end is earnestly pursued.

But the court had devised a more expeditious and summary method of supporting orthodoxy than even the inquisition itself. They issued a proclamation against books of heresy, treason, and sedition; and declared, "That whosoever had any of these books, and did not presently burn them, without reading them, or showing them to any other person, should be esteemed rebels; and without any farther delay, be executed by martial law."[c] From the state of the English government, during that period, it is not so much the illegality of these proceedings, as their violence and their pernicious tendency, which ought to be the object of our censure.

We have thrown together almost all the proceedings against heretics, though carried on during a course of three years; that we may be obliged, as little as possible, to return to such shocking violences and barbarities. It is computed, that in that time two hundred and seventy-seven persons were brought to the stake; besides those who were punished by imprisonment, fines, and confiscations. Among those who suffered by fire, were five bishops, twenty-one clergymen, eight lay gentlemen, eighty-four tradesmen, one hundred husbandmen, servants, and labourers, fifty-five women, and four children. This persevering cruelty appears astonishing; yet is it much inferior to what has been practised in other countries. A great author[d] computes, that, in the Netherlands alone, from the time that the edict of Charles V. was promulgated against the reformers, there had been fifty thousand persons hanged, beheaded, buried alive, or burnt, on account of religion; and that in France the number had also been considerable. Yet in both countries, as the same author subjoins, the progress of the new opinions, instead of being checked, was rather forwarded by these persecutions.

The burning of heretics was a very natural method of recon-

[b] Ibid. p. 246, 247.   [c] Burnet, vol. ii. p. 363. Heylin, p. 79.   [d] Father Paul, lib. 5.

ciling the kingdom to the Romish communion; and little solicitation was requisite to engage the pope to receive the strayed
flock, from which he reaped such considerable profit: Yet was
there a solemn embassy sent to Rome, consisting of Sir Anthony
Brown, created viscount Montacute, the bishop of Ely, and Sir
Edward Carne; in order to carry the submissions of England, and
beg to be re-admitted into the bosom of the catholic church.[e] Paul
IV. after a short interval, now filled the papal chair; the most
haughty pontiff that during several ages had been elevated to that
dignity. He was offended, that Mary still retained among her titles,
that of queen of Ireland; and he affirmed, that it belonged to him
alone, as he saw cause, either to erect new kingdoms or abolish the
old: But to avoid all dispute with the new converts, he thought
proper to erect Ireland into a kingdom, and he then admitted the
title, as if it had been assumed from his concession. This was a
usual artifice of the popes, to give allowance to what they could not
prevent,[f] and afterwards pretend, that princes, while they exercised their own powers, were only acting by authority from the
papacy. And though Paul had at first intended to oblige Mary
formally to recede from this title, before he would bestow it upon
her; he found it prudent to proceed in a less haughty manner.[g]

Another point in discussion between the pope and the English
ambassadors was not so easily terminated. Paul insisted, that the
property and possessions of the church should be restored to the
uttermost farthing: That whatever belonged to God could never
by any law be converted to profane uses, and every person who
detained such possessions was in a state of eternal damnation:
That he would willingly, in consideration of the humble submissions of the English, make them a present of these ecclesiastical
revenues; but such a concession exceeded his power, and the people might be certain that so great a profanation of holy things
would be a perpetual anathema upon them, and would blast all
their future felicity: That if they would truly shew their filial piety,
they must restore all the privileges and emoluments of the Romish
church, and Peter's pence among the rest; nor could they expect,
that this apostle would open to them the gates of paradise, while

[e] Heylin, p. 45.   [f] Ibid. Father Paul, lib. 5.   [g] Father Paul, lib. 5.

CHAPTER XXXVII

they detained from him his patrimony on earth.[h] These earnest remonstrances, being transmitted to England, though they had little influence on the nation, operated powerfully on the queen, who was determined, in order to ease her conscience, to restore all the church lands which were still in the possession of the crown: And the more to display her zeal, she erected anew some convents and monasteries, notwithstanding the low condition of the exchequer.[i] When this measure was debated in council, some members objected, that, if such a considerable part of the revenue were dismembered, the dignity of the crown would fall to decay: but the queen replied, that she preferred the salvation of her soul to ten such kingdoms as England.[k] These imprudent measures would not probably have taken place so easily, had it not been for the death of Gardiner, which happened about this time: The great seal was given to Heathe, archbishop of York; that an ecclesiastic might still be possessed of that high office, and be better enabled by his authority to forward the persecutions against the reformed.

These persecutions were now become extremely odious to the nation; and the effects of the public discontent appeared in the new parliament, summoned to meet at Westminster.[l] A bill[m] was passed, restoring to the church the tenths and first-fruits, and all the impropriations which remained in the hands of the crown; but though this matter directly concerned none but the queen herself, great opposition was made to the bill in the house of commons. An application being made for a subsidy during two years, and for two fifteenths, the latter was refused by the commons; and many members said, that, while the crown was thus despoiling itself of its revenue, it was in vain to bestow riches upon it. The parliament rejected a bill for obliging the exiles to return under certain penalties, and another for incapacitating such as were remiss in the prosecution of heresy from being justices of peace. The queen, finding the intractable humour of the commons, thought proper to dissolve the parliament.

The spirit of opposition, which began to prevail in parliament, was the more likely to be vexatious to Mary, as she was otherwise

21st Octob. A parliament.

9th Dec.

[h] Father Paul, lib. 5. Heylin, p. 45.   [i] Depeches de Noailles, vol. iv. p. 312.   [k] Heylin, p. 53, 65. Hollingshed, p. 1127. Speed, p. 826. [l] Burnet, vol. ii. p. 322.   [m] 2 and 3 Phil. and Mar. cap. 4.

in very bad humour, on account of her husband's absence, who, tired of her importunate love and jealousy, and finding his authority extremely limited in England, had laid hold of the first opportunity to leave her, and had gone over last summer to the emperor in Flanders. The indifference and neglect of Philip, added to the disappointment in her imagined pregnancy, threw her into deep melancholy; and she gave vent to her spleen by daily enforcing the persecutions against the protestants, and even by expressions of rage against all her subjects; by whom she knew herself to be hated, and whose opposition, in refusing an entire compliance with Philip, was the cause, she believed, why he had alienated his affections from her, and afforded her so little of his company.[n] The less return her love met with, the more it increased; and she passed most of her time in solitude, where she gave vent to her passion, either in tears, or in writing fond epistles to Philip, who seldom returned her any answer, and scarcely deigned to pretend any sentiment of love or even of gratitude towards her. The chief part of government, to which she attended, was the extorting of money from her people, in order to satisfy his demands; and as the parliament had granted her but a scanty supply, she had recourse to expedients very violent and irregular. She levied a loan of 60,000 pounds upon a thousand persons, of whose compliance, either on account of their riches or their affections to her, she held herself best assured: But that sum not sufficing, she exacted a general loan on every one who possessed twenty pounds a-year. This imposition lay heavy on the gentry, who were obliged, many of them to retrench their expences, and dismiss their servants in order to enable them to comply with her demands: And as these servants, accustomed to idleness, and having no means of subsistance, commonly betook themselves to theft and robbery, the queen published a proclamation, by which she obliged their former masters to take them back to their service. She levied 60,000 marks on 7000 yeomen, who had not contributed to the former loan; and she exacted 36,000 pounds more from the merchants. In order to engage some Londoners to comply more willingly with her multiplied extortions, she passed an edict, prohibiting, for four months, the exporting of any English cloths or kerseys to the Netherlands; an

The queen's extortions.

[n] Depeches de Noailles, vol. v. p. 370, 562.

CHAPTER XXXVII

expedient which procured a good market for such as had already sent any quantity of cloth thither. Her rapaciousness engaged her to give endless disturbance and interruption to commerce. The English company settled in Antwerp having refused her a loan of 40,000 pounds, she dissembled her resentment, till she found, that they had bought and shipped great quantities of cloth for Antwerp fair, which was approaching: She then laid an embargo on the ships, and obliged the merchants to grant her a loan of the 40,000 pounds at first demanded, to engage for the payment of 20,000 pounds more at a limited time, and to submit to an arbitrary imposition of twenty shillings on each piece. Some time, after she was informed, that the Italian merchants had shipped above 40,000 pieces of cloth for the Levant, for which they were to pay her a crown a piece, the usual imposition: She struck a bargain with the merchant adventurers in London; prohibited the foreigners from making any exportation; and received from the English merchants, in consideration of this iniquity, the sum of 50,000 pounds, and an imposition of four crowns on each piece of cloth which they should export. She attempted to borrow great sums abroad; but her credit was so low, that, tho' she offered 14 per cent. to the city of Antwerp for a loan of 30,000 pounds, she could not obtain it, till she compelled the city of London to be surety for her.[o] All these violent expedients were employed, while she herself was in profound peace with all the world, and had visibly no occasion for money but to supply the demands of a husband, who gave attention only to his own convenience, and showed himself entirely indifferent about her interests.

Philip was now become master of all the wealth of the new world, and of the richest and most extensive dominions in Europe, by the voluntary resignation of the emperor, Charles V.; who, though still in the vigour of his age, had taken a disgust to the world, and was determined to seek, in the tranquillity of retreat, for that happiness, which he had in vain pursued, amidst the tumults of war, and the restless projects of ambition. He summoned the states of the Low Countries; and seating himself on the throne for the last time, explained to his subjects the reasons of his

The emperor resigns his crown.

25th Oct.

---

[o] Godwin, p. 359. Cowper's Chronicle. Burnet, vol. ii. p. 359. Carte, p. 330, 333, 337, 341. Strype's Memor. vol. iii. p. 428, 558. Annals, vol. ii. p. 15.

resignation, absolved them from all oaths of allegiance, and de-
volving his authority on Philip, told him, that his paternal
tenderness made him weep, when he reflected on the burthen
which he imposed upon him.[p] He inculcated on him the great and
only duty of a prince, the study of his people's happiness; and
represented how much preferable it was to govern, by affection
rather than by fear, the nations subjected to his dominion. The
cool reflections of age now discovered to him the emptiness of his
former pursuits; and he found, that the vain schemes of extending
his empire, had been the source of endless opposition and disappointment, and kept himself, his neighbours, and his subjects, in
perpetual inquietude, and had frustrated the sole end of government, the felicity of the nations committed to his care; an object
which meets with less opposition, and which, if steadily pursued,
can alone convey a lasting and solid satisfaction.

1556.   A few months after, he resigned to Philip his other dominions;
and embarking on board a fleet, sailed to Spain, and took his
journey to St. Just, a monastery in Estremadura, which, being
situated in a happy climate, and amidst the greatest beauties of
nature, he had chosen for the place of his retreat. When he arrived
at Burgos, he found, by the thinness of his court, and the negligent
attendance of the Spanish grandees, that he was no longer emperor; and though this observation might convince him still more
of the vanity of the world, and make him more heartily despise
what he had renounced, he sighed to find that all former adulation
and obeisance had been paid to his fortune, not to his person. With
better reason, was he struck with the ingratitude of his son Philip,
who obliged him to wait a long time for the payment of the small
pension which he had reserved; and this disappointment in his
domestic enjoyments gave him a sensible concern. He pursued
however his resolution with inflexible constancy; and shutting
himself up in his retreat, he exerted such self-command, that he
restrained even his curiosity from any enquiry concerning the
transactions of the world, which he had entirely abandoned. The
fencing against the pains and infirmities, under which he laboured, occupied a great part of his time; and during the intervals,
he employed his leisure either in examining the controversies of

[p] Thuan. lib. xvi. c. 20.

CHAPTER XXXVII

theology, with which his age had been so much agitated, and which he had hitherto considered only in a political light, or in imitating the works of renowned artists, particularly in mechanics, of which he had always been a great admirer and encourager. He is said to have here discovered a propensity to the new doctrines; and to have frequently dropped hints of this unexpected alteration in his sentiments. Having amused himself with the construction of clocks and watches, he thence remarked how impracticable the object was, in which he had so much employed himself during his grandeur; and how impossible, that he, who never could frame two machines that would go exactly alike, could ever be able to make all mankind concur in the same belief and opinion. He survived his retreat two years.

The emperor Charles had very early, in the beginning of his reign, found the difficulty of governing such distant dominions; and he had made his brother Ferdinand be elected king of the Romans; with a view to his inheriting the imperial dignity, as well as his German dominions. But having afterwards enlarged his schemes, and formed plans of aggrandizing his family, he regretted, that he must dismember such considerable states; and he endeavoured to engage Ferdinand, by the most tempting offers, and most earnest solicitations, to yield up his pretensions in favour of Philip. Finding his attempts fruitless, he had resigned the Imperial crown with his other dignities; and Ferdinand, according to common form, applied to the pope for his coronation. The arrogant pontiff refused the demand; and pretended, that, though, on the death of an emperor, he was obliged to crown the prince elected, yet in the case of a resignation, the right devolved to the holy see, and it belonged to the pope alone to appoint an emperor. The conduct of Paul was in every thing conformable to these lofty pretensions. He thundered always in the ears of all ambassadors, that he stood in no need of the assistance of any prince, that he was above all potentates of the earth, that he would not accustom monarchs to pretend to a familiarity or equality with him, that it belonged to him to alter and regulate kingdoms, that he was successor of those who had deposed kings and emperors, and that rather than submit to any thing below his dignity, he would set fire to the four corners of the world. He went so far, as, at table, in the presence of many persons, and even openly, in a public consistory, to say, that he would not admit any kings for his companions; they were all his subjects, and he would hold them under these feet: So saying, he stamped on the ground with his old and infirm limbs: For he was now past fourscore years of age.[q]

The world could not forbear making a comparison between Charles V. a prince, who, though educated amidst wars and intrigues of state, had prevented the decline of age, and had descended from the throne, in order to set apart an interval for thought and reflection, and a priest, who, in the extremity of old age, exulted in his dominion, and from restless ambition and revenge was throwing all nations into combustion. Paul had entertained the most inveterate animosity against the house of Austria; and though a truce of five years had been concluded between France and Spain, he excited Henry by his solicitations to break it, and promised to assist him in recovering Naples, and the dominions to which he laid claim in Italy; a project which had ever proved hurtful to the predecessors of that monarch. He himself engaged in hostilities with the duke of Alva, viceroy of Naples: and Guise being sent with forces to support him, the renewal of war between the two crowns seemed almost inevitable. Philip, though less warlike than his father, was no less ambitious; and he trusted, that, by the intrigues of the cabinet, where, he believed, his caution and secrecy and prudence gave him the superiority, he should be able to subdue all his enemies, and extend his authority and dominion. For this reason, as well as from the desire of settling his new empire, he wished to maintain peace with France; but when he found, that, without sacrificing his honour, it was impossible for him to overlook the hostile attempts of Henry, he prepared for war with great industry. In order to give himself the more advantage, he was desirous of embarking England in the quarrel; and though the queen was of herself extremely averse to that measure, he hoped, that the devoted fondness, which, notwithstanding repeated instances of his indifference, she still bore to him, would effectually second his applications. Had the matter indeed depended solely on her, she was incapable of resisting her husband's commands; but she had little weight with her council, still less with her people; and her government, which was every day becoming more odious, seemed unable to maintain itself even during the

[q] Father Paul, lib. v.

CHAPTER XXXVII

most profound tranquillity, much more if a war were kindled with France, and what seemed an inevitable consequence, with Scotland, supported by that powerful kingdom.

An act of barbarity was this year exercised in England, which, added to many other instances of the same kind, tended to render the government extremely unpopular. Cranmer had long been detained prisoner; but the queen now determined to bring him to punishment; and in order the more fully to satiate her vengeance, she resolved to punish him for heresy, rather than for treason. He was cited by the pope to stand his trial at Rome; and though he was known to be kept in close custody at Oxford, he was, upon his not appearing, condemned as contumacious. Bonner, bishop of London, and Thirleby of Ely were sent to degrade him; and the former executed the melancholy ceremony with all the joy and exultation, which suited his savage nature.[r] The implacable spirit of the queen, not satisfied with the eternal damnation of Cranmer, which she believed inevitable, and with the execution of that dreadful sentence, to which he was condemned, prompted her also to seek the ruin of his honour, and the infamy of his name. Persons were employed to attack him, not in the way of disputation, against which he was sufficiently armed; but by flattery, insinuation, and address; by representing the dignities to which his character still entitled him, if he would merit them by a recantation; by giving hopes of long enjoying those powerful friends, whom his beneficent disposition had attached to him during the course of his prosperity.[s] Overcome by the fond love of life, terrified by the prospect of those tortures which awaited him; he allowed, in an unguarded hour, the sentiments of nature to prevail over his resolution, and he agreed to subscribe the doctrines of the papal supremacy and of the real presence. The court, equally perfidious and cruel, were determined, that this recantation should avail him nothing; and they sent orders, that he should be required to acknowledge his errors in church before the whole people, and that he should thence be immediately carried to execution. Cranmer, whether that he had received a secret intimation of their design, or had repented of his weakness, surprized the audience by a contrary declaration. He said, that he was well apprized of the obedience which he owed to his sovereign and the laws; but this duty

Execution of Cranmer.

21st March.

[r] Mem. of Cranm. p. 375. [s] Heylin, p. 55. Mem. p. 383.

extended no farther than to submit patiently to their commands, and to bear without resistance whatever hardships they should impose upon him: That a superior duty, the duty which he owed to his Maker, obliged him to speak truth on all occasions, and not to relinquish, by a base denial, the holy doctrine, which the supreme Being had revealed to mankind: That there was one miscarriage in his life, of which, above all others, he severely repented; the insincere declaration of faith, to which he had the weakness of consent, and which the fear of death alone had extorted from him: That he took this opportunity of atoning for his error, by a sincere and open recantation; and was willing to seal with his blood that doctrine, which he firmly believed to be communicated from Heaven: And that as his hand had erred by betraying his heart, it should first be punished, by a severe but just doom, and should first pay the forfeit of its offences. He was thence led to the stake amidst the insults of the catholics; and having now summoned up all the force of his mind, he bore their scorn, as well as the torture of his punishment, with singular fortitude. He stretched out his hand, and without betraying, either by his countenance or motions, the least sign of weakness or even of feeling, he held it in the flames, till it was entirely consumed. His thoughts seemed wholly occupied with reflections on his former fault; and he called aloud several times, *This hand has offended.* Satisfied with that atonement, he then discovered a serenity in his countenance; and when the fire attacked his body, he seemed to be quite insensible of his outward sufferings, and by the force of hope and resolution to have collected his mind altogether within itself, and to repel the fury of the flames. It is pretended, that, after his body was consumed, his heart was found entire and untouched amidst the ashes; an event, which, as it was the emblem of his constancy, was fondly believed by the zealous protestants. He was undoubtedly a man of merit; possessed of learning and capacity, and adorned with candour, sincerity, and beneficence, and all those virtues, which were fitted to render him useful and amiable in society. His moral qualities procured him universal respect; and the courage of his martyrdom, though he fell short of the rigid inflexibility observed in many, made him the hero of the protestant party.[t]

[t] Burnet, vol. ii. p. 331, 332, &c. Godwin, p. 352.

CHAPTER XXXVII

After Cranmer's death, cardinal Pole, who had now taken priest's orders, was installed in the see of Canterbury; and was thus by this office, as well as by his commission of legate, placed at the head of the church of England. But though he was averse to all sanguinary methods of converting heretics, and deemed the reformation of the clergy the more effectual, as the more laudable expedient for that purpose;[u] he found his authority too weak to oppose the barbarous and bigotted disposition of the queen and of her counsellors. He himself, he knew, had been suspected of Lutheranism; and as Paul, the reigning pope, was a furious persecutor and his personal enemy, he was prompted, by the modesty of his disposition, to reserve his credit for other occasions, in which he had a greater probability of success.[w]

The great object of the queen was to engage the nation in the war, which was kindled between France and Spain; and cardinal Pole, with many other counsellors, openly and zealously opposed this measure. Besides insisting on the marriage articles, which provided against such an attempt, they represented the violence of the domestic factions in England, and the disordered state of the finances; and they foreboded, that the tendency of all these measures was to reduce the kingdom to a total dependance on Spanish counsels. Philip had come to London in order to support his partizans; and he told the queen, that, if he were not gratified in so reasonable a request, he never more would set foot in England. This declaration extremely heightened her zeal for promoting his interests, and overcoming the inflexibility of her council. After employing other menaces of a more violent nature, she threatened to dismiss all of them, and to appoint counsellors more obsequious; yet could she not procure a vote for declaring war with France. At length, one Stafford and some other conspirators were detected in a design of surprizing Scarborough;[x] and a confession being extorted from them, that they had been encouraged by Henry in the attempt, the queen's importunity prevailed; and it was determined to make this act of hostility, with others of a like secret and doubtful nature, the ground of the quarrel. War was accordingly declared against France; and preparations were every where made for attacking that kingdom.

1557.

---

[u] Burnet, vol. ii. p. 324, 325.　[w] Heylin, p. 68, 69. Burnet, vol. ii. p. 327.
[x] Heylin, p. 72. Burnet, vol. ii. p. 351. Sir James Melvil's Memoirs.

The revenue of England at that time little exceeded 300,000 pounds.[y] Any considerable supplies could scarcely be expected from parliament, considering the present disposition of the nation; and as the war would sensibly diminish that branch arising from the customs, the finances, it was foreseen, would fall short even of the ordinary charges of government; and must still more prove unequal to the expences of war. But though the queen owed great arrears to all her servants, besides the loans extorted from her subjects, these considerations had no influence with her; and in order to support her warlike preparations, she continued to levy money in the same arbitrary and violent manner which she had formerly practised. She obliged the city of London to supply her with 60,000 pounds on her husband's entry; she levied before the legal time the second year's subsidy voted by parliament; she issued anew many privy seals, by which she procured loans from her people; and having equipped a fleet, which she could not victual by reason of the dearness of provisions, she seized all the corn she could find in Suffolk and Norfolk, without paying any price to the owners. By all these expedients, assisted by the power of pressing, she levied an army of ten thousand men, which she sent over to the Low-Countries, under the command of the earl of Pembroke. Meanwhile, in order to prevent any disturbance at home, many of the most considerable gentry were thrown into the Tower; and lest they should be known, the Spanish practice was followed: They either were carried thither in the night time, or were hoodwinked and muffled by the guards who conducted them.[z]

The king of Spain had assembled an army, which, after the junction of the English, amounted to above sixty thousand men, conducted by Philibert, duke of Savoy, one of the greatest captains of the age. The constable, Montmorency, who commanded the French army, had not half the number to oppose to him. The duke of Savoy, after menacing Mariembourgh and Rocroy, suddenly sat down before St. Quintin; and as the place was weak, and ill provided with a garrison, he expected in a few days to become master of it. But admiral Coligny, governor of the province, thinking his honour interested to save so important a fortress, threw himself

[y] Rossi, Successi d'Inghilterra. [z] Strype's Eccles. Memorials, vol. iii. P. 377.

CHAPTER XXXVII

into St. Quintin, with some troops of French and Scottish gens-
darmery; and by his exhortations and example animated the soldiers to a vigorous defence. He dispatched a messenger to his
uncle, Montmorency, desiring a supply of men; and the constable
approached the place with his whole army, in order to facilitate the
entry of these succours. But the duke of Savoy, falling on the
reinforcement, did such execution upon them, that not above five
hundred got into the place. He next made an attack on the French
army, and put them to total rout, killing four thousand men, and
dispersing the remainder. In this unfortunate action many of the
chief nobility of France were either slain or taken prisoners:
Among the latter was the old constable himself, who, fighting
valiantly, and resolute to die rather than survive his defeat, was
surrounded by the enemy, and thus fell alive into their hands. The
whole kingdom of France was thrown into consternation: Paris was
attempted to be fortified in a hurry: And had the Spaniards presently marched thither, it could not have failed to fall into their
hands. But Philip was of a cautious temper; and he determined
first to take St. Quintin, in order to secure a communication with
his own dominions. A very little time, it was expected, would finish
this enterprize; but the bravery of Coligny still prolonged the siege
seventeen days, which proved the safety of France. Some troops
were levied and assembled. Couriers were sent to recal the duke of
Guise and his army from Italy: And the French, having recovered
from their first panic, put themselves in a posture of defence.
Philip, after taking Ham and Catelet, found the season so far
advanced, that he could attempt no other enterprize: He broke up
his camp, and retired to winter-quarters.

But the vigilant activity of Guise, not satisfied with securing the
frontiers, prompted him, in the depth of winter, to plan an enterprize, which France, during her greatest successes, had always
regarded as impracticable, and had never thought of undertaking.
Calais was, in that age, deemed an impregnable fortress; and as it
was known to be the favourite of the English nation, by whom it
could easily be succoured, the recovery of that place by France was
considered as totally desperate. But Coligny had remarked, that, as
the town of Calais was surrounded with marshes, which, during
the winter, were impassable, except over a dyke guarded by two
castles, St. Agatha and Newnam bridge, the English were of late

*10th
Aug.*

*Battle
of St.
Quintin.*

*Calais
taken
by the
French.*

accustomed, on account of the lowness of their finances, to dismiss a great part of the garrison at the end of autumn, and to recal them in the spring, at which time alone they judged their attendance necessary. On this circumstance he had founded the design of making a sudden attack on Calais; he had caused the place to be secretly viewed by some engineers; and a plan of the whole enterprize being found among his papers, it served, though he himself was made prisoner on the taking of St. Quintin, to suggest the project of that undertaking, and to direct the measures of the duke of Guise.

1558.   Several bodies of troops defiled towards the frontiers on various pretences; and the whole being suddenly assembled, formed an army, with which Guise made an unexpected march towards Calais. At the same time a great number of French ships, being ordered into the channel, under colour of cruising on the English, composed a fleet which made an attack by sea on the fortifications. The French assaulted St. Agatha with three thousand harquebusiers; and the garrison, though they made a vigorous defence, were soon obliged to abandon the place, and retreat to Newnam bridge. The siege of this latter place was immediately undertaken, and at the same time the fleet battered the risbank, which guarded the entrance of the harbour; and both these castles seemed exposed to imminent danger. The governor, lord Wentworth, was a brave officer; but finding that the greater part of his weak garrison was enclosed in the castle of Newnam bridge and the risbank, he ordered them to capitulate, and to join him in Calais, which, without their assistance, he was utterly unable to defend. The garrison of Newnam bridge was so happy as to effect this purpose; but that of the risbank could not obtain such favourable conditions, and were obliged to surrender at discretion.

The duke of Guise, now holding Calais blockaded by sea and land, thought himself secure of succeeding in his enterprize; but in order to prevent all accident, he delayed not a moment the attack of the place. He planted his batteries against the castle, where he made a large breach; and having ordered Andelot, Coligny's brother, to drain the fossée, he commanded an assault, which succeeded; and the French made a lodgment in the castle. On the night following, Wentworth attempted to recover this post, but having lost two hundred men in a furious attack which he made upon it,[a] he found his garrison so weak, that he was obliged to capitulate. Ham and Guisnes fell soon after; and thus the duke of Guise, in eight days, during the depth of winter, made himself master of this strong fortress, that had cost Edward III. a siege of eleven months, at the head of a numerous army, which had, that very year, been victorious in the battle of Cressy. The English had held it above two hundred years; and as it gave them an easy entrance into France, it was regarded as the most important possession belonging to the crown. The joy of the French was extreme, as well as the glory acquired by Guise, who, at the time when all Europe imagined France to be sunk by the unfortunate battle of St. Quintin, had, in opposition to the English, and their allies, the Spaniards, acquired possession of a place, which no former king of France, even during the distractions of the civil wars, between the houses of York and Lancaster, had ever ventured to attempt. The English on the other hand, bereaved of this valuable fortress, murmured loudly against the improvidence of the queen and her council; who, after engaging in a fruitless war, for the sake of foreign interests, had thus exposed the nation to so severe a disgrace. A treasury exhausted by expences, and burthened with debts: a people divided and dejected; a sovereign negligent of her people's welfare, were circumstances which, notwithstanding the fair offers and promises of Philip, gave them small hopes of recovering Calais. And as the Scots, instigated by French councils, began to move on the borders, they were now necessitated rather to look to their defence at home, than to think of foreign conquests.

After the peace, which, in consequence of king Edward's treaty with Henry, took place between Scotland and England, the queen-dowager, on pretence of visiting her daughter and her relations, made a journey to France, and she carried along with her the earls of Huntley, Sutherland, Marischal, and many of the principal nobility. Her secret design was to take measures for engaging the earl of Arran to resign to her the government of the kingdom; and as her brothers, the duke of Guise, the cardinal of Lorraine, and the duke of Aumale, had uncontrouled influence in the court of France, she easily persuaded Henry, and, by his authority, the Scottish nobles, to enter into her measures. Having also gained

Affairs of Scotland.

---

[a] Thuan. lib. xx. cap. 2.

Carnegy of Kinnaird, Panter, bishop of Ross, and Gavin Hamilton, commendator of Kilwinning, three creatures of the governor's, she persuaded him, by their means, to consent to this resignation;[b] and when every thing was thus prepared for her purpose, she took a journey to Scotland, and passed through England in her way thither. Edward received her with great respect and civility; though he could not forbear attempting to renew the old treaty for his marriage with her daughter: A marriage, he said, so happily calculated for the tranquillity, interest, and security of both kingdoms, and the only means of ensuring a durable peace between them. For his part, he added, he never could entertain a cordial amity for any other husband whom she should choose; nor was it easy for him to forgive a man, who, at the same time that he disappointed so natural an alliance, had bereaved him of a bride, to whom his affections, from his earliest infancy, had been entirely engaged. The queen-dowager eluded these applications, by telling him, that, if any measures had been taken disagreeable to him, they were entirely owing to the imprudence of the duke of Somerset, who, instead of employing courtesy, caresses, and gentle offices, the proper means of gaining a young princess, had had recourse to arms and violence, and had constrained the Scottish nobility to send their sovereign into France, in order to interest that kingdom in protecting their liberty and independance.[c]

When the queen-dowager arrived in Scotland, she found the governor very unwilling to fulfil his engagements; and it was not till after many delays that he could be persuaded to resign his authority. But finding that the majority of the young princess was approaching, and that the queen-dowager had gained the affections of all the principal nobility, he thought it more prudent to submit; and having stipulated, that he should be declared next heir to the crown, and should be freed from giving an account of his past administration, he placed her in possession of the power; and she thenceforth assumed the name of regent.[d] It was a usual saying of this princess, that, provided she could render her friends happy, and could ensure to herself a good reputation, she was entirely indifferent what befell her; and though this sentiment is greatly

---

[b] Buchanan, lib. xiv. Keith, p. 56. Spotswood, p. 92.   [c] Keith, p. 59.
[d] 12th April, 1554.

censured by the zealous reformers,[e] as being founded wholly on secular motives, it discovers a mind well calculated for the government of kingdoms. D'Oisel, a Frenchman, celebrated for capacity, had attended her as ambassador from Henry, but in reality to assist her with his counsels in so delicate an undertaking as the administration of Scotland; and this man had formed a scheme for laying a general tax on the kingdom, in order to support a standing military force, which might at once repel the inroads of foreign enemies, and check the turbulence of the Scottish nobles. But though some of the courtiers were gained over to this project, it gave great and general discontent to the nation; and the queen-regent, after ingenuously confessing, that it would prove pernicious to the kingdom, had the prudence to desist from it, and to trust entirely for her security to the good-will and affections of her subjects.[f]

This laudable purpose seemed to be the chief object of her administration; yet was she sometimes drawn from it by her connexions with France, and by the influence which her brothers had acquired over her. When Mary commenced hostilities against that kingdom, Henry required the queen-regent to take part in the quarrel; and she summoned a convention of states at Newbottle, and requested them to concur in a declaration of war against England. The Scottish nobles, who were become as jealous of French, as the English were of Spanish influence, refused their assent; and the queen was obliged to have recourse to stratagem, in order to effect her purpose. She ordered d'Oisel to begin some fortifications at Eyemouth, a place which had been dismantled by the last treaty with Edward; and when the garrison of Berwick, as she foresaw, made an inroad to prevent the undertaking, she effectually employed this pretence to inflame the Scottish nation, and to engage them in hostilities against England.[g] The enterprizes, however, of the Scots proceeded no farther than some inroads on the borders: When d'Oisel, of himself, conducted artillery and troops to besiege the castle of Werke, he was recalled, and sharply rebuked by the council.[h]

In order to connect Scotland more closely with France, and to

Marriage of the dauphin and the queen of Scots.

[e] Knox, p. 89.   [f] Keith, p. 70. Buchanan, lib. xvi.   [g] Buchanan, lib. xvi. Thuan. lib. xix. c. 7.   [h] Knox, p. 93.

encrease the influence of the latter kingdom, it was thought proper by Henry to celebrate the marriage between the young queen and the dauphin; and a deputation was sent by the Scottish parliament, to assist at the ceremony, and to settle the terms of the contract.

The close alliance between France and Scotland threatened very nearly the repose and security of Mary; and it was foreseen, that, though the factions and disorders, which might naturally be expected in the Scottish government during the absence of the sovereign, would make its power less formidable, that kingdom would at least afford to the French a means of invading England. The queen, therefore, found it necessary to summon a parliament, and to demand of them some supplies to her exhausted exchequer. And such an emergency usually gives great advantage to the people, and as the parliaments, during this reign, had shewn, that, where the liberty and independency of the kingdom was menaced with imminent danger, they were not entirely overawed by the court; we shall naturally expect, that the late arbitrary methods of extorting money should, at least, be censured, and, perhaps, some remedy be for the future provided against them. The commons however, without making any reflections on the past, voted, besides a fifteenth, a subsidy of four shillings in the pound on land, and two shillings and eight pence on goods. The clergy granted eight shillings in the pound, payable, as was also the subsidy of the laity, in four years by equal portions.

The parliament also passed an act, confirming all the sales and grants of crown lands, which either were already made by the queen, or should be made during the seven ensuing years. It was easy to foresee, that, in Mary's present disposition and situation, this power would be followed by a great alienation of the royal demesnes; and nothing could be more contrary to the principles of good government, than to establish a prince with very extensive authority, yet permit him to be reduced to beggary. This act met with opposition in the house of commons. One Copley expressed his fears lest the queen, under colour of the power there granted, might alter the succession, and alienate the crown from the lawful heir: But his words were thought *irreverent* to her majesty: He was committed to the custody of the serjeant at arms; and though he expressed sorrow for his offence, he was not released, till the queen was applied to for his pardon.

*20th
Jan.*

*A par-
liament.*

CHAPTER XXXVII

The English nation, during this whole reign, were under great apprehensions, with regard not only to the succession, but the life, of the lady Elizabeth. The violent hatred, which the queen bore to her, broke out on every occasion; and it required all the authority of Philip, as well as her own great prudence, to prevent the fatal effects of it. The princess retired into the country; and knowing that she was surrounded with spies, she passed her time wholly in reading and study, intermeddled in no business, and saw very little company. While she remained in this situation, which for the present was melancholy, but which prepared her mind for those great actions, by which her life was afterwards so much distinguished; proposals of marriage were made to her by the Swedish ambassador, in his master's name. As her first question was, whether the queen had been informed of these proposals; the ambassador told her, that his master thought, as he was a gentleman, it was his duty first to make his addresses to herself; and having obtained her consent, he would next, as a king, apply to her sister. But the princess would allow him to proceed no farther; and the queen, after thanking her for this instance of duty, desired to know how she stood affected to the Swedish proposals. Elizabeth, though exposed to many present dangers and mortifications, had the magnanimity to reserve herself for better fortune; and she covered her refusal with professions of a passionate attachment to a single life, which, she said, she infinitely preferred before any other.[i] The princess showed like prudence in concealing her sentiments of religion, in complying with the present modes of worship, and in eluding all questions with regard to that delicate subject.[k]

[i] Burnet, vol. ii. Collect. No. 37. [k] The common net at that time, says Sir Richard Baker, for catching of protestants, was the real presence; and this net was used to catch the lady Elizabeth: For being asked one time what she thought of the words of Christ, *This is my body,* whether she thought it the true body of Christ that was in the sacrament; it is said, that, after some pausing, she thus answered:

> Christ was the word that spake it;
> He took the bread and brake it;
> And what the word did make it,
> That I believe and take it.

Which, though it may seem but a slight expression, yet hath it more solidness than at first sight appears; at least, it served her turn at that time, to escape the net, which by direct answer she could not have done. Baker's Chronicle, p. 320.

The money granted by parliament, enabled the queen to fit out a fleet of a hundred and forty sail, which, being joined by thirty Flemish ships, and carrying six thousand land forces on board, was sent to make an attempt on the coast of Britanny. The fleet was commanded by lord Clinton: the land forces by the earls of Huntingdon and Rutland. But the equipment of the fleet and army was so dilatory, that the French got intelligence of the design, and were prepared to receive them. The English found Brest so well guarded as to render an attempt on that place impracticable; but landing at Conquest, they plundered and burnt the town, with some adjacent villages, and were proceeding to commit greater disorders, when Kersimon, a Breton gentleman, at the head of some militia, fell upon them, put them to rout, and drove them to their ships with considerable loss. But a small squadron of ten English ships had an opportunity of amply revenging this disgrace upon the French. The mareschal de Thermes, governor of Calais, had made an irruption into Flanders, with an army of fourteen thousand men; and having forced a passage over the river Aa, had taken Dunkirk, and Berg St. Winoc, and had advanced as far as Newport, but count Egmont coming suddenly upon him, with superior forces, he was obliged to retreat; and being overtaken by the Spaniards near Gravelines, and finding a battle inevitable, he chose very skilfully his ground for the engagement. He fortified his left wing with all the precautions possible; and posted his right along the river Aa, which, he reasonably thought, gave him full security from that quarter. But the English ships, which were accidentally on the coast, being drawn by the noise of the firing, sailed up the river, and flanking the French, did such execution by their artillery, that they put them to flight; and the Spaniards gained a complete victory.[l]

Meanwhile the principal army of France, under the duke of Guise, and that of Spain, under the duke of Savoy, approached each other on the frontiers of Picardy; and as the two kings had come into their respective camps, attended by the flower of their nobility, men expected, that some great and important event would follow, from the emulation of these warlike nations. But Philip, though actuated by the ambition, possessed not the enter-

[l] Hollingshed, p. 1150.

prizing genius of a conqueror; and he was willing, notwithstanding the superiority of his numbers, and the two great victories which he had gained at St. Quintin and Gravelines, to put a period to the war by treaty. Negociations were entered into for that purpose; and as the terms offered by the two monarchs were somewhat wide of each other, the armies were put into winter-quarters, till the princes could come to better agreement. Among other conditions, Henry demanded the restitution of Navarre to its lawful owner; Philip that of Calais and its territory to England: But in the midst of these negociations, news arrived of the death of Mary; and Philip, no longer connected with England, began to relax in his firmness on that capital article. This was the only circumstance that could have made the death of that princess be regretted by the nation.

Mary had long been in a declining state of health; and having mistaken her dropsy for a pregnancy, she had made use of an improper regimen, and her malady daily augmented. Every reflection now tormented her. The consciousness of being hated by her subjects, the prospect of Elizabeth's succession, apprehensions of the danger to which the catholic religion stood exposed, dejection for the loss of Calais, concern for the ill state of her affairs, and, above all, anxiety for the absence of her husband, who, she knew, intended soon to depart for Spain, and to settle there during the remainder of his life: All these melancholy reflections preyed upon her mind, and threw her into a lingering fever, of which she died, after a short and unfortunate reign of five years, four months, and eleven days. *Death of the queen. 17th Nov.*

It is not necessary to employ many words in drawing the character of this princess. She possessed few qualities either estimable or amiable: and her person was as little engaging as her behaviour and address. Obstinacy, bigotry, violence, cruelty, malignity, revenge, tyranny; every circumstance of her character took a tincture from her bad temper and narrow understanding. And amidst that complication of vices, which entered into her composition, we shall scarcely find any virtue but sincerity: a quality, which she seems to have maintained throughout her whole life; except in the beginning of her reign, when the necessity of her affairs obliged her to make some promises to the protestants, which she certainly never intended to perform. But in these cases a weak bigotted woman, under the government of priests, easily finds casuistry sufficient to justify to herself the violation of a promise. She appears also, as well as her father, to have been susceptible of some attachments of friendship; and that without the caprice and inconstancy which were so remarkable in the conduct of that monarch. To which we may add, that, in many circumstances of her life, she gave indications of resolution and vigour of mind; a quality, which seems to have been inherent in her family.

Cardinal Pole had long been sickly, from an intermitting fever; and he died the same day with the queen, about sixteen hours after her. The benign character of this prelate, the modesty and humanity of his deportment, made him be universally beloved; insomuch that, in a nation, where the most furious persecution was carried on, and where the most violent religious factions prevailed, entire justice, even by most of the reformers, has been done to his merit. The haughty pontiff, Paul IV. had entertained some prejudices against him: And when England declared war against Henry, the ally of that pope, he seized the opportunity of revenge; and revoking Pole's legantine commission, appointed in his room cardinal Peyto, an observantine friar and confessor to the queen. But Mary would never permit the new legate to act upon the commission; and Paul was afterwards obliged to restore cardinal Pole to his authority.

There occur few general remarks, besides what have already been made in the course of our narration, with regard to the general state of the kingdom during this reign. The naval power of England was then so inconsiderable, that, fourteen thousand pounds being ordered to be applied to the fleet, both for repairing and victualling it, it was computed that ten thousand pounds a-year would afterwards answer all necessary charges.[m] The arbitrary proceedings of the queen, above mentioned, joined to many monopolies granted by this princess, as well as by her father, checked the growth of commerce; and so much the more, as all other princes in Europe either were not permitted, or did not find it necessary, to proceed in so tyrannical a manner. Acts of parliament, both in the last reign and in the beginning of the present, had laid the same impositions on the merchants of the still-yard as

[m] Burnet, vol. iii. p. 259.

CHAPTER XXXVII

on other aliens: Yet the queen, immediately after her marriage, complied with the solicitations of the emperor, and, by her prerogative, suspended those laws.[n] No body in that age pretended to question this exercise of prerogative. The historians are entirely silent with regard to it; and it is only by the collection of public papers that it is handed down to us.

An absurd law had been made in the preceding reign, by which every one was prohibited from making cloth unless he had served an apprenticeship of seven years. The law was repealed in the first year of the queen; and this plain reason given, that it had occasioned the decay of the woollen manufactory, and had ruined several towns.[o] It is strange that Edward's law should have been revived during the reign of Elizabeth; and still more strange, that it should still subsist.

A passage to Archangel had been discovered by the English during the last reign; and a beneficial trade with Muscovy had been established. A solemn embassy was sent by the czar to queen Mary. The ambassadors were shipwrecked on the coast of Scotland; but being hospitably entertained there, they proceeded on the journey, and were received at London with great pomp and solemnity.[p] This seems to have been the first intercourse, which that empire had with any of the western potentates of Europe.

A law was passed in this reign,[q] by which the number of horses, arms, and furniture, was fixed, which each person, according to the extent of his property, should be provided with for the defence of the kingdom. A man of a thousand pounds a-year, for instance, was obliged to maintain at his own charge six horses fit for demilances, of which three at least to be furnished with sufficient harness, steel saddles, and weapons proper for the demi-lances; and ten horses fit for light horsemen, with furniture and weapons proper for them: He was obliged to have forty corslets furnished: fifty almain revets, or instead of them, forty coats of plate, corslets or brigandines furnished; forty pikes, thirty long bows, thirty sheafs of arrows, thirty steel caps or skulls, twenty black bills or halberts, twenty haquebuts, and twenty morions or sallets. We may remark, that a man of a thousand marks of stock was rated equal

---

[n] Rymer, vol. xv. p. 364.   [o] 1 Mar. Parl. 2. cap. 7.   [p] Hollingshed, p. 732. Heylin, p. 71.   [q] 4 & 5 Phil. & Mar. cap. 2.

to one of two hundred pounds a-year: A proof that few or none at that time lived on their stock in money, and that great profits were made by the merchants in the course of trade. There is no class above a thousand pounds a-year.

We may form a notion of the little progress made in arts and refinement about this time from one circumstance: A man of no less rank than the comptroller of Edward IV.'s household payed only thirty shillings a year of our present money for his house in Channel Row:[r] Yet labour and provisions, and consequently houses, were only about a third of the present price. Erasmus ascribes the frequent plagues in England to the nastiness and dirt and slovenly habits among the people. "The floors," says he, "are commonly of clay, strewed with rushes, under which lies un-molested an ancient collection of beer, grease, fragments, bones, spittle, excrements of dogs and cats, and every thing that is nasty."[s]

Hollingshed, who lived in queen Elizabeth's reign, gives a very curious account of the plain or rather rude way of living of the preceding generation. There scarcely was a chimney to the houses, even in considerable towns: The fire was kindled by the wall, and the smoke sought its way out at the roof, or door, or windows: The houses were nothing but watling plaistered over with clay: The people slept on straw pallets, and had a good round log under their head for a pillow; and almost all the furniture and utensils were of wood.[t]

In this reign we find the first general law with regard to high ways, which were appointed to be repaired by parish duty all over England.[u]

---

[r] Nicolson's Historical Library.   [s] Eras. Epist. 432.   [t] See note [U] at the end of the volume.   [u] 2 & 3 Phil. & Mar. cap. 8.

NOTES TO THE
THIRD VOLUME

NOTE [A], p. 63

Stowe, Baker, Speed, Biondi, Hollingshed, Bacon. Some late writers, particularly Mr. Carte, have doubted whether Perkin were an impostor, and have even asserted him to be the true Plantagenet. But to refute this opinion, we need only reflect on the following particulars: (1) Though the circumstances of the wars between the two roses be in general involved in great obscurity, yet is there a most luminous ray thrown on all the transactions, during the usurpation of Richard, and the murder of the two young princes, by the narrative of Sir Thomas More, whose singular magnanimity, probity, and judgment, make him an evidence beyond all exception! No historian, either of ancient or modern times, can possibly have more weight: He may also be justly esteemed a contemporary with regard to the murder of the two princes: For though he was but five years of age when that event happened, he lived and was educated among the chief actors during the period of Richard: And it is plain, from his narrative itself, which is often extremely circumstantial, that he had the particulars from the eye-witnesses themselves: His authority, therefore, is irresistible; and sufficient to overbalance a hundred little doubts and scruples and objections. For in reality, his narrative is liable to no solid objection, nor is there any mistake detected in it. He says indeed, that the protector's partizans, particularly Dr. Shaw, spread abroad rumours of Edward IV.'s pre-contract with Elizabeth Lucy; whereas it now appears from record, that the parliament afterwards declared the king's children illegitimate, on pretence of his pre-contract with lady Eleanor Talbot. But it must be remarked, that neither of these pre-contracts was ever so much as attempted to be proved: And why might not the protector's flatterers and partizans have made use sometimes of one false rumour, sometimes of another? Sir Thomas More mentions the one rumour as well as the other, and treats them both lightly, as they deserved. It is also thought incredible by Mr. Carte, that Dr. Shaw should have been encouraged by Richard to calumniate openly his mother, the dutchess of York, with whom that prince lived in good terms. But if there be any difficulty in this supposition, we need only suppose, that Dr.

Shaw might have concerted in general his sermon with the protector or his ministers, and yet have chosen himself the particular topics, and chosen them very foolishly. This appears indeed to have been the case by the disgrace, into which he fell afterwards, and by the protector's neglect of him. (2) If Sir Thomas's quality of contemporary be disputed with regard to the duke of Glocester's protectorate, it cannot possibly be disputed with regard to Perkin's imposture: He was then a man, and had a full opportunity of knowing and examining and judging of the truth. In asserting that the duke of York was murdered by his uncle, he certainly asserts, in the most express terms, that Perkin, who personated him, was an impostor. (3) There is another great genius who has carefully treated this point of history; so great a genius as to be esteemed with justice one of the chief ornaments of the nation, and indeed one of the most sublime writers that any age or nation has produced. It is lord Bacon I mean, who has related at full length, and without the least doubt or hesitation, all the impostures of Perkin Warbeck. If it be objected, that lord Bacon was no contemporary, and that we have the same materials, as he, upon which to form our judgment; it must be remarked, that lord Bacon plainly composed his elaborate and exact history from many records and papers which are now lost, and that consequently, he is always to be cited as an original historian. It were very strange, if Mr. Carte's opinion were just, that, among all the papers, which lord Bacon perused, he never found any reason to suspect Perkin to be the true Plantagenet. There was at that time no interest in defaming Richard III. Bacon besides is a very unbiassed historian, nowise partial to Henry: We know the detail of that prince's oppressive government from him alone. It may only be thought, that, in summing up his character, he has laid the colours of blame more faintly than the very facts, he mentions, seem to require. Let me remark in passing, as a singularity, how much English history has been beholden to four great men, who have possessed the highest dignity in the law, More, Bacon, Clarendon, and Whitlocke. (4) But if contemporary evidence be so much sought after, there may in this case be produced the strongest and most undeniable in the world. The queen-dowager, her son the marquis of Dorset, a man of excellent understanding, Sir Edward Woodville, her brother, Sir Thomas St. Leger, who had married the king's sister, Sir John Bourchier, Sir Robert Willoughby, Sir Giles Daubeney, Sir Thomas Arundel, the Courtneys, the Cheyneys, the Talbots, the Stanleys, and in a word, all the partizans of the house of York, that is, the men of chief dignity in the nation; all these great persons were so assured of the murder of the two princes, that they applied to the earl of Richmond, the mortal enemy of their party and family; they projected to set him on the throne, which must have been utter ruin to them, if the princes were alive; and they stipulated to marry him to the princess Elizabeth, as heir to the crown, who in that case was no heir at all. Had each of those persons written the memoirs of his own times, would he not have said, that Richard murdered his nephews? Or would their pen be a better declaration, than their actions, of their real sentiments? (5) But we have another contemporary authority still better than even these great persons, so much interested to know the truth: It is that of Richard himself: He projected to marry his niece, a very unusual alliance in England, in order to unite her title with his own. He knew therefore her title to be good: For as to the declaration of her illegitimacy, as it went upon no proof, or even pretence of proof, it was always regarded with the utmost contempt by the nation, and was considered as one of those parliamentary transactions, so frequent in that period, which were scandalous in themselves, and had no manner of authority. It was even so much despised as not to be reversed by parliament, after Henry and Elizabeth were on the throne. (6) We have also, as contemporary evidence, the universal established opinion of the age, both abroad and at home. This point was regarded as so uncontroverted, that when Richard notified his accession to the court of France, that court was struck with horror at his abominable parricide, in murdering both his nephews, as Philip de Comines tells us; and this sentiment went to such an unusual height, that, as we learn from the same author, the court would not make the least reply to him. (7) The same reasons, which convinced that age of the parricide, still subsist, and ought to carry the most undoubted evidence to us; namely, the very circumstance of the sudden disappearance of the princes from the Tower, and their appearance no where else. Every one said, *they have not escaped from their uncle, for he makes no search after them: He has not conveyed them elsewhere: For it is his business to declare so, in order to remove the imputation of murder from himself. He never would needlessly subject himself to the infamy and danger of being esteemed a parricide, without acquiring the security attending that crime. They were in his custody: He is answerable for them: If he gives no account of them, as he has a plain interest in their death, he must, by every rule of common sense, be regarded as the murderer. His flagrant usurpation, as well as his other treacherous and cruel actions, makes no better be expected from him. He could not say with Cain, that he was not his nephew's keeper.* This reasoning, which was irrefragable at the very first, became every day stronger, from Richard's continued silence, and the general and total ignorance of the place of these princes' abode. Richard's reign lasted about two years beyond this period; and surely, he could not have found a better expedient for disappointing the earl of Richmond's projects, as well as justifying his own character, than the producing of his nephews. (8) If it were necessary, amidst this blaze of evidence, to produce proofs, which, in any other case, would have been regarded as considerable, and would have carried great validity with them, I might mention Dighton and Tyrrel's account of the murder. This last gentleman especially was not likely to subject himself to the reproach of so great a crime, by an imposture, which, it appears, did not acquire him the favour of Henry. (9) The duke of York, being a boy of nine years of age, could not have made his escape without the assistance of some elder persons. Would it not have been their chief concern instantly to convey intelligence of so great an event to his mother, the queen-dowager, to his aunt, the dutchess of Burgundy, and to the other friends of the family? The dutchess protected Simnel; a project, which, had it been successful, must have ended in the crowning of Warwic, and the exclusion of the duke of York! This, among many other proofs, evinces that she was ignorant of the escape of that prince, which is impossible, had it been real. (10) The total silence with regard to the persons who aided him in his escape, as also with regard to the place of his abode during more than eight years, is a sufficient proof of the imposture. (11) Perkin's own account of his escape is incredible and absurd. He said, that murderers were employed by his uncle to kill him and his brother: They perpetrated the crime against his brother; but took compassion on him, and allowed him to escape. This account is contained in all the historians of that age. (12) Perkin himself made a full confession of his imposture no less than three times; once when he surrendered himself prisoner, a second time when he was set in the stocks at Cheapside and Westminster, and a third time, which carries undoubted evidence, at the foot of the gibbet, on which he was hanged. Not the least surmise that the confession had ever been procured by torture: And surely, the last time he had nothing farther to fear. (13) Had not Henry been assured, that Perkin was a ridiculous impostor, disavowed by the whole nation, he never would have allowed him to live an hour after he came into his power; much less, would he have twice pardoned him. His treatment of the innocent earl of Warwic, who in reality had no title to the crown, is a sufficient confirmation of this reasoning. (14) We know with certainty whence the whole imposture came, namely, from the intrigues of the dutchess of Burgundy: She had before acknowledged and supported Lambert Simnel, an avowed impostor. It is remarkable, that Mr. Carte, in order to preserve the weight of the dutchess's testimony in favour of Perkin, suppresses entirely this material fact: A strong effect of party prejudices, and this author's desire of blackening Henry VII. whose hereditary title to the crown was defective. (15) There never was, at that time, any evidence or shadow of evidence produced, of Perkin's identity with Richard Plantagenet. Richard had disappeared when near nine years of age, and Perkin did not appear till he was a man. Could any one, from his aspect, pretend then to be sure of the identity? He had got some stories concerning Richard's childhood, and the court of England: But all that it was necessary for a boy of nine to remark or remember was easily suggested to him by the dutchess of Burgundy, or Frion, Henry's secretary, or by any body that had ever lived at court. It is true, many persons of note were at first deceived; but the discontents against Henry's government, and the general enthusiasm for the house of York, account sufficiently for this temporary delusion. Every body's eyes were opened long before Perkin's death. (16) The circumstance of finding the two dead bodies in the reign of Charles II. is not surely indifferent. They were found in the very place, which More, Bacon, and other ancient authors had assigned as the place of interment of the young princes: The bones corresponded by their size to the age of the princes: The secret and irregular place of their interment, not being in holy ground, proves that the boys had been secretly murdered: And in the Tower, no boys, but those who are very nearly related to the crown, can be exposed to a violent death: If we compare all these circumstances we shall find, that the inference is just and strong, that they were the bodies of Edward the Vth and his brother, the very inference that was drawn at the time of the discovery.

Since the publication of this History, Mr. Walpole *has published his Historic Doubts concerning Richard III. Nothing can be a stronger proof how ingenious and agreeable that gentleman's pen is, than his being able to make an enquiry concerning a remote point of English history, an object of general conversation. The foregoing note has been enlarged on account of that performance.*

NOTE [B], p. 74

Rot. Parl. 3 H. VII. n. 17. The preamble is remarkable, and shows the state of the nation at that time. "The king, our sovereign lord, remembereth, how, by our unlawful maintainances, giving of liveries, signs and tokens, retainders by indentures, promises, oaths, writings, and other embraceries of his subjects, untrue demeanings of sheriffs in making pannels, and untrue returns by taking money, by juries, &c. the policy of this nation is most subdued." It must indeed be confessed, that such a state of the country required great discretionary power in the sovereign; nor will the same maxims of government suit such a rude people, that may be proper in a more advanced stage of society. The establishment of the Star-chamber or the enlargement of its power in the reign of Henry VII. might have been as wise as the abolition of it in that of Charles I.

NOTE [C], p. 77

The duke of Northumberland has lately printed a household book of an old earl of that family, who lived at this time: The author has been favoured with the perusal of it; and it contains many curious particulars, which mark the manners and way of living in that rude, not to say barbarous age; as well as the prices of commodities. I have extracted a few of them from that piece, which gives a true picture of ancient manners, and is one of the most singular monuments that English antiquity affords us: For we may be confident, however rude the strokes, that no Baron's family was on a nobler or more splendid footing. The family consists of 166 persons, masters and servants: Fifty seven strangers are reckoned upon every day: On the whole 223. Two-pence halfpenny are supposed to be the daily expence of each for meat, drink, and firing. This would make a groat of our present money: Supposing provisions between three and four times cheaper, it would be equivalent to fourteen-pence: No great sum for a nobleman's housekeeping; especially considering, that the chief expence of a family, at that time, consisted in meat and drink: For the sum allotted by the earl for his whole annual expence is 1118 pounds seventeen shillings and eight-pence; meat, drink, and firing cost 796 pounds eleven shillings and two-pence, more than two thirds of the whole: In a modern family it is not above a third, p. 157, 158, 159. The whole expence of the earl's family is managed with an exactness that is very rigid, and, if we make no allowance for ancient manners, such as may seem to border on an extreme; insomuch, that the number of pieces, which must be cut out of every quarter of beef, mutton, pork, veal, nay stock-fish and salmon, are determined, and must be entered and accounted for by the different clerks appointed for that purpose: If a servant be absent a day, his mess is struck off: If he go on my lord's business, board wages are allowed him, eight-pence a day for his journey in winter, five-pence in summer: When he stays in any place, two-pence a day are allowed him, beside the maintainance of his horse. Somewhat above a quarter of wheat is allowed for every mouth throughout the year; and the wheat is estimated at five shillings and eight-pence a quarter. Two hundred and fifty quarters of malt are allowed, at four shillings a quarter: Two hogsheads are to be made of a quarter; which amounts to about a bottle and a third of beer a day to each person, p. 4. and the beer will not be very strong. One hundred and nine fat beeves are to be bought at Allhallow-tide, at thirteen shillings and four-pence a piece: And twenty four lean beeves to be bought at St. Helens at eight shillings a piece: These are to be put into the pastures to feed; and are to serve from Midsummer to Michaelmas; which is consequently the only time that the family eats fresh beef: During all the rest of the year they live on salted meat, p. 5. One hundred and sixty gallons of mustard are allowed in a year; which seems indeed requisite for the salt beef, p. 18. Six hundred and forty seven sheep are allowed, at twenty pence a piece; and these seem also to be all eat salted, except between Lammas and Michaelmas, p. 5. Only twenty-five hogs are allowed at two shillings a piece; twenty-eight veals at twenty-pence; forty lambs at ten pence or a shilling, p. 7. These seem to be reserved for my lord's table, or that of the upper servants, called the knight's-table. The other servants, as they eat salted meat, almost through the whole year, and with few or no vegetables, had a very bad and unhealthy diet: So that there cannot be any thing more erroneous, than the magnificent ideas formed of the *Roast Beef of Old England.* We must entertain as mean an idea of its cleanliness: Only seventy ells of linen at eight-pence an ell are annually allowed for this great family: No sheets were used: This linen was made into eight table-cloths for my lord's table; and one tablecloth for the knights, p. 16. This last, I suppose, was washed only once a month. Only forty shillings are allowed for washing throughout the whole year; and most of it seems expended on the linen belonging to the chapel. The drinking, however, was tolerable, namely, ten tuns and two hogsheads of Gascogny wine, at the rate of four pounds thirteen shillings and four-pence a tun, p. 6. Only ninety-one dozen of candles for the whole year, p. 14. The family rose at six in the morning, dined at ten, and supped at four in the afternoon: The gates were all shut at nine, and no farther ingress or egress permitted, p. 314, 318. My lord and lady have set on their table for breakfast at seven o'clock in the morning a quart of beer; as much wine; two pieces of salt fish, six red-herrings, four white ones, or a dish of sprats. In flesh days half a chyne of mutton, or a chyne of beef boiled, p. 73, 75. Mass is ordered to be said at six o'clock, in order, says the household-book, that all my lord's servants may rise early, p. 170. Only twenty-four fires are allowed, beside the kitchen and hall, and

NOTES TO THE THIRD VOLUME

most of these have only a peck of coals a day allowed them, p. 99. After Lady-day, no fires permitted in the rooms, except half-fires in my lord's and lady's, and lord Piercy's and the nursery, p. 101. It is to be observed that my lord kept house in Yorkshire, where there is certainly much cold weather after Lady-day. Eighty chalders of coals at four shillings and two-pence a chalder, suffices throughout the whole year; and because coal will not burn without wood, says the household-book, sixty-four loads of great wood are also allowed, at twelve-pence a load, p. 22. This is a proof that grates were not then used. Here is an article. *It is devised that from henceforth no capons to be bought but only for my lord's own mess, and that the said capons shall be bought for two-pence a piece, lean, and fed in the poultry; and master chamberlain and the stewards be fed with capons, if there be strangers sitting with them,* p. 102. Pigs are to be bought at three-pence or a groat a piece: Geese at the same price: Chickens at a halfpenny: Hens at two-pence, and only for the above-mentioned tables. Here is another article. *Item, It is thought good that no plovers be bought at no season but only in Christmas and principal feasts, and my lord to be served therewith and his board-end, and none other, and to be bought for a penny a piece, or a penny halfpenny at most,* p. 103. Woodcocks are to be bought at the same price. Partridges at two-pence, p. 104, 105. Pheasants, a shilling; peacocks the same, p. 106. My lord keeps only twenty-seven horses in his stable at his own charge: His upper servants have allowance for maintaining their own horses, p. 126. These horses are, six gentle horses, as they are called, at hay and hard meat throughout the whole year, four palfreys, three hobbies and nags, three sumpter horses, six horses for those servants to whom my lord furnishes a horse, two sumpter horses more, and three mill horses, two for carrying the corn and one for grinding it; whence we may infer that mills, either water or wind-mills, were then unknown, at least very rare: Besides these, there are seven great trotting horses for the chariot or waggon. He allows a peck of oats a day, besides loaves made of beans, for his principal horses; the oats at twenty pence, the beans at two shillings a quarter. The load of hay is at two shillings and eight-pence. When my lord is on a journey, he carries thirty-six horsemen along with him; together with bed and other accommodation, p. 157. The inns, it seems, could afford nothing tolerable. My lord passes the year in three country-seats, all in Yorkshire, Wrysel, Leckenfield, and Topclyffe; but he has furniture only for one: He carries every thing along with him, beds, tables, chairs, kitchen utensils, all which, we may conclude, were so coarse, that they could not be spoilt by the carriage: Yet seventeen carts and one waggon suffices for the whole, p. 391. One cart suffices for all his kitchen utensils, cooks beds, &c. p. 388. One remarkable circumstance is, that he has eleven priests in his house, besides seventeen persons, chanters, musicians, &c. belonging to his chapel: Yet he has only two cooks for a family of 223 persons, p. 325.* Their meals were certainly dressed in the

---

* *In another place, mention is made of four cooks, p. 388. But I suppose, that the two servants, called in p. 325, groom of the larder and child of the scullery, are in p. 388. comprehended in the number of cooks.*

slovenly manner of a ship's company. It is amusing to observe the pompous and even royal style assumed by this Tartar chief: He does not give any orders, though only for the right making of mustard; but it is introduced with this preamble, *It seemeth good to us and our council.* If we consider the magnificent and elegant manner in which the Venetian and other Italian noblemen then lived, with the progress made by the Italians in literature and the fine arts, we shall not wonder that they considered the ultra-mountaine nations as barbarous. The Flemish also seem to have much excelled the English and even the French. Yet the earl is sometimes not deficient in generosity: He pays for instance, an annual pension of a groat a year to my lady of Walsingham, for her interest in Heaven; the same sum to the holy blood at Hales, p. 337. No mention is any where made of plate; but only of the hiring of pewter vessels. The servants seem all to have bought their own cloaths from their wages.

NOTE [D], p. 138

Protestant writers have imagined, that, because a man could purchase for a shilling an indulgence for the most enormous and unheard-of crimes, there must necessarily have ensued a total dissolution of morality, and consequently of civil society, from the practices of the Romish church. They do not consider, that, after all these indulgences were promulgated, there still remained (besides Hell-fire) the punishment by the civil magistrate, the infamy of the world, and secret remorses of conscience, which are the great motives that operate on mankind. The philosophy of *Cicero,* who allowed of an *Elysium,* but rejected all *Tartarus,* was a much more universal indulgence than that preached by *Arcemboldi* or *Tetzel:* Yet nobody will suspect *Cicero* of any design to promote immorality. The sale of indulgences seems, therefore, no more criminal than any other cheat of the church of Rome, or of any other church. The reformers, by entirely abolishing purgatory, did really, instead of partial indulgences sold by the pope, give, gratis, a general indulgence, of a similar nature, for all crimes and offences, without exception or distinction. The souls, once consigned to Hell, were never supposed to be redeemable by any price. There is on record only one instance of a damned soul that was saved, and that by the special intercession of the Virgin. See Pascal's Provincial Letters. An indulgence saved the person, who purchased it, from purgatory only.

NOTE [E], p. 149

It is said, that when Henry heard that the commons made a great difficulty of granting the required supply, he was so provoked, that he sent for Edward Montague, one of the members, who had a considerable influence on the house; and he being introduced to his majesty, had the mortification to hear him speak in these words: *Ho! man! will they not suffer my bill to pass?* And laying his hand on Montague's head, who was then on his knees before him: *Get my bill passed by to-morrow, or else to-morrow this head of yours shall be off.* This cavalier manner of Henry succeeded: For next day the bill passed.

NOTES TO THE THIRD VOLUME

Collins's British Peerage. Grove's life of Wolsey. We are told by *Hall,* fol. 38. That cardinal Wolsey endeavoured to terrify the citizens of London into the general loan, exacted in 1525, and told them plainly, that it *were better, that some should suffer indigence, than that the king at this time should lack; and therefore beware and resist not, nor ruffle not in this case, for it may fortune to cost some people their heads.* Such was the style employed by this king and his ministers.

NOTE [F], p. 185

The first article of the charge against the cardinal is his procuring the legantine power, which, however, as it was certainly done with the king's consent and permission, could be nowise criminal. Many of the other articles also regard the mere exercise of that power. Some articles impute to him as crimes, particular actions, which were natural or unavoidable to any man, that was prime minister with so unlimited an authority; such as receiving first all letters from the king's ministers abroad, receiving first all visits from foreign ministers, desiring that all applications should be made through him. He was also accused of naming himself with the king, as if he had been his fellow, *the king and I:* It is reported that sometimes he even put his own name before the king's, *ego et rex meus.* But this mode of expression is justified by the Latin idiom. It is remarkable, that his whispering in the king's ear, knowing himself to be affected with venereal distempers, is an article against him. Many of the charges are general, and incapable of proof. Lord Herbert goes so far as to affirm, that no man ever fell from so high a station, who had so few real crimes objected to him. This opinion is perhaps a little too favourable to the cardinal. Yet the refutation of the articles by Cromwel, and their being rejected by a house of commons even in this arbitrary reign, is almost a demonstration of Wolsey's innocence. Henry was, no doubt, entirely bent on his destruction, when, on his failure by a parliamentary impeachment, he attacked him upon the statute of provisors, which afforded him so little just hold on that minister. For that this indictment was subsequent to the attack in parliament, appears by Cavendish's life of Wolsey, and Stowe, p. 551, and more certainly by the very articles of impeachment themselves. Parliamentary History, vol. iii. p. 42. article 7. Coke's Inst. pt. 4. fol. 89.

NOTE [G], p. 191

Even judging of this question by the Scripture, to which the appeal was every moment made, the arguments for the king's cause appear but lame and imperfect. Marriage in the degree of affinity which had place between Henry and Catherine, is, indeed, prohibited in Leviticus; but it is natural to interpret that prohibition as a part of the Jewish ceremonial or municipal law: And though it is there said, in the conclusion, that the gentile nations, by violating those degrees of consanguinity, had incurred the divine displeasure, the extension of this maxim to every precise case before specified, is supposing the Scriptures to be composed with a minute accuracy and precision, to which, we know with certainty, the sacred penmen did not think proper to confine themselves. The descent of mankind from one common father, obliged them, in the first generation, to marry in the nearest degrees of consanguinity: Instances of a like nature occur among the patriarchs: And the marriage of a brother's widow was, in certain cases, not only permitted, but even enjoined as a positive precept by the Mosaical law. It is in vain to say, that this precept was an exception to the rule; and an exception confined merely to the Jewish nation. The inference is still just, that such a marriage can contain no natural or moral turpitude; otherwise God, who is the author of all purity, would never, in any case, have enjoined it.

NOTE [H], p. 199

Bishop Burnet has given us an account of the number of bulls requisite for Cranmer's installation. By one bull, directed to the king, he is, upon the royal nomination, made archbishop of Canterbury. By a second, directed to himself, he is also made archbishop. By a third, he is absolved from all censures. A fourth is directed to the suffragans, requiring them to receive and acknowledge him as archbishop. A fifth to the dean and chapter, to the same purpose. A sixth to the clergy of Canterbury. A seventh to all the laity in his see. An eighth to all that held lands of it. By a ninth he was ordered to be consecrated, taking the oath that was in the pontifical. By a tenth the pall was sent him. By an eleventh; the archbishop of York, and the bishop of London, were required to put it on him. These were so many devices to draw sees to offices, which the popes had erected, and disposed of for money. It may be worth observing, that Cranmer, before he took the oath to the pope, made a protestation, that he did not intend thereby to restrain himself from any thing that he was bound to, either by his duty to God, the king, or the country; and that he renounced every thing in it that was contrary to any of these. This was the invention of some casuist, and not very compatible with that strict sincerity, and that scrupulous conscience, of which Cranmer made profession. Collier, vol. ii. in Coll. No 22. Burnet, vol. i. p. 128, 129.

NOTE [I], p. 212

Here are the terms in which the king's minister expressed himself to the pope. An non, inquam, sanctitas vestra plerosque habet quibuscum arcanum aliquid crediderit, putet id non minus celatum esse quam si uno tantum pectore contineretur; quod multo magis serenissimo Angliae Regi evenire debet, cui singuli in suo regno sunt subjecti, neque etiam velint, possunt Regi non esse fidelissimi. Vae namque illis, si vel parvo momento ab illius voluntate recederent. Le Grand, tom. iii. p. 113. The king once said publicly before the council, that if any one spoke of him or his actions, in terms which became them not, he would let them know, that he was master. Et qu'il n'y auroit si belle tete qu'il ne fit voler. Id. p. 218.

NOTES TO THE THIRD VOLUME

NOTE [J], p. 236

This letter contains so much nature and even elegance, as to deserve to be transmitted to posterity, without any alteration in the expression. It is as follows.

"Sir, your grace's displeasure and my imprisonment are things so strange unto me, as what to write, or what to excuse, I am altogether ignorant. Whereas you send unto me (willing me to confess a truth, and so obtain your favour) by such an one, whom you know to be mine ancient professed enemy, I no sooner received this message by him, than I rightly conceived your meaning; and, if, as you say, confessing a truth indeed may procure my safety, I shall with all willingness and duty perform your command.

"But let not your grace ever imagine, that your poor wife will ever be brought to acknowledge a fault, where not so much as a thought thereof preceded. And to speak a truth, never prince had wife more loyal in all duty, and in all true affection, than you have ever found in Anne Boleyn: With which name and place I could willingly have contented myself, if God and your grace's pleasure had been so pleased. Neither did I at any time so far forget myself in my exaltation or received queenship, but that I always looked for such an alteration as I now find; for the ground of my preferment being on no surer foundation than your grace's fancy, the least alteration I knew was fit and sufficient to draw that fancy to some other object. You have chosen me from a low estate to be your queen and companion, far beyond my desert or desire. If then you found me worthy of such honour, good your grace let not any light fancy, or bad counsel of mine enemies, withdraw your princely favour from me; neither let that stain, that unworthy stain, of a disloyal heart towards your good grace, ever cast so foul a blot on your most dutiful wife, and the infant princess your daughter. Try me, good king, but let me have a lawful trial, and let not my sworn enemies sit as my accusers and judges; yea let me receive an open trial, for my truth shall fear no open shame; then shall you see either mine innocence cleared, your suspicion and conscience satisfied, the ignominy and slander of the world stopped, or my guilt openly declared. So that whatsoever God or you may determine of me, your grace may be freed from an open censure, and mine offence being so lawfully proved, your grace is at liberty, both before God and man, not only to execute worthy punishment on me as an unlawful wife, but to follow your affection, already settled on that party, for whose sake I am now as I am, whose name I could some good while since have pointed unto, your grace not being ignorant of my suspicion therein.

"But if you have already determined of me, and that not only my death, but an infamous slander must bring you the enjoying of your desired happiness; then I desire of God, that he will pardon your great sin therein, and likewise mine enemies, the instruments thereof, and that he will not call you to a strict account for your unprincely and cruel usage of me, at his general judgment-seat, where both you and myself must shortly appear, and in whose judgment I doubt not (whatsoever the world may think of me) mine innocence shall be openly known, and sufficiently cleared.

"My last and only request shall be, that myself may only bear the burden of your grace's displeasure, and that it may not touch the innocent souls of those poor gentlemen, who (as I understand) are likewise in strait imprisonment for my sake. If ever I have found favour in your sight, if ever the name of Anne Boleyn hath been pleasing in your ears, then let me obtain this request, and I will so leave to trouble your grace any further, with mine earnest prayers to the Trinity to have your grace in his good keeping, and to direct you in all your actions. From my doleful prison in the Tower, this sixth of May;

"Your most loyal and ever faithful wife, Anne Boleyn."

NOTE [K], p. 244

A proposal had formerly been made in the convocation for the abolition of the lesser monasteries; and had been much opposed by bishop Fisher, who was then alive. He told his brethren, that this was fairly showing the king the way, how he might come at the greater monasteries. "An ax," said he, "which wanted a handle, came upon a time into the wood, making his moan to the great trees, that he wanted a handle to work withal, and for that cause he was constrained to sit idle; therefore he made it his request to them, that they would be pleased to grant him one of their small saplings within the wood to make him a handle; who, mistrusting no guile, granted him one of their smaller trees to make him a handle. But now becoming a complete ax, he fell so to work, within the same wood, that, in process of time, there was neither great nor small trees to be found in the place, where the wood stood. And so, my lords, if you grant the king these smaller monasteries, you do but make him a handle, whereby, at his own pleasure, he may cut down all the cedars within your Lebanons." Dr. Bailie's life of bishop Fisher, p. 108.

NOTE [L], p. 255

There is a curious passage, with regard to the suppression of monasteries, to be found in Coke's institutes, 4th Inst. chap. 1. p. 44. It is worth transcribing, as it shews the ideas of the English government, entertained during the reign of Henry VIII. and even in the time of Sir Edward Coke, when he wrote his Institutes. It clearly appears, that the people had then little notion of being jealous of their liberties, were desirous of making the crown quite independent, and wished only to remove from themselves, as much as possible, the burthens of government. A large standing army, and a fixed revenue, would, on these conditions, have been regarded as great blessings; and it was owing entirely to the prodigality of Henry, and to his little suspicion that the power of the crown could ever fail, that the English owe all their present liberty. The title of the chapter in Coke is, *Advice concerning new and plausible Projects and Offers in Parliament.* "When any plausible project," says he, "is made in parliament, to draw the lords and commons to assent to any act, (especially in matters of weight and importance) if both houses do give upon the matter projected and promised their consent, it shall be most necessary, they being trusted for the commonwealth, to have the matter projected and promised (which moved the houses to consent) to be established in the same act, lest the benefit of the act be taken, and the matter projected and promised never performed, and so the houses of parliament perform not the trust reposed in them, as it fell out (taking one example for many) in the reign of Henry the eighth: On the king's behalf, the members of both houses were informed in parliament, that no king or kingdom was safe, but where the king had three abilities; 1. To live of his own, and able to defend his kingdom upon any sudden invasion or insurrection. 2. To aid his confederates, otherwise they would never assist him. 3. To reward his well deserving servants. Now the project was, that if the parliament would give unto him all the abbies, priories, friories, nunneries, and other monasteries, that, for ever in time then to come, he would take order that the same should not be converted to private uses: but first, that his exchequer for the purposes aforesaid should be enriched; secondly, the kingdom strengthened by a continual maintenance of forty thousand well-trained soldiers, with skilful captains and commanders; thirdly, for the benefit and ease of the subject, who never afterwards, (as was projected) in any time to come, should be charged with subsidies, fifteenths, loans, or other common aids; fourthly, lest the honour of the realm should receive any diminution of honour by the dissolution of the said monasteries, there being twenty-nine lords of parliament of the abbots and priors, (that held of the king *per baronium*, whereof more in the next leaf) that the king would create a number of nobles, which we omit. The said monasteries were given to the king by authority of divers acts of parliament, but no provision was therein made for the said project, or any part thereof."

NOTE [M], p. 264

Collier, in his ecclesiastical history, vol. ii. p. 152. has preserved an account which Cromwel gave of this conference, in a letter to Sir Thomas Wyat, the king's embassador in Germany. "The king's majesty," says Cromwel, "for the reverence of the holy sacrament of the altar, did sit openly in his hall, and there presided at the disputation, process and judgment of a miserable heretic sacramentary, who was burned the 20th of November. It was a wonder to see how princely, with how excellent gravity, and inestimable majesty his highness exercised there the very office of supreme head of the church of England. How benignly his grace essayed to convert the miserable man: How strong and manifest reasons his highness alledged against him. I wish the princes and potentates of Christendom to have had a meet place to have seen it. Undoubtedly they should have much marvelled at his majesty's most high wisdom and judgment, and reputed him no otherwise after the same, than in a manner the mirror and light of all other kings and princes in Christendom." It was by such flatteries, that Henry was engaged to make his sentiments the standard to all mankind; and was determined to enforce, by the severest penalties, his *strong* and *manifest* reasons for transubstantiation.

NOTE [N], p. 266

There is a story, that the duke of Norfolk, meeting, soon after this act was passed, one of his chaplains, who was suspected of favouring the reformation, said to him, "Now, Sir, what think you of the law to hinder priests from having wives?" "Yes, my lord," replies the chaplain, "you have done that; but I will answer for it, you cannot hinder men's wives from having priests."

NOTE [O], p. 277

To show how much Henry sported with law and common sense; how servilely the parliament followed all his caprices; and how much both of them were lost to all sense of shame; an act was passed this session, declaring, that a precontract should be no ground for annulling a marriage; as if that pretext had not been made use of both in the case of Anne Boleyn and Anne of Cleves. But the king's intention in this law is said to be a design of restoring the princess Elizabeth to her right of legitimacy; and it was his character never to look farther than the present object, without regarding the inconsistency of his conduct. The parliament made it high treason to deny the dissolution of Henry's marriage with Anne of Cleves. Herbert.

NOTE [P], p. 287

It was enacted by this parliament, that there should be trial of treason in any county where the king should appoint by commission. The statutes of treason had been extremely multiplied in this reign; and such an expedient saved trouble and charges in trying that crime. The same parliament erected Ireland into a kingdom; and Henry henceforth annexed the title of king of Ireland to his other titles. This session, the commons first began the practice of freeing any of their members, who were arrested, by a writ issued by the speaker. Formerly it was usual for them to apply for a writ from chancery to that purpose. This precedent encreased the authority of the commons, and had afterwards important consequences. Hollingshed, p. 955, 956. Baker, p. 289.

NOTE [Q], p. 294

The persecutions, exercised during James's reign, are not to be ascribed to his bigotry, a vice, of which he seems to have been as free as Francis the first or the emperor Charles, both of whom, as well as James, shewed, in different periods of their lives, even an inclination to the new doctrines. The extremities, to which all these princes were carried, proceeded entirely from the situation of affairs, during that age, which rendered it impossible for them to act with greater temper or moderation, after they had embraced the resolution of supporting the ancient establishments. So violent was the propensity of the times towards innovation, that a bare toleration of the new preachers was equivalent to a formed design of changing the national religion.

NOTE [R], p. 345

Spotswood, p. 75. The same author, p. 92. tells us a story, which confirms this character of the popish clergy in Scotland. It became a great dispute in the university of St. Andrews, whether the *pater* should be said to God or the saints. The friars, who knew in general that the reformers neglected the saints, were determined to maintain their honour with great obstinacy, but they knew not upon what topics to found their doctrine. Some held that the *pater* was said to God *formaliter,* and to saints *materialiter;* others, to God *principaliter,* and to saints *minus principaliter;* others would have it *ultimate* and *non ultimate:* But the majority seemed to hold, that the *pater* was said to God *capiendo stricte,* and to saints *capiendo large.* A simple fellow, who served the sub prior, thinking there was some great matter in hand, that made the doctors hold so many conferences together, asked him one day what the matter was; the sub-prior answering, *Tom,* that was the fellow's name, *we cannot agree to whom the paternoster should be said.* He suddenly replied, *To whom, Sir, should it be said, but unto God?* Then said the sub-prior, *What shall we do with the saints?* He answered, *Give them Aves and Creeds enow in the devil's name; for that may suffice them.* The answer going abroad, many said, *that he had given a wiser decision than all the doctors had done with all their distinctions.*

NOTE [S], p. 365

Another act, passed this session, takes notice in the preamble, that the city of York, formerly well inhabited, was now much decayed: Insomuch that many of the cures could not afford a competent maintenance to the incumbents. To remedy this inconvenience, the magistrates were impowered to unite as many parishes as they thought proper. An ecclesiastical historian, Collier, vol. ii. p. 230, thinks, that this decay of York is chiefly to be ascribed to the dissolution of monasteries, by which the revenues fell into the hands of persons who lived at a distance.

A very grievous tax was imposed this session upon the whole stock and monied interest of the kingdom, and even upon its industry. It was a shilling in the pound yearly, during three years, on every person worth ten pounds or upwards: The double on aliens and denizens. These last, if above twelve years of age, and if worth less than twenty shillings, were to pay eight pence yearly. Every wether was to pay two-pence yearly; every yew three-pence. The woollen manufactures were to pay eight-pence a pound on the value of all the cloth they made. These exorbitant taxes on money are a proof, that few people lived on money lent at interest: For this tax amounts to half of the yearly income of all money holders, during three years, estimating their interest at the rate allowed by law; and was too grievous to be borne, if many persons had been affected by it. It is remarkable, that no tax at all was laid upon land this session. The profits of merchandise were commonly so high, that it was supposed it could bear this imposition. The most absurd part of the laws seems to be the tax upon the woollen manufactures. See 2 & 3 Edw. VI. cap. 36. The subsequent parliament repealed the tax on sheep and woollen cloth. 3 & 4 Edw. VI. cap 23. But they continued the other tax a year longer. Ibid.

...lergy taxed themselves at six shillings in the pound to be paid in ...years. This taxation was ratified in parliament, which had been the ...mmon practice since the reformation, implying that the clergy have no legislative power, even over themselves. See 2 & 3 Edw. VI. cap. 35.

NOTE [T], p. 427

The pope at first gave cardinal Pole powers to transact only with regard to the past fruits of the church lands; but being admonished of the danger attending any attempt towards a resumption of the lands, he enlarged the cardinal's powers, and granted him authority to ensure the future possession of the church lands to the present proprietors. There was only one clause in the cardinal's powers that has given occasion for some speculation. An exception was made of such cases as Pole should think important enough to merit the being communicated to the holy see. But Pole simply ratified the possession of all the church lands; and his commission had given him full powers to that purpose. See Harleyan Miscellany, vol. vii. p. 264, 266. It is true, some councils have declared, that it exceeds even the power of the pope to alienate any church lands; and the pope, according to his convenience, or power, may either adhere to or recede from this declaration. But every year gave solidity to the right of the proprietors of church lands, and diminished the authority of the popes; so that men's dread of popery in subsequent times was more founded on party or religious zeal, than on very solid reasons.

NOTE [U], p. 464

The passage of Hollingshed, in the Discourse prefixed to his History, and which some ascribe to Harrison, is as follows. Speaking of the encrease of luxury: Neither do I speak this in reproach of any man; God is my judge; but to shew, that I do rejoice rather to see how God has blessed us with his good gifts, and to behold how that in a time wherein all things are grown to most excessive prices, we do yet find the means to obtain and achieve such furniture as heretofore has been impossible: There are old men yet dwelling in the village where I remain, which have noted three things to be marvellously altered in England within their sound remembrance. One is the multitude of chimnies lately erected; whereas in their young days, there were not above two or three, if so many, in most uplandish towns of the realm (the religious houses and manor places of their lords always excepted, and peradventure some great personage); but each made his fire against a reredosse in the hall where he dined and dressed his meat. The second is the great amendment of lodging: For, said they, our fathers and we ourselves have lain full oft upon straw pallettes covered only with a sheet under coverlets made of dagswaine or hopharlots (I use their own terms), and a good round log under their head instead of a bolster. If it were so, that the father or the good-man of the house had a matrass or flockbed, and thereto a sack of chaff to rest his head upon, he thought himself to be as well lodged as the lord of the town: So well were they contented. Pillows, said they, were thought meet only for women in child bed: As for servants, if they had any sheet above them, it was well: For seldom had they any under their bodies to keep them from the pricking straws, that ran oft through the canvas, and razed their hardened hydes.——The third thing they tell of is, the exchange of Treene platers (*so called, I suppose, from Tree or Wood*) into pewter, and wooden spoons into silver or tin. For so common were all sorts of treene vessels in old time, that a man should hardly find four pieces of pewter (of which one was peradventure a salt) in a good farmer's house. *Description of Britain, chap.* X.——*Again, in chap. xvi.* In times past men were contented to dwell in houses builded of sallow, willow, &c.; so that the use of the oak was in a manner dedicated wholly unto churches, religious houses, princes palaces, navigation, &c. but now sallow, &c. are rejected, and nothing but oak any where regarded; and yet see the change, for when our houses were builded of willow, then had we oaken men; but now that our houses are come to be made of oak, our men are not only become willow, but a great many altogether of straw, which is a sore alteration. In these the courage of the owner was a sufficient defence to keep the house in safety; but now the assurance of the timber must defend the men from robbing. Now have we many chimnies; and yet our tenderlines complain of rheums, catarrhs, and poses; then had we none but reredosses, and our heads did never ach. For as the smoke in those days was supposed to be a sufficient hardening for the timber of the house; so it was reputed a far better medicine to keep the goodman and his family from the quacke or pose, wherewith, as then, very few were acquainted. *Again, in chap.* xviii. Our pewterers in time past employed the use of pewter only upon dishes and pots, and a few other trifles for service; whereas now, they are grown into such exquisite cunning, that they can in manner imitate by infusion any form or fashion of cup, dish, salt, or bowl or goblet which is made by goldsmith's craft, though they be never so curious and very artificially forged. In some places beyond the sea, a garnish of good flat English pewter (I say flat, because dishes and platters in my time begin to be made deep and like basons, and are indeed more convenient both for sauce and keeping the meat warm) is almost esteemed so precious as the like number of vessels that are made of fine silver. *If the reader is curious to know the hour of meals in queen Elizabeth's reign, he may learn it from the same Author.* With us the nobility, gentry, and students do ordinarily go to dinner at eleven before noon, and to supper at five, or between five and six at afternoon. The merchants dine and sup seldom before twelve at noon and six at night, especially in London. The husbandmen dine also at high noon, as they call it, and sup at seven or eight; but out of term in our universities the scholars dine at ten.

Froissart mentions waiting on the duke of Lancaster at five o'clock in the afternoon, when he had supped. These hours are still more early. It is hard to tell, why, all over the world, as the age becomes more luxurious, the hours become later. Is it the crowd of amusements that push on the hours gradually? or are the people of fashion better pleased with the secrecy and nocturnal hours, when the industrious vulgar are all gone to rest? ue ages men have few amusements or occupations but what daylight .ords them.

END OF THE THIRD VOLUME